# International Finance

# International Finance: Text and Cases

George Feiger
*McKinsey and Co.*

Bertrand Jacquillat
*Centre d'Enseignement Supérieur des Affaires*

ALLYN AND BACON, INC.

Boston · London · Sydney · Toronto

*Production Editor:* Margaret Pinette/David Dahlbacka
*Series Editor:* Richard Carle

**Library of Congress Cataloging in Publication Data**

Feiger, George.

   International Finance.

   Includes bibliographies and index.
   1. International Finance.   2. International
finance—Case studies.   I. Jacquillat, Bertrand,
1944–     joint author.   II. Title.
HG3881.F42     332'.042     80-17364
ISBN 0-205-07137- 6
ISBN (International Student Edition): 0-205-07602- 5

10 9 8 7 6 5 4 3 2 1 86 85 84 83 82 81
Printed in the United States of America.

# Contents

# Introduction: Structure and Suggested Use of the Book

## 0.1 THE AUDIENCE WE INTENDED TO ADDRESS

The label "international finance" can be applied to all international trans-actions involving the exchange of currencies, the provision of credit, and the transfer of ownership of assets. The environment of, and the mech-anism for, undertaking these transactions concern different types of or-ganizations and people. In the non-private sector, national governments have wanted to control international financial transactions and induce changes in them to fit their own goals. Both national governments and international organizations make substantial deposits in and substantial borrowings from the international capital markets. Politicians, political appointees, financial administrators, and professional economists all have a hand in these decisions. In the private sector both corporations and individuals make international financial transactions. Individuals travel and import on their own behalf, but most important, as controls on capital movements have been eased in the major market economies in recent decades, individuals have regained the opportunity to diversify their own asset portfolios internationally. The last era of such investment freedom was under the gold-exchange standard system in the quarter-century pre-ceding 1914. Non-financial corporations are involved in international fi-nancial transactions as an inseparable corollary of projecting their business across national borders. They must transact in, and report in, foreign currencies and they can choose to hold cash and to borrow and lend in various currencies. Financial corporations have the opportunity to form asset and liability portfolios in different currencies and are liable to the taxation and administrative conditions prevailing in the home coun-tries of their debtors and creditors. Large corporations employ profes-sional economists who are expert in the operation of the international monetary system. However, even in these companies (and certainly in small organizations and for individuals) the important decisions will be made by people who are not specialists in the international economy.

International finance has been intensively studied by academic econ-omists and there exists an enormous and sophisticated professional lit-erature on the subject. This literature is not fully accessible to people without at the very least an intensive undergraduate concentration in (technically-oriented) economics. On the other hand, the subject, because of its wide practical relevance, is always commented on in the business press and in books written by business figures, government administrators and politicians. Typically, in these courses the level of anecdotal evidence, *ad hominen* argument, simple repetition of the opinion of "experts" and institutional description is high, and the amount of analysis of the operation of the system as a whole is low. Our primary audience is not academic specialists in international monetary affairs. This book will be useful to economists *beginning* a specialization in that area, and to academics and government officials who wish a better understanding of the problems and opportunities the system offers to the private sector. In writing this book, it was our intention to provide an operationally useful analysis of the international financial system to people who make business decisions, and, secondarily, governmental policy decisions. Primarily, we have aimed to provide information of use to people who, individually or in corporations, will make private, profit-oriented business transactions. Within the major market economies, it is the latter group of people whose actions governments seek to control and modify, which explains the potential relevance of the book to government policy makers.

## 0.2   RELEVANT BACKGROUND KNOWLEDGE

The international monetary system is more complex than any single, component domestic monetary system. Exchange rate and balance of payments developments are the product of interaction between the events and circumstances in a number of national economies. International asset markets are connected by diverse arbitrage processes and speculations on real returns and exchange rate changes. International loans are harder to evaluate than otherwise similar domestic loans. This litany of obstacles is recited not to induce the reader to put down the book immediately, but rather to warn that one can't start from scratch—a good amount of background is needed. The financial sectors of the world economy are a superstructure built to facilitate trade in goods and services and in assets, which are claims on goods and services producible in the future. The economic component of human welfare derives from these underlying real transactions, not from transactions in financial claims per se. In general, events in the real economy are the most important influence on financial magnitudes like interest rates and stock prices. So to fully understand the financial system you need a good grasp of the economics of production and exchange, and of interest rates and inflation. To derive the maximum benefit from this book you should have under your belt the equivalent of a solid introductory course in macroeconomics and microeconomics. This is definitely not indispensable. We have taught most parts of the book in executive programs in banks, corporations, and summer schools to line managers and financial executives, with generally positive response. However in this field as in any other, the more you bring to the study of a subject the more benefit you derive from it.

At some places in the text, particularly in Chapters 9, 10, and 11, reference is made to a variety of statistical concepts that have become indispensable for the study of problems involving choices among risky alternatives. These concepts are means, variances, covariances, Taylor approximations, utility maximization, and stochastic calculus. A reader without interest in the techniques by which our results are derived will have no trouble following the text. For those who wish to pursue the subject in greater depth we recommend the following as good sources

A. Mood, F. Graybill, D. Boes, *Introduction to the Theory of Statistics*, Third Edition, McGraw-Hill, 1974.

J. Mossin, *Theory of Financial Markets*, Prentice-Hall, 1973.

D. Cox and H. Miller, *The Theory of Stochastic Processes*, Chapman and Hall, 1965.

## 0.3   THE STRUCTURE OF THE BOOK

The book divides naturally into two parts. The first consists of analysis of the international system of currency exchange and its implications. This culminates in our discussion of exchange-related gains and losses, hedging, and exposure to exchange risk. The second part explains the operation of the international capital markets, spanning the spectrum from short-term money markets through bond and equity markets and on to the problems of international bank lending. This section concludes with a discussion of international taxation regimes. The order in which these two themes are presented is not arbitrary, because all the analysis draws on the core material explaining the level and behavior of exchange rates presented in Chapters 5 and 6.

In terms of analytical difficulty, the hardest parts of the book are found in the exchange rate discussions in Chapters 5 and 6, and in the equity market and international bank lending analysis of Chapters 10 and 11. The exchange rate discussion is demanding not for reasons of technical complexity but because the subject matter itself is inherently complex. Exchange rates are the product of the interaction of many macroeconomic phenomena and it is here that a good background in economics will yield the greatest rewards. Chapters 10 and 11 use the sophisticated analytic methods now spreading among capital market specialists. We are talking about the so-called "capital asset pricing model," the famous "beta" coefficients of common stocks, and the entire philosophy and arsenal of statistical methods that created these ideas. The essential underpinning of

the new approaches to capital market analysis is simple. It is the reali-
zation that the statistical characteristics of a *portfolio* of risky assets or
attributes can be quite different from the statistical characteristics of each
portfolio component taken by itself. This is not mysterious—it is the basis
of the insurance industry. Nothing could be riskier than predicting the
year a person will die, but sell a few hundred thousand life insurance
policies and under "normal" conditions your cash flows will be extremely
predictable. The *portfolio* of life risks is much less risky than any one
policy. Why? Implicitly because all the risks are *uncorrelated*—no common force will cause many people to die simultaneously. That is what
we mean by "normal" conditions. In wartime, many of your policy holders
may die at once at random moments and you lose the benefit of averaging
over many people. The so-called "beta" coefficient measures the extent
to which gains and losses on a particular risky asset occur when gains
and losses occur on assets in general. It is thus a measure of how much
the asset in question contributes to diversifying away all the risk in an
asset portfolio. Intuitively we can ask what makes the default risk of a
bank's loan *portfolio* differ from the default risk on any one loan using
similar methods.[1]

    We now present a chapter-by-chapter summary of the contents of the
book.

**1. The Market for Foreign Exchange.**   In this chapter, the reader is
introduced to the terminology of exchange trading and its institutions. In
addition, we explain a number of arbitrage activities and discuss the
convertibility of currencies, particularly those of the so-called "socialist
bloc."

**2. The Evolution of the International Monetary System.**   We begin by
explaining the need for transactions balances in international business,
and the distinction between commodity money and paper money. Then
we examine the gold exchange standard of the pre-1914 era, monetary
chaos in the 1920s and 1930s, and the Bretton-Woods system of the
1945–1973 period. We also explain the principles of operation of the
International Monetary Fund and the Special Drawing Rights and draw
analogies to the European Monetary System which came into operation
in March of 1979. The chapter is unified by an explanation of events in
terms of the tension between the need for a universal money to facilitate
trade and capital flows and pressure by governments to maintain control
over their own monetary systems, for a variety of reasons.

---

[1] If this is the first time you have heard this story, we strongly urge you to bury your nose
in a good book on basic capital market analysis. We recommend W. Sharpe, *Investments*,
Prentice-Hall, 1978.

**3. Trade in Commodities.** The international monetary system is a superstructure created to facilitate the international exchange of goods and of claims to goods in the future (financial assets). International trade is the basis for specialization and the world-wide raising of aggregate real income through the operation of the principle of comparative advantage. We explain the gains from trade and the internal redistributions of income which can occur using the simplest Ricardian approach, the Heckscher-Ohlin theory and the product cycle hypothesis. We then explain the effect of tariffs, quotas, and subsidies as well as pitfalls in measuring these effects. Government manipulation of exchange rates has the same effects on the real economy as do tariff and subsidy programs.

**4. The Balance of Payments.** The first half of the chapter explains the purpose of balance of payments accounts and how they are constructed, using examples and a long exercise. The second half of the chapter discusses the interpretation of balance of payments statistics. We cover numerical accuracy, the meaning of partial balances (such as the balance of payments on current account), bilateral balances (such as the balance of payments between the United States and Japan) and the meaning of the different definitions of "deficit."

**5. Exchange Rate Behavior in the Long Run.** The exchange rate is the rate at which monies exchange, but people exchange monies because they wish to acquire foreign goods and assets. In the "long run" (the duration of which we explain) the exchange rate must adjust to offset international differences in the cost inflation of traded goods, because if this were not so then asymmetric trade flows would move the rate to such a level. Thus we need to understand the causes of differential cost inflation in the traded goods industries. The relationships we expound connect the prices of traded goods with the general price level and explain the interdependence between money supplies, real output growth, and inflation. We offer different reasons for monetary expansion in the post-1945 period. Finally we introduce empirical evidence on the exchange rate process and explain how to make purchasing power parity calculations.

**6. Near Term Exchange Rate Behavior.** Exchange rates make large oscillations around their long run or purchasing power parity values. We explain what is currently believed about the relationship of these exchange rate movements to short-term capital flows and to speculation. The covered interest arbitrage relationship is central. Next we discuss government exchange market intervention policies in terms of magnitude and motivation. Finally we present evidence on the forward exchange rates as forecasts of future spot rates. This chapter concludes our analysis of the workings of the exchange markets.

**7. Hedging and Exposure to Exchange Risk.** We begin with an extensive discussion of different accounting measurements of exchange-related gains and losses. *Real* gains and losses are, of course, gains and losses in cash flow or potentially realizable capital values, and we explain the economic circumstances under which the accounting rules will yield the correct gains and losses. We then examine the cost of hedging, and how to measure the extent of exposure to exchange risk, based on the connections between prices, exchange rates, and interest rates explained in Chapters 5 and 6. Finally, we consider the fundamental question: *should* a corporation seek to hedge itself against exchange-related gains and losses? In the best traditions of the Ivory Tower we present a number of arguments against such hedging, all implying that the corporation's owners will probably find it a more valuable component of their asset portfolios if it goes unhedged. For small companies the Dozier case provides some food for thought in favor of hedging.

**8. Offshore Financing I: The Eurocurrency Market.** The second part of the book examines international borrowing and lending from the viewpoint of corporate treasurers, international banks, and investors. This first segment discusses the "offshore" short- to medium-term credit markets. We explain how Eurocurrencies are created and what the effects are on the money supplies of the countries whose currencies are being used then describe the institutions of the market. We consider the attitudes of central banks to the offshore markets and compare banking practices and risk of collapse with the American commercial banking system. Finally we explain the methods of pricing loans and arbitrage connections with domestic capital markets.

**9. Offshore Financing II: The Eurobond Market.** In this chapter we look at the (substantially smaller) offshore bond market. World bond flotations are large but the "offshore" component is not because of the absence of large pools of uncontrolled long-term funds and large borrowers outside the influence of governments. We explain the currency preferences of bond buyers, and also the interesting fringe bonds—currency basket bonds and currency option bonds.

**10. Offshore Financing III: Equity Markets Outside the U.S.** This chapter explains how the major foreign equity markets operate and outlines their size and available financial instruments. The tools of modern capital market analysis are applied to examine the "efficiency" of the markets. Finally we demonstrate the stabilizing effects on wealth of an international asset portfolio.

**11. International Bank Lending.** The international bank must not only evaluate the riskiness of individual loans but must make an evaluation of the riskiness of its entire portfolio. We explain the ways in which banks currently make these evaluations. We then apply an entirely different approach to the evaluation of portfolio risk, based on modern capital market theory. This enables us to assess, on a statistical basis, the riskiness of loans to types of projects, loans to several projects in one country, and even loans to governments (to the extent that governmental default risk is determined by capacity to repay). The approach, while new, has been demonstrated to be computationally feasible and illuminating.

**12. *International Aspects of Taxation.*** Throughout the book we emphasize the importance of cash flow, actual and potential. However from the perspective of the corporation or investor only after-tax cash flow is relevant. In our discussion of accounting measurement of exchange-related gains and losses in Chapter 7, we emphasize tax deferral opportunities. In this chapter, we give a more unified approach to the issues of tax havens and tax deferrals. The whole discussion must be essentially illustrative because of the variety and complexity of tax laws. In the area of taxation, after one has a general picture of the available opportunities there is no substitute for a "creative lawyer."

## 0.4 CLASSROOM USE IN FULL AND PART COURSES

The book was constructed from the material used to teach a one-quarter elective course at Stanford, representing 20 classroom sessions of 1¾ hours or so. Generally one lecture is spent on the topic of each chapter with the remainder of the time given to discussion of cases and current events and one visitor per quarter. We have found it to be valuable to students to hear from someone who has had extensive exchange dealings, such as the treasurer of a corporation with international business. The text contains examples and quotations from the press, the most recent ones in our lecture notes. An instructor can easily replace these with up-to-the-minute items from sources like *The Wall Street Journal, Business Week, Fortune,* and the like. Arbitrage calculations shown in Chapter 1 should always be undertaken with contemporary numbers—sources are indicated in Chapter 1.

We have found that a student body with a business orientation prefers lecture material to be immediately relevant to current events. It has proven very easy to redirect the chapter material to respond to this preference, as we will show by two examples.

1. In Chapter 2 we discuss the origin, strengths and weaknesses of the fixed exchange rate system, the IMF and the SDR. The European Monetary System (EMS) with its associated unit of account the European Currency Unit (ECU), is basically the old par-value system implemented

on a west European rather than worldwide scale. The EMS was a topic of discussion through 1978 and was implemented in March of 1979. A lecture on the operation of the system of par values can be based on the EMS with historical parallels drawn to the Bretton-Woods system.

2. In the second part of 1978 and into 1979 the U.S. dollar was depreciating generally and there was a great deal of exchange market intervention to try to slow this decline. After the oil cartel raised its prices the dollar started to appreciate and the Bank of Japan, for instance, immediately began intervention operations to slow the decline of the yen against the dollar. All this was dramatic news and was used in a variety of ways. We chose to emphasize the impact of intervention operations on the capital markets as the central banks rapidly built up and ran down billions of dollars of short-term assets. The body of Chapter 4 contains an abstract discussion of the effects while an appendix contains two newspaper articles from *The Wall Street Journal* describing what was happening on U.S. short-term money markets. A lecture beginning with newspaper material of this type and then delving into the explanation has helped us to hold student interest because it exemplifies the practical worth of the theory.

The cases may be used in many ways. At Stanford students write a 2 to 3 page paper on each case before classroom discussion, and for a final project form small groups and analyze the creditworthiness of designated countries. The usual offering is a choice between lending to the government of a socialist country and to the government of a developing country. Most recently, Hungary and the Philippines were used. If you take a case situation seriously the information in the cases is inadequate, and it is necessary to spend a number of hours in a library and then more hours with a calculator. There are obvious benefits from this approach. First, the exercise becomes much more realistic and quite close to what would be expected in an actual job situation. Second, the practical problems of finding, evaluating, and interpreting information become apparent. Especially in the case of the creditworthiness evaluation, it becomes necessary to compare government statements about the economic situation with the implications of data one collects oneself. The need to consider domestic political stability and related social factors also serves to put the economic analysis in an overall perspective.

We have used the material to teach a number of short courses. On the basis of our experience we have created prototypical reading guides for four different types of audience.

*1. Background Information Course.*   This is a course for people in an international business who do not have direct international finance responsibilities but who need to have sympathy with the general problems facing the organization in this area.

- Chapter 1 for terminology but without lingering on the complex arbitrage questions. The discussion on convertibility should be emphasized.

- Chapter 2 in its entirety, followed by an explanation of the EMS or whatever joint floating arrangement will have replaced it in the EEC countries.

- Chapter 5 to establish the "purchasing power parity" concept. The connection between money supplies and price levels should remain at a more intuitive level and the detailed discussion of empirical testing should be omitted. An example of how to make back-of-the-envelope parity calculations is useful and is a basis for discussing the appropriateness of currently prevailing exchange rates.

- Chapter 4 on the balance of payments is best summarized after the material from Chapter 5 is understood. We emphasize the basis of construction of balance of payments accounts and then move on to interpretation.

The overall aim is to convey the exchange market structure at an intuitive level, so discussion of current international monetary events is more useful than a case requiring detailed calculation.

**2.  Corporate Treasurer/Bank Calling Officer.**   We view this as a course for people basically interested in economic exposure to exchange risk, and hedging. Because they are interested in choosing strategies some amount of calculation can reasonably be required.

- Chapter 1 putting particular emphasis on arbitrage calculations.

- Chapter 5 with less emphasis on monetary theory but a lot of emphasis on deviations from purchasing power parity and how to compute parities. Actual worked examples on an up-to-date basis are very useful here.

- Chapter 6 with clear exposition on the random character and unpredictability of short-term exchange rate movements and on the limits of government intervention policies. If time presses a detailed explanation of the motivations for and results of these interventions can be omitted.

- Chapter 7 ties all these things together and is the capstone of a course of this type.

- Chapter 8 may be used to provide a quick introduction to the offshore capital markets.

A couple of cases involving real calculation like *Dozier* and *Port Arthur Timber Company* should be used. Careful selection allows the lecture material to be covered in 3 to 4 hours, leaving a good 2 or more hours for the cases and examples in what we think would be the shortest useful course.

**3. Investment and Asset Managers.** We can divide this into a course for people interested in long-term foreign investment and those with more day-to-day concerns. We begin with a course for those with shorter horizons.

- Chapter 1, but without the discussion of convertibility.

- Chapter 5, emphasizing the effects of monetary policy on the domestic capital markets as well as on the exchange markets.

- Chapter 6, with emphasis on the domestic capital market effects of intervention activities. The last part of Chapter 4 has useful material for such a discussion.

- Chapters 8, 9 and 10 in their entirety.

People with long-range interests have to have some appreciation for the basic state of the world economy and the world monetary system. For the latter purpose Chapter 2 should be included, and for the former purpose Chapter 3, although without emphasis on the technical explanations associated with the Heckscher-Ohlin theory. In terms of case work, it is of great importance to provide examples of purchasing power parity calculations so that the participants can start to form trend exchange rate projections. After that, relevant application exercises depend on the composition of the group. For portfolio managers appropriate work might involve comparing purely domestic and internationally-diversified portfolios.

**4. International Bank Lending.** For a group like this we can presume very good basic knowledge. Thus we suggest Chapters 5, 6, and 11 for reading. The course should concentrate on actual examples of analysis of creditworthiness, such as that following Chapter 11. The instructor can supplement this with the extremely important political and social issues relevant in any actual lending situation.

## 0.5 USE IN SELF-INSTRUCTION

The sequence of chapters seems to us the best one for a person independently working through the subject. If the reader has a limited background in economics it will be advantageous to have at hand an introductory economics book.[2] Inevitably, a great part of the economics

---

[2] For example P. Samuelson, *Economics*, 10th edition, McGraw-Hill 1978. However there are many good introductory economics books.

book will have to be read. Other references are found in the various chapters. The cases are particularly useful for people teaching themselves and we urge readers to make a several-page long written analysis and recommendation for each case. Useful information sources will in general be found in footnotes in the chapter preceding each case. Almost always these sources will be available in large libraries, and certainly in any decent college library. A classroom practice that can usefully be carried over to self-teaching is explanation of current events. All major periodicals carrying business news frequently publish articles relating to international finance. With all such articles (and with all official statements by governments and central banks), the reader should ask himself the following questions.

1.  Have I understood *all* of the statements made?

2.  Are any of the statements mutually incompatible or logically contradictory?

3.  Are all of the arguments made in conformity to the basic economic principles outlined in the book?

4.  Are there alternative, equally sound interpretations of relevant facts than the ones made in the article? (In Chapter 4 in particular we discuss the multiple possible interpretations of exchange rate statistics.)

For people interested in sub-areas the short courses outlined in section 0.3 are guides to the relevant material. Once again, it is necessary to bring in outside relevant material and a skeptical attitude to what you read.

Finally, a good bibliographical source for further reading on international business matters is J. Tarleton, "Recommended Courses in International Business for Graduate Business Students," *Journal of Business,* October 1977.

## 0.6  ACKNOWLEDGMENTS

This book grew from a variety of sources. Part is based on notes and other materials assembled for courses in "international finance" taught at the Graduate School of Business at Stanford between 1976 and 1979. However, a large part of the contents is due to work with and questions from actual practitioners. Chapter 11, on international bank lending, summarizes a consulting project one of the authors undertook for a major commercial bank. Substantial parts of chapter 2, on the evolution of the international monetary system, were created in response to the questions and interests of participants in an ongoing executive education program at Hewlett Packard. The discussion of exposure to exchange risk in chapter 7 was materially sharpened by a variety of shrewd questions and comments offered in an executive education program at the Security Pacific National Bank. The pressure from bank and treasury personnel for an explanation of exactly how to do things prompted a lot of the detail in chapter 5, on the long-run evolution of exchange rates. In short, we have tried to put together a book which explains why and how things happen, in a manner accessible to people who want to put this information to practical use.

Colleagues at Stanford provided helpful input at many points. We are particularly grateful to Bill Sharpe and Margaret Feiger, and to the late Paul Cootner and Alex Robichek.

Finally, we express our homage to the nimble fingers and editorial sense of Jean Roberts, who prepared the manuscript, and our thanks to Richard Carle, of Allyn and Bacon. Business school professors see royalty negotiations as a forum for bringing all their theories to life, and Richard was kind enough to find this humorous.

G. F.

B. J.

# Chapter 1

# The Market for Foreign Exchange

## 1.1 INTRODUCTION

Currencies are traded against each other on markets, and as for any traded commodity, the prices of the currencies, or *rates of exchange*, are determined by demand for and supply of the currencies by potential and actual users. This chapter describes certain features of currency markets that are indispensable to study of their operations.

Our first concern is why people want to trade moneys, after which we describe some institutional features of exchange markets. Perhaps the single most important exchange market phenomenon is *arbitrage*, the attempt to get something for nothing, which ties together exchange quotations in different markets and has very strong implications for the ability of governments to manipulate exchange markets and domestic money markets. Indeed, the existence of significant apparent arbitrage opportunity is a sign that either exchange markets or international capital flows, or both are limited by some form of governmental regulation. An extreme case of governmental limitation is *nonconvertibility* of a currency and we will explain why such nonconvertibility is actually forced on governments in some situations.

## 1.2 NATIONAL CURRENCIES AND INTERNATIONAL CURRENCIES

For all practical purposes there are only national currencies.[1] Within any country, the national currency is used as a unit of account (that is, for bookkeeping purposes) and as a means of payment for domestic transactions. Sometimes a particular national currency will take on the role of a unit of account, and possibly even means of payment, for transactions

---

[1]Special Drawing Rights (SDRs) as units of account are discussed in Chapter 2 where SDRs and gold are analyzed from a general monetary system perspective.

1

outside its national borders or between two parties, both of whom are nonresidents. In recent times, this role of the *international currency* or *vehicle currency* was played by the British pound and the U.S. dollar. This phenomenon is not accidental. In any national or international context a commodity has effectively become a money if it is generally accepted in exchange. Why would a commodity be generally accepted in exchange? Because so many people use it for trading purposes. Thus the existence of a vehicle currency reflects domination of the volume of trade transactions by one national economy. As the world economic system evolves to have several powerful economies, one expects a decline in the importance of any single vehicle currency. One indication of evolution is the very rapid growth of the nondollar segments of the Eurocurrency markets, a phenomenon quantified in Chapter 8.[2]

The polar opposite situation to a vehicle currency is that of an inconvertible currency, which is effectively untraded on any exchange market. We will return to the inconvertible currencies after we have explained the trading system for the major currencies in which the bulk of all transactions takes place.

## 1.3   THE MECHANICS OF TRADE IN NATIONAL CURRENCIES

The key in understanding foreign exchange markets is the simple principle that foreign exchange transactions are derived from transactions in the markets for commodities and assets (the latter being themselves claims to future commodity purchasing power). The trade in currencies is necessary because people wish to trade the underlying commodities and assets.

### Demand and Supply

The justification for international trade is the increase in consumption that it can bring about compared with an autarkic situation; this is discussed in Chapter 3. But in a monetary world, a trade in national monies is virtually a prerequisite for a trade in goods or assets. To acquire a Mercedes Benz the U.S. importer first buys DM with dollars, and then sends the DM to Stuttgart to pay for this automobile. To acquire a share

---

[2]This discussion raises another point of great interest though perhaps of smaller immediate relevance. Should a small economy have an independent currency at all? As will be shown, the relevant consideration in evaluating currencies is purchasing power. A small country whose output is mainly exported and much of whose consumption is imported has no real domestic base for a currency. Those interested in pursuing this should see R. McKinnon, "Optimum Currency Areas," *American Economic Review*, 53 (September 1963), and K. Chrystal, "International Money and the Future of the SDR," *Essays in International Finance*, No. 128 (June 1978), Department of Economics, Princeton University.

of the common stock of Daimler Benz, the U.S. investor first buys DM and then purchases the stock on one of the six German stock exchanges.[3] There is an obvious general principle here: to every international purchase or sale of commodities or assets, there corresponds an international purchase of sale of currencies. The principle exceptions to this rule occur in trade with the socialist bloc countries with inconvertible currencies. Here a form of barter is often used, or else they deal only in hard currencies (that is, non–socialist bloc currencies).

The foregoing should also have illustrated another point: on the foreign exchange markets a party can never be a demander of one currency without simultaneously being a supplier of another. The U.S. resident purchasing a Mercedes Benz is simultaneously a supplier of dollars and a demander of DM, on the dollar/DM exchange market. Such a simultaneity occurs in all transactions, of course. If you want to buy a Whopper at Burger King you are both a demander of Whoppers and a supplier of dollars, while your smiling attendant is a supplier of Whoppers and a demander of dollars. You can say either that a Whopper costs 75 cents, or that a dollar costs 1⅓ Whoppers. A rate of exchange is a price also; it is the price of one currency in terms of another. It may not seem natural to say the price of a dollar is 1⅓ Whoppers. It is no more natural to say a dollar costs 2DM than it is to say a DM costs 50¢.

### Foreign Exchange Rates

An exchange rate is the rate at which one currency exchanges for another. How many exchange rates are there, then? If you said, "One between every pair of currencies," you've greatly underestimated things. Exchange transactions specify a date of delivery: you can trade exchange for delivery (and payment) at future dates as well as right now, the present. Exchange rates for (virtually) immediate delivery are called *spot rates*. Exchange rates for delivery and payment at specified future dates are called *forward rates*. A 90-day forward rate between the dollar and the DM gives the rate at which you can arrange a sure transaction between dollars and DM 90 days hence. This is commonplace practice for many raw materials and foods: pork bellies (bacon chunks!) are traded in the cash (spot) and futures markets. So are soybeans, silver, copper, orange juice, and many

---

[3]As will be discussed in Chapter 10, this is apparently not always the case. Most of the largest international companies are traded on foreign stock markets as well as on their national stock exchange. Thus a French investor can buy on the Paris Stock Exchange a share of IBM with French francs. However, to develop such a market French dealers in IBM have to buy IBM stock from U.S. brokers and exchange francs for dollars to accomplish these assets transactions. Therefore, although the French investor buys IBM with French francs, it is the intermediary who has to go on the foreign exchange market and for foreign exchange purposes, it is exactly as if the French investor had bought IBM directly.

other goods. The distinguishing characteristic of these forward or futures transactions is that payment is made only on delivery but the price is agreed on at the date the forward contract is sold. Such contracts offer obvious opportunities for speculation and for insuring the rate at which future cash flows can be exchanged, called hedging.

A spot or forward contract in foreign exchange is a financial instrument: along with other financial instruments it is quoted with a *bid-ask spread*. Dealers will quote the price at which they are buying from nondealers (the bid price) and the price at which they are selling to nondealers (the ask price). One anticipates with great confidence that the bid price will lie below the ask. The difference between bid and ask is called the spread. For example on Tuesday, February 28, 1978, the spot dollar quotations on French francs were:

| Bid | Ask | Spread |
|-----|-----|--------|
| .2094 | .2097 | .0003 |

In most cases it is a convention to quote the local currency price of one unit of the foreign currencies. Thus in our example one FF costs just under 21¢. In France the quote would be the reciprocal of this: one US$ would be quoted at a little under 5FF (4.77555 to be precise). The British adhere to another convention: they state the number of units of other currencies that one pound sterling will buy. This is called *indirect* quotation while the more common method is *direct* quotation. Clearly, the British indirect quotations are just the other countries' direct quotations. Finally, for currencies that habitually move closely together (such as the CAN$ and the US$) rates may be quoted in terms of discounts or premia even for spot transactions. Thus if you are told in New York that the CAN$ bid is at a 15% discount, you know the bid price of a CAN$ spot is US$ 0.85.

As a final comment on the quotation of exchange rates, consider the terms *appreciation* and *depreciation*. The dollar appreciates against the DM if it becomes cheaper in dollar terms to buy one DM or, equivalently, if you receive more DM in exchange for one dollar. The dollar depreciates against the DM if it becomes more expensive in dollar terms to buy one DM or, equivalently, if you receive less DM in exchange for one dollar. The two ways of stating these definitions correspond, of course, to the direct and indirect methods of exchange rate quotation.

### Triangular Arbitrage

Obviously there should be virtually exact correspondence between the bid and ask rates quoted on a given currency exchange in different places.

Otherwise *arbitrage* would take place. Arbitrage is the activity of profit making from discrepancies between price quotations on identical items. The rule for arbitrage is very simple—buy in the cheap place and sell in the dear. For example, suppose one observed the following quotations for spot transactions:

|  | Bid | Ask |
|---|---|---|
| FF (New York) | .2100 | .2103 |
| $ (Paris) | 5.000 | 5.003 |

One would take $1 to Paris, obtain FF 5.000, exchange them in New York for $1.05, take them to Paris . . . The taking is done by cable, and so is virtually costless; hence a flood of funds would occur, raising the Paris bid on dollars relative to the New York bid on FF.

This arbitrage also takes place in another form. There's more than one way to obtain US$ with FF. You can take the FF and buy dollars, or you can take the FF and buy, say, pounds sterling, and with these pounds buy dollars. This is the roundabout or triangular route, and we had better find that the exchange rate between US$ and FF is the same by either method. If not, traders would be falling all over themselves trying to buy via the cheap route and sell via the expensive route. This activity is known as triangular arbitrage for obvious reasons. The exchange rates computed in the roundabout fashion are known as *cross rates*.

The activity of triangular arbitrage ensures certain things will be true. One, useful and self-evident, is that one can compute exchange rates by computing cross rates. For example on February 28, 1978, the following spot bid quotations were available on the NY interbank market:

$$FF \qquad \$ \ .2104$$
$$\pounds \qquad \$1.9554$$

We can infer the FF bid price of £1 as follows:

$$FF \text{ per } \pounds = \frac{FF \text{ per } \$}{\pounds \text{ per } \$}$$

$$= \frac{1/.2104}{1/1.9554} = 9.2937$$

A second consequence is as straightforward, but less palatable for intervention-minded government officials. Suppose the government of Canada, say, enters the exchange market along with private parties in order to peg the CAN$ at some desired price against the US$. It does this by buying CAN$ with its reserves of US$ when the CAN$ depreciates from the desired peg, and buying US$ with CAN$ (which it prints) when the CAN$ appreciates from the desired peg. Though this seems to be intervention only in the US$/CAN$ market, the Canadian government will find itself having to peg *all* exchange rates against the CAN$, by its US$ transactions.

To see this, consider the following situation where numbers have been rounded for convenience.

**Preintervention Situation (Markets in equilibrium)**

| CAN$ price of | US$ | DM | £ |
|---|---|---|---|
| | 1.00 | .50 | 2.00 |

Suppose the Canadian government wants to depreciate the CAN$ against the US$ to, say 1.20. This means that the private market will have excess demand for CAN$ in terms of US$. The Canadian government will supply these CAN$.

**Postintervention, prearbitrage**

| CAN$ price of | US$ | DM | £ |
|---|---|---|---|
| | 1.20 | .50 | 2.00 |

In the preintervention situation we can read from the crossrates that 1DM costs US$ .50. This will still be true after the intervention. Thus traders can:

1.   trade CAN$ for DM paying CAN$ .50 per DM.

2.   trade DM for US$ at a cost of 2.00 DM per US$, then obtain CAN$ 1.20 per US$ or, CAN$ .60 per DM.

The result will be a flood of conversions from CAN$ to DM by route 1, and the reverse flow by route 2, which goes through the CAN$/US$ market. Since the Canadian government is pegging the latter rate the arbitrage flow will not alter it. Instead the route 1 outflow will cause the CAN$ to depreciate against the DM until a DM costs CAN$ .60.

If the markets were in equilibrium before, at this rate there will be excess demand for CAN$ in the CAN$/DM market. However, as soon as the CAN$ starts to appreciate there will be an arbitrage flow. Thus, the Canadian government will be supplying the excess demand for CAN$ on the CAN$/DM market through the triangular arbitrage mechanism, route

2. The same argument can be made for the CAN$/£ market, the CAN$/FF market, and so on. Triangular arbitrage converts a peg in any one market into a peg in all markets.

### Trading in Forward Exchange

Quotations in one forward market are made in two different ways. As with the spot market the quotation can be made in terms of the amount of the currency necessary to buy and sell a unit of local currency. This is called the *outright rate;* an alternative way is to quote the forward rate in terms of points of discount or premium from the spot rate. Such a quote is called the *swap rate.* By definition the outright rate is the spot rate adjusted by the swap rate.

A foreign currency is said to sell at a *forward discount* when the forward price of the foreign currency is lower than its spot price (this definition assumes a direct quote). Conversely, a foreign currency is said to sell at a *forward premium* when the forward price of the foreign currency is higher than its spot price. For example, the 30–90–180 day forward prices on the currency futures market on February 28, 1978, and the spot price on the same day for the French franc and the DM are indicated on Table 1.1. (Note that the rates indicated are an average of the bid and ask quotations.)

**Table 1.1** *Spot and Forward Rates and Quotations.*

|  | FF outright rate | swap rate | 1 DM outright rate | swap rate |
|---|---|---|---|---|
| Spot price | .2103 | — | .4970 | — |
| 30-day futures | .2093 | − 10 | .4987 | + 17 |
| 90-day futures | .2073 | − 30 | .5024 | + 54 |
| 180-day futures | .2054 | − 49 | .5084 | + 114 |

The French franc was selling at a discount vis-a-vis the U.S. dollar while the Deutsche mark was selling at a premium. That is, a unit of French francs buys more dollars for immediate delivery than for any future delivery. The situation of the DM is the exact opposite. The quotes are outright while the equivalent swap rates are given in the second and fourth columns. To find the outright rates when the forward rates are given as swap rates (points of premium or discount) the points are added to (subtracted from) the spot when the forward is at a premium (discount).

For reasons that will be clear below, it is convenient to express the discount or premium of a forward rate in percentage terms. This is computed with the following formula:

$$\text{forward premium (discount)} = \frac{\text{forward rate} - \text{spot rate}}{\text{spot rate}}$$
$$\times \frac{12 \text{ months}}{\text{number months forward}}$$

Thus we can enter the discounts and premiums for the French franc and the Deutsche mark for each future delivery from Table 1.1. They are shown on Table 1.2.

**Table 1.2**   *Forward Discount or Premium in %
(FF/$ and DM/$ February 28, 1978 Discounts
are in parentheses.;*

|              | FF/$   | DM/$ |
|--------------|--------|------|
| 30-day futures  | (5.71) | 4.10 |
| 90-day futures  | (5.71) | 4.35 |
| 180-day futures | (4.66) | 4.59 |

As we have indicated previously, dealer's quotes include a bid and an ask price. Dealer's quotes on the French franc as of February 28, 1978, for example, are shown in Table 1.3.

**Table 1.3**   *Bid and Ask by Maturity.*

| Maturity | Bid   | Ask   |
|----------|-------|-------|
| Spot     | .2094 | .2097 |
| 1-month  | .2097 | .2101 |
| 3-month  | .2080 | .2085 |
| 6-month  | .2070 | .2077 |

This dealer might give the quotes indicated on Table 1.3 for the spot and the one-, three-, and six-month rates in the following terms: .2094/7, 3/4, 14/12, 24/20.

The basic principles needed to understand these shorthand quotations are:

- The pair of numbers refers to the bid and ask prices.

- Bid is always below ask.

- The later numbers, i.e., 3/4, 14/12, and 24/20, refer to the forward rate in terms of deviations from the spot rate.

- There is a convention that when the first number (the 3 in 3/4) is below the second, the forward rate is at a premium to the spot rate. Conversely when the first number is above the second (as in 14/12), the figures represent forward currency at a discount.

## 1.4 MARKETS AND MARKET PARTICIPANTS

Foreign exchange markets are generally located in the major financial centers. New York is the major foreign exchange market in the U.S. and the world. For foreign exchange, there is no specific trading location as there is for securities or commodities. Participants simply arrange transactions over the telephones or through telex. The currencies and the extent of participation of each currency in this market depend on trade flows and international investment.

Of the more than 150 member countries of the International Monetary Fund, only a few have established relatively free trade patterns and portfolio investment flows and have full convertibility of their currencies for all transactions. As the foreign exchange markets deal primarily with convertible currencies, the bulk of the volume is made with a few currencies. Since important foreign exchange trading centers are located all over the world, the market never closes.

### Forward Exchange Contracting

A forward or futures contract for any commodity or currency whatsoever has the following components: a quantity of commodity to be delivered, a date of delivery, a place of delivery, and a price agreed upon when the contract is sold. The buyer of a forward exchange contract is obligated to take delivery under the terms of the contract. The seller of a forward exchange contract is obligated to make delivery under the terms of the contract. Thus net buyers are net long and net sellers are net short.

There is a difference between a forward transaction and a futures transaction. The difference is not one of functional content but rather of the institutional arrangements for carrying out the deal.

Any deal that any two persons strike up for delivery of any commodity at some future date, that has the characteristics we have just mentioned, is a forward deal. In such a deal, the parties are free to make any specifications they like. For example, they may make a deal over frozen sheeps' brains packed six to a cardboard box marked "not fit for human consumption," to be delivered at the post office in Yuma, Arizona, on May 1 this year at 4:00 P.M., or you may buy kina 189,225 for delivery in Port Moresby in 29 hours. The parties to a forward transaction must make whatever arrangements they deem adequate to guarantee performance of the obligation. For example, hardly any large U.S. banks will permit individuals not well known to them to take substantial foreign exchange market positions for speculative purposes.

By contrast, a futures market is an *organized exchange market* in which:

- only standardized commodities are traded;

- there is a clearing house that legally takes the opposite side of all transactions, and thus guarantees performance to the holders of contracts even in the event of default by the other party;

- there are formal *margin requirements* to guarantee the performance of the traders; and

- there is daily settlement and payment of gains and losses on all accounts.

The International Monetary Market is the only U.S. currency futures market. It is virtually the only place for small-scale trading. As of February 1979, it traded only six currencies and only a few contracts in each currency as indicated in Table 1.4.

Commercial transactions usually require more variety of contracts than this market provides, and virtually all financial deals of any great magnitude originated by commercial transaction go through the interbank market. The IMM is principally a market for speculation. However, there is arbitrage between the interbank market and the IMM, so that there are no discrepancies between rates which permit profitable trading.[4]

---

[4]That is not exactly the same thing as saying that there are no discrepancies. Futures markets have established limits on daily price movements. Once the price moves to the limit, trading stops for the day. This gives brokers time to call for more margin from their clients. Each exchange will, of course, relax the limit as pressure is maintained. On the IMM the limit is progressively raised over four days and abandoned on the fifth. (Specifically, the normal limit stays in place for two consecutive days. If on the third day a currency once again moves the limit, the limit is raised to 150% of normal. If on the next day the currency hits the 150% limit again the limit goes to 200% of normal. On the fifth day there is no limit.) This allows an equilibrium to be reached and the limit is then applied again. Hence as long as the futures price is up against a limit it can differ from the equivalent interbank forward price. However, precisely because the futures price is at a limit, no trade, and thus no arbitrage, can take place. Another consequence of the existence of limits to daily futures price movements is the possibility of not being able to open or close positions when one desires. Once the price moves by the limit, the market is closed for the day, and it may close you in also.

**Table 1.4**  *IMM Futures Quotations on Thursday, March 15, 1979. Open Interest Reflects Previous Trading Day.*

|  | Open | High | Low | Settle | Change | Lifetime High | Lifetime Low | Open Interest |
|---|---|---|---|---|---|---|---|---|
| | | | BRITISH POUND (IMM)—25,000 pounds; $ per pound | | | | | |
| Mar | 2.0380 | 2.0385 | 2.0335 | 2.0385 | −.0005 | 2.1090 | 1.7530 | 391 |
| June | 2.0300 | 2.0340 | 2.0275 | 2.0310 | −.0005 | 2.0880 | 1.7500 | 2,747 |
| Sept | 2.0270 | 2.0320 | 2.0255 | 2.0320 | +.0010 | 2.1800 | 1.8800 | 372 |
| Dec | 2.0225 | 2.0260 | 2.0220 | 2.0255 | −.0025 | 2.0410 | 1.9310 | 95 |
| Mar80 | .......... | .......... | ......... | 2.0230 | ........... | 2.0300 | 2.0100 | 3 |

Est vol 559; vol Wed 1,314; open int 3,608, −658.

| | | | CANADIAN DOLLAR (IMM)—100,000 dirs.; $ per Can$ | | | | | |
| Mar | .8514 | .8527 | .8509 | .8512 | −.0011 | .9030 | .8305 | 886 |
| June | .8516 | .8531 | .8503 | .8509 | −.0021 | .8765 | .8301 | 4,914 |
| Sept | .8533 | 8543 | .8518 | .8525 | −.0017 | .8775 | .8308 | 1,137 |
| Dec | .8545 | .8552 | .8531 | .8531 | −.0016 | .8570 | .8295 | 256 |
| Mar | ......... | ......... | ........ | .8555 | ........... | .8555 | .8430 | 23 |

East vol 2,052; vol Wed 2,103; open int 7,216, −21.

| | | | JAPANESE YEN (IMM) 12.5 million yen; cents per yen | | | | | |
| Mar | .4844 | .4844 | .4828 | .4830 | +.0005 | .5850 | .4485 | 404 |
| June | .4902 | .4912 | .4888 | .4902 | +.0012 | .5971 | .4860 | 3,594 |
| Sept | .4980 | .4980 | .4960 | .4980 | +.0025 | .6060 | .4935 | 240 |
| Dec | .5050 | .5050 | .5050 | .5050 | +.0005 | .6180 | .5045 | 18 |

Est vol 1,293; vol Wed 2,477; open int 4,256, −930.

| | | | SWISS FRANC (IMM)—125,000 francs-$ per franc | | | | | |
| Mar | .5967 | .5967 | .5949 | .5955 | −.0011 | .7113 | .4625 | 804 |
| June | .6128 | .6132 | .6107 | .6123 | +.0003 | .7286 | .5345 | 2,304 |
| Sept | .6275 | .6278 | .6255 | .6269 | +.0005 | .7460 | .4910 | 768 |
| Dec | .6405 | .6412 | .6395 | .6407 | +.0008 | .7610 | .6330 | 384 |
| Mar80 | .6522 | .6522 | .6520 | .6520 | +.0012 | .6968 | .6072 | 215 |

Est vol 739; vol Wed 685; open int 4,475, −174.

| | | | WEST GERMAN MARK—125,000 marks; $ per mark | | | | | |
| Mar | .5383 | .5384 | .5364 | .5373 | −.0011 | .5993 | .4687 | 816 |
| June | .5473 | .5475 | .5454 | .5462 | −.0009 | .6095 | .4930 | 2,822 |
| Sept | .5556 | .5556 | .5540 | .5541 | −.0014 | .6215 | .5420 | 430 |
| Dec | .5620 | .5620 | .5612 | .5620 | −.0005 | .6380 | .5522 | 185 |
| Mar80 | .5660 | .5675 | .5660 | .5675 | −.0025 | .5990 | .5660 | 22 |

Est vol 860; vol Wed 854; open int 4,275, −195.

### Description of Market Trading

The bulk of exchange trading involves spot exchange. According to the Federal Reserve Bank of New York:[5]

> In April, 1977, 55 percent of all exchange trading was in spot contracts, generally for delivery in two days. Another 40 percent of the total turnover was in swap contracts in which a bank simultaneously buys or sells a currency for one maturity and sells or buys the equivalent amount for a later date. The remaining 5 percent of total turnover was in outright forward contracts which are bought or sold for future delivery.

The ordinary spot contract is actually for delivery in two days. This is to allow for time differences between locations and for processing of documents. It is a convention that if the delivery day is a nonbusiness day in one of the home countries of the currencies involved in the two transactions, delivery takes place on the next business day. For instance a dollar/Swiss franc spot trade made on a Monday would be cleared only on Thursday if Wednesday were a public holiday in either Switzerland or the United States. Immediate delivery is possible but it will not take place at the quoted spot rate. Since one party pays, and the other receives, currency two days in advance, the price is adjusted to reflect the difference in the two countries' interest rates. For example consider a spot trade between U.S. dollars and Swiss francs, which is cleared immediately. The trader surrendering dollars foregoes two days yield on dollars and earns two days yield on Swiss francs. The trader surrendering Swiss francs foregoes two days yield on Swiss francs and earns two days yield on dollars. As section 1.5 explains, to avoid the existence of profits on covered interest arbitrage, the immediate spot will be priced in relation to the spot rate and two-day interest rates so that an interest differential favoring the United States will cause the immediate spot rate to be below the spot rate, and a differential favoring Switzerland will cause the immediate spot rate to be above the spot rate.

The swap rate shown in Table 1.1 gives the terms under which banks can undertake swap transactions. Approximately 70% of the swap contracts involve swapping currencies for one week or less. This provides a source of overnight money analogous to the federal funds market. Banks can exchange their inventory of exchange reserves for much-needed home currency funds to meet liquidity needs or other constraints. The Federal Reserve Bank of New York can also provide some idea of the composition of exchange trading in the United States in April, 1977. The total turnover was $106.4 billion for the 44 financial institutions surveyed. Table 1.5 breaks this trade up by currency maturity and, for spot, whether done through brokers or direct. Large commercial banks make the exchange

---

[5]Federal Reserve Bank of New York, Press Release No. 1202, Tuesday, July 12, 1977.

market, dealing with outside customers on a retail level and with each other at the wholesale level. Transactions between banks in this country are performed through a broker to preserve anonymity.[6] There are about eleven of these brokers. When dealing with foreign banks and industries, banks usually deal directly with each other without going through a broker.

All the brokers[7] belong to the brokers association and the Forex Association (of foreign exchange traders). Brokers cannot join Forex unless they are members of the brokers association. The brokers generally charge the same rates (the minimum commissions they are allowed to charge) and compete on service. The minimum commissions are set in the manner characteristic of bilateral monopoly. The brokers association negotiates with representatives of the banks that have agreed to deal through the brokers. The minimum commissions are a linear function of volume. The charges are shown in Table 1.5.

Table 1.6 shows interbank trade to be 92% of the spot market. In part this reflects double counting in the table: a bank which sells forward exchange to a customer may cover itself by buying forward on the inter-

**Table 1.5**  *Commission Rates by Currency, 1977.*

| Currency | (a) Spot Price | (b) Commission per Unit of Foreign Currency | Commission per $1 million [(1 million a) × b] |
|---|---|---|---|
| German mark | $ .4966 | $.0000125 | $ 25.17 |
| pound sterling | $1.9415 | $.0001 | $ 51.51 |
| Swiss franc | $ .5435 | $.0000125 | $ 23.00 |
| Canadian dollar | $ .8941 | $.00005 | $ 55.92 |
| French franc | $ .2112 | $.0000125 | $ 59.19 |
| Netherlands guilder | $ .4648 | $.0000125 | $ 26.89 |
| Belgian franc | $ .031940 | $.000002 | $ 62.62 |
| Japanese yen | $ .004200 | $.000000125 | $ 28.76 |
| Italian lira | $ .001176 | $.000000125 | $106.29 |
| Swedish krona | $ .2184 | $.0000125 | $ 57.23 |
| Norwegian krone | $ .1895 | $.0000125 | $ 65.96 |
| Danish krone | $ .1800 | $.0000125 | $ 69.44 |

*Source:* Laurie S. Goodman, "Equilibrium of Bank Exchange Trading," unpublished Ph.D. dissertation, Stanford University, 1978.)

---

[6]A small number of U.S. banks do not use the broker system. They call other dealing banks directly, and other dealing banks may reciprocate. If the transaction involves either odd-date transaction or exotic currencies, banks that normally trade through brokers may call each other directly.

[7]We wish to thank Laurie Goodman for information on the brokerage function.

bank market and then liquidating and buying spot two days before delivery to the customer. If both banks that engaged in these trades were in the sample of 44 institutions, all the transactions were counted twice. In part, it represents the importance of arbitrage, as emphasized later in the chapter.

Each bank has a net short or long position in each of the currencies in which it deals. Banks hold balances of spot and forward currency as inventories for their market-making use. However, they also speculate on exchange rate movements and make changes in their net position in anticipation of gains. U.S. banks take relatively small speculative positions, usually within the trading day. European banks are willing to hold very large open speculative positions. As is the case with any market-maker in financial instruments, the position in any currency is altered by adjusting the bid-ask spread quoted to potential traders. To build up inventory the bid is raised (and possibly the ask also). To run it down the bid is lowered and the ask is lowered.

Another class of participants in the foreign exchange market is constituted by the Central Banks. Although the international monetary system is now operated with a system of flexible exchange rates, where Central Banks are not supposed to intervene in the foreign exchange market, they still do intervene to maintain the spot rates of their currencies and their domestic interest rates within a desired range and to smooth fluctuations within that range. The purpose, effect, and extent of success of such government intervention are analyzed in greater detail in Chapter 6.

### Why do the Markets Exist?

The reasons for spot transactions in the foreign exchange market presented in the first part of this chapter, are clear: they represent the counterpart of a trade in commodities or assets.

In this section, we address the question: why do forward contracts exist? There are two reasons: speculation and hedging. Everybody can now speculate on future spot exchange rates using futures contracts on the IMM.

For example, on April 14, 1978, the May 1978 British pound contract closed at $1.8685. The delivery day is the third Wednesday of May, in this case, May 17, 1978. By elaborate calculations, a cunning speculator concluded that on May 17, 1978, the pound will be only $1.76. What should he have done? He should have sold pound contracts. Each one he sold obligated him to deliver on the IMM £25000 for which he received $1.8685 per pound. If he were right, he could have bought the pounds with which to make delivery at the then prevailing spot price of $1.76/£ making a profit of 25,000 (1.8685 − 1.76) = $2712.50 per contract less about a $65 commission.

**Table 1.6**  Foreign Exchange Turnover for 44 U.S. Banking Institutions—April, 1977 (in millions of dollars equivalent).

| | Spot | | | | | Outright Forwards | Swaps | | | Grand Total |
| | Interbank | | | | | | | | | |
| | Through U.S. Brokers | Other | Total | Other | Total | Total | Short* Dated | Other | Total | |
|---|---|---|---|---|---|---|---|---|---|---|
| German mark DM | 7,777.4 | 10,969.1 | 18,746.5 | 833.6 | 19,580.1 | 797.4 | 6,509.7 | 2,155.7 | 8,665.4 | 29,042.9 |
| Pound sterling £ | 2,420.0 | 3,238.1 | 5,658.1 | 820.6 | 6,478.7 | 1,856.9 | 5,730.2 | 4,032.5 | 9,762.7 | 18,098.3 |
| Swiss Franc SF | 4,039.2 | 5,039.1 | 9,078.3 | 340.1 | 9,418.4 | 463.3 | 3,374.5 | 1,387.6 | 4,762.1 | 14,643.8 |
| Can. dollar Can$ | 3,963.6 | 6,345.4 | 10,309.0 | 1,222.8 | 11,531.8 | 1,123.2 | 5,171.8 | 2,564.1 | 7,735.9 | 20,390.9 |
| French franc FF | 1,206.8 | 1,431.8 | 2,638.6 | 173.0 | 2,811.6 | 214.8 | 2,630.4 | 994.7 | 3,625.1 | 6,651.5 |
| Neth. guilder NG | 1,532.2 | 1,636.0 | 3,168.2 | 68.2 | 3,236.4 | 249.9 | 2,132.3 | 425.8 | 2,558.1 | 6,044.4 |
| Belgian franc BF | 124.1 | 252.8 | 376.9 | 95.5 | 472.4 | 148.7 | 809.0 | 180.6 | 989.6 | 1,610.7 |
| Japanese yen Yen | 1,556.9 | 1,276.2 | 2,833.1 | 224.2 | 3,057.3 | 336.8 | 1,587.5 | 669.2 | 2,256.7 | 5,650.8 |
| Italian lira Lit | 151.5 | 211.6 | 363.1 | 103.8 | 466.9 | 142.3 | 459.2 | 147.1 | 606.3 | 1,215.5 |
| All Other | 294.9 | 550.8 | 845.7 | 803.5 | 1,649.2 | 254.6 | 917.1 | 230.5 | 1,147.6 | 3,051.4 |
| Total | 23,066.0 | 30,950.9 | 54,017.5 | 4,685.3 | 58,702.8 | 5,587.9 | 29,321.7 | 12,737.8 | 42,059.5 | 106,350.2 |

*One week or less.

Source: Federal Reserve Bank of New York, Press Release No. 1202, Tuesday, July 12, 1977.

However, hedging rather than simple speculation provides the bread and butter activity for the forward exchange markets.

The simplest type of hedging transaction is of the following type. Suppose a U.S. importer has to make some payments in French francs at some future date because she has imported some item from France and has agreed to pay the French exporter in francs. The dollar cost of these payments is clearly going to vary with the exchange rate between the French franc and the dollar at the payment date. The U.S. importer can substitute a sure cost for this risky cost by buying a FF future contract (or a forward contract through a commercial bank) in the amount and maturing on the dates at which she must make her FF payments. Of course the French exporter, potentially owning a certain amount of dollars, might make the opposite transaction and be on the other side of the market.

Fundamentally, all hedging transactions are speculative in that our U.S. importer of the above example would not hedge if she felt strongly the franc would depreciate against the dollar. Her problem is that she cannot opt out of the foreign exchange business without opting out of her basic business as well. Therefore she will always want access to a forward market in order to adjust her net foreign exchange position resulting from her basic business to that position considered best in the light of her anticipation of the future course of exchange rates. World trade provides the basic volume of forward exchange business, although in the last years of the fixed exchange rate system, there were several currency crises in which straightforward speculation was, briefly, an important component of volume.

## 1.5   ARBITRAGE EQUILIBRIUM IN THE FOREIGN EXCHANGE MARKET

In our simple hedging example, the U.S. importer used a forward contract to guarantee a future exchange rate of the US$ against the FF. There is another way of obtaining French francs at a sure rate at a specific future date.

Suppose another U.S. importer wanted on March 1 to obtain 1 million French francs on June 1, 1978. The option we have examined involves buying a 90-day future contract for 1 million FF. If the forward rate is $.2090, the forward contract will cost him $209,000. If the three-month Euro-French interest rate is 11.98%, to have 1 million FF in three months, he would have to deposit today:

$$\frac{1M}{1 + \dfrac{.1198}{4}} = 970,921 \text{ French francs}$$

The $/FF spot rate on March 1 was $.2113 per franc. So, to obtain 970,921 francs today, the U.S. importer would need $205,156.

So, which route is better? An importer who uses the forward method pays only after three months, whereas with the spot/credit route, one has to pay now. If we discount back $209,000 to its present value, using the eurodollar CD rate for 90 days which was 7.5%, we obtain:

$$\frac{209000}{1 + \dfrac{.075}{4}} = 205,153 \text{ dollars}$$

This numerical example illustrates a consequence of *covered interest arbitrage*: there is no secret bargain waiting out there, or in more graphic terms, there's no free lunch. As was the case in our discussion of triangular arbitrage, two different methods of attaining the same goal cannot have different costs, or people would buy the cheap way and sell the dear way.

Covered interest arbitrage may be summarized by the following steps of the typical arbitrage transaction described above:

1. Borrow Eurodollars for 90 days such that one has to repay $1 after 90 days. If the Eurodollar interest rate is 7.50% one can borrow

$$\frac{1}{1 + \dfrac{.075}{4}} = \$0.9816$$

2. Convert the US$ spot into French francs at .2113/FF:

$$\frac{.9816}{.2113} = \text{FF } 4.6455$$

3. Lend for 90 days via a eurofranc commercial deposit at an annual rate of 11.98%. This yields FF 4.7846 francs after 90 days:

$$\left(1 + \frac{.1198}{4}\right) \times 4.6242 = 4.7846 \text{ francs}$$

4. Sell forward the FF 4.7846 you will have after 90 days, to give a guaranteed number of dollars. The aim, of course, is to obtain more dollars than you started with. Here, unfortunately, one would obtain

$$\$4.7846 \times .2090 = \$0.999988$$

Interest arbitrage involves borrowing at one interest rate and lending the borrowed funds at a higher rate. Doing this between currencies is not arbitrage because it involves risk. If I borrow US$ for 90 days at 7.50% and lend in FF at 11.98%, I will make 4.48% profit (on an annualized basis) only if the spot exchange rate does not alter. I converted my US$

to FF initially, and after 90 days I must repatriate my FF principal and interest. To make this activity an arbitrage, the exchange risk must be eliminated, as is done in Step 4 above, by selling forward the FF principal plus interest.

Since the forward can be at a premium or discount, there are two distinct sources of gain or loss in such a transaction:

- The interest differential. In the example above, it is a positive 4.48% (annualized) if we shift funds from eurodollars to EuroFF. It would be negative 4.48% if we moved funds in the other direction.

- The premium or discount on the forward. In our example we are selling forward 90-day FF, which are at an annualized discount of

$$\frac{.2090 - .2113}{.2113} \times \frac{365}{90} = -4.45\%$$

Speaking roughly, to make money on covered interest arbitrage one moves funds in whichever direction gives positive profit from the sum of these two effects. Thus, one might borrow in the high interest rate currency and lend in the low interest rate currency, if the latter were at a sufficient forward premium.

Our interest differential and premium did not balance exactly, although our calculations showed there to be no profit in this arbitrage. The reason is the imprecision of the comparison—steps one through four of the arbitrage do not simply add the interest differential and the forward premium or discount. Let's do this in more general terms, and consider a $T$-day arbitrage (so far we have used $T = 90$ in our example). Let

$r_T^{US}$ = $T$-day Eurodollar rate[8]

$r_T^{FF}$ = $T$-day EuroFF rate

$F_T$ = dollar cost of $T$-day forward FF

$S$ = dollar cost of spot FF

Then we can go through our four arbitrage steps again.

1.   Borrow $\$1/(1 + r_T^{US})$ for $T$ days, creating a repayment obligation of \$1. Thus, we are going to construct this transaction to give the return on an initial input of $\$1/(1 + r_T^{US})$.

2.   Convert this spot, obtaining FF$\dfrac{1}{S(1 + r_T^{US})}$

---

[8]An annualized interest rate must be reconverted to a $T$-day basis. The correct formula for compound interest is $r_T = (1 + r)^{T/365} - 1$, i.e., $(1 + r_T)^{365/T} = (1 + r)$ where $r$ denotes the annualized interest rate. At various places we have used the approximation $r_T = r \times T/365$.

3.  Lend at $r_T^{FF}$ for $T$ days, to have accruing at the end of that time

$$FF \frac{1 + r_T^{FF}}{S(1 + r_T^{US})}$$

4.  Sell forward all the FF which will accrue, so you will receive, after $T$ days

$$\$\frac{F_T}{S} \times \frac{1 + r_T^{FF}}{1 + r_T^{US}}$$

The net profit is the outcome of step 4 less the $1 owed, or

$$\text{net profit (\$)} = \frac{F_T}{S} \times \frac{1 + r_T^{FF}}{1 + r_T^{US}} - 1$$

We can rearrange this simply to yield

$$\text{net profit (\$)} = \left(\frac{1}{1 + r_T^{US}}\right) \times \left[\left(\frac{F_T - S}{S}\right) + \left(\frac{F_T}{S}r_T^{FF} - r_T^{US}\right)\right]$$

That is, the profit for $1/(1 + r_T^{US})$ initial dollars is equal to the sum of the forward premium or discount and a slightly adjusted interest differential. In terms of the example we have been using, and more accurately

$$1 + r_{90}^{US} = (1.075)^{90/365} = 1.01799$$

$$1 + r_{90}^{FF} = (1.1198)^{90/365} = 1.02829$$

$$\frac{F_{90} - S}{S} = \frac{.2090 - .2113}{.2113} = -.01089$$

$$\frac{F_{90}}{S} r_{90}^{FF} - r_{90}^{US} = .02798 - .01799 = .00999$$

So net profit per $\$1/(1 + r_{90}^{US})$ = $-\$0.00090$, or zero, given that small transactions costs exist.

Neglecting the small transactions costs, it is clear that in a properly functioning market there should be no arbitrage profits lying around for the taking. In other words, the premium or discount should be exactly offset by the adjusted interest differential, or

$$\frac{F_T - S}{S} = r_T^{US} - \frac{F_T}{S} r_T^{FF}$$

for all maturity dates $T$ for which forward contracts exist. This relationship is known as covered interest arbitrage or the interest rate parity theorem; it says that arbitrage ensures equality between interest rate differentials and the forward premium or discount.

Hence, you should be cautious if you think you have found an arbitrage opportunity. The following example illustrates a case where an arbitrage opportunity exists on paper but not in reality, because quoted interest rates on financial instruments are not necessarily accessible.

Let's suppose that we find on a certain date the following quotes on spot and forward Danish krone and the following interest rates on financial instruments in Denmark and the United States:

- Spot krone $.15985/Kr
- 90-day krone $.15900/Kr
- 90-day T-bill U.S. 6.25%
- 90-day T-bill Denmark 7.50%

The covered interest arbitrage formula gives:

$$\frac{F^{90} - S}{S} = \frac{1}{4}\left(r^{US}_{90} - \frac{F^{90}}{S}\, r^{D}_{90}\right)$$

or

$$\frac{.15900 - .15985}{.15985} = \frac{-.00085}{.15985} = -.53\%$$

$$\frac{1}{4}\left(.0625 - \frac{.15900}{.15985} \times .075\right) = -.303\%$$

Thus, the discount on the forward exceeds the adjusted interest rate differential.

So, what should you do? We suggest that you borrow in Denmark and lend in the United States by taking the following steps:

1.  Borrow 100 krone for 90 days→repay 101.875
2.  Buy $ spot→$15.985
3.  Lend for 90 days→$16.235 after 90 days

$$15.985 \times \frac{1.0625}{4} = \$16.235$$

4.  Sell these dollars forward →102.107 krone after 90 days

    Profits = 0.23 krone per hundred transacted

These were real numbers, more or less. So how could a successful arbitrage opportunity exist? Well, you have to get into the mechanics of our get-rich-quick scheme more deeply. We can obviously make the forward currency transactions. However, central to our arbitrage is the ability to borrow at the Danish T. Bill rate. This might prove troublesome.

Can you borrow at the 90-day T-bill rate in the United States? And if so, how might you do it? You have to short a T-bill, i.e., you borrow one from a dealer and sell it for the current price, i.e., the maturity value discounted at the current interest rate, and buy one back at the maturity date or just before it. But, at least in the United States, you can't take the proceeds of this short sale. You can only invest them in another T-bill, thereby speculating on changes in the term structure. We are sure that financial opportunities are much more limited in Denmark, which has a government that practices extensive management of the economy. In fact, we can tell you something even worse: there are no 90-day T-bills in Denmark, only 1-year to 15-year government notes. Fortunately this doesn't totally preclude the operation of our scheme. You can trade in these instruments whenever you find one with 90 days to maturity. However, this doesn't happen every day, or even every week. And, as a final blow, short selling is forbidden in Denmark as an unpatriotic act.

You can still borrow using other instruments, principally bank loans. In the United States, without allowing for compensating balances, the prime rate runs, say, 1½% higher than the T-bill rate. In Denmark, however, the prime rate is below the T-bill rate! So we must explain why people don't simply borrow from banks, invest in T-bills, and get rich without effort. To begin with, only large firms have access to the prime rate. Also, there exists strict credit rationing. Denmark is a socialist paradise and if the government doesn't like your reason for borrowing, you can't borrow.

In reality in the high volume arbitrage markets such as pounds, dollars, and francs, T-bills aren't used. Instead the transactions are carried out in Eurocurrencies (such as Eurodollars, Europounds, and Eurofrancs). These are huge wholesale money markets in which millions of dollars of transactions take place daily over the telephone. Only large trusted banks participate on the wholesale level and their obligations are treated as virtually sure. The Eurocurrency markets are extensively discussed in Chapter 8.

Eurodollar rates run about 1% or so higher than T-bill rates and there is a comparable spread on Europounds and British T-bills. As a result, the actual computation of the arbitrage opportunities may be virtually the same using either rates. Recollect the formula for a 90-day opportunity:

$$\frac{F^{90} - S}{S} = \frac{1}{4}\left(r^{US} - \frac{F^{90}}{S} r^{UK}\right)$$

If the spread between T-bills and Eurocurrency were always the same, say 1%, in both countries, then this calculation is unaffected. The interest differential part becomes:

$$\frac{1}{4}\left[r^{US} + 1 - \frac{F^{90}}{S}(r^{UK} + 1)\right]$$

and if $F^{90}/S \approx 1$ we have no problem. We'll go into this in more detail in a later chapter, but you can see that the calculation in our Danish example assumed that the spread between the T-bill notes and the instruments actually able to be used for arbitrage are the same in the United States and Denmark. In reality, only the Danish Central Bank could undertake the transactions described in our calculations. Perhaps it does.

We will conclude this discussion with some facts. The evidence is clear. As long as there is no government intervention, and allowing for transactions costs, the zero profit condition holds virtually all the time. The transactions costs consist of bid-ask spreads and brokerage fees, and have been estimated to be about 0.15%.[9] The zero profit on covered interest arbitrage condition is one of the most important relationships in the exchange markets. It ties together the spot rate, the forward rates, and corresponding interest rates. These things are therefore not free to move independently. As soon as a profit opportunity appears there will be large fund flows through the capital markets and exchange markets, and something has to give. We will return to this point in explaining short-run exchange rate movements.

## 1.6   INCONVERTIBILITY

Not all currencies can be traded on exchange markets. This is not the same thing as saying that we can't read a quote for every currency in the Wall Street Journal. Some countries are very small and have a low volume of trade with only a couple of major trading partners. Thus, their currencies are not widely quoted. But they will be quoted in the currencies of the relevant trading partner and any bank can buy them for you. This is the case of the Papua-New Guinea kina or the CFA franc of the former French colonies in Africa.

A nonconvertible currency is unquoted not for reasons of obscurity but because, except for very limited and special purposes, it is not traded on markets against other currencies. For example, the Russian ruble, the Chinese renminbi, and the Polish zloty are not traded in the foreign exchange markets. This is not to say that exchange rates don't exist in some sense. If you are a tourist in Eastern Europe or China, you have to pay for things with cash, and the governments of these countries will quote you

---

[9]On the empirical content of the interest rate parity theorem, the reader is referred to Lawrence Officer and Thomas Willett, "The Covered Arbitrage Schedule: A Critical Survey of Recent Developments," *Journal of Money, Credit and Banking*, Vol. 2, May 1970; Tamir Agmon and Saul Bronfeld, "International Mobility of Short Term Covered Arbitrage Capital," *Journal of Business Finance and Accounting*, Vol. 2, Spring 1975; and Jacob Frenkel and Richard Levich, "Covered Interest Arbitrage: Unexploited Profits," *Journal of Political Economy*, Vol. 83, No. 2, April 1975.

tourist exchange rates. Official exchange rates which are different from the tourist rates also usually exist.

However, lots of countries peg exchange rates, and have official exchange rates. And there is a good deal of trade between the United States and the socialist countries, more than with Lebanon, whose currency is quoted. So why does no one make a market in these currencies? The reason is that no one *wants* to buy them, apart from tourists, because having the currency does not entitle you to buy commodities with it. In our market economy possession of money is the same thing as possession of a claim on goods, any goods, equal in monetary value to the money that you possess. The ruling governments of the socialist countries have severed the tie between possession of money and possession of the right to export goods and services. In all these countries, foreign trade is centrally planned. The government decides what and how much they want to export and you can't just go in and buy things. Moreover, when these countries receive payment for their goods, they always want the so-called "hard" or convertible currencies. The last thing the Poles want is zlotys, or Hungarian forints, or Russian rubles. Hence, no one on the outside wants to buy these currencies and there is no market for them.

However, this explanation is not very satisfactory, for Chapter 3 explains briefly why free trade maximizes income and welfare. And the socialist countries are particularly emphatic that socialist planning of production raises the consumption and welfare of the masses. So why don't they allow free trade? The Yugoslavs, the exception to this state of affairs, allow relatively unrestricted trade without having private ownership or capitalism, and the Yugoslav dinar is for most commercial purposes a convertible currency.

The resolution to this paradox lies in the fact that in almost all the socialist countries quoted prices are not scarcity prices, i.e., prices that equate demand and supply. This is because there are no links between prices and production in these countries. The state has a central physical plan which tells all the firms what to produce and they carry out this plan regardless of what might maximize profits at the prices set by the state. Because prices don't ration supply, people and firms stand in line. Food and housing are cheap but hard to get. Taking this situation as given, imagine what would happen if we all bought currency and then went to the head of the line to buy goods for export. We would immediately buy all the foods because their prices are officially low. Thus, the socialist countries could end up exporting for 12¢ things which cost them a dollar to produce. The flow the other way would be just as irrational. Basically once prices don't represent costs and scarcities, you can't use prices to make efficiency calculations for the input and output mix in production. Hence, as long as the governments of these countries maintain central planning, they can never have convertible currencies. The Yugoslav cur-

rency is virtually convertible because the Yugoslavs practice market so-
cialism and not central planning.

However, some foreign exchange markets of limited scope might exist
even with nonconvertible currencies. Thus a market for rubles has got off
the ground in Finland. It was originated by Finnish businessmen wanting
to ensure themselves against changes decreed by Moscow in the value of
the ruble. There are limited, priced-based trade relations between Finland
and the USSR that explain the existence of the market, in conformity with
our analysis.

The situation of the centrally-planned economies is the most extreme
of the nonconvertibility situations. The concept has applicability in more
familiar and accessible surroundings. Let's take as an example the following quotations from the *Wall Street Journal* of February 1, 1978.

| | Bank Transfers Rate | Banknote Rate | |
|---|---|---|---|
| Indian rupee | $ .1245/IR | .07 | .11 |
| New Zealand dollar | $1.0225/NZ¢ | .78 | .95 |

The bank transfer rate is the exchange rate on the interbank market
in the United States. The bid-ask spread on this can be 1/10 of 1% or less.
The banknote rates represent the U.S. dollar prices at which you can buy
or sell, let us say, a New Zealand $100 bill.

With our by now heightened sensitivity to arbitrage situations, we
can visualize a tempting arrangement which both makes us money and
broadens our knowledge of the world.

1.  Buy in the United States $NZ 100,000 in notes at .95
    Cost = US$ 95,000

2.  Take these dollars to New Zealand and sell them for US$ at US$
    1.0225/$NZ
    Revenue = US$ 102,250

Profits amount to $7250 from which one has to deduct the travel
expenses. The same type of argument applies to the Indian rupee. Clearly
this one trip has much more than paid for the purchase price of this book,
and this is only the first chapter!

If it were really such a good deal, we wouldn't have told you about
it. In reality these examples illustrate a situation of partial convertibility
of a currency. The $NZ and the Indian rupee are not convertible for the
purpose of speculative capital flows. It is not legal to bring large sums of
bank notes into New Zealand, and it is not possible to convert more than
limited amounts of $NZ into US$ without a "legitimate commercial pur-

pose," as defined by the central bank.[10] The principal effect of these regulations is to restrict access to these arbitrage opportunities to those able to feign commercial needs.


## 1.7  SUMMARY

This chapter has outlined the mechanics of and motivation for foreign exchange trading.

Exchange rates give the price of one national money in terms of another national money. The spot rate is the price for (virtually) immediate delivery. Exchange rates for delivery at specified future dates (and locations) are known as forward rates. Payment is made only upon delivery, but at a price (rate of exchange) agreed upon at the time the contract was written.

Foreign exchange for spot and forward delivery is traded in all the major financial centers of the world, by a telephone-linked interbank market.

Spot transactions are undertaken because, to buy goods, services, or assets priced in other currencies, one must first buy those currencies. Forward transactions are undertaken for speculative and hedging reasons. Speculators use forward contracts to place bets on the spot rate at the forward contract's maturity date. A short speculator has sold forward—he or she has promised to deliver. A long speculator has bought forward—he or she has promised to receive. A long position is taken by speculators who think ultimate spot rates will exceed the current forward quote. A short position is taken by speculators with the opposite presumption. An individual with a foreign account payable can remove exchange risk by going long. An individual with a foreign account receivable can remove exchange risk by going short. These are hedging transactions.

If forward rates exceed spot rates the foreign currency concerned is said to sell at a premium. If forward rates are below spot rates, the forward exchange is said to be at a discount. Discounts and premiums are often quoted at annualized percentage of spot.

The most important exchange market activity is arbitrage. Arbitrage is the activity of making riskless profit because the same item can be bought and sold at two different prices. One buys cheap and sells dear.

---

[10]You might now be asking yourself why there should be significant numbers of $NZ notes hanging around in the United States and elsewhere. (Taking large numbers out is also illegal, and we have just shown them to be selling at a discount.) Ask yourself what you would do with a large amount of earnings on which you had paid no income tax. It's the same in the United States. For the U.S. connection between cash holdings and tax evasion, see P.M. Gutmann, "The Subterranean Economy," *Financial Analysts Journal*, Nov./Dec. 1977. New Zealanders take vacations and acquire foreign assets with their unreported income because detection is easier in a small country than it is here.

In triangular arbitrage one compares direct and indirect purchase of a currency. Indirect purchase occurs when to buy currency A with currency B (whether forward or spot), one buys C with B and then buys A with C. Covered interest arbitrage involves borrowing in one currency, converting spot and lending in the other currency while simultaneously selling forward the proceeds of the loan in the other currency. The two equivalent items here are methods of acquiring (or delivering) foreign currency at a specific future date. One method is forward purchase (or sale). The other method is to buy foreign currency spot, invest at the foreign currency interest rate and accumulate until the desired sum is attained (borrow against a foreign receivable and exchange the discounted sum spot). There are two distinct sources of gain or loss in covered interest arbitrage: the gain or loss on the interest differential, and the gain or loss on the forward discount or premium. When markets function well, the sum of these is zero (after allowing for transactions costs). Covered interest arbitrage takes place in the Eurocurrency markets because they are free of government controls.

Not all currencies are convertible, or freely tradable on exchange markets. Some governments allow conversion only for "legitimate commercial purposes." Others, almost all socialist bloc countries, find free trade in currencies incompatible with their basic economic structure.

**EXERCISES:**

**Foreign Exchange Mechanics**

1.  On Wednesday, June 20, 1979, the bid rate on the spot market in New York was the following for a sample of currencies:

| | |
|---|---|
| pound sterling | 2.104 |
| Belgian franc | .0326 |
| French franc | .2263 |
| German mark | .5238 |
| Dutch guilder | .4797 |
| Italian lira | .001173 |
| Swiss franc | .578 |
| Japanese yen | .004541 |

   a.  What would you expect the price of the U.S. dollar to be in the respective foreign exchange markets of the currencies listed above?

   b.  What do you expect the price of these currencies to be in England?

   c.  In fact, the following prices were quoted in London that day:

$$\$/£ = \quad 2.104$$
$$BF/£ = \quad 64.48$$
$$FF/£ = \quad 9.295$$
$$DM/£ = \quad 4.019$$
$$DG/£ = \quad 4.404$$
$$L/£ = 1793$$
$$SF/£ = \quad 3.64$$
$$Y/£ = \quad 463.3$$

Explain the differences. Do you see any opportunity for profitable arbitrage?

d. Suppose the French franc were quoted in London 9.0526. What would you suggest to take advantage of this situation? What if the Swiss franc were quoted 3.74?

2. A week later, on Wednesday June 27, a foreign exchange trader was given the following quotes: the pound sterling was quoted at 2.115 and the French franc at .2247 in New York. At the same time in Paris, the pound sterling was quoted at 9.4 and the dollar at 4.45. What transactions should the trader pursue?

3. On June 29, 1979, one could read in U.S. financial newspapers the following quotes for spot and forward foreign currencies:

|  | Pound Sterling | French Franc | Yen | Swiss Franc | German Mark |
|---|---|---|---|---|---|
| Spot price | 2.1765 | .2342 | .004592 | .6039 | .5443 |
| 30-day futures | 2.1705 | .2342 | .004616 | .6092 | .5467 |
| 90-day futures | 2.1585 | .2340 | .004648 | .6187 | .5502 |
| 180-day futures | 2.1465 | .2334 | .004693 | .6310 | .5553 |

a. Indicate for each maturity date the swap rate of each of these five currencies. Which currencies sell at a premium, which at a discount, vis-à-vis the U.S. dollar?

b. Calculate for each maturity the forward premium or discount of each currency.

4. On March 30, one could read the following quotes for foreign exchange spot and future rates as well as the following eurocurrency rates:

| Foreign Exchange Rates | U.K. | France | Japan | Switzerland | Germany |
|---|---|---|---|---|---|
| Spot | 2.0615 | .2329 | .004789 | .5922 | .5357 |
| 30-day futures | 2.0587 | .2334 | .004810 | .5973 | .5384 |
| 90-day futures | 2.0551 | .2344 | 004852 | .6075 | .5432 |
| 180-day futures | 2.0530 | .2352 | .004918 | .6218 | .5502 |

**Eurocurrency
Deposit Rates**

|  | Dollar | Pound Sterling | French Franc | Yen | Swiss Franc | Deutsche Mark |
|---|---|---|---|---|---|---|
| One month | 10.25 | 12.37 | 7.62 | 5.87 | .25 | 4.75 |
| Three months | 10.50 | 12.12 | 8.12 | 6.00 | .37 | 4.94 |
| Six months | 10.56 | 11.75 | 8.75 | 5.56 | .87 | 5.37 |
| Twelve months | 10.56 | 11.62 | 9.25 | 5.87 | 1.44 | 5.50 |

a. We don't want you to try every covered interest arbitrage possibility. Just try a few and see if there is money to be made at no risk with these numbers.

b. Given the twelve-month eurocurrency deposit rates, what would you expect the one-year future rate to be for each of the five foreign countries vis-à-vis the dollar?

c. You have just read a serious and well-informed economic letter which says that short term interest rates in the United States are going to go up by 1%. Is this information valuable? How would you react to it?

# Chapter 2

# The Evolution of the International Monetary System

## 2.1 INTRODUCTION

This chapter presents a history of the evolution of the international monetary system from the gold exchange standard of the late nineteenth century to the dirty float of paper moneys that prevails today. Because we have gone beyond a simple chronology of events and attempted to emphasize why things happened, the chapter is suitable also as a historical *conclusion* to the book. The reader will probably find it fruitful to reexamine this chapter after understanding how international capital markets and currency markets work from later chapters. At various points we have referred to specific following chapters in which ideas mentioned briefly here are developed at greater length.

A one-chapter history of nearly a century of monetary development cannot avoid being highly selective and idiosyncratic. We have tried to highlight those features which we feel are most important to an understanding of the present exchange rate system, and have provided various footnote references for readers seeking more detail or a different perspective. We begin with a general discussion of the role and function of money and monetary policy. We then turn to the operation of the gold exchange standard as the prototype of a fixed exchange rate system. The political and economic chaos arising from the First World War, which was not resolved until the end of the Second World War in 1945, nullified all attempts to create a smoothly functioning international payments system. After explaining these developments, we briefly summarize the rise and fall of the postwar fixed exchange rate system. It foundered because the monetary parities were not adequately adjusted to changes in underlying economic realities. The chapter concludes with an examination of the International Monetary Fund (IMF) and its offspring, the Special Drawing Right (SDR).

## 2.2  MONETARY POLICY AND MONEY CREATION AND USE

Throughout the twentieth century the prevailing international monetary arrangements have been not very permanent compromises between two conflicting forces—the perceived value of a universal money as a medium of exchange, and the desire of national governments to influence their economies by monetary manipulations. Before 1914 the first force was clearly the stronger, but particularly since the 1929 depression and the associated development of acceptable justifications for active government intervention in economies (Keynesian economics), the stability of the monetary order has invariably been sacrificed to domestic policy goals. It has now become dogma in all the advanced economies that governments are not only responsible for the economic welfare of their populations but are capable of affecting this welfare by fiscal and monetary policies. In addition, there are important revenue-raising aspects of monetary policy. These views are not universally held, however. In Germany and Japan a stable monetary order has frequently been declared to be a necessary condition of satisfactory policies for domestic welfare,[1] and the pendulum may be swinging back even in the United States.[2] Certainly the decline and final collapse of the Bretton Woods fixed exchange rate regime in the period 1966–1973 was due to conscious decisions by governments to put short-term domestic goals first.

Chapter 3 explains the substantial increases in economic welfare arising from a shift from autarky to free trade and world specialization. (We measure welfare by increases into total consumable goods available—trade also redistributes income internally). The existence of a sophisticated monetary system, with currencies having predictable value in terms of each other and in terms of real purchasing power, is a prerequisite for a complex trading system.

Traders need money, first for transactions balances; and second, to denominate prices and contracts. Outstanding money stocks are basically held to facilitate transactions, to obviate the need for synchronizing in time and place all income and expense flows.[3] Anyone familiar with the operation of business enterprises and banks realizes that the needed transaction balances are large. Therefore, fluctuations in exchange rates or in

---

[1] See for example O. Emminger, "The D-Mark in the Conflict Between Internal and External Equilibrium, 1948–1975," *Essays in International Finance*, No. 122, June 1977, Department of Economics, Princeton University.

[2] In the area of monetary policy the so-called "rational expectations" school has set out to show that monetary policy has only transitory effects on *real* variables, and that the government controls only the inflation rate. A reasonably accessible reference for people with a good knowledge of economics, but who are not professional economists, is T. Sargent and N. Wallace, "Rational Expectations and the Theory of Economic Policy," Parts I and II, Federal Reserve Bank of Minneapolis, 1974.

[3] It is not very rational to hold money balances as *assets*—they earn no return and depreciate in purchasing power at the rate of inflation.

any measure of general prices impose substantial capital gains and losses on the balance-holders. The risk of capital gain and loss on currency balances is a real cost of undertaking international trade in a multicurrency world. If the risks are large enough, they begin to outweigh the advantages of specialization and, from the viewpoint of real output (size of the available pie), the economic system becomes less efficient. Similarly, contracts are written in money terms, so that fluctuations in exchange rates and price levels impose capital gains and losses on the contracting parties. It is possible to index contracts in various ways, but these schemes mainly transfer risks rather than reduce them. Moreover all inflation indexes are compromises, even at the conceptual level. If *all* prices rise at the same rate, then any index will do. If they do not, then the question of weighting is of paramount importance. Different weights are appropriate to different purposes and people.[4] In summary then, international trade is most encouraged in a system with a universal money and reasonable price stability.

As long as countries used commodity money rather than *fiat money* (paper money), there was little that governments could do to affect the money supply. The amount of gold in circulation depended basically upon the rate of discovery of gold worth mining at the current price of gold in terms of other goods. The only monetary policy available was clipping of coinage—reduction of the size of gold or silver coins of a given nominal metal content. However since scales were widely available these practices devalued the coins and led to the famous *Gresham's Law*—"bad money drives out good." People would hoard full-weight coins and let clipped coins circulate at face value. The same phenomenon occurred in the U.S. when silver dimes were hoarded in the 1960s—the silver content of the coins exceeded their face value so all the silver dimes disappeared from circulation. The introduction of paper money not redeemable in any commodity gives a government control over the nominal money supply. This gives the government a steady source of *monopoly income* and also the possibility of fancy taxation schemes without enabling legislation.

The source of monopoly income is *seignorage*, the name for the profit derived from creating the legal tender currency. When the Federal Reserve prints a dollar bill, the cost is a little paper and ink and the wear on a printing plate, while the result is something that exchanges for one dollar's worth of real goods. This is a highly profitable industry[5] and substantial revenue accrues to national treasuries from the operation of their central banks. The taxation possibilities arising from control of the printing press

---

[4]Unless your buying behavior exactly corresponds to that of the urban family of four on which the U.S. Consumer Price Index is based, the price level changes it measures will not be the ones that affect your real income, that is, the bundle of consumption goods relevant to you.

[5]Forgers are attempting to bring free enterprise to the money market but are relentlessly hounded by the existing monopolist producer.

take two forms. Inflation is involved in both, in one as a byproduct and in the other as a central mechanism. The simple process involves funding budget deficits by money creation. The government buys goods with newly printed money. This leaves less goods and more money in the hands of everyone else, with the result that the price of goods in terms of money rises; inflation occurs.[6] All the belligerents in the war of 1914–1918 financed the bulk of their war expenditures this way, causing in some cases price level increases of several hundred percent. The complex process relies on the existence of a progressive income tax schedule not indexed for inflation. If the money supply expands and prices and incomes rise, individuals will be pushed higher in the tax brackets although their *real* income (nominal income adjusted for any reasonable measure of inflation) has not risen. In this way governments raise the share of national income taken in taxes without the politically unpopular need to vote on increases in tax rates. The Federal Government in the United States and state governments with progressive income taxes, like that in California, have been enormous beneficiaries of these tax increases in recent decades.

Government control of the money supply also gives some control over short-term interest rates, real as well as nominal.[7] If, by open market operations, the government expands the money supply, people will have excessive transactions balances. The first place these go is into short-term financial instruments like Treasury Bills, causing a fall in yields in these instruments. Conversely, by reducing the money supply the government precipitates replenishment of transactions balances via the sale of short-term financial instruments, and a consequent increase in their yields. Even if these effects are transitory they can be very important, for example in manipulating the balance of payments, as discussed in Chapter 4. In the Keynesian world view these interest rate changes are the key to altering the level of national income. We explain this at length in Chapter 6. So for reasons of tax revenue and counter-cyclical policy, governments have an incentive to destabilize the money market to achieve their goals.

In studying the history of the world payments system, one must never leave out of sight the rewards that national governments have perceived to follow from monetary manipulation, and their willingness to exchange immediate electoral and other benefits for long term stability of the system of world trade. It is no exaggeration to say that this conflict of goals is central to all current monetary negotiations, whether it is Turkey trying to borrow from the IMF, or Britain and Italy at loggerheads with Germany about the establishment of parities in the European Monetary System.

---

[6]In Chapter 5, we will discuss at length the connection between monetary expansion and inflation. The skeptical reader should look ahead.

[7]These points are developed in greater detail in Chapters 5 and 6.

## 2.3 THE PRE-1914 GOLD EXCHANGE STANDARD

The gold exchange standard system was the last widespread use of a privately produced commodity as a money. It was a gold *exchange* standard rather than a pure gold standard because pure commodity moneys are awkward to use. For example, carrying gold around is risky and inconvenient. In the pre-1914 era most of the major trading nations issued paper money with a gold backing. Holders of one country's paper money could redeem it for gold from the money-issuing agency, take the gold to another country's money-issuing agency and obtain that country's paper money. The money-issuing agencies[8] redeemed legal tender for bullion at fixed rates per ounce of gold (with a small bid/ ask spread to cover the cost of coining bullion and so forth). In this system the exchange rates between the paper monies were virtually fixed, fluctuating only between the so-called *gold points*. It is worth explaining this phenomenon because it clearly demonstrates the impact of transactions costs on all arbitrage processes. (Of course the exchange rates between notes were fixed by triangular arbitrage between notes and gold.)

Suppose (to choose round numbers) that one ounce of gold exchanged for 4 pounds in Britain, and for 40 dollars in the U.S. This implies one paper pound equaled 10 paper dollars in value. Let us assume that there occurred a departure from this exchange ratio, say, because selling pressure by pound holders eager to obtain dollars caused private bank dealers to mark the rate at 9 dollars per pound. In that case it would pay to:

1. take \$9 and buy one pound;

2. exchange the pound at the Bank of England for 1/4 ounce of gold;

3. ship the gold to America; and

4. exchange 1/4 ounce of gold for \$10.

This arbitrage involves an actual shipment, and thus is costly. Let us say it cost 10¢ to ship one ounce of gold. Then until the exchange rate for the paper moneys fell below \$9.90 per pound, no gold would be shipped from Britain to America. And until the exchange rate rose above \$10.10 per pound, no gold would be shipped from America to England. Hence the exchange rate between the paper dollar and the paper pound would be free to fluctuate between \$9.90 and \$10.10 per pound without any arbitrage at all. These two bounds are known as the gold points.

This system of virtually fixed exchange rates had the characteristic of all true fixed exchange rate systems—there was one universal money,

---

[8]We use this phrase rather than "central bank" because the Bank of England, issuer of the premier currency, was still nominally a private profit-seeking bank.

and changes in the supply of that money affected price levels all over the world, not just in the country of source of disturbance. Suppose that gold was discovered in South Africa. This would raise income, costs, and prices there and lead to an import surplus. The import surplus would be paid for by the conversion of gold, and thus the money supplies of the countries exporting to or selling assets to the residents of South Africa would rise. Alternatively, suppose that some innovation in banking occurred that reduced the need for cash balances, for instance the spread of checking accounts in Britain. The now-surplus cash balances would be used to purchase assets and commodities. As the banking innovation did not in itself raise the GNP these would be foreign assets and commodities, paid for by the conversion of gold. The ripple effects would spread to all countries on the gold exchange standard. The supply of world money would rise and thus the value of that world money in terms of goods would fall—there would be worldwide inflation. For most of the last quarter of the nineteenth century there was worldwide deflation—prices fell slowly throughout the period. The world economy was growing in real terms faster than the supply of gold that was providing the needed transactions balances. At current prices transactions balances were inadequate so people abstained from commodity purchases and prices fell, that is, gold became more valuable in terms of goods. This made the transactions balances adequate. Thus very substantial real economic growth took place with falling price levels or rising value of the commodity money. An essentially similar linkage between paper money supplies and prices exists today, as we explain in Chapter 5. Unfortunately, the money is now falling in value in terms of goods.

One should not exaggerate the short-term automaticity of the gold exchange standard system. The response of price levels to money supplies is a slow process, even today taking one to two years to develop fully. The pre-1914 international monetary system was organized around sterling as the sole vehicle currency and London as the banking headquarters for the great bulk of world trade. Factoring of receivables and discounting of bills from all corners of the world took place there, and trade and loans were denominated in sterling rather than gold. Sterling was convenient because universally used, and was convertible into gold at the Bank of England. But, "it hardly occurred to people in those days to speak of sterling as convertible: there was nothing better to convert it into."[9]

The Bank of England backed this vehicle currency with an absurdly small gold reserve, equal to perhaps 2% or 3% of the total money supply. It maintained this small reserve because it manipulated the *bank rate*, the rate at which it would rediscount commercial paper, to safeguard the gold stock. Gold outflows were met by an increase in bank rate which drew

---

[9]L. Yeager, *International Monetary Relations: Theory, History and Policy*, 2nd edition, Harper and Row, New York, 1976, p. 299.

short-term deposits into Britain. Gold inflows were met by reductions in bank rate.

Nothing was safer than lending in sterling to reputable banks and acceptance houses. Credit conditions in Britain, the focus of the world economy, were thus transmitted worldwide and the Bank of England was in effect the central bank for all countries on the gold exchange standard. Of course it could not control the supply of monetary gold and so had no influence over long-run monetary growth or trends in price levels. Perhaps for this reason there was unmatched stability in the capital markets.

> "... from January 1876 to July 1914, Bank rate moved rather narrowly around an average somewhat above 3%. Never in that period did it stand at or above 5% for longer than 26 consecutive weeks. Long-term interest rates were also remarkably stable. Only twice in the 50 years before 1914 did the rate on Consols move by one-quarter of 1 percent or more within a single year."[10]

Never since has there been such a lengthy period of years with comparable confidence in the currencies or in the economic system generally. Other factors than the managed gold exchange standard contributed to this satisfactory state of affairs, of course.

- The absence of ambitious government taxation and expenditure policies.

- Downward flexibility of prices and wages and no organized social conflict over redistribution.

- Expectations confidently held that the existing order would not be upset.

## 2.4  MONETARY DISORDER: 1914–1945

The World War introduced the first major governmental monetary intervention. The belligerents speedily terminated the convertibility of notes into gold and then obtained resources by printing the paper money to pay for them. However the three decades of monetary chaos that followed were not due to this new form of taxation but rather to the destruction of the European economies and trading networks which this war of unanticipated duration and cost brought about.

The old economic order in Europe was destroyed. Central and Eastern Europe had been very important suppliers of raw materials and foodstuffs, and had been a major market for industrial goods. Now Russia had with-

---

[10]ibid., p. 307, note 23. Consols were perpetual debt securities of the British government, and were the standard for measuring the term structure of interest rates.

drawn from the market trading system, under assault from the anticommunist Allies. Central Europe was devastated, the Austro-Hungarian empire disbanded and in disarray, and Germany was economically prostrate. The war reparations demands by the Allies were staggering and provided a strong disincentive to restoration of order within Germany. The major income gains would have to be shipped off to the victors. In addition the country was the scene of numerous armed conflicts between the private armies of left and right wing factions, which lasted into the early 1920s.

Monetary stabilization, by which is meant restoration of operating markets in national currencies wherein prices were stable and trade was feasible, was clearly only part of the overall problem of restoring production and trade linkages. However this in turn was tied up with a number of ultimately insoluble political problems.[11]

1. Security against a resurgence of German militarism. This particularly concerned the French but also the citizens of the newly created nations of Czechoslovakia and Poland. All French governments between the wars preferred a weak Germany, yet a restoration of economic capacity in Germany was essential to any restoration of pre-World War I economic prosperity and stability.

2. Reparations claims against Germany hindered the willingness of the Allies to allow conditions under which the German economy could be restored—they wanted to skim off all gains. The motives for this were various. In Britain and in particular in France, leading politicians had staked their careers, and their budget plans, on the slogan "the Boche will pay." On the Allied side only the United States and Japan emerged better off than when they entered. The others, particularly France, had suffered catastrophic economic loss. In any case, they didn't have much choice about pushing reparations claims as they needed the revenue to repay their war debts to the United States, which treated them as commercial loans and demanded repayment in full. Indeed even in the depths of the depression, in 1932, 12% of Britain's export revenues were going to the U.S. to meet war debts. Unfortunately this desire to milk the Germans ensured the latter would not play in this game.

3. Anticommunist hostility kept Russia out of the European trading system. A major stumbling block was the renunciation by the communists of Czarist foreign debt. Approximately $3 billion was outstanding, of which French citizens held about $2 billion.[12] The French government insisted on payment of the debt as a prerequisite for reintegration.

---

[11]We should say "insoluble by peaceful means." They were basically settled between 1938 and 1945.

[12]Remember, we're talking about 1914 dollars, not 1979 dollars! This represented a huge loss of wealth.

4. An upsurge of isolationist sentiment in the U.S., the only healthy economy, forestalled any assistance being offered to Europe other than on (shortsighted) commercial terms, and prevented American cooperation in attempts to prevent aggression by Japan, Italy, and Germany from plunging the world into another war.

French and Belgian troops were sent to occupy parts of Germany to accelerate reparations payments in 1923; and part in retaliation, part for reasons of lack of understanding and control, the German economy collapsed in a cataclysmic hyperinflation in 1923. A Reichsmark was worth about 2¢ in 1920. By the autumn of 1923, *one trillion Reichsmarks* exchanged for 23.8 cents. In Germany holders of real assets became wealthy and holders of bonds lost everything, creating an embittered middle class group able to be exploited by extremists. These events brought about some cooperation among the former Allies to scale down reparations demands and a loan was floated to reestablish government in Germany. German municipal and central governments borrowed in the United States in the 1920s and used these funds for municipal projects or to meet debts. These activities did not create export revenues to repay past borrowings so German economic recovery depended on the lenders having enough confidence to roll over the loans.

In the mid-1920s attempts were made to restore the gold exchange standard. But the enormous wartime inflation in all the belligerent countries had not been uniform across them, so that a return to the prewar parities would have rendered uncompetitive the exports and the import-competing goods of those countries that had experienced more inflation.[13] There was some understanding of these ideas but purchasing power parities, that is, exchange rates adequately compensating for different rates of cost inflation, are notoriously hard to compute. Britain seems to have overvalued the pound by about 10% when it returned to the prewar gold parity in 1925. That is, given the new parities selected by Britain's major trading partners, and given the wartime and postwar inflation experienced in all these countries, the adoption of the prewar gold parity caused British traded goods to be about 10% too expensive when compared to the goods of her major trading partners.[14] One way to overcome such a problem is to have British domestic prices fall by 10%. The uncompetitive nature of British goods at the prewar parity encouraged this but it did not happen fast enough. As a result Britain did not really experience an economic boom in the 1920s. France, after some major financial crises in the 1920s, settled on an undervalued rate. Even in the supposed boom

---

[13]Chapter 5 explains at length this "purchasing power parity" theory of exchange rates. However, the basic idea has just been presented.

[14]Exchange rates translate commodity prices. British residents saw imports as about 10% cheaper than comparable domestic goods; foreigners saw British exports as about 10% more expensive than comparable local goods or exports from other countries.

of the 1920s the world economy never attained the stability and prosperity of the prewar years. The gold exchange standard was abandoned permanently after the depression began, and in the 1930s the world saw its first experiment in floating exchange rates.

The economic collapse known as the Great Depression came early in Germany, and by 1931 all reparations had effectively ended. They had been paid via German governmental borrowings on the New York capital market, which effectively terminated in 1928. The United States attempted to force its former allies to keep up their own war debt payments. This caused great resentment and then effective default by the British and French in 1933. This soured the atmosphere at a time when economic cooperation to prevent protectionism and competitive depreciation was vital. The focus of the Roosevelt administration on domestic matters, and the need to appease critics of debt relaxation and tariff reduction to buy their support for the domestic policies, doomed transatlantic economic cooperation. Thus other countries retreated into blocs, like the "sterling area" in which autarky was promoted. This could only lower world income, as will be seen in Chapter 3. These divergent interests, and mutual suspicion between the governments of the United States, France and Britain, were the backdrop to monetary events, economic events and ultimately geopolitical evolution in the 1930s.

Sterling was devalued in 1933, then the dollar, and the famous peg of $35 per ounce of gold was installed in January of 1934. These actions left the currencies of the "gold bloc" countries (France, Switzerland, Netherlands, Belgium, Italy and Poland) overvalued with respect to the dollar and the pound. This caused economic distress and speculation. The governments tried to force internal deflation, which was not beneficial for their citizens and did not occur quickly enough. Belgium abandoned the gold standard in March 1935 and the others in September of 1936. Germany had gone to a regime of state-directed trading, virtually on a barter basis in some cases. From 1936 the major currencies floated against the dollar, with the Exchange Stabilization funds of the U.S., Britain, and France cooperating to smooth exchange movements. The French franc depreciated against the dollar and the pound, while over the period January 1936 through August 1939 the pound was on average constant against the dollar.[15]

The experience of the 1930s was called on as justification for the relative rigidity of the postwar par value system designed at Bretton Woods in 1944. The 1930s were said to show the instability and un-

---

[15]See S. Black, "International Money Markets and Flexible Exchange Rates," Princeton Studies in International Finance, No. 32, Department of Economics, Princeton University, 1973. He reports a mean spot rate of $4.86 with a standard deviation of $0.375, and the same for the forward rates.

workability of a floating exchange rate system. For this reason it is of particular value to examine what did happen. In his fascinating paper, S. Black reports on a careful study of the sterling/dollar market in the 1936–1939 period. He identified fifteen major international crises in this period, which can be expected to have caused short-term capital flows. Several were German expansionary steps, culminating in the invasion of Poland. Others were periodic financial measures taken by the French government to stabilize the franc. Others relate to the eruption of rumors that the U.S. government was going to alter the $35 peg to gold. The political events implied capital outflow from continental Europe, which seems to have first gone to Britain as a way station to the United States.

The results are striking. Almost all the time, speculative transactions acted to stabilize and dampen the exchange rate movements based on these crises. The traders seem to have had quite accurate forecasts of the implications of the events that they observed. From the time of the Munich crisis in 1938 the smart money in Europe was betting on war, and large capital outflows from Britain began. The British Exchange Equalization Account became a heavy supporter of sterling, and by January of 1939 it pegged the sterling/dollar rate and forward speculation was outlawed. This altered speculation to the lead-and-lag variety (which we will explain momentarily). The speculation against the pound of this time was also rational of course, as

- the chosen peg rate overvalued the pound on purchasing power parity grounds; and

- war was imminent and assets in Britain would be at risk.

According to Black, the major instabilities in the market were caused by "rumors . . . fed by incautious or ambiguous official statements." Given the extremely troubled circumstances the floating rate system worked extremely well. There was not the stability which would have existed under the effective dominance of one currency, as in the decades before 1914. But in the economic and political conditions of the 1930s nothing better was possible. Governments pursued purely domestic concerns in a shortsighted way and indulged in tariff wars and other beggar-thy-neighbor policies. No substantial cooperation was undertaken on economic policy.

The lead-and-lag speculation that was a complement to and partial substitute for speculation on the forward markets was undertaken with commercial orders and commercial payments. Business transactions ordinarily involve commercial credit—a time limit within which payment may be made with, perhaps, a discount for prompt payment. Companies normally have established patterns for paying their bills. If the discount for prompt payment is not taken it pays to delay payment as long as possible, everything else being given. Similarly importers normally have inventory procedures that determine when new orders are placed. Lead-and-lag speculation involves the acceleration or slowing down of these payments and orders. For example, an American exporter anticipating a depreciation of sterling against the dollar will offer large discounts for prompt payment if he is invoicing in sterling. An American importer who must pay in sterling will delay payment as long as possible in the hope that it will cost him less dollars to meet his sterling accounts payable. Both these moves have the effect of reducing the demand for sterling and increasing the demand for dollars, thus tending to depreciate the pound against the dollar. Importers in Britain who face dollar payables will pay early, and will order more goods, paying in advance for them. The normal flows of commercial payments are so large that even small changes in timing, across the board, will have very dramatic effects on exchange markets. Throughout the life of the Bretton Woods fixed exchange rate system lead-and-lag speculation was of great importance. In 1949, when no speculative capital flows were permitted, Britain was forced off its exchange rate by lead-and lag speculation alone. In the late 1960s the Bundesbank struggled in vain to prevent lead-and-lag speculation on the appreciation of the DM. An elaborate bureaucracy was set up to monitor ordinary terms of payment. The Bank of Japan has exercised tight control over the terms of commercial payment offered and made by Japanese companies.

## 2.5 THE BRETTON WOODS SYSTEM: 1945–1973

There was strong reaction to the noncooperation of the 1930s. In a series of meetings among the soon-to-be victorious allies late in the war, the basis was laid for a number of organizations designed to foster collective responsibility: in politics, the United Nations; in tariffs and trade, the General Agreement on Tariffs and Trade (GATT); and in international finance, the International Monetary Fund (IMF) and the World Bank. The UN, GATT, and the World Bank are outside our area of interest, but we will discuss the IMF in Section 2.6. In addition there was an agreement on a new exchange rate system. The gold exchange standard was abandoned. Gold was to be used for transactions between central banks, and between central banks and the IMF, but currencies were no longer redeemable in gold. Indeed, in the U.S. it was still forbidden to hold gold as an asset or to denominate contractual payments in gold. Countries were to declare a *par value* for their currency in terms of gold and central banks were obliged to enter the exchange markets to buy and sell their currency, to keep it within 2% up or down from its par value. The two key issues were, then:

- where the central banks were to find resources for the intervention, and

- how the par values were to be set and changed.

The par values were supposed to be in accord with fundamental equilibrium, which means purchasing power parity, or exchange rates chosen to keep the goods of all countries competitive on world markets. There was clear understanding, at the inception of the par-value system, that divergent cost trends due to divergent inflation would require that parities be changed from time to time. In practice, parity changes were infrequent and dramatic, being preceded by accelerating speculation. The par-value system in actual operation was too inflexible to permit adjustment to divergent national monetary policies and the different inflation rates that they implied. As the divergences became more and more substantial in the latter 1960s and early 1970s, the system fell apart and was replaced by a somewhat constrained floating exchange rate regime. Whatever else may be said about it, the current floating exchange rate system has permitted extremely rapid exchange rate changes.

Why was the par value system more inflexible in practice than its founders desired? Some factors were specific to the vehicle currency countries, which were the United States and, to a rapidly diminishing extent, Britain. Others were more general.

1. In general, maintaining the parity of the currency in terms of gold became an indicator of competence of government and a symbol of national pride. It was considered a sign of major economic disaster, or else of bowing to foreign pressure, to alter the parities. Governments were willing to squeeze the domestic economy, impose draconian trade and capital-flow controls, and otherwise impose economic harm on their citizens, before changing the price of foreign currencies.

2. Given the outlook we have just described, the par value system was frequently lauded for imposing monetary discipline on national governments. For the system to work with virtually rigid exchange rates, no country could let its inflation exceed the average for any length of time. Of course things didn't work out this way. Countries whose governments actively worked to keep inflation low, like Germany, found continual speculation on appreciation of their currency. High inflation countries like Italy, France, and Britain did not curb monetary growth. Rather they resorted to a haphazard accumulation of makeshift procedures to maintain parity—trade restrictions, exchange controls, limitations on capital outflow, and, worst of all from the general growth perspective, deliberately induced recessions to reduce import demand. The infamous "stop-go" monetary policies followed in Britain, and to some extent in France, were

a major cause of low investment and technological backwardness. Thus the monetary discipline translated into unwanted speculation on revaluation for low-inflation countries, and government-generated economic inefficiency for the high-inflation countries.

3. The vehicle currency countries both gained and lost from their particular status. The gains came in the form of *seignorage*. The extent that people in other countries were willing to hold dollar balances the Federal Reserve was printing world money. To obtain those dollars the foreigners had to surrender real goods or assets. Even if they cashed in these dollar bills at some later date, the U.S. would have had an interest free or low interest loan[16] for the period in which the foreigners held the dollars. However it was felt that the foreigners would not hold these balances if the dollar or the pound started to fluctuate in exchange value. Moreover very large balances were held by foreign governments, putting great pressure on Britain and the United States not to devalue. These governments could not quickly deploy their balances to other currencies, because moves of such magnitude would certainly precipitate the devaluation that they hoped to avoid. In principal the central banks were obliged to redeem their currencies held by other central banks in gold at the par value. In practice only the French tried this. The others abstained because they could deplete the gold reserves of Britain and the United States so much that general confidence in the par values would be shaken. This is how the 1960s passed—growing awareness of the need for parity changes but a general paralysis of will to make them except when forced.

The resources for central bank intervention in exchange markets came from the IMF, from their own holdings of gold and foreign currency, from "line of credit" agreements with other central banks and from the printing press. The printing press was relevant when a government wanted to hold down the value of its currency in terms of others, for example when the Bundesbank wanted to prevent the DM from appreciating against the dollar. In that case, it printed DM and sold them for dollars on the exchange market. The dollars became part of the Bundesbank's foreign exchange reserves and the DM swelled the German money supply. To understand this, recollect that there is upward pressure on the DM vis-à-vis the dollar if more dollar-holders are trying to buy DM than DM-holders are trying to buy dollars. The dollar-holders try to buy the DM because they want to buy German goods or assets. When the Bundesbank supplies them with DM, they buy the goods and assets and the newly-created DM go straight into circulation in the German economy. On the other hand,

---

[16]If the balances were held in non-interest-bearing checking accounts, the resources would have been lent interest-free. Most were held in highly liquid securities like U.S. Treasury Bills and Eurodollars, the yield on which was below the marginal return on capital in the United States, so that seignorage was profitable.

dollar-holders buying DM from the Bundesbank are writing checks to the Bundesbank on dollar-denominated accounts, so the Bundesbank becomes the owner of these accounts. This process was extremely important for Eurodollar creation in the 1960s, as we explain in Chapter 8.

In 1960 there was heavy speculation on a DM appreciation, and so much foreign exchange flooded in and was converted to DM that the Bundesbank lost control of the money supply. In order to forestall an explosion of inflation, the DM was appreciated by 5% in 1961. After this currency crisis the major central banks created swap-loan arrangements, which rapidly provided deficit countries with large sums of foreign exchange to prop up their currencies. The main result of these very large loan plans was to permit currencies like the pound and the lira to remain overvalued for long periods of time. This prolonged the application of restrictive and inefficient domestic policies, and ensured that the final collapse would be much more dramatic. For very simple, fundamental, economic reasons, exchange rates cannot be allowed to deviate from their purchasing power parity values for very long. We explain this at length in Chapters 5 and 6. Whatever value one might ascribe to governmental exchange market stabilization schemes, they must be coordinated with a policy of keeping rates roughly at their fundamental equilibrium levels. Given the reluctance to alter the parities, all the central bank and IMF loan schemes prolonged an untenable situation at great cost to residents of the deficit countries, of the surplus countries (as we explain in Chapter 6) and to the detriment of world trade.

From the late 1950s onwards most western European countries (exceptions were Britain and Italy) tended to run strong surpluses against the U.S. dollar. In part this was deliberate accumulation of dollars to use as reserves; in part it reflected the growing overvaluation of the dollar as the 1960s progressed. This inflow of foreign exchange caused inflationary pressure. The dollars were converted into local currency, which was pumped into the local economy. The European central banks could not conduct satisfactory open-market operations to sop up the excess liquidity, as there was no equivalent to the huge U.S. Treasury Bill market. The instruments available to them were cruder—bank reserve requirement changes and changes in central bank rediscount rates. Any tightening tended to raise short-term interest rates because it could not be fine tuned exactly to absorb the new money inflow. But rising interest rates precipitated more short-term capital inflow from abroad. So the central banks devised new means to cope with the problem.

### Nonprice Credit Rationing.

By the mechanism of the conventional money multiplier, an initial injection of, say, DM into the German money supply due to exchange rate pegging, was multiplied into a final impact on the money supply. The central banks had to either withdraw money in some way or limit the multiplier process. They undertook the following mandatory allocations of credit:

- They limited their own rediscounts of commercial paper held by the banking system, an important source of funds for banks in all the continental EEC countries in the 1960s.

- Except in Germany, ceilings were placed on the ability of banks to make loans. In the Netherlands variations in these ceilings actually became the principal tool of monetary policy. The central banks thus wound up interfering in the allocation of capital among users because of the fixed exchange rate system. Upon reflection, this must be seen as an astonishing indictment of the system.

### Incentives to Domestic Banks to Alter Foreign Exchange Positions.

In Germany and Italy in particular, the central banks induced commercial banks to make capital outflows at times of balance of payments surpluses, and inflows at times of deficits. In Italy, the central bank simply ordered commercial banks to maintain chosen net foreign asset positions. In Germany, the Bundesbank offered to the domestic banks forward exchange rates unrelated to external market rates and designed to create covered interest arbitrage flows in the desired direction. At times more than 50% of foreign money-market assets owned by German banks were under this arrangement. The Bundesbank also imposed special reserve requirements on nonresident deposits, but allowed these to be offset by outward covered arbitrage flows, giving banks further incentive to move funds out of Germany. At times this offset privilege added as much as 1% to the effective yield on capital outflows.

As the 1960s progressed, all the EEC countries, plus Britain and the United States, imposed more and more restrictions on the ability of their residents to lend or borrow abroad, thus moving away from the substantial degree of convertibility achieved by, say, 1960. Indeed, by the late 1960s, the escalating restrictions on movements of funds, and attempts to oversee trade payments to try to inhibit lead-and-lag speculation, caused informed observers to wonder whether the system of free trade and payments that had sustained postwar economic growth could survive. This too was an extraordinary development.

The monetary system experienced a terminal series of currency crises starting with the devaluation of sterling in 1967. By the end of the 1960s cost inflation in the German tradable goods sector was lower than in the United States, while Britain, Italy, and France experienced much more inflation than either. A fundamental realignment of parities was needed but did not come about. Instead, rumors of changes in parities, and balance of payments deterioration, forced a sequence of speculative incidents. In 1969 the DM was appreciated by 9.3%, and in May 1971 the Bundesbank floated the DM because it once again was unable to prevent the money supply from ballooning. Indeed, in the three days preceding the May floating, the Bundesbank absorbed $2 billion equivalent in foreign exchange (at today's prices about $3 billion or $1 billion per day). The DM floating diverted speculation against the dollar into yen, French francs, Swiss francs, Dutch guilder, and even the pound. In 1971 the United States ran a $30.5 billion deficit (close to $45 billion at current prices), and in August 1971 the United States broke with the par value system and effectively floated the dollar. In December of 1971 new fixed rates were worked out at the Smithsonian Meeting but soon proved to be a dead letter.

From 1969 on, the U.S. money supply had grown very rapidly, supposedly to encourage the economy, and then to encourage reelection of Richard Nixon. Inflation had been rapid in Britain. The pound and the dollar were over valued at the Smithsonian pegs, and speculation on another collapse began. In June 1972 the pound was forced to float and then lack of confidence in the pegs spread to the dollar. The U.S. deficit in 1972, at 1972 prices, was $21 billion. On March 1, 1973, the Bundesbank was forced to purchase $2.7 billion (about $4.8 billion at current prices) of foreign exchange to maintain the peg, and then threw in the towel. The exchange markets closed and opened to a new order. The EEC countries floated as a bloc against the dollar, except for Britain and Italy, which floated separately, as did the yen. It was fortunate that the system collapsed then, since floating rates enabled it to ride out the Arab oil embargo and the subsequent inflation without any currency crises of major importance. In its annual report for 1975, the IMF admitted that "on the whole, exchange rate flexibility appears to have enabled the world economy to surmount a succession of disturbing events, and to accommodate divergent trends in costs and prices in national economies with less disruption of trade and payments than a system of par values would have been able to do."

## 2.6   THE INTERNATIONAL MONETARY FUND

The IMF was organized to be a weak kind of central banks' central bank. Its function was to sustain the fixed exchange rate system by lending to central banks the foreign currencies needed to stabilize exchange rates around their true equilibrium values. In addition, it was to provide economic analysis and policy advice to members. Those members wishing to borrow beyond a certain amount were given no choice about whether to accept the advice. The basic structure of the IMF has changed little since its inception, so we will describe its current status with historical digressions where necessary.

The ability of any country to borrow from the fund is related to the size of its quota.

Each member must pay into the IMF a quota of resources determined essentially by the size of its economy. The current quotas (valued in SDRs) are given in Table 2.1. Each member subscribes 75% of its quota in its own currency and 25% in SDRs or convertible currencies. Before 1974, the 25% share was in gold and was known as the *gold tranche*. The deposits of the national currencies comprise the resources available to lend to borrowing countries. A member's deposit of its own currency makes sense because

- if exchange rates are at their fundamental long-run equilibrium values, every member's currency will at some time be borrowed, and in amounts roughly proportional to the country's importance in world trade; and

- with the demonetization of gold and the reluctance to convert the SDR into a true international money, there is nothing else that can be subscribed or lent.

Indeed, if all currencies were convertible there would no longer be any need for an equivalent to a gold tranche.

Members of the fund borrow by exchanging their own currency for convertible currencies of other fund members. A country is free to do this unconditionally so as to bring the fund's holdings of its currency up to 100% of its quota. Thus it can borrow the gold tranche *plus* the total value of drawings of its currency by other members. These drawings of course have drawn down the fund's holding of the currency in question. The normal maximum for loans is three years. Further borrrowings can be made in four credit tranches, each normally equal to 25% of the member's quota. Borrowing under each successive credit tranche requires that to qualify for the loan the member must meet progressively more restrictive conditions regarding the conduct of its economic policies. Annual interest rate terms for credit tranche loans range from 4 3/8 percent for loans of up to one year to 6 3/8 percent for four- to five-year loans. In addition, there is a service charge of 1/2 percent. When the IMF holds a member's currency in excess of the quota, the member is obliged to repurchase its currency from the IMF. This obligation is fulfilled either when the member purchases its currency with SDRs or the currency of members whose currencies are held by the IMF in amounts below 75 percent of the member's quotas, or when its currency is sold by the IMF to other member countries. Figure 2.1 shows borrowings from and repurchases or repayments to the Fund by members over the period 1974–1978. Note that there are a number of special facilities established by the IMF for specific purposes, as well as general intervention financing. Appendix 2.1 provides a summary of the major modifications to the Articles of Agreement of the IMF, ratified by a majority of fund members on April 1, 1978.

**Table 2.1** *Quotas of Member Countries of the IMF on April 1, 1978*

| Member (currency) | Million SDRs | Percent of Total | Member (currency) | Million SDRs | Percent of Total |
|---|---|---|---|---|---|
| Afghanistan (afghani) | 45 | 0.12 | [a]Ethiopia (birr) | 36 | 0.09 |
| Algeria (dinar) | 285 | 0.73 | [a]Fiji (dollar) | 18 | 0.05 |
| [a]Argentina (peso) | 535 | 1.37 | [a]Finland (markka) | 262 | 0.67 |
| Australia (dollar) | 790 | 2.02 | France (franc) | 1,919 | 4.92 |
| Austria (schilling) | 330 | 0.85 | [a]Gabon (franc) | 30 | 0.08 |
| Bahamas (dollar) | 33 | 0.08 | [a]Gambia, The (dalasi) | 9 | 0.02 |
| [a]Bahrain (dinar) | 20 | 0.05 | [a]Germany, Federal Rep. (deutsche mark) | 2,156 | 5.52 |
| [a]Bangladesh (taka) | 152 | 0.39 | | | |
| [a]Barbados (dollar) | 17 | 0.04 | [a]Ghana (cedi) | 106 | 0.27 |
| [a]Belgium (franc) | 890 | 2.28 | [a]Greece (drachma) | 185 | 0.47 |
| [a]Benin (franc) | 16 | 0.04 | [a]Grenada (East Caribbean dollar) | 3 | 0.01 |
| [a]Bolivia (peso) | 45 | 0.12 | | | |
| [a]Botswana (pula) | 9 | 0.02 | Guatemala (quetzal) | 51 | 0.13 |
| [a]Brazil (cruzeiro) | 665 | 1.70 | Guinea (syli) | 30 | 0.08 |
| [a]Burma (kyat) | 73 | 0.19 | Guinea-Bissau[b] (peso) | 3.2 | 0.01 |
| Burundi (franc) | 23 | 0.06 | | | |
| Cambodia | 31 | 0.08 | [a]Guyana (dollar) | 25 | 0.06 |
| [a]Cameroon (franc) | 45 | 0.12 | [a]Haiti (gourde) | 23 | 0.06 |
| [a]Canada (dollar) | 1,357 | 3.48 | [a]Honduras (lempira) | 34 | 0.09 |
| Central African Empire (franc) | 16 | 0.04 | [a]Iceland (króna) | 29 | 0.07 |
| Chad (franc) | 16 | 0.04 | [a]India (rupee) | 1,145 | 2.93 |
| [a]Chile (peso) | 217 | 0.56 | [a]Indonesia (rupiah) | 480 | 1.23 |
| China, Republic (new Taiwan dollar) | 550 | 1.41 | [a]Iran (rial) | 660 | 1.69 |
| | | | Iraq (dinar) | 141 | 0.36 |
| [a]Colombia (peso) | 193 | 0.49 | [a]Ireland (pound) | 155 | 0.40 |
| Comoros[b] (franc) | 1.9 | 0.01 | [a]Israel (pound) | 205 | 0.53 |
| Congo, People's Republic (franc) | 17 | 0.04 | [a]Italy (lira) | 1,240 | 3.18 |
| [a]Costa Rica (colón) | 41 | 0.11 | [a]Ivory Coast (franc) | 76 | 0.20 |
| [a]Cyprus (pound) | 34 | 0.09 | [a]Jamaica (dollar) | 74 | 0.19 |
| [a]Denmark (krone) | 310 | 0.79 | Japan (yen) | 1,659 | 4.25 |
| [a]Dominican Republic (peso) | 55 | 0.14 | Jordan (dinar) | 30 | 0.08 |
| [a]Ecuador (sucre) | 70 | 0.18 | Kenya (shilling) | 69 | 0.18 |
| Egypt (pound) | 228 | 0.58 | [a]Korea (won) | 160 | 0.41 |
| [a]El Salvador (colón) | 43 | 0.11 | [a]Kuwait (dinar) | 235 | 0.60 |
| Equatorial Guinea (ekuele) | 10 | 0.03 | Lao People's Dem. Rep. (kip) | 16 | 0.04 |
| | | | Lebanon (pound) | 12 | 0.03 |

**Table 2.1**   *Quotas of Member Countries of the IMF on April 1, 1978* (cont'd)

| Member (currency) | Million SDRs | Percent of Total | Member (currency) | Million SDRs | Percent of Total |
|---|---|---|---|---|---|
| [a]Lesotho (rand) | 7 | 0.02 | [a]Rwanda (franc) | 23 | 0.06 |
| [a]Liberia (dollar) | 37 | 0.10 | São Tomé and | | |
| [a]Libya (dinar) | 185 | 0.47 | Principe[b] | | |
| Luxembourg | | | (dobra) | 1.6 | 0.01 |
| (franc) | 31 | 0.08 | [a]Saudi Arabia | | |
| Madagascar | | | (riyal) | 600 | 1.54 |
| (franc) | 34 | 0.09 | [a]Senegal (franc) | 42 | 0.11 |
| [a]Malawi (kwacha) | 19 | 0.05 | [a]Seychelles[b] | | |
| [a]Malaysia (ringgit) | 253 | 0.65 | (rupee) | 1 | 0.003 |
| Maldives[b] (rupee) | 0.7 | 0.002 | [a]Sierra Leone | | |
| [a]Mali (franc) | 27 | 0.07 | (leone) | 31 | 0.08 |
| Malta (pound) | 20 | 0.05 | Singapore (dollar) | 110 | 0.28 |
| Mauritania | | | Somalia (shilling) | 23 | 0.06 |
| (ouguiya) | 17 | 0.04 | [a]South Africa | | |
| [a]Mauritius (rupee) | 27 | 0.07 | (rand) | 424 | 1.09 |
| [a]Mexico (peso) | 535 | 1.37 | [a]Spain (peseta) | 557 | 1.43 |
| [a]Morocco | | | Sri Lanka (rupee) | 119 | 0.30 |
| (dirham) | 150 | 0.38 | [a]Sudan (pound) | 88 | 0.23 |
| [a]Nepal (rupee) | 19 | 0.05 | [a]Swaziland | | |
| [a]Netherlands | | | (lilangeni) | 12 | 0.03 |
| (guilder) | 948 | 2.43 | [a]Sweden (krona) | 450 | 1.15 |
| New Zealand | | | Syrian Arab | | |
| (dollar) | 232 | 0.59 | Republic | | |
| Nicaragua | | | (pound) | 63 | 0.16 |
| (córdoba) | 34 | 0.09 | Tanzania | | |
| [a]Niger (franc) | 16 | 0.04 | (shilling) | 55 | 0.14 |
| [a]Nigeria (naira) | 360 | 0.92 | [a]Thailand (baht) | 181 | 0.46 |
| [a]Norway (krone) | 295 | 0.76 | [a]Togo (franc) | 19 | 0.05 |
| Oman (rial | | | [a]Trinidad and | | |
| Omani) | 20 | 0.05 | Tobago (dollar) | 82 | 0.21 |
| [a]Pakistan (rupee) | 285 | 0.73 | [a]Tunisia (dinar) | 63 | 0.16 |
| [a]Panama (balboa) | 45 | 0.12 | Turkey (lira) | 200 | 0.51 |
| [a]Papua New | | | Uganda (shilling) | 50 | 0.13 |
| Guinea (kina) | 30 | 0.08 | [a]United Arab | | |
| [a]Paraguay | | | Emirates | | |
| (guarani) | 23 | 0.06 | (dirham) | 120 | 0.31 |
| [a]Peru (sol) | 164 | 0.42 | [a]United Kingdom | | |
| [a]Philippines | | | (pound) | 2,925 | 7.49 |
| (peso) | 210 | 0.54 | [a]United States | | |
| [a]Portugal (escudo) | 172 | 0.44 | (dollar) | 8,405 | 21.53 |
| [a]Qatar (riyal) | 40 | 0.10 | [a]Upper Volta | | |
| Romania (leu) | 245 | 0.63 | (franc) | 16 | 0.04 |
| | | | [a]Uruguay (new | | |
| | | | peso) | 84 | 0.22 |

**Table 2.1**  *Quotas of Member Countries of the IMF on April 1, 1978* (cont'd)

| Member (currency) | Million SDRs | Percent of Total | Member (currency) | Million SDRs | Percent of Total |
|---|---|---|---|---|---|
| [a]Venezuela (bolívar) | 660 | 1.69 | Yemen, People's Dem. Rep. (dinar) | 41 | 0.11 |
| Viet Nam (dong) | 90 | 0.23 | Yugoslavia (dinar) | 277 | 0.71 |
| Western Samoa (tala) | 3 | 0.01 | Zaïre (zaïre) | 152 | 0.39 |
| Yemen Arab Republic (rial) | 13 | 0.03 | [a]Zambia (kwacha) | 141 | 0.36 |
|  |  |  | **Total** | **39,041.4** | **100.00[c]** |

[a]Member had consented to quota increase as of March 31, 1978.
[b]Country became a Fund member after Sixth General Review of Quotas.
[c]Due to rounding, components may not add to totals shown.

*Source:* Federal Reserve Bank of Chicago, "International Letter," No. 368, April 28, 1978.

**Figure 2.1**  Purchases and Repurchases of Fund Members

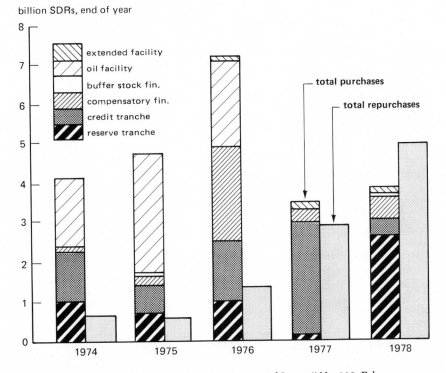

*Source:* Federal Reserve Bank of Chicago, "International Letter," No. 389, February 16, 1979.

For many years the Fund's staff were resistant to the idea of a floating exchange rate system. Perhaps this was because it denied the raison d'etre for their organization, perhaps it was because they preferred the monetary system to evolve instead towards a unified, single money system with the IMF as the central bank. The major step in this direction was the creation of Special Drawing Rights (SDRs), which were viewed by some as the coming world currency. We now examine the history of the SDR.

## 2.7  SPECIAL DRAWING RIGHTS

SDRs were created as a device to increase international liquidity. At their inception in 1969, SDRs were paper claims with a nominal gold value. They were to have the gold value of one pre-1971 U.S. dollar. A certain number were created on the books of the IMF and allocated to member nations on the basis of the members' IMF quotas. The SDRs were to be as good as gold for payments between central banks, and between central banks and the IMF. However, not many were created, and there were quite restrictive limits on how many a country could be obliged to accept before it was free to demand further payments in gold or designated currencies. The leading industrial countries were not willing to countenance the creation of a real international money, freely convertible into all national monies, because that would have deprived them of all power to limit their money supplies. We will return to this subject below. Let us first consider the motivation for the creation of SDRs.

When does one need to create extra international liquidity on top of increases in existing money supplies? Money balances are held to facilitate trade and transactions, whether these transactions are in domestic or foreign commerce. We will become somewhat more precise about the demand for transactions balances in Chapter 5. Here we make the commonsense assertion that demand for balances of money to facilitate transactions should:

- Increase in proportion to inflation, all other things given. If everything costs twice as much, you need twice as many nominal dollars to settle the same transactions as before.

- Increase as real income/real product increase, because economic growth means more transactions.

Just as firms and individuals hold domestic money balances to facilitate domestic transactions, they (or international banks, for convenience) hold balances of foreign currency to facilitate foreign transactions. These balances are balances of the national currencies in which the transactions take place. There is no need for some extra international currency to provide the liquidity needed for trade and production. Moreover there are more than adequate supplies of the domestic currencies of the major trading nations. The excess supplies of these currencies are responsible for the major inflationary trends of the post-World War II period.

What then was the purpose of increasing international liquidity in this way? Effectively, the intention was to increase the resources available to central banks for intervention in foreign exchange markets. The SDRs were to be used only for central bank and IMF settlements in return for currencies purchased to support overvalued rates. As the value of world trade grew, the value of currency input needed to swing the exchange market a given amount grew also. Even so, this growth in the need for intervention resources still would not require the creation of "paper gold" if exchange rates were basically at their purchasing power parity or long run equilibrium values. If the rates were at equilibrium, all interventions would presumably be of a short-run nature. As trade grew, central banks could borrow proportionately more from other central banks, or the IMF, without fear of any problems with repayment. Their borrowings would remain a constant proportion of their export revenues and would be no more risky than at lower levels of world trade. The perceived need for a paper gold reflected other causes than pure stabilization need.

- Sustained departures of exchange rates from their long-run equilibrium values, creating a need for extremely large resources to permit central bank rate pegging.

- Mistrust of the current exchange rates for the British pound, and particularly the U.S. dollar, which were used as vehicle currencies and which were therefore held in very large amounts by institutions in many countries.

The basic problem was that these countries' currencies were overvalued on a purchasing power parity basis, as was confirmed subsequently by a series of depreciations of the pound and the dollar. The collapse of the fixed exchange rate system between 1971 and 1973 effectively ended this need for a paper gold.

Tying the SDR to the U.S. dollar alone made it just another form of dollar, albeit one not created by the Federal Reserve System. After generalized floating in 1973, the SDR had no advantage over dollars, and balances earned no interest. Thus in 1974 the SDR was redefined to be a basket of currencies. The specific basket and the method of construction are shown in Table 2.2. Table 2.3 shows the dollar value of 1 SDR as of noon on January 31, 1979. As the spot exchange rates fluctuate, the value of the SDR in terms of the dollar (or any other currency) will also fluctuate. SDRs defined in this way have not proven any more acceptable as a global money than SDRs tied to gold or to the dollar. However to a limited extent the SDR in its commodity bundle version has found acceptance as a unit of account for setting price. There exist some bond issues whose coupons

**Table 2.2** *Construction of Basket Weights for the Revised SDR*

| | 1 | 2 | 3 | 4 | 5 | 6 | 7 |
|---|---|---|---|---|---|---|---|
| | Exports of Goods and Services (68–72 average) | Share of Total Exports | Share to Total -adj. to US-33% | Actual Weight | $U.S. Value with 1 SDR— $1.20635 (column 4 × 1.20635) | $U.S. exchange rate, 6/28/74 | Currency Unit per SDR (column 5 × column 6) |
| | $U.S. (bill) | percent | percent | percent | $U.S. | $U.S./unit | units |
| dollar (U.S.) | 62.54 | 21.1 | (33.0) | 33.0 | .4000 | — | .40 |
| Deutsche mark | 43.45 | 14.7 | 12.7 | 12.5 | .1508 | .3922 | .38 |
| pound (British) | 36.44 | 12.3 | 10.5 | 9.0 | .1086 | 2.3895 | .045 |
| franc (French) | 25.07 | 8.5 | 7.2 | 7.5 | .0905 | .2065 | .44 |
| yen (Japanese) | 23.99 | 8.1 | 6.9 | 7.5 | .0905 | .003522 | 26.0 |
| dollar (Canadian) | 19.99 | 6.8 | 5.8 | 6.0 | .0724 | 1.03025 | .071 |
| lira (Italian) | 19.70 | 6.7 | 5.7 | 6.0 | .0724 | .001547 | 47.0 |
| guilder (Dutch) | 15.10 | 5.1 | 4.3 | 4.5 | .0543 | .3758 | .14 |
| franc (Belgian) | 12.59 | 4.3 | 3.7 | 3.5 | .0422 | .02681 | 1.6 |
| krona (Sweden) | 8.09 | 2.7 | 2.3 | 2.5 | .0302 | .2272 | .13 |
| dollar (Australian) | 5.80 | 2.0 | 1.7 | 1.5 | .0181 | 1.4925 | .012 |
| peseta (Spanish) | 5.15 | 1.7 | 1.4 | 1.5 | .0181 | .01748 | 1.1 |
| krone (Norwegian) | 4.83 | 1.6 | 1.4 | 1.5 | .0181 | .1839 | .099 |
| krone (Danish) | 4.69 | 1.6 | 1.4 | 1.5 | .0181 | .1664 | .11 |
| schilling (Austrian) | 4.38 | 1.5 | 1.3 | 1.0 | .0121 | .0548 | .22 |
| rand (South African) | 3.99 | 1.3 | 1.2 | 1.0 | .0121 | 1.5025 | .0082 |

**Table 2.3** *Dollar Value of One SDR, January 31, 1979*[a]

| Currency | Number of Units in SDR Basket × | Spot Rate 1/31/79 = | $ Value |
|---|---|---|---|
| dollar (U.S.) | .40 | 1.000 | .40 |
| mark (German) | .38 | .5339 | .2029 |
| pound (British) | .045 | 1.9896 | .0895 |
| franc (French) | .44 | .2330 | .1025 |
| yen (Japanese) | 26.0 | .0049 | .1274 |
| dollar (Canadian) | .071 | .8331 | .0592 |
| lira (Italian) | 47.0 | .0012 | .0564 |
| guilder (Dutch) | .14 | .4948 | .0693 |
| franc (Belgian) | 1.6 | .0340 | .0544 |
| krona (Swedish) | .13 | .2273 | .0295 |
| dollar (Australian) | .012 | 1.1336 | .0136 |
| peseta (Spanish) | 1.1 | .0143 | .0157 |
| krone (Norwegian) | .099 | .1944 | .0192 |
| krone (Danish) | .11 | .1931 | .0212 |
| schilling (Austrian) | .22 | .0729 | .0160 |
| rand (South African) | .0082 | 1.1475 | .0094 |
| | | Total = | 1.2864 |

[a]Computed using noon buying rates in New York City for cable transfers payable in foreign currencies.

are payable in SDRs, and a variety of commodity producers (including oil producers) have toyed with the notion of pricing their goods in terms of SDRs rather than in any one national currency.

To understand why we must raise a basic principle that will recur frequently in the chapters to follow: rational individuals are not interested in nominal wealth but in real purchasing power, the command they have over goods and services. If the price of oil is tied to the U.S. dollar, the purchasing power that the sale of a barrel of oil gives to the producer is tied to the purchasing power of the dollar. As Chapter 5 makes clear, in the long run the producer could vary his U.S. dollar prices to keep them constant in real terms, measured by a U.S. price index, and also have them constant in real terms measured by other price indexes. However there are many short-term exchange rate fluctuations, and all of these reflect on purchasing power. Now suppose the oil producer imported goods in the exact proportions of column 3 in Table 2.2. By pricing his oil in SDRs he is acquiring as revenue a basket of currencies that matches exactly his currency needs for imports. He is thus hedged against short-term purchasing power fluctuations of his export revenues. If the DM appreciates against the dollar then the oil producer's new Mercedes-Benz will rise in price in dollars, but the oil producer has DM revenue that also rises in dollar terms, by the same percentage.

Thus the SDR may have a future as a unit of account for the denomination of contracts. It has no future as a global money unless there is agreement to end the independence of national monetary authorities and found a true world central bank. The forces of nationalism are simply too strong to permit such a development. A single world money would be best for trade and investment. But if this is infeasible a return to the par-value system is the worst alternative. The exchange market is only the reflection of the domestic monetary and fiscal policies of the trading nations. If these policies are not coordinated then exchange rates must change to offset different trends in local currency costs of producing competitive items. A system in which such adjustments do not occur promptly cannot survive.[17]


## 2.8   SUMMARY

This chapter has examined the evolution of the international monetary system from the gold exchange standard of the late nineteenth century to today's dirty float, using as framework the simultaneous evolution of attitudes towards monetary policy. The ever-present tension in the system is derived from the antithesis between the need for a universal money as a medium of exchange to facilitate trade, and the desire of national governments to influence their economies by monetary manipulations.

The pre-1914 gold exchange standard represents one extreme pole of this policy oscillation. In that system most of the major trading nations issued paper money with a gold backing. Holders of one country's paper money could redeem it for gold from the money-issuing agency, take the gold to another country's money-issuing agency, and obtain that country's paper money. Gold shipments would insure that exchange rates between paper moneys stay fixed. We give an example of this phenomenon to illustrate the impact of transaction costs on all arbitrage processes.

As with all true fixed exchange rate systems, there was effectively one universal money, with changes in the supply of that money affecting price levels all over the world, not only in the country which was the source of the disturbance. This period was characterized by a growing world economy and deflation of prices, since gold production could not keep pace with world GNP. There was extraordinary financial stability (by

---

[17]Current attempts to form a European Monetary System (EMS) around a currency basket called the European Currency Unit (ECU) suffers from this defect. All technical details aside, it is a par-value system for EEC members without any formal constraints on divergent monetary policies among the members. There is a central fund (equivalent to the IMF), which is to lend to member central banks to help them maintain the currency pegs, but there is no reason to expect the fund ever to be large enough. An excellent, detailed description of the EMS is available to all free of charge as "International Letter" No. 391, March 16, 1979, Federal Reserve Bank of Chicago, Chicago, Illinois.

comparison with modern times) under the gold exchange standard system. This stability was due not only to the absence of effective governmental monetary policies, but also to the flexibility of prices and wages, and to the general public confidence in the operation of the system.

Between the wars there was neither financial stability nor confidence that stability would be restored. The problems of the monetary system stemmed from the unresolved political conflicts of the war, and the fundamental disruption in the system of production and trade that they caused, such as the exclusion of Russia from trade with western Europe. Countries formed currency blocks and adopted discriminatory tariff regulations and competitive exchange depreciation in an attempt to pass off their problems onto someone else. Whenever the exchange markets were left alone they functioned smoothly, but as the 1930s progressed they were left alone less and less often.

In reaction to the problems of the interwar period, as they were perceived at the time, a new monetary order was established in 1944 and 1945. Its intent was to keep most of the universal currency features of the gold exchange standard system while allowing governments to conduct monetary policy to achieve economic stability and full employment. Governments were to intervene in exchange markets to keep fixed parities between their paper moneys, while the International Monetary Fund was established to aid this price fixing process with analysis and loans. In practice it proved impossible (for political reasons) to alter the fixed parities to allow for new economic circumstances, in particular sustained differences in the rate of inflation which different governments allowed as a matter of policy. Attempts to create a world money in the form of Special Drawing Rights failed, and the various stresses eventually brought down the whole system, the world moving to a floating rate system (with substantial governmental intervention) in the period 1971–1973.

In response to frequent complaints that the current exchange rate variability is harmful to trade, the countries of the European Economic Community have on a number of occasions attempted to fix exchange rates among their currencies by intergovernmental financial cooperation. But the exchange market will always reflect disparities in economic policies followed in the countries in question: as long as such disparities exist no fixed exchange rate system can survive.

### Suggestions for Further Reading

The most comprehensive and generally accessible history of the international monetary system is the book by Yeager cited earlier in this chapter. The next best source is the whole series of special papers published over the years by the International Finance Section of the Department of Economics of Princeton University. This is a famous (and ongoing) series of works. In addition to those cited in the text we recommend:

S.V.O. Clarke, "The Reconstruction of the International Monetary System: The Attempts of 1922 and 1933," *Princeton Studies in International Finance*, No. 33, 1973.

J. Artus and A. Crockett, "Floating Exchange Rates and the Need for Surveillance," *Essays in International Finance*, No. 127, May 1978.

K. Chrystal, "International Money and the Future of the SDR," *Essays in International Finance*, No. 128, June 1978.

## Appendix 2.1  *Amended Articles of Agreement of the IMF*[18]

Reform of the international monetary system that began in 1971 following collapse of the postwar Bretton Woods system was formally completed April 1, 1978, when the Second Amendment to the International Monetary Fund's Articles of Agreement went into force with ratification by the required majority of the 133 member nations.

The Second Amendment contains several major provisions, some of which have been already informally adopted by member nations. Provisions on *exchange rate arrangements* are based on recognition that the essential purpose of the international monetary system is to provide a framework that both facilitates the exchange of goods, services, and capital among countries and sustains sound economic growth for all nations. In ratifying the amendment, members undertake a general obligation to collaborate with the IMF and with other members to ensure orderly exchange arrangements and promote a stable system of exchange rates. Members are required to seek to promote stability by fostering orderly underlying economic and financial conditions and a monetary system that does not tend to produce erratic disruptions. They must avoid manipulating exchange rates or the international monetary system in order to prevent effective balance of payments adjustment or to gain an unfair competitive advantage over other members. Members are free to apply the exchange arrangements of their choice, except that they are not to maintain a value for their currencies in terms of gold. They are required to notify the IMF of the exchange arrangements they intend to apply and of any subsequent changes in these arrangements. The IMF will oversee the international monetary system to ensure its effective operation.

The most important changes with respect to the *role of gold* in the international monetary system are as follows: (1) gold has been eliminated as the unit of value of the SDR and cannot be used as a common denominator for par values of currencies, even if at some future time par values were introduced; (2) the official price of gold has been abolished and members are free to deal in gold in the market and among themselves without reference to any official price; (3) obligatory payments in gold by members between the IMF and its members have been abrogated, and the IMF can accept gold only under decisions taken with an 85 percent majority of the total voting power; (4) the IMF will be required to complete the announced program of disposing of a total of 50 million ounces of gold and will have powers to make further gold sales both on the basis of prices in the market and at the official price in effect before the Second Amendment (SDR 35 per ounce); (5) profits beyond the former official price on any such further sales will be placed in a Special Disbursement Account for use in the ordinary operations and transactions of the IMF or for other uses, including balance-of-payments assistance for the benefit of developing members in difficult circumstances.

---

[18]This summary is reprinted verbatim from Federal Reserve Bank of Chicago, "International Letter," No. 368, April 28, 1978.

   The modifications in the provisions relating to the *Special Drawing Rights* (SDR) are intended to help make the SDR the principal reserve asset in the international monetary system. Under the amended Articles: (1) the method of valuing the SDR can be determined by the IMF by a 70 percent majority; (2) participants can enter into transactions by agreement without general or special decisions by the IMF, and transfers of SDRs in such transactions are not subject to the requirement of need to use reserve assets; (3) the SDR replaces gold in certain payments between the IMF and its members, and its possible use in operations and transactions conducted through the IMF's General Department (formerly the General Account) are to be expanded.

# Chapter 3

# Trade in Commodities: The Ultimate Purpose of International Financial Transactions

## 3.1 INTRODUCTION

We start this discussion of international finance with a subject that at first may seem somewhat removed from our principal sphere of interest. However an understanding of the gains from trade, principles of specialization and efficient mix of production, and the impact of tariffs and quotas is indispensable to an understanding of the operation of exchange markets and to interpretation of events in the international monetary system. It will influence our interpretation of balance of payment statistics in Chapter 4, our understanding of the implications of government exchange markets intervention in Chapter 6, and our evaluation of the creditworthiness of foreign borrowers in Chapter 11. One frequently reads or hears statements claiming that it is always good to export more, or that undervaluation of the yen created export-led growth in Japan, or that greater self-sufficiency in the production of energy, food, clothing (insert the commodity of your choice) is clearly beneficial for the country. In this chapter you will learn how to evaluate these claims. Since an appreciation of the currency is analogous to a tax on exports and a subsidy on imports, while a depreciation is analogous to a tariff on imports and a subsidy on exports, you will see the implications for real economic activity of sustained departures of exchange rates from their natural, or *purchasing power parity*, levels. Purchasing power parity is an equilibrium concept for exchange rates introduced in Chapter 5. It is based on the common-sense statement that trade in goods, services, and assets is the underlying motivator of all international financial transactions.

## 3.2 TRADE IS ALWAYS BETTER THAN AUTARKY: A RICARDIAN EXAMPLE

Trade between countries takes place for two reasons: first, because some countries produce goods which cannot be obtained in other countries; and second, because it is more efficient to export some goods in order to obtain desired commodities than to produce all the desired commodities domestically. It seems safe to say that the great bulk of the world's trade occurs for the second reason rather than the first. It is true that there are rare minerals, and that the Eiffel Tower is only to be found in Paris, and that penguins live only in the southern hemisphere. However, synthetic oil can be created at great cost, and synthetic rubber at lower cost. Probably only for tourism is it absolutely necessary that the same product be un-available domestically.

The "efficiency" explanation of trade (which we will soon label *the theory of comparative advantage*) applies as well to individuals as it does to countries. You could grow all your own food, build your own house, provide your own means of transportation, and write your own textbooks. Invariably it is much more attractive to practice some substantial spe-cialization. You will acquire an occupation and trade the output of that specialization for the goods that you actually want to consume. Of course many people sew buttons on their shirts and darn their own socks, and some even grow vegetables, so that the specialization is never complete. You could all imagine a society in which it was more advantageous to do much more for yourselves. Early pioneer society in the United States was like this. Once again the reason is clear: when one compared the potential results of one's own labors with the cost of having someone else come in to do it, it paid to be a jack-of-all-trades. By building your own house, you had less time to devote to production of grain, but the extra grain you could produce by complete specialization could not be sold for enough to pay the builder in a labor-scarce region. This example isolates all the ingredients of a theory of trade: a technology of producing some mix of goods, and prices at which the goods can be exchanged in trade.[1] Let us now turn to a discussion of trade between countries.

Imagine several countries in an autarkic state. Because these countries

---

[1]We are interested in relative prices, which measure the value of a commodity in terms of the number of units of some other commodity which exchange for it at current nominal prices. For example, before 1973 one hour of minimum wage labor exchanged for one barrel

will have different endowments of productive factors while the populations will have different demands for goods, we can expect that relative prices of goods will differ between countries. We are not discussing prices in arbitrary monetary units, but rather the real terms of exchange, the amount of one good which exchanges for any other good. In general, a consequence of relative prices of *outputs* being different in different countries is that relative prices of *inputs* are different in different countries. If automobiles are more expensive in terms of food, say, in country A than in country B, factors of production specific to the automobile industry will receive more in relation to factors of production specific to the food industry in country A than in country B.

Some factors of production are mobile between industries, especially given a little time. One expects these factors to earn the same reward in all industries, and for them to move to the higher paying industry whenever there is a disequilibrium, thereby eliminating the disequilibrium. This brings us to an important contrast between internal and international trade. Within the United States, say, if returns to land from growing soybeans exceed those from growing corn, farmers will shift their land out of the corn industry and into the soybean industry. If the wages to M.B.A.'s rise relative to those of lawyers, then more young people will go into business school, and fewer to law school, than before. Mobile factors move from industry to industry until returns are equalized.

One could easily imagine such movement occurring between industries in different countries. However, factor mobility is much lower between countries than within countries. Why? It always comes down to cost, of course, but we can make a helpful classification.

- Some factors can be moved, but only at great expense in the present state of technical knowledge: capital equipment, roads, and railways.

- Some factors are effectively immobile: climate for agriculture and sites for tourism.

- Some factors are naturally quite mobile internationally but are prevented from moving by political constraints: human skills, embodied in people, and, to some extent, technology embodied in capital

---

of oil. Now five hours of minimum wage labor exchange for one barrel of oil. A relative price is independent of general inflation trends. It shows the terms on which transactions are really conducted, regardless of monetary units. A monopolist, like the OPEC cartel, who raises prices to make more profit, wants to change the *relative* price of goods, so that other people must surrender more units of their output to obtain one unit of the output of the monopolist, whose command over real resources rises. If general inflation occurs after the relative price change, the monopolist will raise his nominal prices at the inflation rate also, thereby keeping the exploitative relative price constant. Relative prices measure the amount of goods of one type that you must surrender to receive a unit of goods of another type. They are the appropriate prices to use in a discussion of international trade.

equipment, since many developing countries restrict foreign capital inflow.

If all factors of production were perfectly mobile internationally there would be very little trade in outputs. Factors would move until returns to them were equalized, and thus goods would have the same *relative* prices everywhere (if the technology were identical). There would be no incentive to trade, that is, to buy at low prices in one place and sell at high prices in another. Since all factors are not perfectly mobile, relative prices will differ between countries in the absence of trade, providing an opportunity for *all* the participants to gain from trade.

The first systematic demonstration that trade is better than autarky for *all* parties was given by the British economist David Ricardo in 1817. Because it is so clear we will reproduce it in outline here. It uses the commodities wine and cloth, and the countries England and Portugal. If you wish mentally to update it, you might try the commodities computers and steel, and the countries Japan and the United States. Let us begin by considering the production technologies in our two countries. We will assume that only labor can move between industries in each country, but this is inessential.

1. There are 30 man-hours in total available in England

2. There are 27 man-hours in total available in Portugal

3. In England:
   a. 5 man hours make 1 yard of cloth
   b. 6 man hours make 1 gallon of wine

4. In Portugal:
   a. 18 man hours make 1 yard of cloth
   b. 9 man hours make 1 gallon of wine

It is a deliberate characteristic of this hypothetical example that the Portuguese are inferior in production efficiency *in every industry*. This turns out to make them poorer than the English, but it has nothing to do with whether or not it is advantageous for trade to take place between Portugal and England. Because they are poorer they work for lower real wages. In this interpretation our example will show the fallacies in arguments which attempt to prevent imports from "cheap labor" countries.

From the technology we may discern the pretrade, internal prices for goods in the two countries. How do we discern the price of cloth in terms of wine in England? The reasoning proceeds as follows. Labor is mobile between industries and must therefore be paid the same wage in both. Any fixed factors cannot prevent their return being bid down to zero (if the land is not used for growing grapes, it is left vacant, and thus its opportunity cost is zero). So all our relative price calculations can be in terms of labor hours. Thus, a gallon of wine exchanges for 1.2 yards of cloth in England. In arbitrary monetary units, the price of a gallon of wine is 1.2 times the price of a yard of cloth. Similarly, in Portugal a gallon of wine exchanges for half a yard of cloth. So, before trade begins, wine is cheaper in terms of cloth in Portugal than in England.

Once trade begins, the price of wine in terms of cloth must be equal in both countries, neglecting transportation costs. If this were not so, you could always make money just by shipping commodities from the place in which they were cheap to the place in which they were expensive, that is, by undertaking *commodity arbitrage*. At the original price ratios one would buy one yard of cloth in England, promising to pay 5/6 of a gallon of wine. One would ship the cloth to Portugal, obtaining two gallons of wine, which one would then repatriate, and so on. The final, equalized price ratio must be between the two original ones. That is, a gallon of wine will not exchange for less than half a yard of cloth nor more than 1.2 yards of cloth. Outside these limits domestic production will provide both goods more cheaply than will trade. Exactly where it ends up depends upon the tastes and the income and number of consumers in each country. The price ratio will end up at one of the extremes if one of the countries is extremely large relative to the other. When Iceland trades with the United States, Icelandic demand or supply is just a drop in the bucket for the United States, but access to such a huge market means that Icelandic prices must conform to U.S. relative prices (inclusive of tariffs and transportation costs), or arbitrage would swamp Icelandic markets. We will continue on the assumption that the countries are not so extremely mismatched in economic size.

To be concrete, suppose that the price ratio settles at 1.5 gallons of wine per yard of cloth. We can now demonstrate three things, which are true in much more realistic cases also.

1. Both countries have become better off as a result of the opening of trade.

Consider England, and suppose that the English are producing some mixture of the two goods, and they decide that they want more wine. If they produce the wine themselves they must give up 1.2 yards of cloth for each extra gallon of wine. If they trade at our supposed price ratio they must give up only 2/3 of a yard of cloth for each gallon of wine. Similarly, if the Portuguese want another yard of cloth, it costs less in foregone wine to obtain the cloth through trade than through autarkic production. What if the English want more cloth, and the Portuguese want more wine? That can only be answered by looking at the income-maximizing production pattern.

2. Each country exports the good that was relatively cheaper before the opening of trade. This is the principle of comparative advantage.

With the price ratio we have chosen, and with income measured, say, in units of wine, the income maximizing pattern of production is for England to produce only cloth, and for Portugal to produce only wine. Then the English produce six yards of cloth, worth nine units of wine. If they gave up one yard of cloth to produce wine they could produce only 5/6 of a gallon of wine, whereas the foregone yard of cloth was worth 1.5 gallons of wine. Similar calculations show that Portugal should produce only wine. Both countries still consume both goods, of course. Notice that English income (measured in wine) is nine gallons, while Portuguese income is three gallons. On a per man-hour basis, English income is 0.3 whereas Portuguese income is 0.11. As we said, the absolute inefficiency in Portugal makes the Portuguese poorer than the English in this hypo-thetical case; it in no way precludes both parties gaining from trade. The gains come from a change in the rate at which one commodity can be transformed into another, not from anything to do with the absolute amount of commodities in existence, which is connected with absolute efficiency in the use of available inputs. However, notice also that the transition from autarky to trade (more generally, the transition from one pattern of trade to another) involves reallocation of resources. In Ricardo's example the whole English wine industry and the whole Portuguese cloth industry close down; in a less extreme situation we would observe con-traction of some industries and expansion of others. This resource real-location has two types of effects, which explain the opposition to free trade masked by the cheap labor, and other, arguments.

- There are substantial relocation costs as workers must find new jobs in other industries. In Ricardo's example we compared two *stable* situations. During the transition we will have much smaller real income gains. They will occur, and are justifiable on a *present value* basis despite the dislocation in the short term, but this dis-location can be a politically powerful phenomenon.

- There will be a redistribution of income. Even though the pie to be divided will be larger in a free trade situation than under autarky, some people will assuredly receive less under the new market ar-rangements. Again we can see this crudely from Ricardo's example, if we add a small increment of detail about the economies.

Suppose there to be two qualities of land suitable for wine production in England, good land and bad land. The land quality is determined by the number of labor hours required to produce one gallon of wine. On the good land this is 5.0 hours and on the bad land it is 6.0 hours. There is only enough good land to produce one gallon of wine, and to stay with the figures in the original example we can suppose that under autarky more than one gallon of wine was demanded in England, so that the marginal production was on the bad land. Figure 3.1 shows the cost and

**Figure 3.1**  Autarky rent on good British land. The marginal cost curve is the supply curve of wine in England.

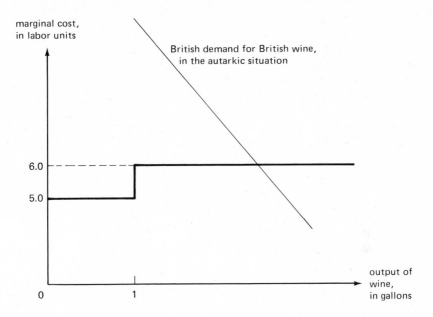

price situation, measuring cost and price in labor units. Under autarky wine must sell in England at a price adequate to cover the variable (i.e., labor) cost of the marginal gallon. Bad land is free. But the good land earns a rent equal in value to one labor hour, because the gallon of wine produced there also sells at a price of 6 labor units, although it costs but 5.0 labor units to produce.

Now let us return to international trade. We saw that English wine production on bad land was at a comparative disadvantage to Portuguese wine production. To obtain one more gallon of wine requires 6 labor units, or 1.2 yards of cloth. In Portugal to acquire one gallon of wine requires 1/2 yard of cloth. On the good English land, to obtain the initial gallon of wine requires 5.0 labor units, or one yard of cloth. So after trade begins, wine production will stop, not only on the bad land but also on the good land. Thus, although the English national income is higher, the landowners are poorer, because land which once commanded a rent will no longer do so. The gains from the opening of trade are broadly distributed over the consumers of wine. The costs are concentrated on the landlords who have an incentive to invest nearly all the present value of their land rent in a political campaign to keep us in autarky.

3. The value of exports always equals the value of imports. Trade not only raises welfare but in itself creates no balance of payments problems.

To see this, we have to do a little accounting. We will establish that the value, in wine, of England's exports must equal the value of England's imports. Since the exports of England are the imports of Portugal, and the imports of England are the exports of Portugal, we are simultaneously proving this for Portugal. Let $p$ denote the after-trade price of a yard of cloth in terms of wine. In the above example we took $p$ to equal 1.5. Let $C_w$ denote the number of gallons of wine the English choose to consume, and let $C_l$ denote the number of yards of cloth the English choose to consume. Let $L$ denote the number of yards of cloth produced in England. In the above example, $L$ was equal to 6. Then

$$\text{English income} = L \cdot p$$

$$\text{English expenditure} = C_w + C_l \cdot p$$

Expenditure can only equal income, so we have

$$L \cdot p = C_w + C_l \cdot p$$

or

$$(L - C_l) \cdot p = C_w$$

The left side is the value of exports, and the right side is the value of imports.

Of course this equality in value holds in situations where there is not complete specialization in production. Let $W$ denote English production of wine. Then we have

$$\text{English income} = W + L \cdot p$$

$$\text{English expenditure} = C_w + C_l \cdot p$$

Once again equating income and expenditure, we obtain

$$(L - C_l) \cdot p = (C_w - W)$$

The left side is the value of exports and the right side is the value of imports.

Although this example is extremely simple, it implies that to a first approximation one should be able to explain which goods a country exports to another, and which it imports from another, by comparing relative labor productivity in the same industries across the two countries. That turns out to be very roughly correct. We may put the proposition this way. Compare two countries which we label the United States and the United Kingdom. Each country should be found to export these goods in which labor productivity—measured by output per worker—is higher in real terms than in the other country. We say "in real terms," because if labor productivity is 50% higher in the production of surfboards in the United States than in Britain, but workers are paid 50% more in the surfboard industry in the United States than in the surfboard industry in the United Kingdom (and if pay in other industries is the same over the two countries) then we have no differences in *relative costs*.

There exists a test using the ratio of U.S. to British exports, and productivity, for twenty industry groups for the year 1937.[2] Its results were as follows:

| U.S. labor productivity<br>U.K. labor productivity | U.K. exports<br>U.S. exports |
|---|---|
| more than 2.0 | 0.12 to   1.0 |
| 1.4 to 2.0 | 2.0  to  18.0 |
| less than 1.4 | 11.0  to 250.0 |

The benchmark for the ratio of productivity is 2.0 because in 1937 U.S. workers received about twice the pay of British workers.

These results are broadly consistent with the Ricardian theory because the ratio of U.K. exports to U.S. exports *rises* as the U.K. productivity advantage *rises*. Only the *changes in the ratio* of exports are important. The absolute size of the ratio reflects something else entirely, namely the difference in the diversity of resources available in Britain and in the United States, which has a large resource base and depends relatively little on imports. Therefore it has relatively small need to export to pay for those imports. Britain is a small country with a narrow resource base. It must import a lot and so must export a lot. Japan is also in this situation.

## 3.3  MORE SOPHISTICATED ANALYSES
## OF PATTERNS OF TRADE

In the Ricardian example we just discussed trade takes place because pretrade relative prices differ, and they differ because technology of producing the two goods is different in the two countries. However, these days engineering textbooks are inexpensive, and in many industries the technology used is the same in numerous countries. This is especially so for modern industrial products. Or consider the following historical example: if one looked at the wheat trade in nineteenth century Europe one could divide nations into two groups:

1.  exporting or self-sufficient countries, which had low ratios of population to land; and

2.  importing countries with high ratios of population to land.

---

[2]D. MacDougall, "British and American Exports: A Study Suggested by The Theory of Comparative Costs," *Economic Journal, 61*, December 1951. Used by permission.

Yet paradoxically from a Ricardian viewpoint the exporting countries had low yields of wheat per acre, while the importing countries had very high yields per acre. In order to explain these and many other phenomena, it is necessary to recognize the existence of many factors of production.

Because a discussion of trade allowing the existence of many factors of production is a more sophisticated exercise than the Ricardian example in section 3.2, we must introduce some new basic analytical constructs. These are the *production possibility frontier,* the *isoquant* and the *indifference* curve. We do not have time to go beyond jogging the reader's memory by defining them. Anyone needing more substantial explanation is referred to a comprehensive textbook on introductory economics; we recommend Samuelson's *Economics.* For simplicity of presentation we take a world of two final, consumable goods (rice and wheelbarrows) and two factors of production (labor, measured in labor-hours, and machinery, measured in machine-hours). Then in either industry (rice or wheelbarrows) the n-unit isoquant shows all combinations of labor-hours and machine-hours that can produce n units of output of the particular good in question. There is thus one isoquant for each level of output of each good. For an economy as a whole, the *production possibility frontier (PPF)* shows all the mixtures of rice and wheelbarrow output that might conceivably be produced with the available labor and machinery resources. Finally, take a consumer and evaluate his or her willingness to change the components of his or her consumption bundle. For each particular level of overall satisfaction, an indifference curve shows all possible substitutions of rice for wheelbarrows in the consumption bundle which keep the consumer at that level of satisfaction. We will tell our story for a trading system composed of two countries, the United States and the United Kingdom. The analysis specific to one country will be for the United States only—exactly parallel reasoning can be developed for the United Kingdom. We start with the PPF (see Figure 3.2).

Suppose the economy is producing at $X$, i.e, it produces $R_x$ rice and $B_x$ wheelbarrows. The slope of the PPF at $X$ tells us the marginal rate of transformation (MRT). This is the rate at which the system can convert one good into another by shifting resources from one industry to another. In the Ricardian example the MRT was constant. In England you could always get one more gallon of wine by giving up 1.2 yards of cloth while in Portugal you could always get one more gallon of wine by giving up 1/2 yard of cloth. As drawn here, the more you specialize in one good the more difficult it is to convert the remaining resources from the other industry to production of the good you are concentrating on.

At point $X$ the MRT is, say, six, that is, to get another unit of rice requires that six wheelbarrows be given up. Alternatively one may say that at $X$ a unit of rice is worth six wheelbarrows. Thus the MRT, six, is also the ratio of the price of rice to the price of barrows.

**Figure 3.2**   PPF of U.S.

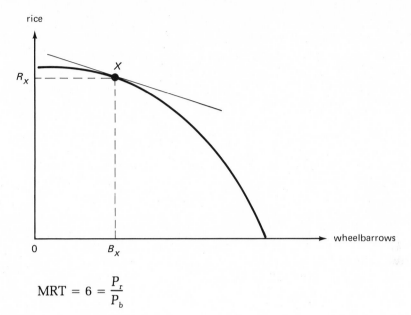

$$\text{MRT} = 6 = \frac{P_r}{P_b}$$

that is,

$$P_r = 6 \cdot P_b$$

Since we are assuming that the economy is competitive this is also the price ratio that individual consumers face when they choose their consumption bundles.

At these prices the value of output is $Y_x = R_x \cdot P_r + B_x \cdot P_b$. All this output is someone's income. The labor that went into it was provided by people, the raw materials were sold by people, the capital is owned by people, and the profits accrue to people. Thus the value of the national product is equal to the value of the national income. Suppose for the sake of argument that there are only two citizens, citizen 1 and citizen 2. From labor, from earning capital, and so on, they receive respective incomes $y_x^1$ and $y_x^2$. We know $y_x^1 + y_x^2 = Y_x$. Even though total output is in the ratio $R_x$ rice to $B_x$ wheelbarrows this of course doesn't mean that Citizen 1 and Citizen 2 consume rice and wheelbarrows in these proportions. The proportions they choose at the given prices and incomes depend on their preferences. We know only that *total* consumption of rice by both will be $R_x$, and of barrows will be $B_x$ (see Figure 3.3).

In our example, the ratio of $P_r$ to $P_b$ is six. This is the slope of the pretrade *budget constraint* for the consumers in the United States. It tells them the rate at which they can substitute rice for wheelbarrows in their consumption bundle without exceeding their income. We indicated that

**Figure 3.3** Consumption Choices of the Citizens Before Trade Begins. We know that $r_x^1 + r_x^2 = R_x$; $b_x^1 + b_x^2 = B_x$.

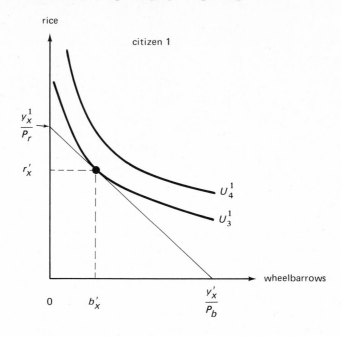

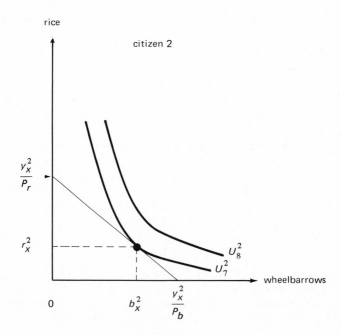

analogous analysis could be carried out for the United Kingdom. Suppose that because of the shape of the PPF and the preferences of the citizens, the MRT turns out to be two before trade begins with the United States. That is, in Britain to get another unit of rice requires that two wheelbarrows be given up. Laying out the pretrade price regimes in the two countries we find:

| U.S. | U.K. |
| --- | --- |
| Pay 6 wheelbarrows for a unit of rice. | Pay 2 wheelbarrows for a unit of rice. |
| Pay 1/6 of a unit of rice for a wheelbarrow. | Pay 1/2 a unit of rice for a wheelbarrow. |

Just as in the simple Ricardian example, the existence of these different transformation/cost ratios before trade means that citizens of both countries will benefit from the opening of trade. After trade begins, the process of arbitrage will equalize the relative price of wheelbarrows to rice in both countries (again, ignoring transportation cost). To be concrete, let's suppose that after the dust settles the common after-trade relative price has five wheelbarrows exchanging for one unit of rice.

What trade pattern does this imply? Comparing the before-trade prices in the two countries we see that the United States will export wheelbarrows and import rice, while the United Kingdom will export rice and import wheelbarrows (see Figure 3.4, next page). Recollect that

$$Exports = production - consumption$$

$$Imports = consumption - production$$

The consequence of the opening of trade is that in the United States, wheelbarrows become *relatively* more valuable so there is more production of them, while in Britain, rice becomes relatively more valuable so there is more production of it. The new production point for both economies is where the local MRT equals the price ratio.[3] Because rice has become relatively cheaper, and wheelbarrows relatively more expensive, less rice and more wheelbarrows will be produced. On the other hand, more rice and less wheelbarrows will tend to be consumed. Figure 3.5 on p. 73 illustrates this, where

---

[3]Why? Because that maximizes income. The price ratio tells you the revenue you get from producing one good or the other. The MRT tells you how many of one you have to give up to get one more of the other. If the two ratios are unequal you can always raise income by altering the production mix.

**Figure 3.4** Old and New Production Patterns (Note: Asterisks denote British values).

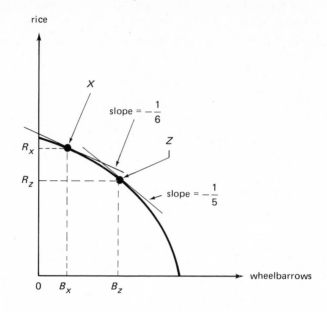

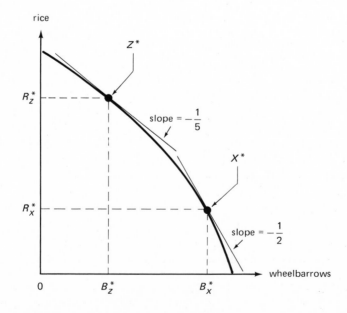

$X$ = old point of both production and consumption.
Before trade one can only consume what one produces.

$Z$ = new point of production. There is more production of
wheelbarrows and less production of rice than at $X$.

$C$ = new point of consumption. As drawn there is more
consumption of rice and less consumption of wheelbarrows
than at $X$. That doesn't have to be the case. Because
real income has risen we could consume
more of both goods.

Once again we find that the value of exports always equals the value
of imports. The imports of one country are the exports of the other, so we
must only show this for one of the countries, say, the United States. The
citizens of the United States can spend their national income on either
rice or wheelbarrows. Let $q_R$ be the after-trade price for rice and $q_B$ the
after-trade price for wheelbarrows, in the United States. We know $q_R$ =
$5q_B$. (Similarly we know $q_R^* = 5q_B^*$ in the United Kingdom.) Thus, national income in the United States is

$$Y_Z = q_R \cdot R_Z + q_B \cdot B_Z$$

**Figure 3.5**  After-Trade Compared with Before-Trade Production
and Consumption in the United States.

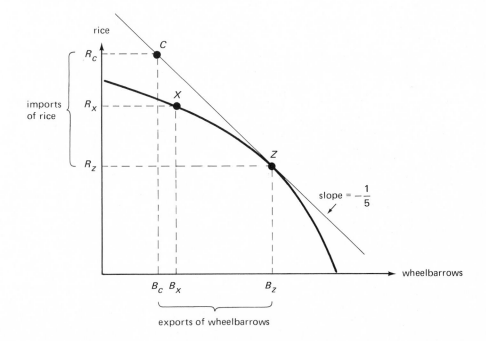

exports of wheelbarrows

while expenditure on consumption goods is

$$E_c = q_R \cdot R_c + q_B \cdot B_c$$

But you can only spend your income, so $Y_Z = E_c$ or

$$q_R \cdot R_Z + q_B \cdot B_Z = q_R \cdot R_c + q_B \cdot B_c$$

or

$$q_B(B_Z - B_c) = q_R(R_c - R_Z)$$

But

$$B_Z - B_c = \text{exports of wheelbarrows by the United States}$$

$$q_B(B_Z - B_c) = \text{value of exports of wheelbarrows by the United States}$$

$$R_c - R_Z = \text{imports of rice by the United States}$$

$$q_R(R_c - R_Z) = \text{value of imports of rice by the United States}$$

We are now in a position to provide more sophisticated analyses of patterns of trade. We begin with the famous *Heckscher-Ohlin theory*, which shows how trade can occur between countries whose citizens have the same tastes and use the same technologies in all industries. Assume that:

1.  The pattern demand is the same in all countries.

2.  All countries use the same technologies to produce goods.

3.  Each country can have different endowments of the various factors of production. As we mentioned earlier, for initial convenience of diagrammatic exposition we will assume only two factors—labor and machines. $L$ denotes the stock of labor and $M$ the stock of machines in the United States; corresponding stocks in Britain are denoted $L^*$ and $M^*$.

Our two goods are still wheelbarrows and rice. Let us make a final and very strong assumption:

4.  At all factor-price ratios, wheelbarrow production is always more machine-intensive than is rice production. This assumption is an assumption about the nature of the technology. We will have more to say about it in due course.

The situation is illustrated in Figure 3.6. Wheelbarrow production is more machine intensive than rice production if, at *all* factor-price ratios (rep-

**Figure 3.6** Isoquants for Rice and Barrows Production Such that all Input-Price Ratios Barrow Production is More Machine Intensive the same factor-price ratio applies to all industries; it defines the cost-minimizing mixture of machines and labor that will produce the output level represented by the isoquants.

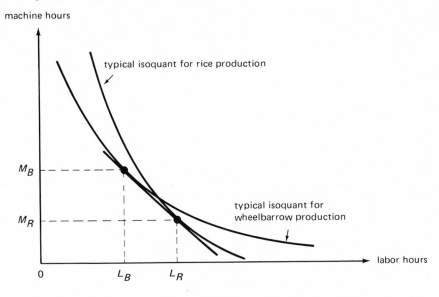

**Figure 3.7** PPF Change When Machines Added. $PPF_2$ describes the economy after more machines are made available.

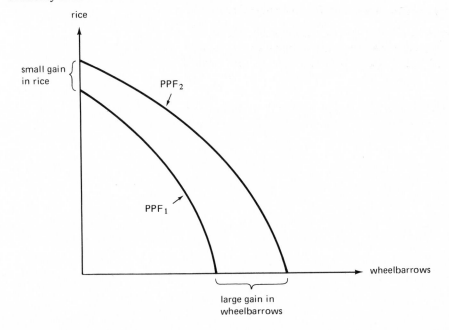

resented by the slope of the tangent lines to the isoquants) the ratio of machine-hours to labor-hours in wheelbarrow production $(M_B/L_B)$ exceeds that for rice production $(M_R/L_R)$.[4]

Now we want to explain the shape of the PPF by the relative supplies of the different factors of production. In Figure 3.7, let $PPF_1$ be the original PPF. Now suppose that more machines become available. This makes possible a greater percentage increase in the output of wheelbarrows than of rice. Thus $PPF_2$ is less steep than $PPF_1$. In general the higher the ratio of $M$ to $L$, the less steep the PPF becomes.

Let us suppose that in the United States machinery is relatively abundant, while in the United Kingdom labor is relatively abundant. This means that

$$\frac{M}{L} > \frac{M^*}{L^*}$$

That in turn means the PPF for the United States is less steep than the PPF for Great Britain. Both PPFs are shown in Figure 3.8.

**Figure 3.8**  PPFs When the United States is Capital-Abundant Country and the United Kingdom is Labor-Abundant Country

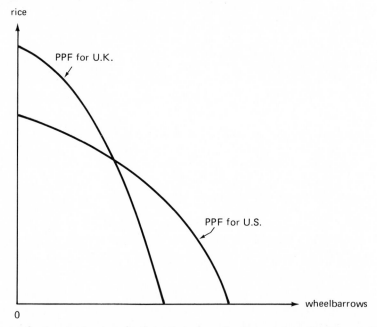

[4]Why use the input mix given by the point where the factor-price ratio is tangent to the isoquant? The factor price ratio tells how much it costs you to substitute one factor for another. The isoquant tells you the feasible substitutions that keep the output level constant. If you produce at a mix other than the one at the point of tangency, you can always lower cost by altering the input mix without changing the quantity of output.

**Figure 3.9** Ratio of Rice Consumed to Wheelbarrows Consumed in Both Countries at a Specific Price Ratio the slope of the line gives the ratio of rice demand to wheelbarrow demand *at a particular price ratio.* Different price ratios imply lines of different slope.

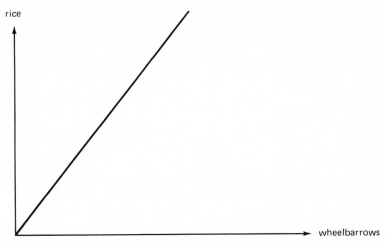

We assumed that demand patterns were the same in both countries. So let us start by supposing that the ratio of the price of rice to the price of wheelbarrows is the same in both countries before trade begins. Then the demands for rice and wheelbarrows must stand in the same ratios in both countries. (Here we omit some important qualifications which are inessential to the basic idea.) This is expressed by saying that the demands lie on a straight line from the origin whose slope is the ratio of rice demanded to wheelbarrows demanded. This is shown in Figure 3.9.

Now we know that in each country production will take place at that point on its PPF at which the MRT equals the price ratio. But this will not imply the same mixture of rice and wheelbarrows for both countries, because the PPF for the United States is less steep than the PPF for the United Kingdom, due to the different factor endowments. Figure 3.10 shows how the relative production of the two goods will appear in the two countries at any common price ratio.

Combining the information in Figures 3.9 and 3.10, we see that at any common price ratio the ratio of demands for rice to demands for wheelbarrows would be the same in both countries, but there would always be a greater supply ratio of rice to barrows in Great Britain than in the United States. Before trade begins demand must equal supply in each country. Thus, at a common price ratio there will tend to be:

- excess supply of rice and excess demand for wheelbarrows in the United Kingdom

**Figure 3.10**   At Any Common Price Ratio U.S. Produces Relatively
More Barrows than U.K.

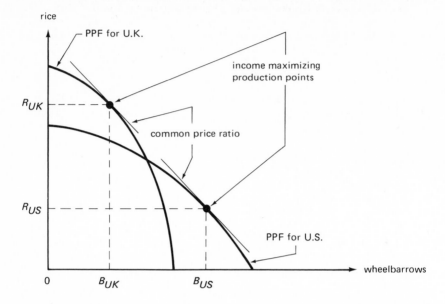

- excess demand for rice and excess supply of wheelbarrows in the
  United States

Hence to bring about equilibrium in both countries the price ratio
$(P_R/P_B)$ will rise in the United States and will fall in the United Kingdom.
So when trade opens rice will be relatively cheap in Great Britain and
wheelbarrows relatively cheap in the United States. This is the pattern
of comparative advantage in the initial example of this section. We have
now established the Heckscher-Ohlin Theory: A country will export the
good which is intensive in its relatively abundant factor.

But this is a simplification, which depends upon common demand
pattern, and not only a common technology but the assumptions on factor
intensity. Let us take first the assumption of the same pattern of demand.
If demand patterns were the same, we saw that at any common price ratio
there would always be supplied a higher ratio of wheelbarrows to rice in
the United States than in Britain. But suppose the U.S. citizens had a real
love for wheelbarrows and quite a marked distaste for rice, compared
with the citizens of the United Kingdom. Then the demand for wheelbarrows in the United States would be high, the demand for rice low, and
the ratio $P_R/P_B$ would be very low in the United States compared with the
United Kingdom. We can see this most easily if we assume there is only
one consumer in the United States, and one in the United Kingdom, so
that we can use indifference curves. The situation would then be as de-

**Figure 3.11** Consumption Tastes Leaning to the Commodity Intensive in the Abundant Factor. The diagram shows indifference curves for the citizens in question. In the United States, the wheelbarrow-lover stays on the same welfare level after the loss of some wheelbarrows only with a large rice compensation. In Great Britain, the rice-lover stays on the same welfare level after the loss of some rice only with a large wheelbarrow compensation.

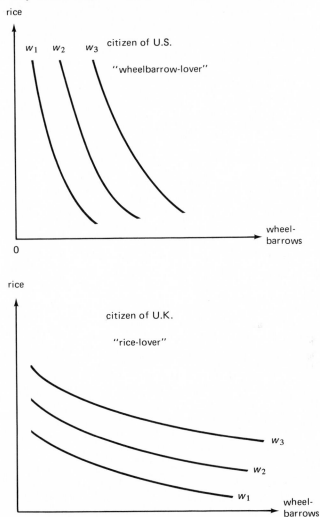

picted in Figure 3.11. If we combine these preferences with the PPFs for the two countries, as is done in Figure 3.12, we see that we can create a situation wherein, before the opening of trade, wheelbarrows are more expensive relative to rice in the United States than in Great Britain. The result is that when trade begins, the United States will export rice and

**Figure 3.12** Pretrade Relative Prices Contradicting the Heckscher-Ohlin Theorem

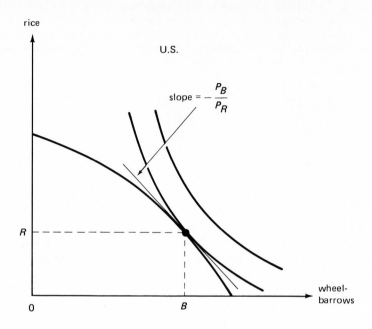

rice

U.S.

slope $= -\dfrac{P_B}{P_R}$

R

0        B

wheel-barrows

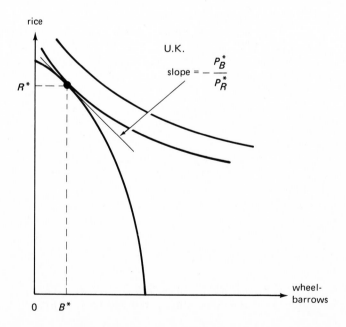

rice

U.K.

slope $= -\dfrac{P_B^*}{P_R^*}$

$R^*$

0   $B^*$

wheel-barrows

the United Kingdom will export barrows. This exactly reverses the Heckscher-Ohlin theory. As drawn $P_B/P_R > P^*_B/P^*_R$, i.e., rice is relatively cheaper in the United States, and wheelbarrows are relatively cheaper in Great Britain, before trade begins.

Now let us again assume demand patterns are the same, and investigate the influence of the factor intensity assumption. The way we drew the PPFs for the United States and the United Kingdom depended upon the assumption that barrows were always more machine-intensive than rice. By this we meant that at any factor-price ratio, more machines per man would be used in wheelbarrow production than in rice production. But this need not be true. Consider the following example: wheelbarrows are produced by a factory process which requires precisely two men per machine. No substitution is possible. The isoquants are right-angled. On the other hand, when labor is cheap relative to machines, rice can be produced in the labor-intensive Asian way. When labor is expensive relative to machines, rice is produced with tractors, pumps, and harvesters in the American way. In Figure 3.13 we have drawn two typical isoquants. As you can see, when labor is cheap wheelbarrow production is more machine-intensive than rice production. But when labor is expensive, rice production is more machine-intensive. Regardless of the price ratio of factors, the machine intensity of wheelbarrow production in both countries is always $\overline{M/L}$. In rice production, if labor is expensive, the machine intensity is $M_1/L_1$, which is greater than $\overline{M/L}$. If labor is cheap, the machine intensity of rice production is $M_2/L_2$, which is less than $\overline{M/L}$.

What does this mean for comparative costs before trade begins? Suppose one country, say the United States, is endowed with a large machine stock per worker, while Great Britain is endowed with a small machine stock per worker. By the Heckscher-Ohlin theory, each country should export the good intensive in its relatively abundant factor. If the machine-rich country, the United States, uses machine-intensive methods to produce rice, it would export rice. And if the labor-rich country, Great Britain uses labor-intensive methods to produce rice, it will export rice also! But of course both countries will not export the same good to each other. The actual outcome will depend upon the technology and the factor supplies in too complex a way for us to bother with here. But it need not be compatible with the Heckscher-Ohlin theory.

Let us now turn to evidence on the ability of the multifactor theory to explain the pattern of exports and imports. We may begin by returning to our historical example of wheat yields in importing and exporting nations in Europe. In importing countries wheat is expensive and land is scarce. Hence large quantities of other factors (labor and capital) are used per acre of land and yield is high (as are costs). In exporting countries wheat is cheap and land is abundant so the land is worked extensively using few cooperating factors. So both yields and costs are low. Modern tests have been carried out and have the following results. First of all,

**Figure 3.13** Factor Intensity Reversal

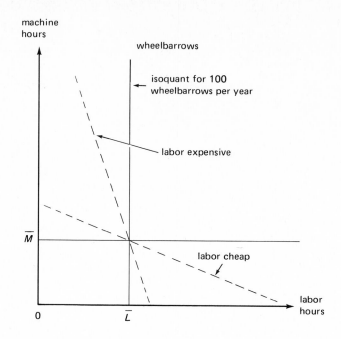

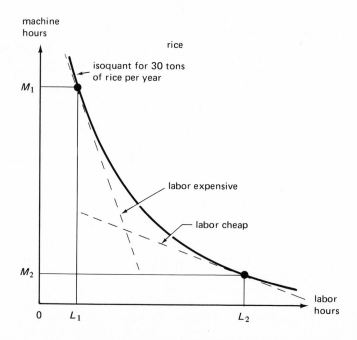

consumption patterns are very similar in most developed countries. Second, one must carefully define and measure factors of production. It is necessary to take account of at least a third factor, natural resources, as well as capital and labor. Moreover in the measure of the stock of capital one must include human capital. Investing a year in the construction of a machine is the same thing as investing a year in the acquisition of a skill. If one does these things, the Heckscher-Ohlin theory explains the bulk of trade of a country like the United States. However, factor-intensity reversals do occur, especially in agriculture versus manufacturing. Our examples of isoquants for wheelbarrows and rice are quite adequate representation. American agriculture is more capital intensive than a lot of American manufacturing. Japanese agriculture is much less capital intensive than a lot of Japanese manufacturing. These facts do not invalidate our theory, but merely imply that in its simplest form it is inadequate. You can still take its predictions as a good first approximation.

Our story explains trade patterns for broad groups of commodities. To explain things in greater detail it is necessary to briefly consider the impact of imperfect competition and of technological change.

Oligopoly is an important phenomenon within national markets, and also affects trade. First turn to the gains from trade. If trade is free, oligopolists in one country must compete with producers from other countries. This competition may force the price nearer to the competitive price with consequent social gain. If one looks at the U.S. automobile industry, it is apparent that the industry was forced to produce smaller cars, which buyers manifestly want, only because of competition from European and Japanese imports. On the other hand, one can also find international collusion of oligopolists. Such collusive arrangements are known as cartels. Important contemporary examples are ocean freight carriage and major oil companies. Cartel agreements generally have the purpose of blocking competition and restricting trade flows by carving up the market. For example, national firms are given exclusive rights to their country's sales and there is no efficient international specialization. This allows price discrimination in different markets—the same good sells at different prices in different countries. A striking example is the manufacture of tungsten carbide in the late 1920s and early 1930s. Krupp sold it in Europe for about $50 per pound. General Electric sold it in the United States for $453 per pound. It cost $8 per pound to manufacture. Finally, we recollect that under imperfect competition product differentiation occurs. Thus a small Japanese car is different from a small European car and so on. Therefore one observes two countries, each exporting small cars to the other. This applies to radios, washing machines, televisions, and so on. Such trade cannot be explained in the competitive framework.

We will discuss one model of trade responding to technological change—Vernon's model of the product life cycle. Among a country's endowment of factors of production we must include also the ability to create new products and techniques—inventiveness and innovative ability. Suppose a country like the United States has a relatively large endowment of this ability. Then its trading pattern would include export of new commodities and import of well-established commodities. When a new good is introduced it is sold first on the U.S. market because that is the one the producers know best. It is exported subsequently, but foreign producers have difficulty imitating it because it is new. Moreover, it is being rapidly improved and the first producer has the greatest amount of information that can be used to carry out these improvements, and often also patent protection. After a sufficient lapse of time, improvements become harder to make, producers in other countries learn how to produce and even to improve the product. Once production is standardized it is often possible to substitute machines plus unskilled labor for the initially-used skilled workers and technicians. Thus comparative advantage in production shifts to other countries. The original innovator now imports the good and must turn out something else new. There is a good deal of evidence that in new industries such as electronics this tale fits the facts extremely well. Of course, our original factor endowment arguments explain why the United States exports wheat and imports oil.

## 3.4  TARIFFS AND OTHER RESTRICTIONS ON TRADE

A *tariff* is a sales tax imposed only on imported goods. A *quota* is a quantitative limit on the volume of imports. The function of tariffs and quotas is to switch domestic demand from foreign to domestic goods, and to encourage industrial production in some sectors rather than others. Rationalizations for such redirections of economic activity are varied, for instance, keeping the money in the country. It has frequently been claimed that, since oil is now so expensive, one should develop expensive domestic oil first, for at least the money goes to other U.S. citizens. In developing countries, it is frequently claimed that the theory of comparative advantage implies that they should produce and sell agricultural materials or minerals. But these are goods with volatile prices and so are risky. Tariffs to protect inefficient manufacturing lead to more stable income. The "keep your money in the country" argument is readily evaluated using the concept of the PPF. At any time the productive resources available to a society are finite. In a situation of free trade the price of one good relative to the price of another gives the relative resources content. This is equally true of the comparison between the price of an imported good and a domestically produced good, since to obtain the import you must surrender a domestically produced export of equal value. If the imported good is cheaper than the domestic good, that means more domestic resources will be available to produce something else consumable

**Figure 3.14**  Demand Curve for Imports

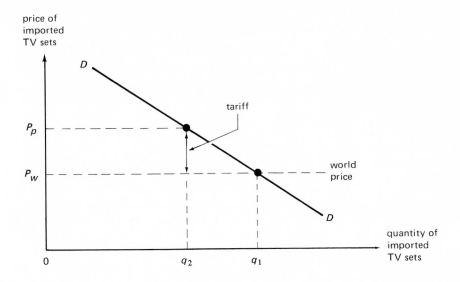

if the import is purchased rather than the domestic good. The reduction of risk argument is only justified if the producers are so stupid as to not realize that they are in a risky industry. Every industry is risky to some extent, and no one is forced to enter one rather than another. People presumably have their own opinion on how they want to trade off risk and return. If you can earn a high average but very risky return producing bananas compared with producing nuts and bolts, although the latter is more stable as a source of income, you may rationally decide to bear the risk. The government can distort the comparison by making nut and bolt production artificially profitable via a tariff, but if it has to do this, it is lowering the welfare of the population. The other usual arguments one hears in favor of trade restrictions are open to equally elementary objections. There are circumstances in which tariffs are justified on efficiency grounds, and we will return to this point after we learn how to analyze the effects of tariffs and quotas.

Consider first of all the relationship between the effects of tariffs and quantitative import controls, which are quite popular in the United States. The purpose of a trade restriction is to restrict trade, and one can always find a quota that is equivalent in its trade restricting effect to any tariff. You can see this immediately by looking at any demand curve for imports, as indicated on Figure 3.14. Before the imposition of the tariff $t$, imported TV sets sold at the world price and the quantity $q_1$ was imported. After the tariff, the price rises to the protected price $P_p = P_w + t$, and the smaller quantity $q_2$ is imported. Now we could have put on a quota saying

**Figure 3.15** National Consumption Opportunities

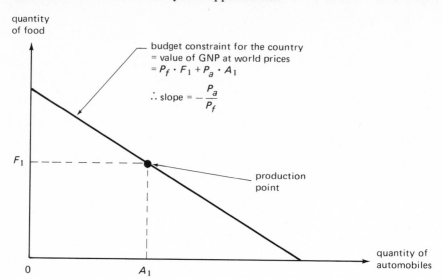

that only $q_2$ TV sets would be allowed in this year. According to the demand curve $DD$, that would cause the price to rise to $P_p$, so the effect on trade is exactly the same.

Well, is there any difference between the tariff $t$ and the quota $q_2$ in the TV industry as is drawn in Figure 3.14? There is an important difference. Although the effect on trade is exactly the same, the effect on the welfare of U.S. consumers is very different. In the case of the tariff, the government at least collects the tariff revenue, $t \times q_2$. But in the case of the quota, the extra revenue is given to the foreign producers.[5] Of course they are probably worse off than without the trade restriction, but not as badly off as if a tariff had been put on.

How does one measure the welfare losses caused by trade restrictions? The traditional division of the costs of protection identifies the consumption costs and the production costs. For expository convenience we will analyze the consumption costs as though the production mix were fixed regardless of the tariff. This doesn't matter because the two effects are additive. Consider a country that produces two goods, food and automobiles (see Figure 3.15). Residents of the country are free to trade at world prices, and can purchase goods equal in value to the value of the

---

[5]The Harvard economist Hendrik Houthakker gave a lecture on this subject several years ago. He mentioned that the United States put on quotas rather than tariffs, and he also pointed out how the United States subsidized its exports through such devices as cut-rate loans from the Export/Import Bank and so forth. Then he allowed a moment of silence and said, "Shrewd Yankee traders; they give their exports away below cost, and pay more than they have to for their imports."

**Figure 3.16**  Determination of Volume of Trade

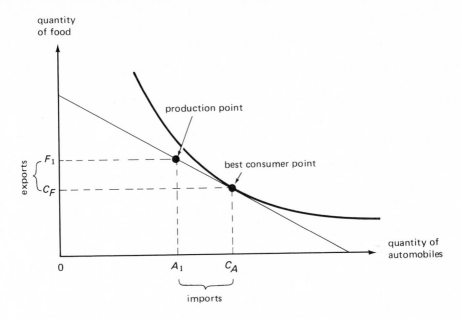

country's production. Thus given the fixed production point we can define a kind of budget constraint for the country, showing all combinations of consumptions that can be afforded on the basis of the fixed production and the given world prices.

Now treat our economy as though there were one big consumer and draw this consumer's indifference curves. Figure 3.16 shows the consumption bundle chosen, and the implied amount of imports and exports. As drawn the country exports food and imports automobiles. Now suppose that the government puts a tariff on automobile imports and gives the tariff revenue back to the consumers; for example, it has more tax revenue and lowers the income tax.

Consumers perceive a new budget constraint thanks to the tariff. The true opportunity locus determined by world prices has slope $-P_a/P_f$. The new one is steeper. It has slope $-(P_a + t)/P_f$ (see Figure 3.17). Note first of all that the tariff does not change world prices (we have assumed that the country does not have monopoly or monopsony power on the world markets). Thus actual consumption must still take place somewhere along the old budget constraint. The public perceives automobiles as being more expensive relative to food than before, and so will consume less automobiles and more food than before. So imports and exports fall. Consumption will take place on the old budget constraint at the point at which it is intersected by an indifference curve with the slope of the new perceived price ratio. Everyone is worse off. The old consumption point

**Figure 3.17**  Consumption Welfare Loss

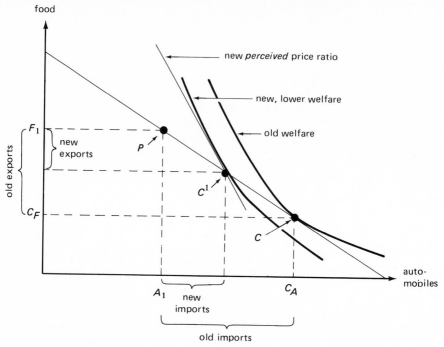

is still feasible (if the tariff is removed) and represents the most preferred consumption (greatest amount of welfare) under the circumstances. The tariff lowers welfare because it causes people to substitute the unprotected for the protected goods in their consumption bundle. The more substitution takes place, the more welfare falls.

To introduce the production costs, we allow for variations in the mix of possible output. The best point of production for the economy is the one that maximizes income, since this provides the economy with the furthest-out budget constraint, in the sense we have just discussed. A profit-maximizing competitive economy always maximizes the value of income (see footnote 3, in this chapter). In Figure 3.18, production alternatives are represented by a production possibility frontier. The best production point is the one which gives the economy the furthest-out budget constraint, the one tangent to the frontier.

When the tariff is placed on automobiles, the relative price of automobiles rises in the domestic economy. This causes resources to be pulled into the automobile industry and out of the food industry. The result is shown in Figure 3.19, a new production point that gives the society an inferior budget constraint. The tariff lowers welfare because it causes producers to substitute the protected for the unprotected goods in production. The bigger is the substitution, the bigger the welfare loss.

**Figure 3.18**  Best Production Mix

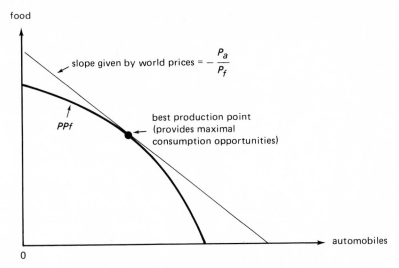

food

slope given by world prices = $-\dfrac{P_a}{P_f}$

PPf

best production point
(provides maximal
consumption opportunities)

0

automobiles

**Figure 3.19**  Production Inefficiency from Tariffs

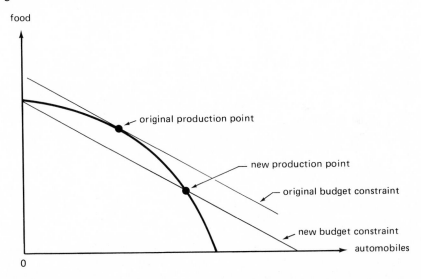

food

original production point

new production point

original budget constraint

new budget constraint

0

automobiles

Now we come to the very practical and important issue of measurement of welfare losses from intervention in trade. Past measurements of the monetary equivalent of the welfare losses from tariff policies have given very low figures.[6] Even when half the goods in the economy bear

---

[6]See H. Johnson, "The Costs of Protection and the Scientific Tariff," *Journal of Political Economy*, August 1960, 327–345; and "The Costs of Protection and Self-Sufficiency," *Quarterly Journal of Economics*, August 1965.

a 50% tariff, the gains from moving to free trade seem to be only in the vicinity of 1% to 2% of GNP. (Is that small? The U.S. GNP is $1800 billion!) Of course average tariffs in the United States are much smaller than this. Thus the gains would seem to be much smaller also.

Given this, why should anyone care about tariffs? Well, the past calculations may be wrong by a factor of two or three, or more. The error is a subtle one, stemming from how aggregated the data are with which one makes the calculation. Remember, the losses come from false substitution of one good for another in consumption and production. Suppose we decided to measure the costs of protection in the United States and aggregated all industries into two categories, e.g., agricultural products and nonagricultural products and services. There is very little substitution in consumption or production between these two categories, and we would measure hardly any cost to having tariffs (and hardly any effect of the tariffs, therefore). But we will have falsely aggregated all the effects away.[7] For example, foreign autos are very good substitutes for smaller U.S. autos, foreign TV sets for U.S. TV sets. Tariffs have large effects there. But we have lumped all these things together in nonagricultural goods and services, and our measure won't pick up any of this.

There is another point. Most of the world's trade is between developed countries, and unless you look very closely, countries seem to be exporting the same goods to each other. That's because the statistics don't discriminate finely between subindustries. Countries specialize in, and obtain increasing returns to scale in different subindustries. Autos aren't just autos. There are small and large, four-cylinder and eight-cylinder, etc. If one disaggregates enough, one finds other cost measures that are significantly larger. The moral of the story is to examine with great care the method by which numerical evidence is constructed.

As is apparent from Figures 3.17 and 3.19, the effect of a tariff is to reduce the amount of trade. Consumers buy less imports and more exportable goods. Producers make more import competing goods and less exportable goods. Many countries subsidize their exports.[8] This does not have any direct consumption effects, because internal prices are world prices. But it pulls productive resources from the importables sector to the exportables sector, and thus increases the amount of trade. From Figure 3.19 it is apparent that this policy also involves a welfare loss, because the society will be on a less favorable budget constraint (one going through a point on the production possibility frontier to the left of

---

[7]Our discussion here draws on a pioneering work: P. Dixon, "The Costs of Protection: The Old and New Arguments," Working Paper No. IP-02, Industries Assistance Commission, Melbourne, Australia, June 1976.

[8]In the United States, the Export-Import Bank provides export financing at below-market rates, thus effectively subsidizing the export of U.S. goods.

the best production point). That is, one can export too much as well as too little.

The implication of our discussion which will stand us in good stead later is the following: there is a right amount of trade; too much trade is as bad as too little. In a competitive environment an unfettered market will generate the optimal amount of trade. Government intervention policies (such as exchange rate manipulation!) which alter perceived prices of foreign versus domestic goods will cause inefficiency and income loss to the economy.

## 3.5   VALID TARIFF ARGUMENTS

This is a very short section. The reason is that, for the most part, even situations in which one has the desire to encourage production of some commodity, say to be self-sufficient for defense reasons, will not require a tariff. Instead the best policy will be a *subsidy*. Tariffs involve inefficiencies, that is, welfare losses, on the consumption side and on the production side, as we saw in Section 3.4. A subsidy which moves the production point a given amount on the PPF will have the same short-term inefficiency effect as a tariff which moves the production point that distance. But there will be no consumption-side losses involved with the subsidy.

Valid tariff arguments, in fact, derive exclusively from the possibility that a country is a large enough consumer of some category of imports to affect the price. That is, collectively the importers may have *monopsony power*. If there are many competing import buyers they will not be able to form a cartel to exploit their potential monopsony power. A tariff imposed by the central government of the importing country reduces import demand and forces down the price of the imported good. (That's what it means to have monopsony power!) The sum of the lowered import costs plus the tariff revenue exceeds the amount needed to compensate the consumers for the inefficiencies caused by the tariff and they are net better off. The parallel argument justifies a central tax on exports when a country's producers of some good have a large enough market share to exercise monopoly power if they could only form a cartel. This is the situation of Brazil in the coffee industry, for instance.[9]

Another good argument for tariffs rests on using them as a short-term retaliatory device, in a struggle to remove all tariffs. If the maneuver succeeds, everyone will be better off under free trade. (By this we mean

---

[9]The world as a whole is always made worse off by the introduction of any of these "optimal tariff" schemes. The global pie shrinks, but the professors of monopoly or monopsony power raise their share more than proportionately.

that the overall pie will have grown in each country. We have already
pointed out in Section 3.2 that there will be market redistributions of
income that make some people within these countries worse off.) If it
does not succeed then a country is still better off moving to free trade all
by itself. If you do not see this, go over the discussions in Sections 3.2
and 3.3 again. The basic point is that if you can't shake the other countries'
tariffs, to you they have to be a fact of nature, and you have to make the
best of the situation; you don't cut off your nose to spite your face.[10]


## 3.6  SUMMARY

The international monetary system is a financial superstructure, built to
facilitate trade in goods, services, and assets. Events in the real economy
are the most important influence on financial magnitudes. Therefore, to
fully understand the world monetary system, one needs a grasp of its
underlying economics of production and exchange.

The chapter starts with a simple example borrowed from Ricardo,
which shows that trade between countries is always mutually beneficial.
This is true even for countries that are able to produce all the goods they
need and/or are more efficient in the production of all goods than are
their trading partners. The principle in question is called the theory of
comparative advantage. It states that all countries will be better off as a
result of the opening of trade between them.

Each country will export the goods that are relatively cheaper to
produce (in which the country is more production-efficient), before the
opening of trade. Although trade raises general welfare, measured by
national income, changes in relative factor prices that result from the
alteration in commodity prices will produce an internal redistribution of
income in each country. In general, factors of production specific to industries that shrink as a result of the opening of trade will lose relative
to factors of production specific to industries that expand.

This simple theory states that trade takes place because pretrade relative prices differ. Ricardo's explanation of the difference in pretrade
relative prices was that the technology of producing the same goods was
different in different countries. To be realistic, we must introduce a large
number of other, and more important, considerations, because in the
advanced economies patterns of commodity demand are all similar, while
all industries have access to roughly the same pool of technology. A
reconciliation of these facts with the necessity of differences in pretrade

---

[10]The most comprehensive reference on justification of tariffs, taxes, and subsidies is J.
  Bhagwati, "The Theory and Practice of Commercial Policy: Departures from Unified Exchange Rates," Special Papers in International Economics, No. 8, January 1968, International Finance Section, Department of Economics, Princeton University.

relative prices has been constructed on the basis of the observation that countries differ in the relative endowments of factors of production (labor, land, physical capital, and human capital, for example). As long as one assumes that at all factor price ratios the production processes of all goods can be ranked by factor intensity, a country will export the goods that are intensive in its relatively abundant factors. The theory just described is known as the Heckscher-Ohlin theory. It provides a good explanation for some of the observed trade patterns, but by no means all.

A fully adequate explanation of observed patterns of trade must take into account imperfect competition, manifested in product differentiation, and must take into account also factors of production not traditionally recognized, such as innovative ability. The so-called "product life cycle" theory of trade is a radically new, but reasonable, explanation of trade in technologically advanced products. It argues that innovative economies pioneer new products and export them until their production becomes routine. Thereafter they import them and are exporting yet other new things.

Finally, government intervention in the form of tariffs, quotas, and other restrictions on trade can explain the existence, or more accurately, the nonexistence of some trade patterns. Whatever may be the professed motives of governments in imposing these restrictions on trade, their outcome is almost invariably production inefficiency and a loss of world income. Virtually without exception, trade restrictions are only beneficial for countries that can use them to exercise monopoly power, and so affect prices of their exports or imports. Even then, world income is lowered by more than the monopolist gains.

### EXERCISES:

### Price Controls on "Old Oil"

The explanation of rent in Figure 3.1 is known as the Ricardian Theory of rent, which says the following: Take any resource available in different qualities (that is, at different marginal costs). The cheapest or best is used first, and then progressively more costly qualities are used. The price of output obviously must cover the cost of the marginal resource. So all the higher quality resources earn a rent equal to the difference between their cost and the cost of the marginal resource.

So, consider the fact that the United States consumes "old oil" from existing wells that were profitable to operate when oil cost $2.00 per barrel, but the marginal supply is imported crude at $25.00. Draw the market situation corresponding to Figure 3.1 in the oil market case, and answer the following questions.

**1.** Do price controls on old oil lower the price of gasoline to retail consumers?

2. There are oil producers and refiners. Do the price controls on old oil prevent the accrual of windfall profits to the oil industry as a whole?

3. If you ran an oil company that did a lot of refining of bought-in oil because you had few U.S. fields, would you be in favor of decontrolling prices of old oil? If you ran an oil company which had more U.S. oil fields than refinery capacity, would you be in favor of decontrolling prices on old oil?

4. Are there any windfall profits *at all* from decontrol of oil prices, or will decontrol merely redistribute the rent?

5. If there are no windfall profts, who will pay the windfall profits tax?

6. What do you think of the members of the executive branch and of Congress who first endorsed price controls and who now endorse a windfall profits tax to accompany decontrol?

## Suggestions for Further Reading

An excellent general reference is R. Caves and R. Jones, *World Trade and Payments*, second edition, Little, Brown and Company, 1977. On the most famous test of the Heckscher-Ohlin theory, see W. Leontief, "Domestic Production and Foreign Trade: The American Capital Position Reexamined," reprinted as Chapter 3 of Richard D. Irwin's *Readings in International Economics*, American Economic Association, 1968. On the product cycle, see R. Vernon, "International Investment and International Trade in the Product Cycle," *Quarterly Journal of Economics*, May 1966.

# Chapter 4

# The Balance of Payments

## 4.1 INTRODUCTION

Balance of payments statistics are compiled retrospectively, for specific periods of time, on a national basis. They provide summary measures of the value of international transactions by residents of the country, during the relevant time period. The international transactions may involve importing, or receipt of interest on holdings of foreign bonds, or a long term investment in a foreign country by a domestic firm. The transactions may have been denominated in local currency or in a foreign currency. By convention, however, balance of payments accounts are always kept in the domestic currency—U.S. dollars for the United States, Deutschemarks for West Germany, and so forth. As exchange rates are now normally subject to quite substantial fluctuations, the same foreign currency transaction can appear to have quite different value in the balance of payments accounts at different times. Value = price × quantity: as long as price is subject to variation, one cannot readily read variations in quantity from variations in value. To people in business, the term "balance of payments" may falsely imply a balance-sheet notion, but the balance of payments is most analogous to an income statement rather than a balance sheet. The emphasis should be on the word "payments". The balance of payments accounts for, say, a quarter, summarize payment flows in and out over that quarter. There is one fundamental difference, however. In an income statement it is desirable to have more flow in than flows out. This is not the case with the balance of payments. By the time you have worked through this chapter and the two succeeding, we hope you will see that it is best to have neither deficit nor surplus. However, if you have to choose, deficits are best because then you consume more (in value) than you produce. To run a persistent surplus is to engage in sustained international charity.

A few more introductory remarks are in order. Since practically everyone is a legal resident of some country, in principle all international transactions occur between the residents of one or more countries and should be recorded twice, once in the account of the legal residence of each of the parties to a transaction. We will see that, for a variety of good reasons, many transactions are lost in at least one of the accounts. Finally, when we speak of the balance of payments in this chapter, we will be referring to the U.S. balance. The reader is free to choose a substitute country instead. All countries adopt a common philosophy and accounting principles in creating their payments statistics, so our analysis will not be institutionally specific.

## 4.2   BALANCE OF PAYMENTS ACCOUNTS AS A SUMMARY OF MARKET TRANSACTIONS

The world of balance of payments analysis breaks neatly into two halves.

Case 1.   The government of the United States[1] makes no direct or indirect intervention in the exchange markets to alter dollar exchange rates.

Case 2.   The government of the United States does attempt to alter exchange rates.

In Case 1 the United States will run neither deficit nor surplus on the balance of payments. In Case 2, the amount of deficit or surplus is a measure of the amount of exchange market intervention. Because there are many methods of exchange market intervention, there are a number of different definitions of the surplus or deficit on the balance of payments. These different definitions attempt to capture the total effect of all the different intervention techniques. At the conceptual level everyone is in agreement—one should try to separate government-contrived international transactions from genuinely private ones. Confusion occurs in practice because this is very hard to do.

Balance of payments statistics give the value in domestic currency of international transactions that pass through exchange markets. We will start with Case 1, and look at the recording of transactions in the exchange markets when there is no own-government intervention. Subsequently we will turn our attention to Case 2, and balance of payments deficits and surpluses. The U.S. dollar is traded in a number of markets against other currencies. For the sake of concreteness we begin our analysis with the dollar-yen market. Figure 4.1 illustrates demand and supply of dollars in exchange for yen for some specific interval of time. In this interval there will be a quantity of dollars transacted for yen, at the indicated equilib-

---

[1] In general, substitute here the government of the country whose balance of payments we are discussing. *Other* governments may attempt to alter the exchange rate of the dollar against their currencies without putting us into Case 2.

**Figure 4.1**   Equilibrium in the Dollar-Yen Market. $1/S_{¥}$ ¥ per $; i.e., the reciprocal of the $ price of ¥.

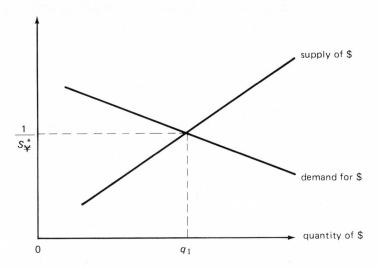

rium price or market-clearing exchange rate. The quantity of dollars transacted at the market-clearing price will be recorded in the balance of payments statistics, but the exchange rate at which the transactions took place will not be. In the period in question, $q_1$ dollars were exchanged for yen at the market-clearing price per dollar of $¥(1/S_{¥}^{*})$.

The salient feature of a market-clearing price is that at this price demand equals supply.[2]

In the dollar-yen market, "demand" means demand for US$ by holders of ¥. Equivalently, it is supply of ¥ in exchange for US$. "Supply" means supply of US$ by dollar holders in exchange for ¥. Equivalently, it is demand for ¥ by holders of US$. This supply of US$ in exchange for ¥ can come from:

- citizens of the United States;

- the U.S. government for noninterventionist motives, for example to pay for military expenditures in Japan;

- foreign private citizens who wish to convert U.S. assets they own into yen; and

- foreign governments holding U.S. assets, who may well be making the conversion to affect the exchange rate between the dollar and the yen.

---

[2]The figure shows a conventional upward sloping supply curve and downward sloping demand curve. In the foreign exchange market there is strong need to justify these assumptions. The question is briefly discussed in the appendix to this chapter.

These holders of dollars wish to acquire yen to hold as cash (for example, tourists), to use to pay for yen-denominated commodities, or to use to acquire yen-denominated assets. Of course a similar classification can be made of the sources of demand for dollars.

For the same interval of time we can similarly represent and classify the outcome of trading the dollar against the other convertible currencies. Sample exchange rates at which demand equals supply of the dollar against other currencies are shown in Figure 4.2. Balance of payments statistics for the trading period represented by our diagrams are lists of the quantities of dollars transacted on all these markets, classified according to certain principles.

**Figure 4.2**   Equilibrium in All Dollar Exchange Markets

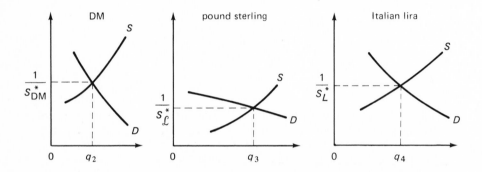

Classifying the numbers one way, we distinguish between balance of payments credits and balance of payments debits. All demands for dollars by holders of other currencies are labelled balance of payments credits. Obviously, another way of saying the same thing is to call all supplies of other currencies in exchange for dollars balance of payments credits. All demands for other currencies by holders of dollars are labelled balance of payments debits. Equivalently, all supplies of dollars in exchange for other currencies are labelled balance of payments debits. We have used

**Table 4.1**   *A First Version of the Balance of Payments*

| supply of dollars (debits) | | demand for dollars (credits) | |
|---|---|---|---|
| to obtain yen | $= q_1$ | by yen holders | $= q_1$ |
| to obtain DM | $= q_2$ | by DM holders | $= q_2$ |
| to obtain £ | $= q_3$ | by £ holders | $= q_3$ |
| to obtain lira | $= q_4$ | by lira holders | $= q_4$ |
| to obtain____ | — | by— | — |
| total debits | $q_1 + q_2 + q_3 + q_4$ $+ \ldots$ | total credits | $q_1 + q_2 + q_3 + q_4$ $+ \ldots$ |

terminology corresponding to our exchange market analysis. Let us draw up a balance of payments at this early point. Table 4.1 is not overly informative, but it focuses attention on one key fact—the balance of payments always balances. This is not an accounting convention but instead reflects the fact that trade in currencies takes place on markets in which the price adjusts to make the quantity supplied equal to the quantity demanded. Even in Case 2 this is true. Only there we will want to subtract transactions inspired by government intervention.

## 4.3  HORIZONTAL CLASSIFICATION OF TRANSACTIONS

The debit/credit distinction gives us the left and right hand columns of our accounts. We now turn to horizontal classification of the debit and credit transactions. In essence, transactions are classified by their *motive*, that is, by the item which the trade in currencies was to facilitate.[3] The overall structure of the horizontal classification is as follows.

- All transactions in commodities and services are placed in the current account.

- All transactions in assets, that is, in financial claims, are placed in the capital account.

- For future reference we mention that there is also an official account, which captures some of the interventionist activities of central banks.

These accounts are divided into finer categories. For example, all transactions in goods are put into the trade account and all services into the service account. The trade and service accounts together comprise the current account. The capital account is divided into short-term capital (assets with life under one year) and long-term capital (the rest of the capital account). The long-term capital account is further subdivided into the direct investment account (purchases of, or establishment of, foreign subsidiaries, branches, etc.) and the portfolio investment account. All these accounts can then be divided up by the country of the transaction. Thus by computing the expenditure of U.S. tourists in Botswana (a debit) and the expenditure of Botswana tourists in the United States (a credit), we could compute the balance of payments on tourist account between Botswana and the United States. When we discuss interpretation of balance of payments statistics, we will consider the extent to which it is worthwhile computing such balances.

We are not finished with the structure of the accounts because balance of payments records are kept on a double-entry basis. The motive for some

---

[3]Recollect that we trade currencies in order to trade in goods, services, and assets.

transaction may be an import. It will be recorded as a debit in the trade account within the current account. But what of the corresponding credit which is the compensating double entry? We are not accountants (we make this remark again and again!), so we will provide the general principle governing the bookkeeping system and then work through a number of examples. The basic philosophy underlying the double-entry structure is the following (and usual) one: one entry records the "motive" of each transaction while the other records the "financial effect."

**Example 1.**   *A U.S. retailer imports $100,000 of cameras from Japan and has 30 days after landing in which to pay.*

This typical commercial transaction has two distinct economic components—an import and a loan. The balance of payments accounts record both these aspects separately, in principle. The import is a current account debit. The loan is a short-term capital credit.[4]

**Example 2.**   *This is the same transaction, except that now the U.S. importer pays the Japanese exporter, and borrows $100,000 from a Japanese bank for 30 days.*

In this case the import and the loan are really two separate transactions and we must have a double entry for each.

    1. *Import and Payment.* This will be recorded as follows:

|                              | debits   | credits  |
| ---------------------------- | -------- | -------- |
| imports                      | 100,000  |          |
| short-term   claims   on foreigners |   | 100,000  |

The first entry is obvious; the second one must be explained. To actually pay the Japanese exporter, we assume the camera dealer has her bank write a check in yen. How did the bank come to have the yen in the first place? It must have opened a checking account with a correspondent bank, or hold similar short-term claims on foreigners. The capital outflow to acquire the short-term claim constituted a debit on the short-term capital account. Now this account is being run down, so we credit the account.

    2. *Loan.* This will be recorded as follows:

|                              | debits   | credits  |
| ---------------------------- | -------- | -------- |
| short-term liabilities to foreigners |  | 100,000  |
| short-term   claims   on foreigners | 100,000 |         |

---

[4]Conceptually, the Japanese exporter buys dollars with yen and lends the dollars to the camera importer. The real counterpart of this implicit transactions is the nonpurchase of yen by the camera importer. Thus the loan is a demand for dollars.

The loan by the bank is a short-term capital inflow, and is thus a credit. The actual cash is paid to an account owned by the U.S. importer; all such foreign accounts are short-term capital outflows, and as such are debits.

Note that when we net out these transactions the outcome is exactly as for Example 1. This is as it should be since the economic content of the transactions is exactly the same.

**Example 3.**   *The U.S. importer in Example 2 now repays the Japanese bank, and pays 1% interest (12% on an annual basis) making a total payment of $101,000.*

This will be recorded as follows:

|                                       | Debits   | Credits |
| ------------------------------------- | -------- | ------- |
| short-term   liabilities   to foreigners | 100,000  |         |
| interest                              | 1,000    |         |
| short-term   claims   on foreigners   |          | 101,000 |

The repayment of the loan wipes off the 100,000 of foreign short-term capital inflow. The 1,000 of interest is debited to services in the current account; it is the payment for the services rendered by the foreign capital for one month. Once again, the actual payment must be from a foreign account owned by a U.S. bank or other entity. The original acquisition is a debit so the running down to make repayment is a credit.

**Example 4.**   *Volkswagen decides to build an assembly plant in the United States. It purchases a facility and related equipment for $100 million. It ships in $80 million of equipment. It finances $75 million of this expenditure by the sale of bonds on the New York capital market.*

This involves direct capital investment, commodity imports, and long-term portfolio capital outflow. We can record it as follows:

|                                 | Debits       | Credits      |
| ------------------------------- | ------------ | ------------ |
| direct investment               |              | 100,000,000  |
| short-term claims on foreigners | 100,000,000  |              |
| direct investment               |              | 80,000,000   |
| imports                         | 80,000,000   |              |
| long-term portfolio investment  | 75,000,000   |              |
| short-term claims on foreigners |              | 75,000,000   |

The first pair of transactions stems from the site acquisition. There is a foreign direct investment in the United States, which is a credit on the capital account, and it is paid for in cash. Thus U.S. citizens come to own $100 million in short-term claims on foreigners. The second pair of transactions treats $80 million of direct investment as being used to pay for $80 million of equipment imports, which are a current account debit item.[5] Finally, the third pair of entries shows payment for the $75 million of Volkswagen bonds by running down of accounts held overseas by U.S. banks or other entities.

As a reward for those who diligently labored to understand these examples, we will conclude our discussion of balance of payments accounts construction by cataloguing the lively (financial) events in the life of Joe Tourist, U.S. citizen vacationing in Europe. Before the statisticians got to him, Joe described these events as follows. He

1. exchanged $250 of traveler's checks for French francs; then

2. was given a diamond tie pin worth $300 by the descendant of a third cousin of his mother's aunt, who lives in Belgium; then

3. purchased a ticket in the Belgian football lottery;

4. which he then won, received a check for BF 50,000;

5. half of which he used to buy a little vacation cottage by the sea; and

6. half of which was stolen from him while he was in a drunken stupor celebrating his success; after which

7. he returned home a sadder but wiser man (see Table 4.2).

**Table 4.2**   *Classification of the Life of Joe Tourist*

|  | Debit | Credit |
|---|---|---|
| 1. short-term claims on foreigners | 250 |  |
| short-term liabilities to foreigners |  | 250 |
| Holding foreign cash is holding a short-term foreign asset. The cash was obtained by selling dollars—i.e., some foreign person has invested in dollars. |  |  |

---

[5]Note that though capital goods are being imported, this is a debit on the current account. The current/capital classification used in the balance of payments accounts is the financial classification. All commodities are current items, all paper claims are capital items.

**Table 4.2** *Classification of the Life of Joe Tourist* (cont'd)

|  | Debit | Credit |
|---|---|---|
| 2. imports | 300 | |
|   unilateral transfers | | 300 |
| 3. travel and tourist expenses abroad | $S \times p$ | |
|   short-term claims on foreigners | | $S \times p$ |
| Here $p$ is the price of the ticket and $S$ is the exchange rate. Buying the ticket runs down the short-term foreign investment in Step 1. | | |
| 4. short-terms claims on foreigners | $S \times 50,000$ | |
|   unilateral transfers | | $S \times 50,000$ |
| Here $S$ = exchange rate. The BF 50,000 is used to purchase an asset, viz: the cash balance. | | |
| 5. short-term claims on foreigners | | $S \times 25,000$ |
|   direct investment | $S \times 25,000$ | |
| Joe has run down his foreign cash asset in order to convert it into a fixed investment—the house. | | |
| 6. unilateral transfers | $S \times 25,000$ | |
|   short-term claims on foreigners | | $S \times 25,000$ |
| Here Joe liquidated the rest of his short-term foreign asset to convert it into a gift to an anonymous foreign person. | | |

## 4.4  VALIDITY OF RECORDED PAYMENTS STATISTICS

Every country that accepts the balance of payments accounting procedures we have described in Section 4.3 will draw up, for every interval for which data are collected, balance of payments tables that appear in main outline as in Table 4.3. The final item, "Official Reserve Transactions," has a net debit balance of $F - F'$. As we will see shortly, this is one measure of the balance of payments deficits for the country in question. Without probing further into why this should be so, let us consider measures of the accuracy with which official statisticians capture international transactions.

Obviously with the huge sums involved there are bound to be omissions and errors, and all nations' accounts have an "errors and omissions"

**Table 4.3**   *Structural Outline of Balance of Payments*

|                                      | Debits | Credits |
|--------------------------------------|--------|---------|
| *current account*                    |        |         |
| trade                                | $A$    | $A'$    |
| services                             | $B$    | $B'$    |
| *capital account*                    |        |         |
| short-term claims                    | $C$    | $C'$    |
| long-term portfolio claims           | $D$    | $D'$    |
| direct investment                    | $E$    | $E'$    |
| *official account*                   |        |         |
| official reserve transactions        | $F$    | $F'$    |
| total      $A+B+C+D+E+F = A'+B'+C'+D'+E'+F'$ |  |  |

item.[6] However is seems clear that a huge volume of transactions is systematically being kept from official statisticians, for a variety of good reasons.[7] One of the principal pieces of evidence for this is the huge value of the whole world's current account deficit. For one country, the current account balance is $(A' + B') - (A + B)$ in Table 4.3. Since one country's imports must be another country's exports, the world as a whole should have a balanced current account. In fact, the cumulative 1978 deficit is estimated at $46 billion, an enormous figure dwarfing the $5 billion West German current account surplus, the $17.5 billion Japanese current account surplus and the $19 billion U.S. current account deficit. In fact, all the current account surpluses and deficits that are officially recorded are rendered suspect. For reasons we will list below, the OECD thinks that most countries have larger surpluses or smaller deficits than official figures show.

Consider first the trade account. The OECD considers that the world trade account is spuriously in surplus most of the time, because exports tend to be recorded when they are shipped, but recorded as imports when they arrive. Thus at times of growing world trade, exports recorded will exceed imports recorded. When the volume of world trade shrinks or grows less fast, current exports will be swamped by recording of earlier, booming exports as imports, so the effect is reversed. To this we should

---

[6]When one of the authors was a graduate student at Harvard University in 1971, he was told the following story by a professor of European origin. The professor had shipped some furniture from Europe and was at the wharf to accompany it on the customs inspection. The inspector wanted to record the source of the imports and asked where the furniture had been shipped from. "Amsterdam," he was told by the professor. The inspector said that he only needed to know the country of shipment, would just write in "Switzerland."
[7]See Richard Janssen, "Gap in World Current Account Indicates Seriously Distorted Statistics, OECD Says," *The Wall Street Journal*, August 14, 1978.

add a factor of great importance for the total volume of world trade, though having unknown importance for the measured balances, namely, smuggling.[8] In parts of Southeast Asia and Africa, the volume of illegal trade can approach 40% and more of the volume of legal trade (estimates only, for obvious reasons). The usual explanations are taxation of earnings from trade, and attempts by governments to confiscate export earnings and ration foreign exchange to importers. Another factor, tending this time to put trade accounts into spurious deficit, is the arranged padding of bills sent from abroad to importers in countries which have strict controls on capital outflow. (Only the true price is recorded as export earnings, of course, or more income tax would have to be paid.) The only way to get substantial capital out of South Africa, for example, is to have your friendly supplier over-invoice you and keep the balance in a foreign account. Such methods are also used for simple income tax avoidance in countries like Italy and Spain.

According to Janssen's article, the OECD thinks that the main source of spurious deficits is the service account where "payments . . . are recorded more punctiliously than receipts." The main motivation here seems to be avoidance of taxation. It is also suggested that intellience agencies channel overseas payments via spurious payments for insurance or advertising services, which are, of course, never recorded in the receiving countries. This may also apply to armaments flows. Finally, since developing countries are often seen as worthier recipients of aid the poorer they are assessed to be, they apparently deliberately exaggerate their current account deficits.

The conclusion seems inescapable that balance of payments figures are useful only for gross magnitude comparisons at best. For this reason alone it seems that much too much attention is lavished on small changes in the current account. We must now turn our attention to interpretation of the statistics and consider what may be wrung from even the best of the numbers.

## 4.5 INTERPRETATION OF PARTIAL BALANCES

As we have noted already, one can compute any partial balance. Earlier we referred to the balance on the tourist account between the United States and Botswana. One frequently reads discussions of the current account balance, the trade account balance, and so forth. Even though the overall balance of payments always balances, it will be an extremely rare event if all the partial balances also come out to zero. If we observe a surplus or deficit on the trade account, this may be an accurate picture

---

[8]See Jorge Dominguez, "Smuggling," *Foreign Policy*, No. 20, Fall 1975.

of the trade account, if the numbers are good. However many people, even in high places, feel an urge to draw conclusions from these partial balances, or to explain them using some causal picture that is supposed to be revealed by looking through the accounts themselves. To be concrete here, we reprint an article from the September 16, 1977, edition of *The Wall Street Journal*, which summarizes certain statements by Canadian government officials about the Canadian current account in the second quarter of 1977.[9]

### Canadian Dollar Declines Only Slightly Despite News of Record Payments Deficit

Canada reported a record deficit of $1.55 billion (Canadian) in its international payments current account for the second quarter, but the Canadian dollar took the news in stride.

The gap, which was the thirteenth consecutive quarterly deficit, widened from a revised deficit of $845 million in the first quarter. The previous record quarterly gap was $1.30 billion in the 1975 first quarter.

Despite the sharp widening of the deficit, the Canadian dollar in Toronto edged down against its U.S. counterpart only slightly, to 93.18 U.S. cents from 93.20 cents. Dealers attributed the small impact to the fact that previously reported trade figures had foreshadowed the deterioration. The current account includes trade plus services and certain financial transactions.

In quiet trading on other international currency markets, the U.S. dollar was mixed.

### Merchandise Trade Surplus Fell

Canada said its record current-account deficit mainly reflects a steep drop in its merchandise trade surplus, which fell to $307 million from $823 million in the first quarter. The deficit was aggravated by bigger deficits in tourism, interest and dividend payments and some service transactions.

Officials said the gap was financed by a heavy inflow of foreign capital from borrowings on foreign markets by Canadian companies and provincial agencies. They added that they don't expect any serious problems from continuing current account deficits as long as interest rates abroad remain lower.

To remove an irrelevant consideration, we will explain the last sentence. It says that higher interest rates in Canada than in the United States are causing speculative capital inflow—speculators are gambling that the interest rate differential will outweigh any future adverse exchange rate movement. Our interest lies in the implied causality behind the current account deficit. The following propositions are asserted.

---

[9]Reprinted by permissions of *The Wall Street Journal*,© Dow Jones & Company, Inc. 1977. All Rights Reserved.

- The record deficit occurred because Canadians bought more imports while foreigners bought fewer Canadian exports. In addition, compared with previous quarters, more Canadian tourists left the country and fewer foreign ones came in.

- Fortunately, this terrible deficit was covered by capital inflow attributable to borrowing by Canadian government agencies and private firms.

This equality of forces kept the exchange rate virtually unchanged.

This explanation implies an independence between the current and capital accounts that cannot occur in a world of market determined exchange rates. What would happen if the capital inflow greatly diminished? Clearly, the Canadian dollar would be forced to depreciate since at the current exchange rate, the supply of Canadian dollars offered in exchange for other currencies would exceed the demand for Canadian dollars by the holders of other currencies. And at the new, lower exchange rate, the current account deficit would again be exactly offset by the now lower capital account surplus, because demand for foreign exchange must equal supply at the market clearing exchange rate. The balance of payments always balances. Thus any deficit in one partial balance must always be exactly equalled by a surplus on the remainder.

Not only can we read nothing into the fact that the capital account surplus offsets the current account deficit, we can also tell another causal story quite at odds with the one attributed to the Canadian officials. Ours runs as follows: through an expansive monetary policy, the Canadian government raised inflation, expectations of future inflation, and thus interest rates in Canada. This simultaneously caused capital inflow through interest rate speculation, and made foreign goods and resorts look relatively more attractive to Canadians while Canadian items looked relatively less attractive to foreigners. The capital inflow kept the exchange rate over-valued on a purchasing power parity criterion (see Chapter 5), and so created the current account deficit. From looking at the accounts alone one cannot detect any causal patterns. Of course in conjunction with some overall theory of exchange rate determination, like purchasing power parity, and with outside evidence such as a knowledge of monetary policy and the inflation rate, one may usefully analyze an economy with these numbers.

A very contemporary partial balance that is often struck is the balance of payments on the oil account. It has frequently been claimed that the US$ has depreciated because of the massive volume of oil imports. This theory is perhaps worth no consideration at all, inasmuch as the Germans and the Japanese import much more oil than does the United States, and we know what happened to their currencies. As is made clear in Chapter 5, the OPEC-induced rise in the price of oil can have affected the value of the US$ only to the extent that it caused or contributed to a differential in inflation between the United States and its trading partners. The OPEC coup lowered real income in many countries, but exchange rates are a monetary phenomenon and explanations of their levels must be sought in price levels and capital flows.

## 4.6   INTERPRETATION OF BILATERAL BALANCES

A bilateral balance is the balance between two countries. Commonly one sees discussion of bilateral partial balances, for example, commentary on the U.S. current account deficit with Japan. As we have said already, even if there is overall bilateral balance there need not be balance on the current account. There may be excellent reasons for countries to run systematic current account deficits, and capital account surpluses, with respect to other countries. Throughout this discussion we maintain the assumption that there is no government intervention in the exchange market, so we are discussing reasons why the private economy should exhibit these deficits and surpluses. We can distinguish two types of reasons.

1.  *Transitory.* For some time one or more countries may be seen as a safe haven for capital. As we noted in our discussion of Canada, any such inflows tend to appreciate the exchange rate and create an offsetting current account deficit.

2.  *Structural.* Wealthy, mature economies generate more savings, and tend to have lower returns to investment, than younger and faster-growing economies. The latter import a great deal, especially capital equipment to facilitate growth. One thus expects fast growing economies to run current account deficits, and capital account surpluses, with wealthier economies.

In addition there is an important and less obvious structural factor. The market approach to the balance of payments shows that there will be no bilateral imbalances between currencies (refer to Section 4.2). However this is not the same as ensuring no bilateral imbalances between countries, because the pattern of trade between countries is determined by the pattern of comparative advantage and by specialization in production and trade. We need an example to make this clear. Let us suppose a world of three countries: Japan, Britain, and Australia. Further, suppose that there are no capital flows so that the balance of payments is just the balance on current account. We will now exhibit a situation of staggering bilateral payments imbalances between countries, combined with perfect, zero bilateral balances between currencies. Moreover this arrangement is the most efficient one possible, and any alteration would make everyone worse off. The essence of the example is given in Figure 4.3, which shows the highly specialized trade flows we presume to exist.

**Figure 4.3** Flows of Commodity Trade

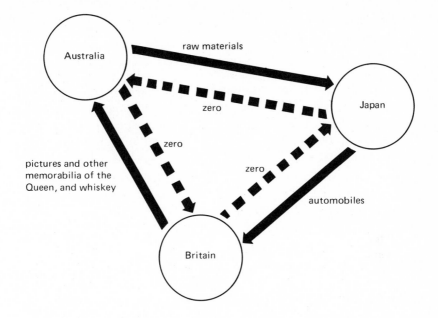

Clearly each country is in gross surplus with one of the others and in gross deficit with the remaining nation. Yet for each, the value of exports can equal the value of imports. Moreover, demand for each currency can equal supply, with respect to exchange against each of the other currencies. We will now work the accounting, on the assumption that each country invoices its exports in its own currency.[10] The firms which export are distinct from the firms which import, so there will exist a market in foreign exchange. We begin by outlining the sources of demand for and supply of each currency.

**Australian dollar**
- Japanese importers wish to buy it in exchange for yen.
- Australian exporters offer to supply it in exchange for pounds.

**British pound**
- Australian importers wish to buy it in exchange for dollars.
- British exporters offer to supply it in exchange for yen.

[10]This seems to be a common practice in world trade. See Sven Grassman, *Foreign Exchange Reserves and the Structure of Foreign Trade*, Lexington Books, 1974. In any event, the reader can confirm that nothing in the example depends on the currency of invoice.

**Japanese yen**  • British importers demand it in exchange for pounds.
                 • Japanese importers supply it in exchange for dollars.

There is thus a source of demand and a source of supply for each currency. Trade flows of equal value will thus balance the currency markets, and also balance the balance of payments for each country. While this example is extreme it should force home the principle that there is absolutely no reason to expect or desire to have each bilateral balance of payments be zero. It would be just as absurd, for the same reason, to expect Boeing, say, to sell each of its many subcontractors and suppliers a number of aircraft equal in value to the parts and assemblies that it buys.

## 4.7  DEFICITS AND SURPLUSES: DIRECT INTERVENTION

The time has finally come to consider the subject of balance of payments deficits and surpluses, which are brought into existence by government attempts to maintain exchange rates that differ from those which would result in the free market. We can distinguish between *open intervention,* whose results will be visible in the official account in the balance of payments, and *indirect intervention,* whose impact on the statistics is much harder to assess.

We commence with open intervention and its consequences. Figure 4.4 reproduces the situation of Figure 4.1. However, we now suppose that the government of the United States wishes to overvalue the dollar in terms of the yen. That is, it wishes to create a lower dollar price of yen than the market would bring about—a price of $\overline{S}_¥$, lower than $S^*_¥$. Our diagram has the yen price of dollars so the government wishes to establish $1/\overline{S}_¥ > /S^*_¥$. If it wishes to do so by open intervention it enters the exchange market as a demander of dollars in exchange for yen. (It must obtain the yen from its reserves, or borrow from the Bank of Japan or the IMF. We return to this point later.) This addition to private demand for dollars in exchange for yen obviously raises the price of the dollar in terms of the yen. By adding enough demand the government may be able to attain the target rate of $1/\overline{S}_¥$[11].

As the figure shows, by demanding the amount $D$ the government bridges the gap between demand and supply at the desired price $1/\overline{S}_Y$. The exchange market still clears, but now it clears as the sum of private plus official transactions. The amount $D$ is the dollar value of the deficit

---

[11]How much is enough? In Chapter 6, we analyze government intervention activities in much greater detail. In the late 1960s the governments of Britain and West Germany learned that they did not have enough resources. They were overrun by speculative waves.

**Figure 4.4**   Creation of a U.S. Deficit in Yen

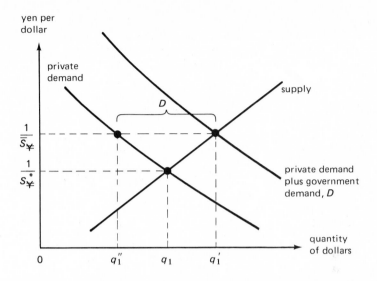

against the yen. A deficit is caused by official open intervention to overvalue the currency. The government loses foreign exchange reserves equal in value to the deficit, because it is the sale of these reserves which creates the deficit, under the open intervention. Had the government attempted to undervalue the dollar in terms of the yen by open intervention, it would have entered the market as a seller of dollars in exchange for yen. (This is easy for the government to do since it prints the dollars.) This extra supply would have driven down the value of the dollar in terms of the yen below $1/S^*_\yen$. The amount of dollars supplied by the government in excess of the private supply at the chosen exchange rate is called the surplus against the yen. The reader should draw the picture analogous to Figure 4.4 that illustrates open intervention to undervalue the dollar against the yen. A surplus is caused by official open intervention to undervalue the currency. The government gains foreign exchange reserves equal in (dollar) value to the surplus, because it is the purchase of these reserves with dollars which creates the surplus, under open intervention. The open interventions of the United States government in all the different currency markets are recorded in the official account, as gain or loss of reserves.

Before we consider indirect intervention and its consequences for the balance of payments, we can draw some simple but compelling conclusions from our study of open intervention. First, the sum of all deficits and surpluses for the world as a whole must be zero (in reality, if not as measured!). One country can run a surplus only if at least one other is running a deficit. Another way of saying the same thing is that not all currencies can be deliberately overvalued or undervalued simultaneously.

Alternatively put, in political terms, all countries cannot pursue independent balance of payments or exchange rate policies, even if for not-altogether-rational reasons they wish to do so. For many years, under the fixed exchange rate system, it was in vogue to undervalue the currency and run surpluses. It was principally the United States that was the passive partner in this game and ran deficits.

Second, countries can only run deficits so long as they have reserves, or borrowing power. When the deficits are brought to a halt by the exhaustion of the resources that create them, the corresponding surpluses terminate also. The market must then revert to the free market exchange rate. Thus, in a period of fixed exchange rates or heavy intervention, the rational speculator will be watching the reserves and borrowing capacity of the deficit countries as a hawk watches its prey. He or she will also be looking at the scope for indirect intervention, which usually is undertaken side by side with direct intervention and is the last resort when reserves and the credit line have run out.

Finally, consider again the situation illustrated in Figure 4.4 where the U.S. government manipulates the exchange market to run a deficit against the yen. The magnitude of the intervention and the deficit appears directly in the case of the United States in the change in reserves—the official U.S. stock of yen-denominated assets has fallen. But a U.S. deficit against the yen must correspond to a surplus of the yen vis-à-vis the dollar in other yen-holding and using countries. If the official U.S. assets that were liquidated were balances held as obligations of the Bank of Japan, then these official short-term liabilities to foreign (i.e., U.S.) monetary authorities will have fallen. Thus the intervention will have its reflection also in the books of the Bank of Japan.

Now suppose that the United States did not have large reserves of yen but, say, Canada did. Let us suppose that the government of the United States arranges a swap to borrow these Canadian reserves of yen for intervention purposes in return for an issue of U.S. Treasury debt. Thus, as the Federal Reserve feeds the Canadian-owned yen into the market of the yen against the US$, U.S. reserves of yen will not fall, but U.S. obligations to Canada will rise, and Canadian reserves of yen will fall. The same intervention now has a different appearance in the U.S. balance of payments statistics. If the Canadian yen were official obligations of the Bank of Japan, then the reflection of the intervention on the latter's books now shows a decrease in official obligations to Canada. In general, if a country's currency is held as official reserves by other countries, all changes in those other countrys' holdings of the currency reflect interventions against the currency of the reserve currency. Because of the possibility of swap operations, the source of these interventions may not be immediately apparent from figures on official reserves.

Consider another possible situation, which is also a common occurrence. A central bank originally acquired foreign currency and invested it in government bonds of the country in question. Let us say that the United States held its yen reserves in official obligations of the Japanese government. However at some stage it may exchange the government bonds for privately issued yen bonds, in order to receive a better return. This would be recorded in the Japanese balance of payments statistics as a portfolio rearrangement in the long-term capital account. When the official bonds are sold there would be a capital outflow, and when the private bonds are purchased, a capital inflow of equal value. Suppose now that to obtain yen to fund appreciation of the dollar, the Federal Reserve sells the yen bonds. What happens? In the U.S. balance of payments statistics, there will be net imports from (plus capital flow to) Japan, offset by outflow of official capital as the Federal Reserve's yen assets are run down to cover the deficit. In Japan there will be a net export surplus to (plus capital flow from) the United States, offset by a capital outflow as the yen assets of the Federal Reserve are liquidated. Note that the actions of the Federal Reserve are recorded in the official account in the U.S. balance of payments, because they involve a rundown of officially held assets to support the dollar against the yen. However in Japan's accounts the counterpart items are all in the private part of the accounts, and moreover do not even involve official obligations of the Japanese government. That is, there is no reason to expect U.S.-inspired intervention in the dollar-yen market to appear in the official account of *both* countries. It will appear in the accounts of the intervening government. It need have no connection with the government of the other country. This point will come up again in our discussion of the Eurocurrency market in Chapter 8.

It should be noted that a major dollar support operation in the dollar-yen market, funded by U.S. rundown of Federal Reserve- and Treasury-owned yen obligations, can have effects on the Japanese economy apart from those directly attributable to the exchange rate being different from its free-market value. The indirect effects come from the implicit portfolio rearrangements consequent on U.S. sale of the yen bonds. The proceeds are paid to the Japanese exporters who are running the net positive balance with the United States (and/or to the dollar holders wanting to invest in yen-denominated assets). The effects on the Japanese economy depend upon what the recipients *want* to do with the funds they receive from the U.S. Suppose

- They want to invest in yen bonds. Then it is as if the United States paid for the deficit by handing over the title to the bonds, and nothing else happens. If the new owners want to hold a different bond mix, then there will be a repricing of yen bonds until the market is content to hold the existing structure of bonds. The general principle is that, collectively, the market cannot alter the outstanding asset stocks. So all that can happen is that the assets are repriced until people are, in the aggregate, willing to hold them.

- They want to invest in common stocks. Again, this desire by the new owners neither raises the aggregate supply of stocks nor lowers the aggregate supply of bonds. So the overall effect will be to raise stock prices relative to bond prices.

- They want to convert to commodities. Once again the general effect must be to drive up the price of commodities relative to bonds. But which commodities? In Chapter 5 we introduce the distinction between goods that are traded internationally and those that are not (such as most personal and government services, for instance). If the new yen-holders wish to acquire nontraded goods in Japan, like housing, there will be a once-for-all jump in these Japanese prices. If they wanted *only* traded goods the whole demand would be satisfied by imports and there would be no deficit for the United States to fund![12] By presuming that the dollar is overvalued through official intervention we have ruled out this case. Thus any desire to switch to commodities will create some jump in the Japanese price level.

Suppose the Federal Reserve sells not private Japanese bonds but government bonds. Then things are as above. If the Federal Reserve lets the bonds roll off and redeems them for cash, the Japanese money supply will have risen as the government will have had to create money to redeem the bonds. However, its stock of bonds outstanding is now smaller, and if it has a fixed borrowing requirement it will issue new bonds and so reabsorb the extra yen cash. Unless we are in Case 1 above, where the new yen-holders want the new government bonds at the old yields, the government will have to raise yields to issue the debt. This involves a different implicit tax obligation for the Japanese taxpayers, to pay the interest. These rather complex effects on yields occur whenever portfolio preferences change for any reason. Major intervention actions cause large asset transfers and make these impacts of immediate concern.

Consider now the money supply effects of exchange market intervention. Take again the case of the United States propping up the dollar against the yen. On balance, dollar holders are writing checks to the U.S. government, which is supplying the deficiency of yen at the officially-desired exchange rate. Thus on balance the Federal Reserve is coming to own dollar-denominated demand deposits, which therefore (by definition) leave the money supply. Thus, deficits reduce the money supply in the deficit country by the amount of the deficit. Suppose the U.S. government were instead undervaluing the dollar against the yen. Then on balance the Federal Reserve is writing dollar checks to meet the excess demand for dollars at the officially supported exchange rate. Thus, sur-

---

[12]Recollect from Figure 4.3 that even if the new yen-holders do not buy *directly* from America, goods of the same value must ultimately be exported from the U.S. to a third country, to make up for the latter's exports absorbed by Japan.

pluses increase the money supply in the surplus country by the amount of the surplus. What happens in the other country, here Japan? We covered that above. Any direct intervention by the U.S. government involves a rundown or buildup of its yen-denominated assets, which has the portfolio pricing effects we have already examined.

## 4.8 DEFICITS AND SURPLUSES: INDIRECT INTERVENTION

Instead of trying to provide yen to meet an excess of private demand over private supply at the desired exchange rate, the government can try to manipulate other markets to increase the private supply of yen, or to decrease the private demand for yen. For example, the U.S. government could suddenly reduce the rate of growth of the money supply, causing a jump in short-term interest rates and a speculative inflow of foreign capital including yen. It could change the tax treatment of U.S. obligations held by foreigners to raise the after-tax return, also inducing a temporary inflow. The reader can think of other measures quite easily, such as unfavorable tax treatment for capital outflows from the United States. Imposing new and/or higher tariffs switches demand from foreign goods to domestic goods and thus also raises the market-clearing price of the country's currency. Import quotas have the same effect. As we made plain in Section 4.7, the purpose of computing balance of payments deficits or surpluses is to determine whether the currency was overvalued or undervalued on the basis of solely private (or at least noninterventionist) transactions. So, if you want to know what the private balance of payments would have been at the official exchange rate, you must work out how to eliminate the effects of these indirect interventions. Certain *ad hoc* balance of payments notions have been created to attempt to deal with this problem.

- *Net Liquidity Balance.* This notion *assumes* that all very liquid short-term inflows and outflows were induced by monetary policy, and so treats the net liquid capital inflow (outflow) as equivalent to a government sale of its reserves (addition to its reserves) when computing the private balance of payments at the current exchange rate.
- *Basic Balance.* This notion goes somewhat further and treats *all* short-term (under one year) capital flows as policy-induced.

Why stop here? We have listed a whole spectrum of government policies aimed at influencing exchange rates. To compile a balance of payments table showing the real private flows of goods and services at current exchange rates is not a matter of accounting conventions but rather a question of the deepest economic detective work. It is almost impossible to disentangle all the channels of government intervention. Fortunately we can provide estimates of equilibrium exchange rates based on the private economy in a much more direct fashion, as we will demonstrate in the next chapter. The balance of payments accounts are useful primarily for forming conjectures on government intervention policies, by examining the resources available to the government. This explains the attention given to the direct intervention or official settlements balance—it shows the net effects of intervention on exchange reserves.


## 4.9  SUMMARY

The balance of payments of a country records, in units of domestic currency, the value of all international payment flows that pass through the exchange markets during some specific time period (usually from a quarter to a year in length) by the residents of that country.

Balance of payments statistics draw in part upon accounting principles, as must any type of financial reporting. Their conceptual base derives from economic theory, since they summarize the financial counterpart of transactions in goods, services and financial claims which take place between residents of different countries.

The accounting principles record transactions in a classification based on motive of the transactions, that is, by the item that the trade in currencies was to facilitate. The accounts are kept on a double entry basis. One entry records the motive of each transaction while the other entry records the financial effect.

All demands for the domestic currency by holders of other currencies are labeled balance of payments credits, while all demands for foreign currency by holders of domestic currency are labeled balance of payments debits. All transactions in commodities are placed in the trade account while all transactions in services are placed in the service account. The sum of the trade and service accounts is called the current account. All transactions in financial claims are placed in the capital account. Direct government interventions in the exchange markets via buying and selling currencies are placed in the official account. The sum of the current account, capital account, and official account is the balance of payments. It always sums to zero (apart from statistical discrepancies), not because of an accounting convention but because this reflects the demand equals supply equilibrium of the markets for foreign exchange.

One can compute partial balances, such as the current account balance or the tourist account balance, or one can compute bilateral balances, such as the balance of payments between the United States and Japan. It is virtually impossible to attribute unambiguous meaning to such numbers without a great deal of outside economic information. For example, bi-lateral imbalances may be a sign of efficient international specialization.

There are a number of concepts of balance of payments deficit or surplus. The aim is to separate the genuinely private transactions from those undertaken or induced by governments to manipulate the exchange markets. If the only form of government exchange market intervention is by open-market purchases and sales of currencies then we can state the following: a balance of payments surplus is caused by, and is equal in value to, the amount of government purchases of foreign currency with domestic currency to undervalue the domestic currency. A balance of payments deficit is caused by, and is equal in value to, the amount of government purchases of domestic currency with foreign currency to overvalue the domestic currency. When indirect exchange market inter-vention occurs, there is no satisfactory concept of deficit or surplus.

Because the sum of all balance of payments deficits and surpluses must be zero, it is obvious that all governments cannot simultaneously run independent balance of payments/exchange rate policies. It's a shame that it is not obvious to the governments.

## Appendix 4.1  Stability of the Market for Foreign Exchange

Consider the upward sloping supply curve of dollars offered in exchange for yen in Figure 4.1. This implies that as $1/S_¥$ rises, that is, as $S_¥$, the dollar price of yen falls, more yen will be demanded. The demand for yen is a derived demand—the yen are wanted because one uses them to acquire commodities and assets which happen to be priced in yen. It is relatively uncontroversial to assert that as the (translated) dollar prices of Kawasaki motorcycles or Sony televisions fall, more of these items will be purchased by Americans. But this does not, in itself, establish that the supply curve in Figure 4.1 slopes upwards. For the supply of dollars in exchange for yen represents the value of import transactions, not the quantity.

$$\text{value} = \text{price} \times \text{quantity}$$

As the price of yen falls in dollar terms (holding all other things constant), the quantity of yen-priced items purchased by Americans will rise. But it is not obvious that the quantity will rise faster than the price falls.

Similarly, the downward sloping demand curve for dollars in exchange for yen represents the value of dollar purchases by yen holders. Yen holders may buy more U.S. products and assets as their (translated) yen price falls, but the reader should be convinced that this need not imply that the value of dollars demanded will rise as the yen price of a dollar falls.

If the demand curves slope upwards and the supply curves slope downwards, markets for foreign exchange will not work. A market is said to work if, when the price is above the equilibrium level, we see supply exceeding demand, whereas if the price is below the equilibrium level we see demand exceeding supply. Since we expect excess demand to raise the price and excess supply to lower it, the market price is forced to move in the "right" direction. The reader should verify that:

- As Figure 4.1 shows, a price $(1/S)$ greater than $(1/S^*_¥)$ leads to excess supply. The dollar is overvalued—dollar holders get more yen per dollar than at the market clearing price. Conversely, at a price $(1/S)$ less than $(1/S^*_¥)$ there is excess demand for dollars because the dollar is undervalued relative to the yen.

- If the labels on the demand and supply curves in Figure 4.1 are switched, the market will not work. A price greater than $(1/S^*_¥)$ leads to excess demand which only drives the price up further; a price lower than $(1/S^*_¥)$ leads to excess supply, which drives the price further down.

We will briefly investigate circumstances in which markets do and do not work.

After the yen had begun its strong rise against the dollar in the second half of 1977, the Japanese government found itself assailed by criticism that the appreciation of the yen was not having the desired effect of reducing the Japanese balance of payments surplus. It was conceded that exports were falling as the yen appreciated, falling to a significant extent, but that imports into Japan were not rising significantly.[13] Let us suppose then that American demand for Japanese goods is very price-elastic, so that as the yen appreciates, the dollar value of American purchases falls. This gives us an upward sloping supply curve of dollars in exchange for yen, shown in Figure 4.5 below. Figure 4.5 also shows a possible implication of the description just given of the Japanese economy. As the dollar depreciates, Japanese buy a smaller value of dollar-priced goods, so that the demand curve slopes upwards also. Note however that the demand curve has been drawn to cut the supply curve from below.

**Figure 4.5**  Upward Sloping Demand for Dollars

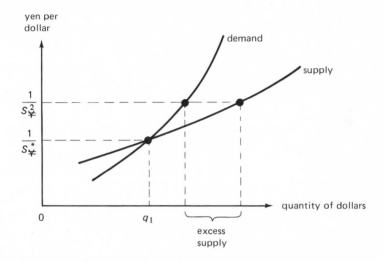

In this case, the reader can see that the market will still work. When the dollar is overvalued relative to the yen (the rate is at $1/S^2_¥ > 1/S^*_¥$) there is excess supply of dollars and the rate will be forced down, despite the clearly perverse behavior of demand. As drawn, the supply response to overvaluation dominates the perverse demand response. Of course, it is possible to construct cases in which the market will not work. (The reader should redraw Figure 4.5 so that the demand curve cuts the supply curve from above—the perverse demand response exceeds the supply response.) There are technical conditions on the demand and supply elasticities which we will not bother to present. However the important point is that these are conditions on the sum of the demand and supply elasticities. As in Figure 4.5, a reasonable supply response can offset a perverse demand effect. So far, there has not been found an unstable or nonworkable foreign eschange market, so that it is reasonable for us to characterize the currency demands and supplies tabulated as the balance of payments as being the results of trading at market clearing prices.

---

[13]See Mike Tharp, "Japan Government Draws Domestic Fire for Strong Yen Rise Against U.S. Dollar," *The Wall Street Journal*, July 11, 1977.

***Appendix 4.2***  *Security-Price Consequences of Liquidation of*
*Central Bank Reserves for Intervention Purposes*

Our discussion of the portfolio rearrangements consequent upon central bank
liquidation of reserves held in the form of marketable foreign securities used the
example of the U.S. government selling yen-denominated bonds to provide resources to appreciate the dollar above its free market value against the yen. This
example was appropriate at the time the first draft of the chapter was prepared
in 1978. By the second quarter of 1979 the tables had turned and foreign central
banks were selling dollar-denominated bonds to provide reserves to prevent their
currencies depreciating too much against the dollar as oil shortages loomed. We
present extracts from two articles published in *The Wall Street Journal* of April
3, 1979,[14] which graphically illustrate the analysis we have developed. The first
describes the circumstances of the exchange market intervention, while the second
shows the consequences for Treasury bill yields.

### Dollar Surges on Most Currency Markets
### As Concerns Over Oil Hurt Japanese Yen

The U.S. dollar soared in Tokyo on news of an oil-well fire off Saudi
Arabia and kept rising throughout the day against most major currencies.

Though the Saudi fire wasn't expected to hurt oil production by Arabian
American Oil Co., the report hit the Japanese yen hard because of concern
about the effects of oil shortages and oil-price boosts on the Japanese
economy, which is totally dependent on imported petroleum.

Central banks in Japan and Europe intervened heavily to support their
currencies against the ebullient dollar. Even the U.S. Federal Reserve
was selling dollars to buy yen yesterday in New York. Trading was hectic
in most markets.

In Tokyo Monday, the dollar zoomed to 211.15 yen despite the active
yen support by the Japanese central bank, which is estimated to have
dumped $700 million in the effort. The dollar continued its rise later in
New York to 211.60 yen, its highest level in New York since mid-June
1978. Last Friday in New York, the dollar was quoted at 209.50 yen.

Reflecting the brisk dollar selling to support the yen, Japan's foreign-
exchange reserves plunged $3.87 billion in March to $28.81 billion, the
lowest since last June 30, when they stood at $27.33 billion.

### Gain Against Mark

On other markets yesterday, the dollar jumped to 1.8830 West German marks in Frankfurt. Though it eased to 1.8790 later in New York,
it was still ahead of its Friday level of 1.8660 marks in New York.

The U.S. currency climbed to 1.7035 Swiss francs in Zurich despite
estimated sales of $200 million by the Swiss central bank to prop the
franc. The dollar dropped back to 1.7010 later in New York, but it was
still up from the Friday level of 1.6830 francs.

---

[14]Reprinted by permission of *The Wall Street Journal,* © Dow Jones & Company, Inc., 1979.
All Rights Reserved.

### U.S. Dollar's Strength in Foreign Trading
### Is Causing Woes for Treasury Bill Market

NEW YORK—The U.S. dollar's surprisingly strong recovery in foreign-exchange trading is causing some woes for the domestic Treasury bill market.

Foreign central banks, led by the Bank of Japan, have been selling massive amounts of U.S. government securities in recent weeks to raise funds to support their own currencies in the international-exchange markets.

By one estimate, the Federal Reserve, acting on behalf of customers, mainly foreign official institutions, sold almost $4.2 billion of Treasury bills on the open market last month. Yesterday, it sold an additional $530 million.

So far, the sales haven't hurt the market too much because dealers' inventories of the securities have been low, partly as a result of Congress's delay in raising the national debt ceiling.

But specialists are worried that the market could begin to feel the pinch. "Sooner or later, it's going to catch up with the market," one trader warned. "The market is underestimating the pressures that could be coming if the dollar remains strong," he added.

Some pressure was evident yesterday. Partly as a result of the sale of $530 million of bills with maturities as distant as August, bill prices declined, pushing rates up.

### Increase Called Limited

The latest 15-week Treasury bill, for example, closed yesterday at 9.53% bid, up from 9.43% last Friday. The companion 26-week issue pressed to a bid of 9.50% from 9.48%.

"The extent of the increase in rates has been limited by the debt ceiling problems and by the general shortage of securities in the marketplace, noted David Jones, an economist for Aubrey G. Lanston & Co., a New York securities firm. "But the pressure could become greater later this year," he warned.

"There's a strong possibility that the effect of this could hit the bill market hard later in the year" if the dollar continues to improve, Mr. Jones said.

The Treasury bill sales, Mr. Jones said, "appear to be related primarily to Japan and other nations trying to keep the dollar from soaring in the foreign-exchange market," where the pressure has been strong. Yesterday, one dollar was fetching 211.60 Japanese yen in the marketplace, up sharply from less than 179 yen at the end of last October.

Foreigners have substantial dollar investments that potentially could be used to support their own currencies. Most of those were acquired when the foreign central banks were moving to prop the dollar in its past slides. According to figures supplied by the Federal Reserve Bank of New York, the Fed held more than $89 billion of marketable U.S. government securities on behalf of central banks and official institutions as of March 28.

These foreign central banks also hold heavy amounts of nonmarketable U.S. government securities purchased directly from the U.S. Treasury. While these issues can't be sold in the marketplace, any reduction in the amounts outstanding could put upward rate pressure on Treasury securities outstanding. That's because the Treasury would be forced to replace the funds lost by offering new securities to the public.

## *Appendix 4.3*   *Recent U.S. Balance of Payments Data*

U.S. balance of payments information is presented regularly in "Survey of Current Business," produced by the Bureau of Economic Analysis, United States Department of Commerce. From the issue of March 1979 (Volume 59, No. 3) we reproduce the actual balance of payments data, without the numerous footnotes (see Table 4.4). All this material can also be found in "Balance of Payments Yearbook," produced annually by the IMF. The IMF data comes from the "Survey of Current Business," but some of the data are reclassified to suit the IMF's conventions. There are no material differences in the outcome.

**Table 4.4** U.S. International Transactions [Millions of dollars]

*Quarterly Data Are Seasonally Adjusted*
(Credits +; debits —)

| |  | | | | | | | | | | | | | | |
|---|---|---|---|---|---|---|---|---|---|---|---|---|---|---|---|
| Exports of goods and services (excl. transfers under military grants) | mil. $ | 171,761 | 184,592 | 221,017 | 44,850 | 46,914 | 46,897 | 45,935 | 48,986 | 54,354 | 56,263 | 61,414 | 64,893 | 67,758 | 74,408 |
| Merchandise, adjusted, excl. military | do. | 114,745 | 120,816 | 142,052 | 29,518 | 31,075 | 30,558 | 29,665 | 30,712 | 35,396 | 36,532 | 39,412 | 41,348 | 42,792 | 47,337 |
| Transfers under U.S. military agency sales contracts | mil. $ | 5,574 | 7,441 | 7,744 | 1,854 | 1,851 | 1,877 | 1,860 | 1,924 | 1,990 | 2,120 | 1,709 | 2,036 | 1,806 | 1,715 |
| Receipts of income on U.S. assets abroad | do. | 29,286 | 32,587 | 43,465 | 7,775 | 8,080 | 8,420 | 8,312 | 9,776 | 10,256 | 10,526 | 12,907 | 14,115 | 15,404 | 17,506 |
| Other services | do. | 22,156 | 23,750 | 27,758 | 5,703 | 5,908 | 6,042 | 6,098 | 6,574 | 6,712 | 7,085 | 7,386 | 7,394 | 7,756 | 7,850 |
| Imports of goods and services | do. | -162,159 | -194,015 | -229,409 | -47,170 | -48,087 | -48,556 | -50,207 | -54,711 | -56,493 | -58,194 | -60,015 | -63,156 | -67,451 | -72,272 |
| Merchandise, adjusted, excl. military | do. | -124,051 | -151,689 | -175,822 | -37,185 | -37,639 | -37,996 | -38,869 | -42,629 | -43,329 | -44,481 | -45,383 | -47,463 | -50,508 | -54,619 |
| Direct defense expenditures | do. | -4,900 | -5,762 | -7,252 | -1,345 | -1,444 | -1,470 | -1,503 | -1,680 | -1,753 | -1,873 | -1,948 | -2,002 | -2,023 | -2,099 |
| Payments of income on foreign assets in the U.S. | mil. $ | -13,311 | -14,598 | -21,820 | -3,192 | -3,519 | -3,686 | -4,201 | -4,537 | -5,402 | -5,574 | -6,308 | -7,251 | -7,939 | -8,712 |
| Other services | do. | -19,896 | -21,967 | -24,517 | -5,448 | -5,485 | -5,404 | -5,634 | -5,866 | -6,009 | -6,266 | -6,376 | -6,440 | -6,981 | -6,842 |
| Unilateral transfers (excl. military grants), net | mil. $ | -4,998 | -4,670 | -5,086 | -1,116 | -1,283 | -1,249 | -1,023 | -1,228 | -1,313 | -1,233 | -1,314 | -1,322 | -1,363 | -1,374 |
| U.S. Government grants (excl. military) | do. | -3,146 | -2,775 | -3,152 | -626 | -811 | -774 | -564 | -765 | -827 | -770 | -790 | -805 | -897 | -870 |
| Other | do. | -1,851 | -1,895 | -1,934 | -490 | -472 | -475 | -459 | -463 | -486 | -463 | -524 | -517 | -466 | -504 |
| U.S. assets abroad, net | do. | -51,269 | -35,793 | -60,957 | -1,683 | -12,272 | -6,625 | -15,213 | -15,188 | -5,466 | -10,049 | -30,254 | -7,637 | -16,165 | -23,325 |
| U.S. official reserve assets, net | do. | -2,558 | -375 | 732 | -420 | -24 | 112 | -43 | 187 | 248 | 115 | 182 | -3,585 | 343 | 2,779 |
| U.S. Gov't assets, other than official reserve assets, net | mil. $ | -4,214 | -3,693 | -4,656 | -1,062 | -885 | -1,001 | -746 | -1,009 | -1,263 | -1,390 | -994 | -1,094 | -1,000 | -756 |
| U.S. private assets, net | do. | -44,498 | -31,725 | -57,033 | -201 | -11,363 | -5,736 | -14,424 | -14,366 | -4,451 | -8,774 | -29,442 | -2,958 | -15,507 | -25,348 |
| Direct investments abroad | do. | -11,949 | -12,898 | -16,670 | -2,365 | -3,873 | -3,090 | -3,570 | -4,856 | -4,386 | -2,782 | -4,646 | -5,755 | -7,280 | -7,281 |
| Foreign assets in the U.S., net | do. | 36,399 | 50,823 | 63,713 | 2,596 | 14,002 | 14,236 | 19,991 | 18,175 | 941 | 15,358 | 29,239 | 1,476 | 6,057 | 23,059 |
| Foreign official assets, net | do. | 17,573 | 36,656 | 33,758 | 5,491 | 7,720 | 8,266 | 15,179 | 15,618 | -5,265 | 4,641 | 18,764 | -9,391 | -10,043 | 5,562 |
| Other foreign assets, net | do. | 18,826 | 14,167 | 29,956 | -2,895 | 6,282 | 5,970 | 4,812 | 2,557 | 6,206 | 10,717 | 10,475 | 10,868 | 16,100 | 17,497 |
| Direct investments in the U.S. | do. | 4,347 | 3,728 | 6,294 | 980 | 965 | 1,023 | 761 | 1,130 | 1,877 | 2,280 | 1,008 | 989 | 2,025 | 2,317 |
| Allocation of special drawing rights | do. | | | | | | | | | | | | 1,139 | | |
| Statistical discrepancy | do. | 10,265 | -937 | 10,722 | 2,523 | 726 | -4,703 | 517 | 3,965 | 7,976 | -2,145 | 930 | 4,606 | 11,163 | -495 |
| Memoranda: | | | | | | | | | | | | | | | |
| Balance on merchandise trade | do. | -9,306 | -30,873 | -33,770 | -7,667 | -6,564 | -7,438 | -9,204 | -11,917 | -7,933 | -7,949 | -5,971 | -6,115 | -7,716 | -7,282 |
| Balance on goods and services | do. | 9,603 | -9,423 | -8,392 | -2,320 | -1,173 | -1,659 | -4,272 | -5,725 | -2,139 | -1,931 | 1,399 | 1,737 | 307 | 2,136 |
| Balance on goods, services, and remittances | do. | 7,752 | -11,317 | -10,326 | -2,810 | -1,645 | -2,134 | -4,731 | -6,188 | -2,625 | -2,394 | 875 | 1,220 | -159 | 1,632 |
| Balance on current account | do. | 4,605 | -14,092 | -13,478 | -3,436 | -2,456 | -2,908 | -5,295 | -6,953 | -3,452 | -3,164 | 85 | 415 | -1,056 | 762 |

# Chapter 5

# Exchange Rate Behavior in the "Long Run"

## 5.1 INTRODUCTION

This chapter and the next introduce the most difficult material dealt with in this book. The difficulty stems from two sources. First, it will become apparent that exchange rate behavior can be understood only in the context of a global macroeconomic perspective. Exchange rates are the product of the interaction of income levels, interest rates, monetary growth, relative prices, and investment patterns across the trading nations. Second, this pattern of interaction is imperfectly understood and is the subject of current research. Understanding is better for the material dealt with in this chapter and not very good for short-run exchange rate behavior analyzed in Chapter 6. In addition, while the picture of exchange rate behavior over the long term that we develop in this chapter accords with intuition and common sense, the reader will find that precise measurement of these common sense relations and variables is a subtle and demanding task.

This chapter deals with long run behavior. How long is the long run? We will discuss this from an empirical point of view when we discuss measurement in Section 5.6 below. A more rigorous examination of the time span over which current theories provide a satisfactory analysis will be undertaken in Chapter 6. Of course all our analysis must flow from the concept of exchange rate itself. Since an exchange rate is the rate at which one national money exchanges for another, to explain the behavior of exchange rates it is necessary to explain what national monies are worth to their holders. Thus, the basic question becomes: what is the price of money? The price of money is the reciprocal of an appropriate price index.[1] As the price index rises higher in the United States, a dollar bill is worth less. Note that the interest rate is not the price of money but the

---

[1]"Which index?" is a question that will occupy us for some time.

price of credit, which is the deferment of present consumption to future periods. This definition of the price of money implies that in the long run, the only value of money is its real value, i.e., the value of the goods and services that you can receive in exchange for it. Everything we have to say on the subject of exchange rate determination derives from elaboration of these ideas.

Section 5.2 develops the overall framework within which we will explain the long-run determination of exchange rates. Subsequent sections take successive components of this framework and explain and elaborate on them. Section 5.3 discusses the law of one price, Section 5.4 examines real factors in the demand for money, and Section 5.5 offers explanations for monetary growth. In Section 5.6 we examine empirical testing of the purchasing power parity theory of exchange rates, which we introduce in Section 5.2. Section 5.7 critically examines some counterhypotheses. One, frequently offered in developing countries, is that rather than inflation explaining exchange rates (as our discussion of the price of money and the purchasing power parity theory imply), it is exchange depreciation that causes inflation. Another counter-hypothesis is that the theory applies better to developed than developing countries. Finally in an appendix, we consider whether countries must have the same bundles of tradable goods for our analyses to apply.

## 5.2   A FRAMEWORK FOR THE EXPLANATION OF LONG-RUN EXCHANGE RATE MOVEMENTS[2]

Exchange rates are market prices—they are determined by demand for and supply of national moneys on the exchange markets. National moneys are demanded so as to be used for the purchase of foreign assets and commodities priced in these moneys. (The supply side, of course, consists of the offer of one's own national money in exchange.) Not all commodities are traded internationally, and it is extremely useful for us to partition the commodities produced and consumed in countries into the categories "tradables" and "nontradables." Tradable goods are goods that are actually exported or imported, or which have as virtually perfect substitutes goods that are actually exported or imported. The goods that fall into the tradables category depend formally on the cost of transportation.

Probably the bulk of United States-produced commodities are nontradables. Virtually all personal services fall into this category—medical attention, legal advice, and the output of municipal, federal, and governmental agencies. Housing and internal transportation are also nontradables. It is clear that any change in the fees charged by general practitioners

---

[2]The stock-equilibrium framework we are using has had substantial recent development and application. Our version conforms to that in R. Dornbusch, "The Theory of Flexible Exchange Rate Regimes and Macroeconomic Policy," *Scandinavian Journal of Economics, 78,* 2 (May 1976).

in Australia will not have an immediate reflection in the fees of U.S. doctors, nor will the charges made for garbage collection by the city of Paris be immediately or necessarily followed by the Palo Alto Sanitation Company. The dissatisfied customers of Palo Alto will find that it does not pay to contract for cleanup with the city of Paris. On the other hand, American wheat is a perfect substitute for foreign wheat, as is American copper and, in an appropriate sense, American machine tools and the like. The closer are other nations and the lower are border restrictions, quotas, and tariffs, the more goods will be tradable. In Monaco virtually all goods are tradable. Since people have to travel but a short distance to obtain medical treatment in France, competition must exert the same market forces on Monegasque doctors as on French doctors.

Obviously if tradables are perfect substitutes, or virtually so, there ought to be a strong connection between their different national-currency prices and the exchange rates between those currencies. The hypothesis of such a connection is the first component of our framework for explaining exchange rates. It is known as *the law of one price*. It says that, in the absence of impediments to trade, all tradable goods must sell at the same price everywhere, allowing for the costs of transportation. For later conceptual and statistical purposes we express this symbolically. Let

$P_T$ = domestic price of some tradable goods

$\overline{P}_T$ = foreign price in foreign currency of the same good

$S$ = spot exchange rate (i.e., \$ per unit of foreign currency)

Then the law of one price says, neglecting transportation costs, that

$$P_T = S \cdot \overline{P}_T \qquad (5.1)$$

We will have more to say on this relationship in Section 3.

We have divided all goods in both countries into the categories tradables and nontradables. A general price index for any country is a weighted average of prices for these two groups of goods. Let the subscript NT denote nontraded goods, let x denote the share of traded goods in national income and let $P$ denote the general price index. Then clearly we can write the two general price indexes

$$P = x \cdot P_T + (1 - x) \cdot P_{NT} \qquad (5.2)$$

$$\overline{P} = \overline{x} \cdot \overline{P}_T + (1 - \overline{x}) \cdot \overline{P}_{NT} \qquad (5.3)$$

We can now consider the price of tradables relative to the price of nontradables in each country. It is convenient to do this by expressing $P_T$ relative to $P$ (and $\overline{P}_T$ relative to $\overline{P}$).[3]

---

[3]$P_T/P = a = P_T/[xP_T + (1 - x)P_{NT}]$
So $1/a = x + (1 - x)P_{NT}/P_T$. For given x, as the relative price of nontradables rises, $a$ falls, and vice versa. The motivation for this will soon be apparent.

$$P_T = a \cdot P, \overline{P}_T = \overline{a} \cdot \overline{P} \tag{5.4}$$

This is the second component of our framework. From Equations 5.1 and 5.4

$$S = \frac{P_T}{\overline{P}_T} = a \cdot \frac{P}{\overline{a}} \cdot \overline{P} \tag{5.5}$$

That is, to explain the exchange rate between these two currencies we must explain the general price levels in the two countries, and the relative price of tradables. Section 5.4 will look at the relative price effects (and some other considerations to be introduced below), while Section 5.5 will examine the causes of general price level changes, or inflation.

The final component of our framework is the demand to hold money balances in each country. Let $M$ denote the domestic money supply, $\overline{M}$ the supply of foreign money and a superscript $D$ the demand for money. Individuals and firms desire to hold money balances because it makes transacting more convenient. The amount of money balances that individuals and firms wish to hold depends upon two factors.

1.   The *nominal* value of transactions. If real income expands, more money balances will be held to facilitate the greater associated volume of transactions. However, if real income is constant but we have inflation, more money will still be needed because each transaction now involves a higher price—more money units. For this reason the demand for money balances is expressed in real terms, or $M^D/P$.

2.   The *opportunity cost* of holding money. If interest rates rise, or if more inflation is expected in the future, it becomes more costly to hold nonearning money, and people will economize more on their money holdings.

Let us write the demand for real transactions balances as

$$\frac{M^D}{P} = L, \quad \frac{\overline{M}^D}{P} = \overline{L} \tag{5.6}$$

where it is understood that $L$ depends upon real income, interest rates and expected inflation.[4]

So much for the demand for money balances. Consider now the supply. This is determined by monetary policy, in a variety of ways that we will consider in Section 5.5. There is one fundamental point that follows from the fact that the government creates the quantity of money. The private sector as a whole cannot get rid of the money supply the govern-

---

[4]Another way of writing (6) is obviously $M^D = P \cdot L$. This says that if all real factors were the same but the price level were 10% higher, we would demand to hold 10% more money balances. Once again, transactions balances are held to facilitate the nominal value of transactions.

ment forces on it. Prices and interest rates must adjust until people are willing to hold the available money. Any one individual can try to convert some cash to goods or securities, but that just passes the cash onto someone else. Collectively, an attempt to reduce money holdings must force up commodity and security prices until, in accordance with Equation 5.6, the private sector is content to hold the money. An attempt to increase money balances must drive down commodity and security prices. Effectively, money demanded must always equal the money supply, for prices adjust to make it so. Symbolically

$$M^D = M, \quad \overline{M}^D = \overline{M}$$

so we may use Equation 5.6 to write

$$P = \frac{M}{L}, \quad \overline{P} = \frac{\overline{M}}{\overline{L}} \tag{5.7}$$

The price levels will have to equal the ratio of money available to money demanded.

By substituting Equation 5.7 into Equation 5.5 we have arrived at an explanation of the long run value of free market exchange rates.

$$S = \frac{\dfrac{a \cdot M}{L}}{\dfrac{\overline{a} \cdot \overline{M}}{\overline{L}}} \tag{5.8}$$

Note what this says:

1.  Other things being equal the country experiencing more rapid monetary growth will experience depreciation of its currency. The more rapid monetary growth raises all prices, and thus tradables prices, faster, and to maintain competitivity the exchange rate must depreciate. See Section 5.3.

2.  Other things being equal the country experiencing a greater increase in real money demands will experience exchange rate appreciation. For instance, the country with greater real output growth absorbs more of its monetary growth into needed transactions balances, and so experiences less inflation.

3.  Other things being equal the country experiencing a lesser increase in the *relative* price of traded goods will experience exchange rate appreciation. For instance, productivity grows faster in the traded goods sector so traded goods prices lag the general inflation rate in one country more than in the other, changing the competitiveness of the two countries' goods.

This explanation of exchange rates thus says that the exchange rate adjusts to make people content to hold the nominal stocks of each currency. Attempts to adjust real balances to desired levels lead to commodity flows and price changes that affect international trade, and so the free market exchange rate. As we will see, many types of real and monetary factors have an impact on the exchange rate.


## 5.3   THE LAW OF ONE PRICE

The relationship between exchange rates and the prices of tradable goods given in Equation 5.1 must be brought about by some actual economic process. The process is known as commodity arbitrage. Whenever Equation 5.1 does not hold, the same good is selling at different prices in different places. Suppose for example that the Mexican peso is overvalued on the law of one price basis or, equivalently, on the purchasing power parity basis. This means that imported goods, after being priced in pesos, are cheaper than domestic substitutes, while Mexican exports, when priced in foreign currencies, are more expensive than foreign-produced substitutes. Hence, imports will rise, exports will fall and the Mexican peso would depreciate on a free exchange market. If the government attempted to peg the over-valued exchange rate, it would find growing balance of payments deficits at this fixed exchange rate. Of course the above situation well describes the Mexican economy in the years prior to the very large devaluation of the peso in 1976. Mexican citizens found it more advantageous to buy groceries for dollars in Texas than to buy Mexican-produced equivalents. The numerous border factories set up to process goods for re-export to the United States were facing closure. The peso costs were rising faster than the dollar value of the output, but at the fixed exchange rate these peso costs became dollar costs rising at the same rate. The Mexican government faced growing deficits and, after exhausting its intervention resources, was forced into a devaluation.

Thus, as a description of a process, the law of one price or purchasing power parity theory of exchange rates makes a good deal of sense. At this stage, however, the discerning reader should raise a fundamental difficulty, highlighted by the Mexican example. The peso-dollar exchange rate was fixed from 1954 to late 1976. Throughout that period Mexican costs rose faster than U.S. costs, with glaring discrepancies in the four years preceding the devaluation. If we use wholesale price indices as a measure of costs, and start the U.S. and Mexican indexes at 100 in 1954, by mid-1976 the U.S. index had risen to 210 while the Mexican index had risen to 350. So, how long does it take for the law of one price to assert itself? The Mexican case is not a test of free market outcomes because the peso was pegged. However, the meaning of the concept "long run" as used in the title of the chapter is to be found in this issue. The long run we are discussing is an interval long enough for the law of one price to take effect. We will return to this question from the empirical side in Section 5.6. At this stage we content ourselves with noting two reasons (not an exhaustive list) why we should not expect to observe undeviating adherence to the law of one price.

1. Commodity shipments take time to arrange in any great quantity. It can take months, at a minimum, to alter import or export patterns to benefit from more favorable prices. Indeed, because of the costs of making such changes, it is rational to wait to see whether the opportunities persist for some time before making commitments.

2. The law of one price refers to the adjustment of exchange rates to compensate for differing local currency costs of production. But trade takes place on the basis of price rather than costs, and it is not true that prices move in lockstep with costs in the short term. (Of course in the long term they must. Slippage means ultimate bankruptcy whereas growing profit margins will attract entry and force down prices.) To the extent that we have less-than-perfect competition in product markets, firms will pay attention to market share and will be willing to manipulate prices to attempt to maintain it. Firms can operate for some time so as to cover only variable cost rather than total cost in an effort to maintain their market position. Thus one might expect prices to move less smoothly than costs, causing commodity flows to respond only imperfectly to cost changes.

Both these considerations imply that even in a situation of free floating, without any sort of deliberate government intervention in the exchange markets, there will be noise in the relationship between inflation and exchange rates. This noise can easily persist for months at a time. (Later in this chapter we present some evidence on the time needed to return to purchasing power parity).

## 5.4 REAL INFLUENCES ON THE DEMAND FOR MONEY AND ON RELATIVE PRICES

To recapitulate our story, over an appropriate interval commodity arbitrage ensures that exchange rates adjust to equate the translated prices of tradable goods. Section 5.2 explained that a search for the determinants of tradable goods prices leads to general inflationary trends and the relative price of tradables and nontradables. The general inflationary trends are explained by variations between the quantity of money the government forces on the system, and the demands for real balances at current price, income, and interest rate levels. In this section we will look at some aspects of price determination more closely, to give the reader a feeling for the kind of phenomena one can expect.

Consider first of all the question of the relative price of tradables and nontradables. Let us say that there is a certain growth of nominal money supply in excess of the rate of growth of real output, generating general domestic inflation. This means that the overall price index for the economy will be growing. Let us take Equation 5.2, the definition of this index, and use it to express the relationship between the rates of change of the general price index and the prices of tradables and nontradables. If we let a dot over a variable denote a rate of change per unit time, some calculus reveals that

$$\dot{P} = \dot{x}(P_T - P_{NT}) + x\dot{P}_T + (1 - x)\dot{P}_{NT} \qquad (5.9)$$

or, in the terms we are seeking

$$\dot{P}_T = \frac{\dot{P} - (1 - x)\dot{P}_{NT} - \dot{x}(P_T - P_{NT})}{x} \qquad (5.10)$$

That is, the change in price of the traded goods equals the change in price of the all-goods index, adjusted for differential in the rate of change of prices in the two sectors, and for changing importance of the sectors in the economy.

Suppose we now introduce two hypotheses that have some reasonable empirical support.

1. High income countries are more productive than low income countries, but the efficiency advantage is not uniform. Productivity grows faster in manufacturing and mechanized agriculture, which tend to be tradables, than in services, which tend to be nontradables.[5]

2. The emphasis in advanced economies is to have the service sectors grow faster than the others.

These hypotheses imply several things. First, the relative price of tradables should be falling in all economies, but fastest where productivity growth is highest. Second, if the price of tradables does tend to be equalized across countries, the relative prices should diverge more as the income disparity grows between the two countries whose currency exchange rate is being analyzed.

Consider now a particular recent example of a changing relationship between money demand and money supply. Our story implies that one of the causes of inflation is an excess of the rate of growth of money supply over money demand. If we look at 1974 we seem to see inflation

---

[5]The evidence for this proposition is discussed in L. Officer, "The Purchasing Power Parity Theory of Exchange Rates: A Review Article," *International Monetary Fund Staff Papers*, XXIII, 1 (March 1976), 18–19, 33–38. As with most empirical work in this area, there is no final resolution to date.

triggered by a rise in the price of one commodity—oil. Can these two things be reconciled? The answer is yes, if we make a careful analysis of the effects of the increase in the price of oil on the demand for money.[6]

The salient feature of the OPEC-induced jump in the price of energy is that it constituted a change in relative prices, not just a jump in nominal prices whose real effects could be eroded by inflation in other goods. The oil producers raised the relative price of oil—the price in terms of other goods. The way a trader with monopoly power makes a real income gain is to increase the quantity of other goods which must be exchanged for a unit of his or her own good. The method is to cut output. With less oil selling at a higher price, demand immediately tended to switch to other energy sources such as natural gas. This demand switch raised their prices also (where price controls existed, supply fell further short of demand). Thus the effect was to raise the price of energy relative to the prices of other goods. This was, we all recollect, an unexpected increase in the relative price of energy. Why is the unexpectedness of importance? Consider firms choosing between different technologies at the time they are inaugurating new production facilities. Speaking roughly (but adequately for our purposes) they will choose to use techniques that have the greatest anticipated present value over the lifetime of the process. This involves economization of the use of inputs that are anticipated to be relatively expensive, and heavier use of those that are anticipated to be relatively cheap. Of course a comparison between anticipated input prices and anticipated output prices determines the overall productivity. So technology is chosen on the basis of anticipations, and after construction flexibility is frequently severely limited. The arrival of unexpected events can thus cause producers to close down certain production facilities which are loss-makers under the new circumstances.

This is what occurred in 1974–75. Any production techniques that were very energy-intensive found input costs rising faster than the market would allow output prices to rise. This must be so if the relative price of energy has risen—energy costs more in terms of other goods, including the goods produced with energy-intensive production processes. The massive relative price change of an unexpected nature rendered a good deal of capital equipment economically obsolete, and capacity was closed down. In fact we observed a 4% to 5% *fall* in real income and capacity in this period. Thus demand for money for transactions purposes fell, while the nominal money supply continued to grow. In accordance with our theory there was a sharp jump in the price level as individuals attempted to unload unwanted real balances. Note further that, holding

---

[6]This discussion draws heavily upon D. Karnosky, "The Link Between Money and Prices—1971–1976," Federal Reserve Bank of St. Louis *Review*, June, 1976, and R. Rasche and J. Tatom, "The Effects of the New Energy Regime on Economic Capacity, Production and Prices," ibid., May 1977.

other things constant, such a phenomenon is associated with relative price changes among commodities, and with different price level jumps in different countries. More energy-intensive goods rose in price relative to less energy-intensive goods. Depending on exact circumstances, this can alter the relative price of tradables and nontradables. Countries whose tradables were more energy intensive would face a jump in $P_T$ relative to countries whose tradables were less energy-intensive, and thus would face currency depreciation.

## 5.5   INFLATION AND MONETARY POLICY

We have so far assumed, and the evidence overwhelmingly confirms, that long-run inflationary trends are caused by money supply outrunning money demand.[7] Speaking roughly, inflation is created by an excess of the rate of growth of the money supply over the rate of growth of real output. Why would any government maintain a long-run policy of having the money supply grow faster than real output? (We obviously wish to abstract from temporary fluctuations due to the government's pursuit of so-called "counter-cyclical policy.") If one is interested in any form of exchange rate prediction activity, the prediction of monetary policy, and thus the answer to this question, must play a key role. We will suggest two explanations for the pursuit of such policies, both of which have historical and current relevance. There are undoubtedly others and our purpose in presenting these examples is not to be exhaustive but to make the reader aware of the types of causal patterns he or she is seeking.

### Budget Deficits and the Inflation Tax

An extremely common explanation for inflation is that the central government runs continual deficit budgets, which it covers not by borrowing but rather by the printing of money.[8] The government does not raise in taxes and public loans as much revenue as it expends. It imposes an inflation tax by obtaining new money and buying goods with it. This leaves a larger money supply but less real goods in the hands of the private sector, with obvious consequences for the price level. This is an efficient (that is, functional) method of taxation as long as the inflation rates do not reach such levels that the monetary system breaks down. If a country

---

[7]For evidence on the strength of the connection between monetary growth and general price levels, see D. Laidler and M. Parkin, "Inflation: A Survey," *Economic Journal*, 85 (December 1975), 741–809.

[8]A frequent legal artifice is to borrow from the central bank, which does *not* resell the Treasury bonds to the public. Thus the central bank buys the bonds with new money, not with voluntary public savings.

is identified as being in this situation, the main factor explaining monetary growth will be the future behavior of the budget deficit, and a forecaster will concentrate on the analysis of sources of revenue and the various pressures of government expenditure.

### Interest Rate Manipulation and Growth Targets

Since 1945 France has had rapid monetary growth and very substantial inflation. Indeed the current franc is a "new franc" having been substituted for the previous one in the 1950s at a rate of 100 old francs to one new franc. However, you will not find a sequence of staggering budget deficits to explain the inflation. Instead the inflation was an unintended by-product of governmental attempts to manipulate interest rates to increase the growth rate of the economy. From 1945 to 1975 the French government followed a policy of attempting to peg nominal interest rates below market-clearing levels. For reasons that will soon be apparent, continual success in these endeavours was impossible, but the rates were held for substantial periods of time. The motivation for pegging interest rates at too-low levels was the notion that lower interest rates encourage investment and thus create economic growth. The method was to increase the money supply in order to create funds for banks and other financial intermediaries to lend to would-be investors.

This strategy was unsatisfactory because it confused money with credit. Creating money is unfortunately not the same as creating credit. The amount of investible resources available for any society is (ignoring capital inflows and outflows, as is reasonable in this case) that part of the national product not absorbed in consumption. Thus the creation of money would only lead to more real investment if it leads to more output or a higher propensity to save. Some people argue that sometimes money creation can raise output as part of a countercyclical policy; it is not accepted or argued that sustained monetary creation raises trend output. Moreover the effect of the interest-pegging policy on the propensity to save was the opposite of the one that would have been desired. As long as the pegs function, the return to savers is below what would otherwise be the case.

What happened instead was substantial inflation as the money supply grew in response to investment demand at the pegged rates. Moreover this process was inherently unstable, implying continual acceleration of the inflation rate. Investment decisions are made in real terms. The real interest rate equals the nominal rate less anticipated inflation. Nominal rates were pegged, so as inflation increased, real interest rates fell. This encouraged more investment demand, which was the signal for more money creation to supply the needed "credit," and which in turn further increased inflation. What stopped the accelerating inflation? A series of financial squeezes imposed on the system for one or two years at a time, the so-called stop-go policies analogous to the better-known British equivalents. At the time of writing, France has abandoned these inflationary policies by going to a system of central control and allocation of credit—at the unrealistic interest rates the demand is officially rationed. The hope is to scrap pegging and allocation and move to a free market capital system.

The purpose of presenting these examples is to illustrate for the reader the diversity of circumstances which may govern monetary policy. Another interesting structural relation among macroeconomic policy, inflation, and depreciation will be explored in Section 5.7.

## 5.6   EMPIRICAL EVIDENCE ON THE PURCHASING POWER PARITY THEORY

In the broadest sense the purchasing power parity theory of exchange rate determination explains exchange rate movements by differences in inflation rates between countries. As Figure 5.1 illustrates, such differences have been substantial in recent years, and casual empiricism confirms the general legitimacy of the idea. There have been a number of attempts to test the precise extent to which the theory applies. These may be conveniently divided into attempts to assess the law of one price at the most disaggregated level possible with the available data, and attempts to explain exchange rate movements by the use of relatively broad indexes of commodity prices. We will briefly outline the results of a number of recent studies, and explain some of the reasons for the great difficulty experienced in empirical testing, or in forecasting, the relations implied by the theory. (In addition to the studies we will cite and the references they contain, the suggestions for further reading at the end of the chapter refer the reader to two extremely good surveys of work in the general area.)

### Disaggregated Tests of the Law of One Price

All empirical research is constrained by the available data. Detailed examination of the law of one price has been undertaken using indexes of prices of goods in the most detailed S.I.C. classifications that are available uniformly for pairs of countries. In general, many different goods are contained in each S.I.C. classification and countries are frequently exporting and importing goods listed within the one classification. We will look at the results of two studies, one examining commodity arbitrage between Canada and the United States,[9] the other examining commodity arbitrage between the United States and a number of developed countries

---

[9] J. Richardson, "Some Empirical Evidence on Commodity Arbitrage and the Law of One Price," *Journal of International Economics*, 8 (1978), 341–351.

**Figure 5.1**   Inflation Differentials 1971–1977. Comparison of rates
of change in consumer price index over corresponding four-quarter
periods. Example: The U.S.–Belgium inflation differential for 1/77 is
computed by subtracting the percentage change in the Belgian CPI
over the 1/76–1/77 period from the percentage change in the U.S.
CPI over the same four-quarter period. Data are seasonally adjusted.
Latest data plotted: Italy–2nd quarter: others–3rd quarter.

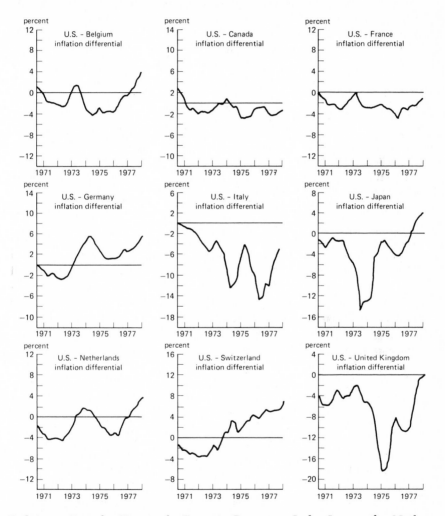

(Belgium, Canada, Denmark, France, Germany, Italy, Japan, the Netherlands, Norway, Sweden, and Britain.[10])

The Canadian study looked at a number of four digit S.I.C. classes

[10]I. Kravis and R. Lipsey, "Price Behavior in the Light of Balance of Payments Theories,"
*Journal of International Economics, 8* (1978), 193–246.

from 1965 through 1973 and attempted to measure the fit of the law of one price relationship, Equation 5.1 on page 125. The chosen method was to test the equation in the form of linkage between rates of change of prices and of the exchange rate. Some of the results were in conformity with the theory and others may raise some doubts. For a number of the chosen commodity groups there seemed to be no commodity arbitrage—these can be called nontradables. They included chewing gum, nonalcoholic beverages, brewing products, cigarettes, malleable pig iron, cement, and petroleum refining products. Other commodity groups had strong evidence of the price linkage given in Equation 5.1—slaughtering and meatpacking products, animal feeds, distilled spirits, biscuits, crackers and cookies, bakery products, leather tanning products, pulp and paper, agricultural implements and tractors, and fertilizers. However, even in the latter cases the fit of the chosen version of Equation 5.1 was not outstanding.[11] Thus this research provides weak support for the story we have told.

Similarly lukewarm conclusions emerge from the more comprehensive study. There was much greater uniformity in the exchange rate translated price movements of tradables than of nontradables, as the law of one price leads one to expect. However the price indexes for the tradable goods categories still exhibited a great deal of divergent motion. As measured, some of these discrepancies seem alarmingly large. For example, comparing 1974 to 1970, German export prices "ranged from 21 to 58 percent higher relative to U.S. export prices than they had been in 1970. If this was an effect of DM appreciation it was not a fleeting one. Most of the 41 percent increase in the dollar price of the mark that occurred between 1970 and 1974 had taken place by 1973; between 1973 and 1974, the increase was only 2 percent."[12] The authors concluded that commodity arbitrage worked quite slowly. They also found evidence consistent with price discrimination between domestic and export markets. Within the same category of goods, export price index numbers and domestic wholesale price index numbers did not have strikingly high correlation either in the United States or in Germany, for instance. Before commenting on these results we will look at the broader analyses.

### Aggregate Price Index Tests of the Law of One Price

Equation 5.1 should hold on a commodity-by-commodity basis. A large number of studies, dating from the period immediately after the First World War, have tested this equation by substituting aggregate price indexes for the variables $P_T$ and $\overline{P}_T$. On the whole these studies have shown

[11]Technically, the law of one price did not hold at the 95% confidence level in any commodity group.
[12]Kravis and Lipsey, op. cit., p. 231.

that over long periods there is not much variation in exchange rates beyond that implied by Equation 5.1 and the two price indexes. Fundamental data limitations ensure that all these studies must be undertaken with the GNP implicit deflator, the wholesale price index or the consumer price index for the countries under study. Studies based on quarterly or monthly data generally cannot use GNP deflator figures since few countries compute them more frequently than at annual intervals.

Table 5.1 gives the results of some purchasing power parity computations where one country at a time is compared with the United States and the relative movement of wholesale prices over the specified time period is compared with the movement of the exchange rate. Let

$$WPI_i(t) = \text{wholesale price index of Country } i \text{ at date } t;$$
$$WPI_{US}(t) = \text{wholesale price index of the United States at date } t;$$
$$S_i(t) = \text{dollar price of a unit of Country } i\text{'s currency at date } t.$$

Then between a pair of dates $t_1$ and $t_2$ we can compute two ratios

$$\frac{WPI_i(t_2)/WPI_i(t_1)}{WPI_{US}(t_2)/WPI_{US}(t_1)} = \text{relative change in the wholesale price indexes}$$
$$\frac{S_i(t_2)}{S_i(t_1)} = \text{change in the exchange rate}$$

If Equation 5.1 held perfectly for the price indexes, we could multiply the first ratio by the second and obtain unity as the result. If the product of the two ratios is greater than unity, the U.S. dollar has depreciated more (appreciated less) than the purchasing power parity calculations imply. If the product is less than unity, the opposite deviation has occurred. Table 5.1 gives these products for a number of countries and periods.

Table 5.1 presented point-to-point estimates on a bilateral basis. In fact, the exchange rates oscillate around the purchasing power parity rates calculated using the price indexes. Moreover at any time a currency will tend to be overvalued against some currencies but undervalued against others, where correct valuation is given by the index number ratio calculation. Thus Table 5.2 reproduces some calculations of the average absolute percentage deviations from purchasing power parity, based upon effective exchange rate, by weighting each bilateral exchange rate by some measure of the base country's trade with it. Table 5.2 uses export shares. So for each country Table 5.2 provides averages over the same period, and over a collection of exchange rates with the currencies of trading partners. Given that it is computed using consumer price indexes, the correspondence with the theory is actually strikingly close.

Evidently the introduction of flexible exchange rates has increased the variability of exchange rates about the calculated purchasing power parity values. According to Genberg's calculations, a band about the pur-

**Table 5.1** *Purchasing Power Parity Indicators Based on Wholesale Prices, Selected Countries and Period, Based on Bilateral Calculations with U.S.*

| Period / Country | 1902 –1965[a] | 1909 –1913[a] | 1919 –1923[a] | 1927 –1931[a] | 1936 –1940[a] | 1949 –1953[a] | 1963 –1967[a] | 1950 –1960[b] | 1960 –1970[b] | 1970 –1973[b] |
|---|---|---|---|---|---|---|---|---|---|---|
| U.K. | 1.03 | .96 | 1.03 | .94 | 1.03 | .87 | 1.02 | 1.15 | .99 | 1.03 |
| Canada | 1.04 | .95 | 1.01 | 1.05 | 1.01 | 1.06 | 1.04 | 1.06 | .99 | 1.13 |
| Japan | 1.26 | 1.05 | 1.39 | 1.23 | 1.07 | 1.19 | 1.26 | 1.22 | .98 | 1.25 |
| Germany | 1.04 | 1.01 | — | 1.08 | 1.64 | 1.00 | 1.04 | 1.06 | 1.07 | 1.29 |
| Switzerland | 1.14 | — | 1.21 | 1.05 | 1.26 | 1.17 | 1.14 | | | |
| Italy | .89 | .97 | 1.03 | 1.06 | 1.29 | .91 | .89 | .92 | 1.10 | 1.11 |
| France | .99 | .99 | 1.00 | .95 | 1.03 | 1.00 | .99 | 1.02 | 1.03 | 1.25 |
| Belgium | | | | | | | | .95 | 1.05 | 1.22 |
| Denmark | | | | | | | | 1.07 | 1.06 | 1.27 |
| Netherlands | | | | | | | | 1.04 | 1.13 | 1.26 |
| Norway | | | | | | | | 1.25 | 1.10 | 1.19 |
| Sweden | | | | | | | | 1.22 | 1.16 | 1.18 |

[a] H. Gailliot, "Purchasing Power Parity as an Explanation of Long Term Changes in Exchange Rates," *Journal of Money, Credit and Banking*, 2 (August 1970), 348–357: Table 1, p. 351; Table 2, p. 352. Computations use five year averages centered on the indicated years.

[b] Kravis and Lipsey, op. cit., Table 5, p. 215. Computations use the index numbers for the cited years.

**Table 5.2** *Average Absolute Percentage Deviations of "Effective" Exchange Rates from Purchasing Power Parity Based on Consumer Price Index Ratio Calculations*

| Period | 1957–66 | 1957–72 | 1957–76 |
|---|---|---|---|
| **Country** | | | |
| U.S. | 1.2 | 1.7 | 3.8 |
| U.K. | 0.5 | 3.1 | 3.8 |
| Austria | 1.3 | 1.5 | 2.0 |
| Belgium | 1.4 | 1.3 | 2.1 |
| Denmark | 1.3 | 1.8 | 2.0 |
| France | 2.5 | 3.0 | 3.0 |
| Germany | 1.3 | 2.1 | 2.7 |
| Italy | 1.2 | 2.3 | 5.8 |
| Netherlands | 0.5 | 1.0 | 1.7 |
| Norway | 0.9 | 1.4 | 2.9 |
| Sweden | 0.7 | 0.8 | 1.4 |
| Switzerland | 0.7 | 1.4 | 5.8 |
| Canada | 2.0 | 3.2 | 3.3 |
| Japan | 1.9 | 2.2 | 3.8 |
| Average | 1.2 | 1.9 | 3.2 |

*Source:* H. Genberg, "Purchasing Power Parity Under Fixed and Flexible Exchange Rates," *Journal of International Economics,* 8 (1978), 247–276, Table 1, p. 260.

chasing power parities wide enough to encompass 90% of the observed actual exchange rates would have to have been ± 2% in 1957–66, ± 4% in 1957–72, and ± 7% for 1957–76. The average absolute deviation rose from 1.2% in 1957–66, to 2.2% in 1967–72, to 4.1% in 1973–76. In the light of the discussion in Section 5.2, if one crudely makes allowances[13] for a change in relative prices in 1974–76 as a result of the increase in the relative price of energy, the average absolute deviation in that period falls to 3.1%. Moreover the calculated average time for the system to get 2/3 of the way back to parity after a disturbance falls from well over two years to a year and a half.

Finally, we present the results of research undertaken by the Commission of the European Communities on purchasing power parities and time taken to revert to the parities.[14] Econometric models of the United Kingdom and of Italy were used to look at the long-run effects of a government-forced devaluation to increase artificially the competitiveness of the countries' tradable goods sectors. Theoretically this should lead to a balance of payments surplus at the fixed (undervalued) exchange rate,

---

[13]The method is to run a time-series regression based on Equation 1, and to use a shift variable for the period 1974–76. Genberg has a lucid discussion of these points.

[14]Our discussion is based on the summary of the studies given in N. Thygesen, "Inflation and Exchange Rates," *Journal of Internation Economics,* 8 (1978), 301–317.

and a net increase in inflation as this surplus is monetized in the course of the pegging operation.[15] This inflation should eventually wipe out the artificial competitive advantage if the exchange rate is not further deliberately depreciated. In the econometric simulations, it was found that all the gains were lost in five to six years, and that 75% would be lost within two years. Thus over even quite moderate horizons, exchange rates are determined by price behavior, and attempts to peg exchange rates merely serve to link price movements across countries.

## 5.7   STATISTICAL PROBLEMS OF PARITY MEASUREMENT

The reader may be surprised that there remains so much uncertainty about the extent to which the law of one price applies. It would seem that simple concepts would be straightforward to test and measure. In reality the problems are immense. We will work through two exercises that reveal the source of the most important discrepancies between what is measured by the usual statistical evidence and what might actually be happening. One shows the implications of comparing prices and exchange rates mismatched in time; the other illustrates the limits of what can be done with price indexes rather than the underlying prices directly.

### Comparing Prices and Exchange Rates Mismatched in Time[16]

Let us begin by supposing the following to be true.

1.  Spot exchange rates follow a *zero-drift random walk*. This means that the expected value of any future spot rate is simply the rate that one currently observes. A spot rate $k$ periods from the present will equal the present rate plus $k$ random increments, each having a zero mean. This implies that exchange rates are uncorrelated over time, and that the variance of the spot rate we anticipate $t$ periods from the present is $k \times \sigma^2$, where $\sigma^2$ is the variance of the random increment.

2.  Forward rates always equal the expected spot rate. By assumption, this is equal to the current spot rate so that one observes neither premium nor discount on all maturities of forwards.

---

[15]Recollect that the central bank undervalues the currency by offering it for sale on the exchange market on top of private supply. The foreign currency the central bank receives in exchange measures the surplus, but of course it has created domestic currency of equal value.

[16]This section draws heavily upon S. Magee, "Contracting and Spurious Deviations from Purchasing Power Parity," Chapter 4 of J. Frenkel and H. Johnson (eds.), *The Economics of Exchange Rates: Selected Studies*, Reading, MA: Addison-Wesley, 1978.

3. Commodity arbitrage is always undertaken on the basis of expected spot rates. Thus for any good with a delivery lag of $i$ periods, we have expected purchasing power parity holding because traders are willing to sign firm delivery contracts on the basis of their exchange rate anticipations. Their contracting ensures that, for any good,

$$P(t + k) = E[S(t + k)] \cdot \overline{P}(t + k) \tag{5.11}$$

where $P(t + k), \overline{P}(t + k)$ are the domestic and foreign prices for the good at $t + k$, and $E[S(t + k)]$ is the expected exchange rate, anticipated when the contracts were signed at date $t$. We rearrange Equation 5.11 to show that, under these circumstances,

$$E[S(t + k)] = \frac{P(t + k)}{\overline{P}(t + k)} \tag{5.12}$$

That is, there is a zero expected deviation from purchasing power parity. The actual deviation from parity will be

$$d(t + k) = S(t + k) - \frac{P(t + k)}{\overline{P}(t + k)} \tag{5.13}$$

The prices are given from the prior contracting so that the variance of $d$ comes only from the variance of $S$. We have already seen that, looking from date $t$, $S(t + k)$ has variance $k \times \sigma^2$. Moreover as the exchange rates are uncorrelated over time, the parity deviations will be uncorrelated over time.

With this elaborate framework in place, let us see how the *measured* parity deviations behave, if we do not realize that shipments arriving on any date were contracted for at some prior date. To be concrete, take trade between Germany and the United States. We are trying to test the law of one price by using an export price index for German goods shipped to the United States, an import price index for imports to the United States from Germany, and monthly values of the spot exchange rate. Our problem is that we compare a ratio of German export prices received to U.S. import prices paid, with a current exchange rate. But the commodity prices were contracted for at a time when the exchange rate, and exchange rate expectations, were different. Let $f_k$ equal the proportion of trade arriving in the United States in any month contracted for $k$ months previously.[17] Then the ratio of tradable goods prices we measure will be a weighted average of past transaction prices, and will at any time $t$ be for each good

$$\sum_k f_k \frac{P(t - k)}{\overline{P}(t - k)} \tag{5.14}$$

---

[17]Magee looked at five product categories—organic chemicals; steel plates and sheets; textile machinery; automobiles; and miscellaneous. The mean delivery lag ranged from 1.07 months for automobiles to 4.93 months for steel plates and sheets, based on recent U.S.-German trade data.

Then the measured deviation from parity $\hat{d}$, will be the same weighted sum of past exchange rate changes.

$$\hat{d}(t) = \sum_k f_k \frac{P(t-k)}{\overline{P}(t-k)} - S(t)$$
$$= \sum_k f_k [S(t-k) - S(t)]$$

(5.15)

using Equation 12 and the fact that $E[S(t+j)] = S(t)$ for all dates $t+j$.

From this fact we can see that the average deviation from parity is still zero—all the exchange rate changes between $t-k$ and $t$ have zero mean. But

1. The measured variance of the deviations will be much larger than the true variance. In the five product categories examined by Magee, the measured variance ranges from 1.09 times the true variance (for automobiles) to 4.17 times the true variance (for steel plates and sheets). True variance is of course the variance under our initial assumptions.

2. There will be a measured serial correlation over time in the parity deviations. They will be observed to have a tendency to persist over time even when, by hypothesis, the true deviations are serially uncorrelated. Once again, as the delivery lags longer, the deviations will be measured to be more persistent. The reader is referred to Magee for sample calculations.

3. There will be no stability in the relationship between the measured and the actual deviations. Different goods have different delivery lags and the commodity composition of trade changes as time passes.

Magee's sample calculations imply that measurement errors of this type might be much too large to be ignored as secondary.

### Problems Deriving from the Use of Price Indexes Rather than Prices

Once again, let us begin by supposing that the law of one price does apply all the time. That is, for say three tradable goods we have

$$P_1 = S \cdot \overline{P}_1, \quad P_2 = S \cdot \overline{P}_2, \quad P_3 = S \cdot \overline{P}_3$$

(5.16)

We measure things with indexes, where the weights are based on use or consumption quantities, or else on production or export quantities. For some sets of weights denoted by $w$ and $\overline{w}$, we have indexes

$$I = w_1 P_1 + w_2 P_2 + w_3 P_3$$
$$\overline{I} = \overline{w}_1 \overline{P}_1 + \overline{w}_2 \overline{P}_2 + \overline{w}_3 \overline{P}_3$$

The parity exchange rate would be approximated by taking the ratio of these two indexes. If we do this and use Equation 5.16 to replace all the $Ps$ by $S \cdot \overline{P}$ we find

$$\frac{I}{\overline{I}} = S \cdot \frac{w_1 \overline{P}_1 + w_2 \overline{P}_2 + w_3 \overline{P}_{3.}}{\overline{w}_1 \overline{P}_1 + \overline{w}_2 \overline{P}_2 + \overline{w}_3 \overline{P}_3} \neq S \tag{5.17}$$

Unless the two price indexes use the same weighting scheme we will obtain a false result.

Can changes in the index ratio give an accurate guide to changes in the parity rate? Well, suppose that in the one country all prices are multiplied by $(1 + m)$ while in the other they are multiplied by $(1 + \overline{m})$. Let $\hat{S}$ be the new exchange rate. From Equation 5.16, if parity is to be maintained in reality we must have

$$P(1 + m) = S \cdot P(1 + \overline{m})$$

or

$$S = \frac{P}{\overline{P}} \cdot \frac{1 + m}{1 + \overline{m}} = S \cdot \frac{1 + m}{1 + \overline{m}} \tag{5.18}$$

We leave it to the reader to compute the new index ratio equivalent to $I/\overline{I}$ in Equation 5.17, to divide it by the ratio in Equation 5.17 and to show that this comparison does indeed reveal $S$ and $\hat{S}$ to differ by the factor $(1 + m)/(1 + \overline{m})$.

However this satisfactory result depends on two questionable hypotheses.

1. *Constancy of index weights in each country.* The comparison gives the right result because the index distortion term cancels out when the ratio of values is computed. But this would not happen if either of the indexes were reweighted in the interval between the two index computations. It might be reasonable to argue that government agencies (and anyone else!) rarely go to the trouble of reweighting published indexes, so this is not likely to be a serious problem. Unfortunately the second problem is unavoidable.

2. *No changes in world relative prices of tradable goods.* Let us leave the index weights unchanged, and consider what happens if world relative prices change. Let Commodity 1 be oil, and suppose that between the period when we first compute the index ratio and the time we recompute it to find $\hat{S}$, not only has there been general inflation, but the relative price of oil has risen. Let $\hat{P}_2$ and $\hat{P}_3$ be $(1 + m)$ times $P_2$ and $P_3$, and $\hat{P}_1$ be $k(1 + m)$ times $P_1$. For parity to be maintained we have to have a comparable relative price change in the other country

$$\hat{\overline{P}}_1 = k(1 + \overline{m})\overline{P}_1, \quad \hat{\overline{P}}_2 = (1 + \overline{m})\overline{P}_2, \quad \hat{\overline{P}}_3 = (1 + \overline{m})P_3$$

Then

$$\frac{\dfrac{\hat{I}}{\bar{\bar{I}}}}{\dfrac{I}{\cdot\bar{I}}} = \frac{S\!\left(\dfrac{kw_1\overline{P}_1 + w_2\overline{P}_2 + w_3\overline{P}_3}{k\overline{w}_1\overline{P}_1 + \overline{w}_2\overline{P}_2 + \overline{w}_3\overline{P}_3}\right)\dfrac{1 + m}{1 + \overline{m}}}{S\!\left(\dfrac{w_1\overline{P}_1 + w_2\overline{P}_2 + w_3\overline{P}_3}{w_1\overline{P}_1 + \overline{w}_2\overline{P}_2 + \overline{w}_3\overline{P}_3}\right)}$$

$$\neq \frac{1 + m}{1 + \overline{m}}$$

which is the correct ratio of new to old parity rates. That is, relative price changes have the same effects on our calculations as index weight changes.

In conclusion, indexes will be poor tools even for the explanation of or prediction of changes in equilibrium parity exchange rates. At best one can hope that there is a tendency for the relative price changes to be cancelled out by changes in the weights. To some extent this happens automatically, if the indexes use consumption weights. As a good rises in relative price, it tends to be consumed somewhat less. (Only in the case of unit elasticity of demand for all tradables, everywhere, would this offset be perfect.) If the indexes use production weights, all relative price effects are magnified, since there tends to be resource pull towards industries whose relative output price has risen. Another corollary is also evident. An extreme instance of different weights in the index occurs when the set of tradable goods being considered is different in the two countries being compared—that is, in each index there are some goods not found in the other.[18] One should, at a minimum, attempt to ensure that the indexes used cover the same commodities. (Appendix 4.1 demonstrates that the possibility that all countries don't produce, or consume, the same set of goods does not affect the PPP principle. Here we are discussing problems with index approximations to PPP exchange rates.)

What, then, do we recommend for people who wish to undertake long-term exchange rate forecasting exercises? The quickest procedure is to project general indices of tradable goods prices. The difficulties we have spelled out above. Probably a better approach is to project local costs for subgroups of traded goods produced domestically, and to compare these with current exchange rate translated cost projections for the other countries in question. A substantial preponderance of higher cost projections for one country implies depreciation of the higher cost country's currency. The projected exchange rate ought to be the one that makes the trade-volume weighted cost discrepancies average out to about zero.

---

[18]If the indices had no goods in common there would be no trade between the countries and no reason for any exchange of currencies.

## 5.8   IS THE STORY WRONG IN A BASIC WAY?

In this section we will consider two of the many objections that might be raised to our analysis of the exchange markets. The first refers to the direction of causality in the relationship between exchange rate changes and inflation. We seem to have implied that the causality runs from inflation to exchange rate changes—it might be argued that we have things backwards. In the second we look at some statistics for Nigeria which seem to imply that even massive inflation has no effect on exchange rates.

### Devaluation and Inflation

In the long run, given what happens in the real economy, the inflation rate is determined by monetary growth. In general, monetary growth is the result of monetary policy (or its absence!). And commodity arbitrage should then bring about parity exchange rates. But of course the monetary policy is not formed in a vacuum but responds to real events in the economy and to a variety of felt political needs. Thus there is room for exchange rate changes to feed back on monetary policy. Consider for example a situation in which a government has held an over-valued exchange rate by gradually using up its exchange reserves. Effectively the community has been consuming more tradables than it has produced. When the reserves run out and a devaluation occurs, real living standards must fall as the price of tradables rises. This is desirable since the original problem was excessive consumption. However, it may be that people are unwilling to take the implied real income cut, and demand higher nominal rewards. Once the reserves have gone there is no way of restoring the former consumption levels. So the income cut must be taken via unemployment. This can precipitate monetary expansion, which leads to inflation and another devaluation, and so on. In effect the inflation is the result of a social conflict over the distribution of wealth. In a crude sense one might caricature the recent economic history of Britain by this example.

Another model of an inflation/devaluation spiral has been constructed by Carlos Rodriguez,[19] and is seen as being relevant to a number of developing countries. It relies on two mechanisms. The first is the absence of any effective sterilization policy so that balance of payments deficits and surpluses (under pegged exchange rates, of course) respectively contract and expand the money supply. The second is that the government runs a fiscal deficit, and creates money in order to finance purchases of imports. (The money is sold on the exchange market, to obtain the foreign currency to buy the imports.)

---

[19]Carlos Rodriguez, "A Stylized Model of the Devaluation-Inflation Spiral," *I.M.F. Staff Papers*, 25, 1, March 1978.

Consider first the situation without any fiscal deficit. The money supply is controlled by the exchange rate. At the rate which exactly equates private demand for and supply of foreign exchange, everything is stable, since the money supply neither grows nor declines and there is no inflation. Call this rate $\overline{S}$. Now allow the deficit. Once we add the government demand for foreign exchange, only a lower exchange rate, say $\hat{S}$, will equate demand for and supply of foreign exchange.

But what exchange rate keeps the money supply constant (and thus precludes inflation)? At the rate $\hat{S}$ there is no payments surplus to be monetized, but the deficit is being funded by new money creation. To keep the money supply constant we need an exchange rate which causes a balance of payments deficit exactly equal to the government budget deficit. For then what is pumped in to fund the deficit is lost in sales to the central bank to buy foreign currency to make up the balance of payments deficit. The required rate is exactly $\overline{S}$, the old exchange rate. For at that rate private demand equals private supply of foreign exchange, so that each budget deficit dollar used to buy imports causes a one dollar increase in the balance of payments deficit. So there is no longer one exchange rate that both clears the foreign exchange market and causes no inflation.

Suppose we start at the rate $\overline{S}$ with no inflation. Then reserves of the central bank are running down all the time. Eventually a devaluation must occur. We assume it is a big one, to allow renewed reserve accumulation. But now that balance of payments surpluses are occurring they augment the deficit as a source of monetary growth and thus of inflation. So the devaluation is followed by rapid inflation. As this inflation erodes the initial competitive advantage given to the tradables sector by the devaluation, the surplus shrinks, and so the monetary growth shrinks. Hence the system moves to price stability but then starts to lose reserves again.

Thus, this is a result of the exchange pegging policies and the monetization of the resulting surpluses and deficits. Under a floating rate regime we would have $S = \hat{S}$ and this rate, $\hat{S}$, would depreciate at the rate of inflation caused by the funding of the budget deficit by money creation.

## Nigeria: A Counterexample?

Table 5.3 gives some figures for the Nigerian money supply. The growth rates are impressive, and had the predictable effect on prices (see Table 5.4). Yet as Table 5.5 shows, rather than depreciating against the dollar, the naira appreciated! How can this be? In essence the answer is that Nigeria's income grew faster that it could be spent on imports, in this period. This is shown in Table 5.6. It grew so fast because Nigeria is a

**Table 5.3** *Nigerian Money Supply (million naira)*

| | 1970 | 1971 | 1972 | 1973 | 1974 | 1975 | 1976 | 1977 | 1978 III |
|---|---|---|---|---|---|---|---|---|---|
| Amount | 608.3 | 628.9 | 747.3 | 925.8 | 1398.5 | 2594.9 | 3752.6 | 5184.1 | 5446.7 |
| % Increase | 3.4 | 18.2 | 23.9 | 51.1 | 85.5 | 44.6 | 38.1 | 5.1 | |

Source: IMF International Financial Statistics, January 1980, 33, 1.

**Table 5.4** *Nigerian Consumer Price Index (Base 1972)*

| 1972 | 1973 | 1974 | 1975 | 1976 | 1977 | 1978 II |
|---|---|---|---|---|---|---|
| 100 | 105.7 | 118.9 | 159 | 194 | 235.6 | 297 |

Source: IMF International Financial Statistics, January 1980, 33, 1.

**Table 5.5** *Naira/Dollar Exchange Rates*

| | 1970 | 1971 | 1972 | 1973 | 1974 | 1975 | 1976 | 1977 | 1978 |
|---|---|---|---|---|---|---|---|---|---|
| SDR per naira | 1.400 | 1.400 | 1.400 | 1.260 | 1.3254 | 1.363 | 1.364 | 1.264 | 1.186 |
| U.S. dollar per naire Dec. | 1.400 | 1.520 | 1.520 | 1.520 | 1.622 | 1.596 | 1.585 | 1.535 | 1.544 |

Source: IMF International Financial Statistics, January 1980, 33, 1.

**Table 5.6**   *Balance of Visible Trade at Current Prices (million naira)*

|  |  | Exports | | | Balance of Trade | | |
|---|---|---|---|---|---|---|---|
|  | Imports | Oil | Nonoil | Total | Oil Sector | Nonoil Sector | Total |
| 1967 | 447.1 | 144.8 | 338.8 | 483.6 | 144.8 | − 108.3 | 36.5 |
| 1968 | 385.2 | 74.0 | 348.2 | 422.2 | 74.0 | − 37.0 | 37.0 |
| 1969 | 497.4 | 261.9 | 374.4 | 636.3 | 261.9 | − 123.0 | 138.9 |
| 1970 | 756.4 | 509.6 | 376.1 | 885.7 | 509.6 | − 380.3 | 129.3 |
| 1971 | 1079.0 | 953.0 | 340.4 | 1293.4 | 953.0 | − 738.6 | 214.4 |
| 1972 | 987.6 | 1152.6 | 259.6 | 1412.2 | 1152.6 | − 728.0 | 424.6 |
| 1973 | 1224.8 | 1893.5 | 383.9 | 2277.4 | 1893.5 | − 840.9 | 1052.6 |
| 1974 | 1737.3 | 5492.5 | 302.3 | 5794.8 | 5492.5 | − 1435.1 | 4057.4 |
| 1975 | 3717.4 | 4629.6 | 358.8 | 4988.4 | 4629.6 | − 3358.6 | 1271.0 |
| 1976 | 5148.5 | 5894.1 | 426.7 | 6320.8 | 5894.1 | − 4721.8 | 1172.3 |
| 1977 | 7159.7 | 7046.2 | 547.6 | 7593.8 | 7046.2 | − 7707.3 | − 661.1 |

*Source: IMF International Financial Statistics, January 1980, 33, 1.*

major oil exporter. And it couldn't be spent very quickly because, in common with a number of other oil exporters, Nigeria faced physical constraints on the ability to absorb imports, starting with basics like harbor capacity. As Table 5.7 makes clear, reality has started to conform with the theory. Thus, this isn't a counterexample to our theories but rather serves to remind us that one must look at countries on a case by case basis to determine the validity of long run models of the exchange rate (or equivalently, of the balance of payments under fixed rates).

**Table 5.7**   *Balance of Payments (million US$)*

| 1972 | 1973 | 1974 | 1975 | 1976 | 1977 | 1978 |
|---|---|---|---|---|---|---|
| − 48 | 200 | 4899 | 189 | − 379 | − 823 | − 1905 |

*Source: IMF International Financial Statistics, January 1980, 33, 1.*

## 5.9   SUMMARY

An exchange rate is the rate at which one national money exchanges for another. To explain the exchange rates we must, therefore, know what moneys are worth to their holders. This principle of exchange rate determination, suitably elaborated, is known as the purchasing power parity principle. From a study of the purchasing power notion we identify three factors affecting long run exchange rate behavior:

1. Relative monetary growth—the country with greater monetary growth will experience exchange depreciation, all other things being equal.

2. Real output growth—the country with greater real output growth, and thus greater absorption of money supply into transactions balances rather than price increases, will experience exchange appreciation, all other things being equal.

3. Growth in productive efficiency—the country with greater relative growth of productive efficiency in the tradables sector will experience exchange appreciation, all other things being equal.

The purchasing power parities are brought about by a process of commodity arbitrage. Buyers choose goods from the cheapest source. This commodity arbitrage process operates only with significant delays, which explains why the purchasing power parity principle gives the long-run trend of exchange rates, but cannot explain day-to-day or even quarter-to-quarter movements. In a floating rate situation the main sources of delay are two:

1.  There are substantial ordering, shipping, delivery, and payment lags in world trade, so that even if buyers respond immediately to the opportunities offered by exchange rate changes, it will take quite a while for these demand changes to be reflected in payments flows. And payments flows affect the spot market.

2.  In the attempt to maintain market share, companies will alter selling prices to prevent the full impact of exchange rate changes being felt by their foreign customers. Companies don't run at a loss forever, but they can for some time.

In reality we must add to these two factors the delaying impact of (sometimes quite prolonged) government exchange market interventions.

Testing and measurement raise severe problems of definition and aggregation. Moreover spurious results arise from using data mismatched in time. Nevertheless the overall weight of evidence supports the purchasing power parity notion, with a return time from major deviations of about 18 months or so.

For further illustration of this material, see Case 3, "Port Arthur Timber Company," at the back of the book.

**EXERCISE[20]**

### Economy of the Netherlands

The economy of the Netherlands is small and open, with its most important structural characteristics its trade dependence and large reserves of natural gas. Despite these features, which subject the Dutch economy to the vicissitudes of

---

[20]Excerpted from "Holland Follows the Rest of Europe," *International Finance*, Chase Manhattan Bank, Vol. XV, No. 5, March 3, 1980, p. 8. Used by permission.

its external sector and the international economy, the country's growth has been stable, ranging between 2% and 3% annually between 1977 and 1979, with an inflation rate for the same period averaging 5.1%, among the lowest in Europe.

[A.]   Exports and imports each account for about half of Holland's $131 billion GNP. This high degree of trade dependence implies that the authorities have only a limited degree of control over aggregate demand. Furthermore, the tradable component of Dutch output (exportables and importables) is even larger than the portion actually traded. This degree of openness means that the Dutch price level is largely determined on world markets through international goods arbitrage. The price level in guilder terms can therefore be changed significantly only if the exchange rate changes. But this option is circumscribed by Holland's membership in the European Monetary System (EMS). Membership in the EMS also restricts the authorities' freedom to target a rate of monetary expansion.

The Dutch economy performed unspectacularly in 1979. Real growth was an estimated 2%, and despite a sharp increase in natural gas output, industrial production registered no growth. The inflation rate was held to some 4.7%, despite a sharp rise in the price of raw materials.

The volume trade balance was strong during the first three quarters of 1979—export volume was up 8.7% as against an import volume increase of only 6.5%. But an unfavorable shift in the terms of trade widened the trade deficit. The Dutch Central Planning Bureau estimates the 1979 current-account deficit at 1.5 billion guilders, compared with a 2 billion guilder gap in 1978.

On the domestic front the Government has not succeeded in reducing the public sector deficit to 4%–4.5% of national income as it had proposed to do. With the sluggishness of the domestic economy, the public sector deficit is now expected to be 5.5% of national income in 1980, roughly unchanged from last year's 5.7%. Wages are expected to rise by some 1.5%–2% in real terms when the current wage freeze expires, and higher costs already in place at the wholesale level point to retail price inflation of 6%–7%. Despite this, corporate profit margins are expected to be squeezed. On balance, real growth in 1980 is forecast to decline to about 1%, with the weakest points, capital investment and export volume.

[B.]   Over the longer run, Holland is faced with several problems. Increasing the price-competitiveness of Dutch exports with a devaluation is difficult because of wage indexation, which would prevent any real reduction in the guilder's exchange value. Thus, in order to make exports more competitive, unit labor costs must rise less quickly in Holland than in its major trading partners.

*Question:* Discuss the analyses in paragraphs A and B.

### Suggestions for Further Reading

L. H. Officer, "The Purchasing-Power-Parity Theory of Exchange Rates: A Review Article," *International Monetary Fund Staff Papers,* XXIII, 1 (March 1976). This gives a comprehensive survey of earlier publications and statistical work. It is the best guide to the antecedents of the theory.

M. H. Lee, *Purchasing Power Parity.* New York: Marcel-Dekker, Inc., 1976. This gives a number of empirical tests of the theory for the period 1900–1972.

J. Frenkel and H. Johnson (Eds.), *The Monetary Approach to the Balance of Payments.* University of Toronto Press, 1976.

***Appendix 5.1:*** *Parity Exchange Rates and Partially Disjoint Bundles of Produced Tradable Goods*

---

The law of one price and the purchasing power parity principle of long run exchange rate determination do not require that a common bundle of tradable goods be produced in all countries so that arbitrage can take place everywhere in all goods. To see this, consider the following simple example of three countries and three goods, where each country specializes in the production of only one good, and imports the other two.

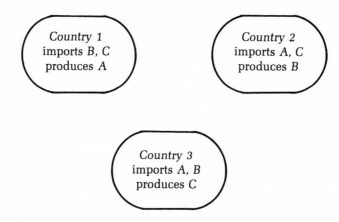

Let $P_{ij}$ = price of good $i$ in Country $j$

$R_{ij}$ = price of $j$'s currency in $i$'s currency

Then from the commodity arbitrage which can take place we have

$$P_{B1} = R_{12}P_{B2}, \quad P_{C1} = R_{13}P_{C3} \tag{A1}$$

$$P_{AZ} = \frac{P_{A1}}{R_{12}}, \quad \mathbf{P}_{C2} = \mathbf{R}_{23}\mathbf{P}_{C3} \tag{A2}$$

$$P_{A3} = \frac{P_{A1}}{R_{13}}, \quad P_{B3} = \frac{P_{B2}}{R_{23}} \tag{A3}$$

These relations simply say that, because of the specialization in production, the local price for an imported good must equal the translated foreign price, the foreign price being that in the place of production.

Now from the second relation in Equation A3, $P_{B2} = R_{23}P_{B3}$. Substitute this in the first part of Equation A1 to obtain

$$P_{B1} = R_{12} \cdot R_{23}P_{B3} \tag{A4}$$

But triangular arbitrage in currencies ensures that at all times $R_{12}R_{23} = R_{13}$. So we have

$$P_{B1} = R_{13}P_{B3}$$

or                                                                                        (A5)

$$R_{13} = \frac{P_{B1}}{P_{B3}}$$

although good $B$ is produced neither in Country 1 nor in Country 3.

# Chapter 6

# Short Term Exchange Rate Movements

## 6.1 INTRODUCTION

The explanation of trend or long-run exchange rate behavior is purchasing power parity or the law of one price applied to the prices of tradable goods. Chapter 5 presented a number of factors that cause the purchasing power parities to change. Moreover, despite a number of very consequential measurement problems, we have seen that exchange rates deviate from the purchasing power parities. Especially when government intervention is present (the cases of Mexico, Britain, Germany, and Japan immediately come to mind) these deviations can persist for a number of years. Even in the absence of government intervention we would expect to see transient variations of spot exchange rates from the parity levels, because the law of one price can operate only over time, not instantaneously. It takes time to alter the pattern of international trade to respond to price differentials. Moreover, as delivery lags exist, even an immediate response will not show up in payments based on trade for several months.[1] Thus short-term exchange rate movements must be explained by something other than the process of commodity arbitrage.

In Section 6.2 we will explain what is currently believed about the shortrun behavior of exchange rates in the absence of government intervention. Our cautious tone in describing this material reflects the relatively poor state of our understanding of these phenomena. They are the subject of active research, and we expect our opinions to evolve substantially in the next few years. Section 6.3 looks at the process of government intervention in the exchange markets. We will examine the motives for these interventions, the methods by which they are carried out, and their results. The latter study requires the use of some of the theory of international trade that was developed in Chapter 3. Our analysis concludes with Section 6.4, which delves into the recent history of short-run exchange movements and into the possibility of forecasting these move-

---

[1] Recollect that Magee found delivery lags of one to five months in U.S.–German trade. See the reference in Section 5.7.

ments. Here we will look at recent studies of the efficiency of the foreign exchange markets and the value of the forward rate as a forecast of future spot rates. We haven't found any method of beating the market—would we tell you if we had?

## 6.2   SHORT-RUN EXCHANGE RATE MOVEMENTS IN A FREE MARKET

The absence of rapid commodity arbitrage responses to exchange rate changes leaves us with the need to find other factors to explain exchange rate movements. It is often claimed that changes in trade flows in response to differential real growth rates determine exchange rate movements over moderate horizons. If U.S. growth exceeds foreign growth, then the United States will suck in imports faster than foreigners are taking U.S. exports, resulting in trade deficits and dollar depreciation. Unfortunately this viewpoint is hard to reconcile with some basic facts about the recent past, as indicated on Tables 6.1 and 6.2.

**Table 6.1**   *Real Output Growth for Selected Countries (% Growth of GNP or GDP)*

| Country | Belgium | Canada | France | Germany | Italy | Japan | U.K. | U.S. |
|---------|---------|--------|--------|---------|-------|-------|------|------|
| Period |  |  |  |  |  |  |  |  |
| 1975I–1976IV[a] | 3.4 | 4.1 | 4.7 | 4.5 | 4.4 | 6.1 | 1.3 | 5.4 |
| 1977I–1978II | 0.4 | 3.6 | 2.9 | 3.1 | 0.5 | 6.1 | 0.2 | 5.1 |

[a]Roman numerals denote quarters

*Source:* D. Mudd, "Movements in the Foreign Exchange Value of the Dollar During the Current U.S. Expansion," *Review*, Federal Reserve Bank of St. Louis, November 1978, Table 1, p. 3.

In 1976 through 1977, the United States grew faster than any economy except that of Japan, and yet the dollar appreciated, by about 8% overall, on a trade-weighted basis. In the later period, the United States again grew faster than any economy except Japan, but the dollar depreciated, by 12½% overall, on a trade-weighted basis.[2] As a crude theory of exchange rate determination, this is inferior to the application of purchasing power parity. As can be seen, U.S. inflation accelerated relative to that of other countries, and the dollar depreciated (except against the Canadian dollar, where the same acceleration phenomenon took place to a more marked extent). We urge the reader to carry out a small graphical pur-

---

[2]The Japanese economy has grown faster than those of all other developed nations for years—the yen has not plummeted. One can make a similar argument for Germany.

**Table 6.2**  *Relative Rates of Price Change [% change in WPI (upper number), CPI (lower number)]*

| Country | Belgium | Canada | France | Germany | Italy | Japan | U.K. | U.S. |
|---|---|---|---|---|---|---|---|---|
| Period | | | | | | | | |
| 1975I–1976IV | 6.1 | 4.8 | 5.2 | 3.5 | 19.6 | 4.5 | 18.1 | 4.9 |
| | 9.1 | 7.7 | 9.6 | 4.7 | 15.7 | 9.2 | 19.3 | 5.9 |
| 1977I–1978II | – 2.7 | 9.2 | 2.4 | 1.1 | 7.7 | – 1.3 | 12.0 | 7.3 |
| | 5.0 | 9.0 | 9.0 | 2.9 | 12.7 | 4.5 | 8.7 | 7.4 |

*Source:* "International Economic Conditions," Federal Reserve Bank of St. Louis, January 1979.

chasing power parity analysis to see the value of the theory over the last few years.[3] It should become apparent that another factor is behind both the exchange rate changes and the inflation (and indeed perhaps behind the short-term growth rate fluctuations as well), namely the relationship between money demand and the growth of the money supply that was extensively discussed in Chapter 5.

Nonetheless, though we may find that purchasing power parity is superior to the growth rate theory, we must still explain the factors acting on the exchange market in the absence of commodity arbitrage responses. There is some degree of consensus among economists that the explanation must be sought in short-term capital flows, which occur for reasons of currency speculation and interest arbitrage. The framework for looking at these flows must be the linkage between exchange rates and interest rates brought about by covered interest arbitrage. Recollect from Chapter 1 that, when there is free flow of capital, competition among arbitrageurs ensures that almost all of the time there will be virtually no profit in covered interest arbitrage. This results in the following relationship between exchange rates and interest rates:

$$\frac{F^t - S}{S} = r_A{}^t - \frac{F^t}{S} r_B{}^t \tag{6.1}$$

where

$F^t$ = price in $A$'s currency of a unit of $B$'s currency deliverable in $t$ days

$S$ = spot price in $A$'s currency of a unit of $B$'s currency

$r_A{}^t, r_B{}^t$ = (Eurocurrency) interest rates for maturity $t$ in currencies $A$ and $B$

---

[3]All the necessary statistics may be found in "International Financial Statistics, International Monetary Fund, which is a monthly publication.

Equation 6.1 may be trivially rearranged to yield

$$S = F^t \left( \frac{1 + r_B^t}{1 + r_A^t} \right) \tag{6.2}$$

This connection between spots, forwards, and interest rates survives to some extent even in the presence of limitations on capital flows, including restriction of international borrowing and lending to credits directly relating to trade.[4] For this reason it will be the focus of our analysis.

We begin with an hypothesis: forward exchange rates are determined by speculation on the relevant future spot rates. That is, $F^t$ in equation 6.2 is determined by speculation. Certain capital market factors, which we will discuss, explain the values of the interest rates. Thus we propose that, in the short-term, the spot rate is simply pulled around by the actions of speculators in the forward exchange markets and by trading on the capital markets. The force that does the pulling is of course the covered interest arbitrage, which acts to maintain Equation 6.2 in an approximate sense almost all the time. For such a story to be more than a mere rearrangement of the variables in Equation 6.1, we require two things:

1. Some basis for believing the hypothesis about the speculative determination of the forward exchange rates. We rest on some common-sense reasoning and some facts. First, forward rates that significantly deviate from anticipated spots provide lucrative speculative opportunities. Second, as we show in Section 6.4 on average the forwards do indeed equal the relevant future spots, an observation compatible with the determination of forward rates by reasonably well-informed speculators.

2. Some explanation for the formation of the forward rates and interest rates, so that the theory can become operational in a predictive sense. It is in the latter requirement that difficulties arise. While we can provide some ideas, our knowledge of the formation of anticipations about future events is extremely limited. As we will see, in part this is because there is always the danger of self-feeding speculative bubbles.

Let us start to see some of the implications for spot exchange rate behavior of the relationship shown in Equation 6.2. For the purposes of discussion, let us assume

- that speculators form forecasts according to purchasing power parity principles; and

---

[4]Appendix 6.1 examines the robustness of this condition under capital flow restrictions. It also looks at the implications of covered interest arbitrage for the term structure of interest rates.

- that interest rates incorporate anticipated inflation using the tradable goods price index; and

- that starting from some initial situation, inflation anticipations are revised by the proportional factors $\Delta_A{}^t$, $\Delta_B{}^t$ for Countries $A$ and $B$ over the horizon to $t$.

Let "hats" over variables denote revised values. Let $\pi_A{}^t$, $\pi_B{}^t$ denote the values of tradable goods price indexes $t$ days from the present (start them at the present for simplicity). Then originally speculators used the anticipated index ratio to forecast the future spot rate, or

$$F^t = \frac{\pi_A{}^t}{\pi_B{}^t} \cdot S$$

Since $\hat{\pi}_A{}^t = \Delta_A{}^t \cdot \pi_A{}^t$, $\hat{\pi}_B{}^t = \Delta_B{}^t \cdot \pi_B{}^t$ we see that we can express the revised forward rate as

$$\hat{F}^t = \frac{\Delta_A{}^t}{\Delta_B{}^t} \cdot F^t \tag{6.3}$$

Similarly, *if* the inflation anticipation factored into the short-term interest rates is the tradable goods inflation, we find[5]

$$(1 + \hat{r}_A{}^t) = \Delta_A{}^t(1 + r_A{}^t), (1 + \hat{r}_B{}^t) = \Delta_B{}^t(1 + r_B{}^t) \tag{6.4}$$

Replacing terms in Equation 6.2 by the revised versions in Equations 6.3 and 6.4, we obtain the new spot rate:

$$\hat{S} = \hat{F}^t \left( \frac{1 + \hat{r}_B{}^t}{1 + \hat{r}_A{}^t} \right) = \frac{\Delta_A{}^t}{\Delta_B{}^t} \cdot F^t \cdot \frac{\Delta_B{}^t}{\Delta_A{}^t} \left( \frac{1 + r_B{}^t}{1 + r_A{}^t} \right) = S \tag{6.5}$$

That is, roughly speaking, under our conditions revisions of expectations about future inflation should have no effect on spot exchange rates.

However our conditions are rather peculiar. Suppose, as is more reasonable, that inflation is not uniform over the traded and nontraded goods sectors, and that there are relative price changes. We discussed this in Chapter 5. To be concrete, imagine that opinions about future inflation in $A$ do not change, but that more inflation is now expected in $B$, with

---

[5]Anticipated real return must equal some anticipated real rate, $\rho$. Thus originally we had $r$ such that

$$\frac{1 + r}{\pi} = \rho \quad \text{or} \quad 1 + r = \rho\pi$$

After the revised anticipations we require $\hat{r}$ such that

$$\frac{1 + \hat{r}}{\Delta \pi} = \rho \quad \text{or} \quad 1 + \hat{r} = \rho \Delta \pi = \Delta(1 + r)$$

stronger effect on the nontradables sector. Then the general or average inflation factor used to mark up $r_B{}^t$ will exceed that used to revise $F^t$. Specifically, $(1 + r_b{}^t)$ will rise by more than $f^t$ falls, so that the spot rate for $B$ will actually appreciate! The relative price change causes an inflow of covered interest arbitrage funds, which appreciate the currency in the short term though it is anticipated to depreciate later on. We suggest that the reader try other combinations of changes in anticipations so as to become more familiar with the variety of possible outcomes.

There are further, subtle connections between revisions of anticipations of inflation and spot and forward exchange rates.[6] What happens to interest rates and prices *right now* if people revise upwards their anticipation of inflation over some future time?

- Nominal yields on bonds must rise, of course. That is the effect we considered immediately above. However, they will not rise as much as the anticipated increment in inflation since anticipated *real* rates of return will fall as a result of money balance adjustments which we must now consider.

- If higher inflation is anticipated, the perceived cost of holding money balances for transactions purposes has risen, and people will attempt to lower their real money balances. As we explained in Chapter 5, the system as a whole cannot dispose of the nominal money supply. So we will observe a jump in asset prices and commodity prices as people attempt to convert some of their money balances into an alternative and preferable form. The jump in asset prices lowers returns, and the jump in commodity prices shows up as *current* inflation.

With this in mind, let us return to our earlier example, on page 161. The appreciation of $B$'s currency was caused by a greater increase in $r_B{}^t$ than in the anticipated price of tradables. But we now see that the tendency for anticipated real returns to fall as asset prices jump tends to offset this effect. It could be that nominal interest rates in $B$ rise initially by *less* than the anticipated increase in tradables goods prices, with the result that $B$'s currency depreciates. Since there will be a burst of contemporary inflation, it would falsely appear that $B$'s currency was depreciating for purchasing power parity reasons.[7] As the theory gives no guide to the relative magnitude of the conflicting effects of a revision in anticipated inflation, one must try to estimate these things on a case-by-case basis.

---

[6]Our discussion of the impact on interest rates and prices of revised inflationary expectations is based on R. Balbach, "The Effects of Changes in Inflationary Anticipations," *Review*, Federal Reserve Bank of St. Louis, April 1977, 10–14.

[7]This is another problem in the measurement of the short-run strength of the law of one price, to be added to those we discussed in Chapter 5.

Let us now turn to another source of changes in interest rates—money supply fluctuations. These always occur as central banks rarely succeed in meeting their money supply targets on a day-to-day basis, or even on a year-to-year basis. Let us suppose that the nominal money supply expands faster than demand to hold real balances, at current prices and interest rates. This means that people will attempt to unload the excess balances. Since the capital markets are more efficient and price responsive than commodity markets, the first effects of the monetary expansion are felt there as investors convert excess money into securities. As a matter of estimation, the short run elasticity of nominal interest rates with respect to changes in the money supply is large enough to cause a given percentage change in the money supply to have an amplified effect on the spot rate via Equation 6.2.[8] Once again the magnitude of the amplifier must be evaluated on a case-by-case basis.

And here we encounter the classical speculative dilemma. For the reasons we have described, spot rates will move away from their purchasing power parity values, which values themselves are extremely hard to measure and forecast. If this is so, it does not make sense for speculators to believe that spot rates will always be at their parity levels. That is demonstrably foolish. But without this anchor, what *should* the speculators expect? They are caught in a chain of circular reasoning. As Equation 6.2 shows, all other things being given, what they expect about future spot rates determines present spot rates. Yet that holds not only now but also at the dates on which today's forward contracts mature. So the speculator today should be trying to estimate what speculators will be anticipating in the future. But the latter will be anticipating what other speculators will be anticipating in the further future and so on. Of course once deviations from parity persist, commodity flows will cumulate, and it is rational to expect a move back towards parity. In such a world there is room for a lot of random movement, and that's what you see.[9]

## 6.3  GOVERNMENT EXCHANGE MARKET INTERVENTION

In a free market one expects a considerable amount of noise about the parity rates, in a manner not yet fully understood and therefore only

---

[8]The derivation of this result seemed a little too complex to be worth placing in the text. The interested reader should consult R. Dornbusch, "The Theory of Flexible Exchange Rate Regimes and Macroeconomic Policy," *Scandinavian Journal of Economics, 78,* 2 (May 1976).

[9]We do not claim that exchange markets are uniquely unstable, or even unstable to any significant extent. The same argument about speculation feeding on itself can be applied to any market for assets or durable goods. There is a lot of noise in all these markets, in part, we conjecture, for the reasons we give. But these reasons do not imply that the government can run the exchange market any better than one anticipates it would run the stock market.

Table 6.3  Exchange Arrangements as of October 31, 1978

| | Currency pegged to | | | | | Exchange Rate adjusted according to a set of indicators[b] | Cooperative exchange arrangements[c] | Other[d] |
|---|---|---|---|---|---|---|---|---|
| US Dollar | Pound Sterling | French Franc | Other Currency | SDR | Other currency composite[a] | | | |
| Bahamas | | | Equatorial Guinea (Spanish Peseta) | | | | | Afghanistan |
| Barbados | Bangladesh | Benin | | Burma | Algeria | Brazil | Belgium | Argentina |
| Bolivia | Gambia, The | Cameroon C. African Emp. | | Guinea | Austria | Colombia | Denmark | Australia |
| | | | | Guinea-Bissau | Cyprus | Peru | Germany | Bahrain |
| Botswana | Ireland | Chad | Lesotho (South African Rand) | Jordan | Fiji | Portugal | Luxembourg | Canada |
| Burundi | Seychelles | Comoros | | Kenya | Finland | Uruguay | Netherlands | |
| China, Rep. of | Sierra Leone | Congo | Solomon Islands | Malawi | India | | Norway | Chile |
| Costa Rica | | Gabon | (Australian Dollar) | Mauritius | Kuwait | | | France |
| Dominican Rep. | | Ivory Coast | Swaziland (South African Rand) | São Tomé & Principe | Malaysia | | | Ghana |
| Ecuador | | Madagascar Mali | | Tanzania Uganda | Malta Mauritania | | | Greece Iceland |
| Egypt | | | | | | | | |
| El Salvador | | Niger | | Viet Nam | Morocco New Zealand Papua New Guinea | | | Iran Israel |
| Ethiopia | | Senegal | | | | | | |
| Grenada | | Togo | | Zaire | Singapore | | | Italy |
| Guatemala | | Upper Volta | | Zambia | Sweden | | | Jamaica |
| Guyana | | | | | | | | Japan |
| Haiti | | | | | Thailand | | | Lebanon |
| Honduras | | | | | Tunisia Western Samoa | | | Mexico |
| Indonesia | | | | | | | | Nigeria |

Iraq
Korea

Lao P.D. Rep.
Liberia
Libya
Maldives

Nepal

Nicaragua
Oman
Pakistan
Panama
Paraguay

Romania
Rwanda
Somalia
South Africa
Sudan

Suriname
Syrian Arab Rep.
Trinidad & Tobago
Venezuela
Yemen Arab Rep.
Yemen, P.D. Rep.

Philippines
Qatar

Saudi Arabia
Spain
Sri Lanka
Turkey
U. Arab Emirates

United Kingdom
United States
Yugoslavia

[a] Comprises currencies which are pegged to various "baskets" of currencies of the members' own choice, as distinct from the SDR basket.

[b] Includes exchange arrangements under which the exchange rate is adjusted at relatively frequent intervals, on the basis of indicators determined by the respective member countries.

[c] Refers to the cooperative arrangement for multicurrency intervention (the "snake") maintained by a group of European countries. Norway withdrew from "the snake" in December.

[d] Covers a heterogeneous group of exchange arrangements, including those of members whose currencies may be deemed to be floating independently, and those which cannot be properly classified under other categories.

Source: "International Letter," Federal Reserve Bank of Chicago, No. 388, February 2, 1979.

poorly predictable (as we will see in the next section). However a further, vast complication is introduced by governmental manipulation of exchange markets. In fact even in the current era of floating exchange rates, most exchange markets are locked into government-maintained pricing relationships. This is illustrated in Table 6.3. In addition, even those countries that do not peg their rates according to some formula will very frequently intervene in exchange markets from time to time in order to push the exchange rates to levels that they consider more desirable. For this reason the period since 1973 has been described by the term "dirty floating."

Almost all central banks keep their intervention activities secret, even from subsequent historians. However the Federal Reserve Board publishes information not only on its own intervention operations but also, in very aggregate, outline form, on those of other major central banks.[10] We can reconstruct the pattern of intervention activities from these data. Until 1978, Federal Reserve intervention amounted, on average, to gross trading of $1 billion annually. In August, September, and October of 1978, exchange market intervention by the Federal Reserve amounted to a record $2.5 billion, consisting of the sale of $2.2 billion worth of DM and $0.3 billion worth of Swiss francs. These funds were mostly drawn from "swap lines," which we will describe shortly. (It should be mentioned that as the decline of the dollar continued, the taxpayers lost a total of $240 million as a consequence of Treasury and federal intervention activities in these three months. The loss comes from the higher dollar cost of repaying the swap borrowings.) Given the current outlook of the government we can anticipate that this (historically) large volume of intervention will continue. How large is this relative to market volume? The most recent available evidence is a survey published by the Federal Reserve Bank of New York, covering the month of April, 1977.[11] About ¼ of the transactions were in DM and 1/5 in Can$. About 92% of the transactions were interbank, the remainder being between the banks and their nonbank customers. The previous survey, in March, 1969, showed total transactions of about $1 billion per business day. It seems that the rate of transaction is very closely tied to the value of trade flows, as one would expect. If we accept a figure of $300 billion–$400 billion as private trading in the New York market for the August–October 1978 quarter, federal intervention came to about 7/10 of 1% of the volume.

The Federal Reserve is undertaking nickel-and-dime work compared to the intervention activities of the European and Japanese central banks.

[10]"Treasury and Federal Reserve Foreign Exchange Operations," appearing in *Federal Reserve Bulletin* in March, June, September, and December of every year.
[11]"Gross Foreign Currency Transactions in April in U.S. Market by 44 Participants Totaled $106.4 Billion or $5 Billion Each Business Day," Federal Reserve Bank of New York, release No. 1202, July 12, 1977.

In 1976, the Swiss National Bank alone carried out about $7.5 billion of exchange market intervention. Non–U.S. central banks carried out $20.5 billion of intervention in the quarter November 1976–January 1977. The Bundesbank has been known to undertake $1 billion of intervention in a single week. Intervention for the whole of 1978 will probably turn out to be a new record, as central banks attempted to stem the depreciation of the dollar against their currencies, and Japan and Switzerland attempted to stem the appreciation of their currencies against all others. According to the Federal Reserve Bank of St. Louis[12] between November 1977 and October 1978 gross foreign exchange market intervention by all major central banks already totalled about $114 billion.

The U.S. government undertakes intervention using its reserves of gold and foreign exchange, supplemented considerably by a number of short-term borrowing or so-called "swap" arrangements with other central banks. Such swap agreements were established in the 1960s as the fixed exchange rate system moved further into disequilibrium. Table 6.4 shows the current status of arrangements in which the U.S. participates.

**Table 6.4**  *Federal Reserve Reciprocal Currency Arrangements (Millions of dollars)*

| Institution | Amount of facility Oct. 31, 1978 | Increases, Nov. 1, 1978 | Amount of facility Nov. 1, 1978 |
|---|---|---|---|
| Austrian National Bank ................. | 250 | — | 250 |
| National Bank of Belgium ............. | 1,000 | — | 1,000 |
| Bank of Canada ............................. | 2,000 | — | 2,000 |
| National Bank of Denmark ............ | 250 | — | 250 |
| Bank of England ............................ | 3,000 | — | 3,000 |
| Bank of France .............................. | 2,000 | — | 2,000 |
| German Federal Bank .................... | 4,000 | 2,000 | 6,000 |
| Bank of Italy ................................. | 3,000 | — | 3,000 |
| Bank of Japan ............................... | 2,000 | 3,000 | 5,000 |
| Bank of Mexico ............................. | 360 | — | 360 |
| Netherlands Bank .......................... | 500 | — | 500 |
| Bank of Norway ............................ | 250 | — | 250 |
| Bank of Sweden ............................ | 300 | — | 300 |
| Swiss National Bank ...................... | 1,400 | 2,600 | 4,000 |
| Bank for International Settlements: | | | |
|   Swiss francs/dollars ................... | 600 | — | 600 |
|   Other authorized European currencies/dollars ...................... | 1,250 | — | 1,250 |
|   Total | 22,160 | 7,600 | 29,760 |

*Source:* "Treasury and Federal Reserve Foreign Exchange Operations: Interim Report," Federal Reserve Bulletin, December 1978, Table 1.

---

[12]"International Economic Conditions," January 10, 1979, p. 1.

The $2.5 billion of intervention in August–October 1978 was almost en-
tirely funded out of the swap agreements. The Federal Reserve drew $1.2
billion from the Bundesbank and $0.3 billion from the Swiss National
Bank, while the Treasury drew about $0.8 billion on its swap line with
the Bundesbank. A complete picture of the U.S. foreign exchange operations for that three-month period is given in Table 6.5.

**Table 6.5**   *U.S. Foreign Exchange Market Intervention
Summary, July 31–October 31, 1978
Millions of dollars equivalent; data are on a transaction-date basis*

| Type of Transaction | Transactions with German Federal Bank |
|---|---|
| Reciprocal currency arrangement | |
| Commitments outstanding | |
| July 31, 1978 ............................................... | 650.5 |
| Drawings or repayments ( − ), | |
| Aug. 1–Oct. 31, 1978 .................................... | { 1,157.5 |
| Commitments outstanding, | − 551.9 |
| Oct. 31, 1978 ............................................... | 1,256.1 |
| U.S. Treasury swap arrangements | |
| Commitments outstanding, | |
| July 31, 1978 ............................................... | 197.0 |
| Drawings or repayments ( − ), | { 796.9 |
| Aug. 1–Oct. 31, 1978 .................................... | − 343.5 |
| Commitments outstanding, | |
| Oct. 31, 1978 ............................................... | 650.4 |

| | Transactions with Swiss National Bank |
|---|---|
| Reciprocal currency arrangements | |
| Commitments outstanding, | |
| July 31, 1978 ............................................... | 22.9 |
| Drawings or repayments ( − ), | |
| Aug. 1–Oct. 31, 1978 .................................... | 294.2 |
| Commitments outstanding, | |
| Oct. 31, 1978 ............................................... | 317.0 |
| Special swap arrangement | |
| Commitments outstanding, | |
| July 31, 1978 ............................................... | 278.8 |
| Repayments, Aug.1–Oct. 31, 1978 ................ | − 91.9 |
| Commitments outstanding | |
| Oct. 31, 1978 ............................................... | 186.9 |
| U.S. Treasury securities (foreign currency series) | |
| Commitments outstanding, | |
| July 31, 1978 ............................................... | 850.4 |
| Issues or redemptions ( − ) | |
| Aug. 1–Oct. 31, 1978 .................................... | − 137.5 |
| Commitments outstanding, | |
| Oct. 31, 1978 ............................................... | 712.9 |

*Source:* "Treasury and Federal Reserve Foreign Exchange Operations: Interim Report," Federal Reserve Bulletin, December 1978, Table 2.

The Federal Reserve indicates that its intervention operations late in 1978 "were fully coordinated with intervention by other central banks in their own markets and in New York for their own account."

Before we consider the motivation for such intervention (and for fixing exchange rates generally) and the long-term consequences, it is worth considering the short-term monetary impact of these large volumes of official capital flows. For purposes of discussion we will take the recent case, in which the central banks were cooperating in an attempt to prevent the appreciation of their currencies against the dollar. This of course involved central bank purchase of dollars with other currencies on a net basis in the exchange markets. We will discuss two alternative intervention procedures.[13]

### Foreign Central Bank Intervention

Let us initially suppose that the sellers of dollars are foreign commercial banks, and that the foreign central banks invest all their purchased dollars in treasury bills. Then the purchase of dollars with foreign currencies raises the reserves of foreign commercial banks. The foreign dollar assets bought by the foreign central banks are claims on U.S. commercial banks. So the latter lose reserves once the foreign central banks purchase treasury bills. However with sales of treasury bills to foreign central banks, less treasury bills need to be sold to domestic residents, and this leaves in the U.S. banking system the amount of the treasury bill sales to foreign central banks. Hence, nothing happens to U.S. bank reserves, and foreign commercial bank reserves rise. Since U.S. residents now hold fewer treasury bills we would expect them to try to purchase more, with the result that treasury bill yields should be lower than without the intervention.

If the foreign central banks purchased dollar-denominated assets other than treasury bills, nothing would be changed. Say they purchased Eurodollar deposits instead. There is a very strong arbitrage connection between Eurodollar rates and equivalent maturity domestic instruments, as illustrated in Figure 6.1. Large Eurodollar deposits drive down Eurodollar yields, causing a flow of funds into the domestic capital market, where the outcome is essentially the same as before. If the sellers of dollars are U.S. commercial banks or the nonbank sector the results are again the same, as the dollars sold are still claims on U.S. commercial banks.

### Intervention by the Federal Reserve

The swap arrangements give the Federal Reserve the power to create foreign money and then put it into circulation by buying dollars with it.

---

[13]A more comprehensive treatment, including a flow-of-funds analysis, can be found in A. Balbach, "The Mechanics of Intervention in Exchange Markets," *Review*, Federal Reserve Bank of St. Louis, February 1978, 2–7.

**Figure 6.1** Selected Eurodollar and U.S. Money Market Rates (Averages for Week Ending Wednesday)

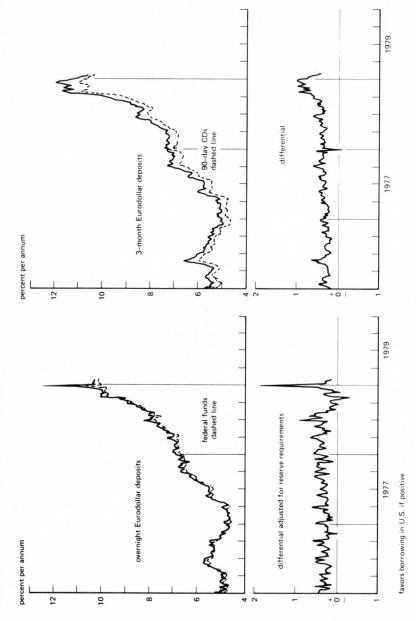

Source: "Selected Interest and Exchange Rates: Weekly Series of Charts," Division of International Finance, Board of Governors, Federal Reserve System, February 5, 1979.

The outcome for foreign commercial bank reserves and U.S. commercial bank reserves is the same as in the previous case—the latter stay the same and the former rise by the amount of the intervention. Moreover, the Treasury now has effectively issued (nonmarketable) securities to the foreign central banks, so it borrows less from the domestic sector than without the intervention so that in this case also treasury bill yields tend to fall.

The bottom line on these calculations is very simple—intervention acts automatically to increase the money supply of the currencies which are being held down by the intervention operation. This has caused the money supplies of the major intervening foreign countries to balloon in 1978 compared with 1977, as is shown in Table 6.6. If the exchange market pressure for appreciation is large enough, a central bank resisting the trend will lose control of its money supply. This happened in Germany in the late 1960s and was instrumental in causing the Bundesbank to abandon its policy of undervaluing the DM. The inflation implications of continual pegging against a strong market pressure should be evident from Table 6.6.

**Table 6.6**  *Comparative Growth of Money Supplies (%)*

| Country | 1977 | 1978 |
| --- | --- | --- |
| Germany | 10.4 | 14.0 |
| Japan | 6.0 | 13.3 |
| Switzerland | 2.0 | 26.0 |

*Source:* "International Economic Conditions," Federal Reserve Bank of St. Louis, January 10, 1979.

Why do governments intervene in exchange markets? We can distinguish two types of intervention, with different motives attached to each. They are short-term or "in-and-out" intervention, and sustained pegging against parity. We commence with the short-term activity.

## In-and-Out Intervention

Perusal of the Federal Reserve Bulletin, or of the comparable publications of other central banks, reveals that central bankers do not have very high regard for the intelligence of private traders. They view private traders as

- inclined to irrational panics and enthusiasms; and

- less capable than the monetary authorities of perceiving the underlying fundamental value of currencies.

The intent of U.S. stabilization efforts is to allow fundamental factors to be reflected in rates but to offset the irrational movement.[14] In Section 6.2 we explained that the dependence of the exchange markets on anticipations of other traders' anticipations does leave the situation without firm ground. We do not care to pursue the question of the appropriateness of the central bankers' perceptions here, and make note only of the following points.

- The fact that the private market could behave peculiarly does not establish that it will, or that on any specific occasion that it has.

- The central banks are also subject to important obstacles to intelligent trading. First, they have yet to show their understanding of economic fundamentals to be superior to that of private traders. And second, they are subject to political pressure to manipulate rates to accord with elections, wage negotiations, and other events. It is not clear whether the irrational pressures emanating from the private or the official sectors are the more disturbing.

**Sustained Intervention**

All sustained exchange market intervention is aimed not at rectifying defects in the exchange market but rather at using exchange rates to affect matters in the domestic economy. We can partition the motivation into Keynesian-type aggregate demand management on the one hand, and resource or income reallocations on the other. The easiest way to understand the demand management motive is to see an argument that justifies it. Therefore we will now develop the so-called "Swan Diagram," named after its inventor, the Australian economist Trevor Swan.

  Let us continue to call $S$ the spot exchange rate, and let $R$ denote the interest rate. Figure 6.2 then shows all combinations of $R$ and $S$ that exactly maintain full employment and price stability. As you can see, higher interest rates require currency depreciation to maintain internal balance. The reasoning is as follows: in the Keynesian perspective, ag-

---

[14]"As has been traditionally the case, the U.S. official intervention during the period (August–October 1978) was not designed to reverse the fundamental market forces at work, but rather to provide for smooth adjustment of the foreign exchange rates to market forces so efficient financing of international flows of commerce could be ensured." "International Letter," Federal Reserve Bank of Chicago, No. 384, December 8, 1978.

gregate demand determines aggregate supply. We start from the well-known income equals expenditure identity for an economy with trade:

$$C + I + G + X = C + S + T + IM^{15}$$

or

$$(I - S) + (G - T) + (X - IM) = 0 \qquad \textbf{(6.6)}$$

Equation 6.6 says that net investment plus net government expenditure must always be offset by a current account deficit of the same amount. So far we have a tautology (for the economy can only draw net resources from abroad). Now let's forget about $G$ and $T$, which the government supposedly controls, and look at the remaining items. We assume that when the nominal interest rate rises, net investment falls. To maintain aggregate demand at a satisfactory level we must now run a bigger current account surplus, which supposedly happens when $S$ rises, that is, when the currency depreciates. Figure 6.2 shows that internal balance can be maintained with high $R$, $S$ pairs, low $R$, $S$ pairs, or appropriate mixtures. The labels for unemployment region and inflation region should now be self-explanatory.

Figure 6.3 shows the combinations of $R$ and $S$ that maintain an exact zero on the balance of payments. The nominal interest rate is supposed

**Figure 6.2** Internal Balance Conditions

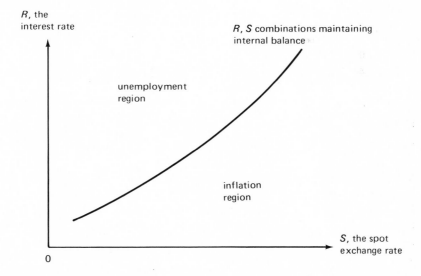

---

[15]$C$ is aggregate consumption, $I$ is investment, $G$ is government expenditure, $T$ is taxes, $X$ is exports, $S$ is savings, $IM$ is imports. These are the standard concepts around which all national income accounts are composed.

**Figure 6.3**   External Balance Conditions

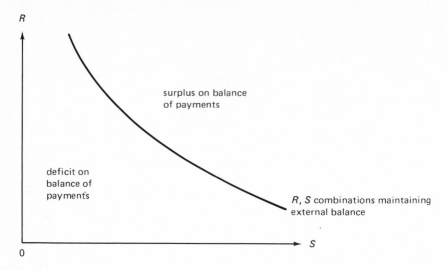

to influence the capital account, and the spot rate influences the current account. If R is low there is capital outflow. For balance we require a surplus on the current account, that is, we need a high S. The reader can now interpret the surplus and deficit regions in Figure 6.3. Figure 6.4 puts the previous two together, and shows the unique combination of R and S that is everywhere balancing. If the economy does not have this blissful combination it will be suffering from one of the diseases listed

**Figure 6.4**   The Entire Economy

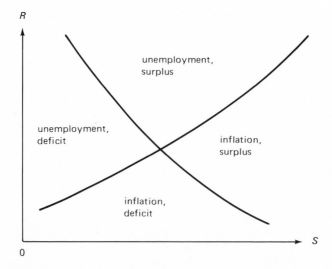

on the chart. The Keynesian view of the world thus requires governments simultaneously to manipulate interest rates and exchange rates to keep the economy in a sound state of health.

This is not a textbook on macroeconomics (at least not more than it needs to be, given the nature of our subject) so we will not analyze this view in depth, but rather leave some questions for the reader to think about.

1. Do nominal or real interest rates affect investment and savings, and can the government affect real interest rates more than transitorily?

2. How do the law of one price and our discussion of inflation square with the supposed relationship between S and the balance of payments on current account?

3. For how long are governments able to control the exchange rate by direct intervention?

In any event, many governments subscribe to some version of this Swan model, and their exchange market reactions vary accordingly.

Consider now the use of the exchange market to effect internal redistributions. From a domestic allocation point of view, the exchange rate has two features. On the consumption side it determines the cost of imports. On the production side it determines the relative attractiveness of the tradables sector vis-à-vis the nontradables sector. Many developing countries maintain an overvalued exchange rate, overvalued, that is, relative to purchasing power parity. Thus exports are too expensive and imports too cheap. This does not seem too good for the economy. The system is running a deficit, which must be funded by the taxpayers whose reserves of foreign exchange are being used up and who must pay the interest on the loans taken out by the government to replenish the reserves. One conjectural explanation is that the function of the overvaluation is to transfer income from the payers of taxes to the consumers of imports, who are often the educated, skilled, landowning, or otherwise wealthy minority.[16]

---

[16]Unfortunately it also transfers the taxpayers' money to foreigners as well. For example, take Mexico in the period 1954–1976 when the peso was pegged at a more and more unrealistic value from a puchasing power parity viewpoint. Suppose you had a Mexican subsidiary producing rubber boots, and suppose further that this subsidiary had no real growth—it produced the same number of boots in 1976 as in 1954. The peso earnings would have risen at the Mexican inflation rate. And as the exchange rate was pegged by the government, the dollar earnings would also have risen at the Mexican inflation rate. All those growing dollar dividends were actually a constant real dividend plus a growing reverse foreign aid from the Mexican taxpayer. This has obvious implications from a corporate control point of view—if you evaluate performance by dollar earnings, at least use parity rates to translate. On a more general note it is ironic and disturbing that developing countries should bestow largesse of this form on corporations from developed countries.

Sometimes governments deliberately undervalue their currencies in the expectation that the tradables sector will expand more and that this will be in some way socially beneficial. The governments of Japan and Germany come to mind. For both of them this process has come to a very unpleasant end, and we should try to understand the reasons.[17] When one looks at things in terms of real consumption power, undervaluation is much harder to defend than overvaluation. At least in the latter case you consume more than you produce (for a time!), whereas the perpetual surplus connected with undervaluation implies continual exchange of real goods in return for IOUs (other countries' moneys) that are never called. In fact this resource transfer is by no means the major cost of such a policy.

Recollect our discussion in Chapter 5, Section 5.6, of the effects of attempts to gain competitive advantage for the tradables sector by maintaining an undervalued exchange rate. As we have made clear, this process expands the money supply, causes inflation, and restores parity by raising the price level to make it appropriate to full parity at the previously undervalued exchange rate. If the undervaluing countries are going to maintain the initially-arranged attractiveness of the tradables sector they will have to impose monetary squeezes to try to contain the inflation which is restoring the original relative prices between tradables and nontradables.[18] These squeezes fall disproportionately on the nontradable goods sector, because its customers are all domestic and are harmed by the tight credit conditions. Because of the active foreign demand at the undervalued exchange rate, the export sector always grows. Thus over time more and more of new investment and employment is found in the tradables sector, as the capital structure of the economy is distorted from its free market (and efficient) configuration.

This could go on forever. The economies of the countries with undervalued exchange rates would produce less than they otherwise would (but more tradables), in addition to which goods are given away in return for pieces of paper. If the governments of Germany and Japan had been willing to make contractual commitments never to cash in the IOUs the deficit countries would have had nothing to fear—they would have had no deficits![19] Without such a commitment, the dollar overhang, sterling overhang, and decline in gold and reserves became frightening. People

---

[17]Our discussion is drawn from R. Dunn, Jr., "Exchange-Rate Rigidity, Investment Distortions, And the Failure of Bretton Woods," *Essays in International Finance,* 97, February 1973, International Finance Section, Department of Economics, Princeton University.

[18]Effectively it would be less trouble (but more blatant) to subsidize all exports and tax all imports. This would draw resources into export- and import-competing production, in response to these false price signals. Using our discussion of trade in Chapter 3, the reader can verify the basic inefficiency of sustained nonparity exchange rates.

[19]From an accounting point of view the deficit on current account would have been offset by an equal entry in the gifts and unilateral transfers account!

started to speculate that the fixed exchange rate constellation would change. The speculation only served to increase the deficits (and corresponding surpluses), and the system did indeed break down, with exchange rates moving decisively in the purchasing power parity direction. This is when the real trouble began for Germany and Japan—the mix of industrial output was no longer appropriate for the new relative prices which emerged. The consequence is economic loss of capital and large-scale structural unemployment. People and resources had to move from old industries into new ones.[20] This phenomenon, together with the increase in the relative price of energy, explains the recent lower real growth rates in these economies.[21] One can apply a symmetrical analysis to economies like Britain in which the currency was overvalued for a sustained period. This caused an inefficient contraction of the tradable goods sector and major adjustment problems subsequently.

As a final point, it should be clear that there is an unfortunate political dynamic in all such structural distortion situations that tends to postpone adjustment as long as possible. Thus when it comes, the impact is extremely severe. The reasoning is simple. The artificially-encouraged sector sees the bulk of the new investment and new employment. This is the source of contributions to political parties, new votes, and new careers. It will be very difficult successfully to advocate proposals harmful to interests in the expanding industries.

## 6.4  SHORT-TERM EXCHANGE RATE BEHAVIOR AND FORECASTING

We have seen that forward and spot exchange rates are in a basic sense speculatively determined prices. They share this characteristic with common stocks, bonds, options, and other financial assets. A minimal requirement for the efficient operation of these markets is that they should generate no "sure things"—that is, it should not be possible to make money by applying some mechanical trading rule based on past prices. In the last few years the intertemporal pattern of spot and forward exchange rates has been intensively studied. We will present a survey of the major results.[22] From our perspective there are two major questions:

1.   How useful are forward rates as predictors of the spot rate on the maturity date of the forward?

---

[20]The Germans disguised their unemployment problem because they were able to send many of the "guestworkers" from other countries back home. Were these included in measured unemployment, Germany would have had an impressive total in the period 1973–1977.

[21]Some very perceptive comment on these issues may be found in the cover story of the April 3, 1978 edition of "International Finance," Economics Group, The Chase Manhattan Bank.

[22]References for further reading will be found at the end of the chapter.

2.    Are there useful predictive models based on perceptible patterns in past forward rate or spot rate movements?

We take these questions in turn.

Tests of the value of the forward rates as forecasts are constructed as follows. Let

$S(t)$ = spot rate at any date $t$
$F^m(t)$ = forward rate with maturity $m$ quoted at date $t$.
    Thus this forward refers to delivery at date $t + m$.

Then after forward contracts have matured we can measure the forecast error at any date $t$ in the past by computing

$$d(t, m) = S(t + m) - F^m(t) \qquad\qquad (6.7)$$

Of course if we had any other forecast $H^m(t)$ of $S(t + m)$ at date $t$ we could, after the event, compute a similar forecast discrepancy. A conventional statistical measure is the mean squared error, where the errors $d(t, m)$ are squared and averaged. This allows us to evaluate the magnitude of the prediction error independent of whether it is a positive (underestimate) or negative (overestimate) error.[23] Of course one also looks at the simple mean, to check for a consistent tendency to overestimate or underestimate.

The results of such testing are as follows. First, forward rates seem to be the approximate mean of the spot rates on the maturity date of the forward contract—there is not sustained over- or underestimation. Second, as one might expect, the quality of the forecasts has deteriorated as we have moved from fixed rates to floating rates. There is now much more dispersion than there used to be. This is shown in Table 6.7. This not an indictment of the floating exchange rate system but principally a reflection of the great instability in the world economy since 1971, and particularly since 1973. Third, and again as one might expect, the quality of the forecasts deteriorates as the forecasting horizon moves further ahead. Taking the example of the DM/$ exchange rate, this is shown in Table 6.8.

It seems that there are no free gains to be made by forecasting future spot rates using some extrapolation of past spot rate behavior. We quote a relatively recent study of the subject.[24]

The market prices forward exchange as if the stochastic process generating exchange rates can be depicted as a diffusion process with a trend. There is some evidence to indicate that such a pricing system ignores

---

[23]For the reader who desires a brief and clear explanation of methods of assessing forecasts along with an interesting application, we strongly recommend M. Prell, "How Well Do the Experts Forecast Interest Rates?", *Monthly Review*, Federal Reserve Bank of Kansas City, September–October 1973.

[24]B. Cornell, "Spot Rates, Forward Rates and Exchange Market Efficiency," *Journal of Financial Economics*, 5, 1977.

**Table 6.7** *Percentage of Three-Month Forward Rate Forecasts Within 0.5%, 1.0%, and 2.0% of Future Spot Rate*

| Country | 1967 0.5 | 1967 1.0 | 1967 2.0 | 1971 0.5 | 1971 1.0 | 1971 2.0 | 1972 0.5 | 1972 1.0 | 1972 2.0 | 1973 0.5 | 1973 1.0 | 1973 2.0 | 1974 0.5 | 1974 1.0 | 1974 2.0 | 1975 0.5 | 1975 1.0 | 1975 2.0 | 1967–1975 0.5 | 1967–1975 1.0 | 1967–1975 2.0 |
|---|---|---|---|---|---|---|---|---|---|---|---|---|---|---|---|---|---|---|---|---|---|
| Canada | 57 | 83 | 100 | 45 | 61 | 100 | 31 | 43 | 92 | 33 | 60 | 87 | 16 | 36 | 92 | 0 | 17 | 83 | 44 | 66 | 90 |
| United Kingdom | 66 | 68 | 70 | 4 | 37 | 50 | 12 | 24 | 34 | 2 | 6 | 14 | 6 | 14 | 38 | 17 | 34 | 67 | 25 | 44 | 61 |
| Belgium | 91 | 100 | 100 | 34 | 38 | 42 | 47 | 68 | 86 | 6 | 14 | 20 | 4 | 8 | 16 | 17 | 34 | 83 | 48 | 60 | 69 |
| France | 57 | 100 | 100 | 53 | 61 | 71 | 22 | 47 | 75 | 4 | 10 | 16 | 2 | 4 | 26 | 0 | 0 | 0 | 28 | 48 | 63 |
| Germany | 54 | 98 | 100 | 8 | 12 | 24 | 29 | 56 | 72 | 6 | 8 | 12 | 4 | 10 | 16 | 17 | 50 | 67 | 28 | 45 | 60 |
| Italy | 98 | 100 | 100 | 36 | 42 | 74 | 59 | 69 | 85 | 10 | 20 | 34 | 8 | 18 | 40 | 0 | 0 | 0 | 48 | 62 | 75 |
| Netherlands | 94 | 100 | 100 | 14 | 28 | 42 | 22 | 42 | 77 | 6 | 10 | 20 | 6 | 10 | 20 | 17 | 34 | 100 | 36 | 56 | 70 |
| Switzerland | 64 | 94 | 100 | 25 | 29 | 56 | 12 | 30 | 72 | 4 | 8 | 16 | 4 | 8 | 14 | 17 | 50 | 67 | 38 | 58 | 70 |
| Japan | — | — | — | 47 | 57 | 57 | 15 | 28 | 43 | 10 | 14 | 31 | 10 | 18 | 30 | 17 | 17 | 34 | 29 | 36 | 46 |
| Average | 73 | 93 | 96 | 30 | 41 | 57 | 28 | 45 | 71 | 9 | 17 | 28 | 7 | 14 | 32 | 11 | 26 | 56 | 36 | 53 | 67 |

*Source:* Richard M. Levich, "Tests of Forecasting Models and Market Efficiency in the International Money Market," from Jacob A. Frenkel/Harry G. Johnson, eds., *The Economics of Exchange Rates,* © 1978, Addison-Wesley, Reading, Massachusetts. Table 4. Reprinted with permission.

**Table 6.8**  *Percentage of Forward Rate Forecast Errors Within Neutral Bands*[a]

| Width of neutral band | 1-month | Horizon 3-month | 6-month |
|---|---|---|---|
| 0.5% | 47 | 28 | 13 |
| 1.0% | 68 | 45 | 26 |
| 2.0% | 80 | 60 | 47 |
| 3.0% | 87 | 66 | 55 |
| 4.0% | 92 | 72 | 59 |
| 5.0% | 94 | 77 | 66 |

[a]Germany only, 1967–1975.

*Source:* Richard M. Levich, "Tests of Forecasting Models and Market Efficiency in the International Money Market," from Jacob A. Frenkel/Harry G. Johnson, eds., *The Economics of Exchange Rates,* © 1978, Addison-Wesley, Reading, Massachusetts. Table 9. Reprinted with permission.

information in past exchange rates in the case of the pound, Canadian dollar and yen. It is also possible that observed auto-correlations for these exchange rates (which are marginal) are the result of random errors and the use of bid prices, and are, therefore, properly ignored by an efficient market.

Are there better forecasts than the forward rate? (By "better" we mean sufficiently improved to make money while playing the forward market, allowing for transactions costs.) Apart from one important circumstance, it is highly unlikely that an improved forecasting method will become public knowledge, let alone appear in a textbook. As long as it is secret it will make money for its investors; once it is public it will be incorporated in the forward rates and cease to be superior.

The one circumstance in which one can beat the forward market is to play against central banks, when the latter are attempting to defend unviable exchange rates. If central banks are pegging spot rates they are also, of course, pegging forward rates because of the covered interest arbitrage tie given in Equation 6.2. This is the way they establish losing gambles for themselves. All speculative forward flows precipitate incipient forward exchange rate changes, leading to covered interest arbitrage flows, which translate these forward speculations into spot market demands that the central banks have committed themselves to satisfy. How do you know when central banks are intervening these days? It is harder, because they announce no week-by-week targets. And for how long can they sustain rates unviable on a purchasing power parity basis? This depends on a number of factors.

1.  The size of reserves and the rate of reserve loss, and the capacity to borrow, for a country overvaluing its rates.

2.  The ability to neutralize money supply impacts, and the considerations in (1.) for its deficit-ridden trading partners, for a country undervaluing its rates. In addition there remains a certain element of arbitrariness. If a pegging policy is basically unviable, a strong-enough perception that it will come unglued can precipitate enough speculative flows to bring the event about. Such a perception can arise from a variety of economic and political factors. Exchange rate speculation is no more of a sure thing than any other commodity futures gambling, for essentially the same reasons.

## 6.5  SUMMARY

Whereas our analysis of long-run exchange rate behavior was both plausible and reasonably in accord with observed events, this chapter has undoubtedly seemed frustrating. We have presented many of the elements which must be included in an adequate analysis of short-run exchange rate behavior, without having tied them together in a coherent story. We are unable to do this because some key elements in any such tale are simply not understood. There are two, both related to the discretion of participants in the exchange market. The first is anticipations of future spot rates. Neither in the field of international finance nor in the fields of stock market and commodity market analysis are the processes of anticipation formation understood. Without this knowledge we cannot give a definitive analysis of the short-term functioning of a free-floating exchange rate system. The second missing ingredient is an explanation for the magnitude and timing of government market interventions. We have indicated the large number of possible motivations and the strong actual or perceived connections with domestic economic and political factors.

Even in the presence of some limitations on capital flows, the covered interest arbitrage relationship links the spot rate with the forward rate for each maturity and the two national interest rates for corresponding maturities. We have put forward the model that assumes that in the short term the spot rate is pulled around by the actions of speculators in the forward markets, and by short-term interest rates. Available evidence is consistent with the assumption that the forward rates are determined by speculators gambling on future spot rates.

While we are not able to predict government exchange market interventions, we can say strong things about the implications of these interventions for the money supply, and therefore for the capital markets. Countries holding down the value of their currencies will experience monetary expansion, and countries holding up the value of their currencies will experience monetary contraction. Governments have no trouble offsetting monetary contraction, but it has proven difficult, in Germany or Switzerland, for example, to adequately sterilize monetary expansions caused by market interventions. Frequently the danger of mushrooming inflation has forced these currencies off the fixed parities their central banks were trying to maintain.

The chapter concluded with an inquiry into the efficiency of the foreign exchange markets, along lines comparable to efficiency studies of markets for common stocks and commodity futures. Intensive study of the monetary system has yielded the following conclusions:

- forward rates seem to be the approximate mean of the spot rates on the maturity dates of the forward contracts—that is, they represent on average correct forecasts of future spot rates; and

- there is no systematic correlation over time in the behavior of spot or forward rates. So forecasting models based on extrapolation of price trends are of no value.

We will have succeeded in our aims if this chapter and the last have given the reader a better intuitive feel for events in the international money markets than he or she previously had. The next step is detailed statistical study of the specific economies in which the reader has an interest, overlaid with a very liberal application of experience.


### EXERCISE

**Forecasting Exchange Rates**

1. Introduction

   The purpose of this exercise is to familiarize the reader with the behavior of spot and forward exchange rates, and with some of the problems of exchange rate prediction. For the most part it involves the charting of data, although the section on short-term forecasts provides equations that allow the generation of rate forecasts using equipment no more sophisticated than a hand calculator. One may carry out the charting exercises for any pair of currencies. We provide short-term forecasting equations only for a number of developed countries.

   There is, potentially, a second and more sophisticated level to this exercise. All the economic forecasting models are incapable of allowing for the discretionary actions of economic policy makers. We have strongly emphasized the importance (at least for short-term movements) of these deliberate acts of policy in the body of Chapter 6. We have also emphasized that many policy actions taken primarily or solely with an eye to domestic repercussions must also have impacts upon the exchange markets. The converse also holds true—many policy actions taken on the basis of developments in the currency markets have internal repercussions. We offer the example of the impact on the U.S. Treasury bill market of the buildup and rundown of dollar-denominated intervention reserves by other central banks, discussed at the end of Chapter 4. We recommend the following as the framework for a much more substantial learning experience.

a. Carry out this exercise for a chosen pair of currencies.

b. Try to explain the various anomalies that are discovered by a detailed look at events in the two economies concerned.

We recommend the following information sources: "International Financial Statistics," IMF; The London "Financial Times"; "The Economist"; "International Finance," published biweekly by the Chase Manhattan Bank; "World Financial Markets," published by the Morgan Guaranty Trust Company; "Euromoney"; "International Letter," published by the Federal Reserve Bank of Chicago; "International Economic Conditions," published by the Federal Reserve Bank of St. Louis; and the press of the countries concerned, to the extent that the language is accessible.

2. Forward Rates As Predictors of Spot Rates

Using historical quotations[25] of forward and futures rates and spot rates, on a daily or last-day-of-week basis, carry out the following exercises in data analysis:

a. Take four or five futures contracts that have recently matured. Using the framework given in Figure 6.5, plot the market quotes relative to the final spot rate, as a function of days to maturity.

b. Take a reasonably large number of 30-, 60-, and 90-day forward or futures quotations, for delivery dates which have already occurred. Do this for a number of currencies. Using the framework of Table 6.9, plot all the 90-day quotations relative to the spot rate that actually occurred 90 days later. Do the same thing for the 30- and 60-day quotations.

**Table 6.9** *Forecast Accuracy as a Function of the Forecast Horizon*

$X$ = day forward quotations plotted relative to the actual spot rate on maturity.

| | < 1% | < 5% | < 10% | < 25% |
|---|---|---|---|---|
| Fraction of Quotations | above | above | above | above |
| Fraction of Quotations | < 1% below | < 5% below | < 10% below | < 25% below |

Does forecast accuracy increase as the horizon is shortened? Does forecast accuracy vary from one currency pair to the next? (It is particularly instructive to compare currency pairs where both are within the European joint float to currency pairs of which at least one is outside the float.)

3. Forward Rates and Purchasing Power Parity Estimates
In this part of the exercise we will see how congruent actual forward rates are

---

[25]These quotations can be found in two convenient locations. One is obviously the *Wall Street Journal*. The other is the annual *Yearbook* series of the International Monetary Market division of the Chicago Mercantile Exchange.

**Figure 6.5**   Convergence of Futures Quotations Do futures rates converge smoothly the closer is the contract to maturity? Would you expect them to?

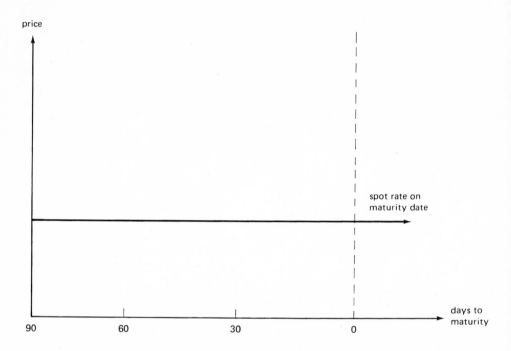

with purchasing power parity estimators that we will construct by simple extrapolation.

a. **Construction of PPP estimators.**  For each pair of currencies, using a base year in the early 1960s, construct monthly wholesale price indexes and from them, construct a PPP exchange rate index. The most convenient data source will be "International Financial Statistics," from the IMF.

To construct an *estimator* we have to somehow project (wholesale) price index behavior into the future, in a relevant manner. Because of shipping lags, trade in any given month is most likely to be affected by the prices of two months earlier (as we discuss in Chapter 5). Thus we can use the existing monthly price indexes to make PPP forecasts 30 days out and 60 days out. To get 90 days out, we must extrapolate the price index by one month. We suggest graph paper, a pencil, and a ruler. Label this "linear time series extrapolative estimator."

b. **Comparison of Forward Rates and PPP Estimators.**  Using the framework of Table 6.8, compare the PPP and forward rates with each other, and then compare each with the spot rate that actually occurred 30, 60, or 90 days later. You have already undertaken the forward rate/spot rate comparison as part 1 of this exercise.

**Table 6.10** *Comparative Evaluation of Forward Rates and PPP Extrapolations as Forecasts*

X-day forward quotations plotted relative to X-day constructed PPP estimators.

| Fraction of Quotations | Within 1% of PPPE | Within 5% of PPPE | Within 10% of PPPE | Within 25% of PPPE |
|---|---|---|---|---|
| | | | | |

X-day constructed PPP estimators plotted relative to the actual spot rate X days later.

| Fraction of Estimates | Within 1% of Spot | Within 5% of Spot | Within 10% of Spot | Within 25% of Spot |
|---|---|---|---|---|
| | | | | |

Which estimator is better? Does this seem to vary from currency to currency?

3.  **Short Term Forecasting Models**
    In this section we provide a number of equations used to make predictions of end-of-month spot rates. In order to use the models for prediction purposes, you must plug in the appropriate values of the explanatory variables. The equations use a one-month lag, so putting in this month's values will generate a prediction for the spot rate at the end of next month. For each equation we give $R^2$, which is the proportion of the total movement in the exchange rate captured by the explanatory variables that we chose, over the historical period we used for estimation purposes. This was the 44 months up to the beginning of 1979.
    Using monthly figures from January 1979 onwards, you should do the following:

    a.  Generate forecasts of the next month's spot rate.

    b.  Obtain from the *Wall Street Journal* or elsewhere the 30-day forward quotes on the same exchange rates.[26]

    c.  Using the general framework of Table 6.8, compare the forward quotes with the forecasts generated by the estimating equations, and compare both with the spot rate that actually occurred.

### Prediction Models

All models take the general form (spot rate, *indirect quotation*) $= a + b.B + c.C + d.D + e.E + f.F + g.G + h.H$ where:

- • lower case letters denote coefficients of the predicting equation, and were estimated by us; and

- • upper case letters denote the variables used to explain the spot rate, whose values for each month you must put in and multiply by the estimated coefficients to generate the spot rate forecast.

---

[26]Recollect that triangular arbitrage allows you to make cross-rate computations of forward rates.

We use the following convention. Indirect quotes are written, for example, "dollars per pound", or "francs per DM". The first currency (dollars, or francs) is the currency of Country 1. The second currency (pounds, or DM) is the currency of Country 2. Then

$B$ = industrial production index for Country 2 minus industrial production index for Country 1, previous month

$C$ = rate of change of money supply between month before last and last month for Country 2, minus the comparable rate for Country 1

$D$ = share price index for Country 2 minus share price index for Country 1, previous month

$E$ = 90-day interest rate for Country 2 minus 90-day interest rate for Country 1, previous month

$F$ = change in CPI between month before last and last month for Country 2, minus that for Country 1

$G$ = change in WPI between month before last and last month for Country 2, minus that for Country 1.

$H$ = change in government bond yield between month before last and last month for Country 2, minus that for Country 1

All data are from the IMF "International Financial Statistics."

*Model 1 United States/United Kingdom* Indirect quote spot rate is dollars per pound, so all explanatory variables are U.K. figures less U.S. figures.

$$(\text{spot rate}) = 2.6116 + .03299. \, B + .09126. \, C + .00316. \, D - .09274. \, E - .0152. \, F - .00286. \, G + .01712. \, H$$
$R^2 = .90$

*Model 2 Netherlands/United States* Indirect quote spot rate is guilders per dollar, so all explanatory variables are U.S. figures less Netherlands figures.

$$(\text{spot rate}) = 2.2918 - .0148 \, B - .2401 \, C + .00761 \, D - .1048 \, E - .00968 \, F - .00701 \, G - .1477 \, H$$
$R^2 = .43$

*Model 3 United States/Japan* Indirect quote spot rate is yen per dollar, so all explanatory variables are U.S. figures less Japan figures.

$$(\text{spot rate}) = 353.4 + .3183 \, B + .5688 \, C + .7688 \, D - 37.817 \, E - 1.3796 \, F - .724 \, G - 3.5058 \, H$$
$R^2 = .92$

*Model 4 France/Japan* Indirect quote spot rate is yen per franc, so all explanatory variables are France figures less Japan figures.

$$(\text{spot rate}) = 71.76 + .497b \, B - 2.4256 \, C + .00299 \, D - 12.1 \, E + .0887 \, F - .802 \, G + .3756 \, H$$
$R^2 = .94$

*Model 5 United Kingdom/Germany* Indirect quote spot rate is DM per pound, so all explanatory variables are U.K. figures less Germany figures.

$$(\text{spot rate}) = 6.2528 + .1448\,B + 3.1087\,C - .018\,D - .5098\,E - .00375\,F + .1194\,G - .004\,H$$

$$R^2 = .75$$

## Suggestions for Further Reading

W. B. Cornell and J. K. Dietrich, "The Efficiency of the Market for Foreign Exchange Under Floating Exchange Rates," *Review of Economics and Statistics, 60,* 1, February 1978.

W. B. Cornell, "Spot Rates, Forward Rates and Exchange Market Efficiency," *Journal of Financial Economics,* 5 (1977).

J. Frankel, "On the Mark: A Theory of Floating Exchange Rates Based on Real Interest Differentials," unpublished Ph.D. dissertation, Department of Economics, M.I.T., June 1978.

D. Kasuman, "The Forward Exchange Rate: Its Determination and Behavior as a Predictor of the Future Spot Rate," *Proceedings* of the American Statistical Association, 1973.

R. Levich, "Tests of Forecasting Models and Market Efficiency in the International Money Market," in J. Frenkel and H. G. Johnson (eds.), *The Economics of Exchange Rates: Selected Studies.* Reading, MA: Addison-Wesley, 1978.

R. Upson, "Random Walk and Forward Exchange Rates: A Spectral Analysis," *Journal of Financial and Quantitative Analysis, 7,* 4 (September 1972).

## Appendix 6.1  More on Covered Interest Arbitrage

The condition for zero profit on covered interest arbitrage is

$$\frac{F^t - S}{S} = r_A^t - \frac{F^t}{S} \cdot r_B^t \tag{A6-1}$$

where

$S$ = price of a unit of $B$'s currency in terms of
   $A$'s currency
$F^t$ = forward rate for maturity $t$
$r^t$ = interest rate for maturity $t$

In this appendix we will look at a number of aspects of this relationship that are worthy of note.

### THE IMPACT OF CAPITAL FLOW CONTROLS

The Swiss franc seems to have often been overvalued on a purchasing power parity basis in recent years. To try to alleviate this problem the Swiss National Bank has frequently resorted to some form of capital flow controls. In 1977, for example, they introduced a flat ban on inflows into instruments of duration $t$ = 30 days or less. This means that Equation A6-1 cannot hold for $t$ less than 30 days. We will consider what remains, taking seven day money in order to be concrete.

Under the Swiss rules, inflow was forbidden but outflow was not. Under what conditions would outflow be desirable?

1. Suppose the Swiss franc is at a discount to the dollar: $(F^7 - S)/S < 0$. This means that if you shift SF into US$ you get less SF back later, in the forward deal. Thus you are willing to make an outflow from Switzerland if: the U.S. interest rate is below the Swiss one, but not by as much as the discount; or, the U.S. interest rate is above the Swiss one. That is, if

$$r_A^7 - \frac{F^7}{S} r_{SF}^7 > \frac{F^7 - S}{S}$$

2. Suppose the SF is at a premium to the US$: $(F^7 - S)/S > 0$. This means that if you shift SF into US$ you get less SF back later, on the forward deal. Thus you are willing to make an outflow from Switzerland if the American interest rate is above the Swiss one by more than enough to cover the premium; or, again

$$r_A^7 - \frac{F^7}{S} r_{SF}^7 > \frac{F^7 - S}{S}$$

So an inequality in this direction will not last. People will take advantage of it and it is not subject to any restriction. However, if

$$r_A{}^7 - \frac{F^7}{S} r_{SF}{}^7 < \frac{F^7 - S}{S} \qquad \text{(A6-2)}$$

it pays to shift money into Switzerland, which is not allowed. Hence the inequality (A6-2) can persist for all the maturities less than 30 days.

## THE ARBITRAGING OF TRADE CREDIT

Even in the cases in which direct arbitrage flows are obstructed by governments, a kind of arbitrage is still possible by those commodity traders who choose to cover their foreign exchange obligations. It occurs through the process of offering trade credit and discounts for early payment. Consider the case of an American firm that imports goods from a Swiss exporter. The Swiss exporter's trade credit means that he is carrying the debt owed to him, either by borrowing in Switzerland, or with the Swiss interest rate as the opportunity cost of his funds. Hence the discount he is able to offer for prompt payment will be closely related to the short-term Swiss borrowing costs. Now look at the American purchaser who has decided to hedge her obligation. She can pay immediately, or pay later. If she pays immediately she has to borrow at the American rate to carry the inventory until it is sold. Thus the opportunity cost is the American short-term rate. On the other hand, she could buy forward Swiss francs and take advantage of the Swiss exporter's credit, at the implicit Swiss cost. In choosing the cheaper alternative, she is choosing to undertake a weak form of covered interest arbitrage.

### Alternative #1

Borrow US$ to hold inventory, buy SF spot, and pay the exporter promptly to earn the trade discount
Let us define

$Z$ = number of SF owed to the Swiss exporter

$r_{SF}{}^{30,D}$ = the interest rate implicit in the Swiss trade discount for 30 days early payment

$r_A{}^{30,B}$ = the interest rate charged in the U.S. to finance the holding of the inventory.

Then the cost of alternative #1, after 30 days, is

$$\frac{Z}{(1 + r_{SF}{}^{30,D})} \cdot S \cdot (1 + r_A{}^{30,B}) \qquad \text{(A6-3)}$$

The first term in A6-3 is the number of SF actually paid when the discount for early payment is taken.[27] S is of course the spot rate on the date at which the early payment is made. The final term is the cost of the inventory when it is financed in the United States.

---

[27]This is how we define $r_{SF}^{30,D}$. If early payment entitles the American importer to pay only Y SF rather than the nominal amount of Z, then we say that $Y = Z/(1 + r_{SF}^{30,D})$ or $r_{SF}^{30,D} = (Z - Y)/Y$

**Alternative #2**

Take the 30 day trade credit, and hedge the uncertainty in the spot rate 30 days hence by purchasing forward SF at the price $F^{30}$. Then the cost at the end of 30 days is just

$$Z \cdot F^{30}$$

The aim is to choose the cheaper alternative. So #1 will be chosen if

$$\left(\frac{Z}{1 + r_{SF}^{30,D}}\right) \cdot S \cdot (1 + r_A^{30,B}) < Z \cdot F^{30} \tag{A6.4}$$

Rearranging A6.4, we find it to be equivalent to the inequality

$$\frac{F^{30} - S}{S} > r_A^{30,B} - \frac{F^{30}}{S} \cdot r_{SF}^{30,D} \tag{A6.5}$$

The reader should now consider the alternative facing a Swiss importer of American goods, and derive an analogous relation to A6.5. Putting them together it will be found that the forward premium or discount must lie within a range, determined by the relevant discount rates and rates for borrowing against inventory in Switzerland and in the United States. The relationship looks a great deal like A6.1. The connection between interest rates, spot rates and forward rates implied by the trade credit process is looser than that implied by arbitrage on the capital markets for two reasons.

1.  Trade discounts are not nearly as flexible as are short-term interest rates.

2.  The financial interest rates are always less than the interest charged to traders on the security of inventory, and the two sets of rates do not move perfectly in parallel.

Nonetheless even in this extreme case where no borrowing and lending unrelated to trade is allowed to occur, we will have quite a strong relationship between forward premiums or discounts and domestic interest rates. So the general outline of the analysis in Section 6.2 will apply, but with much more leeway.

**Interlocking of Short-term Term Structures**

People who are not closely connected with international monetary questions often fail to realize that, in the presence of covered interest arbitrage, the term structures of interest rates of all countries that permit free capital flows are locked together. This connection is through the exchange markets and extends out to the maturity of the most distant forward contract.

Rearrange A6.1 as

$$S = F^t\left(\frac{1 + r_B^t}{1 + r_A^t}\right) \tag{A6.6}$$

and look at two different maturities, say $t = 90$ and $t = 180$ days. Then we must have

$$S = F^{90}\left(\frac{1 + r_B^{90}}{1 + r_A^{90}}\right) = F^{180}\left(\frac{1 + r_B^{180}}{1 + r_B^{180}}\right) \tag{A6.7}$$

We argue in Section 6.2 that forward rates are basically determined by speculation on future spot rates. If that is so, this speculation precisely defines the relationship between the term structures of any pair of countries. Suppose that currency speculators foresee no spot rate changes in the next half year. Then Equation A6.7 says that the two term structures are identical, at least up to 180 days out. If they were not then there would be opportunities to make covered interest arbitrage profits. Attempts to realize these would lead to such large short-term capital flows that interest rates would alter in one or both countries. We urge the reader to confirm this by working through some numerical examples using Equation A6.7 as a framework. If one country is very large relative to the other, the small country's term structure will be locked to that of the large one.[28] (See Table 6.11 and Figures 6.6 and 6.7.)

## *Appendix 6.2*   So You Thought This Was All "Theoretical", Eh?

We have developed at some length a theory of the interaction between exchange rates and inflation, an explanation of the causes of inflation and the effects of exchange market intervention on the money supply, and an (incomplete) discussion of short-term exchange market phenomena. In the United States until recently there was little concern with these phenomena, and some readers may remain skeptical of the value of so complex a tale. We are, accordingly, particularly pleased that the *Wall Street Journal* should publish an article which shows how virtually every one of these things works out in reality, in the case of Argentina.

We leave it to the reader to appreciate the fine points of this story. For example, note that when it is anticipated that Argentinian inflation will outstrip depreciation of the peso against the dollar, it is seen to pay to make short-term, uncovered dollar borrowings and make short-term deposits in pesos. Such flows tend to appreciate the peso against the dollar. This constitutes a perverse move from a purchasing power parity perspective, an outcome that we discussed in Chapter 6.

### KEEPING AHEAD[29]
#### BY EVERETT G. MARTIN
*Staff Reporter of the Wall Street Journal*

BUENOS AIRES—Besides being the world soccer champions, the Argentines can also claim the distinction of having the highest inflation rate in the world—170% last year, 140% or so this year. Yet they don't seem too disturbed about it.

"It's a topic of conversation," a U.S. businessman here says, "but I don't see any riots like you would anywhere else."

In fact, Argentines take a perverse pride in their inflation. Not only has the individual Argentine devised his stratagems for keeping ahead of it, every aspect of economic life is geared to live with it. "It has turned us into an economy of speculation instead of production," an economist says.

---

[28]Can't government monetary policy sterilize these arbitrage flows to maintain control over interest rates? Not if free capital flows are permitted. Even in an economy as large as that of Germany, the central bank lost control of the money supply in the late 1970s, under the pressure of an enormous volume of short-term capital inflow (although, as it happens, based on speculative rather than covered interest arbitrage considerations).

**Table 6.11** Index of Foreign Currency Price of the U.S. Dollar (May 1970=100).

| | 1976 | | | | End of period 1977 | | | | 1978 | | |
| --- | --- | --- | --- | --- | --- | --- | --- | --- | --- | --- | --- |
| | I | II | III | IV | I | II | III | IV | I | II | III | IV |
| Trade-weighted average against 22 OECD currencies[a] | 88.8 | 89.1 | 88.2 | 89.7 | 90.7 | 89.7 | 90.3 | 85.4 | 84.1 | 82.1 | 79.2 | 78.5 |
| Trade-weighted average against 10 currencies[b] | 86.8 | 87.9 | 87.0 | 86.2 | 86.6 | 85.6 | 85.1 | 79.5 | 77.4 | 77.1 | 73.2 | 71.3 |
| Selected currencies:[c] | | | | | | | | | | | | |
| Canada | 91.6 | 90.2 | 90.6 | 94.0 | 98.4 | 98.7 | 99.9 | 101.9 | 105.4 | 104.7 | 110.2 | 110.4 |
| France | 84.6 | 85.9 | 89.3 | 90.0 | 90.0 | 89.1 | 88.8 | 85.2 | 83.0 | 81.6 | 78.5 | 75.7 |
| Germany | 69.9 | 70.9 | 67.1 | 65.0 | 65.8 | 64.4 | 63.5 | 57.9 | 55.7 | 57.1 | 53.4 | 50.3 |
| Italy | 133.6 | 133.7 | 136.7 | 139.1 | 141.1 | 140.7 | 140.3 | 138.6 | 135.5 | 135.9 | 130.9 | 131.9 |
| Japan | 83.5 | 82.9 | 80.1 | 81.6 | 77.3 | 74.6 | 74.0 | 66.9 | 62.0 | 57.0 | 52.7 | 54.2 |
| Netherlands | 74.0 | 75.3 | 70.7 | 67.7 | 68.6 | 68.1 | 67.6 | 62.8 | 59.6 | 61.5 | 58.0 | 54.2 |
| Switzerland | 58.6 | 57.2 | 56.8 | 56.7 | 58.8 | 56.9 | 54.1 | 46.5 | 43.2 | 43.0 | 35.7 | 37.5 |
| United Kingdom | 125.4 | 134.9 | 143.2 | 141.1 | 139.7 | 139.6 | 137.6 | 126.0 | 129.4 | 129.1 | 121.8 | 118.1 |

[a]Australia, Austria, Belgium-Luxembourg, Canada, Denmark, Finland, France, Germany, Greece, Iceland, Ireland, Italy, Japan, the Netherlands, New Zealand, Norway, Portugal, Spain, Sweden, Switzerland, Turkey, United Kingdom. Data: U.S. Department of the Treasury.

[b]Belgium, Canada, France, Germany, Italy, Japan, the Netherlands, Sweden, Switzerland, United Kingdom. Data: Federal Reserve Board. The index has been revised as a result of a change in method of computation; for details, see the August 1978 *Federal Reserve Bulletin*.

[c]Data: International Monetary Fund.

**Figure 6.6**   Covered Interest Arbitrage: Three-Month Funds
Differential: Plus(+), Indicates Favor Dollar Assets Averages for
Week Ending Wednesday)

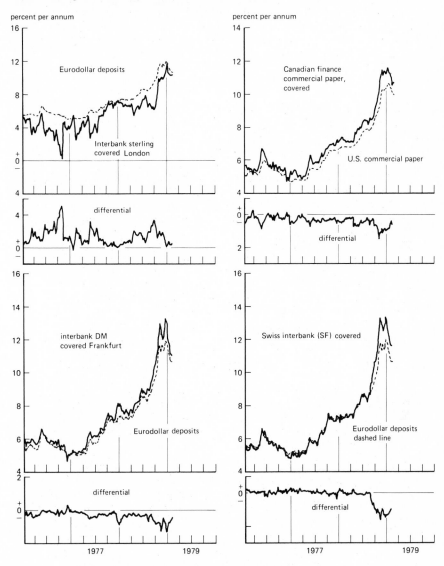

*Source:* "Selected Interest and Exchange Rates: Weekly Series of
Charts," Division of International Finance, Board of Governors,
Federal Reserve System," February 12, 1979, Chart No. 8.

**Figure 6.7**   Indexes of Foreign Currency Price of the U.S. Dollar
(May 1970 = 100) Note: Data are for end of month.

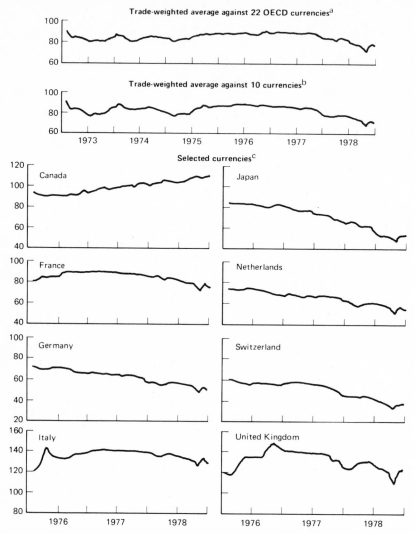

*Source:* U.S. Department of Commerce, Bureau of Economic
Analysis, "Survey of Current Business," March 1979, Chart 2, p. 40.

Watch any Argentine as he courses through the crowded streets of downtown
Buenos Aires and you get some idea of how inflation has programmed his behavior.
No matter how urgent his mission, he can't pass a bank without stopping to check
the latest interest rate on savings. At every money changer's establishment, he
pauses to note how the peso is doing against other currencies.

### Thinking in Real Terms

The foreigner may be completely confused, but Argentines young and old seem able to absorb all the pieces of information and calmly decide what to do next to protect the value of their money.

The editor of a business magazine boasts that "the entire Argentine population has a much better knowledge of financial matters than North Americans." To which a banker adds: "We always think in real terms. You give a worker a 20% raise when the inflation is 25% and he immediately wants to know why you are cutting his salary. And if you want a discussion of the money supply, just ask your cab driver."

Pensions are indexed so that purchasing power isn't lost, and it seems that most retired people own some property anyway. They also have the most free time to go from bank to bank manipulating their money.

Argentines watch the banks because interest rates are uncontrolled and banks may change them at any time. "Each day we look at our loan demand," the banker explains. "If we need more capital, we just push the savings rate up a bit. If the other banks don't counter us, within two days you see people begin switching over to us."

To be ready to make such quick shifts, three-fourths of the savers here buy only certificates of deposit with terms of 30 days or less. A simple passbook account would tie up a saver's money for even less time, but no Argentine would think of opening such an account because it pays far less interest than the CDs.

For all their inflation expertiese, Argentines are at a loss to tell Americans how to deal with their own, much lower inflation rate of 13.4%. "We have financial instruments and special tax provisions to protect us," the banker says. "You have nothing. You put your money in a savings account and you lose because the interest rate is negative compared with inflation, and then your government taxes you as if you had made a profit." Argentine tax laws don't allow that, he points out.

Argentine laws also don't allow inflation to push anyone into a higher tax bracket, and they keep businesses from being taxed on any profits attributable solely to inflation. "You should send people down here to study what we do," a local businessman consultant says, "because you are heading in the same direction."

Since January, very few savers in Argentina have been rushing to switch banks; the interest rates are only about 6.9% a month, which, in effect, is negative. The explanation for this, as anyone on the street can tell you, is that for a variety of economic and political reasons, dollar loans are cheaper than peso loans. Businesses are therefore seeking dollar loans, and the demand for pesos is down.

"The minute the people saw our rates become negative," the banker says, "they started buying hard goods like refrigerators, cars or apartments because they didn't want to hold pesos."

### Playing the Market

They also started playing the stock market with a vengeance. It looked like a reasonable gamble. And with so many people buying stocks, stock prices did move up.

One day in May, 104 stocks climbed and only 25 dropped. The shares of one manufacturing firm tripled that day. Between November and May, the shares of a paper company went to 300 pesos from seven pesos while those of a cement company rose to 1,600 pesos from 300 pesos. The president of a wallboard manufacturing firm said, "We haven't done anything, really, except survive these crazy times, yet the total value of our shares has risen to $27 million from $2 million since January."

Lately, stock prices have dropped a little, eliciting knowing looks for those sophisticated speculators who are wary of the stock market. These speculators engage in more complex financial maneuvers designed to play on the current difference between the rate of inflation and the rate of change in the relationship between the dollar and the peso. (At the moment, there are about 1,330 pesos to the dollar.) Likening the continual turnover of money to a pedaling action, Argentines give these maneuvers such colorful names as the bicycle, the reverse bicycle and the tricycle. "If you stop pedaling," a business consultant says, "you fall off."

Right now, with inflation rates higher than the rate of the dollar's rise against the peso, the reverse bicycle is the thing to do. A well-heeled speculator explains how: "You borrow $500,000 today. Use the dollars to buy a peso bond with principal and interest indexed to the inflation rate, hold it for a month, then liquidate to pay off your dollar loan. You can make $14,300 because the inflation has increased the amount of your pesos by 7% plus increasing the real interest on the bond, while the dollar has gone up less than 5%."

The bicycle involves the same sort of deals starting with the borrowing of pesos. As for the tricycle, it is an even-more-complex transaction involving a financial instrument that somehow makes everything you've earned tax-free. Despite his efforts, the helpful speculator was unable to make the process clear to this correspondent.

Over the years, whenever they could borrow short-term funds at rates that were less than inflation, Argentine manufacturers and many farmers learned that it was better to owe a peso than own one. Any attempt to cut costs has proved hopeless anyway, so a clever financial manager has become more valuable in producing profits than a skilled operations man or a merchandiser.

Retailers, too, have learned to think in terms of speculating instead of selling. "This is a country where retailers will raise prices during a recession to make up for their slower turnover" instead of lowering prices to lure customers, an economist says. "It doesn't matter too much if they sell their merchandise," he says, "because they think they are making money by its increasing value from inflation. One appliance-store owner I know showed a bigger profit, on paper, by closing up and going to the sea shore for a month than his competitor who stayed home trying to make sales."

In Argentina, retailing is done almost entirely through boutiques and corner food stores. "The key thing to remember," says Richard Ahrens, manager of Harrods, Buenos Aires's only department store, "is that people buy those little stores as real-estate investments. Sales don't really matter as long as inflation is pushing property values up."

One result is that many little shops display knit sport shirts for $140, cotton pajamas for $90. None of the shopkeepers seem to mind that customers aren't coming in.

### Blue Collars, Black Wages

Blue-collar workers also seem to be coping with life here. Argentina has full employment—the unemployment rate in Buenos Aires is down to 1.8%—and the military junta decrees frequent wage increases to keep labor peace. But that only tells part of the story. As one manufacturer explains it: "We can't afford to lose our skilled labor, so we have to give them all kinds of special payments under the table."

These so-called black wages make it impossible to determine the real wages of the work force, but they don't stop skilled people from jumping from job to job. In one meatpacking plant, for example, annual job turnover has risen from 10% to 50%.

Also, more factory workers are hiring themselves out on a temporary basis to companies desperate for their skills. One manufacturer whose absenteeism has doubled in recent months suspects that his workers are off somewhere else earning more money at a temporary job.

At least 400 temporary employment agencies have opened in Buenos Aires in the past year. Carlos A. Carril says his seven-month-old Lavantage agency has a registry of 5,000 workers from which he can supply just about any kind of skill.

"We charge for an emergency service," he says. "We haven't any interest in holding down the cost of the product being produced, so a worker can earn from 20% to 50% more with us."

Even at those rates, a temporary worker may be cheaper for an employer than a regular one because Argentine firms pay up to 115% of a regular employee's wages to the government for the various state welfare programs. The employment agency foots that bill for temporary workers, and in their case the payments are based on the minimum wage.

### Does Skill Hurt?

Economics Minister Jose Martinez de Hoz argues that his countrymen's skill at living with inflation is one of the root causes of its continuing fast pace.

Mr. Martinez de Hoz has been guiding the economy ever since the military seized control three years ago from the populist dictator Juan Peron. The Peronists had kicked off the latest binge of inflation with their spending. The military turned to Mr. Martinez de Hoz, a businessman, because he offered a plan to straighten out the mess gradually without causing widespread unemployment. Such unemployment, the military feared, would help the left-wing guerrillas who were terrorizing the country.

Lest he touch off a severe recession, Mr. Martinez de Hoz couldn't resort to drastic cuts in the budget, which accounts for 40% of the country's gross national product. Instead, he increased the state companies' prices for their services and products such as railroad fares, electricity, telephones and gasoline, and he tightened tax collections. He thus brought the deficit down to manageable proportions; it could be financed without printing more pesos as the Peronists had done.

Critics of the economics minister, however, argue that the seize of the budget and of public investment is still so great that it remains a major cause of inflation.

### Imports Wanted

Probably the prime cause, Mr. Martinez de Hoz says, is the foreign-exchange problem. When the military took over, the problem was that Argentina had no foreign reserves and faced default on its international debt. Mr. Martinez de Hoz met that immediate crisis; he ended the Peronist policy of holding down farm prices to subsidize city dwellers and of imposing stiff taxes on farm exports. He thereby allowed farmers to receive higher prices at home and, more important, the world price for their exports of grains and beef. The farmers responded with bumper crops, and now the country's foreign reserves total more than $8 billion.

That solved one foreign-exchange problem, but it created another. "It sounds foolish," an economist says, "but we have a crisis of too few imports or too many exports, however you want to look at it."

For 30 years Argentina has kept its doors closed to manufactured goods to protect its own industry, so that last year exports exceed imports by some $2 billion. The central bank had to create pesos for Argentines to convert all those dollars into. Mr. Martinez de Hoz blames the issuance of all that new currency for 80% of last year's inflation. And with a 52% increase in the wheat harvest this year, the problem could get worse.

Mr. Martinez de Hoz's answer is a five-year program to cut tariffs in stages to encourage imports. This, in fact, is the key to his anti-inflation policy. He wants low-cost imports to force Argentine manufacturers to either produce at competitive prices or go out of business. To give them an incentive to modernize, he has already eliminated tariffs on machine tools.

But Argentina companies are so immersed in debt, because they were following the old rules of operating in an inflation, that only a few can take advantage of these incentives. To make matters more difficult, the government has begun indexing business loans and many companies face serious problems in rolling over their short-term debt.

"They are changing the rules of the game too fast," says an economist who advises several local firms. "We've been conditioned to the old rule for 30 years. People still don't believe that the new rules are going to last."

# Chapter 7

# Economic Exposure to "Exchange Risk"

## 7.1 INTRODUCTION

The combination of the final collapse of the fixed exchange rate system in 1973 and the 1976 implementation of a set of rules for translating foreign exchange gains and losses, without reserve accounts and other disguises,[1] by American companies has made reported profits of international companies fluctuate substantially. Indeed, at times when exchange rates are changing rapidly, corporations with a great deal of foreign business, either through trade or direct investment abroad, may find that potentially large foreign exchange gains or losses dominate the earnings from operations. The investment and business community finds these results distressing. For instance the senior vice-president of a major U.S. manufacturing firm has said "These exchange rate fluctuations, and the unsound formula for recognizing them (FASB No. 8) produce wild swings in the profit and loss statement *which don't necessarily reflect economic realities.*" (our italics).

The only sensible way to take into account exchange-related gains and losses is to measure their effect on actual dollar values, that is, on after-tax cash flow for earnings, and market/replacement value translated into dollars for assets. Liabilities are future cash outflow obligations, of course. Seen from this perspective, FASB 8 is not open to much criticism in its treatment of asset values and earnings, but is peculiar in its representation of the gains and losses on debt obligations dominated in foreign currencies. In section 7.2 we discuss basic accounting measures of exchange related gains and losses. Section 7.3 uses an example to provide cash-flow-related measurements of exposure. Section 7.4 looks at measurement of the gains and costs of hedging. Finally, in section 7.5 we tackle the controversial issue of whether hedging is desirable, and for whom.

---

[1]Financial Accounting Standards Board, "Accounting for the Translation of Foreign Currency Transactions and Foreign Currency Financial Statements," (known as FASB statement No. 8).

Your feelings about the Ivory Tower will be confirmed—we are going to urge you to hedge no part of ongoing operations.[2]

## 7.2   ACCOUNTING EXPOSURE TO EXCHANGE RISK

The extent of accounting exposure to exchange risk rests on the accounting methods used to translate (or convert) balance sheet items and income denominated in different currencies into a single common unit of measurement. Items which must be translated at current exchange rates on balance sheet dates can obviously suffer translation gains and losses. Items which are translated at the exchange rate prevailing when they were originally acquired (the *historical rate*) cannot suffer translation gains and losses. So one problem for designers of accounting rules is to decide which items can be translated at historical rates.

In Europe and the United States, three main accounting methods have been used for the translation of accounts to a common currency. They are respectively:

- the all-current rate method, also called closing rate method

- the working capital method, sometimes called current-noncurrent method

- the monetary and nonmonetary method, (also called historic rate method

The *all-current rate method* brings all balance sheet accounts to a common basis, which is the spot rate as of the balance sheet closing date. The main advantage of this method is its simplicity. It treats everything uniformly. We will see that this method has conceptual appeal if the foreign currency books are constructed using current market value or replacement value. Otherwise the simplicity is bought at too high a price.

The *working capital method* distinguishes for translation purposes between the short-term and the long-term nature of the assets and liabilities. The normal division is one year: assets or liabilities to be received or paid within the year or the working capital of an affiliate are translated at the closing spot rate. They are therefore susceptible to change in terms of the parent currency. Long term assets and liabilities—essentially fixed assets, long term debt, and charges such as depreciation—are translated at their historical rates of booking.

The *monetary-nonmonetary method* is based on the division of assets as to their nature, financial or physical, rather than their maturity. All

---

[2]The only exceptions will be infrequent or one-shot deals for financially weak corporations, and when you are playing against a central bank pegging operation.

physical assets, whether short-term (as is usually the case of inventory) or long-term (as plant and equipment), are translated at their historical rates of booking. On the other hand, all monetary items are translated at the spot rate prevailing at the closing of the balance sheet. The main difference with the previous method is the translation of long-term debt at the current spot rate.

Unlike balance sheet translation, there is more consensus on translation of income. It is to be translated at the average exchange rate prevailing over the reporting period. (This implicitly assumes that profit remittances have been made at the average exchange rate prevailing in the reporting period, or else that some form of compensation has been earned for discrepancies between actual rates on remittance dates and the average rate in the reporting period.)

To overcome wide swings in reported income, whether it comes from operating income or balance sheet accounts adjustments, companies used to establish reserves for foreign exchange gains or losses, which allowed them to smooth out reported earnings from foreign operations over the years. In 1975 the Financial Accounting Standards Board put an end to the discrepancies caused by different translation methods in the U.S. by making compulsory a version of the monetary-nonmonetary method. This version is codified in FASB 8, the main features of which are summarized in Table 7.1.

**Table 7.1**  *Main Features of FASB 8*

| Item | Exchange Rate for Translation |
|---|---|
| Cash, Accounts Receivables, Accounts Payable | Current |
| Inventories | Historical |
| Fixed Assets | Historical |
| Long Term Liabilities | Current |
| Income and Expenses after Depreciation | Average |
| Depreciation and Amortization of Assets | Historical |
| Forward Exchange Positions | Current spot if hedge positions; otherwise, current forward |

The last item on the table is very amusing. Forward contracts have a market price at all times. It gives their immediate cash value. Yet book valuation of the items they hedge force this peculiar treatment. To evaluate the other components from a cash-value perspective, we have to return to the underlying economics of the exchange market.

Consider the following hypothetical situation—Company X, a U.S. company, has an operation in some foreign country. At the beginning of the year the foreign subsidiary confidently projects a certain real domestic currency profit, which is translated into dollars at the current spot rate and reported to the parent company. A week after this planning exercise, however, the government changes in a totally unanticipated way. With the big spenders at the helm, a gross inflation begins. Let us make two assumptions, which are quite critical.

A1   All inflation is "pure" inflation. That is, all prices and wages rise at the same rate and there are no relative price changes.

A2   The law of one price applies all the time. Thus the exchange rate between any pair of currencies will move to exactly offset the difference in the pure inflation rates of the two countries concerned.

Apparently Company X's subsidiary will now be earning profits in a currency that is devaluing against the dollar at a quite unexpected rate. But does this mean that losses are being made that might, perhaps, have been hedged in some way? Of course not. Under our assumptions, local currency costs and prices will rise at the new inflation rate. Profit equals revenue minus cost so it will also rise at the new inflation rate. Thus the extra and unanticipated devaluation of the local currency against the dollar is exactly offset by the extra and unanticipated increase in local currency profits and asset values. As a result, the parent has no economic exposure to exhange risk whatsoever, whether inflation and devaluation are anticipated or not. Our assumptions generate a special case of a fundamental principle, which we will state here:

> Exchange rates do not change without cause. Frequently, the same factors that cause the exchange rate to change, will cause profits and asset values to change also. The true exposure to exchange rate change is the net of these effects. Almost invariably this means that exposure is much less than it seems at first sight.

The FASB 8 rule for translation of income is rationalized by our two assumptions. Translating earnings and assets at historically relevant rates means that they can suffer no exchange related gains or losses. That is, all exchange rate movements must have been compensated for by exactly offsetting changes in local currency values. In Chapter 5 we saw that Assumption A2 was certainly a reasonable description of the trend of things but was invalid in the short term. Assumption A1 seems to be on much shakier ground. It is apparent (at least to us!) that it would be much more informative to present the balance sheet with foreign assets valued at their current market prices or replacement costs, and then translated at current spot rates. Then the extent of washout would emerge from the historical record of the corporation's books, as numbers of such balance sheets were accumulated. Using actual current values would also reflect the actual dollar value of these assets were they to be sold and the proceeds converted to dollars on the balance sheet date. For there are potential gains and losses on assets due to exchange rate changes when A1 and A2 apply at best on average, and not all the time. Let us recapitulate, from Chapter 5, some of the causes of such potential gains and losses.

- Suppose that, once inflation begins, relative prices start to change; not changes that are unrelated to inflation, such as a growing scarcity of unskilled labor that the foreign subsidiary needs, but relative price changes, because the unionized sector is faster to raise its wage claims, and the foreign subsidiary has made previous fixed price contracts without an escalator clause; or any other reason. Then the movement in the price and rate of the foreign subsidiary will not exactly parallel that of the tradable goods index, which is a major cause of the exchange rate change.

- Suppose that the subsidiary operates in the nontraded goods sector. We have seen that this sector can have cost and price trends different from the tradable goods sector, costs which determine the purchasing power parity exchange rate.

- Speculative pressures and short-term monetary phenomena cause spot rates to depart from parity values. Of course on average these effects are not present.

It is worth noting that under some circumstances an automatic hedge may even be present in short-term interest rate movements and exchange rate movements. A short example illustrates this possibility. Suppose we are looking at a foreign subsidiary of General Motors in Germany: General Motors Acceptance Corporation, G.M.B.H., which is a finance company. Whenever interest rates fall in Germany its profits tend to rise, since its revenues come from interest charged to General Motors customers in Germany and the bulk of its operating expenses come from the cost of refinancing, which is short term in nature and cheaper once we have assumed that interest rates were falling. However, unless U.S. interest rates are falling more than in Germany, the interest rate arbitrage mechanism will cause the DM to depreciate relative to the US$. This tends to offset the effects on higher US$ translated profits of the lower interest rates in Germany. Of course, the opposite would happen when interest rates increase more in Germany than in the United States.

Overall, then, the monetary-nonmonetary method gives a satisfactory long-run average picture of fixed and financial assets, inventories, and earnings. The main problems arise with treatment of debts, which are monetary items and translated at the spot rate. We will work through a simple example. Suppose that on January 1, 1980, the AC/DC Corporation headquartered in Polk Street, San Francisco, takes out two long-term loans to finance its domestic and foreign electronic commodity production. One borrowing is in Swiss francs, the other in dollars, as seen in Table 7.2.

**Table 7.2**  *Borrowings of the AC/DC Corporation*

|  | Swiss franc | Dollar |
|---|---|---|
| Date of Borrowing | 1/1/80 | 1/1/80 |
| Amount of Borrowing | 168,265 | 100,000 |
| Interest Rate (annualized) | 1% | 14% |
| Maturity | 2 years | 2 years |
| Coupon Structure | Annual coupon, payable on 12/31; balloon payment of principle | |
| Spot Rate, 1/1/80 | .5943 | — |

We will also make the following assumptions:

A3   Anticipated inflation over the two year period of the loan is zero in Switzerland and 12.88% at an annual rate in the U.S.[3]

Thus in both countries the expected annual real interest rate on two-year loans is about 1%.

A4   Inflation anticipations are exactly realized.

Finally, we repeat A2.

A2   Purchasing power parity applies all the time.

So we have a situation where equal dollar sums are borrowed in two currencies on the same date, with the same coupon structure, and with the same real interest rate. Now let us see how the monetary-nonmonetary method of accounting treats transactions (see Table 7.3).

Reserving comment, consider now the accounting reports in the next

---

[3]Sorry for the spurious precision! However, these examples are specially constructed, and the purpose of the present construction will soon become apparent.

**Table 7.3**   *Income Statement for AC/DC 12/31/80*

|                       | Swiss Franc<br>Loan | Dollar<br>Loan |
|-----------------------|---------------------|----------------|
| Interest Expense      | 1,128.70            | 14,000         |
| Exchange gain (loss)  | (12,870.48)         | —              |
| Total                 | 13,999.18           | 14,000         |

*Notes:* (1) The Swiss Franc appreciated to reflect the 12.88% inflation differential

  spot rate (12/31/80) = .5943 × (1.1288) = .6708

(2) Interest expense on Swiss loan computed as follows:
  SF payment = 1,682.65
  $ equivalent 1,682.65 × .6708 = 1,128.70

(3) Exchange loss on Swiss debt computed as follows:
  $ value (12/31/80)   168,265 × .6708 = 112,870.48
  $ value (1/1/80)                        100,000
  Exchange Loss                            12,870.48

year, when the principle of the loans is repaid. Given Table 7.4 as the accounting record, let us examine the economic aspect, which is *before-tax cash flow* (see Table 7.5).

**Table 7.4**   *Income Statement for AC/DC 12/31/81*

|                       | Swiss Franc<br>Loan | Dollar<br>Loan |
|-----------------------|---------------------|----------------|
| Interest Expense      | 1,273.96            | 14,000         |
| Exchange gain (loss)  | 14,525.75           | —              |
| Total                 | 15,799.71           | 14,000         |

*Notes:* (1) The Swiss franc appreciated to reflect the 12.88% inflation differential.

  spot rate (12/31/81) = .6708 × (1.1288) = .7571

(2) Interest expense on Swiss loan = 1,682.65 × .7571

(3) Exchange loss on Swiss loan computed as follows:

  $ value (12/31/81)   168,265 × .7571 = 127,396.23
  $ value (12/31/80)                      112,870.48
  Exchange Loss                            14,525.75

**Table 7.5**   *Before-Tax Dollar Cash Flow*

|                        | Swiss Franc Loan | Dollar Loan |
|------------------------|------------------|-------------|
| 12/31/80               | 1,128.70         | 14,000      |
| 12/31/81               | 128,670.19       | 114,000     |
| Present value at 14%   | 100,000          | 100,000     |

Neglecting tax, these loans are equivalent. The real interest rate is the same. The differences refer exclusively to the timing of the cash flow. If you take the foreign loan in an appreciating currency you pay back the same present value, but the bulk of the payment is later in time than for the domestic currency loan, reflecting

1.   the growing exchange losses on the coupons; and
2.   the large cumulated loss taken on the balloon terminal payment.

The monetary-nonmonetary accounting rule, exemplified by FASB 8, distorts this cash flow picture in two ways.

1.   It attributes as a cost in Year 1 an actual cash outflow made only in Year 2. In reality the only exchange loss incurred in Year 1 is the small loss on the Swiss franc coupon.

2.   It labels something an exchange loss that is just as much a cost of borrowing as is the dollar interest payment.

So the real impact of FASB 8 interpretation of foreign debt valuation is on cash management and tax liability. If the exchange loss is deductible from income for tax purposes, it is better to take the Swiss franc loan and obtain a $12,870.48 interest-free loan from the tax authorities for one year. If exchange losses are not deductible, on an after-tax basis the dollar loan is preferable.

If one really wanted to record the liability on a cash value basis, we suggest two alternatives.

1.   Compute a present value in Swiss francs and translate at the spot rate. (Of course one uses the Swiss interest rate to compute the present value in Swiss francs.)

2.   Use the forward rate to estimate the future dollar liability, and discount that at the dollar interest rate.

We leave it to the reader to show that these methods give equal dollar value, based on the condition for covered interest arbitrage to offer no profit. Such a valuation shows the number of dollars it would have taken to liquidate the debt on the balance sheet date. It automatically revalues the debt to allow for fluctuations in both interest rates and exchange rates. Thus, changes in this representation of the value of foreign debt are genuine capital gains and losses. This present value approach for liabilities is the counterpart of a market value/replacement value translation at spot rate approach for income and assets. Accounting records prepared on this basis give actual liquidation value of the enterprise on the date of the accounting statements.[4]

As a final concern, we can look at the consequences of the adoption of FASB 8 for U.S. corporations. The rule's great unpopularity has spawned a substantial number of studies of its impact, sponsored by the FASB and by academic researchers. The results of this work have been summarized by Paul Griffin.[5] A number of firms claim to have started to hedge accounting exposure rather than what they conceive of as economic exposure. In most corporations more attention is paid to exchange rate movements (but this period also coincides with a time of increased exchange rate volatility). A number of securities analysts seem confused by the reported gains and losses, and, in one survey study, were inclined to view these reported gains and losses as much more significant than did the companies reporting them. Nonetheless, using the usual statistical techniques for testing for the impact of new information on securities prices, there has been discovered no statistically significant impact of the adoption of FASB 8 on the stock prices of companies with international business. This is what one might hope, as the rule did not require a change in the way business was conducted but only in the reporting of the results of that business. If investors can already see through the accounting veil, then a change in this veil to a different type of lace should have no effect on perceived stock market value. It is true that multinational corporations' stocks fared worse after 1976, but as far as can be ascertained by statistical study this was due to growing problems in the international currency system and not to FASB 8 reporting.

## 7.3  ECONOMIC EXPOSURE—EXAMPLE OF AN IMPORTER

In Section 7.2 various contrasts were drawn between accounting measures of exposure to gains and losses from exchange rate changes, and economic measures, which relate to cash flow. It is useful to consider them all in

---

[4]We aren't accountants (perhaps that has become obvious by now!) but it seems that a balance sheet should show the net worth of the enterprise, which can only be derived by using liquidation values for assets and liabilities.

[5]P. Griffin, "F.A.S.B. Statement No. 8: A Review of Empirical Research on its Economic Consequences," Graduate School of Business, Stanford University Research Paper No. 482, January 1979.

a specific business context. We choose the example of an importer of Mazda automobiles into the United States. From time to time she orders vehicles from the Japanese manufacturer and sells them after they arrive. On each shipment she has the following pattern of payment obligations and possibilities:

1. she orders the automobiles and they arrive 90 days later;

2. she has 90 days from the date of arrival to pay for them; and

3. all payment obligations are in yen.

So for a certain period of time the importer will have both inventory and a yen-denominated payable. As she sells vehicles out of the inventory, she accumulates (dollar) cash from which she will have to meet the yen account payable. If the yen were to appreciate against the dollar between the time the order for vehicles was placed and the time the importer pays Toyo Kogyo for them, would the importer face the prospect of economic loss (loss of cash) as a result? From the discussion in the preceding sections and in Chapters 5 and 6, the answer to this question can be seen to depend upon three things:

1. the effect of the exchange rate change on the dollar price of a Mazda in the United States

2. the amount of inventory held before the exchange rate change

3. what the importer does with the cash she receives from cars as she sells them, and the mechanism for determining interest rates.

The first consideration is the extent to which the exchange rate change was for purchasing power parity reasons. If the dollar depreciates against the yen because of, and to the extent of, the difference in tradable goods inflation in the United States and Japan, the Mazda dealer bears no exchange risk on unsold vehicles in transit or in inventory. She can raise the dollar price of the vehicles by the full percentage of the depreciation and remain just as competitive as before when consumers make price comparisons with domestically-produced vehicles. So the importer's potential problems derive from two sources. First, the prices of U.S.-made automobiles may not rise by the amount of the inflation differential, whether because of a policy of infrequent price adjustments or because the costs of producing automobiles in the United States rose less quickly than those of tradable goods in general. In response to higher inflation rates, U.S. automobile manufacturers raise prices more frequently, so these effects ought to average out over several shipments. Our importer will at some dates be able to make price increases larger than the inflation differential, and at other dates smaller price increases. However if the costs of automobile production in the United States rise less rapidly than general tradable goods costs, this represents a real fall in automobile production costs in the United States. This makes imported vehicles less attractive, and that is the risk the importer faces, not the exchange rate. The second problem is the possibility that the exchange rate will depart from purchasing power parity. This risk is very real. It is the only true exchange risk. Since it seems to be the case that on average exchange rates maintain their parity values, the importer must decide whether she is able to sit out the fluctuations. If not, perhaps she shouldn't be in the import business.[6]

Consider now the cars sold out of inventory. These won't rise in dollar value *to the dealer* up to the time that she must make her yen payment.[7] She can't turn around and ask her customers for more dollars when they bring their vehicles in for the free thousand-mile checkup. That doesn't necessarily matter, because she has converted the inventory to dollars by selling it, and the crucial question is what she did with that cash. It will either have been used to pay off existing debt or invested in some interest-earning asset. Therefore our attention turns to whether interest yields contain an allowance for anticipated inflation, and which inflation rate we mean—tradable goods inflation, consumer goods inflation, general inflation. If interest rates are market prices, set by demand and supply considerations, we can indicate what ought to happen. People in business should be willing to pay more to borrow because the inflation will raise the price of the resulting output. Thus on the demand side the general inflation factor (represented perhaps by the GNP deflator) is relevant. On the supply side, lenders will demand higher interest yields only if they have alternative investments yielding more, the higher is inflation. Principal candidates are real estate and advance purchase of consumer durables—that is, a fall in the savings rate. Empirical investigation seems to show that anticipated inflation has been the main factor explaining changes in short-term interest rates in the United States, and that these predictions do capture the basic trends in short-term interest rates. However there seems to be a lot of noise in the predictions so that substantial short-term errors can occur.[8] There is also some evidence that the more

---

[6]What about staying in the import business by undertaking a policy of forward hedging? Recollect from our discussion in Chapter 6 that, on average, forward rates equal the spot rate on the maturity date of the contract. So on average, the forward rate you pay for yen will equal the spot rate that will occur. You don't get a better rate in the forward market, you get a sure rate. Once again, if you do enough of these transactions the only result of forward hedging will be that more money is paid to the brokerage industry. If you don't do many of the transactions, you can buy certainty at a price equal to the transactions cost of trading in forwards. But if the automobile market in the United States is very competitive, can you afford to pay these insurance premiums?

[7]They do rise in value to the owners, since used cars are priced relative to new cars because they are such close substitutes.

[8]A. Burger, "An Explanation of Movements in Short-Term Interest Rates," *Review*, Federal Reserve Bank of St. Louis, July 1976.

variable is actual inflation, the more divergent are anticipations of future inflation, which may explain the noise in the short-term interest rates as predictors of inflation.[9] Once again, it seems that if our importer has the financial resources to wait out fluctuations, she should on average receive an interest yield on her cash balances that will compensate her for the exchange rate movement.

In conclusion, the importer bears exchange risk on each transaction she undertakes, but the sum of these risky transactions should act for her much like the pooling of individual contracts does for a life insurance company. Therefore, everything else being given, larger[10] participants in the exchange markets have a natural cost advantage over smaller participants. The larger participants can successfully act as their own captive insurer and will experience fewer risks. They receive a benefit from diversifying their portfolio of transactions. This has some obvious implications for hedging policy, a subject we will turn to shortly. Before doing so we wish to note that the arguments made above for short-run interest rates acting as a compensator for exchange rate movements ought to apply also to return on long-term debt. Suppose we assume the following:

- Real interest rates move together and are approximately equal in all countries.

- Nominal interest rates must equal the real rates plus a premium for anticipated inflation.

- The inflation anticipations are on average correct.

- PPP holds on average.

These are the assumptions underlying our example of accounting for translation gains and losses on long-term debt under the monetary-nonmonetary approach. We saw that under these assumptions it was a matter of indifference (on a pretax basis!) in which currency one borrowed or lent. Between the major developed economies, where are assumptions hold quite well, things tend to work out as in the example, on average.[11] Given the long horizon involved in pricing bonds, there is more margin for anticipations to prove incorrect. So it is even more true that diversification of the portfolio of borrowings will have benefits in terms of reduction of exchange-related cash flows gains and losses.

---

[9] A. Cukierman and P. Wachtel, "Differential Inflationary Expectations and the Variability of the Rate of Inflation: Some Theory and Evidence." Working Paper No. 129, Salomon Brothers Center, Graduate School of Business Administration, N.Y.U., November 1977.

[10] By "larger" we mean more individual transactions in more currencies. We do not mean simply larger value transactions with the same frequency in the same exchange markets.

[11] See R. Aliber and C. Stickney, "Accounting Measures of Foreign Exchange Exposure: The Long and Short of It," *The Accounting Review*, January 1975, Tables 2, 3, p. 51.

## 7.4 MEASURING AND RECORDING THE COST OF HEDGING

The Mazda importer could have hedged her yen payable by purchasing forward yen on the date that she placed the order for the vehicles, or she could have undertaken a spot/credit transaction to achieve the same end. Let's recapitulate the circumstances. The importer

- orders the automobiles and they arrive 90 days later.
- has 90 days from the date of arrival to pay for them.
- must pay in yen.
- is allowed to pay promptly and receives a discount for early payment, the discount being linked to Japanese borrowing costs.

If the automobiles are ordered on January 15, they arrive on April 5 and must be paid for by July 15. The importer can choose to pay on April 15 or July 15, let us say. Either payment can be hedged on January 15.

### Forward Hedge

If the importer chooses to pay promptly she can buy 90-day yen at $F_{90}(1/15)$. If she decides to wait until July 15, she can buy 180-day yen at $F_{180}(1/15)$.

### Spot/Credit Hedge

This involves borrowing dollars and converting them immediately to yen, on January 15. If the importer chooses to pay on April 15, she converts the number of dollars which, when invested in a yen-denominated asset, will cumulate to equal the payment obligation on April 15. If she chooses to pay on July 15, the importer will convert the number of dollars which, when invested in a yen-denominated asset, will cumulate to equal her payment obligation on July 15.

Note that one method involves borrowing and the payment of interest and the other does not.

What does it cost to hedge? There are two components to cost—the *transactions cost* and the *opportunity cost*. The transactions cost is straight forward. It is the sum of the brokerage and commission charges involved in the hedge. The opportunity cost derives from the difference between the rate of exchange fixed in the hedge and the actual spot rate which occurs on the payment date. That difference is what you gain or lose by choosing to hedge rather than allowing events to take their course.

The first thing we will examine is whether the importer should be indifferent between the two methods of hedging, given that she decides to hedge.

The forward hedge involves paying the forward rate times the amount of yen owed, on the actual date of payment. That is, the cash outflow of, say, $F_{180}(1/15) \times$ ¥ takes place in 180 days. The spot/credit hedge involves a dollar outlay right now computed as follows.

$$¥ = \text{yen owed on } 7/15$$

$$\frac{¥}{(1 + r_{180}{}^{¥})} = \text{yen deposited on } 1/15 \text{ which will cumulate}$$

$$\text{to ¥ on } 7/15$$

$$S(1/15) \cdot \frac{¥}{(1 + r_{180}{}^{¥})} = \text{dollars needed to be converted now,}$$

$$\text{where } S(1/15) \text{ is the spot rate on } 1/15$$

In order to compare the dollar outlays via the two methods we must discount the forward outlay back to the present. Denoting the relevant interest rate $r_{180}{}^{\$}$ we want to compute the difference in present cost

$$\frac{F_{180} \cdot ¥}{1 + r_{180}{}^{\$}} - \frac{S \cdot ¥}{1 + r_{180}{}^{¥}}$$

Now if $r_{180}{}^{\$}, r_{180}{}^{¥}$ were the interest rates at which covered interest arbitrage took place, this cost difference would be zero, as the reader should confirm. In general a company may be able to lend at the Eurocurrency deposit rate but will not borrow at that rate. Its opportunity cost of cash will not be the arbitrage rate. Thus, given a decision to hedge it is necessary to compute the present dollar outlay under alternative methods. Given the close relationship among all short-term interest rates, the advantage to one method or the other will never be large in percentage terms. An excellent exercise on this topic is Dozier Industries case (Case 4 at the back of this book).

Now let us return to computing the opportunity cost of the hedge.

$$\text{forward hedge } [S(7/15) - F_{180}(1/15)] \times ¥$$

$$\text{spot/credit hedge}^{12} \quad \left[ S(7/15) - \frac{1 + r_{180}{}^{\$}}{1 + r_{180}{}^{¥}} S(1/15) \right] \times ¥$$

Since it will always be approximately true that

$$F_{180}(1/15) = \left( \frac{1 + r_{180}{}^{\$}}{1 + r_{180}{}^{¥}} \right) S(1/15)$$

---

[12]The factor $1 + r_{180}{}^{\$}$ is present because we are making a comparison at 7/15 and the spot/credit transaction involves a dollar outlay on 1/15.

these two approaches to hedging involve approximately the same opportunity cost. The fact that the spot/credit transaction involves a borrowing and interest payments, and the forward hedge does not, is immaterial. Given what we have said about forward rates on average equalling spot rates on the maturity date of the forward contract, the expected opportunity cost in both methods is zero, and the transactions costs is a sure loss. In this sense the transactions cost can be viewed as a kind of insurance premium. The more diversified are a company's foreign exchange transactions, the less insurance do you obtain by hedging, because more gains and losses tend to wash out within reporting periods.

## 7.5  SOME REASONS FOR FINDING EXCHANGE RELATED GAINS AND LOSSES DESIRABLE RATHER THAN UNDESIRABLE

So far we have proceeded as though real dollar capital gains and losses from exchange rate fluctuations were risk and therefore were undesirable. It turns out that only departures from purchasing power parity entail real capital gains and losses. Since these tend to wash out, we concluded that a diversified portfolio of transactions causes this washing-out to be quickly felt in earnings and asset values. But even for very large global concerns, there will remain exchange related gains and losses. In this section we will try to convince you that these gains and losses may be more valued than a smooth dollar earnings stream by the owners of the company. We will take the perspective of the owners rather than that of the international treasurer, who may sleep less well at nights because of the policy we recommend.

Let's slide into our subject with a paradox. Many companies have substantial foreign ownership. A full hedging policy by the U.S. management might go a long way to stabilize the earnings measured in US$. But perhaps the foreign owners would prefer that the earning be stabilized in some other currency. Consider the following example of a company with some German and some American owners, and a receivable denominated in DM. From the viewpoint of the American owners, perhaps it would be desirable to stabilize earnings in terms of U.S. dollars. Thus they would advocate a hedging policy of selling DM forward. If the DM appreciates against the U.S. dollar, the loss on the forward contract is cancelled by the gain on the receivable. But now consider the German owners, whom we presume to want the earnings stabilized in terms of DM. For them of course, there is no risk whatsoever in the DM denominated receivable. Their risks come from the dollar earnings—they should want all of them sold forward for DM. That is, the American owners would want the firm to sell forward for dollars all the DM earnings, while the German owners would want the firm to sell forward for DM all the dollar earnings. We don't suggest a prize fight in the annual meeting as the resolution of the paradox—it is raised only to indicate that in an integrated world capital market, stabilization of earnings and asset values in one currency is unlikely to be of benefit to all the owners.

The situation we have described leads to two points. First, the owners are in principle free to hedge at least the general pattern of earnings from different countries by their own transactions. If a stockholder knows that 30% of earnings come from Germany, he can take a short position in DM, equal to his fraction of the stock times 30% of the estimated earnings. Indeed if one were to push this notion to its extreme, one could argue that stockholders can in any event undo all of a company's hedging actions by their own offsetting transactions.[13] But we don't have to go this far, because to some extent being unhedged is certain to be desirable. We will argue for this from the perspective of stabilization of the value of wealth, and also in more sophisticated form from the perspective of stabilization of real consumption opportunities.

Our argument about the benefits to be derived from exchange-related gains and losses draws upon the modern portfolio theory approach to the valuation of capital assets, in particular the so-called Capital Asset Pricing Model.[14] A very brief summary of the relevant features of this view of asset pricing may be found in Section 11.4 of Chapter 11, where we use it to evaluate the riskiness of the foreign loan portfolios of international banks. The relevant consideration to us is that the risk premium an investor requires to hold a stock is smaller, the less highly correlated are the returns on the stock with asset returns in general (with the return on the market). To the extent that exchange related gains and losses are less than perfectly correlated with returns on assets in general, a firm with foreign operations becomes more desirable in an investor's portfolio. For the earnings of the firm will tend to smooth the earnings on the portfolio as a whole.

It is straightforward to extend this notion to consumption opportunities. The ultimate purpose of having wealth is to acquire commodities— that is, as rational people, investors are concerned with their real wealth, not just their nominal or currency denominated claim. So, saying that people are risk-averse means really that people are averse to risk in their claims on commodities, not to risk in the nominal value of their assets. One might positively welcome risk in the nominal value of assets if it hedges commodity purchasing power. This idea is familiar in the field of real estate. Houses and property are very risky in nominal terms—they experience very sharp movements in prices. Yet people like to hold them

---

[13]We show this in Appendix 7.2.

[14]Knowledge of the concepts embodied in this theory is indispensable for financial analysis. See W. F. Sharpe, *Investments*, Prentice-Hall, 1978. We will use these ideas throughout the remainder of the book.

because the sharp movements are roughly equal to the sharp movements in inflation, that is in the purchasing power of nominal claims. Consider how this has bearing on our problem. In almost all countries, people consume imported goods, either directly or indirectly. Indirect consumption of course occurs when you buy some goods or services that include among their inputs foreign goods or services. Collectively, we consume foreign goods in a proportion equal to the ratio of imports to the national product. The price of this foreign component of consumption varies with exchange rates. Only if there were pure inflation everywhere, and exchange rates never deviated from purchasing power parity, would this not be true. Then no relative prices would change, and all incomes and prices would rise at the same rate, when translated from one currency into another.

But if these conditions do not apply all the time, risk-averse people will want to offset the foreign-exchange-caused risks to their real claims on foreign goods. If the stockholders can find companies whose earnings move with the exchange rates, then they can construct a portfolio whose fluctuations in value hedge the fluctuations in the dollar costs of the imported goods that they buy. This idea seems rather novel in the United States because of the great degree of self-sufficiency until recent years. However, if the United States were in the situation of Belgium, with half of all goods consumed coming from other countries, the importance of having purchasing power in other currencies through possession of an appropriate asset portfolio would be obvious. Once again, this is an argument in favor of thinking that investors will place positive value on exchange-related fluctuations in earnings.

## 7.6  SUMMARY

The chapter began with an extensive discussion of the various accounting methods used in the reporting of exchange-related gains and losses. Items translated at the historical exchange rates at which they were acquired cannot suffer translation gain or loss; only items translated at the spot rates prevailing at statement dates bear such risk. The all-current rate method brings all balance sheet accounts to a common basis, using the closing-date spot rate. The working capital, or current-noncurrent, method distinguishes between the short-term and long-term nature of assets and liabilities, translating the short term at the spot rate and the long term at historical rates. The monetary-nonmonetary method distinguishes between physical and financial items. Physical items are translated at historical rates, while financial items are translated at spot rates. The currently-used translation rules for U.S. firms, given in FASB 8, are based on the monetary-nonmonetary method.

Genuine exchange-related gains and losses must be derived from gains and losses on actual cash flows or potential realizable capital values. The operation of the purchasing power parity principle in the long term makes FASB 8 a reasonable rule for ascertaining the long-term average translated value of assets and earnings. However the rule makes no sense for debt.

The extent of exposure to genuine exchange related gains and losses depends on the actual economic circumstances of the entity concerned. The principles of measurement are explained in Chapters 5 and 6. The basic idea is simple. Exchange rates do not change without cause. Frequently the same forces that are inducing the exchange rates to alter will simultaneously alter the profits and asset values of a firm in the opposite direction. That is, there is always a tendency to be automatically hedged. At its deepest level, this reflects the long-run irrelevance of purely monetary phenomena to the real operation of an economy.

A most fundamental question is whether firms should hedge anything at all. We present a number of arguments which point to the conclusion that the normal presumption should be against rather than for hedging. These arguments are of two types. The first points out that forward exchange markets do not provide bargains, only fair gambles. So if you make enough transactions, the net impact will be the same whether you hedge or not, except that you will save the transactions cost by not hedging. This is an argument for self-insurance, and everything one can say about the self-insurance decision applies here with equal force. The other class of arguments is of a different type. These arguments accept that except for the largest self-insurers, companies will experience real gains and losses from exchange rate changes. But they explain why it might be in the interests of the owners of firms to experience these fluctuations rather than be spared them. The arguments are based on:

1.  ambiguity of the interests of an international shareholder group;

2.  portfolio diversification benefits, since exchange rate fluctuations seem to have only very low correlation with stock market movements; and

3.  the value of having earnings that bear the impact of exchange rate fluctuations to offset the impact of these same fluctuations on consumer purchasing power

Turn to Case 4 at the back of the book, which further illustrates the material in Chapter 7.

### Suggestions for Further Reading

There exist some valuable references on cash control and hedging of commercial transactions.

B. Litaer, *Financial Management of Foreign Exchange Risk: An Operational Technique to Reduce Risk.* Cambridge, MA: M.I.T. Press, 1971.

D. Rutenberg, "Maneuvering Liquid Assets in a Multinational Company," *Management Science*, June 1970.

*Appendix 7.1*  Hedging Contingent Bids

Consider the situation of a firm that submits an international bid, denominated in foreign currency. If management wishes to hedge, it presumably wishes to do so from the time exposure begins, that is, from the date of bid submission. But simply selling forward the foreign currency proceeds that will accrue if the bid is won does not provide a hedge, that is, a sure return. The firm submitting a bid for a contract in a foreign currency and then undertaking a forward transaction will still be exposed to a possible exchange risk. If the firm sold a forward contract in the currency of the bid for the amount it would receive if the contract were to be won and with the maturity corresponding to the payment date, and if it didn't win the contract, it would end up with a speculative position. It would be short in the foreign currency with no offsetting receipt. Conversely, if it conducted no forward transactions and was awarded the contract, it would also have an open exchange position since it would be long in the foreign currency, with the risk that the forward price at the date of the acceptance of the contract is lower than it was when the bid was submitted and the pricing decision was prepared.

Hedging is possible with a more sophisticated strategy, using options on forward contracts, where the options are written at striking prices equal to the current forward exchange rate for the relevant dates. In the situation we have described, one in which a firm has a *contingent* receivable, it is possible to transact in a forward and a call option, or directly in a put option. Consider first the forward plus call. The company can sell a forward contract in the currency of the bid, and for a maturity corresponding to the payment date if the bid is accepted, and at the same time purchase a call option on forward foreign currency with a striking price corresponding to the rate on its forward contract and with the same maturity date as the forward contract. If the contract is not won, the call can be exercised and the firm obtains an offsetting forward contract at the original price. If the contract is won, the call can be abandoned. The only cost is the sure cost of the call premium. A put option entitles the holder to sell a forward contract at a given striking price. If the company were to buy a put, it could exercise the put if it did win the contract. If it did not, it could abandon the put and it will have lost only the (sure) put premium in originally paid.[15]

*Appendix 7.2*  The Modigliani-Miller Theorem Applied to the Forward Currency Positions of Firms

In its domestic version, the Modigliani-Miller theorem says that the debt-equity ratio is irrelevant to the value of the firm because stockholders can lever or unlever the company as they choose. Extended to the international context, one has to

---

[15]For valuation of puts and calls on forward exchange contracts, see G. Feiger and B. Jacquillat, "Currency Option Bond, Puts and Calls on Spot Exchange and the Hedging of Contingent Foreign Earnings," forthcoming in *Journal of Finance*, 34, 5, November 1979.

show that the value of a firm should be independent of the currency denomination of its debt.

The proof is by arbitrage argument, completely parallel to the original Modigliani-Miller proof.

Suppose there to be two firms, with currently quoted values in the currency of the first country of $V_1$ and $V_2$. These values are the sum of the values of the debt ($D$) and the equity of the firms. For simplicity, we assume that these two firms have title to perfectly positively correlated income streams. Let's denote the random value of the income by $X$. For our purposes, the currency of the stream is irrelevant, and we take it to be the currency of country of $V_1$. We will use a single period framework.

Without loss of generality, suppose that Firm 1 has beginning debt of $D_1$ denominated wholly in the currency of Country 1 while Firm 2 has beginning debt of $D_2$ denominated wholely in the currency of Country 2. Then, the end of period payments due to debt and equity owners, as measured in currency of Country 1, are tabulated below.

|         | Equity | Debt | Sum |
|---------|--------|------|-----|
| Firm 1  | $X - R_1 \cdot D_1$ | $R_1 \cdot D_1$ | $X$ |
| Firm 2  | $X - S \cdot R_2 D_2$ | $S \cdot R_2 \cdot D_2$ | $X$ |

where $R_1$ and $R_2$ represent the riskless, one-period nominal rate of return on the Country 1 and 2 bonds, plus unity, and $S$ is the spot exchange rate between the two countries.

Without loss of generality, suppose $V_1 \neq V_2$. Then the following arbitrage is profitable.

1.  Sell short the fraction $\alpha$ of the equity and the debt of Firm 1; this produces income of $\alpha V_1$ and the obligation to pay $\alpha R_1 \cdot D_1$ to owners of the debt, and $\alpha[X - R_1 D_1]$ to owners of equity.

2.  Purchase the fraction $\alpha$ of the equity and the debt of Firm 2; this costs $\alpha V_2$ and produces cash flow $\alpha S \cdot R_1 D_2$ on the debt and $\alpha[X - SR_1 D_2]$ on the equity.

3.  The cash flow from Step 2, total $\alpha X$, matches exactly the obligation to pay under Step 2, total $\alpha X$. But $V_1 > V_2$, so profit on arbitrage is $\alpha(V_1 - V_2) > 0$.

Since this is impossible because of arbitrage, then the market value of any firm is independent of the global structure of its outstanding debt.

If the currency denomination of the capital structure of any firm does not please stockholders, they will be able to buy:

• foreign exchange contracts;

• foreign bonds, i.e., foreign nominal claims

• foreign stocks

so as to effectively hedge or unhedge the position of the companies they own.

# Chapter 8

# Offshore Financing I–The Eurocurrency Markets[1]

## 8.1 INTRODUCTION

This chapter and the three following discuss the operation of the international capital markets, which channel claims on investable resources from net savers to net investors and consumers. The operation of international capital markets conforms in general principle to operation of domestic capital markets—both perform basic intermediary functions. The differences come from the need to undertake foreign exchange transactions in order to consummate the transfer of financial claims, and from the absence of a unified world legal system and associated enforcement mechanism. We have adopted a traditional approach to capital market analysis, dividing the subject into short-term and long-term debt market analysis and equity market analysis. Chapters 8 through 10 are focused on the characteristics of these worldwide markets in financial claims, while Chapter 11 explains how to evaluate credit worthiness and portfolio risk when lending (or borrowing) on the international market. This chapter focuses on the creditworthiness of governments to a much greater extent than the three preceding, which are entirely concerned with transfers of financial claims among private parties. (Such transfers are, of course, strongly influenced by the policies of governments.)

The Eurocurrency markets constitute the short-to-medium-term debt part of the international capital flow structure. The market is made by banks and other financial institutions that accept time deposits and make loans in a currency or currencies other than that of the country in which they are located. The latter characteristic defines the Eurocurrency market—it is a nondomestic financial intermediary. In the light of the rapid growth of similar institutions in Hong Kong and Singapore (and to a lesser

---

[1]We wish to thank Wayne Ferson for research assistance.

extent in the Middle East) the market is new worldwide and is more appropriately called the "offshore" or "external" money market. Growth of this network of intermediaries has been spectacular. From a few million dollars in the early 1960s, the volume of business rose by 1978 to perhaps $475 billion in outstanding credits if we count only transactions between banks and nonbanks, and to perhaps $800 billion if we include interbank transactions. In the period January through September 1978 about $49 billion equivalent of Eurocurrency credits were granted. About 1/3 went to governments, 1/3 to public enterprises of a nonfinancial type, about 1/7 to public financial enterprises, a little over 1/6 to private enterprises of all types, and the remainder to international organizations. Thus nonprivate borrowers dominate the short-term debt markets (as they do the international bond markets).

Wherever the deposit-taking and loan-making banks may be physically located, the main currency of denomination of loans is the US$, as shown in Table 8.1.

**Table 8.1** *Denomination of Eurocurrency Credits, January–September 1978*

| Currency | Equivalent Value (millions US$) | % of Total |
|---|---|---|
| Dollar (U.S.) | 46,889 | 95.24 |
| Deutschemark | 881 | 1.79 |
| Pound (Britain) | 443 | .90 |
| Yen | 322 | .65 |
| Guilder (Netherlands) | 148 | .30 |
| Dollar (Kuwait) | 117 | .24 |
| Ringgit (Malaysia) | 109 | .22 |
| Riyal (Saudi Arabia) | 94 | .19 |
| Lira (Italy) | 57 | .12 |
| Krone (Norway) | 33 | .07 |
| Franc (Switzerland) | 21 | .04 |
| Other | 9 | .01 |
| Total | 49,235 | 100 |

*Source: The Economist,* London, March 24, 1979, p. 26, Table 1.

Almost all the market, both on the deposit and the borrowing sides, is made up of governments and firms from the most advanced economies, the oil producers, and Brazil and Mexico amongst developing nations. This is shown in Table 8.2.

Indeed with the exception of Argentina, Brazil, Korea, Mexico, Peru, and the Philippines, developing countries have made no significant borrowings from the Euromarkets.

**Table 8.2** *Deposits to and Borrowings from Banks of Major Industrial Nations, end of September, 1978*

| Country | Borrowings US$ Billion | % | Deposits US$ Billion | % |
|---|---|---|---|---|
| Britain | 82.4 | 18.33 | 97.3 | 19.21 |
| Benelux | 48.6 | 10.81 | 36.0 | 7.11 |
| U.S. | 48.5 | 10.79 | 85.2 | 16.82 |
| W. Germany | 42.8 | 9.52 | 24.4 | 4.82 |
| France | 40.7 | 9.05 | 43.4 | 8.57 |
| Japan | 33.9 | 7.54 | 11.4 | 2.25 |
| Brazil | 29.8 | 6.63 | 9.3 | 1.84 |
| Mexico | 22.4 | 4.98 | 5.8 | 1.14 |
| Italy | 21.1 | 4.69 | 14.7 | 2.90 |
| Switzerland | 19.7 | 4.38 | 92.2 | 18.20 |
| Canada | 14.9 | 3.31 | 14.8 | 2.92 |
| Oil exporters A[a] | 13.7 | 3.05 | 22.8 | 4.50 |
| Spain | 12.6 | 2.80 | 12.0 | 2.37 |
| Russia | 12.8 | 2.85 | 4.8 | 0.95 |
| Oil exporters B[a] | 5.7 | 1.27 | 32.5 | 6.42 |
| Total | 449.6 | 100 | 506.6 | 100 |

[a]"Oil Exporters A" consists of oil exporting countries showing high capacity to spend oil revenue: Bahrain, Iran, Iraq, Libya, and Oman. "Oil Exporters B" consists of oil exporting countries with a large investible surplus: Kuwait, Qatar, Saudi Arabia, and United Arab Emirates.
*Source: The Economist*, London, March 24, 1979, p. 26, Table 2.

The Eurocurrency market is extremely large and has grown rapidly in a short interval. It has received a bad press from central banks, which continue to call it a major cause of inflation and an obstacle to their control of domestic monetary systems. A number of basic questions and issues crop up as soon as one looks at the offshore capital markets. First, what separates them from domestic markets? Second, why were they needed and how could they grow so fast when sophisticated domestic capital markets already existed? Third, is there a process of offshore money creation analogous to money creation in a domestic banking system, and what effect does this have on world inflation? We will attempt to answer these questions and others in this chapter.

## 8.2 THE CREATION OF EUROMONEY

There are no offshore currencies, only national currencies of different countries. A national currency deposit becomes part of the offshore currency market when it is transferred to a bank outside the controlled national monetary system. This usually means transferred to a bank outside the nation in question. Thus, a US$ deposit held in a bank in Paris qualifies as a Eurodollar deposit; the same deposit in the hands of the Palo Alto branch of Crocker Bank does not. However, for reasons which will become clear when we explain the growth of the offshore capital market, one could conceivably create Eurodollars by a deposit in an American bank in the United States. The bank would merely have to be part of an entirely unregulated banking sector, analogous to a free trade zone. Suggestions have been made that New York City be declared a free trade zone for capital movements. If this happened, the New York City banks would become part of the offshore capital market.[2] An obvious corollary of this definition of Euromoney is that a Eurobank is a financial intermediary that bids for (time) deposits and makes loans in the offshore market. Usually this will mean that it deals in currencies other than those of the country in which it is located. Eurobanks are branches or subsidiaries of large domestic banks in various countries, or else are *consortium banks*. These are joint-venture institutions created especially for offshore operations by partnerships of several major commercial banks.

Offshore deposits can be created in two ways:

1.  One can take the psysical currency of a country and deposit it in a bank in another country. Banks do hold currency of other countries but mainly for the convenience of travellers. And large quantities of currency have been smuggled out of Italy, Spain, or France from time to time in recent years. However this is usually done with the expectations of a depreciation of the currency being smuggled, and the receiving banks quickly convert these balances into some hard currency. So this method is in general of trivial importance as a creator of deposits.

2.  One can transfer deposits from within the country whose currency is in question to an offshore bank. This may well be an overseas subsidiary of the very same bank with which the original deposit was held.

Let us take, for the purpose of illustration, a demand deposit in a German bank, say Dresdner Bank, of DM 1m. owned by Herr Schmidt. Table 8.3 contains an abbreviated balance sheet for Dresdner Bank. Herr Schmidt perceives that the London branch of Banque National de Paris (BNP) is offering a better rate on DM CDs and transfers his money there. He writes a check in DM to the BNP (London). Let us suppose that Dresdner Bank is the German correspondent bank for BNP. Then Dresdner Bank will (initially) experience only a change in ownership of the DM

---

[2]The larger banks have foreign subsidiaries that are part of the market already. We are referring to the domestic assets in New York City itself.

1m. deposit. The initial situation is shown in Table 8.3 and the revised situation is shown in Table 8.4 where a 20% reserve ratio was used for illustrative purposes.

**Table 8.3**  *Original Balance Sheet of Dresdner Bank*

| Assets | Liabilities |
|---|---|
| Reserves (20%) | Demand deposit Herr Schmidt |
| | 1m |
| Loans, etc. (80%) | |

**Table 8.4**  *Balance Sheets After Creation of Euro DM*

| Dresdner Bank | |
|---|---|
| **Assets** | **Liabilities** |
| No change | Demand deposit BNP    1m. |

| BNP (London) | | | |
|---|---|---|---|
| **Assets** | | **Liabilities** | |
| Demand deposit (DB) | 1m. | C. D. Herr Schmidt | 1m. |

By this simple process DM 1m. has been created on the offshore currency market.

What happens next? The BNP is paying interest to Herr Schmidt so it will want to lend his deposit and earn some money on it. It might turn around and lend the 1m. DM at a (slight) profit to another Eurobank, say Kredietbank Luxemburg. The offshore markets have a huge volume of interbank transactions, proportionately many more than a domestic banking system. Each time the money is relent within the offshore system more offshore DM are created. There are no formal reserve requirements in the offshore system and hardly any are kept. Thus, virtually the whole sum can be relent at each stage and in the terminology of simple models of banking, the "Eurodeposit multiplier" seems virtually infinite.[3] Eventually some banks will lend the deposit to a nonbank who wishes to make a DM payment. This is the only way the system as a whole can make

---

[3]For an explanation of the concept of the multiplier in the context of Eurocurrencies, see G. McKenzie, *The Economics of the Eurocurrency System*, John Wiley and Sons, New York, 1976.

money from the deposits that it takes in. Let us cut short the interbank lending process and simply suppose that BNP (London) lends the whole DM 1m. to a Greek importer who owes DM 1m. in trade debts to a German exporter. We will further suppose that the German exporter keeps her balances at Dresdner Bank also. Table 8.5 gives her balance sheet under the assumption that she carries no debt so that all of her accounts receivables are net worth. It copies BNP from Table 8.5, and adds a balance sheet for the Greek importer.

**Table 8.5**   *Balance Sheets Before the Euroloan*

| | | Dresdner Bank | | |
|---|---|---|---|---|
| **Assets** | | | **Liabilities** | |
| Reserves | 0.2m. | | | |
| Loans | 0.8m. | Demand deposit, BNP | 1m. |

| | | BNP (London) | | |
|---|---|---|---|---|
| **Assets** | | | **Liabilities** | |
| Demand deposit (DB) | 1m. | C. D. Schmidt | 1m. |

| | | Greek Importer | | |
|---|---|---|---|---|
| **Assets** | | | **Liabilities** | |
| Goods | 1m. | Accounts payable | 1m. |

| | | German Exporter | | |
|---|---|---|---|---|
| **Assets** | | | **Liabilities** | |
| Accounts receivables | 1m. | Net worth | 1m. |

After BNP makes the DM 1m. loan to the Greek importer, the situation appears as in Table 8.6.

**Table 8.6**   *Balance Sheets After the Euroloan*

| | | Dresdner Bank | | |
|---|---|---|---|---|
| **Assets** | | | **Liabilities** | |
| Reserves | 0.2m. | Demand deposit, exporter | 1m. |
| Cash | 0.8m. | | |

**Table 8.6**  *Balance Sheets After the Euroloan (cont.)*

| BNP (London) | | | |
|---|---|---|---|
| **Assets** | | **Liabilities** | |
| Loan to Greek importer | 1m. | C. D. Schmidt | 1m. |

| Greek Importer | | | |
|---|---|---|---|
| **Assets** | | **Liabilities** | |
| Goods | 1m. | Loan from BNP | 1m. |

| German Exporter | | | |
|---|---|---|---|
| **Assets** | | **Liabilities** | |
| Deposit (DB) | 1.0m. | Net worth | 1m. |

As a result of this sequence of transactions the DM 1m. has left the offshore currency markets and has once again become the property of a German resident. The intermediary role of the offshore banking system is apparent in this example. In effect, if not in terms of legal liability, Herr Schmidt has exchanged his demand deposit at Dresdner Bank for the higher interest yielding accounts receivable of the German exporter. Moreover, using any of the traditional definitions of the German money supply (cash in the hands of the public plus demand deposits plus possibly CDs and time deposits in the domestic banking system), no Euro-DM transactions can possibly affect the money supply. In the above example, ownership of Herr Schmidt's demand deposit was transferred; within the domestic banking system this demand deposit neither grew nor shrank.

The reader might wonder whether this conclusion depended on the fact that none of the DM 800,000 of loans of the Dresdner Bank had been made to the German exporter. After all, had they been, the DM 1m. payment by the Greek importer would have largely gone to wipe out these loans. But this is not the last step, as can be seen from Tables 8.7 and 8.8. Table 8.7 shows how the German exporter's balance sheet would have appeared had she borrowed from Dresdner Bank. Table 8.8 shows her balance sheet and that of Dresdner Bank after the Greek importer has paid the German exporter, who in turn used most of the proceeds to pay off her own debts to the Dresdner Bank.

Table 8.8 seems to imply a reduction in the money supply of DM 800,000. However this can only be transitory, for the Dresdner Bank now carries reserves equal to 100% of its deposit liabilities. As required reserves are only 20%, it will relend the excess Dm 160,000, which, with a multiplier of $1/0.2 = 5$, will recreate the DM 800,000 of *domestic* money.

**Table 8.7**  *Revised Balance Sheet of German Exporter*

| Assets | | Liabilities | |
|---|---|---|---|
| Accounts receivable | 1m. | Loan from DB | 0.8m. |
| | | Net worth | 0.2m. |

**Table 8.8**  *Balance Sheets After Repayment of Loans*

**German Exporter**

| Assets | | Liabilities | |
|---|---|---|---|
| Demand deposit | 0.2m. | Net worth | 0.2m. |

**Dresdner Bank**

| Assets | | Liabilities | |
|---|---|---|---|
| Reserves | 0.2m. | Demand deposit, exporter | |
| | | | 0.2m. |

If we confine our attention to domestic money supplies, the offshore currency markets could only cause inflationary pressure if they could lower statutory reserves against deposits by allowing transformation of deposits from one category to another (and if there were different reserve requirements against the different categories of deposits.) This actually happened briefly in the United States in the late 1960s. While there were reserve requirements against ordinary deposits, there were none against banks' borrowings from foreign branches. When domestic rates came to exceed the CD ceilings, then in effect, funds from domestic U.S. CDs were transferred to the London branches of American banks (which faced no interest rate ceilings) and were then loaned to the parent banks. Since there were no reserve requirements, the same volume of CDs supported more loans than before.

Of course once offshore banking systems exist in tandem with domestic banking systems it is no longer particularly meaningful to measure money supplies according to the domestic banking system exclusively. What are you interested in when you measure the money supply? What purpose do these measurements serve? If our interest is inflation, we are concerned with the demand for and the supply of money balances for transactions purposes, as we explained in Chapter 5. To the extent that they are negotiable, Euromarket CDs are probably used as transactions balances. Analysis of problems involving the money supply should, therefore, embrace a money supply consisting of the domestic monetary aggregates plus the negotiable part of offshore deposits in the currency concerned. If the relevant domestic monetary aggregate includes time deposits, then one should include also Eurotime deposits of the same maturity.

The offshore banking system is outside the control of the central banks whose currencies it uses. We should consider briefly whether this is good or bad, or even, for some purposes, true. Let's consider first the question of whether the central banks have now lost control of the money supply and therefore of inflation. Since every Eurocurrency unit has its origin in a domestic currency deposit or cash unit, this cannot be true. Just as in a system of purely domestic banking, the central bank controls the monetary base[4] and so controls the money supply, up to the vagaries of the money multiplier. The monetary base is multiplied to create the money supply, because deposits are relent except for the portion held as reserves plus the portion held as cash by the public. The offshore currency markets might make the multiplier different in size, or they might make it more variable. A multiplier different in size from that in a purely domestic banking system does not affect the monetary control of the central bank. The latter body must simply know that it is working with a multiplier of size x rather than size y. Hence problems in monetary control arise from variability of the size of the multiplier. For reasons we are about to discuss, variability of the Eurocurrency multiplier cannot be separated from variability of the domestic money multiplier.

The offshore banks face no statutory reserve requirements and hold reserves equal to perhaps 2% of deposits. These reserves are held with domestic commercial banks as deposits, not directly with a central bank. If the domestic statutory reserve ratio is 16.25%, as it is for large U.S. commercial banks, then the effective reserve against Eurodollars with the Federal Reserve is 0.325%. If one inverts this to obtain a classical multiplier, one obtains 307.7, compared to a domestic multiplier in the United States, for M1, of about 2.5! However as best as one can ascertain, the multiplier in the offshore markets is lower than the domestic multiplier, and is somewhere between 1.0 and 2.0. How can this be?

- The multiplier of 307.7 assumes continual redeposit within the offshore market. As our example of the Greek importer shows, borrowers frequently use the loans to purchase items in the domestic economy, so causing a leakage back into the domestic banking system.

- As more loanable funds enter the offshore markets, the yield on these funds tends to fall relative to yields on domestic CDs, and there is a capital outflow back to the domestic banking system. There are extremely strong arbitrage connections between domestic and offshore interest rates. The small size and relative constancy of the spreads are illustrated in Figure 8.1

---

[4]Cash plus reserves held with the central bank.

**Figure 8.1**   Spreads Between Domestic and Offshore Rates:
Interbank rates on three-month Eurocurrency deposits and
differentials over domestic rates (Wednesday figures, in percentages
per annum).

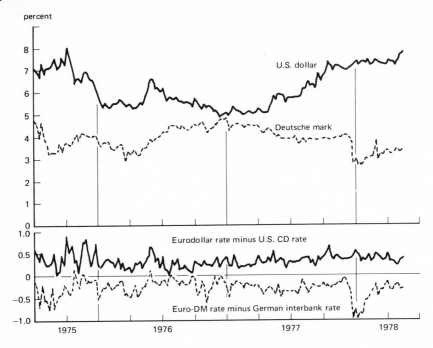

*Source:* B.I.S. Annual Report, 1978. Data for 3 month deposits.

For practical purposes we have one short-term CD cum time deposit
market, and whatever practical problems there are in the conception and
implementation of monetary policy cannot be sensibly described as more
severe in one part of this whole than in another part.

   If this is so, we must explain the hostility central bankers often voice
towards the offshore markets. A number of factors are important here.
First, while the central banks have as much control as they ever had on
creation of money, they have no control over allocation of credit in the
offshore capital market. In the United States there is little overt credit
allocation, although the Federal Reserve does give advice to banks on the
need to limit lending for real estate speculation and the like from time
to time. By contrast, in all the rest of the world active credit allocation
schemes tend to be viewed as an integral part of monetary policy. As
banking business slips away to the offshore markets the capital markets
take up a more laissez-faire hue, with borrowing ability based on capacity
to repay, and remuneration to lenders based on the willingness of borrowers to pay and on the returns on alternative investments, rather than

on official interest rate ceilings. Second, as the Euromarkets are still viewed by the press and the public as mysterious and omnipotent, they make convenient scapegoats for failures of nerve in the handling of domestic monetary policy.[5] Finally, the European central banks made fools of themselves in the 1960s in their Euromarket dealings in a way which they would rather forget, but which is instructive for us to examine.

In the 1960s the European central banks were pegging exchange rates, and absorbing growing dollar deficits. In the early 1960s these dollar deficits, which became dollar reserves of the absorbing central banks, were matched by growth of U.S. official obligations to foreign central banks in the U.S. balance of payments accounts. However, in the late 1960s the European central banks were surprised to observe a growing discrepancy between the change in U.S. official obligations to foreign central banks and their own record of dollar reserves held. The central bankers kept getting more and more dollars than the United States seemed to be losing on the official settlements definition of the balance of payments. The well-known economist Fritz Machlup said of them, "Most magicians who pull rabbits out of their hats know full well that they put them there before the beginning of the show. The magicians in . . . (this) story, however, are more naive, they are just as surprised as the audience by the emergence of the rabbits from their hats."

What happened? Commonly when central banks undervalued their countries' currencies against the dollar they would take the dollars they received in pegging the price and buy U.S. Treasury bills with them. From an accounting viewpoint, the U.S. deficit with Germany, say, equaled in dollar value the German surplus with the United States. A U.S. deficit with Germany meant that more dollar checks were written to purchase DM than DM checks were written to purchase dollars. The Bundesbank became the owner of the excess U.S. demand deposits, which it used to purchase Treasury bills. Thus the U.S. deficit was represented by these excess demand deposits but entered the official settlements balance only when the demand deposits were converted to bills.

Now suppose a foreign central bank decided to earn higher interest on its reserves by converting its acquired U.S. demand deposits to Eurodollar CDs rather than Treasury bills. As we have seen, such an action transfers the ownership of the U.S. demand deposits representing the new foreign reserves to some private, offshore bank. Originally these U.S. deposits were turned into foreign exchange to create the capital outflow that the European central bank absorbed. Subsequently they became the property of the private foreign bank. This was not recorded on the official settlements part of the balance of payments accounts though it certainly

---

[5] Not so long ago the collapse of the pound sterling, and ultimately of the fixed exchange rate system, were blamed by high government officials on the "gnomes of Zurich" (or, as we would call them in these days of equal opportunity, short persons of Swiss nationality).

constituted foreign reserves created by the deficit, just as before. This explains part of the mystery, but the best part is yet to come.

Consider what might have happened to the Eurodollar deposits owned by the foreign central banks. Under the fixed exchange rate system there were periodic exchange crises, during which people would try to switch other currencies into DM or Swiss francs in anticipation of appreciation. Frequently the offshore banks would lend the dollar deposits of the Swiss and German central banks to speculators who converted them into DM or Swiss francs. Under their exchange pegging policies, these tendered dollars had to be absorbed by the central banks, who redeposited in the offshore markets, so that they could be lent again! This is the rabbit in the hat trick of which Machlup was speaking. The central banks came to own very large Eurodollar claims by this circular process, but these large claims were not on the United States but rather (indirectly) on the speculators. To see this it is extremely helpful to conduct another balance sheet exercise. We need four players—a U.S. bank (USB), an offshore bank (OB), a speculator (Spec) and a foreign central bank (FCB). The parenthetic numbers on the balance sheets in Table 8.9 correspond to the steps outlined below. (Each number supersedes all the preceding. Thus at the end of Step 4, for example, only the items numbered 4 should remain.)

1.  As a result of undervaluation of its currency, the FCB comes to own a demand deposit (DD) of amount $X in USB.

2.  The FCB acquires a Eurodollar CD of amount $X$ in OB.

3.  The amount $X$ is lent by OB to the speculator.

4.  The speculator converts his US$ to DM at the fixed rate so that the FCB comes to own the USB DD again.

Thus at this stage the FCB has reserves of $2X, $X of which is the original deficit and a claim on the U.S. demand deposit, while the remainder is a claim on the OB. This bank is securing its liability with its IOU from the speculator.

5.  We can repeat Steps 1 through 4 as often as we like.

They will never create any more claims on the United States but only FCB claims on the OB, secured in turn by IOUs from speculators. When we net out the financial intermediaries (the FCB and the OB), we find that for all practical purposes the monetary authorities have maneuvered the taxpayers into an escalating series of wagers on the exchange rate with the speculators. We know who won in the case of the DM.

These episodes constitute an unfortunate commentary on the fixed exchange rate system and on the central banks. But they do not reflect particularly on the offshore capital markets. As long as the central banks

**Table 8.9** *Balance Sheet Representation of Exchange Rate Wagers Between Taxpayers and Speculators*

| | USB | | | FCB | |
|---|---|---|---|---|---|
| **A** | | **L** | **A** | | **L** |
| Reserves, Loans, etc. | DD FCB(1) | X | USB(1)  X | Taxpayer's burden(1) | X |
| | OB(2) | X | OB(2)  X | | |
| | Spec(3) | X | USB(4)X | Taxpayer's burden(4) | 2X |
| | FCB(4) | X | OB(4)X  2X | | |

| | OB | | | Spec | |
|---|---|---|---|---|---|
| **A** | | **L** | **A** | | **L** |
| USB(2) | XFCB(2) | X | USB(3) | XOB(3) | X |
| Spec(3) | X | | DM(4) | X | |

were willing to deposit their new reserves into private banks that would lend to currency speculators, the same outcome would have occurred and will occur.


## 8.3   EXPLANATION FOR THE GROWTH OF THE EUROMARKETS

The Euromarkets are not a bogeyman but an unregulated financial intermediary. They bring together borrowers and lenders, frequently from the same country. They deal only in the currencies of individual countries and are thus a substitute for the domestic banking system. The incredibly rapid growth of the Euromarkets shows that they were a strongly preferred substitute. But why? To hark back to the example in Section 8.2, why did the Greek importer have to borrow DM from the BNP in London? He could have

- borrowed in DM directly from the Dresdner Bank or some other bank
- borrowed Greek drachmae directly from a Greek bank and converted them spot to DM on the foreign exchange market
- borrowed DM directly from a Greek bank which would have bought them spot to deliver to him

Similarly, if we turn to the case of Herr Schmidt, one must ask why he put his money into a time deposit with the Banque Nationale de Paris in London. Why wasn't he content to put it into a German time deposit, or convert it to French francs and deposit it with the Banque Nationale de Paris in Paris? When posed this way, the question has an obvious answer. An offshore credit market will not exist unless:

- depositors receive better terms than they can receive onshore, and
- borrowers can borrow more, possibly at lower rates, than they can onshore.

That is, banks in the offshore market must operate with a lower spread between the interest rates they charge to borrowers and the ones they pay to lenders.

Now, however, we encounter a problem similar to the one we have just disposed of. Just as there is no such thing as a true offshore currency, there is no such thing as a true offshore bank. The Banque Nationale de Paris in London is just a branch of the BNP of Paris. Citibank's London subsidiary is just a branch of Citibank of New York. It is highly implausible that the lower spread existing in the Eurocurrency system stems from a higher operational efficiency due to superior facilities or superior management. One school of thought links the explanation for the low spread to the explanation of why London is the heart of the system by the following reasoning (written by a Briton, of course).

> The preeminence of London as the Center of the market largely stems from the long tradition of international banking in the United Kingdom, originating from the days when sterling, and not the dollar, was the world's main trading currency and reserve asset. U.K. banks switched over smoothly and easily from financing international financial transactions in sterling to doing the same in dollars; it is the skill of knowing how to do business and having established customers which matters much more than the particular form of currency that is financing the transaction.[6]

The competence of Old Etonians does not seem to us a firm enough foundation for the explanation of so dynamic a phenomenon. A better one also links the lower spread to the pivotal role of London. Put simply, Britain has the least regulation of offshore transactions in foreign currencies (that is, the least regulation in financial intermediation performed for nonresident borrowers and depositors in nonsterling currencies). For a variety of reasons, most countries place various restrictions on short-term capital movements (even in free market economies like Switzerland or Germany) and also constrain banks by reserve requirements, interest ceilings on deposits, and mandatory allocations of bank credit for domestic purposes. However, while Britain's balance of payments problems grew

---

[6]Geoffrey Bell, *The Euro-Dollar Market and the International Financial System*. New York: John Wiley, 1973, p. 13.

in the 1950s and 1960s, the British separated deposit and loan transactions in sterling from those in all other countries. There exists a class of merchant banks, which can be owned by citizens of any country and which is free to accept deposits and make loans in any currency but sterling without any regulation whatsoever. There are no interest ceilings or even reserve requirements but only informal monitoring by the Bank of England. British residents are not free to use these banks, but must go through an extremely restrictive exchange control system. In brief,

> The rapid emergence in the 1960's of a world-wide Eurocurrency market that coexists and competes with traditional foreign exchange banking resulted from the peculiarly stringent and detailed official regulations governing residents operating with their own national currencies. These regulations contrast sharply with the relatively great freedom of nonresidents to make deposits or borrow foreign currencies from these same constrained national banking systems. On an international scale, offshore unregulated financial markets compete with onshore regulated ones.[7]

Standard analysis of unregulated versus regulated financial intermediaries shows why it is not surprising that the former grew rapidly at the expense of the latter.[8] Hence it is not surprising that New York's role as an offshore banking center is virtually nil, and that the offshore banking system is not centered in Germany or Switzerland, which allow free capital movements, but in Britain, which does not.

Although there are no explicit official constraints on external intermediation in New York, a number of factors combine to prevent the development of offshore banking in the United States. First, it has been a policy of the Federal Reserve Board for a long time to discourage U.S. banks from offering time deposits denominated in foreign currencies. This policy dates from the 1960s, when such deposits were believed to disrupt the efforts of the United States to defend the value of the dollar. Second, Federal Reserve regulations on reserve requirements and interest ceilings also apply to foreign-currency deposits. The Bundesbank treats all deposits and loans, whether domestic or foreign, on the same basis. Thus, normal reserve requirements and interest ceilings apply. Moreover, allowing foreign deposits into the domestic banking system tends to dissipate whatever control the central bank may have over the domestic interest rate structure. At various times, Germany and Switzerland have imposed punitive costs on nonresident deposits. Other growing centers

---

[7]R. McKinnon, "The Eurocurrency Market," *Essays in International Finance*, No. 125, Princeton, N.J., December 1977.
[8]See Gurley and Shaw, *Money in a Theory of Finance*, Washington: The Brookings Institution, 1960. Also Milton Friedman, "The Eurodollar Market, Some First Principles," *The Morgan Guaranty Survey*, October 1969.

of offshore capital transactions, such as Hong Kong and Singapore, base their success principally on their virtually unregulated environment. Of course capital market centers must have economic and political stability, an experienced and efficient financial community, and good communications and supportive services. But the most important condition of all is the ability to reduce the bid-ask spread on credit. Figure 8.2 shows that almost all the time in recent years the Eurodollar bid-ask spread has been between the domestic bid-ask spread (where borrowing cost in the latter is prime rate adjusted for a 15% compensating balance). As the U.S. prime rate has become a political number, it undoubtedly understates true borrowing costs when credit becomes tight or inflation accelerates. For the interest of readers, we present in Figures 8.3 and 8.4 similar data for the British pound and the DM. For the DM and the pound we could find no comprehensive Eurolending rate. We are not sure about factors like compensating balances in the case of the German domestic loan rate and for the British prime rate. In any case, as we illustrated in Table 8.1, all the significant business is in dollars.

**Figure 8.2**   Dollar Bid-Ask Spread Comparison

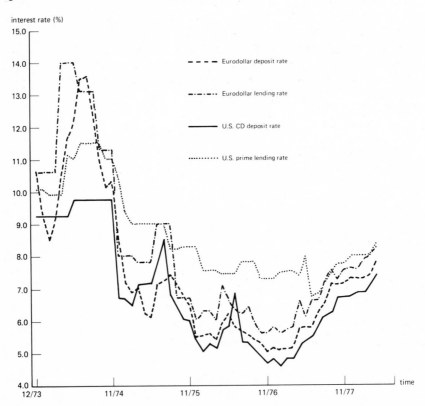

**Figure 8.3** Components of Sterling Bid-Ask Spread Comparisons

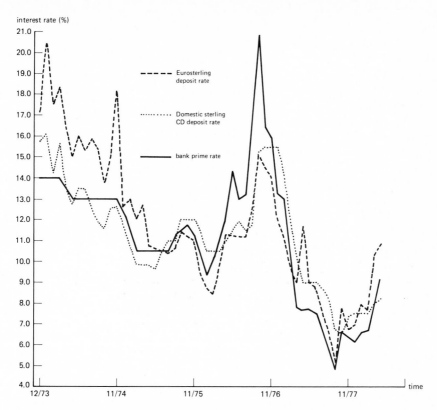

## 8.4 DOMESTIC VS. OFFSHORE BANK INTEREST DIFFERENTIALS

Figures 8.1 and 8.2 both show that, although there is a strong arbitrage connection between the offshore markets and the domestic banking sector, interest differentials persist. The domestic deposit rate remains on average lower than the Eurodollar deposit rate, while the domestic lending rate is on average higher than the Eurolending rate. But how can this be? Surely all potential depositors should hold Eurodollar CDs rather than domestic CDs, and all borrowers should borrow from the offshore rather than the domestic banking system. This argument is reinforced by the fact that many of the Eurodollar banks are branches or subsidiaries of the largest domestic banks, and therefore not strange and unknown either to depositors or borrowers. Already tax haven branches of major U.S. banks are mailbox branches only—all the work and shuttling of funds in the name of these branches is undertaken in the banks' headquarters in New York, Chicago, Los Angeles, or San Francisco. The same personnel run the branch as run the parent. The branches, being branches rather than

**Figure 8.4**   Components of Deutsche Mark Bid-Ask Spread
Comparisons

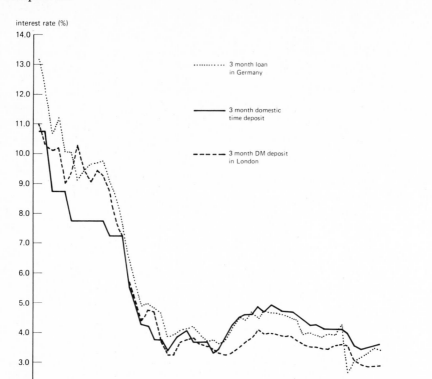

subsidiaries, are backed by the full faith and credit of the parent. Why doesn't the whole large-scale end of the U.S. commercial banking sector transform itself legally into a series of foreign branches of a domestic parent, and thereby escape virtually all federal and state banking regulation?

Perhaps this is happening. Had the offshore banking system not developed, presumably all of that current $500 billion to $800 billion of business would now be in the domestic banking sectors of the United States, Germany, and Britain. When we ask the bankers this question, the answers we receive revolve around two themes:

1.  The customers are still largely unsophisticated in world banking and for the most part would treat a CD from a foreign branch as a different item than a CD from the branch's U.S. parent. However, sophistication is growing.

2.  If widespread action was taken along these lines, the Federal Reserve would try to prevent it.

In our opinion, once enough customers appreciate the facts of the matter the government will find it difficult to stem the tide, just as piece by piece it has been relaxing interest rate ceilings domestically.

At the moment we are in a halfway house, and we can look at the interest differentials, at least on the deposit side, along the lines of modern asset valuation theory. Table 8.10 presents information implying that the short-term deposit instruments having on average higher yields are also riskier, in the sense that offshore yields are more variable, so capital gains and losses due to interest rate changes are larger.

**Table 8.10**  *Return and Risk Relationship of Short-Term Dollar Deposit Instruments*

|  | 5/76–12/76 | 1/77–12/77 | 1/78–6/78 | 5/76–6/78 |
|---|---|---|---|---|
| LIBOR[a] | 5.80 | 6.20 | 7.65 | 6.43 |
|  | (0.42) | (0.86) | (0.28) | (0.96) |
| LIBBR[b] | 5.60 | 6.02 | 7.47 | 6.23 |
|  | (0.39) | (0.82) | (0.34) | (0.94) |
| 90–119-day | 5.47 | 5.72 | 7.17 | 5.99 |
| commercial paper | (0.40) | (0.79) | (0.20) | (0.89) |
| Prime 90-day | 5.44 | 5.77 | 7.30 | 6.04 |
| bankers' acceptances | (0.40) | (0.78) | (0.29) | (0.93) |
| 3-month U.S. CDs, | 5.26 | 5.62 | 7.06 | 5.85 |
| secondary market | (0.38) | (0.77) | (0.25) | (0.90) |
| London dollar | 5.55 | 5.94 | 7.46 | 6.18 |
| CDs | (0.45) | (0.85) | (0.27) | (0.97) |
| 3-month U.S. | 5.19 | 5.43 | 6.70 | 5.67 |
| Treasury bills | (0.35) | (0.67) | (0.20) | (0.78) |

Data show mean yield to maturity, with standard deviation beneath in parentheses.

[a]London Interbank Offer Rate, the wholesale, top name interbank lending rate.
[b]London Interbank Bid Rate, the large-sum deposit rate. See Section 8.6.

Presumably the absence of perfect arbitrage reflects the presence of differential risks of default. As far as a comparison between domestic CDs and foreign-branch CDs of the one U.S. bank is concerned, the default risk must not be related to the overall riskiness of the bank's loan portfolio, but rather to extra default risks on assets booked to the branch, because of the branch's offshore location. There is some chance that the government of the country in which the Eurobank is located might seize the bank or freeze its deposits, or otherwise restrict its transactions through political action.[9] (This has indeed happened to Eurobanks located in Saigon and Beirut, for example. In virtually all cases, depositors were fully repaid by the parent bank or by another branch of the same bank.) Within the same Euromarket center, rates that different banks pay to attract deposits might differ by up to 1%. These differences are due to the usual factors involved in creditworthiness, such as the capital adequacy of the parent and so forth.

## 8.5   DEFAULT RISK OF EUROCURRENCY BANKS

The offshore monetary system is an unregulated banking system with no lender of last resort. Except in a very informal way there are no bank inspections by any central bank to evaluate the soundness of the loan portfolio. Parent banks obviously have a very large stake in the creditworthiness of their subsidiaries but ultimately do not give unconditional guarantees. This contrasts sharply with domestic banking systems, whose very comprehensive regulation has been in large part justified by the need to protect depositors. Yet there have been very few defaults of unregulated offshore banks, despite the immense pressures they have experienced in the 1970s, starting with the oil embargo and the recycling of the petrodollars. We must explain this remarkable record of solvency. The key to any such explanation is the principle that in an unregulated banking system the riskiness of a bank's loan portfolio will be policed by depositors. They have no choice. In a regulated system, especially one with deposit insurance as in the United States,[10] depositors have little or no incentive to care how or to whom their bank lends. The bank inspectors are a necessary corollary of regulation and deposit insurance.

The two principle sources of risk for banks are

1. bad loans; and

2. default due to dependence on maturity transformation and the occurrence of an unfavorable term structure

The bad loan problem is the same for domestic as for foreign banks for the most part. We analyze some of the differences in Chapter 11. The striking thing about the Eurobanking system is its restraint in the matter

---

[9]For an argument that one can explain a number of interest differentials in this way, see R. Aliber, "The Interest Rate Parity Theorem: A Reinterpretation," *Journal of Political Economy*, November/December 1973.

[10]In principle, U.S. deposits are insured to only $40,000, but in practice government agencies almost invariably manage to salvage the funds of all depositors.

of maturity transformation. Tables 8.11 and 8.12 show a comparison between maturity transformation in U.S. commercial banks and U.K.-based Eurobanks as of mid-1977.[11] Moreover, perhaps 90% or more of Eurocredits are on a floating rate basis, regardless of maturity, the usual adjustment being at six-month intervals. Thus the borrower is obliged to compensate the lender for the cost of six-month money and the only effective maturity transformation is from liabilities of less than six months maturity to these six-month assets. By contrast, recent commercial bank practice in the United States involves floating rates on about 50% of short-term commercial and industrial loans, 40% of long-term commercial and industrial loans, and 35% of construction and land development loans. At least in the maturity-transformation dimension, offshore banks are safer than domestic banks. They must be to attract deposits.

## 8.6  OPERATION OF THE EUROMARKETS

There are two levels of offshore currency transactions.

1.  A highly competitive wholesale market centered in London, which determines the basic deposit rates on placements by large non-bank firms and by commercial banks.

These banks sell their funds to each other as need arises, at a basic interest rate called LIBOR (London Interbank Offering Rate). All transactions are undertaken by telephone or telegraph via brokers, so the bank can't be sure which other banks they are negotiating with until after a deal is consummated. The use of such quick means of communications means that a person's word must validate transactions in huge sums of money. Thus only the best "name" banks can transact on this wholesale market.

Certain very large and well known nonbank borrowers have access to the wholesale market, but most do not.

2.  A retail business on loans

Smaller banks, nonbank borrowers, governments of Eastern Europe, or developing countries can acquire loans only after credit investigation. The first to borrow Eurodollars were corporations whose name, size, and good standing enabled banks to make loans to them with a little more than a cursory analysis of credit standing. In recent years and especially

---

[11]Working with slightly more recent and comprehensive data, two analysts at the Federal Reserve Bank of Boston suggest that maturity transformation in Eurobanks is rising. See J. Little, "Liquidity Creation by Eurobanks: 1973–1978," *New England Economic Review*, January/February 1979.

**Table 8.11** *Maturity Transformation by U.K.-Based Eurobanks*

| Maturity | Total | | With Banks (%) | | With Nonbanks | |
|---|---|---|---|---|---|---|
| | Assets | Liabilities | Assets | Liabilities | Assets | Liabilities |
| Less than one month | 33.8 | 38.5 | 37.7 | 37.2 | 22.4 | 36 |
| 1–6 months | 45.6 | 47.9 | 47.3 | 48.8 | 41.1 | 37.2 |
| 6 months–one year | 8.2 | 8.8 | 8.8 | 8.8 | 6.6 | 8.8 |
| Over 1 year | 12.5 | 5.6 | 6.3 | 5.3 | 29.8 | 8.1 |
| All maturities | 100 | 100 | 100 | 100 | 100 | 100 |

Source: Quarterly Bulletin, Bank of England, December 1977. Data for August 17, 1977.

**Table 8.12** *Maturity Transformation by Large U.S. Commercial Banks*

| Maturity | Assets% | Liabilities% |
|---|---|---|
| Less than one year | 47.5 | 78.4 |
| 1–5 years | 10.3 | 11.0 |
| Over 5 years | 36.2 | 10.6 |
| All maturities | 100 | 100 |

Source: Federal Reserve Bulletin, December 1977. Data for June 30, 1977 (classification by authors).

since 1974, the range of corporate and governmental borrowers has spread considerably. Even domestic firms with no international activities are relying on Euroloans when local credit conditions become tight.

In order to explore the lending practices of the Eurocurrency system,[12] it is useful to refer to the hypothetical balance sheet of a Eurobank, presented in Table 8.13.

**Table 8.13**  *Typical Eurobank Balance Sheet Components*

| Assets | Liabilities |
|--------|-------------|
| 1.  Reserve balances | 1.  Interbank deposits |
| 2.  Liquid assets | 2.  Nonbank time deposits |
| 3.  Interbank loans | 3.  London dollar and other currencies CDs |
| 4.  Other loans | 4.  Notes and bonds |
| | 5.  Loans from other branches |
| | 6.  Loans from parent bank |
| | 7.  Equity capital held by parent bank |

An important financial obligation now shown on financial statements of a Eurobank is the loan commitments held with that bank by other financial or nonbank institutions. These involve a commitment by the bank to lend funds at some future date, and therefore can involve a substantial financial liability at a time of tight credit. Conversely, the asset side of the balance sheet does not show the lines of credit that the Eurobank might have contracted for some future date with other Eurobanks and domestic banks.

Interbank deposits, nonbank time deposits, and London dollar CDs represent the bulk of the liabilities of a Eurobank. Interbank transactions bulk particularly large and we will shortly see why. The final depositor in the Eurocurrency market can choose among two major financial instruments. Most funds are raised by fixed time deposits (TDs), the other source being certificates of deposit (CDs). The maturities of time deposits range from one day to several years but most of them are in the one week to six months range (see Tables 8.11 and 8.12). Negotiable certificates of deposit appeared in the London Eurodollar market in 1967. Recently, certificates of deposit denominated in other currencies have started to appear, but they are still infrequent. As in New York, negotiable CDs were issued in the Eurocurrency market to provide a more liquid and therefore appealing money market instrument. Negotiable CDs have appeared in

---

[12]The interested reader is referred to G. Dufey and I. Giddy, *The International Money Market,* Prentice-Hall, 1978.

two different forms: the *top CDs* issued in single amounts by a bank, which remain an interbank financial instrument; and the *tranche CDs*, which are managed issues by several banks and denominated in smaller amounts, so that they can be attractive to corporations and individual investors. The secondary market for London dollar certificates of deposit is now well developed, although this is not true for CDs in other currencies.

While borrowers often want to borrow for longer than five years, CDs are not currently issued for any longer maturities. Thus there have developed forward CDs, whereby a bank will issue and other banks will agree to contract CDs at a fixed or floating interest rate at some given future date. This device allows banks to make medium term loans to corporations or governments which extend beyond five years and be certain of available resources.

Loans in a specific currency are priced according to a "LIBOR plus" principle. Three parameters usually determine the cost: a commitment fee, which is a per annum fee expressed as a percent on the undrawn, uncancelled portion of the loan; a front end fee which is a one-time payment, expressed as a percentage of the amount of the loan, usually paid shortly after the signing of the loan; and a spread which is the percent per annum margin added to the bank's cost of funds, which is LIBOR. The sum of these three pricing elements allows us to determine a total spread, which is annualized and represents the total margin of the loan expressed as an annualized percentage over LIBOR. Under this pricing procedure, the most common in the Eurocurrency market, Euroloans are floating rate loans which depend on the value of LIBOR. The total spread over LIBOR varies with market conditions. Historically it has varied between 1/2% to 3%. If one compares the pricing of Euroloans with U.S. domestic loans, the principle differences are as follows: Euroloans do not involve compensating balances but rather involve commitment fees on the unused part of credit lines, and the front-end fee has become of substantial importance in the Euromarkets. Since credit standing is measured by markup over LIBOR, there has arisen a willingness of weaker borrowers to trade larger front-end fees for lower markups. On a present-value basis the outcome is equivalent, but a lower markup is supposed to have cosmetic advantages.

## 8.7   FUNCTIONS OF THE EUROMARKETS

We can distinguish three distinct functions served by the offshore financial system:

1.   Foreign exchange hedging

In the Eurocurrency markets, commercial banks can take positions that cover the forward commitments they have made vis-à-vis their customers. Let's suppose, for example, that the London branch of Citibank has agreed to loan French francs to a French corporation. It has then acquired a foreign currency asset, which it can turn immediately to a dollar asset by engaging in the forward sale of French francs with the BNP in London, with the maturity of the forward sale corresponding to the maturity of the loan. Conversely, a dollar loan can be converted immediately into any foreign currency asset by a forward purchase of the foreign currency in which the bank wants to have the asset. Also, forward currency commitments can be hedged by offsetting depositing or borrowing transactions. It is only a short step from such activities to covered interest arbitrage, which is an important interbank activity.

2.  Domestic intermediation

The offshore markets can at times partially supplant normal channels of domestic financial intermediation as happened in the United States in the 1968–1969 tight money period and in France in 1974–1975 when the government imposed a severe credit policy on the banking system and at the same time encouraged corporations to seek the necessary financing they needed in the Eurocurrency system.

3.  International intermediation

The offshore markets channel liquid resources from countries with a loanable surplus to those with a desire to borrow. The most striking example of this is the so-called "recycling of petrodollars." When OPEC countries started rolling in cash in 1973, almost everyone predicted a collapse of the world financial system because all those dollars were going to the Arab countries, and everybody wondered how all the importing countries would pay their bills. The dollars were in fact deposited by the OPEC countries in the Eurocurrency system and relent to the importing countries as one might have expected. The real impact of OPEC oil price rise has been a transfer of income it has brought about, not the financial flows that have resulted.

**Why are there so many interbank transactions?**

As was mentioned earlier when we presented the theoretical balance sheet of a Eurobank, interbank transactions represent a large part of the activity of a Eurobank. The actual figures for the size of the Eurocurrency markets vary depending on the source and method of calculation. The most agreed-upon figures are those given by the *Bank for International*

*Settlements* (BIS) annual reports. Other sources include Morgan Guaranty Trust and Bankers Trust. More than a third of the volume of transactions is interbank trade rather than transactions with nonbank depositors or nonbank borrowers (300 of around 800 billion dollars). The BIS figures for the size of the Eurocurrency system net out all the interbank transactions. Table 8.14 presents figures for the size of the Eurocurrency market, both for the gross and the net size as calculated by the BIS. The BIS figures, which are the most commonly reported ones, treat the system only as a financial intermediary, the second and third of the functions with which this section began. If the covered interest arbitrage and foreign exchange hedging aspects of the market are considered, a good part of the interbank transactions represent legitimate economic transactions and not just reshuffling of funds within the network of intermediaries.

## 8.8   SUMMARY

The offshore short- and medium-term capital markets perform the same intermediary functions as domestic capital markets. They differ in two respects.

1.  There is a need to undertake currency exchange to complete some of the financial deals.

2.  The offshore markets are the beneficiaries of the absence of an enforceable world legal framework and world government—they are virtually completely unregulated. Of course they are rigidly controlled by the extreme competitive pressure on both the borrowing and lending sides of the counter.

Eurocurrency deposits are created by the transfer of the ownership of a domestic currency deposit to an offshore bank, in return for a certificate of deposit or time deposit at the offshore bank. Thus the offshore deposit cannot somehow increase the amount of the domestic money supply. It can make it go further, of course, since very little is tied up in reserves. The great number of leakages from the offshore banking system into domestic banking systems means that in practice the Eurocurrency multiplier is extremely low. The offshore banking system does not threaten monetary control, it threatens the profitability of the heavily regulated domestic banking systems.

The threat derives from the greater efficiency possible in the absence of government supervision and control. This has permitted the system to grow from an asset base of zero in the early 1960s to a size of nearly $800 billion today. Moreover the system has survived a number of cataclysmic world monetary crises with hardly any significant defaults. This should provide food for thought for government regulators.

**Table 8.14** *External Liabilities of Reporting European Banks*[9]

| End of December | Dollars | Deutsche mark | Swiss franc | Pound sterling | Dutch guilders | French franc | Others | Total gross size | Total net size |
|---|---|---|---|---|---|---|---|---|---|
| 1967 | 18.1 | 1.7 | 1.4 | 0.8 | 0.1 | 0 | 0.4 | 22.5 | 18 |
| 1968 | 26.9 | 3.0 | 2.3 | 0.8 | 0.3 | 0.2 | 1.5 | 35.0 | 25 |
| 1969 | 46.2 | 4.6 | 4.0 | 0.8 | 0.4 | 0.2 | 1.3 | 57.5 | 44 |
| 1970 | 58.7 | 8.1 | 5.7 | 0.9 | 0.6 | 0.4 | 2.5 | 76.9 | 57 |
| 1971 | 70.8 | 14.6 | 2.8 | 2.1 | 0.9 | 0.4 | 2.7 | 99.3 | 71 |
| 1972 | 96.7 | 19.5 | 8.8 | 2.2 | 1.4 | 1.1 | 3.6 | 133.3 | 92 |
| 1973 | 131.4 | 32.0 | 17.2 | 4.6 | 2.3 | 2.1 | 5.6 | 195.2 | 132 |
| 1974 | 156.4 | 34.4 | 18.3 | 3.6 | 2.8 | 2.3 | 8.1 | 225.9 | 177 |
| 1975 | 189.5 | 39.9 | 15.3 | 3.1 | 3.6 | 3.4 | 6.7 | 261.5 | 205 |
| 1976 | 230.0 | 47.2 | 15.9 | 4.0 | 3.5 | 3.2 | 9.0 | 312.8 | 247 |
| 1977 | 272.9 | 65.0 | 20.9 | 5.9 | 4.9 | 4.4 | 9.5 | 385.5 | 300 |

[a]As of September 1977, Morgan reported a gross size for the Eurocurrency market of 616.2 billion dollars and a net size of 360 billion dollars.

*Source:* Bank of International Settlements Annual Reports.

The dollar is still the dominant currency of transaction, although it has rapidly lost ground to the Deutsche mark and other strong currencies in recent years. The main borrowers are governments, international organizations, public firms, and only last, private enterprises. Loans are priced on a floating rate basis, with credit standing marked by the size of the premium the market demands over LIBOR, the London Interbank Offer Rate, which is the interbank wholesale money rate. For cosmetic reasons, front end fees are being used to lower the apparent premium over LIBOR.

The offshore markets serve three functions.

1. They act as intermediaries within a single currency, allowing borrowers and lenders to bypass the controlled domestic credit markets.

2. They act as international intermediaries, bringing together borrowers and lenders from different countries.

3. They provide the world's banks with a means to offset the forward commitments they have made to their customers, and to undertake covered interest arbitrage.

Turn now to Case 5 at the back of the book.

### Suggestions for Further Reading

The reader may find it useful to look at J. Makin and D. Logue (Eds.), *Eurocurrencies and the International Monetary System*, American Enterprise Institute for Public Policy Research, Washington, D.C., 1976.

# Chapter 9

# *Offshore Financing II–The Eurobond Market*[1]

## 9.1 INTRODUCTION

The Eurobond market is an offshore bond market. Being a bond market, it permits lenders to lend directly to borrowers without the intermediation of a bank that takes the funds from the lenders and itself lends to the borrowers. Eurobonds are simply bonds issued directly by the final borrowers. They have some unusual features. For example, up to 20% of new issues may be floating rate bonds, and much smaller percentages involve currency conversion options and payments in a basket of currencies, features which we will discuss. The designation "offshore" refers to the multinational issue of the bonds. Rather than being issued in only one national capital market, they are underwritten by an international syndicate and distributed worldwide,[2] in a bearer form.

Bond market participants distinguish between Eurobonds, foreign currency bonds, and parallel bonds. A foreign currency bond issue is a bond issue floated in a single country, in the currency of that country, by a foreign borrower. A parallel bond issue is a number of simultaneous foreign currency bond issues, where the borrower raises funds from a number of countries in the currencies of those countries. The Eurobond issue is sold in many capital markets but denominated entirely in one currency (or basket of currencies, etc.). In principle the offshore bond markets could be like the offshore medium and short term credit markets in their freedom from control. Parties would get together to lend and borrow in some currency, away from the control of the monetary au-

---

[1]We would like to thank Wayne Ferson for research assistance.

[2]Except in the United States. It is extremely costly to satisfy the large number of S.E.C. regulations on new issues, so Eurobonds enter the United States only 3 months after issue, as secondary market instruments.

thorities whose currency they were using. This is how the Eurodollar bond market operates, but that constitutes half or less of the annual volume of new Eurobond issues. The ideal state of noncontrol will exist only if

- the national monetary authorities whose currency is being used don't care who borrows and lends in it, and other countries don't bar their nationals from participating; or

- there are large pools of uncontrolled, offshore funds in the currencies concerned so that even if the monetary authorities care about the use made of their currency, there isn't much that they can do about it.

In the case of the dollar, both situations apply. As long as new Eurobonds don't appear on the domestic market (because S.E.C. issue regulations will not have been satisfied), U.S. capital market regulators don't care about the Eurobond market. And the dollar remains a major vehicle currency, large external dollar balances are held, and the U.S. economy is viewed as the last bastion of capitalism. So foreign investors are able and willing to buy dollar-denominated bonds. For the other main currencies there is not really an offshore, unregulated market. The national monetary authorities want to control capital market issues, and there are not large enough outstanding balances of the currencies to conduct a market beyond their reach. The borrowers come largely from the country whose currency is being used, and the lenders do also (with the exception of the Swiss franc). Thus the central banks of these countries have enough leverage to exercise control over many aspects of the market. A committee of the big five West German banks, with the blessing of the Bundesbank, decides each month how many D-mark issues are to be made, who can do the borrowing, and on what terms. The committee stopped new issues by foreign borrowers in May and June of 1978, when borrowers were scrambling for D-mark bonds. Since then, more borrowers have been allowed into the queue, but third-rank borrowers were kept out. The West German banks defended their cartel by saying that, without a queue, these borrowers would have had to wait anyway. They thought that market forces would do the job more messily.

The market for Eurosterling bonds revived at the end of 1977 when the pound had strengthened to $2, but collapsed in 1978. Several issues were launched simultaneously, and the prices of new bonds slumped. Why? Well, who wants to hold sterling bonds? Until recently sterling has been subject to unpredictable and large exchange rate fluctuations which, as we explain in Section 9.3, tends to keep foreign buyers away. British buyers must pay with "external sterling." They must take investment dollars at a premium and buy sterling with it.[3] With the small market for offshore sterling bonds, due to British exchange control regulations and the history of erratic domestic monetary policy, the Eurosterling bond market is weak and easily amenable to official intervention. The Bank of France organizes an explicit queue for would-be issuers of offshore French franc bonds, a practice only made legal in September 1978 after a ban lasting 2½ years. Without central bank approval there would not be enough borrowers and lenders beyond the reach of the Banque de France to keep a market going. The same situation exists in the Euroyen bond market. Issuers of Euroyen bonds are competing for yen funds from Japanese lenders, and the Bank of Japan gives priority to domestic yen bond sales. The Swiss force foreign issuers of Swiss franc bonds to convert the proceeds immediately to foreign currency. But that is what these borrowers want to do anyway. And there are large foreign holdings of Swiss francs that can sustain a market. So it is not clear that Swiss National Bank rules have any real effects on the Euro-Swiss franc bond market. Nonetheless, outside the Eurodollar bond market there is not all that much difference between Eurobond issues in a particular currency and foreign bond issues. The main distinguishing feature is the multinational syndicate of underwriters.

## 9.2 BUYERS, SELLERS, CURRENCY, AND VOLUME

As of the end of 1978 there were about $60 billion worth of Eurobonds outstanding with annual new issues running in the $10 billion to $20 billion equivalent range. Table 9.1 gives the breakdown of new issues for the period 1968–1977 in terms of category of borrower and currency of denomination. For contrast, Table 9.2 shows a breakdown of foreign bond issues in the United States over the same period. For the OECD countries as a group, the total capital raised on domestic markets is running in the $300 billion equivalent range. The Eurobond market began with issues by U.S. companies wishing to avoid the costs of S.E.C. regulation and to bypass U.S. controls on capital outflow. But as Table 9.1 shows, half the new issues are by public sector and international organization borrowers. In the beginning, Eurobonds were primarily sold to individual investors. Bearer bonds are useful to people interested in tax evasion, a categorization of investors that embraces all of western and southern Europe. However, as the market has grown, institutional investors have come to

---

[3]In a futile attempt to improve the balance of payments, the British government until recently forced residents wishing to make foreign investments to buy the needed currency from a pool replenished by sales of foreign investments by other British residents. Foreign currency was at a premium for the most part. Thus it was not sensible to pay more for an offshore sterling bond than a domestic sterling bond.

**Table 9.1** New Eurobond Issues (1968–1977) in Millions of Dollars

| Eurobonds, Total | 1968 3573 | 1969 3156 | 1970 2966 | 1971 3642 | 1972 6335 | 1973 4193 | 1974 2134 | 1975 8567 | 1976 14328 | 1977 17481 | Breakdown 100% | Total 1968–1977 66357 | Breakdown 1968–1977 (%) 100 |
|---|---|---|---|---|---|---|---|---|---|---|---|---|---|
| **By category of borrower** | | | | | | | | | | | | | |
| U.S. companies | 2096 | 1005 | 741 | 1098 | 1992 | 824 | 110 | 268 | 435 | 1130 | 6.5 | 9699 | 15 |
| Foreign companies | 603 | 817 | 1065 | 1119 | 1759 | 1309 | 640 | 2903 | 5323 | 7293 | 41.7 | 22831 | 34 |
| State enterprises | 349 | 682 | 594 | 848 | 1170 | 947 | 542 | 3123 | 4138 | 4508 | 25.8 | 16901 | 26 |
| Governments | 500 | 584 | 351 | 479 | 1019 | 659 | 482 | 1658 | 2239 | 2936 | 16.8 | 10807 | 16 |
| International organizations | 25 | 68 | 215 | 98 | 395 | 404 | 360 | 615 | 2193 | 1614 | 9.2 | 5987 | 9 |
| **By currency of denomination** | | | | | | | | | | | | | |
| U.S. dollar | 2554 | 1723 | 1775 | 2221 | 3906 | 2447 | 996 | 3738 | 9125 | 11525 | 66.0 | 40010 | 60.1 |
| German mark | 914 | 1338 | 688 | 786 | 1129 | 1025 | 344 | 2278 | 2713 | 4029 | 23.1 | 15244 | 23 |
| Dutch guilder | — | 17 | 391 | 298 | 393 | 194 | 381 | 719 | 502 | 361 | 2 | 3256 | 5 |
| Canadian dollar | | | | | | — | 60 | 558 | 1407 | 674 | 4 | 3087 | 4.7 |
| European unit of account | | | | | | 99 | 174 | 371 | 99 | 28 | — | 1156 | 1.8 |
| French franc | | | | | | 166 | | 293 | 39 | — | — | 881 | 1.3 |
| Other | 105 | 78 | 112 | 337 | 905 | 262 | 179 | 610 | 443 | 864 | 5 | 2741 | 4.1 |

Source: Morgan Guaranty's "World Financial Markets," various issues.

**Table 9.2**  *Foreign Bonds Issued (millions of dollars) in U.S.*

| | 1968 | 1969 | 1970 | 1971 | 1972 | 1973 | 1974 | 1975 | 1976 | 1977 | 1977 Breakdown (%) | 1968–1977 (millions $) | Breakdown 1968–1977 (%) |
|---|---|---|---|---|---|---|---|---|---|---|---|---|---|
| **Foreign bonds outside the United States** | | | | | | | | | | | | | |
| *By currency of denomination* | | | | | | | | | | | | | |
| German mark | 674 | 531 | 89 | 308 | 500 | 362 | 253 | 1089 | 1288 | 2096 | 29 | 7190 | 24.2 |
| Swiss franc | 238 | 196 | 193 | 669 | 815 | 1526 | 911 | 3297 | 5359 | 3463 | 48 | 16667 | 56.2 |
| Dutch guilder | 223 | 100 | 17 | 17 | 31 | 0 | 4 | 182 | 597 | 211 | 3 | 1167 | 3.9 |
| Japanese yen | | | 15 | 92 | 311 | 271 | 0 | 17 | 226 | 1271 | 18 | 2311 | 7.8 |
| Other | | | 64 | 452 | 403 | 467 | 264 | 299 | 160 | 144 | 2 | 2360 | 7.9 |
| Total | 1135 | 827 | 378 | 1538 | 2060 | 2626 | 1432 | 4884 | 7630 | 7185 | 100 | 29695 | 100 |
| *By category of borrower* | | | | | | | | | | | | | |
| U.S. companies | 139 | 223 | 55 | 200 | 215 | 546 | 77 | 61 | 28 | 40 | .6 | 1584 | 5.3 |
| Foreign companies | 56 | 128 | 83 | 212 | 345 | 996 | 455 | 1386 | 1654 | 1158 | 16.2 | 6473 | 19.8 |
| State enterprises | 12 | 107 | 16 | 163 | 249 | 446 | 568 | 1314 | 2439 | 1909 | 26.6 | 7223 | 24.3 |
| Governments | 317 | 98 | 53 | 254 | 177 | 297 | 138 | 765 | 1351 | 1834 | 25.6 | 5284 | 17.8 |
| International organizations | 611 | 271 | 171 | 709 | 1074 | 341 | 194 | 1358 | 2158 | 2244 | 31.2 | 9131 | 30.8 |
| Total | 1135 | 827 | 378 | 1538 | 2060 | 2626 | 1432 | 4884 | 7630 | 7185 | 100 | 29695 | 100.0 |
| **Foreign bonds in the United States** | | | | | | | | | | | | | |
| *By category of borrower* | | | | | | | | | | | | | |
| Canadian entities | n.a. | n.a. | 904 | 635 | 986 | 925 | 1962 | 3074 | 6138 | 2946 | | | |
| International organizations | n.a. | n.a. | 300 | 425 | 250 | 0 | 610 | 1900 | 2275 | 1917 | | | |
| Other | n.a. | n.a. | 12 | 44 | 117 | 94 | 719 | 1486 | 2189 | 2423 | | | |

*Source: World Financial Market, March 1978. Reprinted by permission of Morgan Guaranty Trust Company.*

dominate it. Perhaps 80% of Eurodollar bonds are now purchased by insurance companies, central banks, pension funds, and trust funds run by commercial banks, and perhaps 60% of Euro-DM bonds are also absorbed by this group.[4] Institutional investors turn over portfolios in pursuit of superior performance, so the secondary market has blossomed with about 30 major traders, principally located in London. Figure 9.1 shows secondary market turnover through September of 1978.

**Figure 9.1**  Secondary Market Turnover in Eurobonds

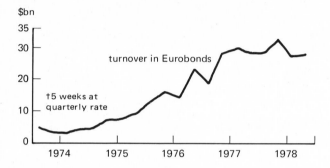

Source: The Economist, London, November 18, 1978, p. 114. Used by permission.

The average maturity of Eurobond issues varies with the degree of perceived stability in the world capital markets. Working with data from the World Bank, the staff of The Economist show the effects of uncertainty on maturity by contrasting 1975 and 1978. This comparison is shown in Figure 9.2. In 1975 when the world was moving into a serious and more or less synchronized recession, borrowers and lenders were very hesitant to make long-term commitments and the maturity of Eurodebt shortened drastically. By 1978 the maturity profile of newly issued debt had returned to its prerecession form.

Table 9.3 gives a more detailed breakdown of Eurobond issues by currency and maturity, and gives also 1977 yield averages.

It is not necessary to dwell on the advantages of the Eurobond market for participants since the relevant points were discussed at length in Chapter 8. To the extent that the markets are really uncontrolled, costs are lower and the whole process is faster. U.S. companies like Beatrice Foods and Texas International Airlines, and the German chemical firm BASF raised money rapidly to finance takeover attempts in the United States in 1978. Lenders have the added advantage of being on their own honor to report interest received to their national tax authorities. In the

---

[4]The Economist, November 18, 1978, p. 114.

**Figure 9.2**   The Effects of Uncertainty on the Maturity of Debt

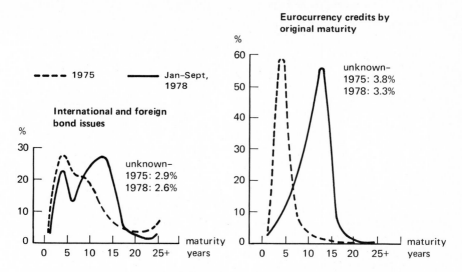

Source: *The Economist,* London, March 24, 1979, p. 25. Used by permission.

rest of this chapter we will discuss currency denomination of Eurobond issues, the unusual fringe bonds with exotic currency features, and implications derivable from comparing the term structure of bonds in different currencies.

## 9.3   CURRENCY DENOMINATION OF EUROBONDS

A large number of factors influence the currency denomination of Eurobonds, some economic and others to do with the official controls which were briefly outlined in Section 9.1. As the market evolves to a less controlled form the economic considerations will take precedence, and it is on these factors that we will focus in this section. We concluded Chapter 7 with a discussion of why corporations might want to avoid hedging exchange risks in a floating rate situation. These arguments were based on the principle that investors would hold asset portfolios providing them a (subjective) optimal pattern of future consumption opportunities. Such asset portfolios involve holding common stocks, bonds, real estate, and other available instruments. We will postpone consideration of the overall optimal portfolio policy until Chapter 10, and confine ourselves to indicating some relevant features here. First, neglecting default risk, we can contrast bonds with other foreign assets as follows. Other assets— stocks, real estate—have returns measured in dollars, which fluctuate with real factors and also with exchange rates. This is equally true if we

**Table 9.3**  *Eurobonds Issued and Announced Between January 1970 and October 1977*
*(In millions of currency units as specified)*

| Currency | Term (Yr.) | 1970 Total | 1970 Yield | 1971 Total | 1971 Yield | 1972 Total | 1972 Yield | 1973 Total | 1973 Yield | 1974 Total | 1974 Yield | 1975 Total | 1975 Yield | 1976 Total | 1976 Yield | 1977 (to end of Nov.) Total | 1977 (to end of Nov.) Yield |
|---|---|---|---|---|---|---|---|---|---|---|---|---|---|---|---|---|---|
| U.S. | 3–8 | 304.5 | 8.38 | 373 | 7.82 | 145 | 7.94 | 320 | 8.77 | 265 | 10.31 | 2180 | 9.71 | 4180 | 8.94 | 4938 | 8.64 |
|  | 9–15 | 1206.5 | 9.17 | 1760 | 8.25 | 2563 | 7.11 | 1308 | 7.29 | 532 | 9.51 | 340 | 9.40 | 2696 | 8.53 | 3405 | 7.95 |
|  | over 15 | 40 | 6.88 | 110 | 7.48 | 365 | 6.47 | 205 | 6.74 | — | — | — | — | — | — | 360 | 7.98 |
| German DM | 3–8 | — | — | — | — | — | — | — | — | 640 | 9.85 | 2315 | 8.91 | 3815 | 7.93 | 3995 | 7.09 |
|  | 9–15 | 1.805 | 8.63 | 2.710 | 7.88 | 3465 | 6.83 | 2330 | 7.34 | 100 | 9.38 | 1320 | 8.95 | 1245 | 7.78 | 4065 | 6.71 |
|  | over 15 | 100 | 8.47 | 100 | 8.04 | 200 | 6.24 | 200 | 7.97 | — | — | — | — | — | — | — | — |
| Dutch guilder | 3–8 | 660 | 7.97 | 850 | 7.07 | 1245 | 6.27 | 580 | 6.25 | 900 | 10.16 | 1390 | 8.80 | 945 | 8.59 | 870 | 7.63 |
|  | 9–15 | 60 | 8.25 | 135 | 7.78 | 50 | 6.11 | — | — | — | — | — | — | 75 | 8.23 | — | — |
|  | over 15 | — | — | — | — | — | — | — | — | — | — | — | — | — | — | — | — |
| Luxemburg franc | 3–8 | — | — | 500 | 7.55 | 6800 | 6.92 | 1300 | 7.01 | — | — | 500 | 9.43 | 1650 | 8.72 | — | — |
|  | 9–15 | — | — | — | — | — | — | 500 | 7.27 | — | — | 2500 | 8.72 | — | — | 2050 | 8.49 |
|  | over 15 | — | — | — | — | — | — | — | — | — | — | — | — | — | — | — | — |
| Canadian dollar | 3–8 | — | — | — | — | — | — | — | — | 25 | 10.05 | 511 | 9.99 | 1075 | 9.77 | 330 | 9.30 |
|  | 9–15 | — | — | — | — | — | — | — | — | 33 | 10.13 | 60 | 9.85 | 220 | 9.94 | 135 | 9.17 |
|  | over 15 | — | — | — | — | — | — | — | — | — | — | — | — | — | — | — | — |
| French franc | 3–8 | — | — | — | — | — | — | 50 | 7.23 | — | — | — | — | — | — | — | — |
|  | 9–15 | — | — | 100 | 7.64 | 2380 | 7.34 | 650 | 7.92 | — | — | 1025 | 10.03 | 12510 | — | — | — |
|  | over 15 | — | — | — | — | 75 | 6.06 | — | — | — | — | — | — | — | — | — | — |
| f | 3–8 | — | — | 15 | 7.93 | 43 | 6.89 | 12.5 | 7.3 | — | — | — | — | — | — | 25 | 9.64 |
|  | 9–15 | — | — | — | — | 20 | 5.17 | — | — | — | — | — | — | — | — | 20 | 9.85 |
|  | over 15 | — | — | — | — | — | — | — | — | — | — | — | — | — | — | — | — |
| EUA | 3–8 | — | — | — | — | — | — | — | — | 43 | 10.11 | 118 | 9.82 | 50 | 9.42 | — | — |
|  | 9–15 | 54 | 8.79 | 166.5 | 7.88 | — | — | 52 | 8.425 | 84 | 9.55 | 149 | 9.64 | 32 | 9.40 | 25 | 8.42 |
|  | over 15 | — | — | — | — | — | — | 30 | 7.41 | 12 | 9.05 | — | — | — | — | — | — |
| ECU | 3–8 | 50 | 7.72 | 135 | 7.37 | 70 | 7.91 | 50 | 8.66 | 60 | 7.83 | 30 | 10.23 | — | — | — | — |
|  | 9–15 | — | — | — | — | — | — | — | — | — | — | — | — | — | — | — | — |
|  | over 15 | — | — | — | — | — | — | — | — | — | — | — | — | — | — | — | — |

| Currency | Maturity (years) | | | | | | |
|---|---|---|---|---|---|---|---|
| Kuwait dinar | 3–8 | — | — | 10 9.20 | 28 8.91 | 42 9.17 | 5 9.45 |
| | 9–15 | — | — | — | 13 8.82 | 21 8.93 | 14 8.91 |
| Danish kroner | 3–8 | 225 6.31 | — | — | — | — | — |
| | 9–15 | — | — | — | — | — | — |
| | over 15 | — | — | — | — | — | — |
| Australian dollar | 3–8 | 30 6.34 | — | — | — | 15 10.74 | 10 10.6 |
| | 9–15 | — | — | — | — | — | — |
| | over 15 | — | — | — | — | — | — |
| Lebanese franc | 3–8 | — | 100 7.9 | — | — | — | — |
| | 9–15 | — | — | — | — | — | — |
| | over 15 | — | — | — | — | — | — |
| Austrian schilling | 3–8 | — | — | 275 9.82 | — | — | — |
| | 9–15 | — | — | — | — | — | — |
| | over 15 | — | — | — | — | — | — |
| SDR | 3–8 | — | — | — | 90 9.51 | — | — |
| | 9–15 | — | — | — | — | — | — |
| | over 15 | — | — | — | — | — | — |
| Norwegian kroner | 3–8 | — | — | — | — | — | — |
| | 9–15 | — | — | — | 200 8.89 | — | — |
| | over 15 | — | — | — | — | — | — |
| Hong Kong dollar | 3–8 | — | — | — | — | — | 650 7.34 |
| | 9–15 | — | — | — | — | — | — |
| | over 15 | — | — | — | — | — | — |
| Japanese yen | 3–8 | — | — | — | — | — | 30000 6.71 |
| | 9–15 | — | — | — | — | — | — |
| | over 15 | — | — | — | — | — | — |
| Bahraini dinar | 3–8 | — | — | — | — | — | — |
| | 9–15 | — | — | — | — | — | 27 8.90 |
| | over 15 | — | — | — | — | — | — |
| Saudi riyal | 3–8 | — | — | — | — | — | 35 9.25 |
| | 9–15 | — | — | — | — | — | — |
| | over 15 | — | — | — | — | — | — |

Source: Euromoney, 1970–1977.

measure their returns in terms of any commodity or bundle of commodities that these returns will buy. On the other hand, the return on a fixed-coupon bond is denominated in currency units and thus will vary in dollar value or in commodity purchasing power solely due to changes in exchange rates and interest rates.

Hence a portfolio containing both real assets and bonds provides investors with an opportunity to hedge away the effects of exchange rate changes on the real purchasing power generated by their wealth. Conceptually, such a hedge is not always required. As we have done before, let us begin with a purchasing power parity base case, and consider deviations from it. Specifically, assume the following:

1.   There is perfectly anticipated, pure inflation in all countries.

2.   Purchasing power parity applies all the time.

Then for investors in any country the translated foreign inflation equals the domestic inflation. Take an example. Let there be anticipated annual inflation of 6% in Country A and 1% in Country B. Then by Assumption 2, B's currency will cost 1.06/1.01 times its New Year's Day value come December 30th. Domestic goods in A will cost 1.06 times their New Year's Day value, and imported goods will cost $(1.06/1.01) \times 1.01 = 1.06$ times their New Year's Day value on December 30th also. The reader can repeat the calculation for Country B to show that there all goods, whether of foreign or domestic origin, will cost 1% more at the end of the year than at the beginning. Under our two assumptions the exchange market is irrelevant.[5] A real portfolio strategy becomes important once we introduce some elements of reality.

- Inflation is not uniform; relative price changes occur. There are many risks in the economy.

- Inflation and relative price changes are not perfectly anticipated.

- The exchange rates deviate from purchasing power parity.

In reality domestic currency and foreign currency do not have the same real purchasing power and there are no sure returns on assets.

In reality then, we can say the following about the role of bonds in an international asset portfolio.

1. *Bonds provide a purchasing power hedge against random departures of exchange rates from purchasing power parity.* Suppose an investor holds a bond portfolio apportioned among currencies according to the

---

[5]Of course with prices of all goods and assets rising at a uniform rate, there are no other risks in the economy either!

proportions in which she buys goods priced in those currencies. Random exchange rate changes will change the cost of the goods she consumes, but she will receive an equal change of opposite sign in the yields on her bond portfolio. A random DM appreciation by 5% will raise the cost of a Mercedes by 5% in dollars, but will also raise the yield on DM bonds by 5% in dollars. If this were the only consideration, we would expect to see investors holding bond portfolios proportional to their consumption of goods from various countries. For the market as a whole we would expect outstanding bond issues to be denominated in different currencies according to the share of world exports contributed by the countries concerned.

2. *Bonds are of no use in hedging against relative price variation (except to the extent that very large price movements cause default of bond-issuing companies).* Holding Treasury bills doesn't hedge you against a rise in the price of real estate compared with goods generally. You would have to hold real estate directly. Similarly if the price of oil rises relative to that of other goods, you could (partially) hedge yourself by holding oil company stocks. This principle applies generally to hedging against relative price changes in foreign goods. Because of this consideration we would expect to see investors holding portfolios of stocks in the tradable goods industries of the countries from which they buy imports. In order to ensure that one is obtaining a relative price hedge that is not complicated by random exchange-related gains and losses, one ought to provide leverage for these foreign real asset holdings by borrowing their initial cost in the foreign currency. Thus exchange gains and losses on the value of the real assets are exactly offset by losses and gains on the debt owed in that currency. If all capital markets functioned equally well, we would expect once again to see bonds issued in currencies proportional to the importance of the countries concerned in world trade. In fact because of limited public ownership of assets in Europe and a variety of exchange controls, disproportionate investment will take place in the United States and therefore there will be disproportionate issue of bonds in U.S. dollars.

3. *Bonds themselves carry risks of capital gain and loss over their life to maturity because interest rates change in an unanticipated way, and inflation is not accurately anticipated.* Unanticipated changes in (anticipation of) inflation are the principal causes of changes in long-term interest rates, and thus of capital gains and losses on bonds. Therefore, all other things being given, we would expect risk averse investors to hold a bond portfolio skewed towards currencies in which the rate of inflation was more predictable. The phenomenon of risk aversion also tends to bias lenders to a preference for their own currency, because of the noise in purchasing power of coupons on foreign currency bonds generated by random deviations from purchasing power parity. In Appendix 9.4 we

show that an investor in Country A will prefer a Country A bond to a
Country B (and currency B) bond if variance (inflation rate in A) < variance (inflation rate in B) + variance (random departure from purchasing
power parity of the A/B exchange rate). An obvious consequence of this
is that periods of great instability in the exchange markets drive lenders
back to their local capital markets, even if these have less predictable
inflation than some foreign markets.

The overall picture of asset holdings we are painting is the following.
Asset holdings should be roughly proportional to import values, with a
bias toward more accessible investments and, at least for bond holdings,
a bias toward currencies with more predictable inflation. Information on
asset holdings by location or currency of the asset is very hard to come
by. Table 9.4 gives composition of U.S. imports by region for 1977, while
Table 9.5 gives the best asset-holding breakdown we could obtain for the
United States. The basic problem with Table 9.5 is that it includes bank
loans, which are a trade item and not true long-term investments held by
or on behalf of final investors. We were not able to obtain asset breakdowns
for the major European economies and Japan.

**Table 9.4**   *United States Imports by Source, 1977*

|  | $ million | | % | |
|---|---|---|---|---|
| **Total** | **193,888** | | **100.0** | |
| Europe | 29,536 | | 15.2 | |
| Germany | | 7,666 | | 4.0 |
| Netherlands | | 1,578 | | 0.8 |
| Switzerland | | 1,125 | | 0.6 |
| U.K. | | 5,391 | | 2.8 |
| Canada | 30,625 | | 15.8 | |
| Latin America | 59,211 | | 30.5 | |
| Bahamas | | 1,094 | | 0.6 |
| Brazil | | 2,342 | | 1.2 |
| Chile | | 291 | | 0.2 |
| Mexico | | 4,759 | | 2.5 |
| Asia | 36,051 | | 18.6 | |
| Japan | 20,274 | | | 10.5 |
| Africa | 13,195 | | | 6.8 |
| All other[a] | 25,270 | | | 13.0 |

[a]Includes Australia, Middle East, and Eastern Europe
Source: *Direction of Trade*, International Monetary Fund.

**Table 9.5** *Estimated Composition of Asset Holdings of U.S. Banking and Nonbanking Concerns, by Region, at end of December 1977*

| Claim on: | $ million | | % | |
|---|---|---|---|---|
| Total foreigners | 110,724 | | 100 | |
| Europe | 24,509 | | 22.1 | |
| Germany | | 1,166 | | 1.1 |
| Netherlands | | 586 | | 0.5 |
| Switzerland | | 834 | | 0.8 |
| U.K. | | 11,842 | | 10.7 |
| Canada | 7,740 | | 6.7 | |
| Latin America | 51,587 | | 46.6 | |
| Bahamas | | 21,804 | | 19.7 |
| Brazil | | 5,290 | | 4.8 |
| Chile | | 923 | | 0.8 |
| Mexico | | 5,401 | | 4.9 |
| Asia | 22,779 | | 20.6 | |
| Japan | | 10,962 | | 9.9 |
| Africa | 3,072 | | 2.8 | |
| Others[a] | 1,338 | | 1.2 | |

[a]Includes nonmonetary international organizations.

*Source:* Federal Reserve Bulletin, July 1978. Sum of banks' own claims on foreigners and short- and long-term claims of large nonbanking concerns, excluding those held through banks.

## 9.4 BONDS WITH UNUSUAL CURRENCY FEATURES

While straight Eurobonds have dominated the Eurobond market, bonds involving more than one currency have come to comprise a not insignificant portion of the Eurobond market, as indicated by the "other" and "European unit of account" listings in Table 9.1. We may classify these multiple currency debt issues into the categories of currency option bonds and various types of indexed bonds.

### Currency option bonds

The holders of currency option (also called multiple currency) bonds are able, prior to each coupon date, to choose the currency of their coupon from among two or more predetermined currencies, at a predetermined exchange rate. The currencies of choice and the exchange rates are part of the original bond contract. This will become clear if you examine Figure 9.3. This is the first page of the prospectus of a 1965 issue by U.S. Rubber

Uniroyal holdings. The two currencies involved are the pound sterling and the Deutsche mark. Because this type of bond was new to the in-

**Figure 9.3.**   Uniroyal Prospectus.

Application has been made to the Council of The Stock Exchange, London and to the Commission of the Luxembourg Stock Exchange for permission to deal in and for quotation for the Bonds of the below mentioned Loan.

This Advertisement is issued in compliance with the Regulations of the Council of The Stock Exchange, London, for the purpose of giving information to the Public with regard to the Loan.   The Members of the Board of Directors of U.S. Rubber UniRoyal Holdings S.A. individually and collectively accept full responsibility for the information given and confirm, having made all reasonable enquiries, that to the best of their knowledge and belief there are no other facts the omission of which would make any statement in this Advertisement misleading.

This Advertisement does not constitute an invitation to the Public to subscribe or purchase any bonds or other securities.

# U.S. RUBBER UNIROYAL HOLDINGS

### SOCIETE ANONYME
*Incorporated with limited liability in the Grand Duchy of Luxembourg*

### SHARE CAPITAL

| *Authorised:* | | | | | | | *Issued and fully paid:* |
|---|---|---|---|---|---|---|---|
| **U.S.$3,000,000** in Shares of U.S.$1,000 each ... | ... | ... | ... | ... | ... | ... | **U.S.$3,000,000** |

## £5,000,000 6 PER CENT. STERLING/DEUTSCHE MARK GUARANTEED LOAN OF 1965

#### UNCONDITIONALLY GUARANTEED BY

# UNITED STATES RUBBER COMPANY

*Incorporated with limited liability in the State of New Jersey, U.S.A.*

Throughout the life of the Loan payments of principal, premium (if any) and interest will be made either in sterling or, at the option of the bearer (subject as mentioned under " Financial Servicing " below), in Deutsche Marks of the Federal Republic of Germany at the fixed rate of DM 11.18 to £1.

| **HAMBROS BANK LIMITED** | **N. M. ROTHSCHILD & SONS** | **S. G. WARBURG & CO. LIMITED** |
|---|---|---|
| LONDON | LONDON | LONDON |

### DEUTSCHE BANK AG
#### FRANKFURT AM MAIN

Hambros Bank Limited, N. M. Rothschild & Sons, S. G. Warburg & Co. Limited and Deutsche Bank AG (" the Banks ") have, under a Subscription Agreement dated 27th July, 1965, agreed to subscribe the £5,000,000 6 per cent. Sterling/Deutsche Mark Guaranteed Loan of 1965 (" the Loan ") of the Company at 97 per cent. (" the Issue Price ") less a commission of 2½ per cent. of the nominal amount of the Loan subject to permission to deal in and quotation for the Bonds of the Loan being granted by The Stock Exchange, London, not later than 4th August, 1965.   Certain bankers, brokers and dealers (" the Selling Group ") are being invited to apply for Bonds of the Loan at the Issue Price less a concession of 1½ per cent. of the nominal amount of the Bonds to be allowed by the Banks. Members of the Selling Group may concede a re-allowance of ½ per cent. to recognised security dealers.   The Banks will not in connection with the distribution of the Bonds offer or sell any Bonds in the United States of America or to persons believed to be residents or nationals thereof.   Sales by the Banks are being made on terms that the Bonds will not in connection with their distribution be re-offered or re-sold in the United States of America or to persons believed to be residents or nationals thereof.

#### KREDIETBANK S.A. LUXEMBOURGEOISE

Kredietbank S.A. Luxembourgeoise has agreed to arrange for quotation for the Bonds of the Loan on the Luxembourg Stock Exchange and to effect, in due course, the exchange of the temporary scrip certificates for Bonds which will be in bearer form and not registrable.   Luxembourg stamp duty (if any) will be paid by the Company.

#### DIRECTORS OF U.S. RUBBER UNIROYAL HOLDINGS S.A.

GEORGE RAYMOND VILA, Windy Hill Farm, Far Hills, New Jersey, Chairman.   (*Chairman and President, United States Rubber Company.*)

ETIENNE ELIOT, Scarswold, Garth Road, Scarsdale, New York, Managing Director.   (*Vice-President, International Finance, United States Rubber Company.*)

SAMUEL EDWARD HARRISON, 2 Avenue Robert De Traz, Geneva.   (*Managing Director, U.S. Rubber Overseas S.A.*)

EDWARD JOHN HIGGINS, 261 Fox Meadow Road, Scarsdale, New York.   (*Divisional President, U.S. Rubber International Company, division of United States Rubber Company.*)

MYRON KALISH, 430 Bryant Avenue, Roslyn, New York.   (*General Counsel, United States Rubber Company.*)

FRANCIS JOSEPH McGRATH, 6 Pinecrest Road, Scarsdale, New York.   (*Financial Vice-President and Treasurer, United States Rubber Company.*)

#### SECRETARY AND REGISTERED OFFICE
ANDRE ELVINGER, 84 Grand' Rue, Luxembourg.

vestment community, an explanatory note, which is reproduced in Figure 9.4, was included with the prospectus.

**Figure 9.4.** Explanatory Note.

EXPLANATORY NOTE

*This note is issued by Hambros Bank Limited, N. M. Rothschild & Sons, S. G. Warburg & Co. Limited and Deutsche Bank AG. It is intended as an illustration only of the application of the proposed currency option, full details of which will be found in the definitive Bonds.*

# U.S. RUBBER UNIROYAL HOLDINGS

Société Anonyme

£5,000,000 STERLING/DEUTSCHE MARK GUARANTEED LOAN OF 1965

UNCONDITIONALLY GUARANTEED BY

# UNITED STATES RUBBER COMPANY

In relation to the currency option available to Bondholders:

1. Throughout the 15-year life of the Bonds, each Bondholder will be entitled to receive, at his own option, payments of principal, premium (if any) and interest

**either in Sterling**

**or in Deutsche Marks at a fixed DM/£ exchange rate**

which will be settled on 22nd July, 1965, and which will not change during the life of the Bonds.

2. Thus, for example, if the rate is fixed at DM 11.20 to £1 and the coupon rate is 6 per cent. per annum a holder of a £100 Bond would be entitled to receive:—

(*a*) on repayment of principal at par either **£100 or DM 1,120**

(*b*) as half-yearly interest on any payment date either **£3 0s. 0d. or DM33.60 irrespective of the actual DM/£ rate of exchange on the payment date.**

3. A decision by a Bondholder to take a particular payment of principal, premium (if any) or interest in one currency will in no way restrict his freedom as to the currency in which he takes any subsequent payments.

4. If a Bondholder requires any particular payment of principal, premium (if any) or interest to be made in Deutsche Marks, the Bond in the case of principal and the appropriate coupon in the case of interest must be deposited with the paying agent from whom payment is required, together with written instructions that such payment is to be made in Deutsche Marks, not less than 21 days before the date on which payment by U.S. Rubber UniRoyal Holdings S.A. becomes due. If such action is not taken by a Bondholder in respect of any payment it can only be made in Sterling.

5. **Thus, in effect, up to 21 days before any payment date, a Bondholder has the option to receive payments of principal, premium (if any) and interest in Sterling or Deutsche Marks, whichever appears to be more advantageous.**

July, 1965.

Most currency option bonds involve only two currencies. However currency option bonds with more than two currencies also exist. The most widely known of these bonds are the five-currency European currency unit (ECU) bonds. As of the beginning of 1978, only two ECU bonds had been issued (by ENEL, an Italian company and by the Republic of South Africa) with the following predetermined exchange rate options:

$$1 \text{ ECU} = 44.8159 \text{ BF/LuxF}$$
$$= 5.11570 \text{ FF}$$
$$= 3.2225 \text{ DM}$$
$$= 3.2447 \text{ guilder}$$
$$= 581.5 \text{ lira}$$

Since the DM has been the strongest currency in the ECU basket, the outstanding ECU issues have for all practical purposes become DM issues.

The currency option strengthens the exchange guaranty for the investor, who will make some gain unless all currencies included in the contract depreciate against the desired currency. Suppose for example that a Kuwaiti investor bought a currency option bond which offered payment in Deutsche marks, French francs, or U.S. dollars. Only when all three currencies depreciate against the Kuwaiti dinar would he lose, and then only in the same proportion as the currency that has depreciated the least among the three. With a currency option clause, therefore, when all currencies in the contract depreciate but in different proportions, the obligations of the borrower fluctuate in the same proportion as the currency that has depreciated the least (this is also the case, as we will see, with the European unit of account bond). However, when all currencies in the contract appreciate, but again in different proportions, the obligations to the issuer appreciate in the same degree as the currency that most appreciated (the European unit of account bond, in this case, appreciates only by the same amount as the currency that least appreciated).

A borrower who issues a currency option bond has effectively created a package consisting of a straight Eurobond plus an option on spot exchange rates with the exercise prices as the rates written into the bond contract. For example, in the Uniroyal issue, the exercise price is the DM 11.20 to the pound rate. Appendix 9.1 presents a comprehensive analysis of the equivalence between a currency option bond and a portfolio of straight Eurobonds plus exchange options. It is possible to find rational prices for currency option bonds along the same general lines as one can find rational prices for options on common stock. Given the advantages of currency option bonds to lenders, we would expect them to carry a price. As with common stocks, investors will pay for the options. Here the payment takes the form of a lower interest rate.

Other types of currency option bonds have been issued recently, but they are not currency option bonds in the sense we have used in this section. They give the lender the option of choosing payments of interest and repayment of principal at an exchange rate corresponding to the spot market rate. Thus, they save brokerage costs on conversion of coupon and principal payments for the investor.

### Currency Basket Bonds[6]

Various currency basket or currency cocktail bonds have been developed to stabilize the purchasing power of coupons. This is accomplished by combining several currencies according to some weighting process. Several forms of currency basket bonds exist: SDRs, EURCOs, B bonds, EEC-EUA, ARCRU, and the European Unit of Account bonds.

The amount of each currency in the basket generally remains fixed, but the value of the basket changes as some of the component currencies depreciate or appreciate relative to each other. Since any one currency constitutes only part of the basket, its fluctuations are reflected in changes in the value of the basket in proportion to its weighting in the basket.

Table 9.6 shows the composition of the first five currency basket bonds cited above.

A unit of account cannot be a means of payment nor an instrument of exchange since no such composite currency exists. Therefore, subscription to these bonds and the payment of interest and principal cannot be made in the denomination unit of the cocktail bonds. The payment currency is generally fixed in the debenture agreement and is a matter of indifference to borrowers and investors alike since no advantage exists in receiving any particular currency aside from the convenience of not having to make an additional exchange transaction into the currency the parties actually want.

The SDR represents the largest cocktail of currencies of all the currency basket bonds (16 currencies). Its historical preeminence derives primarily from its development as the unit of account for the International Monetary Fund. Some banks have agreed to contract for SDR futures (see Appendix 9.1 for the pricing and feature of these futures). The availability of their services allows for possible short-term hedging of the exchange risk related to the SDR bond issues. Up to 1978, few issues have been denominated in SDR.

The European Composite Unit (EURCO), often referred to as the Eurococktail, was an early attempt to arrive at a composite unit of account whose weights would reflect the relative GNPs of the nine member countries of the European economic community. Contrary to initial predictions, EURCO bonds have enjoyed a wide geographical acceptance, well beyond Europe. This acceptance is not at all surprising from an economic viewpoint, as we will see.

---

[6]This part of the chapter draws heavily on A. Robichek and M. Eaker, "Bond Denominations and Exchange Risk in European Capital Markets—A Technical Note," *Financial Management*, 5, 3, Autumn, 1976.

**Table 9.6**   *Composition of Currency Basket Bonds*

|                      | B-Unit | EURCO | EEC-EUA | SDR   |
|----------------------|--------|-------|---------|-------|
| U.S. dollar          | 2.40   | —     | —       | .40   |
| DM                   | 6      | .9    | .828    | .38   |
| United Kingdom pound | 1      | .075  | .0885   | .045  |
| French franc         | 11.50  | 1.2   | 1.150   | .44   |
| Swiss franc          | 7      | —     | —       | —     |
| Italian lira         |        | 80    | 109     | 47    |
| Belgian franc        |        | 4.50  | 3.80    | 1.6   |
| Luxemburg franc      |        | .50   |         |       |
| Danish kroner        |        | .50   | .217    | .11   |
| Irish pound          |        | .20   | .0076   | —     |
| Netherland guilder   |        | .005  | .286    | .14   |
| Japanese yen         |        | .35   |         | 26.   |
| Canadian dollar      |        |       |         | .071  |
| Swedish kronar       |        |       |         | .13   |
| Australian dollar    |        |       |         | .012  |
| Norwegian krone      |        |       |         | .099  |
| Spanish peseta       |        |       |         | 1.1   |
| Austrian schilling   |        |       |         | .22   |
| South African rand   |        |       |         | .0082 |

The ARCRU is composed of the following currencies in equal weights with the two strongest and two weakest currencies eliminated:

| Algerian              | dinar  |
|-----------------------|--------|
| Bahrain               | dinar  |
| Egyptian              | pound  |
| Iraq                  | dinar  |
| Kuwait                | dinar  |
| Lebanese              | pound  |
| Libyan                | dinar  |
| Oman                  | rial   |
| Qatar                 | rial   |
| Saudi Arabian         | rial   |
| Syrian                | pound  |
| United Arab Emirates  | dirhan |

Identical in concept to the EURCO is the European unit of account agreed upon by the EEC finance ministers in March 1975 (EEC-EUA). The difference lies in slightly different weights given to the nine component currencies (see Table 9.6). To avoid confusion, we will refer to the EEC European Unit of Account as EEC-EUA, and refer to the Kredietbank's unit of account (as discussed below) as EUA.

The *B unit* has been suggested by Barclay's Bank as an alternative to the EURCO and especially to the SDR, which is considered to have a cumbersome number of components.

The *ARCRU* was created by Hambros Bank of London. The unit was intended to provide appeal to potential investors from Arab countries. As of 1978, only four issues had been denominated in ARCRU.

The European Unit of Account (EUA) bond is the oldest currency basket denomination formula. The base value is linked to the nine reference currencies of the EEC members and can be altered only if certain events happen. However, for a reference currency to qualify, two conditions must be fulfilled: the currency must have a par value in relation to either gold or SDR, and the price of the currency on foreign exchange markets must be maintained within the 2–1.4% of the European currency snake. It is on the basis of the last requirement that four currencies (the Irish pound, British pound, French franc, and Italian lira) have been disqualified in the fall of 1975 as reference currencies. As of June 1978, the qualified reference currencies and their relation to the EUA are indicated in Table 9.6. The base value of the EUA remains unchanged unless there is a change in the official parity of each of the reference currencies and a majority have changed in the same direction. If each of the reference currencies has been revalued or devalued, then one EUA's issue will be changed in the direction of the majority's movement. The amount of the change will be equal to the least of the changes among the currencies constituting the majority move. Individual currency parity changes do not affect the base value of the EUA; however, they alter the relationship between the respective currency and the EUA.[7] The advantage of the EUA is that borrowers and investors alike are not affected by a change in the parity value of an individual currency unless they happen to be from that country. Since 1961, 78 issues totaling EUA 1.2 billion (over $1.8 billion) have been made for borrowers representing fifteen countries.[8]

Why have there been so few of these basket-bond issues? Recollect our discussion of the currency denomination of Eurobonds in Section 9.3. There we argued that the currency mix of bonds in an investor's portfolio ought to correspond roughly to the mix of consumption expenditure in those currencies. Take now the example of a bond paying coupons in SDRs. The currency weights in the SDR definition roughly correspond to the shares of world trade contributed by the major trading nations. If an investor consumed goods in the typical world trade proportions, holding SDR bonds would spare him or her the trouble of creating a bond portfolio in exactly those proportions. However import patterns vary from country to country and from person to person. Therefore for all but small investors it will be better to purchase straight Eurobonds in whatever proportions are desired. We conjecture that these basket-bond issues have been rare because the market for the consumption-hedging bundle they implicitly create is very small.

---

[7]For practical examples of how exchange rate fluctuations relate to EUA, see Robichek and Eaker, op. cit.

[8]Euromoney, June 1978, p. 145.

## 9.5  INFORMATION CONTENT IN EUROBOND YIELD STRUCTURES

Different Eurobond issues carry different yields. These yield spreads can be explained in a straightforward way as the sum of those factors affecting yield spreads in any domestic bond market, plus factors peculiar to differences in currency of denomination. We have nothing to add to contemporary explanations of domestic yield spreads in terms of time to maturity and default risk. There are a number of good explanations of these factors available to the reader.[9] There are two features which distinguish the Eurobond market from domestic bond markets. First, its international nature has allowed it to escape a substantial amount of government regulation. Second, it provides bonds denominated in different currencies. It is natural to inquire about the relationship between the yields of domestic and Eurobond issues similar in all respects—currency denomination, maturity, and default risk. We might refer to spreads discovered here as the "spatial structure of interest rates." Another natural query concerns the magnitude of spreads attributable solely to differences in currency denomination, which we can call the "currency structure of interest rates."

"Spatial spreads" can be explained by government regulation of capital flows and of the domestic bond market. In the absence of capital flow controls, arbitrage would ensure either that spatial spreads were zero or that the more expensive market would wither away. If the governments are perceived to be capable of severing the arbitrage links, one expects domestic and Euroyields of equivalent bonds to be able to move somewhat independently; that is, one expects to observe spatial spreads of random amount. Whether they should always be of random sign is a trickier question. As we discussed with reference to the spatial differentials observed in the Eurocurrency market (Section 8.4 of Chapter 8), offshore Eurocurrency instruments seem to carry somewhat higher risk of capital gain and loss than do domestic instruments. Such an explanation implies higher average yield on offshore than on domestic instruments. Table 9.7 shows this direction of differential to be the norm for maturities up to 12 months. However the evidence we have been able to gather for bonds is more ambiguous. Guilder, French franc, and dollar bonds do not seem to have higher average yields in the offshore than the domestic market, although DM bonds do. The difficulty of constructing comparable indexes for bonds issued by different entities and with different remaining lives makes all such comparisons extremely sensitive. Only for domestic US$ issues do we even have a clear rating of bonds, and the overall worth of the American ratings as indicators of bond quality has yet to be established. At the moment there is inadequate information to establish definitive conclusions on the direction and magnitude of spatial spreads.

---

[9]We recommend J. Van Horne, *Financial Markets and Flows*. Englewood Cliffs, N.J.: Prentice-Hall, 1978.

**Table 9.7** *Spatial Spreads (Domestic Rate Less Offshore Rate) 1978*

| 3 Mos. Deposits | | January | February | March | April | May |
|---|---|---|---|---|---|---|
| DM | domestic | 3.08 | 2.93 | 2.86 | 2.87 | 2.88 |
| | London | 3.06 | 3.19 | 3.31 | 3.50 | 3.44 |
| | spread | .02 | −.26 | −.45 | −.63 | −.56 |
| US$ | domestic CD | 6.92 | 6.90 | 6.86 | 6.93 | 7.36 |
| | London | 7.47 | 7.50 | 7.50 | 7.69 | 7.94 |
| | spread | −.55 | −.60 | −.64 | −.76 | −.58 |
| SwF | domestic | 1.00 | | .50 | .50 | 1.00 |
| | London | .81 | .38 | .56 | .94 | 1.44 |
| | spread | .19 | | −.06 | −.44 | −.44 |
| FF | domestic | 9.13 | 9.25 | 8.63 | 8.19 | |
| | London | 15.12 | 13.32 | 9.00 | 9.25 | 9.50 |
| | spread | −5.99 | −3.77 | −.38 | −1.06 | |
| L | domestic CD | 6.13 | 6.63 | 6.69 | 8.13 | 9.19 |
| | Paris | 6.94 | 7.94 | 7.69 | 10.31 | 10.81 |
| | spread | −.81 | −1.31 | −1.00 | −2.18 | −1.62 |
| Guilder | domestic | 4.87 | 4.87 | 4.87 | 4.87 | 4.56 |
| | Euroguilders | 5.08 | 5.30 | 5.26 | 4.77 | 4.64 |
| | spread | −.21 | −.43 | −.39 | +.10 | −.08 |
| **6 Mos. Deposits** | | | | | | |
| US$ | domestic CD | 7.25 | 7.20 | 7.25 | 7.70 | 8.00 |
| | London | 7.84 | 7.69 | 7.84 | 8.06 | 8.44 |
| | spread | −.59 | −.49 | −.59 | −.36 | −.44 |
| **12 Mos. Deposits** | | | | | | |
| US$ | domestic CD | 7.50 | 7.50 | 7.50 | 7.80 | 8.20 |
| | London | 7.94 | 7.94 | 8.03 | 8.12 | 8.62 |
| | spread | −.44 | −.44 | −.53 | −.32 | −.42 |
| **Bonds** | | | | | | |
| Guilder | domestic[a] | 7.57 | 7.38 | 7.29 | 7.07 | 7.13 |
| | international[b] | 7.66 | 7.17 | 7.03 | 6.86 | 6.81 |
| | spread | −.09 | .21 | .26 | .21 | .32 |
| FF | domestic[a] | 12.14 | 12.28 | 12.08 | 11.69 | |
| | international[c] | 11.21 | 11.53 | 11.84 | 10.42 | 10.25 |
| | spread | .93 | .75 | .74 | 1.27 | |
| US$ | domestic[d] | 8.45 | 8.60 | 8.60 | 8.80 | 8.90 |
| | international[e] | 7.99 | 7.94 | 7.86 | 7.83 | 7.94 |
| | spread | .46 | .66 | .74 | .93 | 1.04 |
| DM | domestic[f] | 5.76 | 5.75 | 5.68 | 5.71 | 5.76 |
| | international[g] | 6.81 | 6.74 | 6.83 | 6.95 | 6.97 |
| | spread | −1.05 | −.99 | −1.15 | −1.24 | −1.21 |

[a]Private, secondary market, index.
[b]Guilder denominated notes with remaining life over 3 years.
[c]Eurobonds with 7–15 years of remaining life.
[d]Salomon Bros. Aa index, new issues, 5 year call protection.
[e]Morgan Guarantee Index.
[f]FAZ 6% industrials average.
[g]Index of international DM issues.

*Source:* OECD Financial Statistics, Monthly Supplement: Interest Rates, June 1978. Reprinted by permission.

We can do a little better with yield spreads based on currency of denomination. Everything else being constant, one expects changes in the currency structure of yields to reflect changed anticipations about exchange rate movements. This does not have to reflect a conscious arbitrage process. As we explained in Section 7.3 of Chapter 7, bonds are, on average, priced to bring this about. If

1.  bond yields carry an allowance for anticipated inflation;

2.  anticipations are on average realized;

3.  there are no systematic deviations between the countries in real term structures; and

4.  purchasing power parity applies on average,

then yield differentials on comparable bonds denominated in different currencies reflect anticipations of long run inflation differentials, which will translate, more or less, into exchange rate changes, based on the purchasing power parity principle. As a result, comparison of yields on equivalent bonds denominated in different currencies can be used as a forward exchange rate indicator for maturities beyond those quoted on the actual forward exchange market. To do this computationally we must assume that the anticipated real term structure is identical across all capital markets. If we are willing to make this assumption, we can generate forecasts of future spot rates in a way we illustrate using the data in Table 9.8.

**Table 9.8**   *Data for Implied Spot Rate Forecasts*

| Date | Spot | forward quote | DM Bond Matures 1/1/88 (% Yield) | $ Bond Matures 1/1/88 (% Yield) |
|------|------|---------------|----------------------------------|----------------------------------|
| 1/1/78 | .48 | .60 (3 years) | $a_1$ | $b_1$ |
| 1/1/79 | .52 | .65 (2 years) | $a_2$ | $b_2$ |

Assuming $b_1 > a_1$, $b_2 > a_2$ we know the estimated dollar depreciation over 10 years is

$$(1 + b_1)^{10} - (1 + a_1)^{10} - 1$$

over 10 years, as of January 1, 1978. Since the forecast three year depreciation is

$$\frac{.60 - .48}{.48}$$

the estimate of depreciation from year four to year ten is

$$(1 + b_1)^{10} - (1 + a_1)^{10} - 1 - \frac{.60 - .48}{.48}$$

By January 1, 1979, the estimate for years four through ten was revised to

$$(1 + b_2)^{10} - (1 + a_2)^{10} - 1 - \frac{.65 - .52}{.52}$$

If we have available a sufficient sample of comparable bonds of different maturity we can generate an entire implicit forward rate structure.[10, 11]

When would it be appropriate to assume that real term structures are everywhere the same? Only if there were some actual arbitrage process which involved buying bonds in one currency and selling them in another to bring this equality about. Because of the absence of forward exchange markets, there will not be a covered interest arbitrage process to link term structures. However, the covered interest arbitrage analogy should make us cognizant of the role of exchange rate changes. If exchange rates were always roughly at their purchasing power parity values, then the exchange market would always adjust for inflation differentials in the tradables sector. If this tradables sector inflation were always roughly equal to general inflation, in any reasonably long-term perspective the exchange market is irrelevant. In fact inflationary trends in the tradables and non-tradables sectors can vary for periods of reasonable length so that inflation factored into bond yields need not be equivalent to inflation factored into exchange rates. There is leeway for real term structures to move apart, because of the genuine exchange risk any would-be arbitrager faces. Thus we would approach estimates computed as in Table 9.8 as extremely crude approximations only.

## 9.6  SUMMARY

The offshore bond markets are of much less consequence than the offshore banking system. World bond flotations are enormous in volume, but al-

---

[10]This has been explained at length in G. Dufey and I. Giddy. *The International Money Market*, Prentice-Hall, 1978.

[11]Indeed, in a very real sense these are *explicit* forward rates. To obtain a fixed sum of foreign exchange a number of years in the future, one should buy a bond whose cumulative value will equal the required sum on maturity. Conversely, if one has a large receivable due a number of years in the future, one can issue debt in that currency whose cumulative payout value will equal the value of the receivable. The existence of coupons makes this only imperfect hedging. At what yield can the coupons actually be reinvested? At what exchange rate will the coupons actually have to be met? The correspondence would be perfect if one could deal in discount bonds. We examine such hedging strategies in more detail in Appendix 9.2.

most all are made in domestic markets. Probably this is because there are no large pools of investible long-term funds, and large borrowers outside the control of governments.

Market participants distinguish between Eurobonds, foreign currency bonds, and parallel bonds. A foreign currency bond issue is a bond issue floated in a single country, in the currency of that country, by a foreign borrower. A parallel bond issue is a number of simultaneous foreign currency bond issues by the same borrower, who thereby raises funds in a number of currencies. A Eurobond issue is denominated entirely in one currency (or according to some basket formula) and is sold in many countries by an international syndicate of underwriters.

Eurobonds may include unusual currency features. Currency option bonds allow the lender to nominate, before each coupon date, the currency of repayment from a fixed list and at permanently fixed exchange rates. Currency basket bonds pay off in a basket of currencies rather than in only one. A currency option bond is equivalent to a straight one-currency bond plus an option on spot exchange rates at the coupon dates, the striking price being the conversion rate in the original bond indenture. The most popular baskets for denominating bonds have been European Units of Account and SDRs. However the market for these bonds is small and unlikely to grow, as they may be duplicated or "home made" simply by holding a portfolio of single-currency bonds.

The market value of a firm should be independent of the currency denomination of its debt, so the choice of denomination of the currency of bond issues depends on the preferences of lenders. We have argued that these preferences will depend on the composition of the lender's consumption bundle, on the predictability of inflation in the various currencies, and on the magnitudes of deviations from purchasing power parity in the exchange market.

One may use the term structure of interest rates in different currencies to extract forecasts about exchange rates in the more distant future. A corollary of this is that one may construct long term hedges through the bond markets.

Turn now to Case 6 at the back of the book.

## Appendix 9.1   *The Pricing of Currency Option Bonds*[12]

The purpose of this appendix is to show some of the equivalence relationships that exist between currency option bonds and straight Eurobonds on the one hand, and currency option bonds and a straight Eurobond and options on foreign exchange on the other hand. These equivalence relationships allow a rational pricing of options on foreign exchange.

The reader would be justified in wondering why we devote an appendix to a financial instrument that represents a trivial part of the Eurobond market in terms of volume. However, as we indicated in the chapter devoted to economic exposure to exchange risk, we believe that option markets in foreign currencies are likely to develop to allow firms to hedge contingent earnings in international foreign currency bids.

To show the equivalence between currency option bonds on the one hand and a straight Eurobond and options on foreign exchange on the other hand, we use a currency option bond which allows payment to be denominated in either of two currencies. These we take to be the dollar and the yen. To make things more tractable, we deal only with discount bonds (no coupon payments before a single payoff at the terminal date). There is no loss of generality here since a coupon currency option bond is merely a bundle of discount currency option bonds, one discount bond maturing at each coupon date.

The currency option bond we consider pays, at maturity date $T$, either \$1 or ¥y as specified in the prospectus of issue. Thus at date $T$, it has

$$\max \{1, y\, S^{¥}(T)\} \tag{9.1}$$

where $S^{¥}(T)$ denotes the dollar price of yen spot at date $T$ and $C^{¥} = 1/y$ is the explicit exchange rate at $T$ written into the bond contract.

Let $F^{¥}(\tau,T)$ denote the forward price at $\tau$ for delivery of ¥1 at $T$. Let there exist European put and call options on the forward contracts, which may be written at any striking price $E^{¥}(T)$.

Consider now the portfolios containing the following securities:

1.  a pure discount dollar bond, worth \$1 at $T$

2.  y call options on forward ¥ written at the exercise; price: $E^{¥}(T) = 1/y$ $= C^{¥}$

---

[12]This appendix draws heavily on Feiger and Jacquillat, "Currency Option Bonds Puts and Calls on Spot Exchange and the Hedging of Contingent Foreign Earnings," forthcoming in the *Journal of Finance*. For readers unfamiliar with option pricing, we strongly recommend a new book: Mark Rubenstein and John Cox, *Options Markets*, Prentice-Hall, 1981.

At date $T$ this portfolio returns, in dollars,

$$1 + y \, [S^{¥}(T) - C^{¥}]^{+} = \max\left\{1, 1 + y\left[S^{¥}(T) - \frac{1}{y}\right]\right\}$$

$$= \max\{1, y \, S^{¥}(T)\} \tag{9.2}$$

Comparing Equations 9.1 and 9.2 shows that we have reproduced the value of the Currency Option Bond at the terminal date. Note that writing an option on a maturing forward contract is equivalent to writing an option on the spot rate on the maturity date of the forward contract (which is the maturity date of the currency option bond).

Let $P^{\$}[\tau, T; y^{¥}]$ denote the price at $\tau$ of the currency option bond, let $B^{\$}(\tau, T)$ denote the price at $\tau$ of a bond paying \$1 at time $T$ and let $G^{\$}[\tau, T; E^{¥}]$ denote the dollar price at $\tau$ of the call option on forward ¥ at striking price $E^{¥}$. Then we have priced this call option:

$$G^{\$}[\tau, T; E^{¥}] = \frac{P^{\$}(\tau, T; Y^{¥}) - B^{\$})\tau, T)}{y} \tag{9.3}$$

This relationship shows the equivalence between currency option bonds on the one hand and straight Eurobonds and call options on foreign exchange on the other hand. However, as such and for all practical purposes, such a relationship is of limited value for the pricing of options on foreign exchange. The reasons are twofold. First, currency option bonds ($P^{\$}(\tau, T; E^{¥})$ in Equation 9.3 are in too limited a number to offer the necessary amount of data points that would allow a continuous pricing of such options. Second, even if currency option bonds existed in unlimited number, there is no evidence that they would be priced correctly.[13]

The paper cited in footnote 12 on page 273 shows that currency option bonds can be priced by a pure bond arbitrage, which involves, besides the currency option bond, straight Eurobonds; we would need a bond denominated in each currency offered as an option in the currency option bond.

## Appendix 9.2   *Long Range Hedging Using Bonds*

Forward market facilities are available for maturities up to about three years for the major currencies. However, it may be considered desirable to enter into longer hedges. This is feasible through debt transactions.

We will explain to the reader how to obtain one dollar in two years when one can transact in

1. single year discount bonds; and

2. two year bonds with annual coupons

---

[13]There is indeed some evidence that they would be priced incorrectly. When Merrill Lynch, Pierce, Fenner, Smith started to use the Black-Scholes formula for the pricing of options on common stocks, they found discrepancies between the theoretical price of such options and their market price. After a while these discrepancies disappeared, since every trader on the floor was using the Black-Scholes option pricing formula.

Using the method shown here one can arrange at a known present price to receive $1 at any future date for which all maturities of bonds up to and including that date are available. Let

$P_0(2)$ = price today of a two-year bond which has coupon $C_1$
            after 1 year and a final payment of coupon $C_2$ plus
            principal $D_2$

$P_0(1)$ = price today of a one-year discount bond which yields
            $D_1$ after one year

Since we want to obtain $1 after two years, start by buying the fraction $1/(C_2 + D_2)$ of the two-year bonds. This costs us $P_0(2)/(C_2 + D_2)$. In addition to the $1 received in year 2, we are also to receive a coupon of amount $C_1/(C_2 + D_2)$. To eliminate this, sell the fraction

$$\frac{\dfrac{C_1}{C_2 + D_2}}{D_1}$$

of the single period discount bonds. This pays us

$$P_0(1) \times \frac{\dfrac{C_1}{C_2 + D_2}}{D_1}$$

now and obligates us to pay out at the end of a year

$$\frac{\dfrac{C_1}{C_2 + D_2}}{D_1} \times D_1 = \frac{C_1}{C_2 + D_2}$$

an amount exactly equal to our first year's coupon from the two year bond. Thus the price now of $1 two years from now is

$$F_0(2) = \frac{P_0(2)}{C_2 + D_2} - \frac{P_0^{(1)}}{D_1} \times \frac{C_1}{C_2 + D_2}$$

To use a numerical example, let

$P_0(2) = 1000, \quad C_1 = 100, \quad C_2 = 100, \quad D_2 = 1000$

$P_0(1) = 917.43, \quad D_1 = 1000$

That is, the two year bond sells at par at a 10% rate while the one year bond yields 9%. Then

$$F_0(2) = \frac{1000}{1100} - \frac{917.43}{1000}\left\{\frac{100}{1100}\right\}$$

$$= 0.826$$

That is, a price now of 83 cents, approximately, yields $1 with certainty in two years. In this fashion one can construct true long-term hedges that are as reliable as the payments of the bond coupons.

*Appendix 9.3*   *Some Details of Eurobond Flotation*[14]

In the 1960's a standard Eurodollar bond emerged which is now the basis for most new issues on the Eurobond markets. Its principal characteristics are:—

1. Being a bearer instrument, it can be held anonymously.

2. Payments of interest and repayments of capital *are not subject to any withholding tax.*

3. Denominations are usually:

   | | |
   |---|---|
   | Dollar bonds: | $1000 (occasionally $10,000) |
   | Deutschemark bonds: | DM 1,000 or DM 10,000 |
   | Sterling bonds: | £500 or £1,000. |

4. It is *listed on a stock exchange,* usually London of Luxembourg and therefore is subject to the relevant listing requirements. One of these requirements is that a detailed prospectus describing the issuer, the borrower and (if appropriate) the guarantor, should accompany the issue.

5. The issue is otherwise *completely unregulated.*

6. Eurobonds are normally *not secured* on property or assets. The only forms of security offered to the investor are that

   (a) an issue by a nationalised industry, a city or province, may be guaranteed by a sovereign state;

   (b) an issue by a subsidiary company may be guaranteed by its parent;

   (c) an issue by a joint venture company may be guaranteed by all shareholders;

   (d) an issue by a corporate borrower would normally provide lenders with some form of *negative pledge.* This pledge can take many different forms. In essence it provides that if security is given on a subsequent loan (as defined), the same security will be extended to the current issue.

7. For most Eurobonds there is provision for a Trustee to represent the interests of Bondholders.

8. For all issues Paying Agents are appointed in various cities to make interest payments and capital repayments.

## THE MANAGEMENT SYNDICATE

It is the Lead Manager's responsibility to form:

   (a) the Management Group, consisting of itself and a small number of Co-managers. (For a small issue Co-managers may be unnecessary);

---

[14]Source: "An Introduction to the Eurobond Market," Morgan Grenfell and Co. Limited, July 1978, pages 9–24.

(b)  the Underwriting Group; and

(c)  the Selling Group.

All Managers and all Underwriters are members of the Selling Group.

The Lead Manager is primarily chosen for his skill in organising issues. The Co-managers (if any) are normally chosen for their placing power or activity in the secondary market. They may also advise the Lead Manager on terms and timing. Each acquires a direct contractual link with the Borrower by signing the Subscription Agreement for the issue, by which they accept joint and several liability to "subscribe or procure subscribers" for the entire issue.

Underwriters are generally chosen for their financial standing and for their placing power. The names of Managers and Underwriters normally appear in the Prospectus and in the "Tombstone" newspaper advertisement for the issue.

The Selling Group members are normally chosen for their placing power only. The Selling Group per se does not normally appear in the Prospectus or in the Tombstone advertisement.

Selling Group members (including for this purpose Managers and Under-writers) may sell bonds at the issue price to private and institutional investors; or at the issue price less a limited concession to recognised security dealers.

In an average sized issue there might be between one and five Co-managers, up to one hundred Underwriters and (in addition to the Managers and Under-writers) over one hundred members of the Selling Group.

## COMMISSIONS

Commissions are fixed by convention and are expressed as a percentage of the nominal amount of the loan as follows:—

| Term of loan | 5 years | | 7 years | 10–15 years |
|---|---|---|---|---|
| | Others | Can$ | | |
| Management (%) | 3/8 | 3/8 | 3/8 | ½ |
| Underwriting (%) | 3/8 | 3/8 | 3/8 | ½ |
| Selling Group (%) | 1¼ | 1½ | 1½ | 1½ |
| | 2% | 2¼% | 2¼% | 2½% |

For exceptionally large amounts (say $100 million or more) management fees may be less.

## EXPENSES

The Borrower refunds the Managers' out-of-pocket expenses. The principal items are:—

Telex and Telephone
Travel
Postage
Entertaining

The Borrower will bear all other expenses directly. These include:—

The Borrower's legal expenses
The Borrower's accountancy expenses
The Printing of documents
The Printing of the Bonds
The Stock Exchange listing expenses
The Manager's legal expenses
The Trustees legal expenses

## OUTLINE TIMETABLE FOR A EUROBOND ISSUE

### Outline Timetable

"D" is the date on which the borrower receives his funds, known as the CLOSING DAY or COMPLETION DAY. Numbers refer to *calendar* days, not just working days.

| | | |
|---|---|---|
| D minus 46 (approx) | | Preparation of documentation |
| D minus 31 | | Final decision on syndicate members |
| D minus 31 | | Printing of preliminary prospectus |
| D minus 25 | IMPACT DAY | Invitation Telexes received by underwriters and selling group members, and documents mailed to them. *Beginning of selling period.* |
| D minus 24 | | Visits start to underwriters |
| D minus 22 | | Receipt of acceptances of underwriting, subject to approval of final terms by underwriters. |
| D minus 16 | | Receipt of final indications of demand from Selling Group, including Co-Managers and Underwriters. |
| | | Fix terms of issue. |
| | | Telex final terms to Underwriters. |
| D minus 15 | OFFERING DAY | Receipt of final approval of terms from Underwriters |
| | | Execution of Subscription Agreement and Trust Deed. |
| | | Telex allotments of bonds to Selling Group members. |
| | | Printing of Final Prospectus. |
| D minus 14 | | Acceptance of allotments. |
| | | Listing granted. |
| D minus 1 | | Payment by underwriters and Selling Group made to the account of the Managers. |
| D | CLOSING DAY | Payment of subscription moneys to Borrower. |
| | | Delivery of Bonds. |

**Appendix 9.4**   *Inflation Risk and The Choice of*
*Currency of Borrowing*

Define the following notation.

- R is the nominal rate of interest
- r is the "real" rate of interest
- I is the rate of inflation
- S is the rate of change of the exchange rate
- ρ is the real return rate to an investor

Country 1 is the United States and Country 2 is, say, Japan. The investor can buy both U.S. and Japanese bonds. The ex post real return on a U.S. bond is

$$\rho_1 = R_1 - I_1$$

We can suppose that, roughly speaking, the nominal interest rate equals an expected real rate plus an expected inflation rate.[15] Thus

$$\rho_1 = E(r_1) + E(I_1) - I_1$$

Thus the mean and variance of $\rho_1$ can be computed as

$$E(\rho_1) = E(r_1), \operatorname{var}(\rho_1) = \operatorname{var}(I_1) \tag{9.4}$$

Correspondingly for an American investing in Japanese bonds

$$\rho_2 = E(r_2) + E(I_2) - I_1 + S$$

So that

$$E(\rho_2) = E(r_2) + E(I_2) - E(I_1) + E(S)$$

Since $E(r_2)$ and $E(I_2)$ are given and have no variance,

$$\operatorname{var}(\rho_2) = \operatorname{var}(I_1) + \operatorname{var}(S) - 2 \operatorname{cov}(I_1, S)$$

We may express the notion that purchasing power parity holds on average by stating

$$S = I_1 - I_2 + \delta$$

Where δ is some uncorrelated random motion that is on average zero. Then

$$E(S) = E(I_1) - E(I_2)$$

$$\operatorname{var}(S) = \operatorname{var}(I_1) + \operatorname{var}(I_2) - 2 \operatorname{cov}(I_1, I_2) + \operatorname{var}(\delta)$$

$$\operatorname{cov}(I_1, S) = \operatorname{var}(I_1) - \operatorname{cov}(I_1, I_2)$$

---

[15]For those familiar with the Capital Asset Pricing Model, such an outcome could occur only if movements in the real value of a dollar were approximately uncorrelated with real returns on other marketed assets, that is, if in real terms bonds had a beta of zero.

so

$$var(\rho_2) = var(I_2) + var(\delta) \tag{9.5}$$

Thus, given any pattern of departures from purchasing power parity, the risk of which is represented by $var(\delta)$, capital gains and losses are greater in the currency with the more variable inflation rate.

# Chapter 10

# Offshore Financing III: Equity Markets

## 10.1 A GLOBAL PERSPECTIVE ON PORTFOLIO ANALYSIS

In this chapter, as in Chapter 9, we will analyze an international capital market from the viewpoints of both a corporate treasurer and an investment manager or individual investor. There are two questions to be answered:

1. How do the international equity markets function, and what is their structure?

2. How may they be used advantageously?

An answer to the first question must be primarily descriptive and institutional in nature. Appendix 10.1 gives a summary description of the capital markets of major nations that the reader may use as a guide for comparison with the U.S. capital market structure, and provides some references for further reading. Since many U.S. investment banks and brokerage houses have representation in all of these markets, the reader has easy access to up-to-date market information. Our primary concern will be with the use of these markets by corporation and investors.

In modern financial theory, the key to any strategy for using a capital market is an explanation of how assets in this market are priced. To take an example from our context, if national capital markets were not integrated (that is, if the principles on which the assets are priced varied from one national capital market to another), an investor or firm that did have the ability to choose in which market to place funds or obligations would be able to pick up a bargain. In a fully integrated world capital market, there would be no bargains, but there would be guidelines for firms on the expected rate of return particular projects would require if they were to raise a firm's stock market value. And investors would know the terms under which they could construct asset portfolios.

The essential concept in any explanation of the pricing of durable items is stock equilibrium. We encountered this in Chapter 5 when the influence of money creation on the price level was discussed. Recollect that there we argued the inability of the society, as a whole, to dispose of the money stock forced on it by the central bank. As a result, the price level has to adjust until people are willing to hold the existing money supply for transactions purposes. Similarly, durable goods must be priced so that holders are content to hang on to them. This is why current financial theory begins with the question of the optimal portfolio strategy for an investor. The aggregate of these policies defines the market in which the financial assets are traded. Asset prices will then be such that investors, following their optimal strategies, are willing to hold the outstanding supply of each stock and to absorb the full amount of each new issue. Thus the price of the stock depends on those characteristics of its returns that are relevant to the optimal portfolio policies of the investors. The stock equilibrium concept is the basis for the *capital asset pricing model* (CAPM), which in one or another version is the foundation for explaining asset prices not only in the ivory tower but in the investment world. Most of the development of these asset pricing notions has been in the context of a single capital market. While this has proven extremely illuminating, extension to a world context highlights the unresolved difficulties which, for domestic purposes, we have usually been able to ignore. These are

- the potential difference between the motivations of individual investors and institutional investors;

- the inappropriateness of the assumption of a representative investor in a multicountry framework, and the resulting loss of the concept of a universally optimal market portfolio; and

- the possible limitations on market efficiency and the availability of tradable assets outside the United States.

This chapter presents the principles behind any global portfolio analysis and offers a summary of the available data on market returns and portfolio performance. Using this framework one can then extend the usual analysis of capital budgeting.

## 10.2   THE MEANING AND MEASUREMENT OF PORTFOLIO RISK

There are two levels at which we may evaluate the returns on asset portfolios and the riskiness of those returns. The first is in terms of nominal wealth, necessarily denominated in some specific currency (although it is not farfetched to measure one's net worth in ounces of gold or in units of some other homogeneous commodity). This is the frame of reference of almost all the contemporary capital market theory. The second is in terms of real purchasing power, somehow measured. As anyone who has attempted to compute his or her real income knows, purchasing power given by a nominal amount depends on what you spend it on. The prices of all commodities do not move together everywhere in the world. The law of one price does not even hold continually for tradable goods, let alone for the nontradables which in a country like the United States make up half the GNP. For these reasons the real return on an asset portfolio will depend upon the country of residence of the investor and on the currency in which the bulk of that investor's transactions are carried out. We cannot find portfolios optimal for a single representative investor, as is implicitly done in current parables of asset pricing where variation in commodity consumption, and in the location of that consumption, are ignored. There is an obvious problem which arises as a corollary here. If the real return depends on the consumption pattern of the investor, how can an institutional investor ever formulate a portfolio policy? The answer to this question also arises from the considerations we have raised. There is room for many different kinds of managed portfolios, and investors can combine these to form the ultimate portfolios that they prefer. Therefore the rest of the discussion will focus on the individual investor's optimal portfolio policy.

## 10.3 PORTFOLIO POLICY MEASURED IN NOMINAL TERMS

Consider first[1] portfolio return and risk measured nominally in some specific currency. In this context it is a useful simplification to discuss the expected or mean return on the portfolio and its variance or standard deviation as a measure of portfolio risk. The return on a portfolio is the weighted sum of the returns on the assets comprising the portfolio, the weights being the (initial) value shares of the assets in the portfolio. The return on an asset has two components, dividend and capital gain.[2] In principle (that is, speculative bubbles aside) the capital value of an asset represents the stream of anticipated future dividends, appropriately discounted for time and risk. Thus when we discuss asset returns we are basically talking about present and future earnings from economic activity.

From a statistical and portfolio analysis perspective it is extremely useful to divide the considerations explaining earnings into a number of

---

[1]And last really, also! Unfortunately, analysis of real portfolio returns is in its infancy.

[2]Obviously one should consider after-tax return, which is especially important in international investing.

factors, which can be represented by (proxy) variables and actually measured.[3] In general categories these factors include the following:

- global economic trends (for example, the world business cycle);
- national economic trends—the national business cycle—nation-
  wide cost factors such as labor negotiations;
- industry-specific factors, if on the output side (relative price
  changes for inputs);
- firm-specific factors; and
- the currency in which the returns are earned, and the behavior of
  the exchange market.

Without naming empirical proxies for the variables we have identified, it is useful to represent this model of security returns in a formal
way. Let $X_i$ represent the dollar value of the earnings of security $i$. Let
$\delta_i$ represent the dollar price of the currency in which security $i$'s returns
are earned ($\delta_i = 1$ if the security pays in dollars). Finally, let lower case
letters represent logarithms of the respective upper case letters. Then we
write:

$$x_i = s_i + \beta_{i1}\delta_1 + \beta_{i2}\delta_2 + \beta_{i3}\delta_3 + \beta_{i4}\delta_4 + \epsilon_1$$

where

$\delta_1$ = (logarithm of) the world economic factor[4]
$\delta_2$ = (logarithm of) the national economic factor (or factors;
   we can have a number of them)
$\delta_3$ = (logarithm of) the industry-specific factor (or, again, factors)
$\delta_4$ = (logarithm of) the firm specific factor(s)
$\epsilon_i$ = residual, uncorrelated error

If one were to extend this list one could, in principle, capture all the
components that explain earnings. For tractability one tries to keep the
list short, but before turning to actual computational considerations, let
us see what we can explain with this basic structure.

Risk-averse investors will prefer portfolios with lower variance of
return, holding fixed the expected return. Diversification of portfolios will
lower variability unless all the returns are perfectly positively correlated.

---

[3]The exposition here parallels that in the more or less self-contained discussion of the
evaluation of the riskiness of bank loan portfolios in Chapter 11.

[4]The reader seeking an analogy to the standard capital asset pricing model can think of $\delta_1$
as the (logarithm of) world market returns, so that $\beta_{il}$ would be (roughly) related to the
conventional beta of a security.

International diversification will be advantageous as long as (dollar-valued) earnings are not perfectly positively correlated internationally. Obviously, by definition the firm-specific factors like quality of managment, embezzlement, loss through fire, and so on will not be correlated internationally. About these things we can say little. Let us turn to factors more amenable to economic analysis. Will it be beneficial to a risk-averse investor to place some projected investments in steel with domestic firms,[5] and some with foreign firms? Steel is a tradable good and, for specific types of steel, there is worldwide trade and a world market price. However this is not enough to lock together the returns of all steelmakers, regardless of location because:

- *Output* prices received have leeway to vary from country to country, even under free trade. This is because of transportation cost and the fact that steel is a low value-to-weight item. Recollect our discussion of the gold points in Chapter 2. In terms of the statistical model, the steel price variables in $\delta_3$ would not be perfectly positively correlated across countries.

- *Input* prices paid have leeway to vary from country to country, even under free trade. In part this is also because of transportation cost. Inputs like coke and pellets are even lower value-to-weight items than finished steel. In part this is because some of the inputs, like labor and government services, are nontradable internationally so that their costs (wages and taxes) can vary widely over time from one country to another. In the statistical model this would emerge as less than perfect positive correlation internationally of input variables in $\delta_3$.

- Governmental regulation and protection of industries will vary from country to country. Here we refer to tariffs, quotas, employment subsidies, and the like.

- Because the exchange rate deviates from purchasing power parity, and because the prices of tradable goods in any one country are not perfectly positively correlated, the fact that some of the returns are originally denominated in another currency will itself create diversification benefits.

Note however that the last factor is different from the others, because it may be substantially eliminated, reduced, or amplified at the discretion of the investor. This is undertaken by shorting the currency in question to the desired extent, either directly on the forward exchange market, or indirectly, by borrowing via fixed interest obligations in the relevant currencies. This is illustrated concretely by examples.

---

[5] Consider placing with a number of firms to diversify the firm-specific risks.

**Example 10.1**   *Forward Market Offset to Exchange Rate*
*Effects on the Dollar Value of a Portfolio*

In this example and the next the following will be the facts of the case.

- $1 million is to be invested in a portfolio of Japanese stocks with a yen value of $V(t)$ in $t$ months from the date of investment. Of course $V(t)$ is unknown as of the date of investment.

- On the date of investment the spot rate (indirect quotation) stands at ¥200 to the dollar while the 6 month forward rate stands at ¥210 to the dollar. The 6 month Japanese interest rate is denoted $r_6^{¥}$ while the 6 month Treasury bill rate in the United States is denoted $r_6^{\$}$.

- The spot rate (indirect quotation) $t$ months after the investment will be denoted ¥$D(t)$ per dollar. Of course $D(t)$ is unknown at the date of investment.

In our first example the investor sells ¥200 million for 6 months delivery at 210 on the day he makes his investment. *If* he waits 6 months to liquidate the combined stock/forward currency portfolio he will have, *in dollars*, at the end of that time

$$\frac{V(6)}{D(6)} + 200\left(\frac{1}{210} - \frac{1}{D(6)}\right) = \underbrace{\frac{V(6)-200}{D(6)}}_{\substack{\text{unhedged} \\ \text{component}}} + \underbrace{\frac{200}{210}}_{\substack{\text{``sure''} \\ \text{value}}}$$

If the portfolio had not changed in value in Yen, that is, if $V(6) = 200$, then the investor would have \$200/210 million after 6 months. That is, a sure loss of $1 - (200/210) = 4.76\%$ with no exchange implications. Of course in general the value will have changed, so the investor will accrue exchange rate gains and losses on the difference between $V(6)$ and Y200 million.

If the investor expects capital gains of, say, 8% in the 6 month holding period he would sell forward $¥200(1.08) = ¥216$ million and we would have his holding period terminal dollar value as

$$\frac{V(6)-216}{D(6)} + \frac{216}{210}$$

If we make the assumption, shown to be reasonable in Chapter 6, that the 6 month forward rate, 210, is the expected value of $D(6)$, the spot rate 6 months hence, it will be approximately true[6] that the expected gain from this hedge position will be equal to

---

[6]The technically-minded reader can take a Taylor Series expansion of $[V(6) - 216]/D(6)$ to terms of the second order, and take expectations.

$$-\frac{1}{210^2} \times \text{covariance}\,[V(6), D(6)\,]$$

As stock market returns, and exchange rates generally have exhibited negligible correlation, such a hedging procedure will be, on average, extremely satisfactory. Table 10.1 gives a representative sample of such correlation figures.

These results apply if we make the holding period of the stocks equal to the maturity of the forward contracts originally entered into. Suppose the investor liquidates the Japanese investment portfolio after only 3 months. Let $F$ denote the price at that time of his forward delivery contracts, which still have 3 months left to run. Then the investor will receive, in dollars,

$$\frac{V(3)}{D(3)} + 200\left(\frac{1}{F} - \frac{1}{D(3)}\right) = \frac{V(3) - 200}{D(3)} + \frac{200}{F}$$

$$= \underbrace{\frac{V(3) - 200}{D(3)} + \frac{200}{210}}_{} + \left(\frac{200}{210} - \frac{200}{F}\right)$$

forward rate
gamble

By liquidating before the forward contract matures the investor has, effectively, added another gamble.

***Example/Exercise 10.2***   *Borrowing Offset to Exchange Rate Effects on the Dollar Value of a Portfolio*

Instead of selling yen forward the investor might borrow ¥200 million for 6 months at the same time that he makes his stock investment. We leave it to the reader to compute the effect of this hedge on the dollar value of the portfolio, on lines parallel to those in Example 10.1. In practice the deductibility of interest for taxation purposes may make this the preferred alternative. This is analogous to the hedging and exposure issues discussed in Chapter 7.

We have seen, then, that an investor can to a substantial extent control the currency component of portfolio risk. Attempts have been made by a number of researchers to establish the benefits of diversification of the asset portfolio. One line of approach has followed our decomposition of asset returns into a variety of components, while another has constructed sample diversified portfolios and compared them with sample domestic portfolios. Both these approaches are hypothetical from the perspective of a portfolio manager. So after discussing results of these exercises we will look at studies of the actual nature of asset markets.

**Table 10.1** *Correlation Between Exchange Rates and Stock Returns 1966–1974*[a]

| Exchange Rate \ Stock Index | U.K. | Belgium | France | Germany | Netherlands | Switzerland | U.S. |
|---|---|---|---|---|---|---|---|
| U.K. pound | — | .0142 | -.1513 | -.0594 | -.0270 | -.1309 | -.0792 |
| Belgian franc | .0176 | — | -.0829 | -.0061 | -.0954 | -.2757 | -.1399 |
| French franc | -.0233 | .0195 | — | .0781 | -.0394 | -.1377 | -.0563 |
| German mark | .1150 | -.0424 | -.0664 | — | -.1438 | -.2579 | -.1113 |
| Dutch guilder | .0447 | -.0551 | -.0227 | .0434 | — | -.2235 | -.1386 |
| Swiss franc | .1641 | -.0537 | -.0110 | .1142 | .0732 | — | .0143 |
| U.S. dollar | .1336 | .1319 | -.0448 | -.0485 | .0667 | -.1456 | — |

[a]The coefficient in, say, the box with British pound as the row index and French franc as the column index shows the correlation between the returns on a French stock index and the French franc value of a British pound, computed using the sample period 1966–1974.
Source: B. Jacquillat and B. Solnik, "Multinationals are Poor Tool for Diversification," The Journal of Portfolio Management, Winter 1978.

## 10.4 FACTOR DECOMPOSITION OF ASSET RETURNS

To the best of our knowledge there exist only two major studies along these lines.[7] They look not at earnings but rather at asset returns (dividends plus capital gains). Nonetheless the results are suggestive and will be briefly summarized here.

Conventional, single-market models of asset returns usually take the form

$$R_i = \alpha_i + \beta_i R_M + \epsilon_i$$

$R_i$ = returns to asset $i$

$\alpha_i, \beta_i$ = stable parameters specific to asset $i$

$R_M$ = returns on the single-market portfolio

$\epsilon_i$ = well-behaved, white noise error

As Table 10.2 shows, on average only about one-third of individual security returns can be explained by national market indices. Although the sample period is now somewhat dated, the results are similar for more modern data sets. In general, single national market indices leave well over half the total variance of individual stocks unexplained.

A new approach would attempt to explain stock returns by world, national and industry factors. We quote Lessard's article in the *Financial Analysts Journal* (p. 34):

> In order to test for industry elements, returns on the 205 individual stocks were regressed against (1) a world index and (2) the residuals of the country or industry indexes obtained by regressing these on the world index. Four alternative relationships were estimated using two different surrogates for the world factor—one a market value weighted average of the country indexes (MWI), the other an equally weighted average of the country indexes (EWI)—and the residual of either the country or the industry index on the world index used. To summarize, I had

$$R_{it} = \alpha_i + \beta_i (MWI)_t + \gamma_i RC_j(MWI)_t + \epsilon_t, \text{ } i \text{ included in } j, j = 1, J \quad \textbf{(2a)}$$

$$R_{it} = \alpha_i + \beta_i (MWI)_t + \gamma_i RI_k(MWI)_t + \epsilon_t, \text{ } i \text{ included in } k, k = 1, K \quad \textbf{(2b)}$$

$$R_{it} = \alpha_i + \beta_i (EWI)_t + \gamma_i RC_j(EWI)_t + \epsilon_t, \text{ } i \text{ included in } j, j = 1, J \quad \textbf{(2c)}$$

$$R_{it} = \alpha_i + \beta_i (EWI)_t + \gamma_i RI_k(EWI)_t + \epsilon_t, \text{ } i \text{ included in } k, k = 1, K \quad \textbf{(2d)}$$

> where $R_i$ is the return on stock $i$, member of country $j$ and industry $k$ in period $t$, MWI is the market value weighted world index, EWI is the equally weighted world index, $RC_j(\text{ })$ is the residual series remaining after the country $j$ index is regressed on the world index specified in paren-

---

[7] D. Lessard, "World, National and Industry Factors in Equity Returns," *Journal of Finance*, May 1974, 379–391, and "World, Country and Industry Relationships in Equity Returns," *Financial Analysts Journal*, Jan.–Feb. 1976.

**Table 10.2**  *Average Proportion of Variance of Individual Security Returns Explained by National Market Factor*[a]

| Country | 205 Stock Sample 1969–1973 |
|---|---|
| Australia | 0.34 |
| Austria | 0.37 |
| Belgium | 0.49 |
| Denmark | 0.31 |
| France | 0.46 |
| Germany | 0.44 |
| Italy | 0.43 |
| Japan | 0.27 |
| Netherlands | 0.40 |
| Norway | 0.46 |
| Spain | 0.40 |
| Sweden | 0.42 |
| Switzerland | 0.51 |
| U.K. | 0.37 |
| U.S.A. | 0.32 |

[a]Proportions are for returns translated into U.S. dollar equivalents. Monthly data.
*Source:* D. Lessard, "World, Country and Industry Relationships in Equity Returns," *Financial Analysts Journal*, Jan.–Feb. 1976, Table 1, p. 33. Used by permission.

theses, and $RI_k(\ )$ is the residual of the industry $k$ index on the particular world index.

Table 10.3 shows the results.

These results show that the country index is the dominant factor, and for the most part the industry factors are not nearly as important as either the world factor or the national market factor.

Note that without expected return factors one cannot ascertain an optimal portfolio diversification policy from this information. Lessard presents some hypothetical calculations that imply that, on the basis of his sample data, some gains can be expected for all investors, regardless of country of location.[8]

## 10.5   RETURNS FROM HYPOTHETICALLY DIVERSIFIED PORTFOLIOS

Computing the hypothetical returns from international diversification of a stock portfolio is entirely analogous to computing the risk and return

[8]See Table 7, p. 37, of the *Financial Analyst Journal* paper cited in footnote 7.

**Table 10.3** *World, Country and Industry Contributions to Variance of Individual Securities*

Average Proportion of Variance Explained by:

| Stocks Grouped by Country | Market Value Weighted World Index (MWI) | Residual of Country Index on MWI[b] | Residual of Industry Index on MWI | Equally Weighted World Index (EWI) | Residual of Country Index on EWI | Residual of Industry Index on EWI |
|---|---|---|---|---|---|---|
| Australia | 0.107 (11/15)[a] | 0.250 (12/15) | 0.193 (11/15) | 0.168 (14/15) | 0.197 (10/15) | 0.148 (1/15) |
| Austria | 0.013 (0/4) | 0.097 (4/4) | 0.070 (1/4) | 0.131 (3/4) | 0.264 (4/4) | 0.011 (0/4) |
| Belgium | 0.055 (4/11) | 0.444 (11/11) | 0.105 (9/11) | 0.320 (11/11) | 0.180 (10/11) | 0.015 (6/11) |
| Denmark | 0.051 (1/2) | 0.280 (2/2) | 0.037 (0/2) | 0.148 (2/2) | 0.191 (2/2) | 0.002 (0/2) |
| France | 0.028 (2/27) | 0.437 (27/27) | 0.127 (18/27) | 0.256 (27/27) | 0.211 (27/27) | 0.025 (3/27) |
| Germany | 0.086 (17/26) | 0.366 (25/26) | 0.107 (13/26) | 0.275 (25/26) | 0.169 (21/26) | 0.030 (6/26) |
| Italy | 0.012 (0/18) | 0.427 (18/18) | 0.076 (10/18) | 0.062 (8/18) | 0.356 (18/18) | 0.035 (4/18) |
| Japan | 0.088 (23/35) | 0.190 (33/35) | 0.227 (23/35) | 0.129 (28/35) | 0.156 (30/35) | 0.200 (24/35) |
| Netherlands | 0.188 (6/7) | 0.221 (6/7) | 0.097 (4/7) | 0.344 (7/7) | 0.079 (3/7) | 0.034 (3/7) |
| Norway | 0.008 (0/5) | 0.457 (4/5) | 0.077 (2/5) | 0.188 (4/5) | 0.294 (4/5) | 0.013 (0/5) |
| Spain | 0.011 (0/7) | 0.393 (6/7) | 0.046 (1/7) | 0.110 (6/7) | 0.311 (6/7) | 0.012 (1/7) |
| Sweden | 0.069 (5/8) | 0.356 (7/8) | 0.070 (3/8) | 0.165 (6/8) | 0.260 (7/8) | 0.016 (0/8) |
| Switzerland | 0.161 (9/9) | 0.363 (9/9) | 0.139 (8/9) | 0.387 (9/9) | 0.141 (7/9) | 0.017 (0/9) |
| U.K. | 0.084 (20/31) | 0.297 (31/31) | 0.286 (26/31) | 0.100 (20/31) | 0.287 (30/31) | 0.285 (28/31) |
| Simple Average | 0.069 | 0.327 | 0.118 | 0.199 | 0.221 | 0.060 |
| Market Value Weighted Average | 0.075 | 0.290 | 0.192 | 0.164 | 0.212 | 0.154 |

Average Proportion of Variance Explained by:

| Stocks Grouped by Industry | Market Value Weighted World Index (MWI) | Residual of Country Index on MWI[b] | Residual of Industry Index on MWI | Equally Weighted World Index (EWI) | Residual of Country Index on EWI | Residual of Industry Index on EWI |
|---|---|---|---|---|---|---|
| Chemicals | 0.065 (8/19)[a] | 0.350 (18/19) | 0.095 (9/19) | 0.184 (12/19) | 0.239 (15/19) | 0.040 (4/19) |
| Steel | 0.068 (8/19) | 0.381 (19/19) | 0.179 (11/19) | 0.218 (17/19) | 0.228 (18/19) | 0.122 (6/19) |
| Non-Ferrous | 0.062 (8/18) | 0.430 (18/18) | 0.210 (16/18) | 0.233 (16/18) | 0.267 (16/18) | 0.115 (8/18) |
| Buil. Prod. | 0.057 (6/15) | 0.390 (14/15) | 0.156 (11/15) | 0.190 (13/15) | 0.257 (14/15) | 0.079 (4/15) |
| Forest Prod. | 0.065 (7/16) | 0.218 (15/16) | 0.136 (8/16) | 0.138 (13/16) | 0.155 (12/16) | 0.123 (6/16) |
| Electrical | 0.110 (12/14) | 0.403 (14/14) | 0.178 (11/14) | 0.234 (14/14) | 0.282 (14/14) | 0.128 (6/14) |
| Automobiles | 0.064 (7/13) | 0.367 (12/13) | 0.207 (11/13) | 0.248 (12/13) | 0.241 (11/13) | 0.100 (7/13) |
| Tires | 0.041 (3/8) | 0.358 (8/8) | 0.223 (7/8) | 0.158 (6/8) | 0.240 (8/8) | 0.106 (5/8) |
| Food Prod. | 0.052 (5/17) | 0.280 (16/17) | 0.131 (10/17) | 0.132 (11/17) | 0.200 (15/17) | 0.091 (5/17) |
| Breweries | 0.080 (11/19) | 0.214 (17/19) | 0.112 (10/19) | 0.181 (17/19) | 0.131 (13/19) | 0.107 (6/19) |
| Textiles & App. | 0.073 (8/15) | 0.280 (15/15) | 0.103 (5/15) | 0.165 (10/15) | 0.197 (12/15) | 0.072 (5/15) |
| Pharmaceuticals | 0.105 (8/11) | 0.349 (11/11) | 0.125 (6/11) | 0.180 (9/11) | 0.272 (11/11) | 0.105 (5/11) |
| Oil | 0.073 (5/14) | 0.370 (13/14) | 0.182 (7/14) | 0.218 (13/14) | 0.237 (13/14) | 0.114 (4/14) |
| Airlines | 0.097 (4/7) | 0.271 (6/7) | 0.217 (5/7) | 0.283 (6/7) | 0.129 (5/7) | 0.117 (3/7) |
| Simple Average | 0.072 | 0.333 | 0.161 | 0.197 | 0.220 | 0.101 |
| Market Value Weighted Average | 0.075 | 0.290 | 0.192 | 0.164 | 0.212 | 0.154 |

[a] Numbers in parentheses are the number of correlations significantly different from zero at the five per cent level divided by the total number in each group. (Two-tailed t-test with 58 observations, critical value of $r=0.251$, $r^2=0.063$.)

[b] That is, the average proportion variance of the stocks in the indicated country explained by the time series of residual returns remaining after the country index is regressed against the Market Value Weighted World Index (MWI).

*Source:* D. Lessard, "World, Country and Industry Relationships in Equity Returns," *Financial Analysts Journal*, Jan.–Feb. 1976, Tables 3 and 4, p. 35. Used by permission.

consequences of a domestic portfolio diversification. The method is illustrated in the following example.

***Example 10.3***  *Computation of Riskiness of An*
*Internationally Diversified Portfolio*

Consider a portfolio consisting of one mutual fund in each of two countries, distinguished by the subscripts 1 and 2. We express all returns and variances, etc., in the currency of one of the countries.

| Country 1 | Country 2 |
|---|---|
| Stock 1 | Stock 2 |
| Expected Return = $R_1$ | Expected Return = $R_2$ |
| Estimated variance of | Estimated variance of |
|   rate of return = $\sigma\,(R_1)$ |   rate of return = $\sigma\,(R_2)$ |
| Proportion invested in | Proportion invested in |
|   Stock 1: $X_1$ |   Stock 2: $X_2$ |
| Correlation coefficient | |
|   between 1 and 2: $\rho_{12}$ | |

The expected return on the portfolio is:

$$E(R_p) = X_1 E(R_1) + X_2 E(R_2)$$

The variance of the portfolio is:

$$\text{Var}\,(R_p) = \sigma^2(R_p) = X_1{}^2\sigma^2(R_1) + X_2{}^2\sigma^2(R_2) + 2X_1 X_2 \rho_{12}\sigma(R_1)\,\sigma(R_2)$$

Let's suppose for the sake of argument that the portfolio has equal weight in each stock; moreover, the expected return and variance figures are the same for the two stocks.

$$E(R_p) = 0.5\,E(R_1) + 0.5\,E(R_2)$$
$$= E(R_1) = E(R_2)$$
$$\sigma_{R_p}^2 = .25\,\sigma^2(R_1)\,.25\,\sigma^2(R_2) + .50\,\rho_{12}\,\sigma(R_1)\,\sigma(R_2)$$
$$= .50\,\sigma^2(R_1) + .50\,\rho_{12}\,\sigma^2(R_1)$$
$$= .50\,\sigma^2(R_2) + .50\,\rho_{12}\,\sigma^2(R_2)$$

If the markets are perfectly correlated ($\rho_{12} = 1$), forming an equally weighted portfolio of the two stocks is strictly equivalent to putting all the eggs in the same basket (either Stock 1 in Country 1, or Stock 2 in Country 2). However, as soon as $\rho_{12}$, the correlation coefficient between both markets is less than 1, the internationally-diversified portfolio dom-

**Table 10.4** Correlations Among National Stock Market Returns 1974–1976[a]

| Stock Market Returns | U.K. | Belgium | France | Germany | Netherlands | Switzerland | U.S.A. |
|---|---|---|---|---|---|---|---|
| U.K. | 1.000 | .671 | .635 | .387 | .708 | .612 | .578 |
| Belgium | | 1.000 | .717 | .599 | .816 | .798 | .621 |
| France | | | 1.000 | .566 | .740 | .751 | .542 |
| Germany | | | | 1.000 | .632 | .602 | .335 |
| Netherlands | | | | | 1.000 | .807 | .583 |
| Switzerland | | | | | | 1.000 | .685 |
| U.S.A. | | | | | | | 1.000 |

[a]Rows and columns represent stock market returns measured on a monthly basis.
Source: Capital International Perspective and IMF Statistics (various issues).

inates any national portfolio. Indeed, the expected return of the portfolio is the same as the expected return on each of the two stocks, but its risk measured by the variance is less than either variance—note that if $\rho_{12}$ is − 1 (i.e., both stocks are perfectly negatively correlated), the risk of the portfolio is zero. This is an extreme case. If $\rho_{12} = 0$ (no correlation) the risk of the portfolio is half the risk of each of the stocks.

Some evidence of the correlation of returns in recent years is presented in Table 10.4. Table 10.5 provides information on standard deviation of national stock price indexes for the same period.

**Table 10.5**  *Risk Measures for Foreign Market Portfolios*

| Country | Annualized Standard Deviation at Rates of Return |
|---------|:---:|
| France | 26.4% |
| Germany | 20.3 |
| Japan | 20.1 |
| Netherlands | 21.8 |
| Switzerland | 22.7 |
| U.K. | 41.0 |
| U.S. | 18.4 |

*Source:* D. R. Lessard, "An Update on Gains from International Diversification," MIT, unpublished, 1977.

### *Example 10.4*  *U.S./U.K. Equal Weight Portfolio*

Picking up on the principles developed in Example 10.3, let us calculate the riskiness of an equally-weighted U.S./U.K. stock market portfolio using the above data. The variance of such a portfolio would be

$$\sigma_P^2 = (.5)^2\sigma_{US}^2 + (.5)^2\sigma_{US}^2 + 2(.5)(.5)\,\rho_{12}\sigma_{US}\sigma_{UK}$$

with

$$\rho_{12} = .50 \text{ and } \sigma_{US} = 18.4, \sigma_{UK} = 410$$
$$\sigma_P^2 = .25(.184)^2 + (.25)\,(.41)^2 + 2\,(.25)\,(.5)\,(.184)\,(.41)$$
$$= .00846 + .04203 + .01886$$
$$= .06935$$
$$\sigma_P = 26.3\%$$

As an exercise the reader should use the data in the tables to verify the following standard deviation of equally weighted, two-country portfolios.

|  |  |
|---|---|
| U.S./France: | 19.8% |
| U.S./Germany: | 15.8% |
| U.S./Japan: | 15.5% |
| U.S./Netherlands: | 17.9% |
| U.S./Switzerland: | 18.9% |

Finally, what would be the standard deviation of an equally weighted portfolio containing all the national indexes, based on the above tables?

These are hypothetical calculations. The results of these computations depend heavily on the estimates of covariances and standard deviations. As in any security market analysis these estimates must be continually updated. The period 1974–1976 saw unusually synchronized economic changes among the developed countries, a pattern that has since begun to break down. If the world economy returns to the pattern of earlier years there will be much greater apparent gains from diversification. Figure 10.1 is a reproduction of the results of a study spanning the period 1966 through 1971. It indicates that over those years an internationally diversified portfolio containing more than 30 stocks had (in dollar terms) about half the standard deviation of a well-diversified U.S. domestic portfolio.

**Figure 10.1** Diversification Benefits, 1966–1971

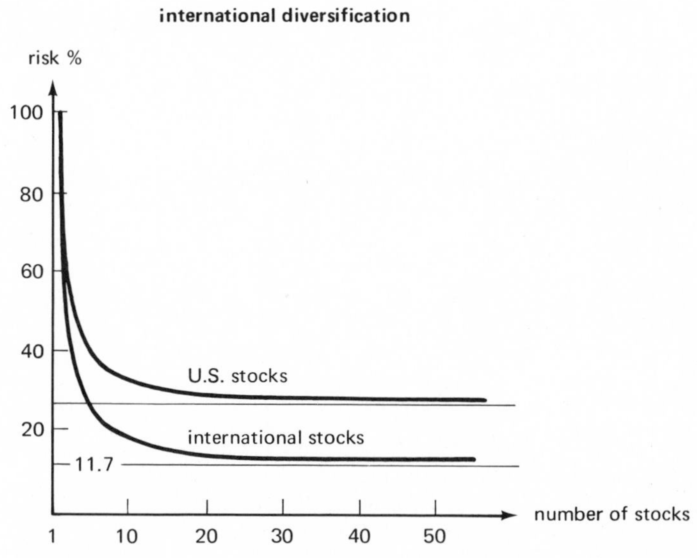

Source: B. H. Solnik, "Why Not Diversify Internationally Rather Than Domestically?" *Financial Analysts Journal*, July–August 1974. Used by permission.

## 10.6   ACTUAL YIELDS FROM DIVERSIFICATION

There have been few studies of the actual benefits to be derived from international, as opposed to purely domestic, portfolio diversifications. A recent, interesting research report examines the experience of 47 British mutual funds which diversified internationally in the favorable period 1960–1970.[9] The funds were all of the same country of origin, quoted in the same currency and subject to the same legal restrictions. On the other hand, they were subject to a number of regulations that made the purchase of foreign currency more expensive than the official exchange rate, and more risky, as measured by rate variability. Principal among these was the need to buy foreign currency from the investment currency pool, in which the pound was more depreciated and much more variable.

The performance of these mutual funds was compared with the performance of random portfolios of British and American securities over the period February 1960 through January 1971. These are hypothetical, internationally diversified portfolios. None of the actual investment trusts outperformed the random portfolios and several trusts were significantly worse. This of course reflects on the ability of managed funds actually to capture diversification benefits. The question remains whether, for British investors, it would have been preferable to invest in the trusts or in a purely domestic portfolio. Using the usual methods[10] for measuring abnormal portfolio performance relative to the London Stock Exchange, none of the mutual funds outperformed the market. It was not clear why the international diversification was not in practice beneficial. Perhaps the funds dissipated the gains in excessive turnover of stocks, incurring the high turnover tax. Two other studies showed more positive results. One is by McDonald,[11] who studied the performance of eight of the oldest mutual funds in existence in France during the period 1964–1969. They exhibited superior risk-adjusted performance, some of which could be attributed to superior skills in analyzing domestic securities and the generally advantageous position of French banks as fund managers, due to their access to current information on French companies;[12] the rest of the

---

[9]James Guy, "An Examination of the Effects of International Diversification from the British Viewpoint on Both Hypothetical and Real Portfolios," *The Journal of Finance*, December 1978, 1425–1438.

[10]The reader should consult J. Treynor, "How to Rate Management of Investment Funds," *Harvard Business Review*, 43 (January–February 1965), 63–75.

[11]John G. McDonald, "French Mutual Fund Performance: Evaluation of Internationally-Diversified Portfolios," *Journal of Finance*, 28, 5, December 1973.

[12]This point is not in contradiction to our claims that most of the foreign stock markets can be considered efficient. To quote Palacios, who studied mutual fund performance in Spain from 1966 to 1971, "Although the average fund performance was clearly superior to that of the market in the first years, the difference has been gradually decreasing over time, consistent with the hypothesis that the market was becoming increasingly efficient." (Juan Palacios, "The Stockmarket in Spain: Tests of Efficiency and Capital Market Theory," unpublished Ph.D. dissertation, Stanford University, August 1973, p. 139.)

superior performance could be attributed to the merits of international diversification through two effects: the pure diversification effect, which would occur even in fully integrated capital markets; and the more favorable return risk ratio in the United States, which would be expected to persist in a fully integrated capital market if the French market had greater total risk and smaller nondiversifiable risk than the U.S. segment of the world market. Another study performed by Farber[13] on internationally diversified European funds also found on average a superior performance for these funds.

## 10.7 INTERNATIONAL CORPORATE FINANCE QUESTIONS

The corporate treasurer uses the capital markets as a source of funds, and as a guide to acceptable new investment projects. Thus from the corporation's perspective there are two important questions to answer.

1. Do foreign stock markets operate efficiently? That is, do they have adequate liquidity and depth so that stock issues there will be attractive to investors, and so that stocks will be rationally priced?

2. Can we identify a "world market line" that gives a better guide to the discount rate to use on new investment decisions than does the national market line?[14]

We will begin with an analysis of the extent to which foreign markets fairly or efficiently price stocks.

Readers familiar with the extensive development of the Capital Asset Pricing Model in the domestic context know that there are three conventional tests of capital market efficiency. These are:

1. tests for the absence of systematic (and thus profitable) price movements in the markets—the *random walk* tests;

2. tests for a positive association between risk and expected return; and

3. tests to see if professionally-managed funds can do better than simple buy-and-hold strategies.

---

[13]Andre Farber, "Systematic Exchange Risk in the International Capital Asset Pricing Model," *Proceedings of the European Finance Association,* North Holland, 1975.

[14]For a brief but excellent explanation of the use of asset pricing theory to determine a hurdle rate for new projects, see Robert Higgins, *Financial Management Theory and Applications,* Science Research Associates, Inc. 1977, Chapter 8 *et seq.*

## Random Walk Tests

Extensive tests have been performed on the major European markets, and recently these same tests have been extended to the major Asian markets. These studies conclude that foreign markets are somewhat less efficient than the U.S. market. However, the magnitude of these departures from randomness is not sufficient to generate gains from strategies based on past prices, as indicated in Table 10.6.

**Table 10.6**  *Summary Statistics of Distributions of Serial Correlation Coefficients for Five Asian and Eight European Countries, and the United States*

| Country | Average serial corr. | Dispersion of sample distribution (S.D.) | Number of terms $\geq 2\sigma$ |
|---|---|---|---|
| *Weekly Log Price Changes* | | | |
| Australia | −.165 | .139 | 5/10 |
| Hong Kong | .030 | .078 | 2/9 |
| Japan | −.065 | .096 | 1/13 |
| Philippines | −.055 | .123 | 1/9 |
| Singapore | −.077 | .111 | 2/13 |
| France | −.049 | .095 | 17/65 |
| Italy | .001 | .086 | 5/30 |
| U.K. | −.055 | .068 | 7/40 |
| Germany | .056 | .072 | 8/35 |
| Netherlands | .002 | .074 | 3/24 |
| Belgium | −.088 | .067 | 5/17 |
| Switzerland | −.022 | .066 | 1/17 |
| Sweden | .024 | .040 | 1/6 |
| U.S.A. | −.038 | .075 | 5/30 |
| *Biweekly Log Price Changes* | | | |
| Australia | −.078 | .255 | 2/10 |
| Hong Kong | .121 | .082 | 3/9 |
| Japan | −.031 | .104 | 0/13 |
| Philippines | .042 | .098 | 0/9 |
| Singapore | −.112 | .187 | 2/13 |
| France | −.050 | .115 | 6/65 |
| Italy | .050 | .100 | 3/30 |
| U.K. | .005 | .098 | 3/40 |
| Germany | .038 | .103 | 4/35 |
| Netherlands | .052 | .104 | 3/24 |
| Belgium | .019 | .116 | 1/17 |

**Table 10.6** *(con't)*

| Country | Average serial corr. | Dispersion of sample distribution (S.D.) | Number of terms $\geq 2\sigma$ |
|---|---|---|---|
| Switzerland | −.063 | .097 | 1/17 |
| Sweden | .070 | .030 | 0/6 |
| U.S.A. | −.053 | .084 | 2/30 |

*Monthly (4 Week) Log Price Changes*

| Country | Average serial corr. | Dispersion of sample distribution (S.D.) | Number of terms $\geq 2\sigma$ |
|---|---|---|---|
| Australia | −.063 | .145 | 1/10 |
| Hong Kong | .009 | .093 | 0/9 |
| Japan | .002 | .123 | 0/13 |
| Philippines | .037 | .132 | 0/9 |
| Singapore | .009 | .125 | 0/13 |
| France | .012 | .104 | 1/65 |
| Italy | −.027 | .110 | 1/30 |
| U.K. | .020 | .108 | 1/40 |
| Germany | .058 | .099 | 2/35 |
| Netherlands | −.011 | .134 | 2/24 |
| Belgium | −.022 | .133 | 1/17 |
| Switzerland | −.017 | .150 | 1/17 |
| Sweden | .140 | .138 | 1/6 |
| U.S.A. | .009 | .099 | 1/30 |

*Source:* Solnik, B., "Note on the Validity of the Random Walk for European Stock Prices," *Journal of Finance,* 5, 1973.

## Tests for a Risk-Return Tradeoff

Extensive tests[15] on the U.S. market have shown that there exists a positive and linear relationship between realized returns and market risk, nearly always what is predicted by capital market theory. Several studies[16] have replicated this test for individual national markets. In all but one country, riskier securities did provide higher realized returns. Although one disturbing finding was that the relationship between risk and return for Germany was negative during an up market, a more recent study for Germany over a longer period of time finds a positive relationship. A

---

[15]See, for example, Michael Jensen (e.), *Studies in the Theory of Capital Markets,* Praeger, 1972.

[16]See S. C. Lau, S. R. Quay, and C. M. Ramsey, "The Tokyo Stock Exchange and the Capital Asset Pricing Model," *Journal of Finance,* May 1974; and James Guy, "The Behaviour of Equity Securities on the Stock Exchange," *Journal of Banking and Finance,* 1, June 1, 1973.

recent study for Japan also finds a positive relationship between risk and return. Therefore, on balance, the risk-return tradeoff appears consistent with modern capital market theory. Such tests are, however, implicitly assuming particular connections among world capital markets, a point we will return to shortly.

### Tests of the Performance of Managed Funds

Such tests have been much more frequently undertaken for the United States than for other countries. However, reasonably carefully designed tests in the French, Spanish, British, and German stock markets imply that superior performance of managed funds is relatively uncommon.

Let us now consider the question of liquidity of foreign markets as measured by the size of these markets relative to the U.S. market. Table 10.7 shows that the U.S. domestic stock market is rapidly losing its dominant position, whether measured by capitalization or by share turnover. Table 10.8 has some information on the global distribution of billion-dollar corporations. As might be expected, the breakdown of the location of these corporations corresponds closely with the size of the various national stock markets.

**Table 10.7**  *Evolution of Foreign Markets*

| Percentage Breakdown of World Stock Market Capitalization | | | |
|---|---|---|---|
| | 1966 | 1975 | March 1979 |
| U.S.A. | 69% | 58% | 54% |
| Japan | 4% | 12% | 17% |
| Europe | 20% | 22% | 20% |
| Other | 7% | 8% | 9% |
| Total | 100% | 100% | 100% |

| Percentage Breakdown of World Share Turnover | | | |
|---|---|---|---|
| | 1966 | 1975 | 1978 |
| U.S.A. | 76% | 55% | 47% |
| Japan | 11% | 21% | 35% |
| Europe | 10% | 20% | 13% |
| Other | 3% | 4% | 5% |
| Total | 100% | 100% | 100% |

*Source:* Tabulated from data in "Capital International Perspective," Capital International, Geneva.

**Table 10.8** *Number of Companies with Stock Market Capitalization in Excess of U.S. $1,000,000,000 (1979)*

| Country | Number | $ of Total |
|---|---|---|
| U.S. | 155 | 49 |
| Japan | 64 | 20.3 |
| Germany | 19 | 6.0 |
| U.K. | 29 | 9.2 |
| Spain | 3 | 1 |
| Switzerland | 8 | 2.5 |
| Netherlands | 4 | 1.3 |
| Australia | 3 | 1 |
| France | 2 | .6 |
| Belgium | 3 | 1 |
| South Africa | 1 | .3 |
| Hong Kong | 2 | .6 |
| Canada | 16 | 5 |
| Italy | 7 | 2.2 |
| Total | 316 | 100 |

*Source: Capital International Perspective (May 1979)*

## National Market Line or World Market Line?

Are world capital markets integrated or segmented? Indeed, what does this question mean? At one extreme the purely segmented market hypothesis is easy to specify: in each country risky assets are priced solely relative to the total asset pool in that country. Investors do not form portfolios incorporating foreign assets. It is this hypothesis (along with a number of others!) that justifies the computation of national market lines and their use in capital budgeting decisions. The alternative is to say that all investors may transact in all capital markets. If one measures returns in nominal terms, as is done in the usual capital asset pricing literature, it can be shown that generally everyone should hold the same risky asset portfolio, which is the market portfolio. This approach can obviously be extended to the international context, and has been so extended in recent work by Richard Stehle.[17] As might be expected, there is no clear resolution—both hypotheses are compatible with the existing evidence because neither fit it very well. Nonetheless, allowing for international factors can help to explain a phenomenon observed on U.S. data when the single-market-line model is tested. This is that stocks with low betas

---

[17]Richard Stehle, "An Empirical Test of the Alternative Hypotheses of National and International Pricing of Risky Assets," *The Journal of Finance*, May 1977, 493–502.

seem to earn higher realized returns than the segmented market theory would predict. As a matter of fact, it turns out that low-beta firms are much larger, on average, than high-beta firms, and tend therefore to have foreign operations. In turn, these have nondiversifiable foreign risks that must command a risk premium. Hence the higher average rate of return that is observed.

The indeterminacy of such tests is unsurprising because they are joint tests of the pricing model and the hypothesis that all returns are measured in nominal units. In section 10.2, we indicated the likely flaws in this reasoning. Thus, the fact that none of the current asset-pricing models fit the data very well needs have no bearing on the extent of integration of world capital markets. The interested reader can pursue these questions in Stehle's paper and the references that he cites.

Why should all this academic investigation be of interest to corporate treasurers? Because it affects their required cost of capital or hurdle acceptance rate. To understand this we will pursue a simple example.

*Example 10.5*  *Cost of Capital Calculations Under Various Hypotheses About World Asset Pricing*

According to the Capital Asset Pricing Model, the required rate of return on any project is the sum of the risk-free rate and a risk premium that is a linear function of the project's systematic risk.

In notational terms:

$$R_j = R_F + \beta_j (R_M - R_F)$$

where $R_j$ and $R_M$ are respectively the required rate of return on the project and the market portfolio, $R_F$ is the rate of return on riskless bonds and $\beta_j$ is the systematic risk of the project.

The systematic risk of the project $\beta_j$ can be expressed as $(\rho_{jM} \sigma_j \sigma_M / \sigma_M^2)$ where $\rho_{jM}$ is the correlation of the returns of the project with the returns on the market portfolio, $\sigma_M$ is the standard deviation of the market portfolio, and $\sigma_j$ is the standard deviation of the project returns.

One can see that there are three factors that contribute to the systematic risk of a project. One is the variance of the market portfolio. The other is the variability of the returns of the project. The last one is the correlation that exists between the variability of returns on the project and the variability on the market portfolio.

*Approach 1: Segmented National Markets*  In this case, the traditional domestic capital asset pricing model can be applied to estimate the minimum expected rate of return that, on a risk adjusted basis, would make a foreign asset attractive from a portfolio management perspective or a foreign project attractive from a corporate perspective. By "attractive," we mean attractive to a U.S. investor, although parallel reasoning would apply for investors in any country. We have the following relationship:

$$E(R_i) = R_F + \beta_{US}^F (E[R_M] - R_F)$$

where

$E(R_i)$ = expected return on stock $i$

$R_F$ = risk-free rate in the United States

$E(R_M)$ = expected rate of return on the U.S. market portfolios

$\beta_{US}^F$ = beta of the foreign market (or stock)

in terms of the U.S. market

From the U.S. perspective an important consideration is the price volatility of the foreign asset or project relative to the volatility of the U.S. asset market, which is the standard of reference. The appropriate risk premium for the foreign asset or project equals its beta, times the risk premium considered by a U.S. investor appropriate for the U.S. market.

$$\beta_{US}^F = \frac{\rho_{US,}^F \cdot \sigma_{US} \cdot \sigma_F}{\sigma_{US}^2} = \frac{\rho_{US,F} \cdot \sigma_F}{\sigma_{US}}$$

Therefore, a low beta of the foreign asset or project means either that the correlation between the U.S. market and the foreign market is low or that the standard deviation of the foreign market or project is low relative to the standard deviation of the U.S. market.

To calculate the average risk premium that must be earned on the foreign asset or project to make it acceptable to U.S. citizens, we need to know the standard deviation of returns of the foreign investment and the correlation coefficient of its returns with the U.S. market, the risk free rate in the United States, and the expected rate of return on the U.S. market portfolio from which we can induce the U.S. risk premium. This and the other data are given in Table 10.9. The risk premium a U.S. investor will require on a foreign investment is the product of the risk premium he or she is asking on the U.S. stock market by the beta of the foreign investment relative to the U.S. market. If we take the example of an average risk investment in France, and if we assume that the risk premium on the U.S. market is 5% (15% expected rate of return on the market minus 10% risk free rate), we find that a U.S. investor would demand a risk premium of 3.90%. Column 4 of Table 10.9 shows the results of similar calculations for other assets or projects having the risk characteristics of the respective national stock market indices.

Of course this approach has treated asset markets as segmented—there is no world capital market line. That is why American investors use their own market betas.

**Table 10.9**   *Risk Measures for Foreign Market Portfolios*

| Country | (1) Annualized Standard Deviation of Returns | (2) Correlation with U.S. Market | (3) Beta of Foreign Market/U.S. Market | (4) Minimum Risk Premium from U.S. Standpoint[a] |
|---|---|---|---|---|
| France | 26.4 | .542 | .78 | 3.90 |
| Germany | 20.3 | .335 | .37 | 1.85 |
| Japan | 20.1 | .450 | .49 | 2.45 |
| Netherlands | 21.8 | .583 | .69 | 3.45 |
| Switzerland | 22.7 | .685 | .85 | 4.25 |
| U.K. | 41.0 | .578 | 1.29 | 6.45 |
| U.S. | 18.4 | — | 1.00 | 5.00 |

[a]This assumes that the risk premium asked by investors is 5%. This column is the product of 5% by column (3).

*Source:* This table is adapted from Lessard, "An Update on Gains from International Diversification," unpublished, 1977, by permission.

***Approach 2: World Capital Markets Fully Integrated on the Basis of Nominal Returns***   If the equity capital markets of the world are integrated, prices and expected returns would be determined by the undiversifiable risk of each investment in the context of the world market portfolio according to the following relation:[18]

$$E(\tilde{R}_I) = i + \beta_I^\omega [E(\tilde{R}_\omega) - i]$$

where:

$E(\tilde{R}_I)$ = the expected return of Country *I* portfolio or project

$i$ = the pure rate of interest

$\beta_I^\omega = \rho_{I\omega} \cdot \sigma_I \cdot \dfrac{\sigma_\omega}{\sigma_\omega^2}$

$\rho_{I\omega}$ = correlation coefficient between the portfolio or project in Country *I* and the world market portfolio

$\sigma_I$ = standard deviation of Country *I* portfolio or project

$\sigma_\omega$ = standard deviation of world market portfolio

Some information for national stock market indices as the relevant assets or projects is contained in Table 10.10. Under the complete integration scenario, the risk premium for the French market increases significantly for two reasons. First, the standard deviation of the world market is less

---

[18]Note that this formula ignores exchange rate questions, because exchange risk can (largely) be hedged away.

than the standard deviations of the U.S. market (16.2% as compared with 18.5%); accordingly, its risk premium is only 4.7%. Indeed, the U.S. beta in terms of the world market is 1.06. Accordingly, the risk premium for the world market is 5.0%/1.06 = 4.7%. Second, the French beta in terms of the world market portfolio is 1.09. Accordingly, 1.09 times 4.7% gives a risk premium of 5.10%. This risk premium is higher than that implied by the segmented market hypothesis. The risk premiums for the other markets are indicated in Column 4 of Table 10.10. Note that for the purpose of all these calculations we continue to assume a 5% required risk premium for the U.S. market.

**Table 10.10** *Expected Returns on Foreign Markets Under Integrated Pricing Hypothesis*

| Country | (1) Annualized Standard Deviation | (2) Correlation with World Market Portfolio | (3) National to World Market Beta | (4) Implied Risk Premium from U.S. Point of View[a] |
|---|---|---|---|---|
| France | 26.4 | .67 | 1.09 | 5.10 |
| Germany | 20.4 | .62 | .78 | 3.70 |
| Japan | 20.1 | .61 | .75 | 3.50 |
| Netherlands | 21.9 | .79 | 1.06 | 5 |
| Switzerland | 22.8 | .78 | 1.09 | 5.10 |
| U.K. | 41.0 | .69 | 1.74 | 8.2 |
| U.S. | 18.5 | .93 | 1.06 | 5 |
| World market portfolio | 16.2 | | | |

[a]This is obtained by multiplying column 3 by 4.7%.

*Source:* This table is adapted from Lessard, "An Update on Gains from International Diversification," Unpublished, 1977, by permission.

## 10.8 SUMMARY

This chapter dealt with equity markets and international investment from portfolio and capital budgeting perspectives. A portfolio manager wants to know the potential benefits and pitfalls of international diversification compared with purely domestic portfolios. As usual, any capital budgeting exercise requires knowledge of the appropriate discount rates to use when considering investment in a new project, domestic or foreign.

To address both of these questions we need an explanation of how assets are priced in world capital markets, in conjunction with floating exchange rates and free commodity and capital flows. Modern portfolio theory says that assets are priced according to their systematic risk; the higher the systematic risk of an asset, the higher should be its expected return. The foundation for the development of these asset pricing notions was laid in the context of single, national capital markets. Extension to a world context has proven difficult and contentious. The main areas of difficulty in extending the domestic models are the following:

- the potential difference between the motivations of individual investors and institutional investors

- the inappropriateness of the usual assumption of a representative investor in a multicountry framework, and the resulting loss of the concept of a universally optimal market portfolio

- the possible limitations on market efficiency and the availability of tradable assets outside the United States

While some of the consequences of these problems are still unresolved we can derive several practical implications for the investor. There is general agreement that covariances between national stock markets are positive and moderate. Thus, with positive excess returns and low covariances, an international mean variance analysis implies that optimal portfolios will be well diversified internationally to reduce risk. Moreover, foreign markets have come of age in terms of size, liquidity, and efficiency. Consideration of exchange risk in a theory of asset pricing might be of limited necessity since

- PPP holds over the long term; and

- national consumption patterns of consumers in developed countries look similar. However, for practical purposes we emphasize in this chapter, as in the preceding, the need for investors to construct internationally diversified portfolios according to the country of origin of the goods they consume.

International corporate finance decisions depend on the existence of a world market line that gives a better guide to the discount rate to use in project evaluation than do national market lines. Whether a world capital market line can be usefully said to exist depends on the degree of integration of world capital markets. At the moment no definite answers exist. Certainly, however, the risk premium required on foreign capital investments should be somewhat lower than if calculation were based on purely domestic considerations.

### Suggestions for Further Reading

M. Adler, "The Cost of Capital and Valuation of a Two Country Firm," *Journal of Finance*, March 1974.

M. Adler and B. Dumas, "Optimal International Acquisitions," *Journal of Finance,*
    March 1975.
F. Grauer, R. Litzenberger, and R. Stehle, "Sharing Rules and Equilibrium in an
    International Capital Market Under Uncertainty," *Journal of Financial Eco-
    nomics,* June 1976.
B. Solnik, *European Capital Markets.* Lexington, MA: Lexington Books, 1973.

## Appendix 10.1   *Equity Markets Outside the United States*

Equity markets outside the United States differ in a number of ways from the American pattern. These differences derive from the methods of financing economic activity and the structure of ownership of firms. These in turn reflect the very different routes these countries followed to industrialization of their economies. Apart from Britain, whose capital markets are very similar to those in the United States, most foreign capital markets may be characterized as follows:

- Very few firms are widely, publicly held. Family holdings and small group holdings dominate, and thus there is reluctance to dilute power and control through the issue of new equity. Such a situation is perpetuated by inheritance tax structures, which, at least de facto, allow these holdings to pass intact from generation to generation.

- Debt financing thus predominates, not only by the issue of bonds but also through continually rolled-over bank loans, which are used to finance long-lived capital assets.

- The role of large commercial banks is great. They underwrite stock issues, manage asset portfolios, vote the stock they hold in trust, provide directors for companies and thus create interlocking directorates, and provide long-term as well as short-term financing through loans. There is no Glass-Steagall Act in Europe.

- Governmental regulation and control of capital flows, the terms on which individuals can buy and sell foreign assets, and the terms on which firms can borrow from banks are of much greater importance than in the United States.

By and large this reflects the governmentally-accelerated pace of industrialization in these countries. Instead of growing slowly with small firms becoming large as their experience increased, in continental Europe and Japan governments channeled capital and resources to small numbers of individuals who would rapidly establish essential industries. The interlocking of banks and firms made direction of capital flows easier and was encouraged. In most of these countries the industrial system emerged as more feudal and paternalistic in structure than in the United States, and much more technologically and organizationally efficient than the capital markets. This is particularly pronounced at the small firm/venture capital end of the markets, as the allocation of risk and seed capital is not well organized by governmental or bank bureaucrats. The multifaceted and less controlled American capital markets have escaped the pressures on governments to allocate scarce capital to socially worthy ends, with the notable exception of mortgage lending. There is more political support in the United States for a laissez-faire capital market than in most other countries. The result is that individual investors and companies seeking funds have much more flexibility and deal in more liquid markets in the United States than elsewhere. The various national equity markets differ substantially, and we offer a brief survey.

## United Kingdom

The British stock markets are most similar to the American. They are self-organized as cooperatives of member firms, and have a jobber system similar to the specialist system on the N.Y.S.E. Because listing requirements are much looser in Britain there is no over-the-counter market in unlisted stocks as there is in the United States and most European exchanges. Some 3000 stocks are listed in London. Institutional holders dominate the market as in the United States, and personal holders turn over their portfolios very slowly. The main obstacle to satisfactory trading is the high level of transactions costs and stamp duties, which can eat up as much as 10% of the value of a transaction. However, there is no compulsion to use the stock exchange and brokers carry out many off-exchange transactions.

## Germany

In Germany the banking system is the most important component of the capital markets, and listed equity issues are relatively small in value while the sale of stock is not a significant source of new resources for firms. Large banks are underwriters of stock issues and retail stocks to the public. Floor brokers do not deal directly with nonbanks. There is a three-tiered equity market. A relatively small number of major stocks are listed. Listing expenses are high, in part because of taxes. At the second level there is a semiofficial market, which also takes place on the exchange floor, for companies that are able to meet much less stringent listing requirements. Finally, the banks run an over-the-counter market in other stocks. Basically, the German financial system channels funds to enterprises via financial intermediaries. Even the bulk of bond issues are by banks, to raise money to lend to corporate customers. Of all new capital raised in 1972–1974, 88% was in the form of bonds and 12% in the form of stocks. Of the bonds, 79% were issued by banks and 20% by public authorities, leaving 1% for corporate issue.

## Belgium

In Belgium the influence of banks on corporations is almost as great as in Germany. The equity market is thin and has few issues. Nearly half of all new issues tend to be made by foreign firms and investment trusts. The market has a couple of features unfamiliar to Americans. First, for actively traded stocks there is not only a spot market (settlement within two days) but also a forward market. On the latter, dealings are made "on account" with settlement every two weeks. In the period 1973 through 1975, two-thirds of market turnover was short-term speculation on the forward market. Second, the bulk of equities are not registered by physically represented by bearer certificates. This is to enable stockholders to avoid declaring dividends for income tax purposes.

### France

In France also, companies tend to be closely held and to raise capital via retained earnings and bond issues. However, there exist a variety of investment trusts encouraging investment by individuals, and the stock market is active. A forward market in stocks exists where accounts are settled monthly. In addition there are two forms of option markets. One is a conventional market in puts and calls, while the other is connected with the forward market. By paying a premium, purchasers of securities on the forward market acquire the right to cancel the transaction on the day before the settlement is due. This is equivalent to a European call option with striking price equal to the forward price of the stock and expiring on the day before settlement. In the French securities markets, brokers hold government appointments and cannot undertake outside business. Recently they have been permitted to become true market makers by trading stocks on their own account. But low capitalization has so far prevented extensive activity of this sort.

### Italy

The situation in the Italian capital markets reflects closely the political structure and problems of the country. For a variety of reasons many firms are government-owned and so do not sell equity. Of the roughly 45,000 or so private firms only 200 or so are quoted publicly. Firms are closely held, and very few individuals in Italy hold common stock. Institutions like pension funds are organized on a transfer basis like the U.S. Social Security system and have no investible resources at hand. Finally, circumstances make it distinctly preferable to raise capital through bank loans. First, for understandable reasons, individuals prefer to hold liquid assets and assets out of the reach of the Italian tax authorities. Second, a vast maze of subsidies and regulations makes it financially advisable for companies to depend on debt finance. Italian bond markets are large and active (mostly with government debt), but the equity markets are neither.

### Netherlands

Stock markets in the Netherlands are worthy of note for two reasons. First, there are five large Dutch multinationals, and trade in their stock is of great importance. (Trade in AK20, Hoogovens, Royal Dutch Shell, Philips, and Unilever makes up about one third of turnover by value.) Second, there is a substantial listing of foreign equities on the Dutch markets—half the stocks listed in Amsterdam are foreign. Large commercial banks are brokers and underwriters, in the usual European fashion.

### Singapore

We mention Singapore because of its growing importance in the Asian currency market. In conformity with its efforts to turn Singapore into a major world financial center, the government has made it extremely easy for foreigners to transact in stocks. There are no exchange controls, remittance restrictions, or capital gains taxes. Listing of foreign stocks and opening of offices by foreign brokers is encouraged. There is a forward market in more active stocks as well as a spot market. The stock market lists a number of Malaysian as well as local companies. However, for the foreign corporation or investor, all this represents more potential than reality as the absolute scale of the market and of equity trading and placements remains small by American or European standards.

### Japan

In Japan as in most of Europe, stock issues have not been the principal or even a very important means of raising capital. Bank loans and bond issues predominate. Nonetheless Japan has a highly developed securities market system, although with a number of parochial characteristics. Government regulation is close and, as in many areas of Japanese economic life, acts to severely limit the participation of foreigners.

There exists a number of stock exchanges and a very small over-the-counter market. The Tokyo Stock Exchange dominates (85% of transactions in 1976) followed by the Osaka Exchange (12% of transactions in 1976). Most of the substantial stocks on the over-the-counter market were listed in "second sections" of the exchanges in the 1960s, and the rate of new public company formation is low. Off-floor trading is permitted and is the basic way of dealing with large blocks of securities. Pricing of new issues and of existing stocks have a number of peculiarities (by U.S. standards). For example only since 1969 have new issues been offered at market, and even in 1976 only 25% of new issues were offered at market price. All the others went to existing stockholders at par plus a premium. Margin trading exists on the U.S. pattern, with the Ministry of Finance setting margin requirements according to its macroeconomic policy goals. Disclosure rules resemble those of the United States in style but are much less stringent, as are accounting rules.

Foreign entities have raised capital in Japan since 1970. In the bond market, foreign issues now exist in substantial number, although these are all by governments or international agencies. Corporations have made private placements in Japan, although on a small scale and subject to substantial governmental restriction. A few foreign companies have made stock issues in Japan, not for very large sums. These things are still at the experimental stage. The government has heavily regulated access of foreign investors to Japanese stocks and bonds, and shows no sign of relinquishing its rights of control. Takeovers of Japanese firms by foreign firms cannot be legally done by stock purchase because of strict limits on the percentage of outstanding stock foreigners are allowed to hold.

# Chapter 11

# International Bank Lending

## 11.1 INTRODUCTION

In this chapter we explain the procedures banks now used to evaluate and control the riskiness of foreign loans. The concept of portfolio risk can be made more precise using modern capital market theory. The decision maker cannot form a policy to cope with risk without first determining the perspective to adopt—we give three distinct concepts and response to each implies different portfolio selection policies. A multi-factor model approach to the assessment of possible portfolio returns allows systematic computation of optimal portfolio policies and, to some extent, an integration of analysis of risks in project lending and in lending to governments. The chapter closes with an exposition of some strategies that can substantially affect the likelihood of default, and a suggestion for further reading along these lines. Appendices look at two interesting questions in more detail. Appendix 11.1 looks at the problem of assessing the adequacy of a country's foreign exchange reserves. Appendix 11.2 explains how to compute the implicit capital market assessment of the portfolio risk.

## 11.2 THE NATURE AND MAGNITUDE OF LENDING ABROAD BY U.S. BANKS

Foreign lending has become extremely important for U.S. banks; for some, it can be as important as their domestic operations. However, what distinguishes it from domestic lending, a field reasonably well explored and well understood? There are two key differentiating features:

1. Repayment of debt must go through the exchange market, so that in addition to assessing the economic potential of the project to which a loan is made, a bank must assess prospects for exchange rates (if the loan was made in another currency) or for controls

on capital flows. In effect, the bank must be prepared to make a global macroeconomic analysis of the environment of the project, as well as an analysis of the project itself.

2. Except in special cases of prior agreement, there is no common legal system and no ultimate arbitrator for the settlement of disputed claims. There is no binding international law, and the governments of developing and eastern bloc nations are particularly unlikely voluntarily to bind themselves to accept the decisions of the international legal fragments that now exist and are very much western-oriented.

The latter point means that collectible collateral for loans is limited to two basic types only: guarantees by U.S. parent or associated companies, and offsetting deposits taken from the country in question. Some major U.S. banks feel it likely that if there is default on a loan to the government of a developing country, they will be able to retain official *and* private deposits taken in that country by branches or subsidiaries of the bank. This is legally questionable and as yet untried. Table 11.1B shows that, in general, guarantees are not of great importance in loans to Eastern Europe and to developing countries. The quality of the loans rests, therefore, on the creditworthiness analysis, the structure of the deals, and on the behavior of the whole loan portfolio.

Banks typically hold a variety of foreign claims. One type is the form of credit traditionally associated with international trade, the most representative activity being discounting of letters of credit guaranteed by foreign banks.[1] Another type is interbank placements.

We saw in Chapter 8 that extremely large sums of capital flow through the offshore money market centers (the principal ones being listed in note h of Table 11.1, plus London). This capital is then eventually lent to final users by offshore banks. For the major banks, forward exchange commitments constitute an important type of foreign claim. They are considered here an item at risk because the possibility exists that the foreign contracting party might default on its obligation to deliver, whether because of its specific business problems or a general restriction on capital outflows by a national government. In the latter eventuality, it is obvious that any forward exchange commitments are as risky a part of the bank's overall foreign claims portfolio as direct loans, which are the final general category of foreign claims held by banks.

Direct foreign loans of any significant size will generally be made by syndicates of banks, with the organizational work and the flow of infor-

---

[1]A particularly brief and lucid explanation of the mechanics of trade financing may be found on pages 158 through 174 of R. M. Rodriguez and E. E. Carter, *International Financial Management* (Englewood Cliffs, NJ: Prentice-Hall, 1976).

mation to the partners being the responsibility of the lead bank. There are two types of syndicated bank loans. The first is a true multibank syndicate, in which there is a separately negotiated agreement between the borrower and each bank in the group. The second is a *participation loan*, in which members of the syndicate pay the lead bank for the right to participate in a large loan and do not have individual agreements with the borrower. These participation loans are the means by which quite moderately-sized U.S. banks become involved in international lending. Only the largest banks have trained staff to evaluate the available lending opportunities. As a result, the smaller banks rely for their information almost solely upon the so-called "placement memorandum", which is the descriptive document (essentially but not legally a prospectus) drawn up by the lead bank to interest other banks. These placement memoranda typically carry disclaimers telling lenders that the lead bank does not guarantee the accuracy of the facts contained therein. Commonly they require the borrower to attest to the facts, but this is not the same, since the borrower is a foreign entity and cannot easily be held to account in a court for any misleading statements. Recently there have been several lawsuits and disputes over alleged failure of a lead bank to make full disclosure of the circumstances of a borrower.[2] Effectively the plaintiffs argued that the lead banks were issuing a form of foreign-project-backed security when they "sold" participations to uninformed partners. The legal grounds for such a claim are flimsy, but it seems clear that for practical purposes that is how these participations were and are treated by small banks.

We should mention a common kind of quasi-guarantee, the *comfort letter*. This is a statement by the parent of a foreign borrower that it fully intends the subsidiary in question to meet all its obligations arising out of a loan. Table 11.2 reproduces a representative comfort letter, while Table 11.3 gives some guidelines used by United California Bank in dealing with such letters of intent.[3] As the UCB policy memorandum makes clear, these letters are not legally binding guarantees. While parents issuing such letters of intent have the obvious strong incentives to maintain their credit rating by ensuring that subsidiaries and affiliates remain solvent, in the event of a large enough corporate crisis the parent can save itself if necessary by abandoning an affiliate or subsidiary. That is, the incentives of the parent are the same whether or not such a letter of intent is written. Hence the title comfort letter.

---

[2] See "Banks vs. Banks—Joint Lending Abroad Loses Some Luster in a Spate of Suits," *Wall Street Journal,* September 14, 1976, and "Hanover Bank Admits Error in Delaying Disclosure of Opinion in Hong Kong Loan," *Wall Street Journal,* December 3, 1976.

[3] We are extremely grateful to Mr. Richard Wickstrom, vice-president, United California Bank, for providing us with this information.

**Table 11.1**   *Foreign Claims of U.S. Banks, June 1977*
(million US$)

### A.   Cross-Border and Nonlocal Currency Claims by Residence of Borrower

| Country | Claims on Banks (Placements) | Public Borrowers | Other Private | Maturity Distribution one year and below | over one year |
|---|---|---|---|---|---|
| Group of 10 and Switzerland[a] | 38,140 | 6,709 | 23,711 | 50,861 | 17,698 |
| Other developed[b] | 3,215 | 5,538 | 8,285 | 8,094 | 8,940 |
| Eastern Europe[c] | 1,236 | 3,996 | 754 | 2,233 | 3,751 |
| Oil exporting countries[d] | 954 | 6,377 | 4,832 | 6,742 | 5,420 |
| Latin America, Caribbean[e] | 1,253 | 13,009 | 14,391 | 12,359 | 16,292 |
| of which | | | | | |
| Brazil | 331 | 3,748 | 6,510 | 3,321 | 7,267 |
| Mexico | 423 | 5,910 | 4,989 | 5,459 | 5,864 |
| Asia[f] | 1,002 | 3,426 | 5,185 | 6,253 | 3,361 |
| of which | | | | | |
| Taiwan | 112 | 1,198 | 1,009 | 1,541 | 778 |
| South Korea | 293 | 929 | 1,993 | 2,274 | 942 |
| Philippines | 279 | 522 | 1,060 | 1,055 | 805 |
| Africa[g] | 96 | 1,366 | 419 | 955 | 925 |
| Offshore banking centers[h] | 12,369 | 446 | 4,016 | 13,945 | 2,889 |
| Other | 405 | 1,129 | 1,951 | 1,932 | 1,555 |
| **Total** | 58,670 | 41,996 | 63,544 | 103,374 | 60,831 |

### B.   Cross-Border and Nonlocal Currency Claims by Country of Guarantor

| Country | Total claims by residence | Claims guaranteed by residents of other countries | Claims on residents of other countries guaranteed by these countries | Total claims by country of guarantor |
|---|---|---|---|---|
| Group of 10 and Switzerland[a] | 68,557 | 15,445 | 14,293 | 67,405 |
| Other developed[b] | 17,037 | 808 | 1,481 | 17,710 |
| Eastern Europe[c] | 5,982 | 221 | 179 | 5,940 |
| Oil exporting countries[d] | 12,163 | 763 | 540 | 11,940 |
| Latin America, Carribbean[e] | 28,652 | 1,661 | 968 | 27,959 |

**Table 11.1**  *(cont'd)*

### B.  Cross-Border and Nonlocal Currency Claims by Country of Guarantor

| Country | Total claims by residence | Claims guaranteed by residents of other countries | Claims on residents of other countries guaranteed by these countries | Total claims by country of guarantor |
|---|---|---|---|---|
| Asia[f] | 9,615 | 469 | 529 | 9,675 |
| Africa[g] | 40,148 | 2,405 | 1,563 | 39,308 |
| Offshore banking centers[h] | 16,834 | 13,010 | 619 | 14,443 |
| Other | 3,487 | 533 | 342 | 3,296 |
| **Total** | 164,208 | 33,185 | 19,017 | 150,040 |

### C.  Claims Stemming from Letters of Credit and Other Contingencies

| Country | Public Borrowers | Banks and Other Private |
|---|---|---|
| Group of Ten and Switzerland[a] | 1,622 | 15,103 |
| Other developed[b] | 1,521 | 4,564 |
| Eastern Europe[c] | 1,011 | 364 |
| Oil exporting countries[d] | 1,805 | 3,004 |
| Latin America and Caribbean[e] | 1,398 | 2,672 |
| Asia[f] | 1,722 | 2,621 |
| Africa[g] | 3,621 | 5,724 |
| Offshore banking centers[h] | 360 | 2,110 |
| Other | 536 | 826 |
| **Total** | 10,476 | 31,695 |

[a]Belgium/Luxemburg, France, Germany, Italy, Netherlands, Sweden, Switzerland, United Kingdom, Canada, Japan

[b]Austria, Australia, Finland, Greece, Iceland, New Zealand, Norway, Portugal, Spain, South Africa, Turkey, Denmark, Ireland

[c]Bulgaria, Czechoslovakia, East Germany, Hungary, Poland, Romania, U.S.S.R., Yugoslavia

[d]Algeria, Ecuador, Indonesia, Iran, Iraq, Kuwait, Libya, Nigeria, Qatar, Saudi Arabia, United Arab Emirates, Venezuela

[e]Argentina, Bolivia, Brazil, Chile, Costa Rica, Dominican Republic, El Salvador, Guatemala, Honduras, Jamaica, Mexico, Nicaragua, Paraguay, Peru, Trinidad and Tobago, Uruguay

[f]Taiwan, India, Israel, Jordan, South Korea, Malaysia, Pakistan, Philippines, Thailand

[g]Egypt, Ghana, Ivory Coast, Morocco, Sudan, Tunisia, Zaire, Zambia

[h]Bahamas, Bahrain, Caymans, Hong Kong, Panama, Singapore, Liberia, Lebanon

*Source:* "Country Exposure Lending Survey," Board of Governors, Federal Reserve System, January 16, 1978

**Table 11.2**   *A Comfort Letter*

---

A B C  Corporation                          New York, NY 10020
_____

March 1, 1979


United California Bank

Gentlemen:

We understand that you are contemplating a line of credit for loans in
maturities up to 180 days that you make available to ABC (Belgium) in the
amount of BF 150,000,000.

In order to induce you to provide the aforementioned financing to our
subsidiary, we hereby agree with you as follows:

   1)  During the period this line of credit is outstanding, or any
renewal or modification thereof is outstanding, we will not transfer or
otherwise dispose of any of the shares of capital stock of our subsidiary now
or hereafter owned by us, and we will not cause our subsidiary to issue any
additional shares of capital stock except to us.

   2)  We will take all necessary steps and do such acts and things as may
be necessary to insure that our subsidiary promptly and completely fulfills
all of its obligations and liabilities to you under this line of credit, or
any extension (up to 60 days), renewal, or modification thereof.

   3)  Our agreements contained herein shall remain in full force and effect
until all of our subsidiary's obligations to you under this line of credit or
any extension (up to 60 days), renewal, or modification thereof are satisfied
in full.

   4)  This line of credit, when available, shall be deemed to have been
made by you in reliance upon this agreement.  Notice of acceptance of this
agreement is hereby waived.

                                   Sincerely,


                                   *Nicholas Jessemen*

                                   Vice President of Finance

---

*Source:* United California Bank. Used by permission.

**Table 11.3**   *UCB Guidelines for Use of Comfort Letters*

---

**Definition—Comfort Letter**

A "Comfort Letter" must constitute an engagement on the part of the parent company to assure that its subsidiary/affiliate will repay its borrowing from our bank. Such an engagement to qualify as a "Comfort Letter" may range from the extreme of being slightly less than the contractual legal commitment of a guarantee to one in which the parent states that it will see to it that their subsidiary conducts its affairs in such a manner so as to enable it to honor its obligations to our bank.

1.  From time to time the bank may be asked to accept comfort letters in lieu of guarantees as a form of support for credit granted to subsidiaries of major concerns. The use of comfort letters is not intended to be encouraged by inclusion in this manual. At this time, U.S. corporations appear generally willing to provide guarantees for their U.S. subsidiaries; however, the use of such letters in foreign lending is growing. All lending officers should be aware of the possibility of shareholder suits seeking to prevent performance by management of U.S. corporations and strive to avoid the erosion of our bank's traditional reliance on guarantees in domestic lending practice. Nevertheless, guidelines for the acceptance of such a letter in lieu of a guarantee will be conditioned upon the following:

    A.  The issuer of a comfort letter must be the parent company, or a major subsidiary thereof, whose ability to perform as a guarantor of its subsidiary is absolutely unquestioned. Because such letters provide an uncertain basis for legal pursuit of the issuer by the bank, it should not be accepted when potential financial problems of the issuer could lessen the management's resolve to meet the moral obligation which had been clearly understood at the time of issuance.

    B.  Such letters are to be accepted only with the signature of senior financial officers of the parent, except with prior approval of the Senior Credit Officer.

    C.  Maturities of loans so supported are not to exceed five years.

    D.  Acceptance of such letters will be avoided altogether when severe country risk or exchange risks exist and when there is essentially no support on the part of the borrower.

---

*Source:* UCB, "International Banking—Credit Administration Guide," UCB, Los Angeles. Used by permission.

## 11.3   CURRENT BANKING PRACTICE IN THE ANALYSIS AND CONTROL OF FOREIGN PORTFOLIO RISK[4]

Broadly speaking, major American banks classify their risks according to the following categories (in descending order of importance):

1. by country of exposure

2. by maturity of the loan

3. by nature of the loan

There is a general presumption that long-term lending leaves a bank more exposed to risk than do short-term commitments. It is also generally considered that loans to finance trade or directly add to productive capacity, especially in export or import substituting industries, are less risky than purely domestically oriented loans, for example for real estate or to governments. The strategies banks use to manage their portfolio risks revolve around geographical diversification and maturity management.[5] The main analytical problems are to measure exposure by country, and then to set so-called "country limits."

It is not straightforward in practice to allocate risks by country. In the case of shipping loans the legal borrower will usually be a shell company in Liberia or Panama. The actual owners may be residents of Greece, but the ships may be on long-term charter to a multinational corporation. Interbank placements to money center banks offer similar problems. On the one hand, the loan will be made to a subsidiary of a foreign bank, and the country of domicile of the foreign bank might then be an appropriate classification. On the other hand, the legal structure of the flow is through the money center and conceivably the government there could in some way hamper repayment. On a conceptual level there are two classification schemes which could be used:

1. The legal classification: attribute all claims to the country of domicile of the guarantor or ultimately responsible party for the claim. This procedure would attribute the shipping loan to Greece, and a deposit with an offshore branch bank to the country of domicile of the parent.

---

[4]This section is based on published and unpublished documents and statements from major banks and the Federal Reserve Board. Banking practices in this area have experienced particularly rapid modification in the past decade, and we anticipate continuing increases in the degree of sophistication of analysis. The second part of the chapter indicates our view of the appropriate direction in which to travel.

[5]See John C. Haley, "A Hard Look at Lending Abroad," in *Business in Brief*, No. 133, April 1977, Chase Manhattan Bank.

2. The economic or functional classification: attribute all claims to the country or countries in which the cash flow needed to meet the claim is generated. To a considerable extent this classification will coincide with the first. However, one can conceive of circumstances in which they would differ. For example, a loan guaranteed by a British corporation whose main assets are in Canada has to be met, if worst comes to worst, by the Canadian cash flow and assets. The business environment in Canada thus controls the value of the guarantee. Of course it also remains true that the British government can itself impose controls on this corporation.

In practice there is substantial divergence in the principles of allocation, especially with respect to interbank placements. Thus interbank comparisons of country exposure can be made only with extreme caution. The estimates most affected are those for exposure in the industrialized countries and the offshore financial centers. There are few interbank placements with banks in developing countries and eastern bloc countries, so comparisons for these areas are reliable. However to the extent that money center banks have re-lent the placements into these areas, the economic principal of allocation of claims would require appropriate adjustment to the exposure figures. Table 11.4 is a composite construction representative of exposure reports prepared for the internal use of major American banks.

**Table 11.4** *Loss Potential in Popular Republic of Bengoslavia as of March 31, 1979 (million US$)*[a]

| | | |
|---|---|---|
| Loans | | 200 |
| Acceptances | | 20 |
| Letters of credit | | 5 |
| Deposits in local banks | | 10 |
| Loan to our Bengoslavian subsidiary | | 20 |
| Book value of investment in subsidiary | | 6 |
| | | 261 |
| | | |
| Less offsetting assets in our grasp | | |
|     Redeposits from Bengoslavian subsidiary | 40 | |
|     Parent's liabilities to Bengoslavian | | |
|       banks and other entities | 60 | 100 |
| Net maximum exposure | | 161 |

[a]A typical report also carries other information. For example, the Bengoslavian subsidiary may have liabilities to third countries. Should capital controls be imposed in Bengoslavia, these liabilities might become claims on the parent. Open forward exchange commitments to individuals and entities domiciled in Bengoslavia would also be recorded.

Despite the substantial effort banks have devoted to this activity in the 1970s, the setting of exposure limits by country remains much more of an art than a science. The purpose of the exercise is to ensure sufficient diversification of the asset portfolio so that expropriation, capital controls, or other forms of default will not have major adverse effects on the bank. Since interest returns are higher in the riskier places, there is an obvious tradeoff to be made. Table 11.5 summarizes the topics studied by one major American bank in assessing the creditworthiness of borrower countries.

**Table 11.5**   *The Basic Parameters of Creditworthiness*

---

**A.   Policy factors**

    1.   quality of economic team; strength of central bank; impact on political leadership

    2.   monetary/budget policies; wage/price policies

    3.   current account adjustment policies; exchange rate policies; import restraint policies

    4.   relations with IMF; willingness to cooperate with international banking community in providing necessary data, projections, and other information

**B.   Basic economic factors**

    5.   growth strategy: whether it is balanced; policy toward agriculture; appropriateness and efficiency of industrial investment

    6.   natural resource base

    7.   human resource base: population growth, educational level, entrepreneurial ability

    8.   financial resource base: policy toward stimulating domestic savings; financial market development; relative importance of foreign capital in total domestic investment

    9.   export diversification by commodity and region

**C.   External Finances**

    10.   external debt, level and maturity structure; debt service burden

    11.   reserves

    12.   potential access to medium-term official finance, e.g., IMF

    13.   balance-of-payments prospects and outlook for external debt service burden

**D.   Politics**

    14.   domestic and regional political stability

---

In this bank, the primary focus is on the quality of the economic policy followed by the government of a country. It is viewed as being primarily responsible for inflation and economic growth, or at least for managing them. Substantial attention is given to the realism of the policy targets. For example, is the government trying to sustain a hopelessly overvalued exchange rate, or trying to accelerate industrial growth behind tariff walls when agricultural productivity and the levels of available skills cannot sustain this? Policies like these are sure to lead to marked calamities at some future date. Ultimately the aim is to assess the external financial situation in order to evaluate the ability to service debt. Additional short-term factors are access to IMF, World Bank, and foreign official credits, and the adequacy of the foreign exchange reserves. Banks work on a rule of thumb of three to four months coverage of imports for a satisfactory reserve level.[6] Using this sort of data, the area heads then decide

1.  an overall country exposure limit;

2.  a limit for exposure with maturity over one year;

3.  general areas in which it is desirable to concentrate future lending. The division here is by nature of borrower and type of activity, for example, loans to governments, loans to banks, loans to private nonbanks, and loans to projects generating hard currency versus loans to projects generating local currency. It is considered that in most developing countries, the creditworthiness of governments and banks is much higher than that of nonbanks. Also, hard currency generating projects and trade finance are preferred to local projects or general-purpose loans to governments.

## 11.4  A MODERN PORTFOLIO THEORY-ORIENTED APPROACH TO ASSESSMENT OF THE RISKINESS OF A BANK'S FOREIGN CLAIMS

In the following sections we will attempt to apply to analysis of the foreign claim portfolios of banks the theory and the statistical analysis that has transformed perceptions of markets for common stocks and other forms of assets.[7] In the final section we will raise some interesting strategic issues that are already understood by corporate managers making equity investments in developing countries. Our aim is to answer the following questions:

- How can one determine the extent to which each new country represented in the asset portfolio adds to the diversification of the

---

[6]For a systematic approach to analysis of the adequacy of reserves, see Appendix n.1.
[7]The reader is referred to W. F. Sharpe, *Investments*, (Englewood Cliffs, NJ: Prentice-Hall, 1978) for a complete exposition of the modern theory of the valuation of risky returns.

portfolio? What distinguishes countries for this purpose? What are the probable sources of covariation among countries?

- How can one determine the extent to which lending into various industries in various foreign countries represents meaningful diversification or more concentration?

Meaningful diversification spreads out the portfolio to reduce risk. However, it will soon become apparent that there are different types of risk, and that strategies that cope well with one type do not necessarily perform well in terms of the others.

We are interested in the earnings or value of a bank's portfolio of investments. It is convenient to proceed as follows. We are now at some date $t_0$, and we wish to consider the bank's activities over the period from $t_0$ to $t_1$. At date $t_0$ the bank's portfolio has value $V(t_0)$. At date $t_1$ it will have value $V(t_1)$ determined by cumulated cash flow over the interval $t_0$ to $t_1$, and by the characteristics of the assets in the portfolio at date $t_1$. Since we have a situation of uncertainty we can represent the distribution $V(t_1)$ as in Figure 11.1.

What do we mean by the riskiness of the distribution in Figure 11.1? There is no all-purpose characterization of risk. One has to ask: *riskiness to whom?* One can suggest at least three perspectives, each of which implies a different measure of risk.

1. A hypothetical, undiversified owner, or anyone else whose career is intimately bound up with the earnings of only this one bank

**Figure 11.1**   Probability Distribution of the Value of the Bank's Claim Portfolio at Future Date $t_1$

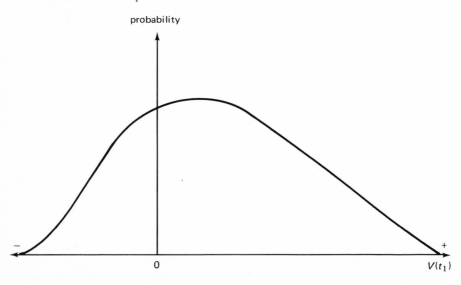

In this case some summary measures of the dispersion in Figure 11.1 provide the relevant notion of risk. For example, one might want to use the variance of the returns or terminal value. But note that such a measure is not really comparable across banks. What do we do if we find on comparison of Bank $A$ with Bank $B$ that Bank $A$'s terminal value has higher variance, but also a higher mean? On an intuitive basis, riskiness is supposed to be bad, but in the case of such a comparison the hypothetical owner of Bank $A$ is not necessarily worse off than the hypothetical owner of Bank $B$.

Clearly *sometimes* it is possible to make comparisons across banks. In our example, if Bank $A$ had a higher variance than Bank $B$ but a mean value the same or lower, we might feel confident in stating that Bank $A$'s portfolio was unambiguously riskier than Bank $B$'s portfolio. There is a general name for such comparisons: we say that the random returns $V_B$ *stochastically dominate* the random returns $V_A$ if every risk averse individual would prefer the returns $V_B$ to the returns $V_A$. From the empirical perspective, the most useful form of this principle remains the mean-variance approximation. But note what we have just seen—a stochastic dominance ranking cannot compare *all* distributions of returns. Only if $V_A$ has mean no higher than $V_B$, and has variance higher than $V_B$, can we say $V_A$ is riskier.

2. A hypothetical stock market investor, who holds a well-diversified portfolio of assets

Such an individual views the bank's earnings and value in conjunction with the earnings and value of all the other assets in his or her portfolio. The investor exhibits risk aversion toward the returns from the whole portfolio but not necessarily toward the returns from any one constituent part. To understand this, consider a portfolio containing many small investments, all distributed independently. A greater number of such small investments in a portfolio (holding the mean return on the whole portfolio fixed) lessens the dispersion of the sum of returns. In the limit such a portfolio is riskless, because all the little independent gains and losses cancel out. Thus the holder of a diversified portfolio experiences risks from correlation or nonindependence of the returns. If the portfolio of investments held by the bank happens to be distributed independently of the returns on the assets in the portfolio of the investor, the investor will treat the bank as though it yielded its expected value with certainty: i.e., he or she will not demand a risk premium to hold it. If we use the capital asset pricing model as an approximation to the state of affairs in the world of investment, the risk premium exacted by investors is a linear function of the correlation of the value of the bank's earnings with those of the universe of assets, i.e.,

$$E(r_B) - p = \beta_B[E(R) - p]$$

where

$r_B$ = (random) rate of return to an investor in the equity of the bank

$R$ = (random) rate of return to a portfolio of all market assets

$p$ = risk-free rate of return

$\beta_B = \dfrac{\text{cov}(r_B, R)}{\sigma^2(r_B)}$ is the measure of yield

correlation for the bank and the market

In this case we can take the beta of the bank's portfolio as a measure of its riskiness relative to the risk of the market portfolio. Which market portfolio? The classical works on the subject use the U.S. domestic market portfolio. However, in truth, U.S. firms are owned in part by foreign stockholders. So one wants a broader context than the U.S. market for assets. We examined international asset pricing in Chapter 10. This is a field of current research. However, from a practical standpoint, the capital asset pricing model works quite well in the U.S. context, and for the moment we recommend its use in calculations of portfolio value.

3. A regulatory agency, like the FDIC, which has the liability for the net debts of the bank should it happen to go bust. In the most general sense, we are interested in the likelihood of the bank's going bad, and in the magnitude of the losses that it incurs should it go bad.

We can approach the measurement of riskiness from this viewpoint in two ways. The first is a general characterization of the bankruptcy tail in Figure 11.2, and the second is estimation of the liability incurred by an agency like the FDIC if it must make up any losses which result from bankruptcy. The second approach obviously combines the information generated by the first in one particular way.

We will begin with the general characterization. The bankruptcy tail in Figure 11.2 is that part of the distribution to the left of the $V(t_1) = 0$ point. Different portfolios imply tails of different shape. Sometimes it is easy to determine that one distribution is riskier for the FDIC than another. This is when, on plotting the two distributions, the tails do not cross. Tail $B$ is strictly less risky than Tail $A$, because the probability of any magnitude of bankruptcy loss is smaller on Tail $B$ than on Tail $A$. If the tails cross, we must compare a distribution having low probability of large losses with one having higher probability of small losses. There is no universally acceptable ranking by riskiness in such a situation. In Appendix 11.2 we show that the capital market implicitly places a value on the bankruptcy tail. This capital market value is a natural way to compare and rank bankruptcy risks.

**Figure 11.2**   A Simple Analysis of Relative Bankruptcy Risk

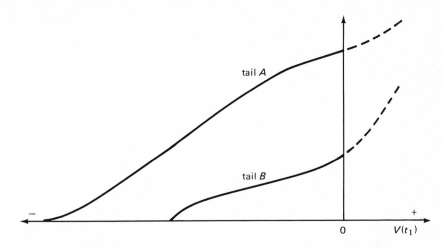

What are the practical conclusions to be derived from this discussion? First, whatever the notion of riskiness we choose, we must construct the portfolio return distribution used in Figure 11.1, or its cumulative analogue, given in Figure 11.4. Second, the notion of riskiness we adopt dictates which characteristics of the return distribution we wish to operate on by a policy of diversification. If we adopt notion 1, above, we want to affect the general dispersion of the distribution. If we adopt notion 2, we want to affect the correlation of the return on the bank's portfolio with the returns on the universe of traded assets. If we adopt notion 3, we focus only on the lower tail of the return distribution. The contribution of any given project loan or government loan to the reduction of the risk of the portfolio will vary with the notion of risk which is being used. Thus until a decision has been made on the concept of risk that is applicable, no proper answers to the questions posed at the beginning of this section can be provided. The remainder of the section establishes the building blocks for all possible risk analyses. Using these building blocks one can then assess the effect of a portfolio change on *any* risk measure. You, the decision maker, must decide the appropriate measure of risk.

## 11.5   HOW TO GENERATE THE DISTRIBUTION OF PORTFOLIO RETURNS

Consider now how to construct a distribution like that shown in Figure 11.1 for an actual bank portfolio. We will exhibit a method of generating an estimate of this distribution that also allows immediate evaluation of

the impact on any desired measure of risk of adding another project to
the portfolio. In principle, if one had a choice of which projects to accept,
one could tailor the portfolio to have any desired characteristics.[8] Let us
begin by considering the sources of portfolio risk for a bank. Initially we
will assume all flows are measured in dollars. Subsequently we will explain how to add an exchange risk component. It is convenient to discuss
risks of project lending first, and then to discuss loans to governments.

For convenience we assume that the bank has no equity participation
in any projects and is entitled to receive payment of principal and interest
if things proceed well, and to liquidate the project at market value in case
of default. In order to permit the use of diagrams, we also assume that the
projects pay all their returns on one future date, like discount bonds.
(This is in no way essential for the calculations.) Let

$X_i$ = total return on project $i$, measured in dollars

$D_i$ = total payment of principal plus interest due to the bank
    from project $i$, a dollar-denominated sum

If the total return exceeds $D_i$, the bank will be repaid. If the return, $X_i$, is
less than $D_i$, the bank will have to settle for $X_i$. This is shown in Figure
11.3, where the thick line shows the probability distribution of the bank's
return on the loan. The bank bears risk only when $X_i < D_i$. To compute
the bank's risk carrying from a project loan we must first estimate a distribution for $X_i$, and then superimpose the cutoff, $D_i$.[9]

In order to consider the overall distribution of $X_i$ it is extremely useful
to partition the risk into various sources of factors that contribute to it.
Thus, divide projects into a number of categories (for example, copper
mining, textile production, logging, plywood production, and so forth).
To be useful, the categories must be broad enough to embrace numerous
existing and past projects in order to provide a statistically significant
sample. Then we may view the returns $X_i$ to a project in category $i$ as
being generated by a statistical model of the form:

$$X_i = \beta_{i1}\delta_1 + \beta_{i2}\delta_2 + \beta_{i3}\delta_3 + \epsilon_i$$

where

$\delta_1$ = world economy factor. A good proxy for this might
    be an index of the real GNP of the major
    trading nations.

---

[8]Looked at before the event, of course! As presented here, we are obviously discussing a
problem very closely related to the staple tasks of investment portfolio management. The
multifactor model approach we apply here to lending is now coming into use in analysis
of stock and bond markets in the United States.

[9]For a project with a sequence of annual returns and payment obligations, one must do this
on a year-by-year basis.

**Figure 11.3**  Cumulative Distribution of Bank Return

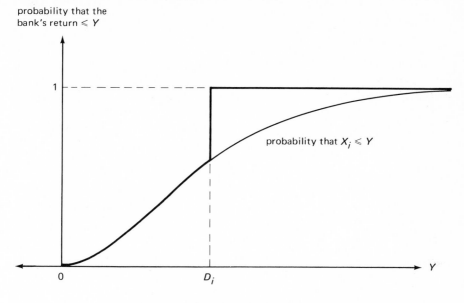

$\delta_2$ = industry factor. A good proxy for this might be world market price for a raw material, or rate of expansion of world capacity for some manufactured good.

$\delta_3$ = national factor. One could use an index of GNP of the country in which the project was located, or other suitable variables.

$\epsilon_i$ = residual, uncorrelated error.

$\beta_{i1}, \beta_{i2}, \beta_{i3}$ = impact of the factors on the returns to projects in category $i$.

Models of this form say that the randomness in $X_i$ is derived from the delta factors. Once the sensitivities $\beta$ are estimated, forecasts and characteristics of the randomness in the delta factors automatically generate the characteristics of the distribution of $X_i$. For example, the forecast variance of $X_i$ is a weighted average of the variances and covariances of the delta factors, the weights being the beta factors specific to category $i$. Or consider how to estimate the reduction in overall portfolio variance from loans to automobile assembly operations in two different countries. Obviously the world and industry factors and their weights are the same for both. Diversification value can arise only from lack of correlation or negative correlation between the two country factors. It will only be important if the beta impact measures for the country factors are high for the automobile industry. Moreover, if the countries in question are heavy raw material exporters to the major trading nations, their GNPs may have high positive correlation. These considerations become tractable when analysis of this sort is performed.

It should by now be clear how to incorporate exchange rate effects here, if the project is not yielding dollars directly. As we have explained in Chapters 5 and 6, the exchange rate is a random variable that can also be explained in a multifactor model. In the long run the purchasing power parity is the only significant factor, but other things always have transitory effects. One can estimate short-run multifactor equations for exchange rates. These do not provide results sufficiently superior to forward market quotations to permit speculative profits (unfortunately), but they provide forecasts in a form which can be readily integrated with the project factor models. Using these methods one can make a comprehensive analysis of the risk characteristics of a portfolio of pure project loans. We next turn our attention to loans to governments.

## 11.6   LOANS TO GOVERNMENTS AND SOVEREIGN RISK

In this section our concern will be with default on governmental loans, or the use of governmental pressure or policy to force private parties to default on loans. Such risks are sometimes called *sovereign risks*, for obvious reasons.

The notion of default on a project loan is clear cut—payments do not meet promised levels, and in the extreme case the whole project is worth less than the debt outstanding. Dealings with governments involve much vaguer calculations. In principle a government can command the entire resources of the country, particularly the foreign exchange resources. In practice it not only cannot, it *will* not. A government will refuse to pay (which means, "will demand to renegotiate") long before it is unable to pay in any financial sense. Beyond some point, deprivation of the non-governmental sector causes substantial economic and political problems. One of the main aims of analysis of governmental loans is to identify such a point or range for each country. Another aim is to explain what moves the economy towards this point and to observe the correlation among these causal factors between countries. Finally, on the way to the region of major problems the government will typically attempt to secure more resources from the private sector to meet its own needs by a variety of devices—exchange controls, quotas, restrictions on repatriation of dividends, and so forth. These have obvious implications for realized returns on project investments in that country.

The first point to consider is the extent to which a government is able to obtain purchasing power and foreign exchange from the private sector. In obtaining resources generally and foreign exchange in particular from the private sector, a government may operate by market means or nonmarket means. Market means consist of borrowing from the public, general taxation of the public, and purchase of foreign exchange on a free exchange market in competition with private parties. Nonmarket means consist of regulations which force certain transactions to go through the government, principally allocation of capital at arbitrary interest rates, and the establishment of the central bank as the monopoly trader in foreign exchange. In developing countries and some developed countries—Spain, Italy, France—there are fundamental limits to the government's ability to command resources via taxation. These limits are determined by tax evasion, smuggling, and unrecorded currency transactions, as well as simple lack of sufficient skilled manpower in the relevant government agencies. These national limits to collection powers are nation-specific and do not, by themselves, contribute to any covariation of risks between countries.

If the government is to take resources to pay debts, the private sector must make do with less. The ability of the private economy to withstand squeezing, especially of access to imported commodities, depends on its structure and the extent of forced import substitution that has already taken place. Economies that are very open to trade will be much more dependent on access to imports. An exception to this principle occurs with economies which would be much more open to trade were it not for artificial import-substitution policies. In such economies the maximal domestic substitution has already taken place and imports are confined primarily to raw materials and capital goods and parts not locally available. Such economies are very vulnerable to a squeeze on the remaining permitted imports. Since projects depend upon some imported goods, in general, public sector squeezes carry over to the private sector.

Let us suppose then that we can tentatively identify for each country in the portfolio the maximal amount of resources a government will be willing to squeeze out of the private sector. If it needs to squeeze this much or more to meet its obligations it will turn to renegotiation or default (which from our perspective are synonymous). What then determines whether this will happen?

Governments receive resources from two types of sources—the domestic economy, and foreign borrowings and grants. As output and exports become greater, a government can command more resources without entering the critical region. It is very straightforward to analyze the stochastic pattern of resources available from the domestic economy, since we can use a version of the multifactor model. If $y_i$ denotes income or foreign exchange availability in Country $i$ we may write the regression model

$$y_i = \bar{\theta}_i + \gamma_{1i}\theta_1 + \gamma_{2i}\theta_{2i} + \gamma_{3i}\theta_{3i} + \mu_i$$

where $\mu_i$ is a zero-mean, uncorrelated error, $\theta_1$ is a measure of world trends, $\theta_{2i}$ (possibly a vector) is a measure of specifically national variables such as aggregate investment and so forth, and $\theta_{3i}$ is a vector of industrial variables. In this context the multifactor model is simply a reduced form of a macroeconometric model.

If we have identified a critical level below which the government cannot drive $y_i$, we want to compute the probability that fulfillment of the government's repayment commitments, allowing for likely official aid and so forth, will force $y_i$ beyond the critical point. Effectively, we are defining a kind of bankruptcy tail for $y_i$, analogous to our discussion in the preceding section. This tail can be generated by the statistical methods outlined above. Of even greater value, this approach clarifies the extent to which the same factors that put a project into difficulty put a government into difficulty, because the private economy is the ultimate source of government revenue. This effect is most marked where the main income generators for the government are a small number of large projects financed by foreign capital.

## 11.7   SOME STRATEGIC CONSIDERATIONS

It would be false to say that default by governments is an entirely economically determined event over which lenders perforce exercise no control. It may be possible to raise the perceived cost of default, or make it more difficult and thereby lessen its likelihood. Default is made more difficult in a variety of ways. We suggest two:

1. If the loan is in conjunction with actions of agencies like the IMF and the World Bank, a default on the commercial part of the loan may jeopardize very important commitments for aid from these agencies. Banks are always eager to involve aid agencies in some way in their lending, because their retaliatory power is thereby greatly increased.

2. It may be possible to structure cash flows in such a way that substantial sums of money pass through the hands of the bank consortium on the way to the governmental borrower. A similar scheme, often used, involves doling out the loan in parts rather than all at one time. The obvious intent is to hold hostage some valuable consideration for as long as possible.

Another set of actions aims to raise the cost of default. Some of this is automatic. Creditworthiness tends to suffer as a result of nonpayment of debts. In addition it may be possible to pull in organizations with more influence on the defaulting country. If the loan was insured by a governmental agency, there will have to be some form of official response. If the governmental agency cannot afford to pay the claim without a modification in the national budget, the response will be more intense. One should think of the insurance as a ticket to external involvement, worthwhile even if only part of an obligation is covered. Finally, it may be possible to coerce the home government of the bank into some official action. This may be because the bank can present the default as a political ploy, or perhaps because the bank can frighten the home government by speaking of folding up if something is not done. Certainly there is a great amount of room for creative thinking in this area.


## 11.8  SUMMARY

Two things distinguish international bank lending from domestic bank lending.

1.  Repayment of debt must frequently go through the exchange markets, so that a bank must not only assess creditworthiness of a potential borrower but also prospects for currencies or for capital flow controls; and

2.  there is no accepted and enforced world legal system and no ultimate arbitrator for the settlement of disputed claims.

Banks must evaluate not only the riskiness of individual loans but also the riskiness of loan portfolios. Current banking practice provides much more satisfactory methods for the first task than for the second. Currently major world banks classify risks by country of exposure and by maturity of the loan. The main control approach is to set country limits on lending, based on long lists of factors such as quality of economic policy, political stability, and similar subjective and nonquantifiable factors.

We have suggested that these methods should be supplemented (not supplanted) by a radically new approach to the evaluation of portfolio risk based on modern capital market theory. This approach enables us to assess, on a statistical basis, the riskiness of loans to projects of various types, to a number of projects in one country, and even, to some extent, of loans to governments. (On the last point, we are limited to consideration of government defaults related exclusively to capacity to repay rather than for political reasons.) In the extensive analysis of Peru in Case 7 at the back of the book, the reader may see a real-life application of some of our methods to a borrower who has been in financial difficulties for a number of years.


### Suggestions for Further Reading

For an excellent summary of the current methods of evaluating creditworthiness for international borrowers, see "Standard and Poor's Approach to International

Ratings," Standard and Poor's Corporation, New York (no date). The best place to begin consideration of strategic aspects of loan making is with T. C. Schelling, *The Strategy of Conflict*, Oxford University Press, 1962.

Foreign exchange reserves are used by central banks to maintain exchange rates at nonequilibrium levels. As we saw in Chapter 4, when the exchange rate is being overvalued through central bank trading on the exchange markets, reserves are falling, while undervaluation of the exchange rate through central bank trading on the exchange market increases foreign exchange reserves. In Chapter 4 we saw that exchange rates cannot deviate permanently from their purchasing power parity values. No reserves are adequate to sustain such deviations. Let us suppose that we are dealing with a government whose aim is to use its reserves and other tools to hold exchange rates at their PPP levels. Then the assessment of an adequate level of reserves becomes an interesting policy problem of determining the optimal inventory of a good that has random inflows and outflows. In this case the desirable inventory size will depend on:

1.   the likely amplitudes of the random inflows and outflows;

2.   the other tools available for stabilization of the exchange rate; and

3.   speculative reaction to the use of the reserves and the other tools.

We start with point 2. It is clear that a government can impose import controls, or export controls, to affect exchange markets. It can also manipulate short-term interest rates to induce capital inflows and outflows, if it has a well-developed capital market open to international transactions. In the heyday of the gold exchange standard system, the quarter century before the first world war, the Bank of England managed nicely with gold reserves less than 3% of the (gold-guaranteed) money supply. By manipulating its rediscount rate ("Bank Rate") the Bank brought about very large inflows and outflows that proved entirely satisfactory in the maintenance of liquidity. Such interest rate changes affect the domestic economy of course, but as we emphasized in Chapter 4, there are many tools capable of affecting the balance of payments. One must look at the available tools, including reserves, as a package. Obviously the same ratio of reserves to exports or whatever means quite a different thing in Britain than in Zambia.

We have already drawn the analogy between the adequacy of reserves issue and the problem of holding optimum inventory in a warehouse, or of holding optimal cash balances to meet unequal transactions inflows and outflows. The (justly) best known works on the transactions demand for money are: W. Baumol, "The Transactions Demand for Cash: An Inventory Theoretic Approach," *Quarterly Journal of Economics*, 66 (November 1952); and M. Miller and D. Orr, "A Model of the Demand for Money by Firms," *Quarterly Journal of Economics*, 80 (August 1966). An adaptation of this notion to official reserves is given in: P. Clark, "Optimum International Reserves and the Speed of Adjustment," *Journal of Political Economy*, 78 (March/April 1970). Clark relates the "optimal" size of intervention reserves to domestic monetary and fiscal policies, which also affect the exchange markets, and the reader is referred there for computational approaches.

We remain somewhat skeptical of this whole approach because of point 3. The existence of private speculation on future exchange rates seems to nullify the notion of optimal government reserves. If speculators anticipate a successful return to parity, they will trade to take advantage of this and so force the currency towards parity purely by their private transactions. In this case the optimal reserve is zero. One might argue that reserves must be sufficiently large to give speculators confidence in a return to parity. But how large is that? It varies with the times, and is not derivable from an inventory formula.

## Appendix 11.2   *Capital Market Valuation of Bankruptcy Risk in a Bank's Claim Portfolio*

The capital market places an implicit value on the bankruptcy potential in a bank's portfolio of claims.[10] The valuation method in question is best illustrated by the following example. Consider a bank which issues a certificate of deposit which promises a payment of $P$ at date $t_1$ and nothing in the interim. The cash from this certificate, plus the initial equity of the bank's owners, is used to purchase a portfolio of assets. The current price at which the certificate of deposit is sold is $D$, the current equity is $C$ and the current price of the asset portfolio is $A$. The initial balance sheet of the bank, at date $t_0$, is

| assets = A | deposits = D |
|---|---|
|  | capital   = C |

$$A = D + C$$

At date $t_1$ the portfolio $A$ will have a risky value the distribution of which is given by Figure 11.1. Figure 11.4 shows the cumulative distribution obtained from Figure 11.1.

As long as $V(t_1) \geq P$ the depositors receive the full face value of the certificate of deposit. If $V(t_1) < P$ the depositors can only receive $V(t_1)$ from the assets of the bank. Thus in Figure 11.4 the line $HJKM$ gives the cumulative probability distribution of the value of the deposits at date $t_1$, derived from the riskiness of the value of the portfolio $A$.

Now let $r(t_0, t_1)$ denote the default-free interest rate applicable to securities maturing at $t_1$. Then we can write the default-free value of the certificate of deposit at $t_0$ as

---

[10]See W. F. Sharpe, "Bank Capital Adequacy, Deposit Insurance and Security Values (Part I)," N.B.E.R. Working Paper No. 209, Stanford, October 1977.

**Figure 11.4**   The Cumulative Distribution Derived from Figure 11.1

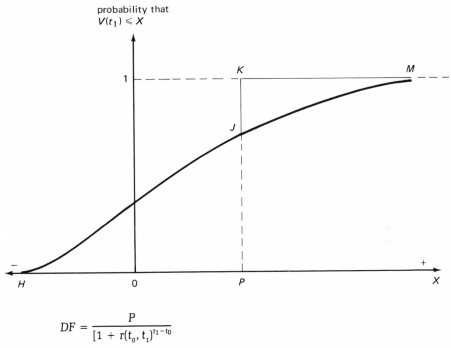

$$DF = \frac{P}{[1 + r(t_0, t_1)]^{t_1 - t_0}}$$

We will be interested in the percentage difference between the true value of the deposits, $D$, and the default-free value, $DF$. That is, the default cost to depositors, in percentage terms, is

$$\frac{(DF - D)}{DF}$$

This spread is the market's valuation of the impact of the defaulting tail, $HJ$, on Figure 11.4. It is the discount for risk of default on the deposits, as assessed in the capital markets.

## *Appendix 11.3*   *Glossary of Exposure Management Terms*[11]

The Glossary contains approximately 75 technical terms. It is arranged in alphabetical order. From a conceptual standpoint, however, it is convenient to classify these terms into four general areas:

• Basic Country Risk Terms

---

[11]From *Country Exposure Management and Reporting Practices of Member Banks*, Association of Reserve City Bankers, 1977. Used by permission.

- Transfer of Country Exposure
- Balance Sheet Items
- Off-Balance Sheet Items

Within their respective definitions, all of the terms are classified as appropriate, into one or more of the above subsets. For example, all technical terms which are used in support of the definitions of country risk and country exposure are categorized within their respective definitions as "Basic Country Risk Terms." Other terms having to do with the mitigation of country risk or the transfer of country risk from one country to another (e.g., by types of guarantees: "full and unconditional", keepwells, etc.) are classified as "Transfer of Country Exposure" terms.

Finally, the remaining terms are referred to as "Balance Sheet" and "Off-Balance Sheet" items as appropriate. For these terms, standard banking reference sources have been consulted and relied upon.


## GLOSSARY


*Accrued Interest Receivable.*   (A Balance Sheet Item). Interest earned by the bank on its claims against third parties which remains uncollected due to administrative and other reasons.

*Advances.*   (A Balance Sheet Item). Short-term loan, i.e., maturity less than one year.

*Advised Line of Credit.*   (An Off-Balance Sheet Item). Credit facility confirmed in writing as to the terms and conditions under which the bank is prepared to grant credit. These facilities are normally of three types:

1. *Good Until Cancelled*—wherein the bank may terminate the line of credit at will, and prior to such termination the beneficiary may draw at will.

2. *Annual Review*—wherein the line of credit terminates one year from date of confirmation, during which period the beneficiary may draw at will.

3. *As Offered*—wherein the bank must be consulted prior to each drawing.

*Annual Review.*   (An Off-Balance Sheet Item). See "Advised Line of Credit."

*Arranged Overdraft.*   (A Balance Sheet Item). A debit balance in the client's account arranged by the banker at the request of the client. It is a common European method of short-term lending comparable to a line of credit.

*As Offered.*   (An Off-Balance Sheet Item). See "Advised Line of Credit."

*Assets.*   (Basic Country Risk Term). Anything owned by a bank which has commercial or exchange value. Assets usually consist of specific property or claims against others.

*Bankers Acceptance.*   (A Balance Sheet Item). A time bill of exchange (frequently called a Time Draft) drawn on and accepted by a banking institution. By accepting the draft, the bank signifies its commitment to pay the face amount at maturity to anyone who presents it for payment at that time. In this way the bank provides its name and credit and enables its customer, who pays a commission to the accepting bank for this accommodation, to readily secure financing. When a bankers acceptance is discounted, the discounting bank acquires a debt investment (i.e., a claim against a third party) which appears on the balance sheet. Such acceptance can subsequently be sold to another bank or investor, although the accepting bank continues to guarantee payment on maturity.

***Bareboat Charter.***   (The Transfer of Country Exposure). See "Shipping Guarantees."

***Bills Discounted.***   (A Balance Sheet Item). Written debt instruments evidencing the obligation of one party (the drawer) to pay another a certain sum of money at a given time. (Transfer of Country Exposure). Refers to written debt instruments drawn on a payor (the borrower) by a third party (the drawer) who in turn discounts the draft with a bank. The bank may discount the draft either with or without recourse to the drawer. When there is full and unconditional recourse to a drawer who is a resident of a country than that of the payor (i.e., the ultimate obligor) country exposure is generally transferred from the country of the payor to the country of the drawer.

***Cash.***   (A Balance Sheet Item). This definition of cash is restricted to "cash on hand" and noninterest bearing deposits held by non-affiliated banks. More frequently, cash held by non-affiliated banks is considered to be exposure to the country where such banks are domiciled. For the most part, given the nominal amounts, cash on hand is only infrequently tabulated as country exposure.

***Casual Overdraft.***   (A Balance Sheet Item). A debit balance in a client's account. An overdraft is created when checks, drafts, money transfers or other transactions are drawn or charged against demand deposit accounts in excess of the available balance in the account. Such an overdraft is not by prearrangement.

***Charter Party.***   (The Transfer of Country Exposure). See "Shipping Guarantees."

***Charter Party Assignment.***   (The Transfer of Country Exposure). See "Shipping Guarantees."

***Collateralized Loan.***   (The Transfer of Country Exposure). A loan granted to a customer upon the pledge of (1) liquid assets, e.g. registered shares of stock, bonds, or (2) illiquid assets (mortgage on a building, etc.). If the borrower is unable to repay the loan, the lender can then sell the security to satisfy the claim. Generally, when liquid collateral is offered a bank, country exposure is often transferred from the country of the obligor to the country where the liquid collateral is held provided, however, the latter is denominated in the same currency as the loan.

***Comfort Letter.***   (The Transfer of Country Exposure). A written instrument issued by a third party whereby that party agrees to make every effort to assure the maker's compliance with the terms of a contract in the event the maker is unable to fulfill his obligation thereunder, but by which instrument that party is not itself obligated to perform. For the most part, ARCB banks do not transfer exposure from the country of the obligor to the country of the issuer of the comfort letter in part due to the uncertain legal status of such instruments.

**Confiscation.** (Basic Country Risk Term). Seizure of private property by a government without any compensation to the owner. Also, a seizure of assets without *fair* compensation.

**Contingent Liabilities.** (Basic Country Risk Term and An Off-Balance Sheet Item). The term applies to the obligations of a bank when acting as a guarantor or accommodation endorser of a negotiable instrument. The guarantor or endorser has no benefit from the negotiable instrument involved, but is required by law to make good the payment of the instrument if the maker defaults. The actual liability exists *with* the maker of the note (the borrower). The contingent liability exists for the duration of the instrument, and is passed to the guarantor as a primary liability only if the borrower dishonors the instrument upon presentation and request for payment. Once the guaranteeing bank meets the liability involved, it then has a claim (i.e., asset) against the borrower. Because there is the potential for an actual claim to arise from a contingent liability, ARCB banks include all contingent liabilities issued on behalf of foreign customers as exposure to the domicile of the customer-unless the transaction is fully and unconditionally counter-guaranteed by an external obligor in which case exposure is allocated to the country of the counter guarantor. In addition, the term contingent liabilities includes legal commitments to extend credit, forward exchange contracts and guarantees whether or not reflected in the financial statements of the bank.

**Contract of Affreightment.** (The Transfer of Country Exposure). See "Shipping Guarantees."

**Country Exposure.** (Basic Country Risk Term). A term of measurement which refers to the volume of "assets" held and "off-balance sheet items" considered to be subject to the "country risk" of a given country. In practice, one important aspect of this measurement is based on identifying the country of domicile of the entity ultimately responsible for the credit risk of a particular transaction.

**Country Risk.** (Basic Country Risk Term). Refers to a spectrum of risks arising from the economic, social and political environments of a given foreign country (including government policies framed in response to trends in these environments) having potential favorable or adverse consequences for foreigners' debt and/or equity investments in that country, e.g.,

Events which may adversely affect profitability and/or recovery of equity investments in a given foreign country include:

* Confiscation;
* Nationalization;
* Branching Limitations;
* Restrictions on earnings remittances;
* Higher local taxes levied on earnings;
* Market Conditions (Deflation);
* Devaluation; etc.

Events which affect profitability of debt investments in a given foreign country include:

* Withholding and other special taxes which impact on existing Outstandings;

- Interest rate controls;
- Government-imposed delays on the liquidation of private and/or public sector external obligations;

Events which often affect potential recovery of debt investments include:

- Certain types of foreign exchange controls including government-imposed restrictions on the liquidation of public and/or private sector external obligations;
- Domestic policies often imposed in a sudden, unpredictable manner which affect client's ability to generate the necessary cash flow to repay loans. Examples are:
  - fiscal policy, (e.g., increase in taxes)
  - restrictive monetary policy and/or
  - price controls; etc.

The above types of country risk are incurred as a result of activities undertaken in a foreign country and are distinct from considerations relating to a given borrower's credit-worthiness. In varying degrees, the above examples of events can affect both local and foreign currency investments.

In the above context, the term "investments" is often used synonymously with exposure.

***Cross-Border Exposure.***   (Basic Country Risk Term). Exists when any subsidiary or branch of the holding company/bank, irrespective of location, lends to; invest in; places with; or otherwise extends any form of credit or credit commitment to any entity (including any holding company/other bank entity) that is *located outside* the booking unit's national borders, irrespective of currency.

***Deflation.***   (Basic Country Risk Term). A reduction in the level of economic activity in an economy. Deflation will result in lower levels of national income, employment, and imports, and lower rates of increase of wages and prices. It may be brought about by monetary policies, such as increases in rates of interest and contraction of the money supply and/or by fiscal policies, such as increases in taxation (direct and indirect) or reductions in government expenditure.

***Devaluation.***   (Basic Country Risk Term). The reduction of the official rate at which one currency is exchanged for another.

***Exchange Controls.***   (Basic Country Risk Term and An Off-Balance Sheet Item). Any regulation or action taken by a government or authorized government agency which restricts the free flow of domestic or foreign currency into or out of its country. During recent years, such regulations have taken many forms, e.g.,

*Blocked Exchange.* The condition which exists when importers and others (e.g., borrowers) desiring to make payments abroad are prohibited from doing so by their government; that is, they are blocked from purchasing required foreign currencies. Under such conditions deposits in local currency are sometimes made to cover the prospective remittances, but foreign creditors must wait until the block is removed or they find some way of using the local currrency credited to them.

*Multiple Currency System.* Involves the establishment by law of different exchange values for the national currency, the applicable value in any exchange transaction depending upon the type of commodity or service purchased abroad for which exchange is desired.

*Rationing of Foreign Exchange.* A means of controlling foreign exchange by requiring that all holders of bills of exchange relinquish them to the government in return for domestic currency at a stipulated legal rate, and that all importers apply for bills of exchange to the government. The government then allocates such exchange to importers and/or other claimants (i.e., those with external debt commitments) whose activities it wishes to encourage and denies it to others whose activities are considered less essential or perhaps harmful to the government's plan for foreign trade equilibrium.

**Expropriation.**  (Basic Country Risk Term). Governmental seizure of assets owned by a foreign entity, with or without compensation.

**Federal Funds Sold.**  (A Balance Sheet Item). An amount due a bank for all transactions involving the disposal of immediately available funds, enabling other U.S. domestic commercial banks, *including U.S. branches of foreign banks*, to maintain their reserve requirements at the Federal Reserve Bank.

**Fiduciary Accounts.**  (An Off-Balance Sheet Item). A relationship between two or more parties whereby one party, such as a bank, gives advice, manages, controls, or holds in safekeeping assets, including foreign assets, owned by another.

**Finance Lease.**  (A Balance Sheet Item). See "Lease."

**Fiscal Policy.**  (Basic Country Risk Term). That part of government policy which is concerned with raising revenue through taxation and other means and deciding on the level and pattern of expenditure. It is through the level and pattern of budgetary surpluses or deficits (and their means of financing) that the government can control the level of demand in the economy.

**Fixed Assets.**  (A Balance Sheet Item). Those assets of a permanent nature required for the normal conduct of a business and which will not normally be converted into cash during the ensuing fiscal period.

**Foreign Currency Exposure.**  (Basic Country Risk Term). A term of measurement which refers to the volume of assets and other non-balance sheet items that are deemed to be subject to the country risk of a given country and denominated in a currency other than the currency of the country.

**Forward Exchange Contracts.**  (An Off-Balance Sheet Item). An example of a contingent liability, i.e., a contract calling for delivery at a future date of a specified amount of one currency with the exchange rate fixed at the time the contract is made.

**Good Until Cancelled.**  (An Off-Balance Sheet Item). See "Advised Line of Credit."

**Guarantee.**  (The Transfer of Country Exposure). A written promise by one party, the guarantor, to be liable for the debt of another party, the principal debtor, should the latter be unable to meet his obligations. A guarantor can be resident of the same country as that of the debtor, or he can reside in a different country in which case he is often referred to as an external guarantor. In the latter case, the ARCB member banks almost unanimously transfer country exposure from the country of the debtor to the country of the guarantor where "hard," i.e., "full and unconditional" guarantees are involved covering the bank against all risks—commercial and political. Less frequently, the ARCB member banks will also transfer country exposure from the country of the debtor to the country of the guarantor where certain types of "soft" guarantees are involved, e.g., Keepwell arrangements. The term "soft" guarantee is generally applied to comfort letters, i.e., letters of Assurance, Awareness, Indemnity, Keepwell Agreements, etc.

*Guidance Line of Credit.*   (An Off-Balance Sheet Item). Credit facility used to facilitate extension of credit to a given entity, the existence of which facility and its terms and conditions are not formally advised to that entity.

*Indigenization.*   (Basic Country Risk Term). Any action by a government agency which forces the transfer of controlling interest in an entity located within that government's country from foreign to private domestic interests of individuals.

*Intrabank Transactions.*   (Basic Country Risk Term). Refers to asset acquisitions that take place within a holding company/bank, its branches, subsidiaries and affiliates which are eliminated in consolidated financial statements.

*Intra-Country Foreign Currency Exposure.*   (Basic Country Risk Term). Exists when any subsidiary or branch of the holding company/bank lends to; invests in; places with; or otherwise extends any form of credit or credit commitment to entities (including any holding company/other bank entity) that are located within the same country as the booking unit but in a currency foreign to the country where the obligor and the booking unit are located.

*Items In the Process of Collection.*   (A Balance Sheet Item). A payee's means of receiving payment wherein a check or clean draft is presented to a bank and settlement is completed only when payment in full is received by said bank.

*Keepwell.*   (The Transfer of Country Exposure). One of the stronger types of comfort letters whereby a provision is made by a parent of a borrowing subsidiary in which the parent specifies that its subsidiary will conform to certain requirements. Generally, these requirements are stated in financial terms. Although there are numerous potential requirements, some examples are that the subsidiary will:

- maintain a minimum working capital or current ratio;
- maintain a minimum net worth;
- restrict the amount of capital expenditures;
- not increase the current dividend rate or will not increase it by some stated amount.

In addition, the parent may further provide assurances of on-going interest in the subsidiary by incorporating the following:

- maintenance of a certain percentage of ownership of the credit taker;

- undertake to maintain the credit taker in a financial condition which would allow it to honor its debt.

A keepwell should be distinguished from a "letter of assurance" which is less specific than a keepwell and normally only acknowledges that a loan has been made to a subsidiary. The parent "assures" that its subsidiary's financial condition will meet the standards of the parent. Letters of assurance are not legally binding on the issuer whereby keepwell, depending on their wording, may be binding on the parent. According to many ARCB members, a strong keepwell may be justification to transfer exposure from the country of the borrower to the country of the issuer.

**Lease.**  (A Balance Sheet Item). A contract by which one (e.g., a bank) conveys the use of property for a period of time for a specified rent. There are two types of leases: Finance and Operating.

*Finance Lease.*  A sales and financial term designating a lease which is recognized in law as providing the lessor with full ownership rights in the underlying asset but that for *tax purposes* is treated as if the lessee were "owner." In a finance lease, the lessee pays to the lessor over the term of the lease a stream of payments that cover the full cost of the asset, the cost of administering and financing the asset and a return on investment.

*Operating Lease.*  A lease in which the lessor provides specific services such as insurance or maintenance. The contract terms usually do not guarantee the lessor full recovery of the cost of the asset, the cost of administering and financing the asset and a return on the investment. In such cases, the lessor assumes the "economic risk" of ownership.

**Legal Commitment to Lend.**  (An Off-Balance Sheet Item). A contractual agreement which is legally binding on both lender and borrower defining terms and conditions of a loan.

**Letter of Credit.**  (An Off-Balance Sheet Item). A contingent liability, i.e., a written instrument issued by a bank whereby the bank substitutes its more widely known credit for that of the lesser known credit of a buyer, addressed to a seller (beneficiary), authorizing an individual or firm to draw drafts on the bank or one of its correspondents for its account under certain conditions stipulated in the credit.

*Sight Letter of Credit.*  Letter of credit calling for drafts payable upon presentation to the drawee at sight.

*Standby Letter of Credit.*  Letter of credit against which the beneficiary can draw only if another business transaction is not completed. In other words, when a promissory note is given, sometimes a letter of credit is issued to back up the note; the credit will only be used if the maker of the promissory note defaults.

**Line of Credit.**  (An Off-Balance Sheet Item). An arbitrary decision made by a bank regarding the maximum amount of credit which may be extended to a customer under an uncommitted facility, advised or unadvised. See "Advised Line of Credit."

**Loan.**  (A Balance Sheet Item). Refer to "Advances," "Arranged Overdraft," "Casual Overdraft," "Federal Funds Sold," "Loans to Consortium Banks," "Loans to Multilateral Agencies," and "Term Loan."

***Loans to Consortium Banks.***   (A Balance Sheet Item). The consortium bank is generally established in an international money center as a financial multiproduct institution owned by two or more parents. Ownership in such banks generally is for the specific purpose of participating in cross-border Eurocurrency financings. To leverage their sales force, the parents are usually from different countries. ARCB banks assign exposure emanating from their loans to consortium banks to the domicile of the bank rather than that of its parents.

***Loans to Multilateral Agencies.***   (A Balance Sheet Item). Multilateral agencies are supranational organizations such as the World Bank, International Monetary Fund, Bank for International Settlements, Comecon, Inter-American Development Bank, etc. For the most part, exposure to multilateral agencies is monitored separately by the ARCB banks and is not allocated to any specific country.

***Local Currency Exposure.***   (Basic Country Risk Term). Refers to the level of assets and other non-balance sheet items that are deemed to be subject to the country risk of a given country, and are denominated in the local currency of that country. Eurocurrency assets are often not included in the measurement of local currency exposure, even when the currency in question is the Euro-version of the local currency.

***Marketable Securities—Trading Account.***   (A Balance Sheet Item). Securities held by an institution as inventory for business of trading, i.e., maintaining a secondary market, in such securities. These instruments may represent claims against public and/or private sector issuers.

***Minimum Risk Assets.***   (A Balance Sheet Item). Cash or assets whose conversion to cash at a future date is virtually assured and on which the probability of loss is virtually zero.

***Monetary Policy.***   (Basic Country Risk Term). That part of economic policy which regulates the level of money or liquidity in the economy in order to achieve some desired policy objective, such as the control of inflation, an improvement in the balance of payments, a certain level of employment, or growth in the gross national product. It contrasts with more direct measures of control.

***Money Market Transactions.***   (A Balance Sheet Item). Refer to the purchase of foreign and/or domestic bills in a given country where the interest rate on such instruments is closely tied to prevailing, well publicized day-to-day domestic and international market rates.

***Nationalization.***   (Basic Country Risk Term). Ownership and operation by the central government of a nation of some enterprise previously a private or local government undertaking. Also, the act of taking over assets owned by either local or foreign entities or individuals, with compensation.

***Operating Lease.***   (A Balance Sheet Item). See "Lease."

***Performance Bond.***   (An Off-Balance Sheet Item). A contingent liability, i.e., a written instrument which substitutes a strong financial risk (usually of an insurance, bank or bonding company) for a lesser known risk, and which warranties compensation for non-performance in accordance with certain conditions stipulated in the bond.

**Placement.**   (A Balance Sheet Item). An interbank interest bearing time deposit.

**Price Control.**   (Basic Country Risk Term). The fixing of prices by government statute in order to prevent price rises in an inflationary situation.

**Redeposit.**   (A Balance Sheet Item). See "Placement."

**Risk Assets.**   (A Balance Sheet Item). All assets of a bank except cash and minimum risk items.

**Shipping Guarantees.**   (The Transfer of Country Exposure).

>   *Charter Party.*   An agreement by which a shipowner agrees to place an entire ship, or part of it, at the disposal of a merchant or other person, for the conveyance of goods, binding them to a particular place, for a sum of money which the merchant undertakes to pay as freight for their carriage. Charters are either time, affreightment, or demise (bareboat). See "Charter Party Assignment."

>   *Charter Party Assignment.*   A contractual arrangement whereby the contract existing between the shipowner and the charterer (specifically, the rents payable) is assigned to a bank as security for its loan to a shipowner. In theory, the bank actually takes possession of the rents that are due the shipowner from the charterer. These amounts are paid by the charterer directly to the bank to reduce the shipowner's loan. The ARCB member banks use three basic treatments in dealing with loans to shipowners collateralized by charter party assignments:

>   * Most commonly, ARCB members consider shipping loans collateralized by bareboat and/or time charters to be "special situations" because political and/or economic developments in the country of the owner or registration may not necessarily impact the flow of funds from the charterer to the bank. In such cases, shipping transactions are monitored separately from the other types of country exposure;

>   * Alternatively, banks may assign country exposure to the country of the charterer, especially if the bareboat and/or time charterer is deemed to generate relatively little foreign exchange from countries other than his country of residence;

>   * Finally, banks may consider that the country exposure belongs to the country of the shipowner, especially where unguaranteed loans to national flag carriers (including government maritime agencies) are involved and/or to the country from which the carriage of goods takes place in the case of contracts of affreightment. See below: "Bareboat," "Time" Charters, and "Contract of Affreightment."

>   *Bareboat Charter.*   A charter in which the bare ship is chartered without crew; the charterer, for a stipulated sum, taking over the vessel with a minimum of restrictions. Also called bare-pole charter, bare-hull charter.

>   *Contract of Affreightment.*   A contract of affreightment is one with a shipowner to hire his ship or part of it for the carriage of goods. Such a contract generally takes the form of a charter party or bill of lading.

>   *Time Charter.*   A form of charter party issued when the vessel is chartered for an agreed period of time. It places the vessel in the possession of the

charterer. It may, however, provide that the owner shall man and provision the vessel.

***Sight Letter of Credit.***   (An Off-Balance Sheet Item). See "Letter of Credit."

***Standby Letter of Credit.***   (An Off-Balance Sheet Item). See "Letter of Credit."

***Term Loan.***   (A Balance Sheet Item). Usually a long-term loan with a maturity from one to ten years, extended by large commercial banks to large well-established business enterprises and repayable according to a specified schedule (for the most part in periodic installments) under a legal agreement between the bank and the borrower.

# Chapter 12

# Some Brief Notes on Taxation of International Transactions[1]

## 12.1 INTRODUCTION

This chapter is very short. It is relatively straightforward to black in the outline of the international taxation problem. Beyond that point we enter the maze of diverse national tax rules, and for a guide you need a good tax lawyer.

Taxes have two possibly complimentary functions. They raise revenue, and they alter incentives to undertake certain actions. These actions might be the location of production, transfer prices, and the amount exported. They might also involve the choice of how much of the outflow to the parent from a foreign subsidiary will be called dividends, and how much will be called royalties and fees for the use of the parent's technology and facilities. We will not concern ourselves very much with governmental tax schemes to reallocate resources, as the more basic problem comes from the revenue-raising goal. We are concerned with corporations and individuals who earn income in more than one tax jurisdiction.[2] Each taxation authority wishes to tax at least the income it sees as derived from local activity, and sometimes seeks to tax all income earned anywhere by taxpayers who pay local tax. The various arrangements made among countries to avoid double taxation, and differences in tax rules and rates, provide the opportunity temporarily to shelter income from taxation, thus obtaining an interest-free loan from the tax authorities.

---

[1]We are grateful for the assistance of Jacques Favier, tax partner at Arthur Andersen in Paris.
[2]National borders demarcate tax jurisdictions, but so do regional boundaries within federal states like the United States, where the regions, here the states, retain substantial taxation rights.

The key issue in taxation is the definition of taxable income. Closely allied is the fact that rates of taxation will vary with the nature of the income earned—whether it is production profits, dividends, royalties and fees, and so on. Taxes which attempt to reallocate resources will vary according to the industry and location of the earnings, and also according to the legal structure of the corporation (for example the Domestic International Sales Corporation, DISC, in the United States).

The basic legal framework for avoidance of double taxation is given by the roughly 30 tax treaties between the United States and the major trading nations. These treaties allocate tax sovereignty between the relevant pairs of countries. Specifically, they

- define the taxes coming under the aegis of the treaty;

- define who is a resident for tax purposes;

- provide a procedure for resolution of disputes;

- define the types of income which are subject to taxation; and

- allocate between the countries the rights to levy the various types of taxes.

## 12.2 TAXATION ON WORLDWIDE INCOME

Taxes may be levied either on worldwide income of a resident for tax purposes, or within the territorial jurisdiction of the tax authority. In this section we will elucidate the principle of taxation on worldwide income, which is the system in use in the United States. In the United States, all citizens plus all other taxable resident entities must pay tax on income wherever earned, subject to certain credit provisions for foreign taxes paid. Foreign income earners in the United States who are not treated as residents for tax purposes are taxed only on their U.S. income, at U.S. tax rates. This set of procedures distinguishes the United States from most other countries, which tax solely on the basis of some definition of residence rather than on the basis of citizenship. Almost invariably the place of residence of corporations is the tax jurisdiction in which they are legally incorporated. Innovations in this area tend to originate with developing countries. Recently in one such country the government attempted to tax all the foreign participants in a large construction project, including the banks which were providing the debt financing! The interest paid by the construction consortium was taxed, on the grounds that this interest cost was included in the price of the project and so was ultimately paid by the developing country.[3]

---

[3]The tax was applied, although in conventional thinking the justification for it is absurd. As we emphasized in Chapter 11, when dealing with governments the question of power is paramount.

Under the system of taxing worldwide income, the U.S. government avoids double taxation by allowing a certain amount of credit for taxes already paid on this income in other countries. Basically two approaches may be followed.

1.  A total U.S. tax obligation on income earned worldwide may be calculated, and then foreign taxes paid may be deducted from the resulting tax obligation.

2.  Foreign taxes paid may be deducted from worldwide taxable income, and U.S. taxes are then paid on this adjusted income.

Obviously the second method pays if, according to U.S. definitions of taxable income, the foreign tax paid exceeds 100% of the income.

There are at least four major complications in this basic scheme. The first has already been alluded to. U.S. firms owe U.S. tax on worldwide income as defined by U.S. tax codes. Income will be defined differently in different countries, so that one will not receive an exact offset of taxes paid. The second problem is that the allowable tax credit in the United States has an upper bound. It cannot exceed the tax that the company would hypothetically pay under U.S. income definitions and at U.S. tax rates. Whenever the foreign tax obligation exceeds the U.S. figure that would apply, the excess is not able to be credited against U.S. tax owed.

The third problem relates to the definition of ultimate ownership of foreign subsidiaries and affiliates. Which earnings are to be consolidated with those of a U.S. parent for tax purposes?[4] As one might expect, the definition of an effectively-owned subsidiary varies from country to country. As far as the United States is concerned, beneficial ownership of 10% or more of the stock of a foreign corporation requires consolidation of the (pro rata share of the) earnings. If a foreign subsidiary itself has subsidiaries, the (pro rata share of the) earnings must be consolidated if:

1.  one subsidiary holds at least 10% of the stock of the other; *and*

2.  the parent itself holds at least 5% of the stock of each.

## Example 12.1

Consider a U.S. parent with two wholly-owned European subsidiaries, denoted *A* and *B*, and measure all items in dollars. We will assume that the applicable U.S. tax rate is 48%. The earnings and payouts of the subsidiaries, according to U.S. definitions, are given in Table 12.1. U.S. tax law then requires that taxable income be computed as in Table 12.2.

---

[4]Unconsolidated earnings will be taxed eventually, on repatriation, but in the meantime the corporation receives an interest-free loan of the amount of the ultimate tax obligation.

In our hypothetical example there is excess tax credit. It may be possible to carry forward such credit, depending on circumstances.

**Table 12.1** *Earnings and Payouts of European Subsidiaries, Using U.S. Definitions and Measured in Dollars*

|  | Subsidiary A | Subsidiary B |
|---|---|---|
| Before-tax earnings | 100 | 100 |
| Income taxes | 60 | 50 |
| After-tax profit | 40 | 50 |
| Dividends | 40 | 30 |
| Withholding tax | 4 | 2 |
| Dividend payout Ratio | 40/40 = 1 | 30/50 = .6 |
| Dividend withholding Tax rate | 4/40 = 10% | 2/30 = 6 2/3% |

**Table 12.2** *Calculation of Applicable U.S. Corporate Tax*

|  | Subsidiary A | Subsidiary B |
|---|---|---|
| Dividends received by parent | 36 | 28 |
| Add withholding tax | 4 | 2 |
| Dividend payout ratio times foreign tax paid | 1 × 60 = 60 | .6 × 50 = 30 |
| Taxable income | 100 | 60 |
| U.S. tax obligation | .48 × 100 = 48 | .48 × 60 = 28.8 |
| Less tax credit |  |  |
|   Income tax[a] | 60 | 30 |
|   Withholding | 4   64 | 2 |
| Excess credit | 16 | 3.2 |

[a]The only foreign tax allowed is the dividend pay-out ratio times foreign tax paid.

The final complication in the crediting of foreign taxes paid arises from considerations of timing. The credit may be taken in the tax period in which the income is earned by the subsidiary or in the tax period in which the dividends are remitted to the parent. Since dividend payments can be deferred indefinitely, resulting in an interest free loan of the tax owed, U.S. tax law ensures a certain minimum tax will be paid in the tax period in which earnings occur. This is the provision for "Subpart *F*" income. Tax is payable on undistributed base income of controlled foreign corporations. Computation of the base income is complex but is meant to capture strategies used to minimize U.S. tax obligations.

The system of taxing worldwide income has the unpleasant and costly side effect of virtually requiring the tax authorities to minutely scrutinize intracompany matters such as pricing and the timing of remittances. Moreover the Internal Revenue Service is empowered to make its own allocation of overhead expenses among parent and subsidiaries for the purpose of computing taxes. The result is frequent occurrences of incidents of the following type. After audit the I.R.S. reallocates some overhead expenses from parent to foreign subsidiaries. This does not alter consolidated pretax profit but is still prejudicial. For the parent now has more taxable income and is taxed more. The subsidiaries have less taxable income by U.S. rules but not by foreign rules. So their taxes paid, and the resulting tax credit, do not change.

## 12.3  TAXATION BASED ON TERRITORIALITY

Under the territoriality principle tax is payable only on income generated within the tax jurisdiction. As with all legal concepts relating to taxation, the concept of "generated within" is specified at length. For example, a company incorporated in France owes French tax on all income it earns, wherever the source. But if it sets up a German subsidiary that operated outside France, no French tax is owed on that subsidiary's earnings (although undoubtedly German tax is owed). Evidently, in such a system transfer pricing and other methods of shuttling recorded earnings among subsidiaries have their greatest rewards. This evident scope for evasion has led to a large number of limitations on the operation of the basic principle. We give some examples.

- There is generally limited deductibility from domestic taxable income of losses incurred in foreign business. Some countries allow such deductions only for the first few years after foreign business begins while others limit deductions to a certain amount and allow carry-forwards.

- In almost all countries using this system it is applied only to corporations. Individuals pay taxes on worldwide income.

- In general, foreign subsidiary income kept safe from tax in a foreign tax haven becomes taxable upon distribution to the domestic owner. Corporations also owe tax on dividends, interest, royalties, fees, and so forth received from foreign corporations.

## 12.4   OTHER TAX-RELATED AREAS

### Capital Gains

Under U.S. tax law, assets meeting a minimum holding period qualification generate, upon sale, earnings that are taxed at a capital gains rate that is lower than the applicable rate on incomes. However, all gains made from sale of a stock interest in a controlled foreign corporation are taxed at the rate for ordinary income.

### Exchange Gains and Losses

Surprising as it may seem, U.S. tax law has no clear approach to this subject. Disputed decisions have been settled on a case-by-case basis and have involved contradictory judgments. In other countries, such as Britain, there exist whole networks of laws defining the circumstances under which exchange gains and losses, realized or unrealized, are to be added to or subtracted from taxable income.

### Bribes

Since 1958 the I.R.S. has disallowed bribes as legitimate, deductible costs of doing business. This point of view is not shared by many foreign governments. Bribery and facilitating tax evasion for one's suppliers and customers are normal features of international business.[5]

### DISCs

As an example of a tax law designed to encourage a particular pattern of commodity flow we take the example of the Domestic International Sales Corporation in the U.S. The DISC law was intended to encourage export of products produced in the U.S., by lowering taxes paid on earnings from these export activities. A DISC is a specially-incorporated entity (frequently a subsidiary of another firm) wherein:

1.   at least 95% of its assets are used to generate exports; and

2.   at least 95% of its income comes from exporting.
     DISCs are not taxed but are deemed to distribute to their parent 50% of their income. The parent is taxed on this whether or not this distribution actually occurs. A DISC may lend its 50% tax deferred income to its parent without tax consequences for the parent, if the income is used by the parent to increase U.S. exports. In essence, then, the DISC legislation halves the corporate tax payable on exports.

---

[5]Of course the frequency with which it is undertaken does not establish the morality of the act.

# Trade Expansion Act of 1962

## STATEMENT OF B. C. DEUSCHLE IN HEARINGS BEFORE THE EIGHTY-SEVENTH CONGRESS, SECOND SESSION COMMITTEE ON WAYS AND MEANS, HOUSE OF REPRESENTATIVES[1]

*Mr. Keogh (presiding):* You are recognized, Mr. Deuschle.

*Mr. Deuschle:* Thank you, Mr. Chairman.

Mr. Chairman and members of the Committee on Ways and Means, my name is B. C. Deuschle.

I am vice president of the Acme Shear Company, located in Bridgeport, Connecticut. I appear before this committee as president of the Shears, Scissors and Manicure Implement Manufacturers Association, the only national trade association of domestic manufacturers of scissors and shears.

The scissors and shears industry is a distinct industry and should not be confused with the larger industry and flatware industries.

The association respectfully wishes to record with this committee its strong opposition to H. R. 9900 in its present form. This bill could destroy industries such as ours and add to the unemployment problem.

During the past 15 years representatives of our association have appeared before this committee and other congressional committees, the Committee for Reciprocity Information and the Tariff Commission, to present our views on the impact of imported scissors and shears on our domestic industry.

We have never requested or suggested that a complete embargo be placed on the import of scissors and shears. All that we have asked for and desire is a fair competitive opportunity, not an advantage.

To date we have not obtained relief in any form.

We believe that H. R. 9900 would make matters worse. H. R. 9900 provides for new presidential authority to reduce or eliminate duties. We realize that title III of H. R. 9900 provides for adjustment assistance, but the criteria are general and too much is left to the discretion of the president in granting assistance.

Terms such as "significant," "prolonged," and "reasonable," used in title III to determine if a firm or an industry should receive assistance are subject to many interpretations.

[1]Reprinted from Hearings Before the Committee on Ways and Means, 1962, pp. 1656–1659, U.S. Government Printing Office, Washington, D.C.

Injury or threat of injury as it is written into our present escape clause cannot be properly defined. When 42 manufacturers out of 50 cease manufacturing and go out of business within 12 years as a direct or indirect result of excessive imports, and the Tariff Commission as well as the president decide that there is no injury or threat of injury, something should be done.

Imports of shears and scissors valued over $1.75 per dozen import value have reached the proportion that they represent 95% of domestic production of scissors and shears in this category.

This category represents 75% of total sales of all scissors and shears in the domestic market. Would you honestly say, under these circumstances, that there is no injury or threat of injury to our industry?

The Secretary of Commerce in his presentation to this committee passed over industries such as ours by stating that they accounted for only a minute part of our gross national product.

We realize that the domestic scissor and shear industry with its 1,000 plus employees accounts for only a fraction of 1% of the gross national product, but we see this as no justification for letting the industry be completely destroyed by imports produced with low-cost labor.

The workers in the domestic scissor and shear industry do not want to become wards of the state; they want to use their skills, which have taken years to develop. These workers are not interested in retraining; over many years they have developed a skill they are proud of and want to continue the work they are happy doing.

If the scissors and shears imported during 1961 had been manufactured in the United States, it would have provided over 2 million man-hours of factory work, or full-time employment for over 1,000 American employees.

Domestic manufacturers of scissors and shears have modernized and automated their operations in an effort to meet foreign competition. But foreign manufacturers also have modern equipment and with their lower wage rates are underselling domestic firms in the U.S. market at today's rate of duty.

H. R. 9900 would give the president unrestricted authority to reduce duties and thereby reduce the cost of imported scissors and shears in our market. Under the provisions of this bill, scissors and shears would be buried in a category with many other items and the duty cut 50%.

This would mean a reduction of at least 20¢ per pair at the retail level for scissors and shears now being retailed at $1 to $1.29 per pair.

If this is permitted, we do not need a crystal ball to see the results. There are only eight domestic firms now remaining of the 50 operating in the United States prior to the 50% reduction in import duty during 1950–51.

A list of these is attached to my statement, which we would very much like to have included in this record.

*Mr. Keogh:* Without objection, it will be placed at the conclusion of your testimony.

*Mr. Deuschle:* These few remaining manufacturers would be forced to close their doors and discharge their employees. The United States would then become wholly dependent on imported scissors and shears.

We cannot understand how it could be in the national interest to permit such a loss. We would lose the skills of the employees and management of the industry as well as the capital investment in production equipment. In the event of a national emergency and imports cutoff, the United States would be without a source of scissors and shears, basic tools for many industries and trades essential to our defense.

The scissor and shear industry is one of the oldest in the world. The skill was brought to the United States from Germany at a time when the United States needed new industry, and a scissor and shear industry in particular.

Scissors and shears of all sizes and types are used in every school, retail establishment, office, factory, hospital, and home in the United States. Scissors cannot be classified as a luxury, gimmick, or novelty.

Scissors are used to separate us from our mothers at birth; to cut our toenails; to trim the leather in our shoes; to cut and trim the materials used in every piece of clothing that we wear.

They are used to cut our fingernails, to trim our mustaches, the hair in our ears and nose, and to cut the hair on our heads—even down to the end of the road when our best suit or dress is cut down the back so that the undertaker can dress us for the last ride. Scissors are truly used from birth to death. They are essential to our health, education, and general welfare.

I ask you gentlemen, is this an industry that should be permitted to become extinct in this country?

*Mr. Knox:* Then, in your opinion, and in many other people's opinion, the industry itself would be unable to operate in competition if the duty was cut by 50%?

*Mr. Deuschle:* Yes, sir. You see, in any commodity with a high labor content, foreign competition definitely has the edge.

In Germany, where, incidentally, our own company has a financial interest and we are well aware of what is going on, wages there in our industry are approximately 50% or less of ours.

The labor content in our product is very high. In comparing import dollars with export dollars, the economic imbalance comes in the amount of labor content of the product, not in the dollars.

If we export wheat, which has low labor content, cigarettes, which have low labor content, and we import high labor content products, we create an imbalance that cannot be compared in terms of dollars and cents.

*Mr. Betts:* Does your industry enjoy any export business?

*Mr. Deuschle:* Our export business was quite substantial at one time, but
we lost it back in 1950 and 1951. It diminished to practically nothing.
I have had some conversations with people in the Commerce
Department who claim that there was $1,400,000 worth of cutlery
exported from this country, but on investigation we find that the bulk
of it is made up of commodities other than scissors and shears.

*Mr. Betts:* Mr. Knox asked you about our tariffs on imports. How does it
compare with the tariff of other countries on these items?

*Mr. Deuschle:* I did not quite hear you.

*Mr. Betts:* How does our tariff on these products compare with the tariff
that other countries have on these products?

*Mr. Deuschle:* On scissors and shears?

*Mr. Betts:* Yes.

*Mr. Deuschle:* To tell you the truth, I have never checked them because all
of the foreign countries could manufacture scissors and shears so
much cheaper than we could, and they were all exporting them into
this country.

I did not find any need to check their duty restrictions or monetary
restrictions or quota restrictions, whatever they might have. There is
no need for it. The foreign countries, as I learned on my last trip to
France, England, and Italy, feel that they are going to protect their
industries, and that is the purpose of the Common Market, to protect
their own industries and set up external tariffs to keep damaging
competition out of those countries.

It is one of the principal reasons for the Economic Community of
Europe. They feel that the time has to come when our wage rates and
their wage rates are comparable and that we have a common currency.

They feel that there will probably be further revaluations of foreign
currency, and, of course, they would like to see a devaluation of
American currency which, in turn, would help bring us to a more
common level.

If this does not happen, it looks as though the administration will
force American industry to become competitive on an international
basis. There is only one way that it can become competitive on an
international basis, and that is if we can reduce our cost to a point
where we are competitive.

How do you do that? You have to reduce your cost by automation,
mechanization, elimination of labor. This is a wonderful concept, but
the large labor unions in this country do not favor this sort of program.

They would like to see wages increased. Unless the administration
stops inflation in other quarters, how in the world can they expect
American industry to cut costs and automate and get their costs down
to a point where they can compete with foreign countries?

Mr. *Keogh:* Mr. Deuschle, I would like to ask you briefly this question: You indicated in your direct testimony or in response to a question that the wage rate of your industry in Germany is about 50% of the wage rate here.

Mr. Deuschle: Approximately.

Mr. Keogh: My question is: What has been the trend in the wage schedules in Germany over the last 10 years, say? Have they been going up?

Mr. Deuschle: Up until a year or two ago, there was not too much increase. There was not very much increase in wage rates in Germany, but it has accelerated in the last year or year and a half. However, so have ours. We are in an area, our factories are in areas, I should say, where we are forced to compete with large manufacturers.

If we do not keep raising our wage rates, we do not get any help. We are competing with people like Sikorsky, General Electric, Westinghouse. These are the companies that we have to compete with for labor. So our wage rates and our fringe benefits have increased just as well as theirs. In fact, probably equal.

# Orion Bank—Loan to Government of Malaysia[1]

The loan committee of Orion Bank met to discuss the bank's role as syndicator of a participation loan to the government of Malaysia.[2] The loan was to be for $400 million and was to be used for general purposes of the government, such as exchange market intervention, commonly called "balance of payments financing." Thus it was to be secured by the good will and guarantees of the government itself and not by any specific project revenues or assets. This made it of great importance to assess the capacity of the government to generate enough foreign exchange to service the debt over its seven-year life, and to repay the principal.

This was not the first governmental loan in which Orion had participated and the bank had built up a small staff whose job it was to evaluate the creditworthiness of governments. Four people worked in the headquarters in London—two with advanced training in economics and two with M.B.A.'s. Their job was to combine statistical analysis of reports generated by governments and by international agencies like the International Monetary Fund and the Bank for International Settlements, with on-the-spot reports from the bank's regional loan officers. The loan officers worked by feel, basing their evaluations on the many business and governmental contracts they developed in their region.

Although its record in credit evaluation was not spotless, the bank was willing to commit its own funds on the basis of favorable reports from the team in London. The problem it faced was its potential liability to the numerous smaller banks that would provide the bulk of the funds for the loan. These banks would invest on the basis of the placement memorandum drawn up by Orion to attract co-lenders. Most of the banks were too small to have full-time staff involved in evaluation of the resources available to the governments of 80 or more developing countries. Thus they relied heavily on Orion's researches, as evidence in the placement memorandum. It was always the practice, in preparing placement memoranda, to be as scrupulous as possible but ultimately to disclaim

---

[1]This case has been constructed to highlight certain major issues in balance of payments analysis. The incidents and characters are fictional.

[2]For the definition of a participation loan and for evaluation of creditworthiness, see Chapter 11.

responsibility for the accuracy of the facts they contained. Commonly the borrower attested to the accuracy of his or her own facts. For many years this practice had proceeded without difficulties. Recently, however, lawsuits had been filed against lead banks in participation loans who had allegedly failed to make full disclosure in the relevant placement memoranda. The plaintiff banks had asserted that placement memoranda were essentially prospectuses and that the participations were securities, which should be subject to S.E.C. disclosure requirements. These suits were filed in 1976, and the main issue had never been ruled upon, but the bank's directors were resolved to be as careful as possible to ensure that they had made all good efforts to obtain information.

While the bank took a large number of factors into account in assessing creditworthiness, such as political stability, consistency of economic policy, and so forth, the primary consideration remained whether the country could generate adequate foreign exchange to meet its debt servicing requirements. Orion's research team had undertaken a very comprehensive analysis of the Malaysian balance of payments, as a basis for its placement memorandum. The loan committee was meeting to discuss a problem with this analysis namely that substantial smuggling occurred, which was obviously not recorded in the official statistics. Their problem was to decide whether the existence of the smuggling vitiated the balance of payments analysis based on the official data. The London research team was inclined to dismiss the issue. They made the following arguments. First, the smuggling transactions escaped the government's revenue net, and so were not available as potential sources of funds to offset government debt obligations. What one saw on the official tables was what was there, for all purposes relevant to the bank. Second, the smuggling had gone on for many years and would presumably continue. The situation was stable, with no reason to expect an increase or decrease in the importance of smuggling relative to observed trade.

The directors were uncomfortable with sophisticated arguments about the merits of different statistics. They preferred to listen to their expert on Malaysia who indicated, as did the London research team, that the Malaysians seemed able to meet the debt service requirements without problems. They were restrained from approving the syndication and the memorandum by the vehement opposition of board member Dr. David Bell. Dr. Bell was not a banker but a professor of political science. He was brought onto the board to provide some detailed high-level knowledge of the developing countries whose borrowing needs formed so large a part of Orion's business. Dr. Bell was an expert on political allegiances in developing countries rather than on economics. The basis for his opposition was a recent article on smuggling in the widely-read journal *Foreign Policy*. The author of the article was very strongly of the opinion that smuggling constituted a major problem for the economy and the balance of payments. Dr. Bell had distributed selected excerpts from the article to the directors, the members of the loan committee, and to the London research team. He disliked the latter group because, in his words, "They don't have a broad perspective; they look at things only from the point of view of cash flows coming in and cash flows going out."

**Exhibit 1**   *Selected Excerpts from "Smuggling," by Jorge Dominguez, in Foreign Policy, No. 20, Fall 1975*[3]

Smuggling destabilizes relations with allies. It is a source of frustration in areas ranging from industrial protection to population growth. It dulls the effectiveness of foreign policy instruments such as trade and immigration acts. And it can affect the internal structure of a society by creating new actors, power bases, and patterns of consumption. Smuggling may be the extreme instance of loss of state control. . . .

How much smuggling actually goes on? Obviously the precise answer is not known. One country with a reputation for a good deal of smuggling is Indonesia. From 1958 to 1962, prior to the confrontation between Malaysia and Indonesia, Indonesia's average unrecorded exports were between 18 per cent and 24 per cent of its average recorded exports; Indonesia's average unrecorded imports were about 27 per cent of its average recorded imports. During the period of confrontation, Indonesia's recorded trade with Malaysia-Singapore was zero. Other information, however, suggests that while recorded trade fell, smuggling increased.[4] . . .

The basic procedure for smuggling is universal. Country *A* has a prohibition, quota, or tariff on the import of various goods (or people or services). Country *A* may also have export duties. Country *B*, which may be its neighbor or an international smuggling center, has much lower import or export duties, no prohibitions or quotas, and probably a low tax on goods in transit. Goods (or people or services) flow in and out of country *A* through country *B*, where such transactions are legal. The flow into country *B* is fully regulated and legal, and goods in transit leave country *B* under supervision. Country *B* asserts that it is not responsible for investigating what occurs beyond its borders. . . .

*Why Smuggle?*

Legal and illegal trade were born simultaneously. Smuggling is, and always has been, a serious problem. It is a particularly difficult problem for developing countries. Whereas the industrial countries can more competently control smuggling and are less affected by it, the developing countries do not have this control—and the poorest of them often benefit from smuggling. Trade is crucial to these developing countries, whose governments benefit from its growth through taxation and tariffs. The

---

[3]Reprinted with permission from *Foreign Policy* #20 (Fall 1975). Copyright 1975 by the Carnegie Endowment for International Peace.

[4]C. G. F. Simkin, "Indonesia's Unrecorded Trade," *Development Digest*, vol. 9, no. 2, April 1971, pp. 41, 45, and passim.

relatively weak bureaucratic capabilities of developing countries, however, make possible and often encourage the rise of smuggling. Thus smugglers have been active throughout history, not only for their own personal benefit but also as instruments of states and revolutionary movements—though rarely acknowledged by their patrons. Smuggling, therefore, has often been politically motivated.

There are those in power who, although not personally dishonest, may find sufficient reason to tolerate smuggling as a solution to other problems. Take, for example, a country with a balance-of-payments problem which has made international lending institutions unwilling to extend credit. One solution would be to impose prohibitive tariffs on imported products, thus reducing imports and improving the balance of payments. The demand for the imports would still exist, however, and therefore a portion of the import trade would shift from recorded (legal) to unrecorded (illegal) trade. But the offending items would disappear from the balance-of-payments accounts, and the country would thus have shown a willingness to meet its international obligations and exercise financial responsibility through belt-tightening. The country's international financial standing would thereby be improved, while the effective inflow of goods continued—through smuggling.

A government is more likely to control smuggling if demand is diffuse than if it is focused on one commodity. Should a government suppress the importation of a popular product, it may fuel its political opposition. Shifting importation from legal to illegal channels insures a continued supply of the product and avoids political suppression. Weak governments thus choose corruption through smuggling over political suppression. The enforcement of laws against smuggling is too politically costly. . . .

Smuggling can also have more orthodox economic and political benefits. For example, if a country establishes high tariffs to protect an infant industry, it may also result in producer sovereignty, leading to high prices and poor quality. Smuggling provides a degree of foreign competition for these local manufacturers. Because smuggling usually brings in fewer goods than if trade were free and legal, a significant measure of effective protection continues. The inflow of smuggled goods strengthens supply, helps curtail inflation, and sets a minimum quality threshold.

The main difference between import smuggling and normal trade is that the importing country's government receives no revenues. If the exporting country has export taxes, its government may still receive such revenues; and there may be an intermediary country through which goods flow, also receiving benefits. The original producer has no obvious economic preference if he can market his goods. The effects on employment in the target country are probably the same; the only difference being that part of the marketing system is illegal. Thus it is the importing country's government which loses the most. Should there be an intermediary country, its government gains the most. . . .

Note, however, that is these cases of export smuggling, there is a very negative effect on the balance of payments of the country whose exports are being smuggled. *Whereas import smuggling offers gains for all participants, export smuggling approaches a zero-sum game, where the intermediary country's gains are the exporting country's losses.* . . .

Who benefits most from smuggling? The smuggler. The actual smuggling network is not designed to benefit the poorest countries but to enrich a few individuals. Though smuggling may achieve a measure of redistribution of wealth between countries, it does not redistribute wealth from the elite to the poor within countries. Even in the poorest countries, the benefits to smugglers outweigh any benefits to the country as a whole. The middle-income (and still poor) countries tend to lose the most though they benefit some. The high-income countries, though they also benefit in some respects, have too much to lose from the flow of narcotics and illegal aliens, and from the disruption of the norms of international relations. . . .

Successful enforcement against smuggling, in short, is unlikely because so many agree with Adam Smith: "A smuggler is a person who, although no doubt blameable for violating the laws of the country, is frequently incapable of violating those of natural justice, and would have been, in every respect, an excellent citizen had not the laws of his country made that a crime which Nature never meant to be so."

# 'Port Arthur Timber Company'[1]

## 1. THE OPPORTUNITY

Shortly before the end of December 1962, Mr. Zaven Demarchek, president of the Port Arthur Timber Company (PATCO), had received a letter from a Brazilian lumber company concerning a proposed venture. The Brazilian company, Cascamon–Industrial Madeireira S.A., wanted to build a large new sawmill with facilities for producing finished lumber and construction materials. The management of Cascamon proposed that as a partner in the joint venture PATCO would supply the milling equipment and an expert operating manager for the mill. In return PATCO would be given limited exploitation rights for a period of five years. At the end of the five-year period, the ownership of all the equipment was to pass to Cascamon.

Mr. Demarchek found that the required machinery would be available for delivery in Brazil within 45 days after the order date. The cost of this equipment was estimated to be 175 million cruzeiros. At the present buy rate for cruzeiros in terms of Canadian dollars, 437.6 cruzeiros per Canadian dollar, this investment amounted to approximately $400,000. In return for this investment PATCO would be allowed to cut 15,000 cubic meters, equivalent to 6,361,000 board feet, of lumber each year for five years. The revenues from the sale of this lumber would become the property of PATCO. Any other earned revenues would belong to Cascamon. Cascamon did not guarantee the lumber supply but owned or had cutting rights on much more forest than would be needed to allow PATCO its board feed limit. Because of his extensive Canadian experience, Mr. Demarchek was unworried by any problems of actual operation. His interest was in analyzing the financial worth of the proposition. The remaining details of the proposal stated that Cascamon would provide all needed working capital and that operating costs, including the salary of the operating manager, would be divided in proportion to the amount of lumber cut. As the owner of the mill equipment, PATCO would be allowed to depreciate its investment fully for tax purposes during the first five years. The joint-venture agreement permitted remittance of funds to the parent company only at the end of each calendar year, after division of operating

---

[1]This is a revised version of a case written by the late Alexander Robichek, and originally copyrighted in 1974 by l'Institut pour l'Étude des Méthodes de Direction de L'Entreprise (IMEDE), Lausanne, Switzerland.

expenses between the two companies and payment of taxes. Thus, intermittent cash flows would be part of the operating working capital until released for remittance.

## 2. TAX, DEPRECIATION, EXCHANGE AND REMITTANCE FEATURES

Brazilian regulations on these subjects were rather involved. They are summarized in Exhibit 1. Because of the government's encouragement of joint ventures, the allowable straight line depreciation for equipment had been doubled to 20%. The high and variable inflation in Brazil forced the government to allow for depreciation from inflation-adjusted values. The chosen correction factor was an officially-compiled general price index. For calculation of depreciation for tax purposes, the amount of depreciation at book value could be marked up by the amount of inflation that had taken place between the year the asset was purchased and the tax year in question. An example of such calculation for the period 1957 through 1962, using a price index based at 1.00 in 1962, is shown in Exhibit 2.

## 3. THE COMPANIES INVOLVED IN THE PROPOSED VENTURE

PATCO operations extended from central Canada eastward into the Maritime Provinces. The company was formed in 1948 by the three Demarchek brothers in the southern part of the province of Ontario, near Lake Superior. Port Arthur became the company's headquarters, and even today PATCO's largest single milling facility was just outside that city. Zaven Demarchek's older brother was killed in a logging accident in 1950, and in 1955 his younger brother left the company to join a construction firm in Toronto. Thus, it was under the sole leadership of Zaven that the company grew to have annual sales in excess of $30 million Canadian. Since the beginning of 1961 he had shared the responsibility of running PATCO with his new partner, Mr. Harold Zablocki. Zablocki had worked as a government bank inspector before joining PATCO and brought a knowledge of accounting and finance to the company.

Cascamon–Industrial Madeireira S.A., the Brazilian company that proposed the joint venture, had been directed to contact PATCO by the Canadian consul in Sao Paulo. This lumber and land development company was located in southern Brazil, not far from the town of Cascavel in the state of Paraná. This region was the center of the Brazilian lumber industry. Cascamon had timber rights for more than 50,000 square kilometers (in excess of 1,250,000 acres) of previously uncut land. While pursuing several other means for speeding the development of its lumber operations, Cascamon decided to approach PATCO with a plan for a joint venture.

## 4.  PATCO'S ANALYSIS OF THE PROPOSAL

Zablocki had introduced project evaluation using the concept of discounted cash flow analysis to PATCO. He and Demarchek had decided that PATCO should not undertake projects that were expected to return less than 15 percent after taxes. Neither of the partners had experience in international business or finance, and viewed it as intrinsically riskier than domestic operations. For this reason they decided that the Brazilian venture would be accepted only if it could clear a 20% hurdle rate. Their problem was to forecast the Canadian dollar returns to them over the next five years. Zablocki had made a first pass by assuming that all the relevant numbers (see Exhibit 3) would remain as they had been in late 1962. This led to an income statement shown in Exhibit 4. Since the internal rate of return under these assumptions was less than 20%, the implied outcome was rejection.

Demarchek was dissatisfied. On the one hand, he wanted to undertake the project. On the other hand, it was unlikely that things would stay as they had been in late 1962, and he was worried about the volatile inflation rate. If the past was to be a guide, perhaps they ought to forecast by extrapolating recent events in some way. Demarchek suggested that the whole calculation should be rerun under the assumption that inflation would affect lumber prices, wage rates, costs, and exchange rates in the same relative way as during the past five years. This meant that the rate of inflation between the end of 1962 and the end of 1963 would correspond to that between December 1957 and December 1958, that the rate in 1964 would be the same as in 1959, and so on for the rest of the five-year period. The specific simplifying assumptions were:

1. The price of lumber during the next five years will be a function of the lumber price index for the past five years (Exhibit 3).

2. Labor costs will rise according to the past five-year trend of the labor wage rate index for the lumber industry (Exhibit 3).

3. General and administrative costs will be a function of the past general price index (Exhibit 3).

4. Depreciation will be adjusted according to the amount of capital revaluation that is allowed by the Depreciation Adjustment Index (Exhibit 2).

5. The tax rate will remain at 30% of profits before taxes. Taxes were payable shortly after the end of the operating year.

6.  Exchange rates between the cruzeiro and the Canadian dollar will change as they did during the past five years as shown in the index of exchange rate movements (Exhibit 3).

7.  A full year's cutting could be taken in 1963.

8.  Average figures for costs and prices would be used. For example, Zablocki estimated that the average selling price of lumber in 1963 would be 28,590 cruzeiros per cubic meter. This represents the average lumber price index for 1958 (i.e., five years before) of 105.9 (from 100.00 to 111.8) times the December 1962 estimated selling price of 27,000 per cubic meter (see Exhibit 2). Similarly, for labor and general expenses he planned to use an average index of the year-end figures as an approximation of that year's experience.

**Exhibit 1**   *Taxation Provisions in Brazil*[2]

### Inventories

3.21  The determination of the cost of sales element of gross profits is indirectly prescribed in the Regulations. Raw materials and work in process must be valued at cost. Finished goods and goods purchased for resale also must be valued at cost, except that market value, if lower than cost, must be used for commodities which are regularly traded on an exchange. In the determination of cost, the average cost, first-in first-out and standard cost methods may be used. It is not clear whether the retail method of inventory valuation is permitted, and it is doubtful whether the last-in first-out method is acceptable. The cost of manufactured goods must include appropriate elements of raw material, direct labor and overhead expenses. Such items as customs duties and freight-in must be included in the cost of purchased inventory. Arbitrary write-downs of inventory are prohibited, and valuation reserves may not be deducted in the determination of taxable income, even though it is permissible to record such reserves on the books.

### Depreciation of Property, Plant and Equipment

3.22  Brazilian tax and accounting concepts allow a provision for depreciation as a cost or charge each year. Any properly and consistently applied method of depreciation may be used. This, however, usually infers the straight-line method. The Regulations empower the National Institute of Technology to set standards for the determination of useful life; however, the Institute has as yet taken no action. The following straight-line rates are examples of those normally allowed:

| | |
|---|---|
| Real property (buildings) | 2% |
| Office furniture and equipment | 10% |

---

[2]*Tax and Trade Guide: Brazil.* Arthur Andersen and Co., January 1972. Reprinted by permission.

| | |
|---|---|
| Industrial and agricultural machinery, equipment, tools and accessories | 10% |
| Automobiles and other vehicles | 20% |

The Regulations provide for a 50% increase over normal depreciation if property is used for two eight-hour shifts and a 100% increase in the case of use for three eight-hour shifts.

### Interest and Monetary Correction

3.35   Interest and monetary correction expenses (see 3.38) on debt contracted for business purposes is deductible, including interest and monetary correction on loans, advances and current accounts between an owner or partner and the business entity. If the debt runs to an owner or partner, it must have fixed conditions of interest and monetary correction similar to the most expensive loans taken out by the corporate entity, or it must have similar conditions to those of the current financial market.

### Exchange Losses

3.36   Exchange losses incurred on obligations in foreign currency (or in cruzeiros, subject to monetary correction) are a deductible expense only when actually realized. Losses on debts contracted to finance fixed assets are handled as follows: the unrealized portion of the loss is added to the outstanding debt balance payable, offsetting the annual monetary restatement of the fixed assets, and the realized portion is partly deducted as an expense and partly added to the fixed asset account. The part to be deducted as expense is determined by the proportion of accumulated depreciation to the fixed asset value. On obligations contracted to finance current assets (working capital), losses realized are deductible, and unrealized losses are recorded as a deferred charge.

### Monetary Correction Received

3.38   Brazilian legislation provides for two types of monetary correction in the financial market:

1. Prefixed monetary correction- which estimates the inflation rates over the period the debt will be repaid, and

2. Official monetary correction- which is published monthly by the government, based on the actual inflation rate.

3.39   Prefixed monetary correction received by business entities constitutes taxable income. Monetary correction received, to the extent it is equal to the official monetary correction indexes published by the government (not prefixed), will not be subject to corporate income tax provided the correction is utilized in capital increases by the receiving company. Tax at the source must be withheld only on commercial paper which has prefixed monetary correction. The tax is retained at the source when the taxpayer buys the security (bill of exchange, debenture, or certificate of deposit). If the taxpayer is an individual, the monetary correction received will be taxed only at the source. In the case of corporate taxpayers, the tax withheld at the source may be deducted from the income tax liability computed on the annual tax return.

### Reserve for Maintenance of Working Capital

3.40   Business entities may deduct from taxable income an allowance for monetary restatement of their working capital. This deduction is computed through the application of a corrective index to the value of the company's working capital. The deduction is limited to 20% of taxable income and the company applying for it must have accounting profit sufficient enough to support the value of the reserve in the year it is established. The value of the reserve for maintenance of working capital must be capitalized, and is free from income tax. There is no time limit on the capitalization of this reserve.

### Loss Carry-Forward

3.41   A loss sustained in one base year may, with limitations, be carried forward to the three succeeding years. The principal limitation on availability of a loss carry-over is that it may only be utilized in the event of the nonexistence of reserves, such as the reserve for tax contingencies, the reserve for indemnities, etc., earned surplus or capital surplus. This limitation does not affect sole proprietorships and branches of foreign firms, which by their nature do not have capital surplus and, pursuant to the theory that earnings are distributed by operation of law at the end of a fiscal period, cannot have reserves or earned surplus.

3.42   A carry-over loss may be applied against income of any of the three succeeding years in any manner the taxpayer sees fit. The carry-over period may not be extended by applying a carry-over to create a loss and then carrying forward the latter loss. A carry-over loss may also be offset against the net result of monetary restatement of fixed assets (see 3.67).

### Distributed Profits Tax

3.43   Besides the normal 30% corporate tax, an additional levy of 5% is payable on distributed profits, except for: stock dividends, profits distributed by open capital companies (see 2.39), and companies the net worth of which does not exceed Cr $316,800 (U.S. $63,360 at 1972 rates).

### General Exchange Controls

5.01   Foreign currency is bought and sold at the official rate by all authorized commercial banks or exchange houses. They must report all transactions daily to the Bank of Brazil (Banco do Brasil) which operates in the exchange market as an agent of the Central Bank to maintain a uniform exchange rate. Trade and payment transactions are effected at the official rate.

5.03   Investments and reinvestments are registered in local (Cr $) and foreign currency. Incorporations into capital of amounts derived from monetary correction are registered only in local currency.

### Remittance of Profits

5.04   In the event of an unfavorable balance of payments situation or in anticipation of such a situation, annual profit remittance can be limited to 10% of registered capital and reinvestment. The Profit Remittance Law also established a supplementary tax of 40–60% on annual profit remittances in excess of 12% of registered capital plus capital in process of being registered.

5.06   Remittances of principal and interest on foreign loans must be registered with the Central Bank. Interest rates in excess of those prevailing in the country of origin may be disallowed.

### Price Controls

5.09   The Interministerial Price Council (C.I.P.) is the body which regulates wholesale and retail price controls over most industrial products. The C.I.P. is composed of the Ministers of Finance, Industry and Commerce, Agriculture, Planning and General Coordination. The C.I.P keeps statistics of the evolution of prices and costs of products and services by drawing up corresponding indexes for each sector of economic activity. These indexes are the bases for calculating the rates of price adjustments.

5.10   A company applying for price increases must fill out a statement prepared by the C.I.P. Through this statement, based on direct and indirect costs, the company can justify the increase being applied for. Price adjustments that have not been reviewed and decided upon within 45 days from the date of presentation of the documents and information judged necessary for examination by C.I.P. are considered to be automatically approved. However, in practice, notification is usually given the applicant of the lack of a decision within the prescribed time and the period begins again.

5.11   Price increases applied for as a consequence of cost increases derived from exchange devaluation, general salary increases or tax increases are automatically justified and the companies have only to file the statements mentioned above, demonstrating the new price structure.

**Exhibit 2**   *Brazilian Depreciation Adjustment*

| Year | Official Price Index | Age of Investment (from 1957) | Depreciation Markup Factor[a] |
|---|---|---|---|
| 1957 | .200 | 0 | 1.00 |
| 1958 | .229 | 1 | 1.15 |
| 1959 | .328 | 2 | 1.64 |
| 1960 | .433 | 3 | 2.17 |
| 1961 | .622 | 4 | 3.11 |
| 1962 | 1.000 | 5 | 5.00 |

$$\text{depreciation markup factor} = \frac{\text{index for year of calculation}}{\text{index for year of purchase}}$$

[a]In the final column, we took the year of purchase to be 1957. Thus the depreciation markup factor for, say, 1960, is computed as .433/.200 = 2.17. Book value depreciation would be marked up 2.13 times for tax purposes in computing tax obligations for 1960.

**Exhibit 3**　*A History of Relevant Prices*

| | Lumber Price Index in Brazil | | Labor Wage Rate Index for the Brazilian Lumber Industry | | General Price Index for Brazil | |
|---|---|---|---|---|---|---|
| | Year-end figure | Mid-year average | Year-end figure | Mid-year average | Year-end figure | Mid-year average |
| 1957 | 100.0 | | 100.0 | | 100.0 | |
| | | 105.9 | | 106.2 | | 107.4 |
| 1958 | 111.8 | | 112.4 | | 114.9 | |
| | | 135.4 | | 121.9 | | 139.6 |
| 1959 | 159.0 | | 131.4 | | 164.4 | |
| | | 191.8 | | 146.4 | | 190.8 |
| 1960 | 225.6 | | 161.4 | | 217.2 | |
| | | 267.4 | | 197.4 | | 264.4 |
| 1961 | 310.3 | | 233.3 | | 311.5 | |
| | | 398.9 | | 272.8 | | 406.3 |
| 1962 | 487.2 | | 312.4 | | 501.0 | |

*Source:* MMP Statistic

*Exchange Rates Between Cruzeiros and Canadian Dollars*
*(cruzeiros per Canadian dollar)*

| | Year End | | Index of Change in Exchange Rates |
|---|---|---|---|
| | Buy Rate | Sell Rate | |
| 1957 | 91.42 | 92.34 | 100.0 |
| 1958 | 143.0 | 144.4 | 156.4 |
| 1959 | 213.2 | 215.4 | 233.0 |
| 1960 | 204.8 | 206.9 | 224.1 |
| 1961 | 304.7 | 307.8 | 333.3 |
| 1962 | 437.6 | 442.0 | 478.7 |

*Source:* IMF International Financial Statistics

**Exhibit 4**　*PORT ARTHUR TIMBER COMPANY*
*Initial Projected Annual Income Statement for Proposed Joint Venture*

| | |
|---|---|
| Lumber cut | 15,000M³ |
| Price/M³ | 27,000 CRZ |

*Income Statement*
*(thousands of cruzeiros)*

| | |
|---|---|
| Sales | 405,000 |
| Operating Expenses | |
| Labor | 260,000 |
| General Administration and Other | 80,000 |
| Total Operating Expenses | 340,000 |

| | |
|---|---:|
| Operating Revenues Before Depreciation | 65,000 |
| Depreciation | 35,000 |
| Net Operating Income Before Taxes | 30,000 |
| Taxes | 9,000 |
| Profit After Taxes | 21,000 |
| | |
| Cash Flow (Profit After Taxes + Depreciation) | 56,000,000 |
| Exchange Rate (Sell Rate from Exhibit 4) | 442.0 |
| Return in Canadian Dollars | $    126,700[a] |

[a]Cash flows of $126,700 per year for five years discounted at 20% equal 378,909.
Cash flows of $126,700 per year for five years discounted at 15% equal 424,724.
Approximate discounted cash flow rate of return equals 18%.

**Exhibit 5**  *Central Bank Discount Rates (end of period; annualized per cent)*

| | 1953 | 1954 | 1955 | 1956 | 1957 | 1958 | 1959 | 1960 | 1961 | 1962 IV |
|---|---|---|---|---|---|---|---|---|---|---|
| Canada | 2.00 → | | 2.75 | 3.92 | 3.82 | 3.74 | 5.37 | 3.50 | 3.24 | 4.00 |
| Brazil | 6.00 ———————————→ | | | | | 8.00 ———————————→ | | | | |

*Source:* IMF

**Exhibit 6**  *Money Supply Growth Index Numbers: December 1958 = 100 End of December*

| | 1953 | 1954 | 1955 | 1956 | 1957 | 1959 | 1960 | 1961 | 1962 |
|---|---|---|---|---|---|---|---|---|---|
| Canada | 75 | 81 | 86 | 85 | 89 | 97 | 102 | 114 | 118 |
| Brazil | 35 | 43 | 50 | 62 | 82 | 142 | 196 | 295 | 482 |

*Source:* IMF

**Exhibit 7**  *Consumer Prices Index Numbers: December 1958 = 100 December Data*

| | 1953 | 1954 | 1955 | 1956 | 1957 | 1959 | 1960 | 1961 | 1962 |
|---|---|---|---|---|---|---|---|---|---|
| Canada | 92 | 93 | 93 | 95 | 98 | 101 | 103 | 103 | 105 |
| Brazil | 38 | 47 | 55 | 72 | 82 | 143 | 189 | 271 | 436 |

*Source:* IMF

**Exhibit 8**   *Wholesale Prices Index Numbers: 1958 = 100*

|  | 1953 | 1954 | 1955 | 1956 | 1957 | 1958 | 1959 | 1960 | 1961 | 1962 |
|---|---|---|---|---|---|---|---|---|---|---|
| Canada | 97 | 95 | 96 | 99 | 100 | 100 | 101 | 101 | 102 | 105 |
| Brazil |  |  |  |  |  |  |  |  |  |  |
| (including coffee) | 45 | 59 | 66 | 79 | 89 | 100 | 138 | 180 | 249 | 383 |
| (excluding coffee) | 42 | 53 | 63 | 76 | 87 | 100 | 143 | 188 | 263 | 396 |

*Source:* IMF

**Exhibit 9**  *Gross National Product*

| | 1953 | 1954 | 1955 | 1956 | 1957 | 1958 | 1959 | 1960 | 1961 |
|---|---|---|---|---|---|---|---|---|---|
| Canada (billions of Can $) | 25.0 | 24.85 | 27.11 | 30.57 | 31.88 | 32.91 | 34.78 | 35.42 | 36.81 |
| Brazil (Billions of cruzeiros) | 425.2 | 550.6 | 685.9 | 877.5 | 1049.9 | 1300.0 | 1774.3 | 2363.6 | 3499.0 |

Source: IMF

**Exhibit 10**  *Brazilian Balance of Payments (million US$)*

| | 1953 | 1954 | 1955 | 1956 | 1957 | 1958 | 1959 | 1960 | 1961 | 1962 |
|---|---|---|---|---|---|---|---|---|---|---|
| Goods and Services | — | — | −27 | 15 | −295 | −267 | −337 | −538 | −291 | −475 |
| Trade Balance (fob) | — | — | 320 | 436 | 107 | 64 | 72 | −24 | 111 | −90 |
| Freight and Insurance | — | — | −143 | −130 | −139 | −117 | −105 | −95 | −91 | −99 |
| Investment Income | — | — | −117 | −146 | −137 | −114 | −150 | −194 | −184 | −195 |
| Other Services | — | — | −87 | −145 | −126 | −100 | −154 | −225 | −127 | −91 |
| Transfers: Private | — | — | −11 | −17 | −17 | −9 | −10 | −13 | −1 | 1 |
| Government | — | — | 3 | 4 | 4 | 3 | 5 | 8 | 5 | |
| Capital n.i.e.: Private | — | — | 63 | 240 | 341 | 275 | 251 | 196 | 242 | 234 |
| Government | — | — | | 22 | −41 | −23 | −29 | −2 | 154 | |
| Commercial Banks: | | | | | | | | | | |
| Assets (line 12a) | — | — | 7 | −43 | 27 | 16 | −3 | 5 | −37 | −9 |
| Liabilities (line 12b) | — | — | −11 | 15 | −4 | −9 | 1 | 11 | −25 | −2 |
| Monetary Authorities | — | — | −57 | −173 | 116 | 175 | 88 | 376 | −49 | 388 |
| Net IMF Position | — | — | | −28 | 38 | 38 | −20 | 15 | 40 | −18 |
| Monetary Gold (line 10a) | — | — | −1 | −1 | | −1 | −1 | 40 | 2 | 10 |
| Other Claims (line 10z) | — | — | −14 | −119 | 135 | −6 | 27 | −42 | −143 | 86 |
| Other Liabilities | — | — | −42 | −25 | −57 | 144 | 82 | 363 | 52 | 310 |
| Net Errors and Omissions | — | — | 33 | −63 | −131 | −161 | 34 | −43 | 2 | −137 |

Source: IMF

**Exhibit 11** Canadian Balance of Payments (million Can$)

| | 1953 | 1954 | 1955 | 1956 | 1957 | 1958 | 1959 | 1960 | 1961 | 1962 |
|---|---|---|---|---|---|---|---|---|---|---|
| Goods and Services | — | — | — | -1,264 | -1,322 | -969 | -1,376 | -1,103 | -855 | -777 |
| Exports-Imports | — | — | — | -709 | -567 | -122 | -422 | -148 | 173 | 155 |
| Nonmonetary Gold | — | — | — | 150 | 147 | 160 | 148 | 162 | 162 | 165 |
| Travel Receipts | — | — | — | 337 | 363 | 349 | 391 | 420 | 482 | 560 |
| Travel Payments | — | — | — | -498 | -525 | -542 | -598 | -627 | -642 | -610 |
| Investment Income | — | — | — | -391 | -472 | -474 | -489 | -480 | -561 | -570 |
| Other Services | — | — | — | -153 | -268 | -340 | -406 | -430 | -469 | -477 |
| Transfers: Private | — | — | — | -72 | -93 | -109 | -56 | -79 | -71 | -39 |
| Government | — | — | — | -30 | -40 | -53 | -72 | -61 | -56 | -32 |
| Capital n.i.e. | — | — | — | 1,414 | 1,350 | 1,240 | 1,493 | 1,204 | 1,272 | 1,003 |
| Direct Investment in Canada | — | — | — | 583 | 514 | 420 | 550 | 650 | 515 | 525 |
| New Issues: | | | | | | | | | | |
| Central Government | — | — | — | -41 | 8 | 42 | -59 | -39 | -9 | 83 |
| Local Government | — | — | — | 303 | 210 | 241 | 417 | 152 | 51 | 178 |
| Private | — | — | — | 264 | 447 | 236 | 91 | 69 | 194 | 152 |
| Outstanding Securities | — | — | — | 202 | 74 | 109 | 215 | 110 | 45 | -48 |
| Balancing Item | — | — | — | 103 | 97 | 192 | 279 | 262 | 476 | 113 |
| Monetary Authorities | — | — | — | -48 | 105 | -109 | 11 | 39 | -290 | -155 |
| Net IMF Position | — | — | — | -15 | — | — | -59 | — | -61 | 372 |
| Special Short-term Borrowing | — | — | — | — | — | — | — | — | — | 10 |
| Foreign Assets | — | — | — | -33 | 105 | -109 | 70 | 39 | -229 | -537 |

Source: IMF

**Exhibit 12** *International Economic Indicators for Brazil*
*Total Reserves Available for Exchange Market Intervention*
*(End of Period: millions US$)*

| 1953 | 1954 | 1955 | 1956 | 1957 | 1958 | 1959 | 1960 | 1961 | | | 1962 | | |
|---|---|---|---|---|---|---|---|---|---|---|---|---|---|
| | | | | | | | | III | IV | I | II | III | IV |
| 605 | 483 | 491 | 611 | 476 | 465 | 438 | 428 | 459 | 563 | 516 | 504 | 466 | 417 |

Source: IMF

**Terms of Trade Components (1958 = 100)**

| | 1953 | 1955 | 1956 | 1957 | 1958 | 1959 | 1960 | 1961 | 1962 |
|---|---|---|---|---|---|---|---|---|---|
| Export Prices | 119 | 111 | 106 | 198 | 100 | 85 | 83 | 85 | 80 |
| Import Prices[a] | 97 | 96 | 98 | 100 | 100 | 102 | 104 | 106 | 118 |
| Terms of Trade | 1.23 | 1.16 | 1.08 | 1.08 | 1.0 | .83 | .80 | .80 | .68 |

[a]No import price series constructed for Brazil at this time; the index used here is for Venezuela.

Source: Computed from "International Financial Statistics," IMF.

**Exhibit 13** *Canadian Trade by Value (million US$)*

| | 1953 | 1954 | 1955 | 1956 | 1957 | 1958 | 1959 | 1960 | 1961 | 1962 |
|---|---|---|---|---|---|---|---|---|---|---|
| Exports (fob) | 4,576 | 4,413 | 4,765 | 5,254 | 5,404 | 5,386 | 5,663 | 5,837 | 6,107 | 6,231 |
| Imports (cif) | — | 4,433 | 5,020 | 6,110 | 6,188 | 5,638 | 6,242 | 6,150 | 6,193 | 6,367 |

Source: IMF

**Exhibit 14** *Brazilian Trade by Value (million US$)*

| | 1953 | 1954 | 1955 | 1956 | 1957 | 1958 | 1959 | 1960 | 1961 | 1962 |
|---|---|---|---|---|---|---|---|---|---|---|
| Exports (fob) | 1,539 | 1,562 | 1,423 | 1,482 | 1,392 | 1,243 | 1,282 | 1,269 | 1,403 | 1,214 |
| Imports (cif) | — | 1,630 | 1,306 | 1,234 | 1,488 | 1,353 | 1,374 | 1,462 | 1,460 | 1,475 |

Source: IMF

**Exhibit 15** *Exchange Rates*

| | 1953 | 1954 | 1955 | 1956 | 1957 | 1958 | 1959 | 1960 | 1961 | 1962 |
|---|---|---|---|---|---|---|---|---|---|---|
| Crz per US$ (free rate) | 55.0 | 76.0 | 66.8 | 65.6 | 90.5 | 138.5 | 203.8 | 205.1 | 318.5 | 475.0 |
| Can$ per US$ | .9744 | .9663 | .9991 | .9597 | .9847 | .9641 | .9528 | .9962 | 1.0431 | 1.0778 |

Source: IMF

**Exhibit 16**  *Brazilian Government Finance*

| | 1953 | 1954 | 1955 | 1956 | 1957 | 1958 | 1959 | 1960 | 1961 | 1962 |
|---|---|---|---|---|---|---|---|---|---|---|
| | | | | | | | Billions of Cruzeiros: December 31 | | | |
| Deficit (−) or Surplus | — | — | — | — | — | — | — | −76.7 | −137.5 | −280.9 |
| Revenue | — | — | — | — | — | — | — | 219.8 | 317.5 | 497.9 |
| Expenditure | — | — | — | — | — | — | — | 296.4 | 455.0 | 778.8 |
| Financing | | | | | | | | | | |
| Net Borrowing: Bank of Brazil | — | — | — | — | — | — | — | 75.4 | 128.9 | 246.7 |
| On Treasury Bills | — | — | — | — | — | — | — | 2.2 | 1.5 | 22.8 |
| Use of Cash Balances | — | — | — | — | — | — | — | −1.0 | 7.1 | 11.4 |
| Debt: Cruzeiros | 36.8 | 42.9 | 51.3 | 75.7 | 114.7 | 145.2 | 197.3 | 292.8 | — | — |
| Held by: Monetary Authorities | 27.7 | 33.8 | 42.1 | 66.5 | 105.3 | 126.3 | 167.9 | 259.2 | — | — |
| Commercial Banks | 1.4 | 1.3 | 1.5 | 2.0 | 2.3 | 11.0 | 18.7 | 21.5 | — | — |
| Others | 7.7 | 7.8 | 7.7 | 7.2 | 6.2 | 7.9 | 10.7 | 12.1 | — | — |
| Intragovernmental Debt | 19.8 | 27.2 | 36.7 | 52.9 | 64.4 | 95.6 | 123.1 | 152.2 | — | — |
| Held by: Social Insurance System | 13.3 | 16.9 | 22.1 | 29.5 | 40.6 | 55.1 | 75.6 | 97.2 | — | — |

Source: IMF

**Exhibit 17**  *Canadian Government Finance*

| | 1953 | 1954 | 1955 | 1956 | 1957 | 1958 | 1959 | 1960 | 1961 | 1962 |
|---|---|---|---|---|---|---|---|---|---|---|
| | Millions of Canadian Dollars: Year Beginning April 1 | | | | | | | | | |
| Deficit (−) or Surplus | 309 | 107 | 116 | 490 | −199 | −1,257 | −402 | −242 | −725 | — |
| Revenue | 4,530 | 4,270 | 4,683 | 5,463 | 5,168 | 4,818 | 5,755 | 5,925 | 6,183 | — |
| Expenditure | 4,221 } | 4,289 | 4,424 | 4,851 | 5,039 | 5,354 | 5,719 | 5,958 | 6,563 | — |
| Net Lending | } | −126 | 143 | 122 | 327 | 721 | 438 | 209 | 344 | — |
| Advances to Exchange Fund (−) | 15 | −25 | 30 | −71 | 46 | −20 | 36 | −64 | 241 | — |
| Financing | −323 | −82 | −146 | −149 | 152 | 1,279 | 367 | 306 | 484 | — |
| Net Borrowing | −209 | −211 | 193 | −518 | −12 | 1,445 | 325 | 235 | 887 | — |
| Canadian Dollars | −142 | −130 | 257 | −513 | −11 | 1,466 | 328 | 238 | 889 | — |
| Foreign Currency | 76 | −81 | −63 | −4 | −1 | −21 | −3 | −3 | −2 | — |
| Use of Cash Balances | −104 | 128 | −340 | 99 | 165 | −166 | 42 | 71 | −401 | — |
| Canadian Dollars | −95 | 137 | −325 | 78 | 158 | −166 | 33 | 88 | — | — |
| Foreign Currency | −9 | −9 | −15 | 20 | 7 | — | 8 | −16 | — | — |
| Debt: Canadian Dollars | 14,234 | 14,104 | 14,361 | 13,848 | 13,837 | 15,303 | 15,631 | 15,869 | — | — |
| Foreign Currency | 291 | 210 | 147 | 143 | 142 | 121 | 118 | 115 | — | — |

Source: IMF

# Dozier Industries

MARK R. EAKER[1]

Richard Rothschild, the chief financial officer of Dozier Industries, returned to his office after the completion of his meeting with two officers
of Southeastern National Bank. He had requested the meeting in order to
discuss financial issues related to Dozier's first major international sales
contract, which had been confirmed the previous day, January 13, 1976.
Initially, Rothschild had contacted Robert Leigh, a vice president at the
bank who had primary responsibilities for Dozier's business with Southeastern National. Leigh had in turn suggested that John Gunn of the bank's
international division be included in the meeting since Leigh felt that he,
himself, lacked the international expertise to answer all the questions
Rothschild might raise.

The meeting had focused on the exchange risk related to the new
sales contract. Dozier's bid of £425,000 for the installation of an internal
security system for a large manufacturing firm in the United Kingdom
had been accepted. In accordance with the contract, the British firm had
transferred by cable £42,500 (i.e., 10 percent of the contract amount) as
deposit on the contract with the balance due at the time the system was
completed. Dozier's production Vice-President, Mike Miles, had assured
Rothschild that there would be no difficulty in completing the project
within the 90-day period stipulated in the bid. As a result, Rothschild
was planning on receiving £382,500 on April 13, 1976.

## HISTORY OF THE COMPANY

Dozier Inc. was a relatively young firm specializing in electronic security
systems. It had been established in 1963 by Charles L. Dozier who was
still President and the owner of 78 percent of the stock. The remaining
22 percent of the stock was held by other members of management. Dozier
had formerly been a design engineer for a large electronics firm. In 1963
he began his own company to market security systems for small firms and

---

[1]Reprinted from *Stanford Business Cases 1976* with the permission of the Publishers, Stanford University Graduate School of Business, © 1976 by the Board of Trustees of the Leland
Stanford Junior University.

households. By 1966, Dozier had begun to concentrate on military sales and the company's growth paralleled the growth of U.S. expenditures in Vietnam. As the U.S. involvement in Vietnam and military expenditures in general began to decrease, Dozier's military sales slumped and the company sought increased business in the private sector. During the period of transition from being primarily a military contractor to relying on private sales, Dozier experienced severe reductions in revenues and profits. (See Exhibit 1.) In 1975 the company showed a profit for the first time in three years, and management was confident that the company had turned the corner.

By early 1976, military sales were only about 20 percent of Dozier's total revenue. The Company's management believed that the best prospects for future growth were sales to companies in countries that were experiencing terrorist activity. Therefore, in the spring of 1975 Dozier launched a marketing effort overseas. The selling effort had not met with much success until the confirmation of the contract discussed above. The new sales contract, although large in itself, had the potential of being expanded in the future since the company involved was a large multinational firm with manufacturing facilities in many countries.

## FOREIGN EXCHANGE RISK AND HEDGING

On January 13, the day the bid was accepted, the value of the pound was $2.0320. However, the pound had been weak for the past six months (See Exhibit 5). Rothschild was concerned that the value of the pound might depreciate even further during the next 90 days and it was this worry that prompted his discussion at the bank. He wanted to find out what techniques were available to Dozier to reduce the exchange risk created by the outstanding pound receivable.

Gunn, the international specialist, had explained that Rothschild had several options. First, of course, he could do nothing. This would leave Dozier vulnerable to pound fluctuations which would entail losses if the pound depreciated, or gains if it appreciated versus the dollar. On the other hand, Rothschild could choose to hedge his exchange risk.

Gunn explained that a hedge involved taking a position opposite to the one that was creating the foreign exchange exposure. This could be accomplished either by engaging in a forward contract or via a spot transaction. Since Dozier had an outstanding pound receivable, the appropriate hedging options would be to sell pounds forward 90 days or to secure a 90 day pound loan. By selling pounds forward Dozier would incur an obligation to deliver pounds 90 days from now at the rate established today. This would insure that Dozier would receive a set dollar value for its pound receivable, regardless of the spot rate that existed in the future.

The spot hedge works similarly in that it also creates a pound obligation 90 days hence. Dozier would borrow pounds and exchange the proceeds into dollars at the spot rate. On April 13, Dozier would use its pound receipts to repay the loan. Any gains or losses on the receivable due to a change in the value of the pound would be offset by equivalent losses or gains on the loan payment.

Leigh assured Rothschild that Southeastern National would be able to assist Dozier in implementing whatever decision Rothschild made. Dozier had a $1.5 million line of credit with Southeastern National. John Gunn indicated that there would be no difficulty for Southeastern to arrange the pound loan for Dozier through its correspondent bank in London. He felt that such a loan would be at 1½ percent above the U.K. prime rate. In order to assist Rothschild in making his decision, Gunn provided him with information on interest rates, spot and foreign exchange rates, as well as historical and forcasted information on the pound. (See Exhibits 4, 5, and 6.)

Rothschild was aware that in preparing the bid Dozier had allowed for a profit margin of only 6 percent in order to increase the likelihood of winning the bid and hence developing an important foreign contact. The bid was submitted on December 3, 1975. In arriving at the bid, the company had estimated the cost of the project, added an amount as profit, but kept in mind the highest bid that could conceivably win the contract. The calculations were made in dollars and then converted to pounds at the spot rate existing on December 3 (See Exhibit 5), since the U.K. company had stipulated payment in pounds.

Rothschild realized that the amount involved in the contract was such that an adverse move in the pound exchange rate could put Dozier in a

**Exhibit 1**   *Sales and Income Summary*

| Year Ended<br>31 December | Sales<br>($000) | Net Income<br>($000) |
|:---:|:---:|:---:|
| 1963 | 314 | 28 |
| 1964 | 397 | 34 |
| 1965 | 521 | 43 |
| 1966 | 918 | 86 |
| 1967 | 2,127 | 179 |
| 1968 | 3,858 | 406 |
| 1969 | 5,726 | 587 |
| 1970 | 7,143 | 702 |
| 1971 | 9,068 | 857 |
| 1972 | 8,646 | 309 |
| 1973 | 5,471 | (108) |
| 1974 | 5,986 | (16) |
| 1975 | 6,427 | 82 |

loss position for 1976 if the transactions were left unhedged. On the other hand, he also became aware of the fact that hedging had its own costs. Still, a decision had to be made. He knew that "no action" implied that an unhedged position was the best alternative for the company.

**Exhibit 2**   *Balance Sheet as of December 31, 1975*

| Assets | |
|---|---:|
| Current Assets: | |
| Cash and Securities | $   147,286 |
| Accounts Receivable | 859,747 |
| Inventories | 1,113,533 |
| Total Current Assets | $2,120,566 |
| | |
| Properties, Plants, and Equipment: | |
| At Cost | $4,214,906 |
| Less: Accumulated Depreciation | 1,316,702 |
| Net plant: | $2,898,204 |
| | |
| Other Assets: | |
| Investments and loans | $   225,000 |
| Total Assets | $5,243,770 |

| Liabilities and Equities | |
|---|---:|
| Current Liabilities: | |
| Accounts Payable | $   467,291 |
| Notes Payable—Bank | 326,400 |
| Total Current Liabilities | $   793,691 |
| | |
| Long-Term Liabilities: | |
| Notes Payable | $   275,000 |
| | |
| Common Equity | |
| Common Stock | $1,126,705 |
| Reserves | 313,622 |
| Retained Earnings | 2,734,752 |
| Total Equity | $4,175,079 |
| | |
| Total Liabilities and Equity | $5,243,770 |

**Exhibit 3**   *Bid Preparation*[a]

| | |
|---|---:|
| Materials | $414,250 |
| Direct labor | 208,410 |
| Shipping | 35,000 |
| Direct overhead[b] | 104,205 |
| Allocation of indirect overhead | 50,246 |
| Total Cost | $812,111 |
| Profit Factor | 48,726 |
| Total | $860,836 |

[a]Spot pound rate on December 3: 2.0255
 Pound value of the bid: £425,000

[b]Based on 50% of direct labor.

**Exhibit 4**   *Interest and Exchange Rate Comparisons January 14, 1976*

| | United States | United Kingdom |
|---|:---:|:---:|
| Three month money[a] | 5 1/8 | 10.22 |
| Prime Lending Rate | 7.00 | 11.50 |
| Three month deposits (large amounts) | 5.00 | 10.16 |
| Eurodollar 3 month | | 5 3/8 |
| Europound 3 month (Paris) | 10.50 | |
| Other key London rates: | | |
|    91-day treasury bills | | 10.28 |
|    Local authorities three-month fixed deposit | | 10 1/8 |
|    Finance houses three-month fixed deposit | | 10 9/16 |
| The spot rate for the pound: | 2.0290 | |
| Three-month forward pound: | 2.0032 | |

[a]Prime commercial paper in the United States; interbank rates in the United Kingdom.
*Source: The Economist*

**Exhibit 5**  *Historical Spot and Forward Pound Rates in U.S. Dollars*

|  | Spot | Three-Month Forward Rate |
|---|---|---|
| 7/9 | 2.2020 | 2.1864 |
| 7/16 | 2.1855 | 2.1682 |
| 7/23 | 2.1800 | 2.1570 |
| 7/30 | 2.1650 | 2.1445 |
| 8/6 | 2.1360 | 2.1137 |
| 8/13 | 2.1075 | 2.0865 |
| 8/20 | 2.1100 | 2.0940 |
| 8/27 | 2.1105 | 2.0948 |
| 9/3 | 2.1120 | 2.0947 |
| 9/10 | 2.1120 | 2.0942 |
| 9/17 | 2.0830 | 2.0665 |
| 9/24 | 2.0550 | 2.0350 |
| 10/1 | 2.0430 | 2.0245 |
| 10/8 | 2.0470 | 2.0242 |
| 10/15 | 2.0560 | 2.0315 |
| 10/22 | 2.0780 | 2.0500 |
| 10/29 | 2.0730 | 2.0470 |
| 11/5 | 2.0660 | 2.0396 |
| 11/12 | 2.0640 | 2.0388 |
| 11/19 | 2.0430 | 2.0184 |
| 11/26 | 2.0330 | 2.0088 |
| 12/3 | 2.0255 | 2.0021 |
| 12/10 | 2.0240 | 2.0008 |
| 12/17 | 2.0240 | 2.0000 |
| 12/23 | 2.0225 | 1.9965 |
| 12/30 | 2.0250 | 1.9918 |
| 1/7/76 | 2.0350 | 2.0032 |
| 1/14/76 | 2.0290 | 2.0032 |

Source: *The Money Manager*

**Exhibit 6**

### *Sterling: Going going . . .*

PADRAIC FALLON

The prospects of a major recovery of sterling between now and Christmas are now so thin that they hardly exist. Since our last currency review in August, confidence in the pound has continued to decline. That decline in confidence has been masked to some extent by the renaissance of the dollar; when these trappings of disguise were whipped away during the recent reversal in the dollar's strength, the weakness of sterling stood out stark and clear as the effective rate breached new lows to nudge the 30% depreciation barrier.

It should decline further. The Labour Government, far from initiating the £1 billion cuts in public spending that were deemed necessary if overseas holders' confidence in sterling were to be maintained, have actually announced that they are not considering any major measures to cut government spending in the short-term; there is a widespread conviction that they will not cut expenditure in the medium or long-term either, but it is the immediate future that concerns the foreign exchange markets.

In the immediate future the Government's policy of allowing the exchange rate to take the strain of keeping unemployment to a minimum is likely to become more obvious, a policy that is likely to show an increasing divergence from the views of the Bank of England. The Bank is displaying increasing signs of alarm over the scale of public spending and the public sector deficit, and so it should: It is widely believed that the government's borrowing requirement in the current financial year has risen by a third over last April's estimate of £9 billion.

The Chancellor of the Exchequer announced the Government's decision not to cut public spending during 1975 at the same dinner that the Governor of the Bank made it clear that the Bank is becoming increasingly concerned over public spending.

Sterling will be weaker against some currencies than others in coming months, but the British may find themselves celebrating Christmas with a currency worth less than $2 even if the dollar does not regain its strength. There is not much consolation in that.

*Source:* Reprinted from *Euromoney*, November, 1975.

# Chemical Bank–INI Facility[1]

Late in June 1975 Mr. Arthur V. Smith, head of the Project Finance and Loan Syndications Group of Chemical Bank, London, in conjunction with the officers responsible for Spanish business, was considering the pricing of a $110 million syndicated loan to INI (Instituto Nacional de Industria) in Spain. There had already been four rounds of negotiations and he hoped the next round would close the deal.

Mr. Smith faced the task of determining a final bid acceptable to the borrower and at the same time meeting the investment requirements of Chemical and the other banks in the market. The concept of present value was central to the discussion of pricing of the INI facility, as there were many variables affecting the "all in yield" to the bank, including front-end fees, commitment fees, the spread, and the loan amortization schedule. The so-called pricing decision actually entailed the design of the credit facility.

## Background

During calls on INI from their office in Madrid, officers of Chemical Bank had determined that the borrower would have an external requirement during 1975 for $100+ million. As soon as this need had been identified and appropriate internal approval obtained, Mr. Smith had been called in London to design a credit facility to fulfill INI's requirements, if at all possible.

INI is an autonomous agency of the Spanish State, established in 1941 and headquartered in Madrid. INI acts as a holding company and makes investments, in the form of loans and equity commitments, in the industrial and commercial sectors of the Spanish economy. The assets of INI totalled nearly $5 billion as of 1974, with approximately one-half of the assets in loans and the remaining half in equity and other investments. The INI group accounted for 16 percent of total Spanish exports in 1974, with important positions in oil, petrochemicals, gas, electricity, iron and steel, coal and manufacturing.

---

[1]This case was written by Professor John G. McDonald of Stanford University and Mr. Thomas J. Harrington, Vice-President of the Chemical Bank. The negotiation in the case represents the general sequence of bids, with some details changed for purposes of discussion. The case is reproduced here with the permission of the authors and of INI.

In 1974 and the first half of 1975 there had been a large volume of loans to Spanish borrowers, but an organized "queue" had not been established to ensure orderly and timely entry into the market. In 1974 Spain had been one of seven countries with borrowings in excess of $1 billion. Observers of the Eurocurrency syndicated loan market estimated that four countries would borrow in excess of $1 billion in 1975: Brazil, Mexico, Indonesia and Spain. There was, however, some concern in 1975 over the future political environment in Spain as Generalissimo Franco had recently been seriously ill.

Typical maturities in the Eurocurrency syndicated loan market had shortened from the historic highs in the 8–10 year range in 1973–74 to 5–7 years in 1975. Loans in excess of $100 million in size had been common in 1974 but in the first half of 1975, following the Herstatt and Franklin National Bank failures, large loans had not been easy to place. The Chemical Bank's staff had made a summary of market conditions for 1973–75, shown in Appendix C at the end of the case.

A Spanish borrower, regarded as being in the same risk category as INI, had recently come to the market with a $150 million, 5-year maturity loan believed to be priced with a 5/8% or 3/4% front-end fee and a 1–1/2% spread (as defined below). The pricing of this loan was considered to be generally indicative of the terms which the market would consider appropriate for the INI loan.

### Borrower's Objectives and the Bank's Objectives

INI wished to match cash flows from their long term capital investment program with those of the financing. For this reason they regarded a 10-year maturity as an essential element in the loan, despite the prevailing market conditions which suggested a shorter maturity. It was believed, however, that if any Spanish borrower could qualify for such terms it would be INI. The Eurobond market, as an alternative source, was not available to the borrower for a number of reasons. INI made it clear that they did not expect any cost element of the loan (fees, etc.) to deviate greatly from the terms of similar loans recently in the market.

A key objective of the Bank was to increase its penetration of the Spanish market, preferably through a large customer in either the government or quasi-government category. In addition, the Bank was looking for a lead management position in a major credit to enhance its visibility as an important factor in the Eurocurrency syndicated loan market. Finally, the Bank placed a high priority on increasing its fee income.

### Structure of the Loan: Initial Proposal

Mr. Smith was concerned by the obvious disparity between INI's requirements for a 10-year credit and lenders' current preferences for 5–7 year credits. He felt that the real task was to try to find a proposal acceptable to INI which might be sold to other banks in the market.

The innovative solution which Mr. Smith and his group came up with was a two-part facility. The first part would be a 6-year loan of $110 million to be amortized as follows: 7 equal semi-annual installments commencing 30 months after drawdown, each of 1/16th of the original principal amount, followed by a final installment of 9/16th of the original amount at the end of year 6. This final installment would comprise a regular 1/16th installment plus a "balloon" payment of 50 percent of the original principal. The second part would be a refinancing facility of $55 million, for the sole purpose of refinancing the entire amount of the balloon payment—the principal to be amortized in 8 equal semi-annual installments over the final 4 year period.

### Pricing of the Loan

Mr. Smith's group sent INI executives an outline of proposed terms for this two-part facility. There were three parameters of the loan pricing:

1.  *Commitment Fee:* A per-annum fee, expressed as a percent, (payable semi-annually in arrears) on the undrawn, uncancelled portion of the facility. The commitment fee would only be payable on the $55 million refinancing facility, not on the original amount of $110 million which was to be drawn within 30 days of signing. For example, with a 1/2 percent commitment fee, the payment at the end of each 6 month period would be $139,410 (.005 × $55 million × 182.5/360).[2]

2.  *Front-end fee:* A one-time payment, as a percentage of the amount of the loan, usually paid shortly after signing. For example, a 7/8 percent front-end fee on the proposed facility would be $962,500 paid to the manager to be used at his discretion to induce other lenders to participate in the financing, so as to raise $110 million.

3.  *Spread:* The percent per annum margin added to the bank's cost of funds in determining the interest rate charged to the borrower for each period. The bank's cost of funds is defined as LIBOR, as explained in Appendix A. Interest is due and payable at the end of every 6-month period, beginning 6 months after drawdown of the initial amount.

Chemical Bank's first bid (Bid No. 1 shown in Exhibit 1) included a 1/2% commitment fee, a 7/8% front-end fee, and a 1-3/4% spread.

---

[2]It had been common practice in the syndicated loan market to translate annual rates to charges for a particular period by using the actual number of days in the period as a fraction of a 360 day year. For example, a 31-day loan was charged at 31/360 times the annual rate, and a half-year loan was charged at 182.5/360 times the annual rate.

Mr. Smith's group had pioneered in the use of a measure referred to as the *equivalent spread*. Equivalent spread is a time-weighted measure of the bank's "all in yield" which combines commitment fees, front-end fees, and spread into one figure, summarizing the profit to the bank of the facility. It also represents the "all in cost" to the borrower in excess of LIBOR. A description of the calculations of equivalent spread, using an example of a simple 2-year loan, is given in Appendix B.[3]

## Pricing of the Loan: Counter Proposals and Negotiations

INI executives in Madrid responded to the Bank's Bid No. 1, with an invitation to come down and discuss the matter further. At the meeting they outlined INI's proposal, Bid No. 2 (see Exhibit 1), which shaved the commitment fee, the front-end fee and the spread by 1/4 percent each. The net result of this counter proposal was to reduce the equivalent spread by 43.1 basis points.

Mr. Smith regarded the latter proposal, Bid No. 2, as "unsellable in the market," and he felt that it would be impossible to raise $110 million for 10 years in the current market with these terms. His group countered with Bid No. 3 (see Exhibit 1), holding the line on fees and splitting the difference on the spread by reducing it from 1-3/4% to 1-5/8%.

The borrower responded with Bid No. 4 (see Exhibit 1). They again insisted on a 1/4% commitment fee; they split the difference on front-end fee with a 3/4% proposal; and they accepted the 1-5/8% spread. In addition, the INI officials specified that an "all in cost" in excess of 2 percent over LIBOR was unacceptable.

With Mr. Smith's knowledge of the market, he knew that the 2 percent above LIBOR "all in cost" suggested as an upper limit by INI represented the lower limit of terms sellable to other banks. With the INI executives facing him at the negotiating table, Mr. Smith wondered how they would respond to his final bid.

## Thoughts on Mr. Smith's Mind

In considering his final bid, Mr. Smith was thinking: The refinancing facility at the end of year 6 may never be used, because the borrower may have the option of going to the bond market or some other source to finance the balloon at that point to pay off the 6-year lenders. Why not split the 1/2% commitment fee into two components: the first payable semi-annually during the first 6 years, and the second paid retroactively

---

[3]Mr. Smith used a 5% discount rate on semi-annual cash flows (based on a 10% per annum discount rate).

*at the end of year 6* only if the $55 million refinancing facility is actually used? He decided to include a two-part commitment fee in his final bid. To keep matters simple he felt that the retroactive portion should not be adjusted to reflect the time value of its receipt. For example, if 1/4% per annum is the retroactive commitment fee component, INI would pay $0.0025 \times \$55$ million $\times 182.5/360 \times 12$ at the end of the 12th semi-annual period.

During these negotiations Mr. Smith had to respond quickly to counter-proposals. He and his group had developed an "Equivalent Spread Contribution Matrix" which showed the contribution to equivalent spread of various levels of fees and spread with this loan structure. Shown in Exhibit 2, this Matrix was a tool which Mr. Smith planned to use in responding with a final bid.

**Exhibit 1**   *Negotiation*

|  | Bid No. 1 (of Bank) % | Bid No. 2 (of INI) % | Bid No. 3 (of Bank) % | Bid No. 4 (of INI) % |
|---|---|---|---|---|
| Commitment fee | 1/2 | 1/4 | 1/2 | 1/4 |
| Front-end fee | 7/8 | 5/8 | 7/8 | 3/4 |
| Spread | 1-3/4 | 1-1/2 | 1-5/8 | 1-5/8 |

**Exhibit 2** *Equivalent Spread Contribution Matrix[a]*

|  | 1/8 | 1/4 | 3/8 | 1/2 | 5/8 | 3/4 | 7/8 | 1 |
|---|---|---|---|---|---|---|---|---|
| **Commitment fee (two-part)** | | | | | | | | |
| Current (per annum) | .06256 | .12512 | .18768 | .25024 | .3128 | .37536 | .43792 | .50048 |
| Retroactive (per annum) | .04716 | .09432 | .14149 | .18865 | .23581 | .28298 | .33014 | .37731 |
| Management fee (one time) | .02784 | .05569 | .08354 | .11139 | .13923 | .16708 | .194932 | .22278 |
| Spread (per annum) | .1250 | .2500 | .3750 | .5000 | .6250 | .7500 | .8750 | 1.0 |

*Hypothetical Examples to Assist in Reading Matrix:*

A 1/2 management fee would contribute .11139 to equivalent spread in the INI loan structure.

A 1 1/2 spread would contribute 1.5000 to equivalent spread. A 1/4 current commitment fee would contribute .12512 to equivalent spread.

A 1/4 per annum retroactive commitment fee, all payable at the end of year 6, would contribute .09432 percentage points per annum to equivalent spread.

[a]This matrix obviously applies only to the loan structure of this INI facility.

***Appendix A***   *The Eurodollar Syndicated Loan Market and LIBOR*

---

Syndicated loans are loans made by a group of banks, i.e. a syndicate, co-operating with each other to provide the funds requested by a borrower. The groups are usually formed ad hoc for each new loan transaction. There is no single standard form for these groups and the terminology for the different roles may vary somewhat. It is usual, however, for a group to consist of: a "lead manager" who generally has established the relationship with the borrower and been asked to form a bidding syndicate; a number of "co-managers" who have each agreed to provide a significant portion of the total amount of the loan and work actively on its preparation; and a greater number of "participants" who provide smaller amounts of money and are interested in the loan largely for portfolio reasons. The Eurocurrency syndicated loan market refers to the several hundred institutions which are active to various degrees in this type of lending.

Syndicated Eurocurrency loans are priced to reflect the fact that the banks must themselves raise the money they are lending (i.e. "fund" the loan) and pay interest to their source of funds. The borrower agrees to pay the funding cost plus an additional percentage or "spread" which compensates the banks for the credit risks and costs associated with the loan and provides a margin of profit. Rather than funding a loan at the beginning for its entire life, and hence paying the interest rate appropriate for such a maturity, it is agreed that the loan will be periodically refunded for shorter periods, usually 3, 6, 9 or 12 months. At the end of each period the lending bank pays off its funding from new funding for the next period and from repayments by the borrower.

Banks generally fund their Eurodollar syndicated loans by borrowing an amount equal to their shares of the loan in the London interbank Eurodollar "market." This market is not a physical place of exchange, such as the New York Stock Exchange, but rather an informal communication network among banks and brokers whereby institutions with excess Eurocurrency deposits may lend them to other institutions which require them for lending to final customers. The original source of Eurodollar funds is time deposits made by corporations, governments and individuals; the maturity of such deposits reflects the needs and preferences of these depositors. While maturities range from overnight to 10 years, most deposits have maturities of 12 months or less. The funds tend to be "on-lent" for periods close to the original deposit's maturity. That is, these banks tend to match the maturities of their financing (deposits) and their investment (loans).

There are more than 300 institutions which are active in the London interbank market; the volume of trading is such that the market is usually described as very competitive. Market practice is that quotations for deposits are made in a manner which does not disclose the quoting bank's intention. For example, "6-month $6-1/16%–6-1/8%" means "I will take from the market deposits at 6-1/16% or I will place deposits in the market at 6-1/8%." These rates are known as the bid and offered rates: that is to say, "I bid 6-1/16% for deposits and I offer deposits at 6-1/8%." It is this offered rate (London Interbank Offered Rate, LIBOR) which is taken as the cost of funds to the lending bank when calculating the rate to be charged to the borrower. When a group of banks are involved in a loan it is usual that a few of them will be designated as "reference banks." The average of the rate offered to them for deposits of the specified maturity is used as LIBOR for the whole group. In that context, the LIBOR rate is the marginal cost of funds of the agreed maturity to the lending bank.

## Appendix B   *Equivalent Spread Analysis: An Example*

### EQUIVALENT SPREAD DEFINED

A loan represents an investment on the part of the Bank, with associated cash outflows (e.g. advances to the borrower and payments for funding) and cash inflows (e.g. front-end fees, commitment fees, interest payments and repayments of principal) over the life of the loan. By varying the different pricing elements of a loan, i.e. the interest rate and the level of commitment and front-end fees, the cash flows from the investment are altered. Each different pricing structure may be viewed as an alternative (mutually exclusive) investment which the bank could undertake. The net present value concept is suited to the comparison of such alternative investments.

The net present value method of comparing two investments consists of discounting the *net* cash flows at the end of each period to some common point of time, usually that of the first cash flow, and comparing the values. The concept of *equivalent spread* extends this comparison to loans, viewed as investments. Rather than referring directly to the net present monetary value of a particular loan, equivalent spread analysis determines a proxy for this number. This proxy is the spread which a hypothetical loan of the same amount and amortization pattern as the actual loan would have to have, in the absence of any pricing element other than spread, to give the same net present value as the actual loan. For a loan of a given amount and amortization pattern the equivalent spread is defined by the present value of the net cash flow. Two alternative pricing possibilities for a loan of a particular amount and amortization may therefore be compared as alternative investments, by comparing their equivalent spreads.

While the concept of equivalent spread is obviously closely akin to net present value, it has at least one practical advantage. It reduces all of the various pricing parameters associated with a loan to a single number which has meaning to the market—the spread associated with a very simple loan which is "equivalent" for purposes of investment comparison with the given loan. It is this spread, which represents the net cash flow to the bank after LIBOR costs, which is considered the "all in yield." If the market determines that a certain "all in yield" is required for a loan to a particular borrower, the equivalent spread concept allows the determination of different pricing strategies which are equivalent in the sense that they give the same "all in yield."

### EXAMPLE

Assume a 2-year loan of $100 million with semi-annual principal payments of $25 million, the first due 6 months after the initial drawdown. The front-end fee at time zero is 1/2% of the total amount of the loan.

**Symbols (figures for this example are in parentheses):**

$f$ = front-end fee (1/2%)

$c_t$ = commitment fee payable at the end of period $t$, (0 for all $t$)

$s$ = spread (1-1/2% per annum)

$A$ = initial principal ($100 million)

$O_t$ = outstanding principal during period $t$ ($25 million payable at end of each 6-month period)

$\quad O_1 = 100 \quad O_2 = 75 \quad O_3 = 50 \quad O_4 = 25$

$r$ = discount rate (5% per semi-annual period)

$E$ = equivalent spread, percent per annum

The net cash flows associated with the loan in this example are as follows:

| Time | Net Interest Cash Flows[a] | Front-end Fee | Commitment Fee |
|------|----------------------------|---------------|----------------|
| $t = 0$ | | $f \times A = (.005)(100) = .50$ | 0 |
| $t = 1$ | $s \times O_1 \times \left(\dfrac{182.5}{360}\right) = (.015)(100)\left(\dfrac{182.5}{360}\right) = .760$ | | 0 |
| $t = 2$ | $s \times O_2 \times \left(\dfrac{182.5}{360}\right) = (0.15)(75)\left(\dfrac{182.5}{360}\right) = .570$ | | 0 |
| $t = 3$ | $s \times O_3 \times \left(\dfrac{182.5}{360}\right) = (0.15)(50)\left(\dfrac{182.5}{360}\right) = .380$ | | 0 |
| $t = 4$ | $s \times O_4 \times \left(\dfrac{182.5}{360}\right) = (.015)(25)\left(\dfrac{182.5}{360}\right) = .190$ | | 0 |

[a]These cash flows in millions of dollars are net of funding (i.e. LIBOR) costs. They represent the net amount of each interest payment which accrues to the bank after the bank pays its interest charges on the deposits borrowed for the period.

A hypothetical loan with the same amortization pattern but only the, as yet unknown, "equivalent spread" of the above loan would have the following cash flows:

| Time | Net Interest Cash Flows | Front-end fee | Commitment Fee |
|------|-------------------------|---------------|----------------|
| $t = 0$ | | 0 | 0 |
| $t = 1$ | $E \times O_1\left(\dfrac{182.5}{360}\right) = 50.694E$ | 0 | 0 |
| $t = 2$ | $E \times O_2\left(\dfrac{182.5}{360}\right) = 38.021E$ | 0 | 0 |
| $t = 3$ | $E \times O_3\left(\dfrac{182.5}{360}\right) = 25.347E$ | 0 | 0 |
| $t = 4$ | $E \times O_4\left(\dfrac{182.5}{360}\right) = 12.674E$ | 0 | 0 |

To find the equivalent spread $E$, equate the present values of the cash flows associated with the two loans: The *Example Loan* defined on page 396 and the *Hypothetical Loan* defined above on page 397:

Time   Present Value of Example Loan (p. 396) = Present Value of Hypothetical Loan (p. 397)

0:   $f \times A$                0

$$
\begin{aligned}
1:&\quad \frac{182.5}{360} \times s \times \frac{O_1}{1+r} \\[4pt]
2:&\quad \frac{182.5}{360} \times s \times \frac{O_2}{(1+r)^2} \\[4pt]
3:&\quad \frac{182.5}{360} \times s \times \frac{O_3}{(1+r)^3} \\[4pt]
4:&\quad \frac{182.5}{360} \times s \times \frac{O_4}{(1+r)^4}
\end{aligned}
\quad=\quad
\begin{aligned}
&\frac{182.5}{360} \times E \times \frac{O_1}{1+r} \\[4pt]
&\frac{182.5}{360} \times E \times \frac{O_2}{(1+r)^2} \\[4pt]
&\frac{182.5}{360} \times E \times \frac{O_3}{(1+r)^3} \\[4pt]
&\frac{182.5}{360} \times E \times \frac{O_4}{(1+r)^4}
\end{aligned}
$$

## Summary and Simplification

$$
f \times A + \frac{182.5}{360} \times s \times \left\{ \frac{O_1}{1+r} + \frac{O_2}{(1+r)^2} + \frac{O_3}{(1+r)^3} + \frac{O_4}{(1+r)^4} \right\}
$$

$$
= \frac{182.5}{360} \times E \left\{ \frac{O_1}{1+r} + \frac{O_2}{(1+r)^2} + \frac{O_3}{(1+r)^3} + \frac{O_4}{(1+r)^4} \right\}
$$

## Solution for Equivalent Spread, $E$

$$
E = f \times A \times \left[ \frac{\dfrac{360}{182.5}}{\left\{ \dfrac{O_1}{1+r} + \dfrac{O_2}{(1+r)^2} + \dfrac{O_3}{(1+r)^3} + \dfrac{O_4}{(1+r)^4} \right\}} \right] + s
$$

That is, equivalent spread here equals management fee contribution plus the spread. A senior colleague of Mr. Smith commented, "I thought you said this was going to be a *simple* example."

Before doing the numerical substitution to determine the actual value of the equivalent spread of the particular loan, it is important to notice a few general features. First, it can be seen that the equivalent spread depends on each component (e.g. front-end fee and commitment fee) of the pricing and is equal to the sum of the "equivalent spread contributions" of each. Furthermore, the contribution of each pricing component is directly proportional to the level of that component; if the front-end fee rate were doubled its contribution to the equivalent spread of the loan would also be doubled. Second, as long as each pricing component is expressed as a percentage of the total loan, the actual amount of the loan does not affect the equivalent spread. As the size of the loan changes, both the numerators and denominators in the above fractions change proportionately so the net effect cancels out.

## *Appendix C:*   *General Market Conditions, 1973–75;*
## *Eurocurrency Syndicated Loans*[4]

1. *Market volume:* Continuous growth through 1974 despite slowdown in second half of 1974. First-half 1975 volume down, showing first decline since beginning of Eurodollar market.

2. *Borrower Class:* 1974 vs. 1973—Great increase of borrowings by western industrialized countries for balance of payments and energy related uses. Reduced OPEC borrowings reflecting excess liquidity. 1975 vs. 1974—Decreased western borrowings as the BOP situation normalizes. Increased developing country borrowings both for general development uses and for BOP reasons. The developing countries' increased need for funds reflects higher energy costs, desire for rapid development (particularly among OPEC borrowers), and decreased export earnings due to the recession.

3. *Typical Loan:* Progressive easing of terms for borrowers through 1973, as shown by decreasing spreads and increasing maturities. Some tightening of conditions in 1974, reflected in higher spreads and shorter maturities, but deal sizes still increased, due in part to the very large loans extended to governments for energy related finance. First half of 1975 brought a retrenching of the market and a more critical attitude of lenders; loan maturity and size both diminished, and spreads increased considerably.

Recent shortening of maturities reflects not only changing attitudes toward borrowers in general but also the changing composition of the set of borrowers in the market. This implies that the figures for 1974 would have shown a more conservative attitude versus 1973, had not the set of borrowers included so many western government financings as prime credits. Hence, the extreme tightening of terms for 1975 reflects not only changing attitudes but also the shift in lending toward developing countries.

---

[4]Beyond the brief written summary given here, Appendix C of the original case contains substantial descriptive and statistical material on Eurolending. We have covered this in the body of Chapter 8.

# International Metals, Ltd.[1]

On Friday, September 26, 1975, Sir John Carthright, the managing director of International Metals, Ltd., Ellis Pines, the company's financial director, and several representatives of the company's merchant banks met in order to reach a final position on a number of aspects concerning the company's proposed £20,000,000 bond issue. On September 29, Sir John was scheduled to present his recommendations to the Finance Committee of the Board.

## HISTORY OF THE COMPANY

International Metals, Ltd. (IML) was founded on September 5, 1867 and was among the first European firms to utilize modern methods in the processing and production of various metals. Along with its subsidiaries and affiliates, IML was one of the largest producers of non-ferrous metals in the world. The company operated along the whole spectrum of the business—mining, smelting, semi-finished and finished products. Its properties, plants, and operations were located in thirty countries.

The company's headquarters was the 30 story IML-Tower in the City of London. Its shares were widely owned and actively traded on a number of leading exchanges in the UK and abroad. The company had no majority shareholder. The largest single block of stock was held by the Carthright Trust, which owned approximately 5.3 percent of outstanding shares.

The company began its operations in Northern England, but by early 1900's it had already expanded into Latin America and Scandinavia. Beginning in the late 1950's, the company committed increasing amounts of capital in E.E.C. countries, United States, Canada, and Australia (See Exhibit 4).

## THE PROPOSED BOND ISSUE

The proposed bond issue was to be for £20,000,000. This amount was considered appropriate for the company's intermediate-term needs and

---

[1]Reprinted from Stanford Business Cases 1976 with the permission of the Publishers, Stanford University Graduate School of Business, © 1976 by the Board of Trustees of the Leland Stanford Junior University.

had been approved by the Finance Committee at its July 1975 meeting. The proceeds of the issue were to be used by IML to repay a portion of its existing debt maturing in 1976 (See Exhibit 3) and for general corporate purposes related to IML's worldwide activities of developing new sources of raw materials, ore extraction, smelting, and fabrication.

The Finance Committee's approval in July pertained only to the aggregate amount of the issue and the need to proceed with such an issue by approximately October 1975. The Committee had requested Sir John to contact the company's merchant bankers and to investigate the possible financing alternatives. The final evaluation and approval of the issue and the relevant financial terms were to be made at the Committee's September 29 meeting.

Between late July and mid-September, Sir John and Ellis Pines had met on a number of occasions with the principals of Harrison Orpham & Co. and J. Scott & Co., two of the company's merchant banks. By late September, most of the financial questions pertaining to the issue appeared resolved. The issue was to have a maturity of ten years, with no repayment of principal until the sixth year. During years six through nine the company would repay £2,000,000 per year leaving a balloon maturity of £12,000,000. A five year "no-call" provision would be required with call possible in year six at 104, with the call price declining annually to 100 by the maturity date. The bond would have the normal requirements pertaining to subsequent issues of bonds, but would otherwise be free of financial restrictions.

The difficult issue, still unresolved as of September 26, was the choice of the currency denomination for the bond issue. Given the foreign exchange limitations imposed on the UK pound, IML had no option but to float the issue in the Eurobond market. Moreover, the uncertain foreign exchange status of the pound made it impossible to denominate the issue in that currency since foreign investors were unwilling to commit long-term funds to pounds. Sir John and Ellis Pines were well aware that the choice of the denomination would also strongly influence the rate of interest on the issue.

Until 1975, IML had borrowed in various currencies, but all the obligations were in specific currencies (See Exhibit 3). After a number of meetings with the merchant bankers, Sir John became convinced that IML should at least consider the possibility of denominating the issue in one of the so-called "currency cocktails." The company's merchant bankers had suggested specifically either a Special Drawing Rights (SDR) indexed issue or a European Units of Account (EUA) issue.[2] By September 26, the feasible denominations and their respective approximate interest costs were narrowed to the following five:

---

[2]See Technical Notes on SDRs and Bond Denomination and Exchange Risk in European Markets.

| Denomination | Approximate Interest Rate |
|---|---|
| 1. Special Drawing Rights (SDR) | 9.00% |
| 2. European Units of Account (EUA) | 9.25% |
| 3. US dollars ($) | 9.25% |
| 4. German mark (DM) | 8.50% |
| 5. Three-Currency ($,DM,£) | 8.00% |

The purpose of the meeting on September 26 was to reach a decision as to which of the above five denominations Sir John would recommend to the Finance Committee on September 29. In preparation for the meeting, Ellis Pines had prepared Exhibit 6 and had called Sir John's attention to the information in Exhibit 7.

As 6 pm began to approach, Sir John became concerned. The individuals at the meeting seemed unable to reach consensus. Cedric White, the partner of Harrison Orpham & Co., was strongly in favor of an SDR-indexed issue. In his opinion, "the risk to the company was low, and the prospects for a successful market reception high." Albert Scott, the partner of J. Scott & Co., favored the EUA issue. He had close contacts with the Kredietbank of Luxembourg (the originators of the EUA denomination) and felt that "the time was particularly well suited for an EUA issue." In Scott's opinion, the US dollar was likely to strengthen against most of the European currencies and therefore the EUA issue would be less costly to the company in the long run. Moreover, he felt that the value of the EUA would be more "stable" than the value of the SDR. Ellis Pines shared Scott's opinion regarding the future strength of the US dollar, but his recommendation was to issue a DM-denominated bond so as to take advantage of the spread in interest rates. Sir John's own views initially favored the US dollar denomination because the $ proportion of IML's revenue flows was rising and additional revenue flows could probably be converted most easily to dollars. But, the more he listened to the discussion, the more he wondered whether the three-currency denomination may not be the best one given the 1.25 percent differential in interest rates versus the straight dollar denomination.

The meeting adjourned shortly after 6 pm. After filling his briefcase, Sir John decided to cancel his planned weekend trip to Majorca so that he could resolve the question satisfactorily in his own mind prior to the Finance Committee meeting.

**Exhibit 1** *Comparative Consolidated Balance Sheet (Millions of Pounds Sterling)*

| Assets | Dec. 31, 1974 | Dec. 31, 1973 |
|---|---|---|
| Current Assets: | | |
| Cash and Securities | 71.3 | 56.9 |
| Accounts Receivable | 128.4 | 68.5 |
| Inventories | 156.7 | 80.6 |
| Total Current Assets | 356.5 | 206.0 |
| Properties, Plants, and Equipment: | | |
| Raw material plants | 206.1 | 210.7 |
| Power Stations | 55.0 | 21.5 |
| Reduction Plants | 146.2 | 103.6 |
| Fabricating Plants | 167.2 | 97.4 |
| Miscellaneous Plants | 135.6 | 50.1 |
| at Cost | 710.1 | 483.3 |
| Less: accumulated depreciation | 303.2 | 187.6 |
| Net Plant | 406.9 | 275.7 |
| Other Assets: | | |
| Investments and loans | 95.7 | 102.5 |
| Miscellaneous | 5.2 | 3.6 |
| Total Other Assets | 100.9 | 106.1 |
| Total Assets | 864.2 | 587.8 |

| Liabilities and Equities | Dec. 31, 1974 | Dec. 31, 1973 |
|---|---|---|
| Current Liabilities: | | |
| Accounts payable | 56.8 | 34.1 |
| Notes payable to banks | 77.1 | 63.2 |
| Long-term debts due within one year | 6.2 | 10.8 |
| Provisions and deferred items | 25.3 | 21.2 |
| Miscellaneous | 15.7 | 8.4 |
| Total Current Liabilities | 181.1 | 137.7 |
| Long-Term Liabilities: | | |
| Bonds | 126.2 | 98.7 |
| Other long-term debt | 180.5 | 101.4 |
| Provisions | 24.8 | 21.3 |
| Total Long-term Liabilities | 331.5 | 221.4 |
| Minority Interest | 36.2 | 2.6 |
| Common Equity: | 75.0 | 62.5 |
| Common Stock | 75.0 | 62.5 |
| Reserves | 45.1 | 44.2 |
| Additional Net Worth | 195.3 | 119.4 |
| Total Equity | 315.4 | 226.1 |
| Total Liabilities and Equity | 864.2 | 587.8 |

**Exhibit 2**   *Comparative Statements of Consolidated Net Income*

| | 1974 | 1973 | 1972 | 1971 | 1970 |
|---|---|---|---|---|---|
| | | Years ended December 31 (Millions of pounds sterling) | | | |
| Sales | 639.6 | 288.1 | 276.5 | 249.3 | 278.9 |
| Other Income | 12.7 | 7.2 | 6.9 | 7.8 | 7.5 |
| Total | 652.3 | 295.3 | 283.4 | 257.1 | 286.4 |
| Cost of sales | 488.7 | 206.2 | 203.1 | 184.3 | 200.8 |
| General Expenses and taxes | 67.3 | 38.1 | 37.8 | 34.2 | 34.3 |
| Depreciation | 42.9 | 21.8 | 21.3 | 19.1 | 22.1 |
| Interest | 30.7 | 15.6 | 12.9 | 10.8 | 12.1 |
| Total | 629.6 | 281.7 | 275.1 | 248.4 | 269.3 |
| Net Income | 22.7 | 13.6 | 8.3 | 8.7 | 17.1 |

**Exhibit 3**   *Denominations and Maturities of Long-term Debt (Millions of Pounds Sterling)*

| Denomination of Debt | 1976 | 1977 | 1978 | 1979 | 1978 | 1981–1995 | Total |
|---|---|---|---|---|---|---|---|
| UK pounds | 2.5 | .6 | 1.5 | 8.6 | 4.3 | 28.9 | 46.4 |
| US dollars | 4.6 | .5 | 2.5 | 2.1 | 1.1 | 35.4 | 46.2 |
| German marks | 1.8 | 1.3 | 1.0 | 1.0 | 1.1 | 7.4 | 13.6 |
| Swiss francs | 1.2 | .8 | .6 | .3 | — | 4.6 | 7.5 |
| Canadian dollars | .4 | — | — | — | — | 5.1 | 5.5 |
| Other | .3 | .4 | 1.8 | 2.6 | .8 | 1.1 | 7.0 |
| Totals | 10.8 | 3.6 | 7.4 | 14.6 | 7.3 | 82.5 | 126.2 |

**Exhibit 4**   *Capital Investments Made During 1970–1974, By Geographical Region (Millions of Pounds Sterling)*

| Year | U.K. | Other Western Europe | USA Canada | Other Countries | Total |
|---|---|---|---|---|---|
| 1970 | 15.2 | 16.1 | 33.8 | 3.9 | 69.0 |
| 1971 | 12.4 | 25.8 | 30.5 | 2.7 | 71.4 |
| 1972 | 5.8 | 20.4 | 35.7 | 1.5 | 63.4 |
| 1973 | 5.2 | 6.3 | 25.1 | 1.2 | 37.8 |
| 1974 | 11.5 | 37.1 | 39.2 | .4 | 88.2 |
| | 50.1 | 105.7 | 164.3 | 9.7 | 329.8 |
| Percent of Total | 15.2% | 32.0% | 49.9% | 2.9% | 100.0% |

**Exhibit 5**  *Geographical Distribution of Consolidated Sales, 1970–1974 (Percent of Total Sales)*

| Year | U.K. | Other Western Europe | USA Canada | Other Countries | Total |
|------|------|----------------------|------------|-----------------|-------|
| 1970 | 18.4 | 56.7 | 18.8 | 6.1 | 100.0 |
| 1971 | 15.6 | 59.0 | 14.1 | 11.3 | 100.0 |
| 1972 | 14.3 | 60.8 | 12.6 | 12.3 | 100.0 |
| 1973 | 13.1 | 59.4 | 14.9 | 12.6 | 100.0 |
| 1974 | 12.0 | 44.6 | 34.2 | 9.2 | 100.0 |

**Exhibit 6**  *Selected Balance of Payments Statistics 1974 (Millions of US$)*

| | Balance of Trade | Current Balance | Change in Reserves from 1973 |
|------|------------------|-----------------|------------------------------|
| Australia | − 2181 | − 2697 | − 1428 |
| Austria | − 535 | − 486 | 557 |
| Belgium | 1214 | 880 | 245 |
| Canada | − 2229 | − 1673 | 57 |
| Denmark | − 1145 | − 987 | − 388.7 |
| France | − 3466 | − 5849 | 322 |
| Germany | 16159 | 9676 | − 773 |
| Italy | − 7286 | − 7817 | 505 |
| Japan | − 4365 | − 4650 | 1273 |
| Netherlands | 1951 | 1648 | 411 |
| Norway | − 945 | − 1062 | 353.7 |
| South Africa | − 122 | − 103 | − 75 |
| Spain | − 4355 | − 3137 | − 287 |
| Sweden | − 577 | − 1008 | − 793 |
| United Kingdom | − 7613 | − 8573 | 463 |
| United States | − 4044 | − 3,362 | 1,680 |

*Source: International Financial Statistics*

**Exhibit 7**

## QUARTERLY CURRENCY REVIEW

### *Watch relative inflation rates*

DAVID KERN[a]

*Manager, Economic Analysis Section, National Westminster Bank*

One of the more beneficial effects of the world-wide recession has been the strong dampening effect it has had on inflationary pressures throughout most industrialized countries. The slowdown in inflation has been particularly sharp in the last six months, and the continued sluggishness in output throughout the industrialized world will undoubtedly continue to exert a strong dampening effect on inflation over the next year. In the longer term, however, there is a serious danger that premature reflation and other political pressures will help to reintroduce a strong inflationary bias in the world economy. In any case, not all major countries have shared equally in the recent favourable trends and the continuing wide disparity in the inflation performance of the various countries is one of the key factors influencing the currency outlook. At the low end of the inflation spectrum we have countries whose current rate of price increase is running at some 10% or less; this group includes the US, Netherlands, Switzerland, Sweden and, most notably, Germany, where the rate of inflation is now around 6%. In the middle range we have countries such as Japan, France, Belgium and Denmark, where inflation is now running at a rate of some 12 to 14%, while at the high end of the inflation spectrum we have Italy and the UK, where prices are now rising at a rate of 20% or more.

There has been a great deal of comment during recent months about the alleged weakness of the US dollar. The decline in the value of the dollar from the autumn of last year to the end of February 1975 was largely, though not exclusively, due to the tendency of short-term US rates to move ahead of comparable interest rates in other countries. As expected, once the rate of decline in American rates slackened during the spring, while interest rates in Japan and in Western Europe started to fall more sharply, the dollar recovered some of the ground it had lost previously and, on a trade-weighted basis, it now stands roughly at its end-1974 level. The misleading impression of weakness has been reinforced by the tendency to focus particular attention on the relationship between the dollar and a small number of Western European currencies, particularly the Swiss franc and the German mark. However, the US dollar has remained strong against many currencies, including the Ca-

---

[a]Mr. Kern writes in a personal capacity.
*Source:* Reprinted from *Euromoney,* August 1975, pp. 49–56.

nadian dollar and the Japanese yen, which are very important in terms of US trade.

Nevertheless, there can be little doubt that the very large overhang of dollars outside the US, including oil funds, can be an important source of weakness because it makes possible sudden and abrupt speculative pressures against the dollar, particularly during periods of international tension. A related factor depressing the dollar is the asymmetry between countries with weak balance-of-payments positions which tend to sell dollars to support their own currencies and the reluctance of strong countries to purchase dollars. While it would be unwise to ignore the importance of these factors in the short term, the fundamental long-term factors indicate that the dollar is likely to remain strong against most major currencies, reflecting a strong economic and industrial base, a relatively low rate of inflation and relatively limited dependence on imported energy.

The only important exception to the above statement is the German mark, where the elimination of a massive current account surplus would probably require a large-scale upward adjustment in the value of the mark against all major currencies, including the US dollar. There can be little doubt that in the medium to long term the German mark appears the strongest major currency, reflecting the lowest rate of inflation among the major countries and a very buoyant export performance. However, a substantial upward adjustment in the value of the mark could well be delayed, both by the current recession and by EEC considerations.

## 1   US dollar

### *Getting stronger*

GEORGE W. MCKINNEY

*Senior vice-president, Irving Trust Company*

The US dollar strengthened at mid-year, having traded within a fairly narrow range against most other major currencies since early April. Given the favourable performance of several important US economic indicators during this period, it may seem surprising that the dollar did not show even more strength. The rate of inflation in the United States slowed markedly, signs of an impending economic recovery grew more and more numerous, a large and unexpected trade surplus was run up and interest rates began to firm. Many of these fundamental trends are likely to continue to be favourable for some time, and the stage now seems set for a further moderate recovery in the dollar.

A year ago the US was in the upper half of the OECD inflation league, with consumer prices rising at an annual rate of more than 12%. Now the US has cut its inflation rate by more than half to 6%, one of the lowest in the OECD. This relatively good price performance is likely to be maintained, even though the economy is moving out of recession. With capacity utilization in major materials industries at just over 70%, major bottlenecks are not likely soon. Wage claims are likely to be moderated by a continued high level of unemployment and productivity gains will be strong, as is typical of recovery periods. Finally, federal tax receipts have been running well above expected levels, which means a smaller federal deficit, less fiscal stimulus and less risk of price pressures from this source than had originally been anticipated.

Interest rate trends, too, point to a stronger dollar. The dollar strengthened in March largely because of a rise in US interest rates, which resulted from fears that massive federal borrowing would crowd out private borrowers. Crowding out did not materialize, however, and it became clear that over the next few months Treasury borrowing needs would be lower than originally anticipated. Yet it now seems that the ensuing downward drift in interest rates has practically run its course. Fed policy has tightened moderately in recent weeks.

## 2   Sterling

### *Tempered pessimism*

PADRAIC FALLON

Inflation in Britain has probably turned the corner, but there will be few major net buyers of sterling until the Wilson government cuts public spending and that is now not expected until the autumn. Even if the government's expenditure cuts match foreign exchange dealers' hopes, sterling will probably continue to decline because of the inflation rate differential between the UK and other industrial countries, but the decline may be more gentle than it was and it may also be punctuated by some sharp rallies.

The outlook is one of tempered pessimism. It is pessimistic because wildcat strikes could still make a nonsense of the government's voluntary-but-backed-by-statutory-powers-if-necessary £6 a week pay limit, it is pessimistic because the government may have neither the courage nor the conviction to cut its spending by the £1 billion or more that is needed to restore confidence in sterling, and it is pessimistic, but less so, because inflation must continue to run at a rate considerably higher than Britain's trading competitors.

The facts that have tempered this pessimism have already led to a recovery in sterling. On a trade-weighted basis, it fell to a low of 29.3% below its Smithsonian parity on June 30 and closed at 28.9% on the same day, but has since recovered because of the government's pay measures.

Apart from the new pay policy which carries the endorsement of the higher echelons of the trades unions (but not necessarily that of the entire rank and file) holders of sterling have been encouraged by the encouraging trend of the trade figures. The government is making much of the narrowing of the trade gap in the first five months of this year but the June current account was £49 million in deficit and any further worsening in the exchange rate may make that worse before it gets better.

The trend is still infinitely better than it was. Against a £2 billion deficit in the second half of 1974, the current account's shortfall was only £458 million in the first six months of this year. Opinion is on the side of that deficit narrowing further.

Financing a deficit of this size is possible without recourse to the International Monetary Fund or the activation of swap arrangements, provided that the capital account continues to run at a healthy surplus; and the latter, of course, depends on maintaining a certain degree of confidence in the currency. Both the Prime Minister and the Governor of the Bank of England are believed to have done their best to provide Kuwait, a large overseas holder of sterling, with a great deal of reassurance when Kuwait's Finance Minister, Sheik Abdul el Atiqi visited London last month. There is a widespread conviction that the government's policies are now more strongly influenced by overseas concern with sterling than they were, but the rate of deposits flowing in from the Middle East has certainly slowed down by a greater degree than the oil producers' income.

Overseas holders of sterling will now be more concerned with the UK rate of inflation than before. In the April–June quarter, the annual rate slowed slightly to 23.2% compared with nearly 29% for the year to January.

### 3   Yen

#### *Strong in the autumn*

SACHIO KOHJIMA
*Bank of Tokyo*

Having held its ground for a few months, the Japanese yen eased appreciably in mid-June on the Tokyo foreign exchange market, with the dollar rate jumping from ¥291–292 to ¥295–296. This pronounced easing of the yen has altered the optimistic outlook.

The change in prospects stems from (1) expectations of a strengthening dollar, based on the possibility of improvement in the United States balance of payments and a leveling-off of short-term interest rates in the US and (2) growing concern over the recent sharp decline in Japanese exports.

Japan's balance of payments, despite a dramatic improvement, was still adverse in the first half of 1975, indicating that the yen would weaken. But the reverse occurred. The yen rate continued buoyant on the strength of the massive inflow of foreign capital, attributable to (1) expectations of a high yen rate in the period ahead, (2) a drop in Euro-dollar rates and (3) high domestic interest rates compared with rates abroad. The expected dollar shortage was thus covered by the inflow of foreign capital. The channels through which foreign capital flows into Japan are now limited to investment in Japanese securities and placement of non-resident free yen deposits. A huge amount of foreign capital flowed into the country through these channels.

The outlook for the yen is still by no means clouded. True, exports and imports have slackened noticeably recently. But the downtrend is more pronounced in imports than in exports, resulting in a growing trade surplus. What is more, the world economy seems likely to recover in the autumn. Recovery from the recession will spread from the United States to Japan and West Germany. In this setting it is expected that Japanese exports and imports will regain momentum in the autumn.

With world trade in 1975 expected to expand by about 9% at best, Japan's export growth will be constrained to around this figure in the fiscal year ending next March. Growth in imports, on the other hand, will be limited to 1 to 2% in value, even if domestic production should resume expansion early this autumn, because it is now running some 20% below last year and stocks of raw materials continue at an unprecedented level. Consequently, the trade balance will widen to $8 to $9 billion, swinging the current account into a surplus for the first time in three years.

These forecasts indicate that the yen, despite its current weakness, will gain strength in the autumn.

## 4  Deutschemark

### *Rising*

HERBERT PETERS

*Manager, Commerzbank, Frankfurt*

The Deutschemark's value is governed by very different factors. The economy of the United States, which appears to be gathering momentum again, and the interest differential in favour of the dollar, have been causing that currency to harden. In terms of foreign trade and payments it is still the safest currency, so it may tend to rise against other European currencies. For the dollar a Deutschemark equivalent of 2.40 still appears to be a level that is unlikely to be lastingly surpassed.

During the past few months the Bundesbank has consistently continued its policy of monetary relaxation. As a result of several lowerings of the discount rate which followed each other comparatively quickly we have now, at 4.5%, reached again the level of early 1973, i.e. before the beginning of the sharply restrictive course. Simultaneously the rates for Lombard loans which were available to the banks without interruption were lowered. Several decreases of the minimum reserve ratio, whose effect was partly compensatory and partly liquefying, paralleled the interest policy of the Bundesbank.

This shows the level at which interest rates will remain during the coming months. Apart from technically induced fluctuations of rates for day-to-day money, rates will continue on the present level or even go slightly down. Whether the Bundesbank will support possible impellents on the part of the Government in the early autumn by another lowering of rates cannot yet be said.

The recession has proved to be more enduring than at first assumed, and significant growth signals are not yet in sight. Incisive structural adjustment processes at home, intensification of the world-wide economic setback, combined with a painful decrease of foreign demand, and still no great propensity of industry to invest, which could not even be noticeably improved by the 7.5% investment grant which expired on June 30, make it necessary to revise earlier forecasts for the whole of 1975. For instance, a decline of GNP by 2 to 3% is more probable than zero growth which had been hoped for a short while ago.

## 5  Guilder

### *Weaker position*

M. H. P. STARREN
*Algemene Bank, Amsterdam*

The strong position taken by the guilder on the foreign exchange markets during the greater part of the first six months of 1975 seemed to weaken somewhat by the end of that period. This was due to, among other things, the greater easiness of the money market, which caused the rate for three-month fixed deposits to fall to about 3% per annum. However, less favourable developments of the economy, the Government budget and the political situation as well have no doubt played a part.

While most of the Dutch were already preparing their holidays, the Government was still absorbed in the budget plans for the next year. Although preparing a budget is naturally a difficult matter, in the present case the Government was confronted with a number of special problems. So, when this became known, it led to some cautiousness vis-à-vis the guilder.

First, the fact that the forecast of the budgetary deficit for 1975 had to be raised from 4,000 million to 9,300 million guilders. The size of this rise, which is largely accounted for by the deterioration of the economic situation, necessitates the Government to adopt inflationary financing. Up to the middle of July only 4,400 million guilders of the overall amount of 9,300 million had been covered, so that the amount to be financed had become too big to be borrowed in its entirety on the capital market. The fact that inflationary financing has become unavoidable has aroused the fear abroad that the inflation—which had failed against expectations to decline in the first half-year—will be on the increase again. As a result, the guilder lost something of its strong position. The latter development was also caused by the disappointing economic situation; the figures for the first six months have been more unfavourable than was expected.

Industrial production in the first four months of the year was over 8% less than a year ago, while inventories and order inflow—particularly with respect to foreign countries—continued their unfavourable development. In view of this, the central planning bureau had to reduce its forecast for the growth of gross national product in 1975 from + 2% to − 1%. This development, of course, also affected revenues from taxation, while new measures to stimulate the economy (in February and April) were required, resulting in the budgetary deficit referred to above. However, the disappointing economic situation did not only have an impact on the budgetary deficit; it also showed that, apart from the balance of payments supported by natural gas, the Netherlands does not take that exceptional position against other countries that it has been thought to take for a considerable length of time. Finally, the position of the guilder was also impaired by an increase in political uncertainty.

## 6   Swiss franc

### *Tending easier*

DR. HANS J. MAST
*Executive vice-president, Credit Suisse*

Turnover on the Swiss foreign exchange market, which was extraordinarily heavy a few months ago, has declined markedly since spring; swings in rates have become less violent, with the trend of rates showing a basic change. This is illustrated by the US dollar, which after sinking to an all-time low of Sw f2.39 in February, gradually recovered, with certain fluctuations to Sw f2.52 at the beginning of July. Other currencies, with the exception of the weak pound sterling, followed a similar course. The export-weighted appreciation of the Swiss franc, which reached a record 52.7% in February, has meanwhile been reduced to 45.8%.

This easier trend should predominate on balance for the next few months. Since the recession in Switzerland is likely to persist at least until the spring of 1976, the decline in Swiss interest rates should continue for the time being, whereas in the United States and other countries money costs are expected to rise with the anticipated economic recovery, at least in the short-term sector. The interest differential between Switzerland and abroad will therefore probably widen, which, together with intensified export financing, should lead to a further increase in capital outflow. Under these conditions the firmer trend of the US dollar against the Swiss franc is likely to persist for a while. However, its appreciation will hardly be spectacular. Switzerland's surplus on current account, which will continue to grow in the short run partly owing to the reduction in wage transfers by the declining foreign labour force, will operate against any dramatic upward movement.

## 7 Belgian franc

### *Shaky*

MICHEL GROSFILS

*Manager, Banque de Bruxelles*

The balance of payments of the Belgo-Luxemburg Economic Union (BLEU) showed a surplus of B f25.1 billion in 1974, compared with the record B f34.3 billion surplus attained in 1973. The increase in the cost of oil imports was partly compensated by higher exports, while there was a reduction in net outflows of capital on the part of companies and private individuals.

During the first quarter of 1975 the surplus continued to be impressive.

As a result the National Bank's foreign exchange reserves rose by more than 13% from the beginning of this year until the end of May. On the foreign exchange markets, and especially within the snake, the Belgian franc has been very firm.

However, a crucial problem is emerging in the form of a rapid increase in wages and prices, despite the fact that the business and general economic climate has sharply deteriorated since the beginning of the summer of 1974.

Inflation is still raging: on account of its relatively small size and its high degree of dependence on foreign trade, Belgium is, more so than other OECD countries, very much the child of international fortune. And clearly inflation, which in 1974 was partly related to international monetary phenomena, the oil crisis and the general commodity price boom has not been curbed very much in 1975. Compared with a consumer prices rise of about 16% last year, the present growth rate of the cost-of-living index is still 12.5% on a yearly basis, and this in spite of a two months' price freeze. Even if it means an actual slowing of inflation, the Government will fail to realize its intention of curbing the inflation rate this year to less than 10%.

Despite the rise in unemployment, wages and salaries have increased very substantially. At end-March 1975 they were, in industry, 26.7% above their March 1974 level. Given the present rate of unused productive capacity—which means no gain in productivity—it is resulting in a worsening of industrial costs per unit of output, feeding cost-push inflation.

## 8 French franc

### *Hot money's target*

DAVID EDWARDS

*First National City Bank*

What appears to be another strong recovery has made the dollar the belle of the ball in the European money markets. Its rise from 4.00 to 4.18

in the last two weeks has eclipsed the ascent of the French franc and its calculated re-entry into the European float at its old parities.

The sudden resurgence of the French franc has been a rather surprising development. Having been weak for so long, the franc, like the dollar, was disregarded by many international operators. What was overlooked was a conscious drive by the government to reinstate the franc into the system of which they were the prime architects.

The reasons for the strength of the French franc are multiple. Three months ago the Banque de France started a concerted support operation in the foreign exchange markets to forcefully move the French franc into striking range of the snake. This action accomplished two additional benefits. It put dollars into the reserves of the central bank while it attracted attention in the international capital markets to the domestic improvements in the French economy.

The government's shrewd dealing with the OPEC countries has had a twofold advantage. One, the use of technology and munitions as barter in the Middle East has reduced her crude bill significantly: and two, created an *entente cordiale* favouring massive Arab investment. All this plus the political courage of Monsieur Fourcade to continue the tight monetary policy and the restrictive credit controls initiated in the summer of 1974 has tended to push the interest rate structure up against the Deutschemark, thus attracting interest-sensitive hot money. In short, Minister Fourcade has done a remarkable job of managing the French economy. His actions, considering the existing conditions, must be interpreted as making the very best of a bad situation. Last, and not sought after, a windfall for the French has resulted from the industrial problems in the United Kingdom. The flight out of sterling has created a large capital inflow directly into France.

Yet, what must be stressed in predicting the future of the franc over the next six months is neither economic nor political in nature. It is rather the menace of becoming the market leader.

# Assessing the Debt Servicing Capacity of Peru

A. JAVIER ERGUETA AND RICHARD SHRIEVE[1]

## A. BACKGROUND

Vowing to re-establish the national dignity and independence through vigorous development, in 1968 Peru's military initiated an economic strategy which at first soared to success only then to plummet to disaster. Although Peru's leaders asserted the country's need for foreign capital, their policies actually alienated both private investors and traditional "soft" lenders, forcing them to rely strongly on private commercial credits and loans. Awash with liquidity and lulled to confidence by a few years of Peru's favorable trade balances, multinational banks evidenced little concern over Peru's ability to service its debt. Each side indulged in strategies to secure the best terms possible from the other, by offering and demanding special advantages. When bust inevitably followed boom, both were over-exposed and suffered accordingly.

Fortune at first appeared to smile upon the military government of Juan Velasco Alvarado. Although avowedly leftist, by 1974 its economic policies had achieved remarkable success. They provided solid growth, won foreign lenders' confidence, and bought valuable time to consolidate the new regime's social problems. (See Exhibit 1 and the glowing reports in the Annual Report of the U.N. economic Commission for Latin America, 1969–1974.) The underlying economic strategy seemingly responsible for this was nationalist. One pillar was an industrialization program to establish in Peru an independent manufacturing sector to reduce manufactured imports and to fuel future growth. Another was a "Peruvianization" plan to claim ownership and control of the country's traditional primary export industries.

---

[1]This is not a case but rather the "solution" to a case, written by two MBA students at the Stanford Graduate School of Business in the Winter Quarter of the 1978/79 academic year. (Mr. Shrieve is currently with the Bank of America.) This is an excellent creditworthiness analysis, especially when the other study constraints on the authors are considered! We include it because, firstly it admirably illustrates the benefits derivable from the approach we take in Chapter 11; and secondly, it suggests similar analyses for other countries and raises a host of interesting and open-ended questions.

A prerequisite of both plans was foreign resources. As Velasco put it,[2] "Latin American development requires foreign capital." To industrialize, Peru needed foreign machinery, equipment and intermediate inputs. To "Peruvianize," it needed large sums to compensate the current foreign owners of the country's export sector and to further reinvest. At first, the government saw no incompatibility between the broader goals of its economic program and their prerequisite, attracting the needed resources from abroad. Its five-year plan optimistically called for net foreign direct investment of $700 million and loans of another $1,800 million.[3] Government policy proved attractive enough to banks, but not to investors.

The investors were frightened away by the vigorous expropriation policies followed by the military government. A selection of these nationalizations is given in Exhibit 2. The compensation was inadequate because (i) it was based on book values which were generally well below economic values; (ii) the compensation was often heavily taxed; or (iii) compensation was often paid in local currency and forcibly re-invested in government-stipulated projects. There were important new foreign investments in these years, for instance by Southern Peru Copper in the Cuajone mine, and by Marcona Mining. However unpublished analyses of these projects seem to imply a more complex motivation than might seem to be the case.[4] In both cases, it appears the risk factor was such as to make either project unattractive on its own merits. The companies involved stayed in Peru only because they considered they already had recouped their investments and were "playing on the bank's money" (Marcona) or because some reinvestment was necessary to continue to be allowed to enjoy the profitability of previous investments (Southern Peru Copper). As for the numerous oil companies which had been exploring in Peru in 1968, despite the undeniability of substantial oil reserves, virtually all left Peru by the end of 1975. Generally, the Peruvian government undertook a large variety of measures to limit the scope of private enterprise.[5]

Under the terms of the Hickenlooper amendment to the Foreign Aid Act of 1962, the United States government could not ignore the nationalization of U.S. companies which were not awarded "prompt, fair compensation." It immediately threatened the Peruvian sugar quota, froze

---

[2]Speech of April 6, 1970. Cited in S. Hunt, "Direct Foreign Investment in Peru: New Rules for an Old Game," in A. Lowenthal (ed.), *The Peruvian Experiment*, 1975.

[3]L. Guasti, "Peruvian Industrialization Within the Global Economy, 1968–1976," paper presented at the "Conference on the Peruvian Experiment Revisited," organized by the Woodrow Wilson International Center for Scholars.

[4]C. Jackson, "Southern Peru Copper," and Brad Buermann, "Marcona Mining in Peru," papers submitted in the Joint Venture Investments seminar at the Graduate School of Business in 1978 and 1979.

[5]D. M. Schydlowsky and J. J. Wicht, "The Anatomy of an Economic Failure: Peru 1968–1978," paper presented to the "Peruvian Experiment Revisited," section I, pp. 20, 21.

foreign aid, denied further EXIM credits, and moved against Peru within international "soft" lending organizations such as the World Bank and the Inter-American Development Bank. No loans or credits came from these sources from 1969 to 1972.[6]

The policy of enforced Peruvianization cost Peru dearly by cutting off most of its traditional sources of foreign capital: private investment, aid, soft loans, and official credits. For its foreign exchange reinvestment needs, the country was largely on its own resources, namely on the strength of demand abroad for its goods and services. Fortunately, 1969 to 1974 were good years for Peru's main export industries. The continuing worldwide boom, heightened by the war demands of the American economy, drove primary resource prices upward. The upshot was a favorable trade balance throughout accompanied by the accumulation of international reserves.

On the strength of this record, Peru had little trouble financing its current needs directly through credits granted by foreign suppliers. By the end of 1973, two-thirds of the country's new finance and half its outstanding public debt was in this form.[7] Financing large new projects requiring major investments proved a different matter. Behind the Cuajone copper proposal which languished on the drawing boards from 1969 to 1974, waited a long line of other extraction and manufacturing projects.

Some of the first of these to get off the ground were in oil exploration and development. Following the discovery of petroleum in northeastern Peru by the state company Petroperu, over fifteen foreign oil companies accepted the government's exacting conditions for granting concessions. Foreign oil companies agreed to foot the entire investment for exploration and development in exchange for half the resulting crude (the other half would go to Petroperu), driven largely by their concern to diversify their sources of crude in the face of tightening Middle East situation. Private as well as official—though unpublicized—estimates slated Peru to become a significant oil exporter in the late 1970s. (This included in-house estimates by the World Bank upon which the Peruvians relied implicitly.) Recognition of its growing global status was quickly accorded, even before the 1973 hike in the price of oil by the OAPEC countries. Its first big break came from the international finance community.

Peru finally lined up a loan to finance Cuajone in the fall of 1973, with a consortium of U.S. banks led by Chase Manhattan. In retrospect, the merits of the project itself were not such as to ensure Cuajone's ability to support a trouble-free loan, and good financial analysis should have recognized this. Yet the question why the consortium agreed to the loan

---

[6]G. Ingram, *Expropriation of U.S. Property in South America*, pp. 64–66, 83–86. (New York: Praeger, 1974)

[7]E. V. K. Fitzgerald, *The State and Economic Development: Peru Since 1968*, p. 71. (New York: Cambridge University Press, 1976.)

at all is eclipsed by another one: why among the preconditions set by the consortium there featured the stipulation that no loan would be consummated unless Peru compensated previously expropriated U.S. companies, including IPC?

This requirement seems removed from maximizing the wealth of the banks' stockholders, and so it was. The motivation was political and even ideological. The banks argued that unless Peru demonstrated its commitment to the private property norms underlying the system, the viability of a joint venture with a private company such as Southern Peru was open to question. The banks' strategy succeeded. Peru badly wanted the loan and acceded to a compensation of $76 million—to come directly out of the loan proceeds for the Cuajone project. Most of it was expected to go to IPC, but Peru saved face at home by declaring that none of the money it was giving over to the U.S. government to distribute was intended for IPC.[8]

Again Peru showed how far it was willing to go to keep the banks' favor. On the other hand, the banks revealed a few interesting matters about themselves. Chase and the rest evidently did not regard the loan to Cuajone primarily as a project loan, grounded on the individual venture's repayment capacity and collateral, but rather as a loan to Peru itself, to be used and repaid on the authority of the Peruvian government. This suggests the need to go beyond the analysis of the creditworthiness of the Cuajone project in isolation to analyzing the debt servicing capacity of the entire country, as we attempt below. Chase and the others seemingly harbored few doubts about Peru's overall capacity to repay. In effect, they pushed on Peru an added—and unrequested—liability to themselves, and thought themselves the wiser.

A bumper year for Peru's balance of payments in 1974 encouraged further optimism on both sides. Although Peru reported its first trade deficit ($326 million) since before the revolution, this was attributed partly to bad luck, partly to its need to import petroleum before its own production came on stream. Other imports and repatriation of profits brought the current account deficit to $603 million. This was more than made good by a net capital inflow of $935 million, of which loans to development projects (including Cuajone) totaled $520 million. Short-term loans totaled $336 million. The country's international reserves increased to $332 million. Concern over the imposing trade deficit nevertheless prompted the government to clamp on a policy prohibiting the importation of anything but capital goods and food items, and then only ac-

---

[8]Guasti, *op. cit.*, p. 32. With this compensation paid, U.S. and multilateral agencies recommenced lending to Peru, but by this time Peru's need of funds was voracious, and it maintained its previous rate of borrowing from the private sector. Between 1974 and 1976 Peru's outstanding debt more than doubled.

cording to government quotas.[9] The other leg of the strategy called for maintenance in the growth of export revenues.

Spurred doubtlessly by the increase in the relative prices for commodities, the government undertook massive new investments. In 1974 spending shot up 44% over the previous year in agriculture, 88% in oil development, 139% in mining, and 1,016% in steel. Peru based its development plan for 1975–1978 largely on the happy experience of the years immediately preceding. Exports were expected to grow at an annual rate of 14%, whereas imports would be held to 5% increases.[10] However, the growth in export values was predicated entirely on continued increases in world prices. The Peruvianization schemes involved taking over the "essential and primary" export sectors. The government was indifferent to considerations of efficiency and economic rationality so that the spread of nationalization led to a fall in real output in the nationalized industries. The state-encouraged import-substitution firms made the situation for exporters worse by preempting large amounts of investible resources and foreign exchange needed by exporters to pay for intermediate inputs.[11]

Everything started to fall apart in 1975, when general mining production fell by 11%, copper production fell by 16%, the anchovies on which the fishmeal industry was based disappeared as they had in 1972 and raw material prices fell sharply. Copper prices fell by 40%, silver by 7%, fishmeal by 36% and lead by 10%. The government was desperate for revenue and expropriated Marcona while attempting to squeeze the oil companies. However all but two of the latter then pulled out, and Velasco was replaced by Morales Bermudez. He negotiated with a bank consortium headed by Manufacturers Hanover for balance of payments deficit financing. The consortium lent the money after extracting a government promise to compensate Marcona. To go to the banks instead of to the IMF for what was *prima facie* a balance of payments problem in itself resulted from a decision of cabinet members to avoid the ill-famed "IMF treatment." Instead, they asked the banks to draw up a regimen similar to but less rigid than what the IMF would require to which they would agree to adhere. In this way they won time and political support but also lost valuable opportunities to confront the nation's spreading economic ills. In 1975, Peru was a net borrower in the amount of $625 million. In 1976, the debt level rose $685 million. By September of 1976, the government was so far out of line with its own standard, the banks refused further entreaties and called in the IMF. Since 1976, GNP has declined and loans have again and again been rescheduled.

---

[9]Fitzgerald, *op. cit.*, p. 63.
[10]*Plan Nacional de Desarello 1975–1978*, Republica Peruana, Oficina de la Presidencia, p. 90.
[11]See Schydlowsky and Wicht, *op. cit.*, pp. I-11, I-22, 24, II-1–8.

## B.   CREDIT ANALYSIS OF A NEW TYPE

As Peru re-discovered only too late, its rosy capital account surplus could not long survive its first trade deficit. Once foreign lenders and investors perceived the country's export earnings could not cover its own import needs, they became concerned about its long-term ability to service and repay their capital. We take a portfolio theory approach (as outlined in the text of Chapter 11).

Our objective is to forecast the foreign exchange available to service foreign debt. For Peru's undiversified economy, it is reasonable to assume that virtually all foreign exchange becomes available through its export of seven basic commodities. These are copper, fishmeal, iron, silver, sugar, zinc, and coffee. (In fact, the analysis *defines* Peru's "export portfolio" as these seven.) For the purpose of this study, we will also assume that the primary source of earnings variability is the movement of world prices. Peru is a price taker in all these industries. (See Exhibit 3, 4 and 5.) Our efforts will attempt to forecast the foreign exchange available from this export portfolio. Let $X_i$ equal foreign exchange generated by these seven exports in year $i$. Then:

$$X_i = [1 + \sum_{j=1}^{n} \beta ij\ \delta ij]\ E_{(i-1)}$$

$\beta ij$ = percentage of total exports which commodity $j$ makes up in year $i$. For example, copper comprised 36% of total exports in 1978, and thus its beta would be 0.36.

$\delta ij$ = the growth rate of the price of the commodity $j$ in year $i$. (We used the log [price/price( −1)] for delta.)

$E_{(i-1)}$ = Last year's total exports expressed in dollars.

$n$ = The number of exports in the portfolio.

For example, imagine a portfolio consisting of the two commodities, $A$ and $B$, where $A$ comprises 20% of the total and $B$ 80%. If $A$'s price were to go up 10% next year and $B$'s 5%, the weighted growth rate of the portfolio would be:

$$.2 * .1 = .02$$
$$.8 * .05 = .04$$
weighted growth = .06 (or 6%)

If last year's exports were $1,000, then we would expect this year's to equal $1,060 (1.06 × 1,000). However, our interest lies not so much in estimating the growth of the export portfolio as a whole but in the growth of foreign exchange available to repay foreign debt. Two additional factors are necessary to complete the formulation.

First, each export industry requires some minimum rate of reinvestment of its foreign exchange earnings to maintain output at current levels. We label this factor *theta*, the required rate of reinvestment, expressed as a decimal. If, for example, export industry $A$ (20% of total portfolio and with a 10% growth in price next year) required a reinvestment rate of 20%, the rate of growth of the portfolio due to $A$ alone would be:

$$\beta_A \delta_A (1 - \theta_A)$$

$$.2 \times .1(1 - .2)$$

$$.2 \times .1 \times .8 = .016 \text{ or } 1.6\%$$

Similarly, the weighted growth of the *total portfolio* earnings after reinvestment can be expressed:

$$\sum_{j=1}^{n} \beta_{ij}\, \delta_{ij}\, (1 - \theta_{ij})$$

There is a second additional factor that must be included in the model before we have truly focused in on the growth rate of foreign exchange *available to pay foreign debt*. In practice, even where debtors have a genuine willingness to repay and there is a free market for foreign exchange, they may find themselves outbid by those who consider the acquisition of foreign exchange vital to their economic and political survival. (In Peru, as in many developing countries, there was not a free market in foreign exchange at this time. The central bank retained a monopoly on foreign exchange.) Quite frequently, these groups include import-substitution firms, which are commonly dependent on imported inputs to maintain any output at all, and the government. In the case of Peru, in 1974 about 22% of its imports were food and fuel and 65% were industrial supplies and capital goods. It would not have been possible for the government to cut off these sectors of the economy from all foreign exchange without extreme social hardship and political risk. Consequently, the model must deduct the amount required for these sectors to arrive at that which is available for debt service. We call this factor *lambda* ($\lambda$). It is expressed as the number of dollars of foreign exchange *required* by sectors of the economy other than the seven in the export portfolio.

The formulation for forecasting foreign exchange available for debt service, $X_i$, is:

$$X_i = [1 + \sum_{j=1}^{n} \beta_{ij}\, \delta_{ij}\, (1 - \theta_{ij})]E_{(i-1)} - \lambda_i$$

The primary issues from this point on deal with methods for forecasting *beta*, *delta*, *theta* and *lambda*. In practice, an economist and lending officers would be required to perform fundamental analysis to forecast these factors. In this paper, we have made some simplifying assumptions. The procedure we used is as follows:

1. Choose a base year in which the loan is to be (or was) made. In analyzing a current loan request, the analysis should employ all relevant information available to the present. In analyzing a past loan syndication, use only information available to the lenders up to the time of the loan.

2. Choose the export sectors/industries which generate the majority of the LDC's export revenues. Choose the main source of variability of the export revenues, which in the case of most LDC's is the *price* of its primary resource exports.

3. Acquire the appropriate data. Exhibit 6 shows the world prices of the seven commodities we are analyzing for the period from 1950 to 1978. Calculate each export's year-to-year price change over the desired time range. We used the log (price/price[−1]) to represent "change." We then calculated the mean change, the standard deviation of the change, and the correlation coefficients of the seven commodities' price changes. (This was obviously the work of a computer.) Exhibits 7 and 8 show these statistics for Peru's exports.

4. Treat the probability distribution of each price change as an independent random variable. Using a Monte Carlo simulation routine, simulate a large number of combinations of the individual prices holding the commodity weights (*betas*) and the *thetas* constant. (Two of our simplifying assumptions.) The simulation generates a large number of estimates of the growth rate of the export portfolio as a whole.

5. Calculate the mean growth rate and its standard deviation from the large number of simulations. (See Exhibit 8.)

6. Estimate *lambda* for each of the years of the forecast period. The model is very sensitive to the level of *lambda*. We would, therefore, recommend running it several times at different levels of *lambda* to obtain a *range* of foreign exchange available for debt service.

7. Using the mean price change of the portfolio as a whole (the bottom line of the Monte Carlo simulation) and a standard deviation expanding for each year of the forecast period, calculate the maximum debt service Peru could manage for each year of the forecast period. We assumed a "random walk" model with a drift. This model implies that the most recent growth rate of the export portfolio is the best predictor of future rates. However, the *standard deviation* of the growth trend is calculated on the formula $(\sigma_n = S\sqrt{n})$. The meaning of the increasing standard deviation is that the interval within which we can predict debt servicing capacity at a given confidence level increases each year.

8. Consider the debt servicing amounts proposed for each year of the loan. Using a Z-table, calculate the probability that export earnings in any given year will suffice to cover the proposed payment. (Or, alternatively, read from the table the maximum debt servicing, ex *ante*, which the country will be able to handle.)

9. To derive the cumulative probability of a trouble-free loan calculate the joint probability of a trouble-free loan for every individual year.

## Results of the Model

To check the model's results we decided to examine three periods corresponding to three actual periods of commitments of loans by the banks to Peru. Two of these have been discussed already. We look at the time of the 1974 Cuajone project loan which, we suggested, should have been analyzed from the country's overall debt servicing capacity. We look at the 1976 balance of payments bailout, when the banks very explicitly extended credit to the government to allow it not to resort to the IMF. Finally, we look at the most recent restructuring of the debt in 1978 when realistic debt service payments were supposedly agreed upon. To what degree were (and are) the size and terms of these loans reasonable, given sound estimates of Peru's export earnings?

Our model provides one way of answering this question by allowing a calculation of the maximum amount of debt Peru could have on its books and be able to service—at a specified confidence level. This is shown for each of our three chosen examples in Exhibits 9, 10 and 11. The export revenues have a probability distribution whose mean level grows at the specified rate for the exhibit. The mean exports are shown in column 1. We must subtract the $\lambda$ sum from the mean to indicate precommitted revenues. Now using the standard deviation from column 2 we can calculate the export revenues we will have with probability 99% (giving the 1% confidence figure) and 95% (giving the 5% confidence figure). The latter revenues are available to service debt, with respective default probabilities of 1% and 5%. The next question is how much debt can be serviced by export revenue flows of these magnitudes. That depends on the interest rate on the debt. It floats at about 2% over the LIBOR, so for illustrative purposes we take LIBOR of 10% and 15%. The maximum debt that the designated export flows can service at these rates is shown in the exhibits. Exhibit 12 contains a recent history of LIBOR.

The model's estimate contrasts markedly with the amounts outstanding each year. In brief, at the 5% confidence level, in millions of dollars of public debt:

|      | Calculated maximum | Actual Outstanding |
|------|--------------------|--------------------|
| 1974 | $   939–1,064      | $1,441             |
| 1976 | 1,244–1,423        | 3,468              |
| 1978 | 2,069–2,420        | 6,300              |

*Source:* Model, World Bank Debt Tables, and Banco Nacional de la Reserva: *Ayuda Memoria.*

According to our model, it was not advisable to add to Peru's debt in any of the years selected. The table speaks for itself: the gap between the maximum Peru could confidently repay and what it was obligated to pay grew over the entire period.

There are limitations to the forecasts resulting from the assumptions in our model. These are best clarified by retracing the steps taken in the analysis, following the sequence presented in the methodological section.

1. The base years we used in these runs were 1973, 1975 and 1978 (1978 rather than 1977 because, unlike the 1974 and 1972 loans, the 1978 loan was made late in the year when more current period data was available).

2. As already mentioned, for our purposes Peru's export portfolio consisted of copper, fishmeal, silver, sugar, coffee, iron ore and zinc. We discuss the limitations of this assumption below.

3. Price data going back to 1952 was acquired and analyzed as described. For example, in 1973 the value of Peru's export portfolio was growing at a mean rate of 3%, with a standard deviation of 12%.

4. We chose a *lambda* of $300 million a year to represent the unavoidable drain of foreign exchange to other sectors. This figure is, in fact, wildly conservative, since in 1974 alone such expenditures amounted to about $750–1,000 million. But a Peruvian economist, Daniel Schydlowsky, advised us that the $300 million figure could serve as an absolute floor. Similarly, he advised us that the extractive industries in Peru had a very low need for the re-investment of foreign exchange in order to maintain capacity at current levels. Consequently, we used *thetas* (the re-investment rate) of only 5% of the export earnings of each industry.

5. The results, listed in Exhibits 9 through 11, are, for example, that Peru could have handled about $242.9 million of debt servicing in 1976 at the 5% confidence level and is based on the following calculation:

$$X = [B(1 + g)^n - \lambda] - B(1 + g)^n * \sigma_o n * 1.645$$
$$= [755(1 + .03)^3 - 300] - 755(1 + .03)^3 * .12 \sqrt{3} * 1.645$$

$B$ = base year exports ($755 million in 1973)
$g$ = estimated growth rate of the portfolio
$n$ = number of years from the base year
$\lambda$ = amount of foreign exchange demanded for other sectors
$\sigma_o$ = standard deviation of the growth of the export portfolio up to the base year
1.645 = number of standard deviations from the mean which encompasses a 5% confidence interval for a normal distribution

Columns 6 through 9 of the exhibits discount debt service to the present at both 10% and 15%. The 10% figure is that now used by the Peruvian Banco Central de la Reserva in its own forecasts. If LIBOR averages higher than 15%, our estimates of debt-servicing capacity are generous; if below 10%, they are conservative. The bottom line sums of these columns represent the maximum level of debt Peru could have on its books at present and be able to repay at the confidence level specified. They are the figures we used at the beginning of this section in comparing our model's estimate of Peru's repayment capacity and its actual debts.

Another way to assess the wisdom of the loans actually extended in 1974, 1976 and 1978 using our model is to analyze the probability of a trouble-free repayment of an existing debt service schedule. The underlying procedure is the same as above until almost the end. Instead of calculating the debt service amount lying at the edge of a 95% confidence interval in any given year, we calculate the probability of a trouble-free loan given a debt service schedule outstanding. Because we were unable to locate satisfactory data on the debt servicing schedules as it existed at the 1973 and 1975 decision points, valid analysis is only possible of the 1978 situation. The results can be summarized as follows:

|  | Level of Debt Service with 95% Confidence Level of Trouble-Free Repayment | Actual | |
|---|---|---|---|
|  |  | Debt Service | Probability of Trouble-Free Repayment |
| 1979 | $576 | $900 | 36% |
| 1980 | 512 | 796 | 52% |
| 1981 | 473 | 649 | 75% |
| 1982 | 442 | 444 | 95% |
| 1983 | 415 | 300 | 96% |

Cumulative probability of a trouble-free repayment history: 12.9%.

Clearly, the current structure of the debt servicing is unrealistic. So are some of the assumptions of our model, to be sure. But the difference between our reasonable confidence level and the actual probability of trouble-free repayment is too large to be shrugged off. Bankers' optimism that they have finally settled on the debt schedule that will return their principal to them in a specified time is almost certainly unfounded. No doubt, they are reluctant to admit their Peruvian loans will actually have a maturity longer than the normal five to seven years. Nevertheless, that will probably have to be the case.

Our model also has the capability of allowing the analyst to experiment with different debt service schedules until he finds one with the lowest acceptable risk. For example, a multinational banker or official of the Peruvian central bank in 1978 might have been curious to see what the probabilities were of a trouble-free repayment given a schedule of $600 million the first year, $500 the next two years, and $400 million after that. Using our model, this could be estimated, but we did not believe the information at our disposal allowed such estimates on our part to have much interest. This is, though, one feature of the model that could be of great use to practitioners.

Many such capabilities could, of course, be incorporated into the model should its underlying approach prove useful. We are all too aware of the roughness of some of the techniques and assumptions we had to fall back on. Some possible ways to refine the model might include:

1. Expanding the sources of risk modelled. Probably our most glaring simplification is the assumption that uncertainty derives exclusively from the unpredictable movement of world commodity *prices*. Obviously, there are other sources: movements in costs (though these are probably reflected in prices over the long run); changes in exchange rates; effects of delays in supplies; labor unrest; climactic and tidal changes (such as affected Peru's anchovy industry). In theory, probability assessments can be made of each of these, if not through statistical extrapolations of past trends then by informed estimates based on fundamental analysis. The important point is to develop a model that uses a probability *distribution*, not merely a point estimate. The resulting distributions can be included in the model at the stage of the Monte Carlo simulation where previously only price variability was simulated and combined into a comprehensive portfolio. As always, the benefits of such refinements depend on the quality of the additional inputs. However, we believe that any competent economist specializing in Peru or the Andean area will be able—far better than we— to develop the basic inputs to the model.

2. Altering the weighting procedure. Our current method of weighting each export commodity within the portfolio according to its percentage of the total dollar value of exports in the preceding year is biased. The bias lies in the fact that last year's *prices* entered into the calculation of the weights. A better method would be to estimate based on the *volume* of exports in each commodity. Either fundamental analysis—taking new mines into account, for example—or continuation of the current year's level of output volume might provide more accurate results than our approach. In any case, this is a problem a good credit and economic staff can easily deal with.

3. Elasticities of supply and demand ought to be considered. With the prices of the commodities in this analysis rising and falling as precipitously as they do, both output and demand may change. In addition, it is also likely that Peru would be required, for political reasons, to continue production even though the world price of a given commodity had fallen below the level of marginal costs.

4. The model needs to be updated continuously. For example, in 1979 it is anticipated that Peru will become a significant exporter of oil. Some official forecasts project earnings on petroleum exports to be over $500 million annually. Clearly, this will be an important element to include in the model.

## CONCLUSION

The Peruvian experience over the past ten years will long be remembered as an example, for LDC's and lenders, of the financial, social and political risks of ill-defined criteria for estimating debt-servicing capacity. Country risk analysis can derive useful tools from some of the techniques of modern portfolio theory—techniques which help to define risk far more specifically than any analysis of macroeconomic variables or cross-country comparisons based on such variables. Peru, like many LDC's, can reasonably be viewed as an "undiversified investor" holding a "portfolio" of highly "risky investments"—the risk of which taken together is substantially less than that of any of its pieces. Surely the interests of both the shareholders of multinational banks and the people of the LDC's are better served when debt is managed within realistic levels.

**Exhibit 1**   *Average Annual Growth Rates: 1960–73 (% change at 1963 prices)*

|               | 1960–64 | 1965–68 | 1969–73 | 1960–73 |
|---------------|---------|---------|---------|---------|
| Agriculture   | 3.8     | −0.5    | 2.1     | 1.8     |
| Fishing       | 17.1    | 1.5     | −16.8   | 0.6     |
| Mining        | 2.9     | 2.6     | 1.4     | 2.3     |
| Manufacturing | 9.2     | 5.3     | 7.1     | 7.2     |
| Construction  | 6.4     | −2.2    | 10.0    | 4.7     |
| Services      | 9.2     | 3.8     | 8.9     | 7.3     |
| GNP           | 7.6     | 2.9     | 6.3     | 5.6     |
| GFCF[a]       | 10.3    | −1.2    | 9.0     | 6.0     |
| Prices[b]     | 7.4     | 13.7    | 7.3     | 9.5     |

*Source:* Eric Fitzgerald, *The State and Economic Development*, p. 17, Table 9. Cambridge, England: Cambridge University Press, 1975. Used by permission.

*PERU: Main Short-Run Economic Indicators (Percentage annual growth rates)*

|                                   | 1971–1973 | 1974  | 1975    |
|-----------------------------------|-----------|-------|---------|
| Gross domestic product            | 6.0       | 6.6   | 4.0     |
| Gross income[a]                   | 6.3       | 8.7   | 1.9     |
| Per capita gross domestic product | 3.0       | 3.5   | 1.0     |
| Gross fixed investment            | 9.0       | 25.8  | 18.1    |
| Value of exports                  | 3.7       | 36.4  | −9.9    |
| Value of imports                  | 13.5      | 78.6  | 21.3    |
| Terms of trade                    | 1.5       | 18.3  | −15.1   |
| Balance on current account[b]     | 114       | −851  | −1567   |

|                                              | 1971–1973 | 1974 | 1975  |
| -------------------------------------------- | :-------: | :--: | :---: |
| Variation in international reserves[b]        |    15     | 242  | −543  |
| Consumer price index[c]                       |    8.5    | 19.1 | 24.0  |
| Money                                        |   22.4    | 41.6 | 28.3  |

[a]Gross domestic product plus terms-of-trade effect.
[b]Absolute values in millions of dollars at current prices.
[c]December to December
Source: Economic Survey of Latin America 1975 (E/CEPAL/1014/Rev.1) published by the Economic Commission for Latin America (CEPAL). Used by permission.

**Exhibit 2**  *Selected Peruvian Nationalizations, 1968–1975*

*International Petroleum Company (Canadian)*
(100% owned by Exxon [U.S.])
10.1968 New government immediately nationalizes part of IPC property. Total value of assets eventually nationalized is $190 million. Government claims company owes Peru over $600 million for past exploitation.
2.1974 As part of Greene Agreement, IPC receives a payment of about $68 million.

*Various mining firms, including Anaconda*
1969 Government announces that all foreign firms holding concessions in Peru must either develop them or surrender them. Most leave, but Southern Peru tries to develop Cuajone.

*Cartavio, Paramunga sugar estates*
(100% owned by W. R. Grace and Co. [U.S.])
6.1969 Government expropriates all large agricultural estates, gives 15% value in cash and the rest in long-term government debt.
2.1974 Greene Agreement results in Grace getting to divide around $7 million with other firms.

*Compania Peruana de Telefonos*
(69% owned by ITT [U.S.])
10.1969 Government announces expropriation of ITT's shares. Grants $14.8 million; book value is $18.5 million. Only $4 million is paid in dollars, the rest in soles, with the stipulation that ITT has to build and operate a $12 million hotel.

*Banco Continental*
(80% owned by Chase Manhattan [U.S.])
5.1970 Government buys out Chase shares at 586 soles/share; book value was at 188. Chase gets $6.3 million on 1964 investment of $1.7 million.

*Cerro de Pasco Corporation*
(100% owned by Cerro Co. [U.S.])
12.1971 Cerro offers to sell properties to government, which responds

with offer to buy at $12 million. Book value is estimated at $145 million, market value at $250 million. Cerro charges bad faith.
1.1974 Government expropriates.
2.1974 Green Agreement earmarks $67–79 million for Cerro.

*The Peruvian Corporation*
(Privately held, British)
1971 As main creditor, Government drives company into bankruptcy and then auctions off and purchases for $21 million—just enough to pay outstanding indebtedness.

*Refineria Conchan Chevron S.A.*
(100% owned by Standard Oil of California [U.S.])
5.1972 Government claim for $2 million in back taxes leads to company refusal to pay, confiscation, and government purchase for amount equal to its tax claim. Company evaluated at $6 million.

*Fish meal industry*
(Gold Kist, Star Kist, Cargill, General Mills, and International Protein comprise 40%—all U.S. owned)
5.1973 Government nationalizes firms, giving 10% in cash, the rest in 6% bonds maturing in 10 years.

*Marcona Mining and Smelting*
(100% owned by Utah Mining and Cypress Springs Corp. [U.S.])
6.1975 Government expropriates.
3.1976 Compensation of over $50 million agreed on.
*Sources:* Various, including G. Ingram, *Expropriation of U.S. Property in South America* (New York: Praeger, 1974) S. Hunt, "New Rules for an Old Game," in A. Lowenthal, *The Peruvian Experiment: Continuity and Change Under Military Rule* (Princeton, NJ: Princeton University Press, 1975).

**Exhibit 3** *Peruvian Traditional Exports (thousand tons)*

|  | Average 1961–1963 | Average 1967–1969 | Average 1973–1975 |
|---|---|---|---|
| Cotton | 127 | 76 | 45 |
| Sugar | 607 | 475 | 492 |
| Coffee | 37 | 46 | 43 |
| Wool | 7 | 7 | 4 |
| Fish products | 1,104 | 2,040 | 563 |
| Oil | 606 | 464 | 222 |
| Copper | 178 | 201 | 176 |
| Gold (thousands of kg) | 2 | 1 | 2 |
| Silver (thousands of kg) | 1,028 | 1,018 | 1,131 |
| Lead | 136 | 153 | 152 |
| Zinc | 192 | 305 | 412 |
| Iron | 3,370 | 5,571 | 4,769 |

*Source:* B.C.R., Lima, Memoria 1975, Anexo 25. Used by permission.

**Exhibit 4**  *GDP by Sector, 1970–1975 (in billions of soles, at constant [1970] prices Annual Rates of Growth in %)*

| | 1970 | 1971 | 1972 | 1973 | 1974 | 1975 | 1950-60 | 1960-70 | 1970-75 |
|---|---|---|---|---|---|---|---|---|---|
| Agriculture | 36.2 | 37.3 | 37.6 | 38.5 | 39.4 | 39.8 | 4.3 | 2.0 | 1.9 |
| Fishing | 6.6 | 5.7 | 3.0 | 2.3 | 3.1 | 2.6 | 16.3 | 9.3 | -17.0 |
| Mining | 19.8 | 19.0 | 20.4 | 20.3 | 21.0 | 18.7 | 10.0 | 4.0 | -1.1 |
| Manufactures | 57.2 | 62.1 | 66.7 | 71.6 | 77.0 | 80.6 | 7.2 | 7.5 | 7.1 |
| Other Sectors | 120.9 | 128.9 | 140.1 | 151.7 | 163.4 | 172.3 | 4.2 | 6.3 | 7.3 |
| G.D.P. | 240.7 | 253.0 | 267.8 | 284.4 | 303.9 | 314.0 | 5.3 | 5.6 | 5.5 |

Source: B.C.R., Lima, Memoria 1973 and 1976, Anexo 38. Used by permission.

**Exhibit 5** *Percentage of World Exports of Selected Commodities Supplied by Peru in 1975*

| SITC Category | Item | Percentage Supplied by Peru |
|---|---|---|
| 03201 | Fish, prepared, preserved[a] | 5.5 |
| 071 | Coffee | 1.0 |
| 061 | Sugar | 2.6 |
| 28311 | Copper ores | 7.7 |
| 68211 | Copper metal | 3.3 |
| 2813 | Iron ore, excluding pryites[a] | 0.6 |
| 672 | Iron, steel primary forms[a] | 0.03 |
| 68111 | Silver, unworked, worked not rolled | 5.9 |
| 2835 | Zinz ores, concentrates | 14.8 |
| 6861 | Zinc, alloys unwrought | 3.7 |

[a]1974 figures

Source: *United Nations Yearbook of International Trade Statistics, 1977*, Vol. II, "Trade by Commodity" tables. Used by permission.

**Exhibit 6** *Unit Price of Peruvian Exports by Commodity*

| | Copper | Fishmeal | Iron ore | Silver | Sugar | Zinc | Coffee |
|---|---|---|---|---|---|---|---|
| 1950 | 22.40 | 88.49 | 4.99 | 74.20 | 4.98 | 13.88 | 44.80 |
| 1951 | 27.60 | 93.08 | 5.46 | 89.40 | 5.67 | 17.99 | 50.60 |
| 1952 | 32.60 | 94.62 | 6.09 | 84.90 | 4.17 | 16.21 | 51.30 |
| 1953 | 30.10 | 92.65 | 6.76 | 85.20 | 3.41 | 10.86 | 52.70 |
| 1954 | 31.20 | 93.95 | 6.99 | 85.30 | 3.26 | 10.69 | 65.70 |
| 1955 | 43.80 | 105.29 | 7.12 | 89.10 | 3.24 | 12.30 | 52.20 |
| 1956 | 41.00 | 109.98 | 7.75 | 90.80 | 3.48 | 13.49 | 51.20 |
| 1957 | 27.40 | 107.50 | 8.33 | 90.80 | 5.16 | 11.40 | 57.30 |
| 1958 | 24.80 | 110.73 | 8.39 | 89.00 | 3.50 | 10.31 | 48.90 |
| 1959 | 29.80 | 113.83 | 8.69 | 91.20 | 2.97 | 11.46 | 37.60 |
| 1960 | 30.80 | 77.00 | 8.79 | 91.40 | 3.14 | 12.95 | 36.90 |
| 1961 | 28.80 | 69.80 | 8.99 | 92.40 | 2.91 | 11.55 | 36.30 |
| 1962 | 29.30 | 94.50 | 8.84 | 108.40 | 2.98 | 11.63 | 34.40 |
| 1963 | 29.30 | 100.60 | 9.22 | 127.90 | 8.50 | 12.01 | 34.50 |
| 1964 | 44.00 | 100.50 | 9.52 | 129.30 | 5.87 | 13.57 | 47.90 |
| 1965 | 58.80 | 110.00 | 9.33 | 129.30 | 2.12 | 14.50 | 45.10 |
| 1966 | 69.10 | 139.50 | 9.49 | 129.30 | 1.86 | 14.50 | 41.40 |
| 1967 | 50.90 | 108.70 | 9.92 | 155.00 | 1.99 | 13.85 | 38.40 |
| 1968 | 55.80 | 98.30 | 10.21 | 214.50 | 1.98 | 13.50 | 37.60 |
| 1969 | 66.60 | 117.10 | 10.34 | 179.10 | 3.37 | 14.65 | 40.80 |

| | Copper | Fishmeal | Iron ore | Silver | Sugar | Zinc | Coffee |
|---|---|---|---|---|---|---|---|
| 1970 | 63.80 | 155.10 | 10.80 | 177.10 | 3.75 | 15.32 | 55.70 |
| 1971 | 49.30 | 157.70 | 11.55 | 154.60 | 4.52 | 16.14 | 46.10 |
| 1972 | 48.60 | 144.20 | 12.20 | 168.50 | 7.43 | 17.73 | 54.40 |
| 1973 | 80.90 | 385.10 | 12.84 | 256.00 | 9.61 | 20.84 | 67.60 |
| 1974 | 91.40 | 321.60 | 16.34 | 470.80 | 10.73 | 35.94 | 70.20 |
| 1975 | 55.10 | 205.60 | 21.41 | 442.00 | 34.24 | 38.89 | 67.80 |
| 1976 | 63.00 | 284.10 | 17.90 | 435.40 | 17.63 | 37.38 | 122.80 |
| 1977 | 59.40 | 343.00 | 14.90 | 462.20 | 12.41 | 34.38 | 219.50 |
| 1978 | 57.90 | 321.90 | 14.00 | 457.60 | 9.33 | 29.44 | 136.40 |

**Exhibit 7**   *Year-to-Year Price Changes for Peruvian Exports* (log [Price at *t*/Price at *t* − 1])

| | Copper | Fishmeal | Iron ore | Silver | Sugar | Zinc | Coffee |
|---|---|---|---|---|---|---|---|
| 1951 | 0.2088 | 0.0505 | 0.0900 | 0.1864 | 0.1298 | 0.2594 | 0.1217 |
| 1952 | 0.1665 | 0.0164 | 0.1092 | − 0.0516 | − 0.3073 | − 0.1042 | 0.0137 |
| 1953 | − 0.0798 | − 0.0211 | 0.1044 | 0.0035 | − 0.2012 | − 0.4005 | 0.0269 |
| 1954 | 0.0359 | 0.0139 | 0.0335 | 0.0012 | − 0.0450 | − 0.0158 | 0.2205 |
| 1955 | 0.3392 | 0.1140 | 0.0184 | 0.0436 | − 0.0062 | 0.1403 | − 0.2300 |
| 1956 | − 0.0661 | 0.0435 | 0.0848 | 0.0189 | 0.0715 | 0.0923 | − 0.0193 |
| 1957 | − 0.4030 | − 0.0228 | 0.0722 | 0.0000 | 0.3939 | − 0.1683 | 0.1126 |
| 1958 | − 0.0997 | 0.0296 | 0.0072 | − 0.0200 | − 0.3882 | − 0.1005 | − 0.1585 |
| 1959 | 0.1837 | 0.0276 | 0.0351 | 0.0244 | − 0.1642 | 0.1057 | − 0.2628 |
| 1960 | 0.0330 | − 0.3909 | 0.0114 | 0.0022 | 0.0557 | 0.1222 | − 0.0188 |
| 1961 | − 0.0671 | − 0.0982 | 0.0225 | 0.0109 | − 0.0761 | − 0.1144 | − 0.0164 |
| 1962 | 0.0172 | 0.3030 | − 0.0168 | 0.1597 | 0.0238 | 0.0069 | − 0.0538 |
| 1963 | 0.0000 | 0.0626 | 0.0421 | 0.1654 | 1.0481 | 0.0322 | 0.0029 |
| 1964 | 0.4066 | − 0.0010 | 0.0320 | 0.0109 | − 0.3702 | 0.1221 | 0.3282 |
| 1965 | 0.2900 | 0.0903 | − 0.0202 | 0.0000 | − 1.0184 | 0.0663 | − 0.0602 |
| 1966 | 0.1614 | 0.2376 | 0.0170 | 0.0000 | − 0.1308 | 0.0000 | − 0.0856 |
| 1967 | − 0.3057 | − 0.2495 | 0.0443 | 0.1813 | 0.0676 | − 0.0459 | − 0.0752 |
| 1968 | 0.0919 | − 0.1006 | 0.0288 | 0.3249 | − 0.0050 | − 0.0256 | − 0.0211 |
| 1969 | 0.1769 | 0.1750 | 0.0127 | − 0.1804 | 0.5318 | 0.0818 | 0.0817 |
| 1970 | − 0.0430 | 0.2810 | 0.0435 | − 0.0112 | 0.1068 | 0.0447 | 0.3113 |
| 1971 | − 0.2578 | 0.0166 | 0.0671 | − 0.1359 | 0.1868 | 0.0521 | − 0.1892 |
| 1972 | − 0.0143 | − 0.0895 | 0.0547 | 0.0861 | 0.4970 | 0.0940 | 0.1656 |
| 1973 | 0.5096 | 0.9823 | 0.0511 | 0.4182 | 0.2573 | 0.1616 | 0.2172 |
| 1974 | 0.1220 | − 0.1802 | 0.2411 | 0.6093 | 0.1102 | 0.5450 | 0.0377 |
| 1975 | − 0.5061 | − 0.4474 | 0.2702 | − 0.0631 | 1.1604 | 0.0789 | − 0.0348 |
| 1976 | 0.1340 | 0.3234 | − 0.1791 | − 0.0150 | − 0.6638 | − 0.0396 | 0.5940 |
| 1977 | − 0.0588 | 0.1884 | − 0.1834 | 0.0597 | − 0.3511 | − 0.0837 | 0.5808 |
| 1978 | − 0.0256 | − 0.0635 | − 0.0623 | − 0.0100 | − 0.2853 | − 0.1551 | − 0.4758 |

**Exhibit 8**   *Statistical Properties of the Prices of Peru's Exports*

| Growth Rate | Mean | Standard Deviation |
|---|---|---|
| Copper | .055832 | .221107 |
| Fishmeal | .06394 | .252655 |
| Iron ore | .041092 | .034776 |
| Silver | .053844 | .134665 |
| Sugar | .028581 | .394236 |
| Zinc | .01767 | .136012 |
| Coffee | .017887 | .159452 |

*Correlation Matrix*

| | copper | fishmeal | iron ore | silver | sugar | zinc | coffee |
|---|---|---|---|---|---|---|---|
| Copper | 1.000 | | | | | | |
| Fishmeal | 0.510 | 1.000 | | | | | |
| Iron ore | −0.235 | −0.054 | 1.000 | | | | |
| Silver | 0.271 | 0.374 | 0.003 | 1.000 | | | |
| Sugar | −0.270 | 0.089 | 0.234 | 0.188 | 1.000 | | |
| Zinc | 0.539 | 0.242 | −0.250 | 0.214 | 0.150 | 1.000 | |
| Coffee | 0.176 | 0.255 | 0.217 | 0.156 | 0.189 | 0.093 | 1.000 |

**Exhibit 9** Debt Service Capacity of Peru at Selected Confidence Levels Under the Assumption of a Total Export Portfolio Growth Rate of 3% and Base Year (1974) Estimated Standard Deviation of 12%

| | 1 | 2 | 3 | 4 | 5 | 6 | 7 | 8 | 9 |
|---|---|---|---|---|---|---|---|---|---|
| | | | | Maximum Debt Service | | PRESENT VALUE | | | |
| | | | | | | 1% CONF. INT. | | 5% CONF. INT. | |
| | Trend | $\sigma n$ | $\lambda n$ | 1% C.I. | 5% C.I. | 10% LIBOR+2 | 15% LIBOR+2 | 10% LIBOR+2 | 15% LIBOR+2 |
| 1974 | 777.7 | 0.1200 | 300 | 260.8 | 324.1 | 236.9 | 226.6 | 294.7 | 281.9 |
| 1975 | 801.0 | 0.1697 | 300 | 184.8 | 277.4 | 152.7 | 139.7 | 229.2 | 209.7 |
| 1976 | 825.0 | 0.2078 | 300 | 126.1 | 242.9 | 94.7 | 82.9 | 182.5 | 159.7 |
| 1977 | 849.8 | 0.2400 | 300 | 75.3 | 214.3 | 51.5 | 43.1 | 146.4 | 122.5 |
| 1978 | 875.3 | 0.2683 | 300 | 28.9 | 188.9 | 18.0 | 14.4 | 117.3 | 93.9 |
| 1979 | 901.5 | 0.2939 | 300 | -14.9 | 165.6 | -8.4 | -6.5 | 93.5 | 71.6 |
| Maximum Level of Current Debt: | | | | | | 545.3 | 500.2 | 1063.6 | 939.4 |

**Exhibit 10** *Debt Service Capacity of Peru at Selected Confidence Levels Under the Assumption of a Total Export Portfolio Growth Rate of 4.84% and Base Year (1976) Estimated Standard Deviation of 15.27%*

| | 1 | 2 | 3 | 4 | 5 | 6 | 7 | 8 | 9 |
|---|---|---|---|---|---|---|---|---|---|
| | | | | Maximum Debt Service | | PRESENT VALUE | | | |
| | | | | | | 1% CONF. INT. | | 5% CONF. INT. | |
| | Trend | σn | λn | 1% Level | 5% Level | 10% LIBOR+2 | 15% LIBOR+2 | 10% Libor+2 | 15% LIBOR+2 |
| 1976 | 969.6 | 0.1527 | 300 | 325.1 | 426.0 | 295.6 | 282.7 | 387.3 | 370.4 |
| 1977 | 1016.5 | 0.2160 | 300 | 205.8 | 355.4 | 170.1 | 155.6 | 293.7 | 268.7 |
| 1978 | 1065.7 | 0.2645 | 300 | 110.0 | 302.0 | 82.6 | 72.3 | 226.9 | 198.6 |
| 1979 | 1117.3 | 0.3054 | 300 | 23.5 | 256.0 | 16.1 | 13.4 | 174.8 | 146.4 |
| 1980 | 1171.3 | 0.3414 | 300 | −59.1 | 213.4 | −36.7 | −29.4 | 132.5 | 106.1 |
| 1981 | 1228.0 | 0.3740 | 300 | −140.5 | 172.4 | −79.3 | −60.7 | 97.3 | 74.5 |
| 1982 | 1287.5 | 0.4040 | 300 | −222.5 | 131.8 | −114.2 | −83.7 | 67.6 | 49.6 |
| 1983 | 1349.8 | 0.4319 | 300 | −306.4 | 90.8 | −142.9 | −100.2 | 42.4 | 29.7 |
| Maximum Level of Current Debt: | | | | | | 191.3 | 250.2 | 1422.6 | 1244.0 |

**Exhibit 11** Debt Service Capacity of Peru at Selected Confidence Levels Under the Assumption of a Total Export Portfolio Growth Rate of 3.62% and Base Year (1979) Estimated Standard Deviation of 11.38%

| | 1 | 2 | 3 | 4 | 5 | 6 | 7 | 8 | 9 |
|---|---|---|---|---|---|---|---|---|---|
| | | | | Maximum Debt Service | | PRESENT VALUE | | | |
| | | | | | | 1% Level | | 5% Level | |
| | Trend | $\sigma n$ | $\lambda n$ | 1% Level | 5% Level | 10% LIBOR+2 | 15% LIBOR+2 | 10% LIBOR+2 | 15% LIBOR+2 |
| 1979 | 1066.2 | 0.1138 | 300 | 484.0 | 566.6 | 440.0 | 420.9 | 515.1 | 492.7 |
| 1980 | 1104.8 | 0.1609 | 300 | 391.2 | 512.3 | 323.3 | 295.8 | 423.4 | 387.4 |
| 1981 | 1144.8 | 0.1971 | 300 | 319.9 | 473.6 | 240.3 | 210.3 | 355.9 | 311.4 |
| 1982 | 1186.3 | 0.2276 | 300 | 258.2 | 442.1 | 176.3 | 147.6 | 302.0 | 252.8 |
| 1983 | 1229.2 | 0.2545 | 300 | 201.6 | 414.7 | 125.2 | 100.2 | 257.5 | 206.2 |
| 1984 | 1273.7 | 0.2788 | 300 | 147.8 | 389.7 | 83.4 | 63.9 | 220.0 | 168.5 |
| 1985 | 1319.8 | 0.3011 | 300 | 95.4 | 366.1 | 49.0 | 35.9 | 187.9 | 137.6 |
| 1986 | 1367.6 | 0.3219 | 300 | 43.6 | 343.5 | 20.3 | 14.2 | 160.2 | 112.3 |
| | | | | | | | Maximum Level of Current Debt: | | |
| | | | | | | 1457.8 | 1288.8 | 2422.0 | 2068.9 |

**Exhibit 12**   Six-Month LIBOR Plus 2 Points, Quarterly Average of Daily Figures for 1963 Through 1978[a]

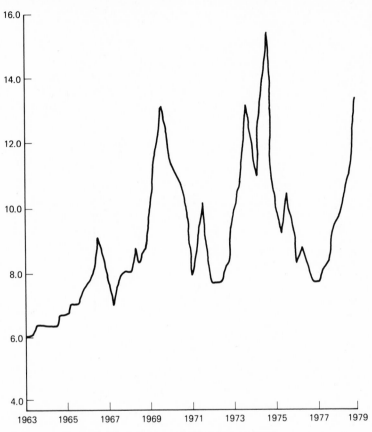

[a]Minimum = 5.9%, Maximum = 15.3%, Mean = 9.0%

# Index